Cascading Style Sheets
The Definitive Guide

Cascading Style Sheets
The Definitive Guide

Eric A. Meyer

O'REILLY®

Beijing · Cambridge · Farnham · Köln · Paris · Sebastopol · Taipei · Tokyo

Cascading Style Sheets: The Definitive Guide
by Eric A. Meyer

Copyright © 2000 O'Reilly & Associates, Inc. All rights reserved.
Printed in the United States of America.

Published by O'Reilly & Associates, Inc., 101 Morris Street, Sebastopol, CA 95472.

Editor: Richard Koman

Production Editor: Melanie Wang

Cover Designer: Ellie Volckhausen

Printing History:

May 2000:	First Edition.

Library of Congress Cataloging-in-Publication Data

Meyer, Eric A.
    Cascading style sheets: the definitive guide/Eric A. Meyer.--1st ed. p. cm.
    ISBN 1-56592-622-6
    1. HTML (Document markup language) 2. Web sites--Design. 3. Computer graphics.
       I. Title.
QA76.76.P98 H94 M47 2000
005.7'2--dc21

00-035694

ISBN: 1-56592-622-6
[M]

[1/01]

Table of Contents

Preface

The subject of this book is, as you might have guessed by the cover, Cascading Style Sheets (CSS). There are two "levels" to CSS; these are referred to as CSS1 and CSS2. The difference between the two is that CSS2 is all of CSS1, plus a lot more. This book attempts to cover all of CSS1, and CSS positioning, which is a part of CSS2. The rest of CSS2 is excluded because, at the time of this writing, nobody had implemented most of it. Rather than cover a lot of theoretical territory, we chose to stick to what was currently usable.

If you are a web designer or document author interested in sophisticated page styling, improved accessibility, and saving time and effort, then this book is for you. All you really need before starting the book is a decent knowledge of HTML 4.0. The better you know HTML, of course, the better prepared you'll be. You will need to know very little else in order to follow this book.

It is important to remember something about web standards and books: the former are continually evolving, while the latter are frozen in time (until the next edition comes out, anyway). In the case of HTML and CSS, there are a great many changes afoot even as these words are being written. The recent formalization of XHTML 1.0 as a full W3C Recommendation, for example, is a major milestone in the evolution of the World Wide Web. There are likely to be even more levels to CSS, further extending the ability to style documents; major web browsers are approaching full CSS1 support, and robust CSS2 implementations can be seen lurking on the horizon. This is an exciting time to be a designer, and learning CSS now will give you a leg up on the future.

Typographical Conventions

The following typographical conventions are used in this book:

`Constant width`
>   is used to indicate code examples, HTML tags and CSS elements.

`Constant width italic`
>   is used for replaceables that appear in text.

Italic
>   is used to introduce new terms and to indicate URLs, filenames, and path-
>   names.

     The owl indicates a note or tip relating to the nearby text.

     The turkey indicates a warning.

Property Conventions

Throughout this book, there are boxes that break down a given CSS property. These have been reproduced practically verbatim from the CSS specifications, but some explanation of the syntax is in order.

Throughout, the allowed values for each property are listed with a syntax like the following:

>   Value: [<length> | `thick` | `thin`]{1,4}
>   Value: [<family-name> ,]* <family-name>
>   Value: <url>? <color> [/ <color>]?
>   Value: <url> || <color>

Any words between < and > give a type of value, or a reference to another property. For example, the property `font` will accept values which actually belong to the property `font-family`. This is denoted by using the text "<font-family>." Any words presented in constant width text are keywords that must appear literally, without quotes. The forward slash (/) and the comma (,) must also be used literally.

Several keywords strung together means that all of them must occur—in the given order. For example, `help me` would mean that the property must use those keywords in that exact order.

If a vertical bar (X | Y) separates alternatives, then any one of them must occur. A vertical double bar (X || Y) means that either X or Y, or both, must occur, but they may appear in any order. Brackets ([...]) are for grouping things together. Juxtaposition is stronger than the double bar, and the double bar is stronger than the bar. Thus "V W | X || Y Z" is equivalent to "[V W] | [X || [Y Z]]."

Every word or bracketed group may be followed by one of the following modifiers:

- An asterisk (*) indicates that the preceding value or bracketed group is repeated zero or more times. Thus, `bucket*` means that the word `bucket` can be used any number of times, including zero. There is no defined upper limit on the number of times it can be used.

- A plus (+) indicates that the preceding value or bracketed group is repeated one or more times. Thus, `mop+` means that the word `mop` must be used at least once, and potentially many more times.

- A question mark (?) indicates that the preceding value or bracketed group is optional. For example, `[pine tree]?` means that the words `pine tree` need not be used (although they must appear in that exact order if they are used).

- A pair of numbers in curly braces ({M,N}) indicates that the preceding value or bracketed group is repeated at least M and at most N times. For example, `ha{1,3}` means that there can be one, two, or three instances of the word `ha`.

Following are some examples:

`give || me || liberty`

At least one of the three words must be used, and all of them can be used in any order. For example, `give liberty`, `give me`, `liberty me give`, and `give me liberty` are all valid interpretations of this example.

`[ I | am ]? the || walrus`

Either, but not both, of the words `I` or `am` may be used, but use of either is optional. In addition, either `the` or `walrus`, or both, must follow. Thus, you could construct `I the walrus`, `am walrus the`, `am the`, `I walrus`, `walrus the`, and so forth.

`koo+ ka-choo`

One or more instances of `koo` must be followed by `ka-choo`. Therefore, `koo koo ka-choo`, `koo koo koo ka-choo`, and `koo ka-choo` are all legal. The number of `koo`s is potentially infinite, although there are bound to be implementation-specific limits.

`I really{1,4}* [love | hate] [ Microsoft | Netscape ]`

The all-purpose web designer's opinion-expresser. This can be interpreted as `I love Netscape`, `I really love Microsoft`, and similar expressions.

Anywhere from zero to four `reallys` may be used. You also get to pick between `love` and `hate`, even though only `love` was shown in this example.

`[[[ Alpha || Baker || Cray ],]{2,3} and ] Delphi`

This is a potentially long and complicated expression. One possible result would be `Alpha, Cray, and Delphi`. Another is `Alpha Baker, Cray Alpha, Baker Cray Alpha, and Delphi`. The comma is placed due to its position within the nested bracket groups.

How to Contact Us

We have tested and verified the information in this book to the best of our ability, but you may find that features have changed (or even that we have made mistakes!). Please let us know about any errors you find, as well as your suggestions for future editions, by writing to:

O'Reilly & Associates, Inc.
101 Morris Street
Sebastopol, CA 95472
(800) 998-9938 (in the U.S. or Canada)
(707) 829-0515 (international/local)
(707) 829-0104 (fax)

You can also send us messages electronically. To be put on the mailing list or request a catalog, send email to:

info@oreilly.com

To ask technical questions or comment on the book, send email to:

bookquestions@oreilly.com

We have a web site for the book, where we'll list errata and any plans for future editions. You can access this page at:

http://www.oreilly.com/catalog/css/

For more information about this book and others, see the O'Reilly web site:

http://www.oreilly.com/

Acknowledgments

This book was written with a single goal: to make Cascading Style Sheets (CSS) easy to learn, understand, and use. Of course, there is much more to this goal than meets the eye. Trying to translate tersely defined algorithms into comprehensible English isn't always as easy as it sounds.

In my work on this book, I found myself crawling through the various nooks and crannies of CSS, creating test suites, and banging my head against myriad problems, not to mention the aforementioned web browser limitations. Along the way, I encountered a number of people whom I'd like to thank.

First, of course, are Håkon Wium Lie of Opera Software and Bert Bos of the W3C for their efforts in creating Cascading Style Sheets, and for answering many of my questions on the *www-style* mailing list, even the foolish ones. I'd also like to thank Chris Lilley, also of the W3C, for encouraging my attempts to help make the web more stylish. His words of praise for some of my earliest efforts came at exactly the right moment to spur me on, and it was he who made it possible for me to join the World Wide Web Consortium's CSS&FP Working Group.

Tim O'Reilly took a big chance in giving me my first shot at a major professional publication, for which I will always be grateful. My editor at O'Reilly, Richard Koman, was more than patient with me during the writing process, and I probably should have shown my gratitude by sending in more rough drafts. Tara McGoldrick, also of O'Reilly, was a great help in sorting out figures, smoothing out communications, and generally making my life much easier. Dale Dougherty of Songline Studios gave me my first real break into professional writing, and Chuck Toporek (now at O'Reilly) was my long-suffering first editor at *Web Review*, managing to weather my totally random article submission schedule with good grace. My friend and colleague Peter Murray was gracious enough to contribute some of his time and expertise to assist me in the creation of one of the Case Studies, and Ron Ryan gets a gold star and a whole bucket of "attaboys" for being the best supervisor I've ever known.

The gang from the Usenet group *comp.infosystems.www.authoring.stylesheets* has been a huge help over the years, both in answering questions and providing feedback. Within that group, Todd Fahrner, Alan Flavell, Anthony Boyd, and Jan Roland Eriksson have been generally clueful and helpful, and Sue Sims deserves special mention for being just as helpful plus willing to assist (and occasionally defend) someone she'd never met—namely, me. Ian Hickson and David Baron deserve thanks for not only being as expert on the subject of CSS as anyone else I know, but also for applying their raw energy to interpreting the specification, ferreting out browser bugs, and generally being helpful in spreading the CSS gospel. Their comments and insights were extraordinarily helpful in the writing of this work.

And, of course, a hearty "hikeeba!" to the CSS Samurai: Todd Fahrner, Liam Quin, David Baron, Ian Hickson, Sue Sims, Jan Roland Eriksson, John Alsopp, and Braden McDaniel. Yes, many of those names are repeats. What can I say? It's a small web.

Please note that none of these people should be blamed for any errors contained herein. They should instead be credited for helping me correct a vast number of mistakes, even if they didn't always know they were doing so.

At this point, I believe it's appropriate for me to thank Tim Berners-Lee for inventing the World Wide Web. I don't know Tim, and he doesn't know me, but it's pretty much required that authors of books related to the Web thank Tim for his fundamental contribution. I think this might actually be an international law by now; call it the Berners Convention.

And, finally, personal thanks to: Michelle, for being a friend through thick and thin; Randy, who has always gladly been both teacher and confidant; Steve, who helped me survive college and the years succeeding it; Dave, for all the years of making me laugh, especially when I most needed it, and for being the voice of sanity when I least expected it; and Tina, who helped me to stand when I wanted to stay down.

I'd also like to thank my wonderful wife, Kathryn, for her boundless support and for meritorious valor in putting up with me, particularly when my deadlines loomed, and for her inexhaustible belief in me and my abilities; and humble thanks to my parents, Art and Carol, and my sister, Julie, all of whom have always been there for me and never did learn to tell me when to quit. Well, guys, I guess it's too late now.

Thanks for everything.

—Eric A. Meyer
23 February 2000

1

HTML and CSS

In many ways, the Cascading Style Sheets (CSS) specification represents a unique development in the history of the World Wide Web. In its inherent ability to allow richly styled structural documents, CSS is both a step forward and a step backward—but it's a good step backward, and a needed one. To see what is meant by this, it is first necessary to understand how the Web got to the point of desperately needing something like CSS, and how CSS makes the web a better place for both page authors and web surfers.

The Web's Fall from Grace

Back in the dimly remembered early years of the Web (1990–1993), HTML was a fairly lean little language. It was almost entirely composed of structural elements that were useful for describing things like paragraphs, hyperlinks, lists, and headings. It had nothing even remotely approaching tables, frames, or the complex markup we assume is a necessary part of creating web pages. The general idea was that HTML would be a structural markup language, used to describe the various parts of a document. There was very little said about how these parts should be displayed. The language wasn't concerned with appearance. It was just a clean little markup scheme.

Then came Mosaic.

Suddenly, the power of the World Wide Web was obvious to almost anyone who spent more than ten minutes playing with it. Jumping from one document to another was no harder than pointing the mouse cursor at a specially colored bit of text, or even an image, and clicking the mouse button. Even better, text and images could be displayed together, and all you needed to create a page was a plain text editor. It was free, it was open, and it was cool.

Web sites began to spring up everywhere. There were personal journals, university sites, corporate sites, and more. As number of sites increased, so did the demand for new HTML tags that would allow one effect or another. Authors started demanding that they be able to make text boldfaced, or italicized.

At the time, HTML wasn't equipped to handle these sorts of desires. You could declare a bit of text to be emphasized, but that wasn't necessarily the same as being italicized—it could be boldfaced instead, or even normal text with a different color, depending on the user's browser and their preferences. There was nothing to ensure that what the author created was what the reader would see.

As a result of these pressures, markup elements like <B> and <I> started to creep into the language. Suddenly, a structural language started to become presentational.

What a Mess

Years later, we have inherited the flaws inherent in this process. Large parts of HTML 3.2 and HTML 4.0, for example, are devoted to presentational considerations. The ability to color and size text through the FONT element, to apply background colors and images to documents and tables, to space and pad the contents of table cells, and to make text blink on and off are all the legacy of the original cries for "more control!"

If you want to know why this is a bad thing, all it takes is a quick glance at any corporate web site's page markup. The sheer amount of markup in comparison to actual useful information is astonishing. Even worse, for most sites, the markup is almost entirely made up of tables and FONT tags, none of which conveys any real semantic meaning to what's being presented. From a structural standpoint, these pages are little better than random strings of letters.

For example, let's assume that for page titles, an author is using FONT tags instead of heading tags like H1, like this:

```
<FONT SIZE="+3" FACE="Helvetica" COLOR="red">Page Title</FONT>
```

Structurally speaking, the FONT tag has no meaning. This makes the document far less useful. What good is a FONT tag to a speech-synthesis browser, for example? If an author uses heading tags instead of FONT tags, the speaking browser can use a certain speaking style to read the text. With the FONT tag, the browser has no way to know that the text is any different from other text.

Why do authors run roughshod over structure and meaning like this? Because they want readers to see the page as they designed it. To use structural HTML markup is to give up a lot of control over a page's appearance, and it certainly doesn't allow for the kind of densely packed page designs that have become so popular over the years.

So what's wrong with this? Consider the following:

- Unstructured pages make content indexing inordinately difficult. A truly powerful search engine would allow users to search just page titles, or only section headings within pages, or only paragraph text, or perhaps only those paragraphs that are marked as being important. In order to do this, however, the page contents must be contained within some sort of structural markup— exactly the sort of markup most pages lack.

- A lack of structure reduces accessibility. Imagine that you are blind, and rely on a speech-synthesis browser to browse the Web. Which would you prefer: a structured page that lets your browser read only section headings so you can choose which section you'd like to hear more about; or a page so lacking in structure that your browser is forced to read the entire thing with no indication of what's a heading, what's a paragraph, and what's important?

- Advanced page presentation is only possible with some sort of document structure. Imagine a page in which only the section headings are shown, with an arrow next to each. The user can decide which section heading applies to him and click on it, thus revealing the text of that section.

- Structured markup is easier to maintain. How many times have you spent long minutes hunting through someone else's HTML (or even your own) in search of the one little error that is messing up your page in one browser or another? How much time have you spent writing nested tables and FONT tags, just to get a sidebar with white hyperlinks in it? How many line-break tags have you inserted trying to get exactly the right separation between a title and the following text? By using structural markup, you can clean up your code and make it easier to find what you're looking for.

Granted, a fully structured document is a little plain. Due to that one single fact, a hundred arguments in favor of structural markup wouldn't sway a marketing department away from the kind of HTML so prevalent at the end of the twentieth century. What was needed was a way to combine structural markup with attractive page presentation.

This concept is nothing new. There have been many style sheet technologies proposed and created over the last few decades. These were intended for use in various industries and in conjunction with a variety of structural markup languages. The concept had been tested, used, and generally found to be a benefit to any environment where structure had to be presented. However, no style sheet solution was immediately available for use with HTML. Something had to be done to correct this problem.

CSS to the Rescue

Of course, the problem of polluting HTML with presentational markup was not lost on the World Wide Web Consortium (W3C). It was recognized early on that this situation couldn't continue forever, and that a good solution was needed quickly. In 1995, they started publicizing a work-in-progress called CSS. By 1996, it had become a full Recommendation, with the same weight as HTML itself.

So what does CSS offer us? As of this writing, it offers us two levels of itself. The first level is Cascading Style Sheets, Level 1 (CSS1), which was made a full W3C Recommendation in 1996. Soon thereafter, the W3C's Cascading Style Sheets and Formatting Properties (CSS&FP) Working Group got to work on a more advanced specification, and in 1998 their work paid off when Cascading Style Sheets, Level 2 (CSS2) was made a full Recommendation. CSS2 builds on CSS1 by extending the earlier work without making major changes to it.

The future is likely to see further advances in CSS, but until then, let's go over what we already have.

Rich Styling

In the first place, CSS allows for much richer document appearances than HTML ever allowed, even at the height of its presentational fever. CSS contains the ability to set colors on text and in the background of any element; it permits the creation of borders around any element, as well as the increase or decrease of the space around them; it allows authors to change the way text is capitalized, decorated (e.g., underlining), its spacing, and even whether or not it is displayed at all; and many other effects.

Take, for example, the first (and main) heading on a page, which is usually the title of the page itself. The proper markup is:

```
<H1>Leaping Above The Water</H1>
```

Now, suppose you want this title to be dark red, use a certain font, be italicized and underlined, and have a yellow background. To do all of that with HTML, you'd have to put the H1 into a table and load it up with a ton of other tags like FONT and U. With CSS, all you need is one rule:

```
H1 {color: maroon; font: italic 1em Times, serif; text-decoration: underline;
    background: yellow;}
```

That's it. As you can see, everything we did in HTML can be done in CSS. There's no need to confine ourselves to only those things HTML can do, however:

```
H1 {color: maroon; font: italic 1em Times, serif; text-decoration: underline;
    background: yellow url(titlebg.png) repeat-x;
    border: 1px solid red; margin-bottom: 0; padding: 5px;}
```

Now we have an image in the background of the H1 that is only repeated horizontally, plus a border around the H1 that is separated from the text by at least five pixels, and we've removed the margin (blank space) from the bottom of the element. These are things which HTML can't even come close to matching—and that's just a taste of what CSS can do.

Ease of Use

If the depth of CSS doesn't convince you, then perhaps this will: style sheets can drastically reduce a web author's workload.

Style sheets can do this by centralizing the commands for certain visual effects in one handy place, instead of scattering them throughout the document. As an example, let's say you want all of the headings in a document to be purple. (No, I don't know why you would want this, but assume with me.) Using HTML, the way to do this would be to put a FONT tag in every heading tag, like so:

```
<H2><FONT COLOR="purple">This is purple!</FONT></H2>
```

This has to be done for every heading of level two. If you have forty headings in your document, you have to insert forty FONT tags throughout, one for each heading! That's a lot of work for one little effect.

But let's assume that you've gone ahead and put in all those FONT tags. You're done, you're happy—and then you decide (or your boss decides for you) that headings should really be dark green, not purple. Now you have to go back and fix every single one of those FONT tags. Sure, you might be able to find-and-replace, as long as headings are the only purple text in your document. If you've put other purple FONT tags in your document, then you *can't* find-and-replace, because you'd affect them too.

It would be much better to have a single rule instead:

```
H2 {color: purple;}
```

Not only is this faster to type, but it's easier to change. If you do switch from purple to dark green, all you have to change is that one rule.

Let's go back to the highly styled H1 element from the previous section:

```
H1 {color: maroon; font: italic 1em Times, serif; text-decoration: underline;
    background: yellow;}
```

This may look like it's worse to write than using HTML, but consider a case where you have a page with about a dozen H2 elements that should look the same as the H1. How much markup will be required for those 12 H2 elements? A lot. On the other hand, with CSS, all you need to do is this:

```
H1, H2 {color: maroon; font: italic 1em Times, serif; text-decoration: underline;
    background: yellow;}
```

Now the styles apply to both H1 and H2 elements, with just three extra keystrokes.

If you want to change the way H1 and H2 elements look, the advantages of CSS become even more striking. Consider how long it would take to change the HTML markup for all H1 and 12 H2 elements, compared to changing the previous styles to this:

```
H1, H2 {color: navy; font: bold 1em Helvetica, sans-serif;
    text-decoration: underline overline; background: silver;}
```

If the two approaches were timed on a stopwatch, I'm betting the CSS-savvy author would handily beat the HTML jockey.

In addition, most CSS rules are collected into one location in the document. It is possible to scatter them throughout the document by associated styles to individual elements, but it's usually far more efficient to place all of your styles into a single style sheet. This lets you create (or change) the appearance of an entire document in one place.

Using Your Styles on Multiple Pages

But wait—there's more! Not only can you centralize all of the style information for a page in one place, but you can also create a style sheet that can then be applied to multiple pages—as many as you like. This is done by a process in which a style sheet is saved to its own document, and then imported by any page for use with that document. Using this capability, you can quickly create a consistent look for an entire web site. All you have to do is link the single style sheet to all of the documents on your web site. Then, if you ever want to change the look of your site's pages, you need only edit a single file and the change will be propagated throughout the entire server—automatically!

Consider a site where all of the headings are gray on a white background. They get this color from a style sheet that says:

```
H1, H2, H3, H4, H5, H6 {color: gray; background: white;}
```

Now, let's say this site has 700 pages, each one of which uses the style sheet that says headings should be gray. At some point, it's decided that headings should be white on a gray background. So the site's webmaster edits the style sheet to say:

```
H1, H2, H3, H4, H5, H6 {color: white; background: gray;}
```

Then he saves the style sheet to disk, and the change is made. That sure beats having to edit 700 pages to enclose every heading in a table and a FONT tag, doesn't it?

Cascading

And that's not all! CSS also makes provisions for conflicting rules; these provisions are collectively referred to as *the cascade*. For instance, take the previous scenario in which you're importing a single style sheet into a whole bunch of web pages. Now inject a set of pages that share many of the same styles, but also have specialized rules that apply only to them. You can create another style sheet that is imported into those pages, in addition to the already existing style sheet, or you can just place the special styles into the pages that need them.

For example, you might have one page out of the 700 where headings should be yellow on dark blue instead of white on gray. In that single document, then, you could insert this rule:

```
H1, H2, H3, H4, H5, H6 {color: yellow; background: blue;}
```

Thanks to the cascade, this rule will override the imported rule for white-on-gray headings. By understanding the cascade rules and using them to your advantage, you can create highly sophisticated sheets that come together to give your pages a professional yet easily changed look.

This ability is not confined to just the author. Web surfers (or *readers*) can, in some browsers, create their own style sheets (called *reader style sheets*, oddly enough) that will cascade with the author's styles as well as the styles used by the browser. Thus, a reader who is color-blind could create a style that makes hyperlinks stand out:

```
A:link {color: white; background: black;}
```

A reader style sheet could contain almost anything: a directive to make text large enough to read, if the user has impaired vision; rules to remove images for faster reading and browsing; even styles to place the user's favorite picture in the background of every document. (This isn't recommended, of course, but it is possible.) This lets readers customize their web experience without having to turn off all of the author's styles.

Between importing, cascading, and its variety of effects, CSS becomes a wonderful tool for any author or reader.

Compact File Size

Besides the visual power of CSS and its ability to empower both author and reader, there is something else about it that your readers will like. It can help keep document sizes as small as possible, thereby speeding download times. How? As we've mentioned, a lot of pages have used tables and FONT tags to achieve nifty visual effects. Unfortunately, both of these methods create a lot of HTML markup, and that drives up file sizes. By grouping visual style information into central areas and representing those rules using a fairly compact syntax, you can remove the FONT tags and other bits of the usual tag soup. Thus, CSS can keep your load times low and your reader satisfaction high.

Preparing for the Future

HTML, as I previously pointed out, is a structural language, while CSS is its complement: a stylistic language. Recognizing this, the World Wide Web Consortium (W3C), the body that debates and approves standards for the Web, is beginning to remove stylistic tags from HTML. The reasoning for this move is that style sheets can be used to create the effects that certain HTML tags provide, so who needs them?

As of this writing, the HTML 4.0 specification has a number of tags that are deprecated; that is, they are in the process of being phased out of the language altogether. Eventually, they will be marked as obsolete, which means that browsers will be neither required nor encouraged to support them. Among the deprecated tags are <FONT>, <BASEFONT>, <U>, <STRIKE>, <S>, and <CENTER>. With the advent of style sheets, none of these HTML tags are necessary.

As if that weren't enough, there is the very strong possibility that HTML will be gradually replaced by the Extensible Markup Language (XML). XML is much more complicated than HTML, but it is also far more powerful and flexible. Despite this, XML does not, of itself, provide any way to declare style tags such as <I> or <CENTER>. Instead, it is quite probable that XML documents will rely on style sheets to determine the appearance of documents. While the style sheets used with XML may not be CSS, they will probably be whatever follows CSS and very closely resembles it. Therefore, learning CSS now will give authors a big advantage when the time comes to make the jump to an XML-based Web.

Limitations of CSS

There are a few areas that CSS1 does not address, and therefore are not covered in detail in this book; some of these topics are touched upon in Chapter 10, *CSS2: A Look Ahead*. Of course, even a full-blown CSS implementation, covering all of CSS1 and CSS2, would not meet every request from every page designer in the world. It's worth going through some of the boundaries of CSS.

Limited Initial Scope

When you get right down to it, CSS1 is not an overly complicated specification. The entire thing can be printed out in less than 100 pages, and it contains about

70 properties. It is still a very sophisticated and subtle engine, but some areas of web design were omitted from CSS1.

In the first place, CSS1 had almost nothing to say about tables. You might think that you can set margins on table cells, for example—and a web browser might even let you do so—but margins should not be applied to table cells under any circumstances. CSS2 introduced a new set of properties and behaviors for dealing with tables, but as of this writing, few if any of these are supported.

 To a certain degree, the omission of tables from CSS1 says a great deal about the feeling many have that tables should never be used to lay out pages. It is felt that floated and positioned elements should do all of the work tables used to do, and more. Whether this premise can be supported is not a discussion I intend to undertake here.

In a similar way, CSS1 contains nothing in the way of positioning. Sure, it's possible to move elements around a little bit, but mostly with negative margins and floating. Everything is, in a sense, relative. CSS2, on the other hand, has three chapters devoted to the visual rendering model, which includes the positioning of elements.

CSS1 makes no provision for downloadable fonts. This leads to a good deal of discussion about how to account for user system configurations and available fonts. CSS2 introduces some font-handling, but even there the issue is not resolved, mostly due to the lack of a widely supported font format. It may be that Scalable Vector Graphics (SVG) will solve some or all of this problem, but it is impossible at this point to say with any certainty.

Finally, there is a lack of media types in CSS1. In other words, CSS1 is primarily a screen-device language, intended to be used to put content onto a computer monitor. There is some thought toward paged media, like printouts, but not much. (Despite this, CSS1 is not a pixel-perfect control mechanism.) In an effort to overcome this limitation, CSS2 introduces media types, which makes it possible to create separate style sheets that are applied to a document depending on its display media. CSS2 also introduces properties and behavior specifically aimed at paged media and aural media.

Implementations

Sadly, the major drawback to using CSS is that it was so poorly implemented at first. Through a combination of miscommunication, misinterpretation, confusion, and poor quality control, the first browsers to attempt support of CSS did a rather poor job of it.

The worst offenders are Microsoft Internet Explorer 3.x and Netscape Navigator 4.x. The first in their respective lines to attempt CSS support, these browsers have incomplete, bug-ridden, and quite often contradictory implementations of CSS1, never mind CSS2. These implementations are so bad that it is difficult to consider them CSS-supporting at all. Some of their flaws are bad enough to cause the browser to crash, or even lock up an entire system, when trying to handle some styles.

With Internet Explorer 4.x and 5.x, things did improve. Although not perfect by any means, these browser versions did at least stomp out many of the bugs that plagued IE3, and also added some support for previously unrecognized CSS properties in both CSS1 and CSS2.

Opera 3.5, on the other hand, came out of the gate with impressive CSS support. Confining itself to CSS1, this browser did quite well with the properties that it supported, suffering only a few minor bugs. When 3.6 was released, almost all of these bugs were eliminated, although support did not move past CSS1. Before version 3.5, Opera did not support CSS at all.

As for Netscape's products, the Navigator 4.7 is not significantly better at CSS support than was version 4.0, although it's at least less crash-prone. The only real hope for good CSS support out of Netscape is their Gecko rendering engine. As this was being written, the latest builds of Gecko were quite excellent, and were in fact used (along with Internet Explorer 4.5 and 5.0 for Macintosh) to create many of the figures in this book.

Since CSS is not intended to provide total control over document display, and should allow the page's content to come through no matter what browser is being used, this general state of affairs should not be considered a barrier to the use of CSS. You may wish, however, to warn your users that if they are using browsers of a certain vintage (Explorer 3.x, and perhaps Navigator 4.x) that they go into their preferences and disable style sheets. That way, they'll at least be able to read the content of your pages, even if it isn't styled the way you might have hoped.

Bringing CSS and HTML Together

We keep visiting the point that HTML documents have an inherent structure. In fact, that's part of the problem with the Web today: too many of us forget that documents are supposed to have an internal structure, which is altogether different than a visual structure. In our rush to create the coolest-looking pages on the Web, we've bent, warped, and generally ignored the idea that pages should contain information that has some structural meaning.

However, that structure is an inherent part of the relationship between HTML and CSS; without the structure, there couldn't be a relationship at all. In order to understand it better, let's look at an example HTML document and break it down by pieces. Here's the markup, shown in Figure 1-1:

```
<HTML>
<HEAD>
    <TITLE>Eric's World of Waffles</TITLE>
    <LINK REL="stylesheet" TYPE="text/css" HREF="sheet1.css" TITLE="Default">
    <STYLE TYPE="text/css">
        @import url(sheet2.css);
        H1 {color: maroon;}
        BODY {background: yellow;}
        /* These are my styles! Yay! */
    </STYLE>
</HEAD>
<BODY>
    <H1>Waffles!</H1>
    <P STYLE="color: gray;">The most wonderful of all breakfast foods is
    the waffle-- a ridged and cratered slab of home-cooked, fluffy
    goodness...
    </P>
</BODY>
</HTML>
```

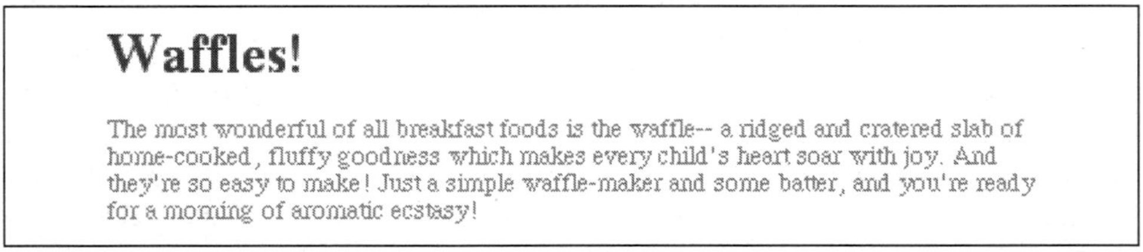

Waffles!

The most wonderful of all breakfast foods is the waffle-- a ridged and cratered slab of home-cooked, fluffy goodness which makes every child's heart soar with joy. And they're so easy to make! Just a simple waffle-maker and some batter, and you're ready for a morning of aromatic ecstasy!

Figure 1-1. A simple document

Now, let's examine each portion of the document.

The LINK Tag

```
<LINK REL="stylesheet" TYPE="text/css" HREF="sheet1.css" TITLE="Default">
```

First we consider the use of the LINK tag. The LINK tag is a little-regarded but nonetheless perfectly valid tag that has been hanging around the HTML specification for years, just waiting to be put to good use. Its basic purpose is to allow HTML authors to associate other documents with the document containing the LINK tag. CSS1 uses it to link style sheets to the HTML document; in Figure 1-2, a style sheet called *sheet1.css* is linked to the document.

These style sheets, which are not part of the HTML document but are still used by it, are referred to as *external style sheets*. This is due to the fact that they're style sheets but are external to the HTML document. (Go figure.)

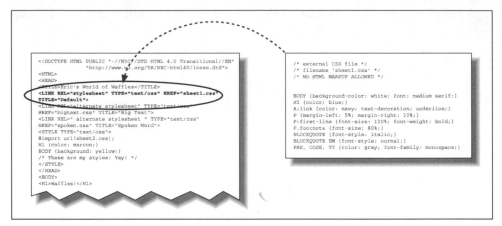

Figure 1-2. A representation of how external style sheets are applied to documents

In order to successfully load an external style sheet, **LINK** must be placed inside the **HEAD** element but may not be placed inside any other element, rather like **TITLE** or **STYLE**. This will cause the web browser to locate and load the style sheet and use whatever styles it contains to render the HTML document, in the manner shown in Figure 1-2.

And what is the format of an external style sheet? It's simply a list of rules, just like those we saw in the previous section and in the example above, but in this case, the rules are saved into their own file. Just remember that no HTML or any other markup language can be included in the style sheet—only style rules. Here's the markup of an external style sheet:

```
H1 {color: red;}
H2 {color: maroon; background: white;}
H3 {color: white; background: black; font: medium Helvetica;}
```

That's all there is to it—no **STYLE** tags, no HTML tags at all, just plain-and-simple style declarations. These are saved into a plain text file and are usually given an extension of *.css*, as in *sheet1.css*.

The filename extension is not required, but some browsers won't recognize the file as containing a style sheet unless it actually ends with *.css*, even if you *do* include the correct **TYPE** of `text/css` in the **LINK** element. So make sure you name your style sheets appropriately.

LINK attributes

For the rest of the **LINK** tag, the attributes and values are fairly straightforward. **REL** stands for "relation," and in this case, the relation is "stylesheet." **TYPE** is always set to `text/css`. This value describes the type of data that is to be loaded using the **LINK** tag. That way, the web browser knows that the style sheet is a CSS style sheet, a fact that will determine how the browser deals with the data it imports. After all, there may be other style languages in the future, so it will be important to say which language you're using.

Next we find the `HREF` attribute. The value of this attribute is the URL of your style sheet. This URL can be either absolute or relative, depending on what works for you. In our example, of course, the URL is relative. It could as easily have been something like *http://www.style.org/sheet1.css*.

Finally, there is the `TITLE` attribute. This attribute is not often used, but it could become important in the future. Why? It becomes important when there is more than one `LINK` tag—and there can be more than one. In these cases, however, only those `LINK` tags with a `REL` of `stylesheet` will be used in the initial display of the document. Thus, if you wanted to link in two style sheets with the names *basic.css* and *splash.css*, the markup would look like this:

```
<LINK REL="stylesheet" TYPE="text/css" HREF="basic.css">
<LINK REL="stylesheet" TYPE="text/css" HREF="splash.css">
```

This will cause the browser to load both style sheets, combine the rules from each, and apply the result to the document (see Figure 1-3). We'll see exactly how the sheets are combined in the next chapter, but for now, let's just accept that they're combined. For example:

```
<LINK REL="stylesheet" TYPE="text/css" HREF="sheet-a.css">
<LINK REL="stylesheet" TYPE="text/css" HREF="sheet-b.css">

<P CLASS="a1">This paragraph will be gray only if styles from the
stylesheet 'sheet-a.css' are applied.</P>
<P CLASS="b1">This paragraph will be gray only if styles from the
stylesheet 'sheet-b.css' are applied.</P>
```

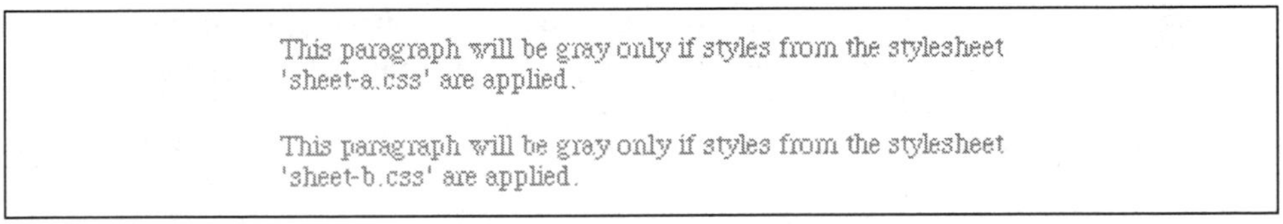

This paragraph will be gray only if styles from the stylesheet 'sheet-a.css' are applied.

This paragraph will be gray only if styles from the stylesheet 'sheet-b.css' are applied.

Figure 1-3. Combining linked style sheets

It's also possible to define alternate style sheets. These are marked with a `REL` of `alternate stylesheet` and come into play only if they're selected by the reader.

Alternate style sheets

Unfortunately, as of this writing, browsers don't make it very easy to select alternate style sheets, assuming that they can do so at all. Should a browser be able to use alternate style sheets, it will use the values of the `TITLE` attributes to generate a list of style alternatives. So you could write the following:

```
<LINK REL="stylesheet" TYPE="text/css"
 HREF="sheet1.css" TITLE="Default">
```

```
<LINK REL="alternate stylesheet" TYPE="text/css"
 HREF="bigtext.css" TITLE="Big Text">
<LINK REL=" alternate stylesheet " TYPE="text/css"
 HREF="spoken.css" TITLE="Spoken Word">
```

Users could then pick the style they wanted to use, and the browser would switch from the first one (labeled "Default" in this case) to whichever the reader picked. Figure 1-4 shows one way in which this selection mechanism might be accomplished.

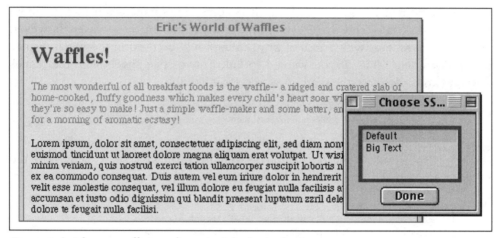

Figure 1-4. A browser offering alternate style sheet selection

Alternate styles sheets are only supported by one browser as of this writing—Internet Explorer for Macintosh—and that only with a Java-Script widget, which does not ship with the browser. None of the three major browsers natively supports the selection of alternate style sheets (shown in Figure 1-4).

As of this writing, the one browser that does recognize alternate style sheets (Internet Explorer for Macintosh) will not apply the styles from any LINK element with a REL of `alternate stylesheet` unless that style sheet is selected by the user.

The STYLE Element

The STYLE element, which is a relatively new element in HTML, is the most common way to define a style sheet, since it appears in the document itself. STYLE should always use the attribute TYPE; in the case of a CSS1 document, the correct value is `text/css`, just as it was with the LINK tag. So, the STYLE container should always start with `<STYLE TYPE="text/css">`. This is followed by one or more styles and finished with a closing `</STYLE>` tag.

The styles between the opening and closing `STYLE` tags are referred to as the *document style sheet* or the *embedded style sheet*, since this style sheet is embedded within the document. It contains styles that apply to the document, but it can also contain multiple links to external style sheets using the `@import` directive.

The @import Directive

Now for the stuff that is found inside the `STYLE` tag. First, we have something very similar to `LINK`: the `@import` directive. Just like `LINK`, `@import` can be used to direct the web browser to load an external style sheet and use its styles in the rendering of the HTML document. The only real difference is in the actual syntax of the command and its placement. As you can see, `@import` is found inside the `STYLE` container. It must be placed there, before the other CSS rules, or else it won't work at all.

```
<STYLE TYPE="text/css">
@import url(styles.css); /* @import comes first */
H1 {color: gray;}
</STYLE>
```

Like `LINK`, there can be more than one `@import` statement in a document. Unlike `LINK`, however, the style sheets of every `@import` directive will always be loaded and used. So given the following, all three external style sheets will be loaded, and all of their style rules will be used in the display of this document:

```
@import url(sheet2.css);
@import url(blueworld.css);
@import url(zany.css);
```

 Only Internet Explorer 4.x/5.x and Opera 3.x support `@import`; Navigator 4.x ignores this method of applying styles to a document. This can actually be used to one's advantage in "hiding" styles from these browsers. See Chapter 11, *CSS in Action*, for more details.

Actual Styles

```
H1 {color: maroon;}
BODY {background: yellow;}
```

After the `@import` statement in our example, we find some ordinary styles. What they mean doesn't actually matter for this discussion, although you can probably guess that they set H1 elements to be maroon and BODY elements to have a yellow background.

Styles such as these comprise the bulk of any embedded style sheet—style rules both simple and complex, short and long. It will be only rarely that you have a document where the STYLE element does not contain any rules.

For those of you concerned about making your documents accessible to older browsers, there is an important warning to be made. You're probably aware that browsers ignore tags they don't recognize; for example, if a web page contains a BLOOPER tag, browsers will completely ignore the tag because it isn't a tag they recognize.

The same will be true with style sheets. If a browser does not recognize <STYLE> and </STYLE>, it will ignore them altogether. However, the declarations within those tags will *not* be ignored, because they will appear to be ordinary text so far as the browser is concerned. So your style declarations will appear at the top of your page! (Of course, the browser should ignore the text because it isn't part of the BODY element, but this is never the case.) This problem is illustrated in Figure 1-5.

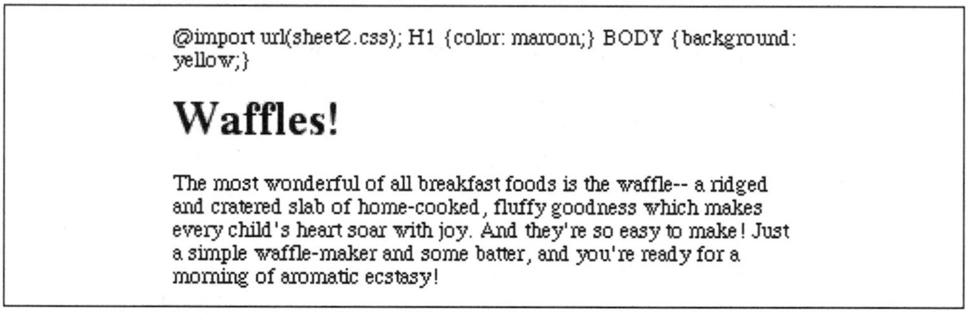

@import url(sheet2.css); H1 {color: maroon;} BODY {background: yellow;}

Waffles!

The most wonderful of all breakfast foods is the waffle-- a ridged and cratered slab of home-cooked, fluffy goodness which makes every child's heart soar with joy. And they're so easy to make! Just a simple waffle-maker and some batter, and you're ready for a morning of aromatic ecstasy!

Figure 1-5. Older browsers will literally display your style sheets

In order to combat this problem, it is recommended that you enclose your declarations in a comment tag. In the example given here, the beginning of the comment tag appears right after the opening STYLE tag, and the end of the comment appears right before the closing STYLE tag:

```
<STYLE type="text/css"><!--
@import url(sheet2.css);
H1 {color: maroon;}
BODY {background: yellow;}
--></STYLE>
```

This should cause older browsers to completely ignore not only the STYLE tags but the declarations as well, because HTML comments are not displayed. Meanwhile, those browsers that understand CSS will still be able to read the style sheet.

There is one drawback to this strategy. A few versions of older browsers, such as very early versions of Netscape Navigator and NCSA Mosaic, had some trouble with comments. The problems ranged from mangled display to browser crashes. This happened with only a very few browser versions, and it's safe to say that very few of these browsers are still being operated. Be aware that there are some people out there using these particular browsers, and they may well have major problems viewing your page if you use these comment tags.

CSS Comments

```
/* These are my styles! Yay! */
```

CSS also allows for comments, but it uses a completely different syntax to accomplish this. CSS comments are very similar to C/C++ comments, in that they are surrounded by /* and */:

```
/* This is a CSS1 comment */
```

Comments can span multiple lines, just as in C++:

```
/* This is a CSS1 comment, and it
can be several lines long without
any problem whatsoever. */
```

It's important to remember that CSS comments cannot be nested. So, for example, this would not be correct:

```
/* This is a comment, in which we find
another comment, which is WRONG
    /* Another comment */
and back to the first comment */
```

However, it's hardly ever desirable to nest comments, so this limitation is no big deal.

If you wish to place comments on the same line as markup, then you need to be careful about how you place them. For example, this is the correct way to do it:

```
H1 {color: gray;}    /* This CSS comment is several lines */
H2 {color: silver;} /* long, but since it is alongside */
P {color: white;}    /* actual styles, each line needs to */
PRE {color: gray;} /* be wrapped in comment markers. */
```

Given this example, if each line isn't marked off, then most of the style sheet will become part of the comment, and so will not work:

```
H1 {color: gray;}    /* This CSS comment is several lines
H2 {color: silver;}    long, but since it is not wrapped
```

```
P {color: white;}    in comment markers, the last three
PRE {color: gray;}   styles are part of the comment. */
```

In this example, only the first rule (H1 {color: gray;}) will be applied to the document. The rest of the rules, as part of the comment, are ignored by the browser's rendering engine.

Moving on with our example, we see some more CSS information actually found inside an HTML tag!

Inline Styles

```
<P STYLE="color: gray;">The most wonderful of all breakfast foods is
the waffle-- a ridged and cratered slab of home-cooked, fluffy goodness...
</P>
```

For cases where you want to simply assign a few styles to one individual element, without the need for embedded or external style sheets, you'll employ the HTML attribute STYLE to set an *inline style*. The STYLE attribute is new to HTML, and it can be associated with any HTML tag whatsoever, except for those tags which are found outside of BODY (HEAD or TITLE, for instance).

The syntax of a STYLE attribute is fairly ordinary. In fact, it looks very much like the declarations found in the STYLE container, except here the curly brackets are replaced by double quotation marks. So <P STYLE="color: maroon; background: yellow;"> will set the text color to be maroon and the background to be yellow *for that paragraph only*. No other part of the document will be affected by this declaration.

Summary

In order to facilitate a return to structural HTML, something was needed to permit authors to specify how a document should be displayed. CSS fills that need very nicely, and far better than the various presentational HTML elements ever did (or probably could have done). For the first time in years, there is hope that web pages can become more structural, not less, and at the same time the promise that they can have a more sophisticated look than ever before.

In order to ensure that this transition goes as smoothly as possible, HTML introduces a number of ways to link HTML and CSS together while still keeping them distinct. This allows authors to simplify document appearance management and maximize their effectiveness, thereby making their jobs a little easier. The further benefits of improving accessibility and positioning documents for a switch to an XML world make CSS a compelling technology.

As for user agent support, the LINK element has been universally supported, as have both the STYLE element and attribute. @import didn't fare so well, though, being ignored outright by Navigator 4. This is not such a major tragedy, annoying though it might be, since the `LINK` element will still let you bring external style sheets into play.

In order to fully understand how CSS can do all of this, authors need a firm grasp of how CSS handles document structure, how one writes rules that behave as expected, and most of all, what the "Cascading" part of the name really means.

2

Selectors and Structure

The life of a web designer can be pretty rough at times. How many times have you slaved over a new design, guided it through 17 committees and 4 major revisions, and finally come up with something that everyone seems to like, when a vice-presidential voice suddenly says, "I'm concerned about the shade of green we're using for our headings. Could we see some versions of the site using a few lighter shades, and maybe a couple of darker shades as well?"

Well, now you're faced with the necessity of scheduling another meeting so you can go back to your computer and produce new versions of the design, replacing all of your `<FONT COLOR="green">` tags with new ones that have different shades of green. Meanwhile, all the other administrators have started to think of their own ways to nitpick the design to death. Maybe the headings should be dark blue instead of green, or perhaps the sidebar's background is the wrong color, or maybe the company logo ought to be used for list-item bullets instead of those little black dots that everyone else uses.

So, at the next design meeting, after everyone's agreed that such-and-so shade of green is a good one, all these new revision ideas start popping up, and all the administrators are nodding gravely and saying, why yes, maybe we should see a design which uses shades of red, not green. The downward spiral has begun.

Even if you're lucky enough to work in a place where you don't have to tolerate such nonsense, you probably pose similar questions to yourself while you're working on your design. Does the particular blue you're using for your sidebar's background contrast enough with your yellow links? Would the headings all look better if they were red instead of green? What if the paragraphs were in one font and the headings in another? The only way to find out is to fiddle with `FONT` tags and `BGCOLOR` attributes. That can take forever if you have a lot of documents, or a really complicated design, and if you suddenly head in a different direction, you can spend almost as much time cleaning up the residue of your old assumptions as you do on actual creative design work.

Style sheets offer an easy, convenient, and powerful way to break out of this morass. One of the primary advantages that CSS offers to designers is its ability to easily apply a set of styles to all elements of the same type. This may not sound like much, but consider: with the edit of a single line of CSS, you can change the colors of all your headings. Don't like the blue you're using? Change that one line of code, and the headings can all be purple, or yellow, or maroon, or any other color you desire. Design time is reduced by cutting out the grunt work, allowing you to focus on being creative. The next time you're in a meeting and someone wants to see headings with a different shade of green, just edit your page's styles and hit reload. *Voilà!* The results of that change are right there for everyone to see, and it only took seconds to accomplish, instead of requiring another meeting.

Of course, CSS can't solve all your problems—you can't use it to change the color of your GIFs, for example—but it can make your life a lot easier than it has been. It does this with selectors and structure, the first of which is used to make changes that take advantage of the second.

Basic Rules

Central to CSS is the ability to apply certain rules to the same types of elements in a document, which can drastically reduce the amount of work an author has to undertake. For example, let's say that you wish to make the text of all H2 elements appear gray. Using straight HTML, you'd have to do this by inserting <FONT color="gray">...</FONT> tags in all your H2 elements, something like this:

```
<H2><FONT COLOR="gray">This is H2 text</FONT></H2>
```

If you have a document with a lot of H2 elements, this can become very tedious to type. If you later decide that you want to change all the H2s to be green instead of gray, then the task becomes even worse because you have to find all of those H2s and change the value of each and every FONT tag to be gray.

In CSS, you can avoid all that hassle, and still get the effects you want in a way that makes them easy to change. In the document's style sheet, you need only define the following to get the same result:

```
H2 {color: gray;}
```

Altogether, this is known as a *rule*. This single rule is enough to cause all H2 elements to be colored gray. If you want to change this to another color, then the alteration of this single rule will affect all H2s in the document:

```
H2 {color: silver;}
```

Rule Structure

In order to understand this in more detail, let's break down the structure of a rule.

Each rule has two parts, the *selector* and the *declaration*. At a finer level, each declaration is actually a combination of properties and values. Every style sheet is made up of a series of rules, but rules do not always appear in style sheets.

First, however, let's break down our example rule into its various parts, as shown in Figure 2-1.

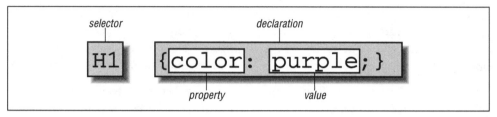

Figure 2-1. The structure of a rule

As you can see, on the left side of the rule, we find the selector. A selector is simply the part of the rule that selects the parts of the document to which the styles should be applied. In this case, H1 elements are selected. If the selector shown here were P, then all P (paragraph) elements would be selected, and H1 elements would not.

On the right side of the rule, we have the declaration. This is a combination of a CSS property and a value of that property. In Figure 2-1, the declaration says that this rule will cause parts of the document to have a **color** of **purple**. The parts that will be purple are those shown in the selector (in this case, all H1 elements).

Simple Selectors

A selector is most often an HTML element, but it can be other things. For example, if a CSS file contains styles for an XML document, it might look something like this:

```
QUOTE {color: gray;}
BIB {color: red;}
BOOKTITLE {color: purple;}
MYElement {color: red;}
```

In other words, the most basic kind of selector for a document is one of the elements of that document. In XML, this could be anything. If you're styling an HTML document, on the other hand, then you will generally use one of the many HTML elements such as P, H3, EM, A, or even BODY, like this:

```
BODY {color: black;}
H1 {color: purple;}
```

```
H3 {color: gray;}
STRONG {color: red;}
EM {color: maroon;}
```

The results of this style sheet are shown, with the obvious limitations imposed by grayscale printing, in Figure 2-2.

Figure 2-2. Simple styling of a document

This ability to apply styles to elements is obviously very powerful. It also makes it simple to shift styles from one type of element to another. Let's say we have a page design where H2 elements arc gray:

```
H2 {color: gray;}
```

Okay, not bad, but the more you look at this, the less you like it. You eventually decide that you actually want your paragraph text to be gray, not your H2 text. No problem! All you have to do is change the selector from H2 to P, and you'll have shifted the style from H2 elements to P (paragraph) elements:

```
P {color: gray;}
```

For the moment, that takes care of the left side of CSS rules. Let's examine the right side, where the declaration lives, before we return to selectors for some added features.

Declarations

A declaration is always formatted as a *property* followed by a colon, and then a *value*. Finally, the declaration is terminated with a semicolon (;). The value can be a single *keyword*, or a space-separated list of one or more *keywords* that are permitted for that property. If an incorrect property is used in a declaration, the entire declaration is ignored. Thus, the following declaration would be ignored because, while the value is correct, the property is not:

```
brain-size: 2cm;
```

If an incorrect value is used, then in most cases, only that value should be ignored—although it is possible to invalidate an entire rule with an incorrect value. This is less likely with many browsers, however, because most of them are fairly tolerant of mistakes in CSS: they'll just drop unrecognized values and use the rest of the declaration, instead of ignoring the whole thing. (While this sounds like a polite thing to do, it unfortunately makes it much easier for authors to pick up bad authoring habits.)

In an instance where you can use more than one keyword for a property's value, then the keywords are usually separated by spaces. Not every property can accept multiple keywords, but many can: for example, the `font` property. Should you wish to define paragraphs to use medium-size Helvetica for their text, then the rule would be as follows:

```
P {font: medium Helvetica;}
```

Note the space between `medium` and `Helvetica`, each of which is a keyword (the first for the font's size and the second for the actual font name, of course). The space allows the user agent to distinguish between the two keywords and apply them correctly. The final semicolon indicates that the rule has been concluded.

The reason we refer to these space-separated words as keywords is that, taken together, they all form the value of the property in question. For instance, consider the following fictional rule:

```
rainbow: red orange yellow green blue indigo violet;
```

There is no such property as `rainbow`, of course, and many of the colors used aren't valid either, but it will be useful for illustrative purposes. What we have is a case where the value of `rainbow` is `red orange yellow green blue indigo violet`. The seven keywords add up to a single, unique value. We can redefine the value for `rainbow` as follows:

```
rainbow: infrared red orange yellow green blue indigo violet ultraviolet;
```

Now we have a different value for `rainbow`, but this time it's composed of nine keywords instead of seven. Despite their seeming similarity, these two values are as unique and different as the values zero and one.

There are a few instances where keywords are separated by something other than a space. `font` is an excellent example of this, as it happens: there is exactly one place where a forward-slash (/) can be used to separate two specific keywords. Here's an example:

```
H2 {font: large/150% sans-serif;}
```

The slash separates the font size and the line-height. This is the only place the slash can appear in the `font` declaration. All of the other keywords allowed for `font` are separated by spaces.

That's basically all there is to simple declarations, just as there wasn't much to say about simple selectors. We aren't limited to such simple operations, though. In fact, let's find out just how powerful CSS can be.

Grouping

So far, things have been pretty simple—as long as you only want to apply a single style to a single selector, that is. No doubt you'll want to go further than that, though: sometimes you'll want the same style to apply to multiple elements, which means you'll want to use more than one selector, and other times, you'll want to apply more than one style to an element or group of elements.

Grouping Selectors

Let's say you have a document in which both H2 elements and paragraphs should have gray text. The easiest way to accomplish this is to use the following.

```
H2, P {color: gray;}
```

By placing both the H2 and P selectors on the left side of the rule and separating them with a comma, we've defined a rule where the style on the right (`color: gray;`) is applied to both selectors. The comma tells the browser that there are two different selectors involved in the rule. Leaving out the comma would give the rule a completely different meaning, which we'll explore later, in the section titled "Contextual Selectors."

It is possible to group any number of selectors together. If you wanted to make sure that every element in your document had a color of gray, you might use the following rule:

```
BODY, TABLE, TH, TD, H1, H2, H3, H4, P, PRE, STRONG, EM, B, I {color: gray;}
```

As you can tell, grouping allows an author to drastically compact certain types of style assignments which might otherwise result in a very long style sheet. The following two alternatives will have exactly the same result, but it's pretty obvious which one is easier to type:

```
H1 {color: purple;}
H2 {color: purple;}
H3 {color: purple;}
H4 {color: purple;}
H5 {color: purple;}
H6 {color: purple;}
```

or:

```
H1, H2, H3, H4, H5, H6 {color: purple;}
```

Grouping can make for some interesting choices. For example, all of the style sheets in the following example are equivalent—each merely shows a different way of grouping both selectors and declarations—and any of them will yield the result shown in Figure 2-3:

```
H1 {color: purple; background: white;}
H2 {color: purple; background: green;}
```

```
H3 {color: white; background: green;}
H4 {color: purple; background: white;}
B {color: red; background: white;}

H1, H2, H4 {color: purple;}
H2, H3 {background: green;}
H1, H4, B {background: white;}
H3 {color: white;}
B {color: red;}

H1, H4 {color: purple; background: white;}
H2 {color: purple;}
H3 {color: white;}
H2, H3 {background: green;}
B {color: red; background: white;}
```

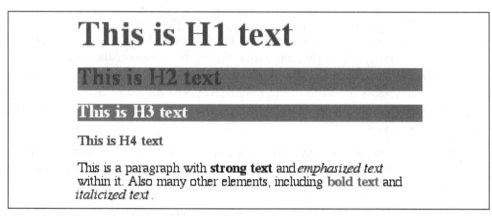

Figure 2-3. The result of equivalent style sheets

Grouping Declarations

Since it is possible to group selectors together into a single rule, it makes sense
that you can also group declarations. The importance of using the semicolon to
end each declaration becomes even more clear once we consider the fact that
there can be more than one declaration in a given rule. This helps keep style
sheets compact, organized, and easier to read. For example, assume that you want
all H1 elements to have purple text on an aqua background, and use 18-point Helvetica for the font. You could write your styles like this:

```
H1 {font: 18pt Helvetica;}
H1 {color: purple;}
H1 {background: aqua;}
```

That's rather inefficient, though—imagine having to do this for an element to
which you're assigning 10 or 15 styles! Instead, you can group your declarations
together:

```
H1 {font: 18pt Helvetica; color: purple; background: aqua;}
```

This will have exactly the same effect as the three-line style sheet shown before, yielding the result shown in Figure 2-4.

This is H1 text

Figure 2-4. Grouping declarations

When you group declarations together into a single rule, the semicolons are used to separate the declarations. This is especially important since whitespace is ignored in style sheets, so the user agent (UA) must rely on correct syntax to parse a style sheet. There is nothing wrong with formatting your styles like this:

```
H1 {
    font:       18pt Helvetica;
    color:      purple;
    background:   aqua;
}
```

If the second semicolon is omitted, the user agent will interpret the style sheet as follows:

```
H1 {
    font: 18pt Helvetica;
    color: purple background: aqua;
}
```

Since **background:** is not a valid value for `color`, and also since `color` can be given only one keyword, the entire statement should be ignored completely. A user agent in this case might incorrectly render H1s as purple text without an aqua background. However, since only a single keyword is permitted for `color`, the user agent should ignore the entire declaration as being invalid, meaning that you won't even get purple H1s; instead, they'll be the default color (usually black) with no background at all. The declaration `font: 18pt Helvetica` will still take effect, since it was correctly terminated with a semicolon, but the other styles shouldn't work at all.

 While it is not technically necessary to follow the last declaration of a rule with a semicolon, it is generally good practice to do so. In the first place, it will keep you in the habit of terminating your declarations with semicolons, the lack of which is one of the most common ways to cause errors in rendering. Second, if you decide to add another declaration to a rule, you don't have to worry about forgetting to insert an extra semicolon. Finally, some older browsers such as Internet Explorer 3.x have a greater tendency to become confused if the semicolon is omitted from the final declaration in a rule. My advice is to avoid all these problems and always follow a declaration with a semicolon.

As with selector grouping, declaration grouping is a convenient way to keep your style sheets short, expressive, and easy to maintain. The following example shows two ways of assigning six different styles to H1 elements. The first uses a separate rule for each property, and the second uses declaration grouping to apply all six styles to a single selector. The primary advantage of the second method is that it allows you to change the element to which the styles are applied by editing one selector, instead of six. Either way, though, you'll get the result depicted in Figure 2-5:

```
H1 {color: gray;}
H1 {background: white;}
H1 {border: 1px solid black;}
H1 {padding: 0.5em;}
H1 {font: 20pt Charcoal,sans-serif;}
H1 {text-transform: capitalize;}
```

```
H1 {color: gray; background: white; border: 1px solid black; padding: 0.5em;
    font: 20pt Charcoal,sans-serif; text-transform: capitalize;}
```

Figure 2-5. With or without grouping, the results are the same

Grouping Everything

All right, so we can group selectors, and we can group declarations. By combining both kinds of grouping in single rules, it is possible to define very complex styles using only a few statements. Let's assume that we wish to assign some complex styles to all of the headings in a document. Thus:

```
H1, H2, H3, H4, H5, H6 {color: gray; background: white; padding: 0.5em;
    border: 1px solid black; font-family: Charcoal,sans-serif;}
```

The grouping of the selectors means that the styles on the right side of the rule will be applied to all the headings listed, and the grouping of declarations means that all of the listed styles will be applied to the selectors on the left side of the rule. The result of this rule is shown in Figure 2-6.

This approach is obviously preferable to the alternative, which would start out something like this and would continue for quite a while:

```
H1 {color: gray;}
H2 {color: gray;}
H3 {color: gray;}
H4 {color: gray;}
H5 {color: gray;}
```

```
H6 {color: gray;}
H1 {background: white;}
H2 {background: white;}
H3 {background: white;}
```

You can write your styles like this, of course, if that's what you really want to do—but I wouldn't recommend it. The problems you'd face in trying to edit your styles would be almost as bad as if you were back to using FONT tags everywhere!

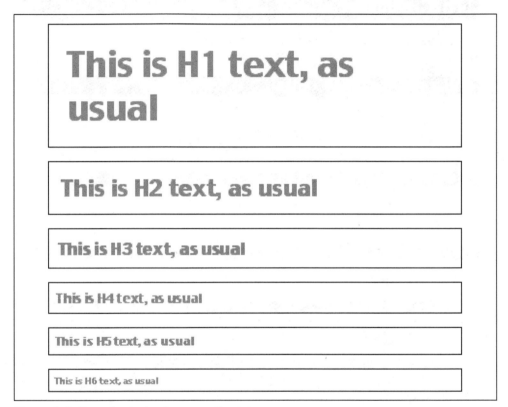

Figure 2-6. Grouping both selectors and rules

It's largely thanks to grouping that CSS files look the way they do. Here is a typical style sheet, with Figure 2-7 showing the result:

```
BODY {background: white; color: gray;}
H1, H2, H3, H4, H5, H6 {font-family: Helvetica, sans-serif;
  color: white; background: black;}
H1, H2, H3 {border: 2px solid gray; font-weight: bold;}
H4, H5, H6 {border: 1px solid gray;}
P, TABLE {color: gray; font-family: Times, serif;}
PRE {margin: 1em; color: maroon;}
```

For all the power and complexity we've introduced, there is even more with regard to selectors. It's possible to add more expression to selectors, and in so

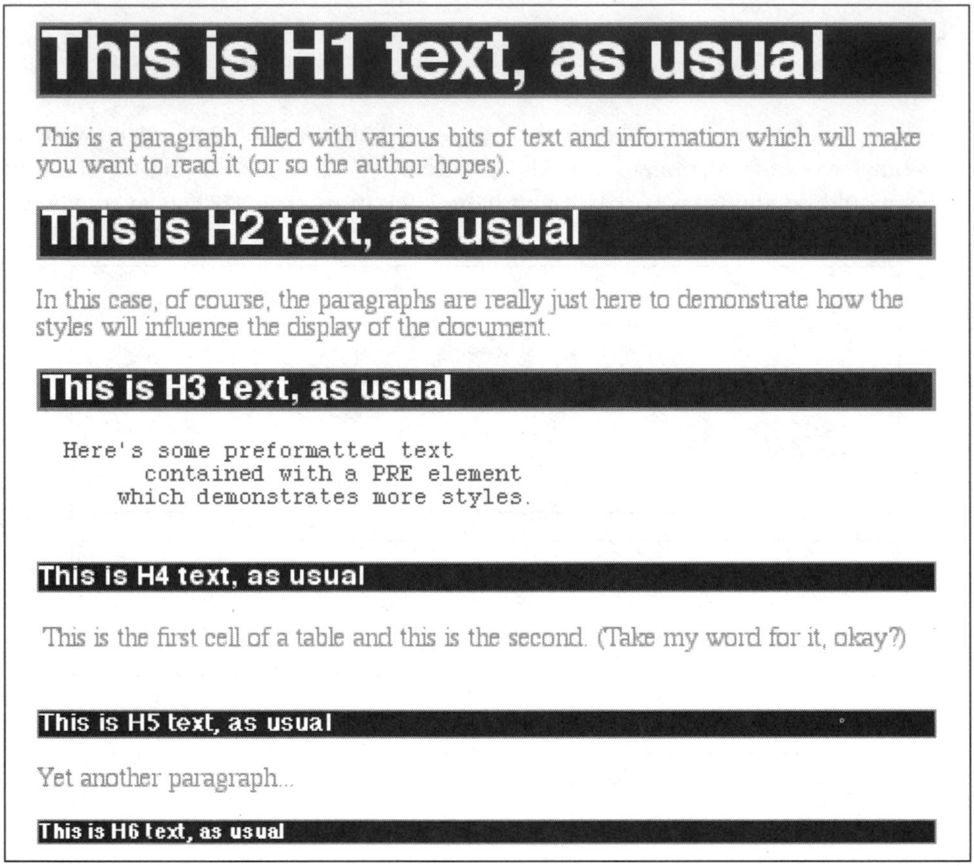

This is H1 text, as usual

This is a paragraph, filled with various bits of text and information which will make you want to read it (or so the author hopes).

This is H2 text, as usual

In this case, of course, the paragraphs are really just here to demonstrate how the styles will influence the display of the document.

This is H3 text, as usual

```
    Here's some preformatted text
            contained with a PRE element
        which demonstrates more styles.
```

This is H4 text, as usual

This is the first cell of a table and this is the second. (Take my word for it, okay?)

This is H5 text, as usual

Yet another paragraph...

This is H6 text, as usual

Figure 2-7. The result of a typical style sheet

doing, apply styles in a way that cuts across elements in favor of types of information. Of course, to get something so powerful, you'll have to do a little work in return, but it's well worth it.

Class and ID Selectors

So far, we've been grouping selectors and declarations together in a variety of ways, but for all that, the selectors we've been using are very simple ones. They only refer to document elements, and while that's often just what you need, there are times when something a little more specialized is required.

In addition to raw document elements, there are two other kinds of selectors: *class* and *ID* selectors, which allow the assignment of styles in a way that is independent of document elements. These selectors can be used on their own or in conjunction with element selectors. However, they only work if you've marked up your document appropriately, so using them generally involves a little forethought and planning.

Of course, you probably want to know why you should go to the effort. What will it get you? Let's consider a document about the handling of plutonium, in which there are various warnings on things to do (or not do) while working with such a dangerous substance. You want to make each warning use boldface text so that it will stand out from everything else.

However, you don't know what kind of elements these warnings will be. Sometimes there will be a whole paragraph of warning text, but other times there might be a single warning list item out of a lengthy list, or just a given section of a paragraph. In any case, you can't define a rule using simple selectors of any kind. If you did this:

```
P {font-weight: bold;}
```

then *all* paragraphs will be bold, not just those that contain warnings. You need a way to only select the paragraphs that are warnings, or more precisely, a way to select only those *elements* that are warnings.

Another scenario involves ways of styling different kinds of links. You might wish to set a different color for links that point to pages not found on your site. Once more, you can't just write:

```
A {color: maroon;}
```

because that will select *all* anchors, regardless of whether they point to pages on your site or off it.

So what we need is a way to apply styles to parts of the document that have been marked in a certain way, independent of the elements involved—and that's just what CSS gives us.

Class Selectors

The most common way to apply styles without worrying about the elements involved is to use *class selectors*. Before you can use them, however, you need to modify your actual document markup so that the class selectors will work. Why? Since we aren't going to be selecting according to the elements, we need something else to grab onto. Enter the CLASS attribute:

```
<P CLASS="warning">While handling plutonium, care must be taken to avoid
the formation of a critical mass.</P>
<P>During this step, <SPAN CLASS="warning">the possibility of implosion is
very real, and must be avoided at all costs</SPAN>. This can be accomplished
by keeping the various masses separate...</P>
```

In order to associate the styles of a class selector to an element, that element must have the appropriate value set to a CLASS attribute. In the previous code, we've assigned a class value of `warning` to two elements: the first paragraph and the `SPAN` element in the second paragraph.

All we need now is a way to apply styles to these classed elements. Here it is:

```
.warning {font-weight: bold;}
```

That simple rule will have the effect shown in Figure 2-8, when combined with the example markup shown earlier. In fact, given the style sheet shown, the style of `font-weight: bold` will be applied to *any* element with a `CLASS` attribute with a value of `warning`.

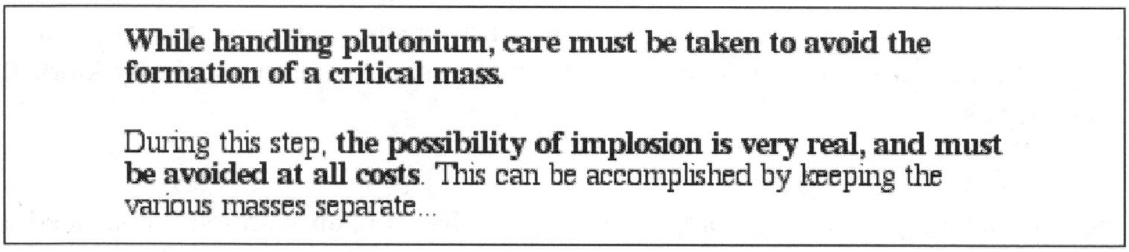

> **While handling plutonium, care must be taken to avoid the formation of a critical mass.**
>
> During this step, **the possibility of implosion is very real, and must be avoided at all costs**. This can be accomplished by keeping the various masses separate...

Figure 2-8. Results of using a class selector

As you can see, the class selector works by directly referencing a value that will be found in the `class` attribute of an element. This reference is *always* preceded by a period (`.`), which marks it as a class selector. The period is necessary because it helps keep the class selector separate from anything with which it might be combined—like an element selector. For example, maybe we only want boldface text when an entire paragraph is a warning. Thus:

```
P.warning {font-weight: bold;}
```

As you can see in Figure 2-9, only the first paragraph is bold, whereas the text in the second paragraph is no longer bold, because it no longer matches the `SPAN` element. The simplest way to translate the selector `P.warning` is like this: "Any paragraph whose `CLASS` attribute has a value of `warning` will take the following styles." Since the `SPAN` element is not a paragraph, the rule's selector doesn't match, and so its text is not made bold.

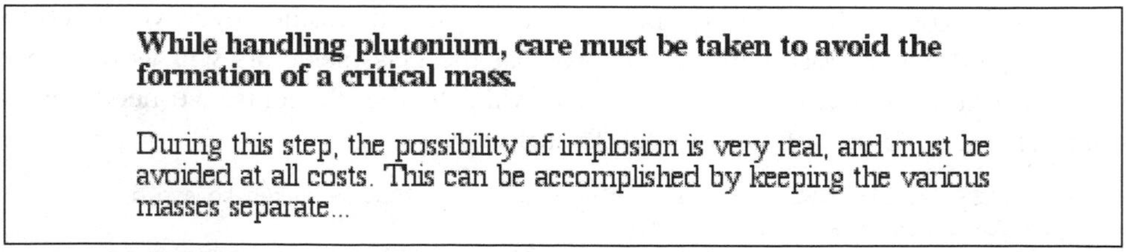

> **While handling plutonium, care must be taken to avoid the formation of a critical mass.**
>
> During this step, the possibility of implosion is very real, and must be avoided at all costs. This can be accomplished by keeping the various masses separate...

Figure 2-9. Combining a class selector with an element selector

Of course, you could use the selector `SPAN.warning` to assign different styles to that element. See Figure 2-10 for the results of these styles:

```
P.warning {font-weight: bold;}
SPAN.warning {font-style: italic;}
```

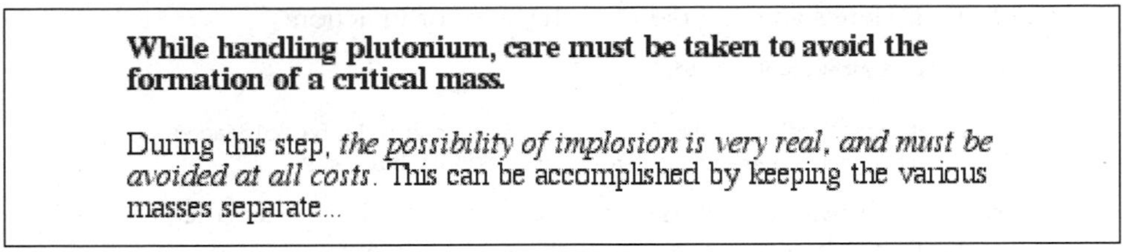

> **While handling plutonium, care must be taken to avoid the formation of a critical mass.**
>
> During this step, *the possibility of implosion is very real, and must be avoided at all costs.* This can be accomplished by keeping the various masses separate...

Figure 2-10. Making selectors more specific

In this case, the warning paragraph is boldfaced, while the warning SPAN is italicized. Each rule applies only to a specific type of element-class combination, and so does not "leak over" to other elements.

In addition, you could use a combination of a general class selector and an element-specific class selector to make the styles even more useful, as shown in Figure 2-11:

```
.warning {font-style: italic;}
SPAN.warning {font-weight: bold;}
```

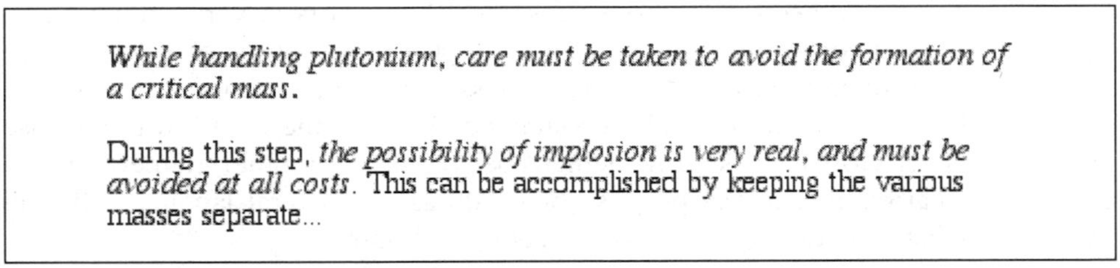

> *While handling plutonium, care must be taken to avoid the formation of a critical mass.*
>
> During this step, *the possibility of implosion is very real, and must be avoided at all costs.* This can be accomplished by keeping the various masses separate...

Figure 2-11. Using generic and specific selectors to combine styles

Now we have a situation where any warning text will be italic, but only text within a SPAN element with a class of warning will be boldface as well.

ID Selectors

In many ways, ID selectors are just like class selectors—but there are a few crucial differences. The first difference is the fact that ID selectors are preceded by an octothorpe (#)—otherwise known as a pound sign, hash mark, or tic-tac-toe board—instead of a period. Thus, you might see a rule like this one:

```
#first-para {font-weight: bold;}
```

This will apply boldface text to any element whose ID attribute has a value of first-para.

That's the second difference: instead of referencing values of the CLASS attribute, ID selectors refer to values found in ID attributes. This likely does not come as a surprise to you. Here's an example of an ID selector in action:

```
#first-para {font-weight: bold;}

<P ID="first-para">This is the first paragraph, and will be boldfaced.</P>
<P>This is the second paragraph, which will NOT be bold.</P>
```

As Figure 2-12 shows, the paragraphs are rendered just as the text within describes: the first is boldfaced, whereas the second is not.

This is the first paragraph, and will be boldfaced.

This is the second paragraph, which will NOT be bold.

Figure 2-12. Using an ID selector

Note that the value `first-para` didn't have to be applied to a paragraph. It could have been assigned to any element within the document.

Class? ID? What's the Difference?

Up until now, we've been using both class and ID selectors in very similar ways. In effect, we've been using both to usurp the structural nature of HTML, since styles can be applied to any element, regardless of its function in the structure of the document. This is not generally recommended, since one could in theory use class and ID selectors to make any element behave like any other element, which runs somewhat counter to the purpose of HTML as a structural language. But all this aside, what's the difference between classes and IDs?

In the first place, classes may be assigned to any number of elements, as we saw earlier—the class warning was applied to both a paragraph and some SPAN text, and it could have been applied to many more elements. IDs, on the other hand, are supposed to be used once, and only once, within an HTML document. In this way, they're somewhat similar to the values of the attribute NAME in form elements like INPUT. Each value of NAME should be unique, and so it is with IDs.

In the real world, browsers don't usually check for the uniqueness of IDs in HTML, which means that if you sprinkle an HTML document with several elements, all of which have the same value for their ID attributes, you'll probably get the same styles applied to each. This isn't correct behavior, but it happens anyway. Note, by the way, that I was careful to say that this is incorrect for HTML documents. Other markup languages may not have the same restrictions on ID values, although there's no way to know that until you actually go look at a given language's specification. In HTML, it is forbidden to have ID values that are identical to other IDs within the same document.

The other difference between class and ID is that IDs carry a higher weight when trying to determine which styles should be applied to a given element. This is explained in greater detail in the section, "The Cascade," later in this chapter.

Like classes, IDs can also be declared independently of an element, although since they are supposed to be unique anyway, this generally makes less sense. Still, there may be circumstances in which you know that a certain ID value will appear in a document, but not the element on which it will appear, so it is useful to be able to declare standalone ID selectors. For example, you may know that in any given document, there will be an element with an ID value of `mostImportant`. You don't know whether that most important thing will be a paragraph, a short phrase, a list item, or a section heading. You know only that it will exist in each document, that it will be on an arbitrary element, and that it will appear no more than once in a given document. In that case, you would write a rule like this:

```
#mostImportant {color: red; background: yellow;}
```

This rule would match any of the following elements (which, as noted before, should *not* appear together in the same document, because they all have the same ID value):

```
<H1 ID="mostImportant">This is important!</H1>
<EM ID="mostImportant">This is important!</EM>
<LI ID="mostImportant">This is important!</LI>
```

Pseudo-Classes and Pseudo-Elements

Even more interesting, at least in terms of syntax, are the *pseudo-class* and *pseudo-element* selectors. These allow the author to assign styles to structures that don't necessarily exist in the document, or to things that are inferred by the state of certain elements, or even the state of the document itself. In other words, the styles are applied to pieces of a document based on something other than the structure of the document, and in a way that cannot be precisely deduced simply by studying the document's markup.

This may sound like we're applying styles at random. Not at all! Instead, the styles are applied based on somewhat ephemeral conditions that can't be predicted in advance. Nonetheless, the circumstances under which the styles will appear are well-defined. This is sort of like saying, "During a sporting event, whenever the home team scores, the crowd will cheer." You don't know exactly when during a game this will happen, but when the right conditions occur, the crowd will do just as predicted. The fact that you can't predict the exact second (or inning, or quarter) in which this will happen doesn't make the behavior any less expected whenever the home team does score.

Pseudo-Class Selectors

First we'll look at pseudo-class selectors, since they're better supported by browsers and therefore more widely used. Let's use an example to see how they work; this will take a minute before I reach the actual point, so bear with me.

Consider the anchor, which is used to set up a link from one document to another. Anchors are always anchors, of course, but some anchors refer to pages that have already been visited, while others refer to pages that haven't been visited yet. You can't tell which are which by simply looking at the HTML markup, because in the markup, all anchors look the same. Only by comparing the links in a document to the user's browser history is it possible to tell which links have been visited and which have not. So, in a certain sense, there are two basic types of anchors: visited and unvisited. In fact, these types are known as *pseudo-classes,* and the selectors that use them are called *pseudo-class selectors*. These cause, in a certain sense, ghostly classes to be applied to elements.

To see what I mean, let's consider for a moment how browsers behave with regard to links. The Mosaic convention was that links to pages you hadn't visited were blue, and links to already visited pages were red (this was modified to purple in succeeding browsers such as Internet Explorer). If you could only insert classes into anchors, such that any anchor you had visited would have a class of, say, "visited," then you could write a style to make such anchors red:

```
A.visited {color: red;}
```

```
<A HREF="http://www.w3.org/" CLASS="visited">W3C Web site</A>
```

Such an approach, however, would require that the classes on anchors change every time you visited a new page, which is a little silly. Instead, CSS defines pseudo-classes that make the anchors to visited pages act as though they have classes of "visited." Thus:

```
A:visited {color: red;}
```

There you have it—any anchor that points to a visited page will now be red, and you don't even have to add CLASS attributes to any of the anchors. Note the colon (:) in the rule. The colon separating the A and the visited is the calling card of a pseudo-class or pseudo-element. All pseudo-class and pseudo-element keywords are preceded by a colon.

Here's another example:

```
A:visited {color: silver;}
```

```
<A HREF="http://www.w3.org/">W3C Web site</A><BR>
<A HREF="http://www.nowhere.net/">Nowhere in particular</A>
```

As you can guess from Figure 2-13, the first anchor points to an already visited page, and so it's silver, whereas the second anchor is still blue, since the browser hasn't loaded that page before.

W3C Web site
Nowhere in particular

Figure 2-13. Pseudo-classes in action

In CSS1, there are only three pseudo-classes. We've already seen `:visited`, and in addition, there are `:link` and `:active`. Each refers to a different kind of anchor, as shown in Table 2-1.

Table 2-1. Pseudo-classes

Name	Description
`:link`	Refers to any anchor that is a hyperlink (i.e., has an **HREF** attribute) and that points to an address that has not been visited. Note that some browsers may interpret `:link` to refer to any hyperlink, visited or unvisited.
`:visited`	Refers to any anchor that is a hyperlink to an already visited page.
`:active`	Refers to any anchor that is in the process of being activated (e.g., clicked). In CSS1, this applies only to hyperlinks, whereas in CSS2, `:active` can theoretically apply to any element.

The first of the pseudo-classes in Table 2-1 may seem a little bit redundant. After all, if an anchor hasn't been visited, then it must be unvisited, right? Therefore, all we should need is the following:

```
A {color: blue;}
A:visited {color: red;}
```

That seems reasonable, but actually it's not quite enough. The first of the rules shown here will apply not only to unvisited links, but also target anchors such as this one:

```
<A NAME="section4">4. The Lives of Salmon</A>
```

The text shown would be blue, because the A element will match the first rule shown before. Therefore, in order to avoid applying your link styles to target anchors, use the `:link` pseudo-class:

```
A:link {color: blue;}     /* unvisited links are blue */
A:visited {color: red;}   /* visited links are red */
A:active {color: yellow;} /* anchors turn yellow while clicked */
```

As you may have already realized, the `:link`, `:visited`, and `:active` selectors are functionally equivalent to the **BODY** attributes **LINK**, **VLINK**, and **ALINK**. In the case of the CSS pseudo-classes, of course, you can apply more than just colors.

Assume that an author wishes to create a page in which all anchors are purple if the linked pages haven't been visited, red if they have been, and yellow as the user clicks them. In HTML, this could be done as follows:

```
<BODY LINK="purple" VLINK="red" ALINK="yellow">
```

In CSS, this would be accomplished as:

```
A:link {color: purple;}
A:visited {color: red;}
A:active {color: yellow;}
```

This is a good place to bring class selectors back in and show how they can be combined with pseudo-classes. For example, let's say you wish to change the color of any link that points outside your own site. If you assign a class to each of these anchors, it's easy. For example:

```
<A HREF="http://www.mysite.net/">My home page</A>
<A HREF="http://www.site.net/" CLASS="external">Another home page</A>
```

In order to apply different styles to the external link, all you need is a rule like this:

```
A.external:link, A.external:visited {color: maroon;}
```

This will have the effect of setting the second anchor in the preceding markup to be maroon, while the first will be the default color for hyperlinks (usually blue).

Real-world issues

There are some interesting issues with the anchor pseudo-classes. For example, it would be possible to set visited and unvisited links to one font size, and active links to have a larger size:

```
A:link, A:visited {font-size: 12pt;}
A:active {font-size: 18pt;}
```

As you can see in Figure 2-14, the user agent has increased the size of the anchor as it's being clicked. A user agent that supports this behavior is forced to redraw the document as an anchor is being clicked. However, the CSS specifications specifically state the user agents are not required to do redraw a document once it's been drawn for initial display, so you can't absolutely rely on this happening. Whatever you do, avoid designs that depend on such behavior!

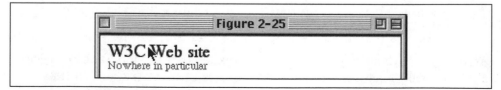

Figure 2-14. Resizing elements based on their state

The `:active` pseudo-class isn't supported in Navigator 4.x or Opera 3.x, although it is supported in Explorer 4.x and 5.x.

Pseudo-Element Selectors

In a fashion similar to the way that pseudo-classes cause ghostly classes to be assigned to anchors, pseudo-elements trigger the insertion of fictional elements into a document in order to achieve certain effects.

In CSS1, there are two pseudo-elements, called `:first-letter` and `:first-line`. These are used to apply styles to the first letter or first line, respectively, of a block-level element such as a paragraph. For example:

```
P:first-letter {color: red;}
```

This will cause the first letter of every paragraph to be colored red, which is pretty straightforward. Another possibility is to make the first letter of each H2 twice as big as the rest of the heading, with the result seen in Figure 2-15:

```
H2:first-letter {font-size: 200%;}
```

T his is an H2 element

This, on the other hand, is a paragraph. Lorem ipsum, dolor sit amet, consectetuer adipiscing elit, sed diam nonummy nibh euismod tincidunt ut laoreet dolore magna aliquam erat volutpat. Ut wisi enim ad minim veniam, quis nostrud exerci tation ullamcorper suscipit lobortis nisl ut aliquip ex ea commodo consequat. Duis autem vel eum iriure dolor in hendrerit in vulputate velit esse molestie consequat, vel illum dolore eu feugiat nulla facilisis at vero eros et accumsan et iusto odio dignissim qui blandit praesent luptatum zzril delenit augue duis dolore te feugait nulla facilisi.

Figure 2-15. The :first-letter pseudo-element in action

In a like way, `:first-line` can be used to affect the first line of text in an element. For example, we could make the first line of each paragraph in a document gray:

```
P:first-line {color: gray;}
```

In Figure 2-16, we see the style is applied to the first displayed line of text in each paragraph. This is true no matter how wide or narrow the display region may be. If the first line contains only the first five words of the paragraph, then only those five words will be gray. If the first line contains the first 30 words, then all 30 will be gray.

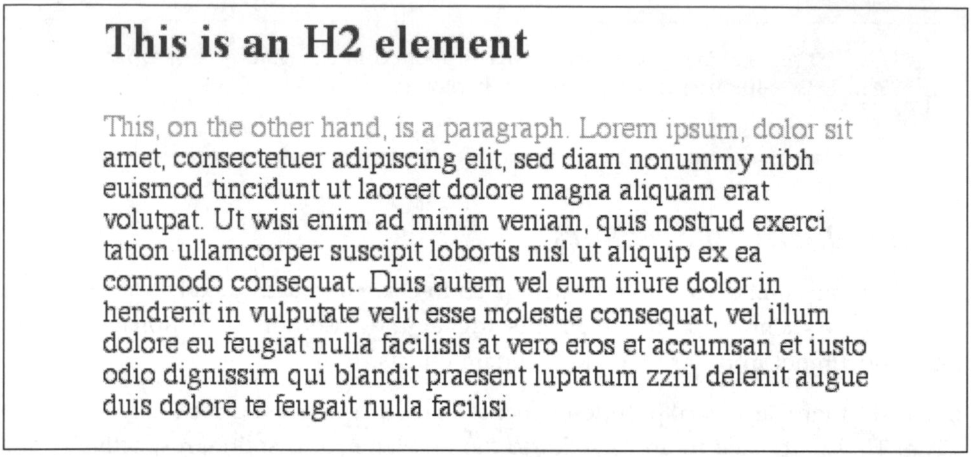

This is an H2 element

This, on the other hand, is a paragraph. Lorem ipsum, dolor sit amet, consectetuer adipiscing elit, sed diam nonummy nibh euismod tincidunt ut laoreet dolore magna aliquam erat volutpat. Ut wisi enim ad minim veniam, quis nostrud exerci tation ullamcorper suscipit lobortis nisl ut aliquip ex ea commodo consequat. Duis autem vel eum iriure dolor in hendrerit in vulputate velit esse molestie consequat, vel illum dolore eu feugiat nulla facilisis at vero eros et accumsan et iusto odio dignissim qui blandit praesent luptatum zzril delenit augue duis dolore te feugait nulla facilisi.

Figure 2-16. The :first-line pseudo-element in action

The reason `:first-line` and `:first-letter` are referred to as *pseudo-element selectors* is that they cause, in effect, a temporary element to appear within the document structure. This is most easily visualized with an example employing "fictional tags," as the CSS1 specification calls them.

Assume the following markup:

```
P:first-line {color: gray;}

<P>This is a paragraph of text which has only one style applied to it. That
style causes the first line to be gray. No other text in the paragraph is
affected by this rule (at least, it shouldn't be).</P>
```

Assume further that a user agent displays the text like this:

```
This is a paragraph of text which has only
one style applied to it. That style causes
the first line to be gray. No other ...
```

and so forth. Since the text from "This" to "only" should be gray, the user agent employs a fictional markup that looks something like this:

```
<P><P:first-line>This is a paragraph of text which has only</P:first-line>
one style applied to it. That style causes the first line to be gray. No other ...
```

This fictional tag sequence causes the effect seen in Figure 2-17.

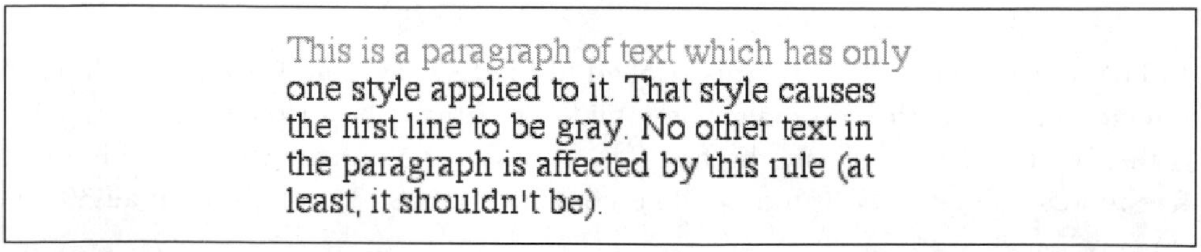

This is a paragraph of text which has only one style applied to it. That style causes the first line to be gray. No other text in the paragraph is affected by this rule (at least, it shouldn't be).

Figure 2-17. How the pseudo-element selector :first-line works, in a theoretical sense

This `<P:first-line>` element does *not* appear in the document source. It isn't even a valid element at all. Instead, its existence is constructed on the fly by the user agent and used to apply the `:first-line` style(s) to the appropriate block of text. In other words, `<P:first-line>` is an element that isn't really an element, but is instead a pseudo-element. Remember, you don't have to add any new tags. The user agent will do it for you.

The `:first-letter` pseudo-element causes something similar to happen:

```
P:first-letter {font-weight: bold;}

<P><P:first-letter>T</P:first-letter>his is a paragraph of text which has
another style sheet applied to it. This time it uses a first-letter effect.
```

Restrictions on Pseudo-Class and Pseudo-Element Selectors

There are limits to the CSS properties that may be applied to `:first-line` and `:first-letter`. These are given in Table 2-2.

Table 2-2. Properties Permitted on Pseudo-elements

:first-letter	:first-line
all font properties	all font properties
all color and background properties	all color and background properties
text-decoration	word-spacing
vertical-align (if float is set to none)	letter-spacing
text-transform	text-decoration
line-height	vertical-align
all margin properties	text-transform
all padding properties	line-height
all border properties	clear
float	
clear	

Under CSS1, pseudo-classes and pseudo-elements cannot be combined within a single selector. As we will see, this changes to some degree in CSS2. It *is* possible to combine pseudo-class and -element selectors with class and ID selectors, although the syntax for doing so is fairly rigid. The pseudo-class or pseudo-element is always the very last thing in the selector, coming after the element, class, and/or ID portions of the selector:

```
A.external:link {color: gray;}
A#link721:visited {color: purple;}
```

Structure

As I've mentioned before, CSS is powerful because of the way in which it uses the structure of HTML documents to determine which styles should be applied in what ways. That's really only a part of the story, though, since it implies that the only way CSS uses document structure is to determine which rules apply to which elements.

The truth is that structure plays a much bigger role in the way styles are applied to a document. In order to understand this role, we need to understand how documents are structured. Take the "tree" view in Figure 2-18 of the simple HTML document listed here:

```
<HTML>
<HEAD>
<BASE HREF="http://www.meerkat.web/">
<TITLE>Meerkat Central</TITLE>
</HEAD>
<BODY>
<H1>Meerkat <EM>Central</EM></H1>
<P>
Welcome to Meerkat <EM>Central</EM>, the <STRONG>best meerkat web site
on <A HREF="inet.html">the <EM>entire</EM> Internet</A></STRONG>!</P>
<UL>
<LI>We offer:
<UL>
<LI><STRONG>Detailed information</STRONG> on how to adopt a meerkat</LI>
<LI>Tips for living with a meerkat</LI>
<LI><EM>Fun</EM> things to do with a meerkat, including:
<UL>
<LI>Playing fetch</LI>
<LI>Digging for food</LI>
<LI>Hide and seek</LI>
</UL>
</LI>
</UL>
<LI>...and so much more!</LI>
</UL>
<P>
Questions? <A HREF="mail to:suricate@meerkat.web" >Contact us!</A>
</P>
</BODY>
</HTML>
```

Much of the power of CSS is based on the *parent-child relationship* of elements. HTML documents, and indeed most structured documents of any kind, are based on a hierarchy of elements, which is visible in the "tree" view of the document in Figure 2-18. In this hierarchy, each element fits somewhere into the overall structure of the document, and every element is either the *parent* or *child* of another element, and often both.

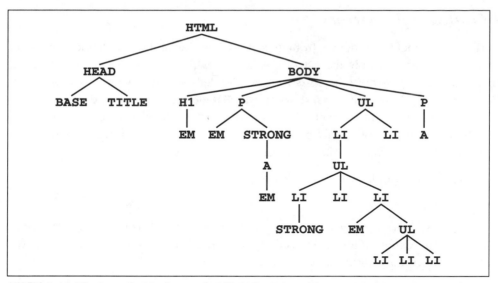

Figure 2-18. The "tree view" of a simple HTML document

An element is said to be the *parent* of another element if it encloses the other element. For example, in Figure 2-18, the P element is parent to an EM and a STRONG element, while the STRONG is parent to an anchor element which is itself parent to another EM element. Conversely, an element is the *child* of another element if it is enclosed by the other element. Thus, the anchor element in Figure 2-18 is a child of the STRONG element, which is in turn child to the paragraph, and so on.

The terms *parent* and *child* are often generalized to the terms *ancestor* and *descendant*. There is a difference: in the tree view, if an element is exactly one level above another, then they have a parent-child relationship. (Of course, the child is also a descendant, and the parent is an ancestor.) If, however, the path from one element to another moves through two or more levels, then the elements have an ancestor-descendant relationship. In Figure 2-18, the first UL element is parent to two LI elements and a UL, but the first UL is also the ancestor of every element within its child UL, all the way down to the most deeply nested LI elements.

If we continue to examine Figure 2-18, we see that, for example, the anchor is a child of STRONG, but also a descendant of the paragraph element as well as of the BODY and HTML elements. The BODY element is an ancestor of everything the browser will display, of course, and the HTML element is ancestor to the entire document. For this reason, the HTML element is also sometimes called the *root element*.

Contextual Selectors

The first benefit we derive from this model is the ability to define *contextual selectors*. This is simply the act of creating rules that operate in certain structural circumstances but not others. As an example, let's say you want to set EM text to be gray, but only if it's found within an H1 element. You could put a CLASS attribute in every EM element within an H1, but that's almost as bad as using the FONT tag. It would obviously be far better to declare rules that only match EM elements which are found inside H1 elements.

To do so, you would write the following:

```
H1 EM {color: gray;}
```

This rule will make gray any text in an EM element which is the descendant of an H1 element. Other EM text, such as that found in a paragraph or a block quote, will not be selected by this rule, as Figure 2-19 makes clear.

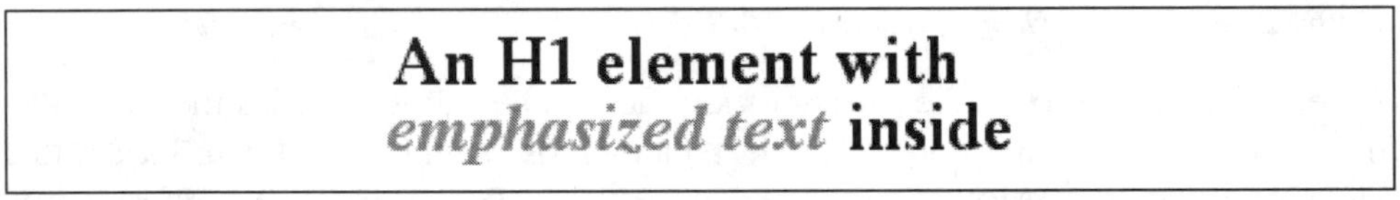

An H1 element with
emphasized text inside

Figure 2-19. Selecting an element based on its context

In a contextual selector, the selector side of a rule is composed of two or more space-separated selectors. Each space can be translated as "found within," "which is part of," or "that is a descendant of," but only if you read the selector *backwards*. Thus, H1 EM can be translated as, "Any EM element that is a descendant of an H1 element." (If you insist on reading the selector forwards, then you might phrase it something like, "Any H1 that contains an EM will have the following applied to the EM.")

You aren't limited to two selectors, of course. For example:

```
UL OL UL EM {color: gray;}
```

In this case, as Figure 2-20 shows, any emphasized text that is part of an unordered list that is part of an ordered list that is part of an unordered list will be gray. This is obviously a very specific selection criterion.

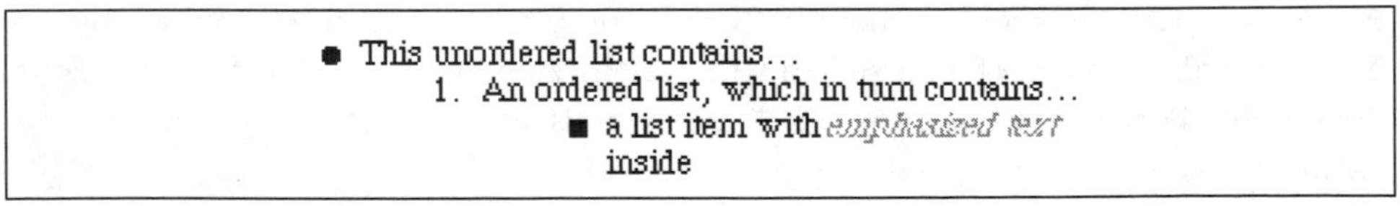

- This unordered list contains...
  1. An ordered list, which in turn contains...
     - a list item with *emphasized text* inside

Figure 2-20. A very specific contextual selector

Contextual selectors can be very, very powerful. They make possible what could never be done in HTML—at least not without oodles of FONT tags. Let's consider a common example. Assume you have a document that has a sidebar and a main area. The sidebar has a blue background, and the main area has a white background. You have a list of links in the sidebar, but you also have links which appear in the main text. You can't set all links to be blue, because they'd be impossible to read in the sidebar (blue text on a blue background).

The solution? Contextual selectors. In this case, you set the table cell that contains your sidebar to have a class of sidebar, and the main area to have a class of main-page. Then you write styles something like this:

```
TD.sidebar {background: blue;}
TD.main-page {background: white;}
TD.sidebar A:link {color: white;}
TD.main-page A:link {color: blue;}
```

Figure 2-21 shows the result: white hyperlinks on a blue background in the sidebar, with blue links on a white background in the main area of the page.

Figure 2-21. Using contextual selectors to apply different styles to the same type of element

Here's another example: let's say that we want gray to be used as the text color of any B (boldface) element that is part of a BLOCKQUOTE, and also for any bold text that is found in a normal paragraph:

```
BLOCKQUOTE B, P B {color: gray;}
```

The result, shown in Figure 2-22, is that while the boldface text in paragraphs and block quotes is gray, boldface text in lists is not colored gray.

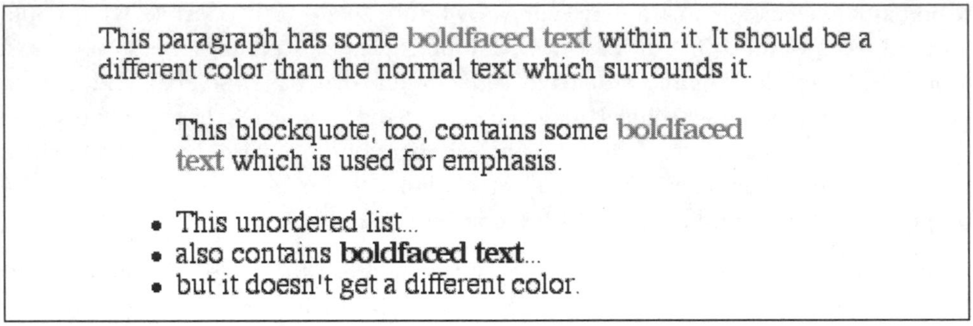

This paragraph has some boldfaced text within it. It should be a
different color than the normal text which surrounds it.

> This blockquote, too, contains some boldfaced
> text which is used for emphasis.

- This unordered list...
- also contains **boldfaced text**...
- but it doesn't get a different color.

Figure 2-22. Context and style

Thankfully, contextual selectors are one of the things that almost
everyone got right the first time they tried—although there are some
minor random quirks to be found in Navigator 4.x that defy analysis. In general, though, like grouping, contextual selectors are as safe
and stable an operation as you're going to find.

Inheritance

Viewing a document as a tree is very important for one other reason: a key feature of CSS is *inheritance*, which relies on the ancestor-descendant relationship to
operate. *Inheritance* is simply the mechanism by which styles are applied not only
to a specified element, but also to its descendants. If a color is applied to an H1
element, for example, then that color is applied to all text in the H1, even the text
enclosed within child elements of that H1:

```
H1 {color: gray;}

    <H1>Meerkat <EM>Central</EM></H1>
```

As shown in Figure 2-23, both the ordinary H1 text and the EM text are colored
gray because the value of color inherits into the EM element. This is very likely
what the author intended, which is why inheritance is a part of CSS.

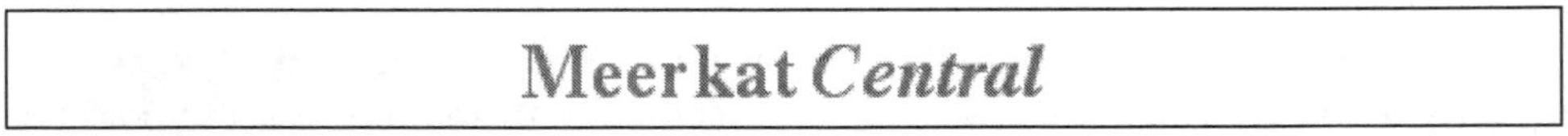

Meerkat *Central*

Figure 2-23. Inheritance of styles

The alternative would be a hypothetical situation where inheritance does not operate; in that case, the EM text would be black, not gray.

Another good example of how inheritance works is with unordered lists. Let's say
we apply a style of color: gray for UL elements. What we expect is that a style

that is applied to a `UL` will be applied to its list items as well, and to any content of those list items. Thanks to inheritance, that's exactly what does happen, as Figure 2-24 demonstrates:

```
UL {color: gray;}
```

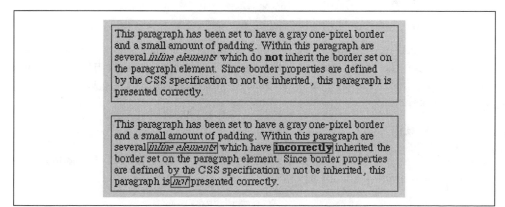

The list items figure:

- The list items of...
- this unordered list...
- inherit the grayness...
- applied to the 'UL' element.

1. The list items in...
2. this ordered list...
3. do not.

Figure 2-24. Inheritance of styles

Inheritance is one of those things about CSS that are so basic that you almost never think about them unless you have to—rather like the way we tend to take the convenience of the highway system for granted until part of it is closed or otherwise rendered difficult to use. However, there are a few things to keep in mind about inheritance.

Limitations of Inheritance

As with any great thing, there are a few blemishes if you look closely enough. First off, some properties are not inherited. This may be for any number of reasons, but they generally have to do with simple common sense. For example, the property **border** (which is used to set borders on elements, oddly enough) does not inherit. A quick glance at Figure 2-25 will reveal why this is the case. Were borders inherited, documents would become much more "cluttered" unless the author took the extra effort to turn off the inherited borders.

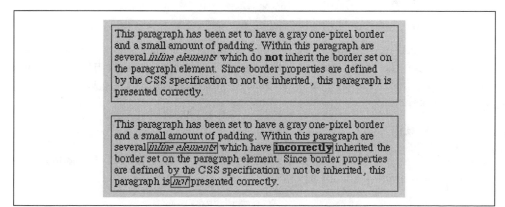

Figure 2-25. Why borders aren't inherited

As it happens, most of the box-model properties, including margins, padding, backgrounds, and borders, are not inherited for this very reason.

Inherit the Bugs

Inheritance can be a tricky thing, unfortunately. Thanks to problems in various browser implementations, an author cannot always rely on inheritance to operate as expected in all circumstances. For example, Navigator 4 (and, to a lesser extent, Explorer 4) does not inherit styles into tables. Thus the following rule would result in a document with purple text everywhere outside of tables:

```
BODY {color: purple;}
```

Even that isn't quite true, as some versions of Navigator 4 will forget about styles altogether once a table has been displayed; thus, any text after a table, as well as the text within it, would not be purple. This is not technically correct behavior, but it does exist, so authors often resort to tricks such as:

```
BODY, TABLE, TH, TD {color: purple;}
```

This is more likely, although still not certain, to achieve the desired effect. Despite this potential problem, the rest of this text will treat inheritance as though it operated perfectly in all cases, since an exhaustive documentation of the ways and reasons it might fail could be a book in itself.

Specificity

Given the existence of inheritance, one might well wonder what happens in a circumstance such as this:

```
.grape {color: purple;}
H1 {color: red;}
```

```
<H1 CLASS="grape">Meerkat <EM>Central</EM></H1>
```

Since the selectors `H1` and `.grape` can both match the `H1` element shown, which one wins? As it happens, `.grape` is the correct answer, and so the `H1` element will be colored purple. This happens because of the *specificity* of the two rules, and the rules CSS has to deal with such situations.

Specificity describes the relative weights of various rules. According to the specification, a simple selector (e.g., `H1`) has a specificity of 1, class selectors have a specificity of 10, and ID selectors a specificity of 100. Thus the following rules would have the noted specificity:

```
H1 {color: red;}            /* specificity = 1 */
P EM {color: purple;}       /* specificity = 2 */
```

```
.grape {color: purple;}            /* specificity = 10 */
P.bright {color: yellow;}          /* specificity = 11 */
P.bright EM.dark {color: brown;}   /* specificity = 22 */
#id216 {color: blue;}              /* specificity = 100 */
```

Thus, the rule for #id216 has a much higher specificity, and therefore more weight, than any of the others listed. In cases where more than one rule can apply to an element, the styles with the higher weight win out.

Inheritance and Specificity

Within the framework of specificity, inherited values have, effectively, a specificity of 0. This means that any explicitly declared rule will override an inherited style. Therefore, no matter how much weight a rule might have, it is only inherited if no other rule can be applied to the inheriting element.

For example, consider the following:

```
BODY {background: black;}
LI {color: gray;}
UL.vital {color: white;}
```

You would likely expect that all list items would be gray except for those which are found in lists with a class of vital, in which case they'll be white. However, as Figure 2-26 demonstrates, this is not the case.

Figure 2-26. Apparently incorrect behavior

Why does this happen? Because the explicit declaration with the selector LI wins out over the value which might have been inherited from the UL.vital rule.

Let's look at this process in a little more detail. Given the following markup, the emphasized text will be gray, not black, since the rule for EM outweighs the value inherited from the H1:

```
H1#id3 {color: black;}   /* specificity = 101 */
EM {color: gray;}        /* specificity = 1 */

<H1 ID="id3">Meerkat <EM>Central</EM></H1>
```

This is because the specificity of the second rule (1) is higher than the specificity of the inherited value (0). The fact that the original specificity of the H1#id3 rule is 101 has no effect on the inherited value, whose weight is still 0.

If the intention is to have H1s be consistently black, while EM text in all other circumstances should be red, then the following would be a good solution:

```
H1, H1 EM {color: black;}    /* specificity = 1, 2 */
EM {color: red;}             /* specificity = 1 */
```

Given these rules, EM text in any circumstance except within an H1 will be red. However, EM text inside H1 elements will be black, because the specificity of their selector (2) is greater than that of the second rule (1). Note that since, due to selector grouping, there are effectively two rules in the first statement (one for H1 and one for H1 EM), there are also two specificities—one for each rule.

Elements with a STYLE attribute are defined under CSS1 to have a specificity of 100, just as though they were ID selectors such as #id3. In practice, however, this specificity value is somewhat higher, since the value of a STYLE element seems to outweigh most normal rules, even those which technically have a higher specificity (such as H1#id3 EM). In other words, the following markup will generally have the result shown in Figure 2-27:

```
H1#id3 EM {color: gray;}

<H1 ID="id3">Meerkat <EM STYLE="color: black;">Central</EM>!</H1>
```

Meerkat *Central!*

Figure 2-27. Inline styles have high specificity

You might choose to treat STYLE value as having a specificity value of, say, 1,000, although this interpretation is not supported by the CSS specification and so cannot be relied upon. Finally, pseudo-elements are ignored altogether when calculating specificity, but pseudo-classes are treated like regular classes.

There is one other wrinkle in the specificity picture, which is a way to pretty much override the entire specificity mechanism.

Importance

Ever felt like something is so important that it outweighs all other considerations? Well, it's possible to mark certain rules as being more important than others. These are called *important rules* due to the way in which they are declared and also because of their very nature. An important rule is marked by inserting the phrase !important just before the terminating semicolon in a rule:

```
P.dark {color: #333 !important; background: white;}
```

Here, the color value of #333 is marked !important, whereas the background value of white is not. If you wish to mark both rules as important, then each rule will need its own !important:

```
P.dark {color: #333 !important; background: white !important;}
```

It is important to ensure that you place the !important correctly, or else the rule can be invalidated. The !important *always* goes at the end of the declaration, right before the semicolon. This is especially important—no pun intended—when it comes to properties that allow values which contain multiple keywords, such as font:

```
P.light {color: yellow; font: 11pt Times !important;}
```

If the !important were placed anywhere else in the font declaration, then that entire declaration would very likely be invalidated and none of the styles applied.

Rules that are marked !important do not have a defined specificity value, but authors can assume that they have a conveniently high value, such as 10,000—in other words, a value that outweighs all others. Note that while author-defined styles are treated as having a greater weight than reader-defined styles (see the section "The Cascade," later in this chapter), the reverse is true of !important rules: important reader-defined rules take precedence over author-defined styles, even those marked !important.

Indeed, an !important rule will override the contents of an inline STYLE attribute. Thus, given the following code, the result will be gray text, not black:

```
H1 {color: gray !important;}
```

```
<H1 STYLE="color: black;">Hi there!</H1>
```

There is one last scenario to consider. Consider the following:

```
P#warn {color: red ! important;}
EM {color: black;}
```

```
<P ID="warn">This text is red, but <EM>emphasized text is black.</EM></P>
```

Remember that inherited values always have a specificity of 0. This is true even if the rule from which the value comes has an !important attached. All of its importance is lost outside the elements which match that rule.

As of this writing, very few browsers implement !important. Internet Explorer 5 and Opera 3.6 have it right, but that's all. On the other hand, !important is expected to be supported in Navigator 6.

The Cascade

Through all this, we've skirted one rather important issue: what happens when there are two rules of equal specificity that apply to the same element? How does the browser resolve the conflict?

For example, let's say we have the following rules:

```
H1 {color: red;}
H1 {color: blue;}
```

So which one wins? Both have a specificity of 1, so they have equal weight and should both apply. That simply can't be the case, though, because the element can't be both red and blue. It has to be one or the other. But which?

This is where the name "Cascading Style Sheets" finally makes some sense. CSS is based on a method of causing styles to cascade together—a method that is made possible by the rules of inheritance and specificity, as it happens. The cascade rules are simple enough:

1. Find all declarations that contain a selector that matches a given element.

2. Sort by explicit weight all declarations applying to given element. Those rules marked !important are given higher weight than those that are not. Also sort by origin all declarations applying to a given element. There are three origins: author, reader, and user agent. Under normal circumstances, the author's styles win out over the reader's styles. !important author styles win out over important reader styles in CSS1, but in CSS2, !important reader styles are stronger than any other styles. Either author or reader styles will override user agent styles.

3. Sort by specificity all declarations applying to a given element. Those elements with a higher specificity have more weight than those with lower specificity.

4. Sort by order all declarations applying to a given element. The later a declaration appears in the style sheet or document, the more weight it is given. Declarations that appear in an imported style sheet are considered to come before all declarations within the style sheet that imports them, and declarations within STYLE attributes come later than those in the document's embedded style sheet.

In order to be perfectly clear about how this all works, let's consider an example that illustrates each of the four cascade steps. The first one is simple enough: find all rules whose selectors match a given element.

Under the second step, if two rules apply to an element, and one is marked !important, then the important rule wins out. Thus:

```
P {color: gray !important;}

<P STYLE="color: black;">Well, <EM>hello</EM> there!</P>
```

Despite the fact that there is a color assigned in the **STYLE** attribute of the paragraph, the `!important` rule wins out, and the paragraph is gray, as shown in Figure 2-28. This gray is inherited by the **EM** element as well.

Well, *hello* there!

Figure 2-28. Sorting styles by their importance

Furthermore, the origin of a rule is considered. If an element is matched by styles in both the author's style sheet and the reader's style sheet, then the author's styles are used. For example, assume that the following styles come from the indicated origins:

```
P EM {color: black;}     /* author's style sheet */

P EM {color: yellow;}    /* reader's style sheet */
```

In this case, we have the result shown in Figure 2-29, where the emphasized text is black.

Well, **hello** there!

Figure 2-29. Sorting styles by origin

As it happens, the browser's default styles—which are often influenced by its preferences—are figured into this step. The browser's default styles are the least influential of all. Therefore, if an author-defined rule applies to anchors (e.g., declaring them to be **white**), then this rule overrides the user agent's defaults. If readers wish to enforce certain rules at all costs, then they must define them in a local style sheet and declare them to be `!important`, so that they will win out under step 1 of the cascade rules. In this case, though, it will be a case of the reader's styles overriding both the author's and browser's styles due to their importance.

According to the third step, if multiple rules apply to an element, then they should be sorted by specificity, with the most specific rule winning out. For example:

```
P#bright {color: silver;}
P EM {color: gray;}
P {color: black;}

<P ID="bright">Well, <EM>hello</EM> there!</P>
```

As we can see from Figure 2-30, the text of the paragraph is silver, except for the **EM** text, which is gray. Why? Because the specificity of **P#bright** (101) overrode the specificity of **P** (1), even though the latter rule comes later in the style sheet.

> Well, *hello* there!

Figure 2-30. Sorting styles by specificity

However, the **EM** text does not inherit the value `silver`, because it has an explicit rule associated with it, and the rule's specificity (2) overrides the inherited value of `silver`.

This is not a trivial point. For example, assume that a style sheet has been written such that all text in a toolbar is to be white on black:

```
#toolbar {color: white; background: black;}
```

This will work so long as the element with an ID of `toolbar` contains only plain text. If, however, the text within this element is all hyperlinks (**A** elements), then the user agent's styles for hyperlinks will take over—because despite the fact the they're imported, they are explicit style assignments, so they override any inherited values. Usually, this means that they'll be colored blue, since the browser's style sheet probably contains an entry like this:

```
A:link {color: blue;}
```

In order to overcome this problem, the author would need to declare:

```
#toolbar A:link {color: white; background: black;}
```

By targeting the rule directly to the **A** elements within the toolbar, the author will get the result shown in Figure 2-31.

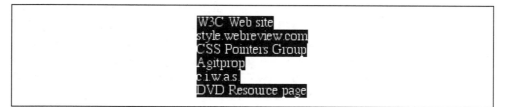

Figure 2-31. Using contextual selectors to overcome specificity

Lastly, under the fourth step, if two rules have exactly the same weight, origin, and specificity, then the one that occurs later in the style sheet wins out. Thus, let us return to our earlier example, where we find the following two rules in the document's style sheet:

```
H1 {color: red;}
H1 {color: blue;}
```

The value of `color` for all **H1** elements in the document will be `blue`, not `red`.

Any rule that is contained in the document, having a higher weight than the imported rule, wins out. This is true even if the rule is part of the document's style sheet and not part of an element's **STYLE** attribute. Consider the following:

```
P EM {color: purple;}  /* from imported style sheet */

P EM {color: gray;}     /* rule contained within the document */
```

In this case, the second rule shown, since it is a part of the document's style sheet, will win out over the imported rule.

For the purposes of this rule, styles that are given in the STYLE attribute of an element are considered to be at the end of the document's style sheet, which places them after all other rules. In addition, a STYLE attribute has a weight equivalent to that of an ID selector. Thus, the following code would result in black text, as shown in Figure 2-32:

```
#hello {color: red;}

<P ID="hello" STYLE="color: black;">Hello there!</P>
```

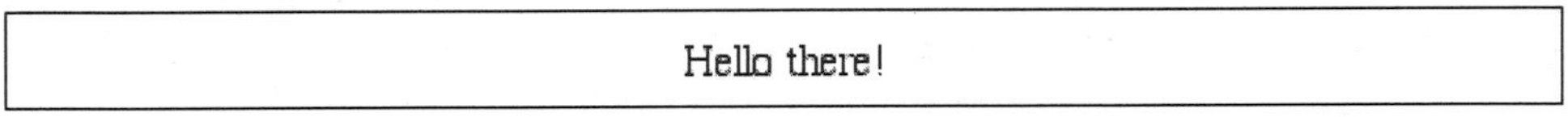

Hello there!

Figure 2-32. Sorting styles by their position

Here, the weight of the inline style (100) is equal to the weight of the rule #hello (100), so the winner is the rule that occurs later in the document.

Classification of Elements

As we have already discussed, elements in a document occur in a sort of hierarchy. At the most basic level, block-level elements contain other block-level elements, inline elements, and replaced elements. A part of this hierarchy scheme depends on the relationships between these types of elements; for example, while inline elements can be children of block-level elements, the reverse is not true.

In CSS, elements are grouped into three types:

Block-level elements

> Elements such as paragraphs, headings, lists, tables, DIVs, and BODY. Replaced elements, such as images and form inputs, can be block-level elements but usually are not. Each block-level element is displayed on a line by itself, so to speak, beginning on a new line and forcing any element after it to do the same. Block-level elements can only be children of other block-level elements, and then only in certain circumstances.

Inline elements

> Elements such as A, EM, SPAN, and most replaced elements, such as images and form inputs. They do not force anything to start on a new line, not even themselves, and can be the children of any other element.

List-item elements

Elements that in HTML pretty much include only the LI element. These are specially defined to have presentation aspects such as a "marker" (a bullet, letter, or number) and a certain sense of ordering, if such an element appears within an ordered list of some kind. Thus, list items within such a list can be automatically numbered, based on their context within the document.

These terms are, as it happens, the basic three of the four values for the property display.

---

display

Values	block | inline | list-item | none
Initial value	block
Inherited	no
Applies to	all elements

Unlike almost every other property in CSS, display is often evaluated to a value other than its default. Instead, the value of display for a given element is defined in the document type definition* (DTD) for the language being used. Thus, in HTML, the H1 and P elements are defined to be block-level elements by the document type definition for HTML. A and EM, on the other hand, are inline elements, and of course LI is a list item. Thus, the default display values for these elements would be:

```
H1, P {display: block;}
A, EM {display: inline;}
LI {display: list-item;}
```

Replaced elements may be one or the other, depending on their context and how they are placed within the document flow. A floated image is considered to be block-level, for example, but images are usually inline.

In theory, display makes it possible to completely upset the structural definitions of a markup language. In traditional HTML, paragraphs always have blank

---

* A *document type definition* is a formal description of a markup language such as HTML. The DTD provides a rigorous way of defining what elements mean and how they fit into the language's hierarchy. It's similar to describing English as a collection of nouns, verbs, adverbs, and so on, but with the added bonus of describing what each of the parts means and how they relate to each other. DTDs are not easily readable by the untrained eye.

space between them, and two paragraphs cannot appear "on the same line," so to speak. This can be changed with the following rule:

```
P {display: inline;}
```

With this simple declaration, a `P` element becomes no different than a `SPAN` element, for example. If this rule were applied to a document with several paragraphs, they would all suddenly run together in a single, rambling mass of text. Figure 2-33 shows the result.

This is a paragraph, which is ordinarily block-level. This is a second paragraph. As you can see the paragraphs in this document are no longer block-level. Here's the third paragraph. The setting of inline for the display property has made the paragraphs all inline elements, which is why they're "running together." This is the fourth paragraph. There really are <P> elements in this document. The elements are still here, and the structure of the document is preserved. It's just that the display is not quite what we're used to.

Figure 2-33. Inline paragraphs

Note that the styles applied to each paragraph, such as font and color, still hold sway, even over inline paragraphs. Only those properties that can only apply to block-level elements will cease to work with an inline paragraph.

The reverse of this is to change a normally inline element to a block-level element. Let's say you wish to make sure all images in a document appear on their own lines. All you need is the following rule, which has the effect shown in Figure 2-34:

```
IMG {display: block;}
```

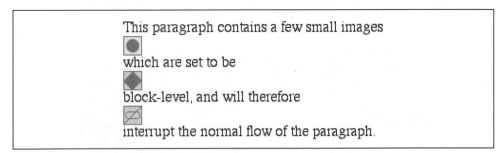

Figure 2-34. Block-level images

On the other hand, you might want to simply turn off all of the images in a document, so that they aren't displayed at all:

```
IMG {display: none;}
```

If you set the `display` of an element to `none`, the element's existence is completely ignored by the user agent, as we can see in Figure 2-35.

This paragraph contains a few small images which are set to be not displayed, and will therefore not interrupt the normal flow of the paragraph-- indeed, they don't appear at all.

Figure 2-35. Suppression of images using display: none

Not only is it not displayed, but the space it would have otherwise occupied is closed up. The document will be displayed as though the suppressed element had never existed in the first place, even though it's still in the source document:

```
<P>This is the first paragraph in the document.</P>
<P STYLE="display: none;">This will not be displayed,
nor will it affect the layout of the document.</P>
<P>This is another paragraph in the document.</P>
```

This can be useful for creating little warnings which only non-CSS browsers will display:

```
<P STYLE="display: none;">This page was designed with CSS, and
looks best in a CSS-aware browser--which, unfortunately, yours is not.
However, the document should still be perfectly readable, since that's
one of the advantages of using CSS.</P>
```

The only way this warning will be seen is on a browser that doesn't understand `display: none`—in other words, a browser that doesn't understand CSS at all, since every CSS-aware browser known supports `display: none`.

There is one other value for `display`, and that's `list-item`. This value is used to declare that an element is, well, a list item. This should, in theory, make the element behave as though it is part of a list. List items already have this display type by default, of course.

 Of course, `none` is one value of `display` that most browsers get correct right off the bat, while ignoring nearly everything else. (After all, the vendors don't want you claiming to the world that they don't have CSS-capable browsers, now do they?) `none` is the only value of `display` that you can reliably assume will work in any CSS-capable browser. Internet Explorer 5.x for Windows was the first browser to really support values of `display` other than `none`, but even it isn't perfect: it doesn't seem to handle `list-item` correctly.

Why Does the display Property Exist?

The `display` property can be used to completely upset the structure of HTML documents, as you may have realized. Try to imagine the havoc caused by a style sheet like this one:

```
H1, H3, P, DIV {display: inline;}
IMG, B, STRONG, EM, A {display: block;}
A:link {display: none;}
H2, I, TABLE {display: list-item;}
```

Depicting this is not even possible with current browsers, nor should we wish to try.

So why have this property at all? First of all, the `display: none` trick can be very useful. Assume for a moment that you have a browser that supports alternate style sheets. You could define a style sheet called "No Images" in which you set the following style:

```
IMG {display: none;}
```

This rule will turn off the display of all images within the document, as we saw earlier.

More to the point, however, is that `display` becomes very useful when CSS is linked to an XML document. XML contains next to no information regarding the display of its elements, mostly because XML has no predefined element types. Therefore, once you have finished writing an XML document, you can work up a CSS style sheet that describes which elements are block-level, which are inline, and so forth. Without such a style sheet, a browser would have no idea which XML elements were to be displayed as list items, which were block-level, and so forth.

It's worth noting that CSS1 has no way to describe parts of tables, such as cells or rows, so the formatting of tables can't really be described using CSS1. Table-related `display` values were first introduced in CSS2, and a brief look at these values can be found in Chapter 10, *CSS2: A Look Ahead*.

Summary

By using selectors based on the document's language, authors can create CSS rules that apply to a large number of similar elements just as easily as they can construct rules that apply in very narrow circumstances. The ability to group together both selectors and declarations keeps style sheets compact and flexible, which incidentally leads to smaller file sizes and faster download times. Thanks to inheritance and the cascade, authors are able to create sets of interlocking rules which, taken together, result in sophisticated document styles. This is all thanks to the fact that CSS is very deeply bound to the structure of documents, and that it uses this structure to determine how rules are applied, which rules should apply, and what elements should assume styles from their ancestors.

Selectors are the one thing that user agents almost have to get right, because the inability to correctly interpret selectors pretty much prevents a user agent from using CSS. However, the cascade and inheritance are different stories, and there have been some flaws in how they're implemented. Navigator 4.x, for example, has a rough time with inheritance into tables, as well as other structures such as lists. You can clear up many of these problems by using very strictly correct HTML, but not all of them.

There are many CSS rules describing lengths, colors, or other things that can be expressed using specific units and values—and this is the subject (and title) of the next chapter.

3

Units and Values

In this chapter, we study the basis for almost everything that can be done in CSS: the units that affect the color used or the distance set for a whole host of properties. Without units, it wouldn't be possible to declare that a paragraph should be purple, or that an image should have ten pixels of blank space around it, or that a heading should be a certain size. By understanding the concepts put forth here, you'll be able to learn and use the rest of CSS much more quickly.

However, that's the good news. The bad news is that this chapter will contain a good many caveats, warnings, and discussions of browser bugs and inconsistencies between operating systems. Remember, though, that CSS is not supposed to be a totally precise layout language—and besides, many of the issues discussed in the chapter are not the fault of CSS but are more fundamental issues that you'll encounter no matter what you try to do with a computer. So, once you've finished this chapter, you will have a grasp not only of how CSS units work, but perhaps also of a few basic issues that you previously were unaware of.

Above all, though, regardless of how bleak things may seem, keep going! Your perseverance will be rewarded.

Colors

Of course, the one thing that almost every beginning web author wants to know is, "How do I set colors on my web page?" Under HTML, there were two choices: use one of a small number of colors with names, like `red` or `purple`, or employ a vaguely cryptic method using hexadecimal codes. Well, both of those methods for describing colors can be found in CSS, as well as some other methods that are only moderately complex.

Named Colors

Assuming that you're happy with picking from a small, basic set of colors, then the easiest method is to simply use the name of the color you want. These are referred to, unsurprisingly enough, as *named colors*.

Contrary to what some browser companies might have you believe, you are limited in the range of named colors available. For example, setting a color to "mother-of-pearl" isn't going to work, because it isn't a defined color. (Well, not yet, at any rate.) Technically speaking, there are *no* defined colors, but there are 16 colors that are suggested by the specification and that all major browsers recognize:

aqua	gray	navy	silver
black	green	olive	teal
blue	lime	purple	white
fuchsia	maroon	red	yellow

If these seem like odd color names, it's because—well, they are. In my opinion, anyway. So where do they come from? These colors were taken from the original sixteen basic Windows VGA colors, and browsers are supposed to generate colors that at least come close to matching those original 16. They may be a fairly motley collection of colors, but they're what we have.

So let's say we want all first-level headings to be maroon. The best declaration would be:

```
H1 {color: maroon;}
```

Simple, straightforward, and difficult to forget. It doesn't get much better than that. Here are a few more examples:

```
H1 {color: gray;}
H2 {color: silver;}
H3 {color: black;}
```

Of course, you've probably seen (and maybe even used) color names besides the ones listed earlier. For example, if you specify:

```
H1 {color: orange;}
```

you're likely to see all of your H1 elements colored orange, despite the fact orange isn't on the list of named colors. This is due to the fact that most web browsers recognize as many as 140 color names, including the standard sixteen. There are two problems associated with using these extra names, though. The first is that not all browsers will recognize them; Opera, for example, sticks with the standard 16 colors, at least in the Opera 3.x series. Far from being a failure on their part, this represents a remarkable commitment to standards support, even though it might confuse or annoy many web designers.

The second problem is a little more fundamental: there are no standard color values for these names. Declaring that an element should be colored **orange** doesn't mean that different browsers, or even the same browser running on different platforms, will produce exactly the same shade of orange. With the sixteen standard colors, there is at least some hope that they will appear as similar as possible, because the color values for these sixteen are defined. Beyond those, all bets are off. Browsers may implement similar shades for the same color name, or they may not; the differences may be imperceptible to the eye, or so obvious that they're almost jarring.

Reproducing Colors

Consistent color reproduction is, as it happens, a major issue unto itself. As we'll soon see, all colors can be specified in a consistent manner, which would seem to solve the issue of whether two different user agents will display the same color. In fact, the situation is much more complicated. In the first place, human perception is relative. The same color displayed on the same monitor may appear to change due to changes in lighting, ambient brightness, adjacent colors, and many other factors. You can experiment with this effect simply by changing the background color of your computer's desktop. The colors of your icons will appear to subtly shift as you do so.

In an attempt to address this situation, displays such as monitors usually have a default *gamma value* set; this is a factor that modifies colors to account for display conditions. The gamma is typically set via the operating system, although more expensive monitors may have their own gamma settings. The problem is that different systems have different gamma values. Thus, if you were to create a web page with a color background and then display it on Windows and Macintosh machines side by side under identical lighting conditions, the background color would look different on each machine. This also crops up in graphics created for the Web, in that graphics created on Windows machines tend to appear darker to Macintosh users, whereas images created on a Macintosh look lighter for Windows users.

The situation degrades even further when colors are printed, since factors as diverse as the stock and color of the paper used, and even the temperature of the printing mechanism, can affect how well colors are reproduced on paper.

In effect, this is yet another area where you must remember that total control over document appearance is simply not possible. In this case, it's due to a combination of inconsistent operating system settings and the vagaries of human perception, which is an obstacle no computer is going to overcome any time soon.

It is left to individual authors to decide what chances they wish to take with using named colors, but at least with the specified sixteen colors, there is some moderate hope of consistency.

Okay, so that was the easiest way to specify color—scary as that may seem, it's true. The other four ways are a bit more complicated. The advantage is that with these methods, you can specify any color in the 8-bit color spectrum, not just sixteen (or however many) named colors. This is accomplished by taking advantage of the way colors are generated by computers.

Colors by RGB

Computers create colors by combining different levels of red, green, and blue, which is why color in computers is often referred to as *RGB color*. In fact, if you were to open up a computer monitor, or even a television, and you got far enough into the projection tube, you would discover that there are three "guns." (Remember, however, that actually looking for these guns will pretty much void your monitor's warranty.) These guns shoot out beams of light in varying levels of light and dark, in one of the three RGB colors, at each point on the screen. The brightnesses of each of these beams combine at each point to form all of the colors you see on your screen. Each point, by the way, is known as a *pixel*, which is a term to which we'll return later in the chapter.

Given the way colors are created on a monitor, it makes sense that a good way to let you set colors is to give you direct access to those color levels, thereby determining your own mixture of the beams. This method is a bit more complex, obviously, but the payoffs are worth it because you aren't limited to whichever colors have been named.

Percentage colors

There are, in fact, four ways to affect RGB color. The first way we'll examine is perhaps the easiest to grasp because it uses percentages. Here's an example:

```
rgb(100%,100%,100%)
```

This color declaration sets the level of red to its maximum, blue to maximum, and green the same. These combine to create white, which is, after all, the combination of all colors. Alternatively, in order to specify black—the absence of color—all three would be set to 0%. Here are a few more color declarations:

```
H1 {color: rgb(0%,0%,0%);}        /*black*/
H2 {color: rgb(50%,50%,50%);}     /*medium gray*/
H3 {color: rgb(25%,66%,40%);}
```

The general syntax of this type of color value is:

```
rgb(color)
```

where *color* is one of two ways to specify the color. The first way is to use percentages, and the second, which uses numbers, is discussed later in this section.

Perhaps you want your H1 elements to be colored a shade of red somewhere between the values for red and maroon. **red** is simply `rgb(100%,0%,0%)`, whereas **maroon** is more like `(50%,0%,0%)`. In order to get a color between those two, you might try this:

```
H1 {color: rgb(75%,0%,0%);}
```

This makes the red component of the color lighter than that of **maroon**, but darker than that of **red**. If, on the other hand, you wished to create a pale red color, then you would want to raise the other two values:

```
H1 {color: rgb(75%,50%,50%);}
```

The easiest way to visualize how these percentages correspond to color is to create a table of gray values. Besides, grayscale printing is all we can afford for this book, so that's what we'll have to do:

```
P.one {color: rgb(0%,0%,0%);}
P.two {color: rgb(20%,20%,20%);}
P.three {color: rgb(60%,60%,60%);}
P.four {color: rgb(80%,80%,80%);}
P.five {color: rgb(100%,100%,100%);}
```

Figure 3-1 shows what the various percentage values will yield.

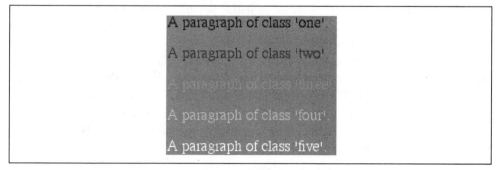

Figure 3-1. Grayscale values

Of course, since we're dealing in shades of gray, all three RGB numbers are the same in each statement. If any one of them was different from the others, then a color would start to emerge. If, for example, `rgb(50%,50%,50%)` were modified to be `rgb(50%,50%,60%)`, the result would be a medium gray with just a hint of blue.

The equivalents for the various rainbow primaries, plus a few others, are presented in Table 3-1.

Table 3-1. Percentage RGB Equivalents for Common Colors

Color	Percentage Equivalent
red	`rgb(100%,0%,0%)`
orange	`rgb(100%,40%,0%)`
yellow	`rgb(100%,100%,0%)`
green	`rgb(0%,100%,0%)`
blue	`rgb(0%,0%,100%)`
indigo	`rgb(20%,0%,100%)`
violet	`rgb(80%,0%,100%)`
medium gray	`rgb(50%,50%,50%)`
dark gray	`rgb(20%,20%,20%)`
tan	`rgb(100%,80%,60%)`
gold	`rgb(100%,80%,0%)`
purple	`rgb(100%,0%,100%)`

It is also possible, at least in theory, to use fractional values. For example, you might want a color to be exactly 25.5% red, 40% green, and 98.6% blue. Not a problem:

```
H2 {color: rgb(25.5%,40%,98.6%);}
```

Actually, there is a problem. Some user agents may not recognize decimal values, and still others could interpret them as if the decimal wasn't there, which would lead them to think the preceding value is actually `rgb(255%,40%,986%)`. In that case, assuming the user agent behaves correctly, the out-of-range values will be "clipped" to the nearest legal value—in this case, `100%`. Thus, a user agent which ignores the decimal points should act as if the declared value is `rgb(100%,40%,100%)`. Whether it does so is, of course, another story altogether. Also, negative values aren't allowed, so any value set to be less than `0%` should be clipped to that amount. For example, the following values would be clipped as demonstrated in Figure 3-2:

```
P.one {color: rgb(300%,4200%,110%);}
P.two {color: rgb(0%,-40%,-5000%);}
```

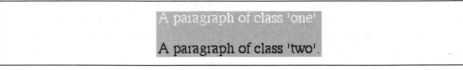

Figure 3-2. Out-of-range values are clipped

Going by numbers

Closely related to percentages is a method of setting color using raw numbers. These numbers are on a scale from 0 to 255, where `rgb(0,0,0)` represents black and `rgb(255,255,255)` represents white. Most of you will recognize this number range from other sources: it's the decimal equivalent of an 8-bit binary number. If you don't recognize this, then it's enough to know that computers employ binary values (on/off) for everything, including representations of numbers and colors, and 255 is one of the numbers that just naturally fall out of that sort of setup.

Anyway, this is almost exactly the same as setting percentage values: only the scale is different, going up to 255 instead of 100%. Accordingly, the values in Table 3-2 correspond to our usual list of colors.

Table 3-2. Numeric RGB Equivalents for Common Colors

Color	Numeric RGB Equivalent
red	`rgb(255,0,0)`
orange	`rgb(255,102,0)`
yellow	`rgb(255,255,0)`
green	`rgb(0,255,0)`
blue	`rgb(0,0,255)`
indigo	`rgb(51,0,255)`
violet	`rgb(204,0,255)`
medium gray	`rgb(128,128,128)`
dark gray	`rgb(51,51,51)`
tan	`rgb(255,204,153)`
gold	`rgb(255,204,0)`
purple	`rgb(255,0,255)`

As expected, any value outside the range of 0–255 is clipped, just as with percentages—although in this case, of course, the values are clipped to 0 and 255:

```
H1 {color: rgb(0,0,0);}              /* black */
H2 {color: rgb(127,127,127);}        /* gray */
H3 {color: rgb(255,255,255);}        /* white */
P.one {color: rgb(300,2500,101);}    /* white */
P.two {color: rgb(-10,-450,-2);}     /* black */
```

If you prefer percentages, you can use them, and it's actually easy to convert between percentages and straight numbers. If you know the percentages for each of the RGB levels you want, then you need only apply them to the number 255 to get the resulting values. Let's say you have a color of 25% red, 37.5% green, and 60% blue. Multiplying each of those percentages by 255, we get 63.75, 95.625, and 153. We need to round those off to `rgb(64,96,153)`, however, because only integers (whole numbers) are permitted when using numbers. Percentages can have decimals, but these numbers can't.

Of course, if you already know the percentages, there isn't much point in converting them into straight numbers. This notation is more useful for people who use programs such as Photoshop, which produce such color values, or for those who are familiar enough with the technical details of color generation to already think in terms of 0–255 values.

Then again, such people are probably more familiar with thinking in hexadecimal notation, which is what we turn to next.

Hexadecimal colors

If you've done any web authoring in the past and have ever set a color in the course of that authoring, then this part will be a snap. You can set a color using the same hexadecimal notation so familiar to web authors:

```
H1 {color: #FF0000;}    /* set H1's to red */
H2 {color: #903BC0;}    /* set H2's to a dusky purple */
H3 {color: #000000;}    /* set H3's to be black */
H4 {color: #808080;}    /* set H4's to be medium gray */
```

If you aren't familiar with this notation, here's a quick primer. First, *hexadecimal* means base-16 counting, so the basic unit is groups of 16, not the groups of 10 to which we're accustomed. In hexadecimal numbering, the valid digits are 0 through 9 and A through F. Once you've reached F, the next number is 10. Thus, a child learning to count in hex would learn this basic progression:

```
00, 01, 02, 03, 04, 05, 06, 07, 08, 09, 0A, 0B, 0C, 0D, 0E, 0F,
10, 11, 12, 13, 14, 15, 16, 17, 18, 19, 1A, 1B, 1C, 1D, 1E, 1F,
20, 21, 22, 23, ...
```

I realize that it may be a bit weird to think of letters as numbers, but that's how it works in hex. The digits A through F are actually just symbols—they could have been anything. Someone just decided that letters would be easier to remember than invented symbols...plus nobody would have to invent new names for letters.

How this corresponds to our regular decimal (base 10) numbering is fairly straightforward. 05 is equal to 5, 0C is equal to 12, 0F is the same as 15, and 10 is equal to 16. No, really. 1F is equal to 31, 20 to 32, and so on. It goes like this:

```
01, 02, 03, 04, 05, 06, 07, 08, 09, 0A, 0B, 0C, 0D, 0E, 0F,
01, 02, 03, 04, 05, 06 ,07, 08, 09, 10, 11, 12, 13, 14, 15, 16,

10, 11, 12, 13, 14, 15, 16, 17, 18, 19, 1A, 1B, 1C, 1D, 1E, 1F,
17, 18, 19, 20, 21, 22, 23, 24, 25, 26, 27, 28, 29, 30, 31, 32,

20, 21, 22, 23, ...
33, 34, 35, 36, ...
```

Computers have been using hex notation for quite some time now, and typically programmers either are trained in its use or pick it up through experience. Either way, most programmers are comfortable with hex notation—some of them even think in it—and so it's part of the CSS specification. Why? Because the specification was written and edited by programmers. It makes sense that they'd put in color schemes to which they could relate.

So, by stringing together three hex pairs, you can set a color. A more generic description of this method is:

```
#RRGGBB
```

Viewed in this way, the hex-pair method is a lot like the method we previously discussed—the one involving numbers from 0 to 255. In fact, 255 in decimal is equivalent to FF in hexadecimal, which explains a lot about how this method works. It's really the same as the last method: it just uses a different number system. If you have to pick between the two, use whichever makes you more comfortable.

So, similar to the way you can specify a color using three numbers from 0 to 255, you can specify one using three hex pairs. If you have a calculator that converts between decimal and hexadecimal, then making the jump should be pretty simple. If not, it might be a little more complicated. (Of course, you could just not use this method, but that would be too easy.)

Once again, we present some color equivalents in Table 3-3.

Table 3-3. Hexadecimal Equivalents for Common Colors

Color	Hexadecimal Equivalent
red	#FF0000
orange	#FF6600
yellow	#FFFF00
green	#00FF00
blue	#0000FF
indigo	#3300FF
violet	#CC00FF
medium gray	#808080
dark gray	#333333
tan	#FFCC99
gold	#FFCC00
purple	#FF00FF

Believe it or not, though, there's a way to set colors that involves even fewer keystrokes.

Short hexadecimal colors

Now, finally, the last method. Again, let's look at an example and then explain it:

```
H1 {color: #000;}    /* set H1s to be black */
H2 {color: #666;}    /* set H2s to be dark gray */
H3 {color: #FFF;}    /* set H3s to be white */
```

As you can see from the markup, there are only three digits in each color value. However, since hexadecimal numbers between 00 and FF need two digits each, and we only have three digits total, how does this method work?

The answer is that the browser takes each digit and replicates it. Therefore, #F00 would be equivalent to #FF0000—and it's as simple as that. Otherwise, this method is the same as the #RRGGBB method we just discussed, only shorter. #6FA would be the same as #66FFAA, and #FFF would come out #FFFFFF, which is the same as white. This approach is sometimes called *shorthand hex notation*.

One thing to watch out for is that with the hexadecimal methods, unlike the numeric methods, there are no defined clipping methods for the hex-pair systems. If you enter an invalid value, the browser's response could be unpredictable. A well-written browser will perform clipping so that out-of-range values are assumed to be whichever limit they exceed, but you can't necessarily count on this. As an example, Netscape Navigator 4.x will not ignore or clip an invalid color value, but will instead perform some sort of magic translation to yield a totally unexpected color.

Bringing the colors together

Table 3-4 presents an overview of the colors we've discussed. Italicized color names are those that can be legally used as values of a color declaration. Those without italics might not be recognized by browsers and therefore should be defined with either RGB or hexadecimal values (just to be safe). In addition, there are some shortened hexadecimal values that do not appear at all. In these cases, the longer (6-digit) values cannot be shortened, because they do not replicate. For example, the value #880 expands to #888800, not #808000 (otherwise known as olive). Therefore, there is no shortened version of #808000, and the appropriate entry in the table is left blank.

Table 3-4. Color Equivalents

Color	Percentage	Numeric	Hex Pair	Short Hex
red	rgb(100%,0%,0%)	rgb(255,0,0)	#FF0000	#F00
orange	rgb(100%,40%,0%)	rgb(255,102,0)	#FF6600	#F60
yellow	rgb(100%,100%,0%)	rgb(255,255,0)	#FFFF00	#FF0
green	rgb(0%,100%,0%)	rgb(0,255,0)	#00FF00	#0F0

Table 3-4. Color Equivalents (continued)

Color	Percentage	Numeric	Hex Pair	Short Hex
blue	rgb(0%,0%,100%)	rgb(0,0,255)	#0000FF	#00F
indigo	rgb(20%,0%,100%)	rgb(51,0,255)	#3300FF	#30F
violet	rgb(80%,0%,100%)	rgb(204,0,255)	#CC00FF	#C0F
aqua	rgb(0%,100%,100%)	rgb(0,255,255)	#00FFFF	#0FF
black	rgb(0%,0%,0%)	rgb(0,0,0)	#000000	#000
fuschia	rgb(100%,0%,100%)	rgb(255,0,255)	#FF00FF	#F0F
gray	rgb(50%,50%,50%)	rgb(128,128,128)	#808080	
lime	rgb(0%,100%,0%)	rgb(0,255,0)	#00FF00	#0F0
maroon	rgb(50%,0%,0%)	rgb(128,0,0)	#800000	
navy	rgb(0%,0%,50%)	rgb(0,0,128)	#000080	
olive	rgb(50%,50%,0%)	rgb(128,128,0)	#808000	
purple	rgb(50%,0%,50%)	rgb(128,0,128)	#800080	
silver	rgb(75%,75%,75%)	rgb(192,192,192)	#C0C0C0	
teal	rgb(0%,50%,50%)	rgb(0,128,128)	#008080	
white	rgb(100%,100%,100%)	rgb(255,255,255)	#FFFFFF	#FFF
dark gray	rgb(20%,20%,20%)	rgb(51,51,51)	#333333	#333
tan	rgb(100%,80%,60%)	rgb(255,204,153)	#FFCC99	#FC9

Web-safe colors

You may recall the earlier discussion about how colors aren't always the same across different operating systems, user agents, and so forth. There is one way to partially beat this problem, although once again it means restricting your color choices. There is a set of 216 colors that are considered "web-safe," which means they should look the same on all computers and browsers, without any dithering or color-shifting. Note that I say "should"—this is not a guarantee. It generally seems to work, however.

Web-safe colors are those colors that are expressed in multiples of the RGB values 20% and 51, and the corresponding hex-pair value 33. Also, 0% or 0 is a safe value. So, if you use RGB percentages, then make all three values either 0% or a number divisible by 20; for example, rgb(40%,100%,80%) or rgb(60%,0%,0%). If you use RGB values on the 0–255 scale, then values should be either 0 or divisible by 51, as in rgb(0,204,153) or rgb(255,0,102).

With hex pairs, the appropriate values are 00, 33, 66, 99, CC, and FF. Any hex-pair triplet using those values in any combination is considered to be web-safe. Examples are #669933, #00CC66, and #FF00FF. This means the shorthand hex values that are web-safe are 0, 3, 6, 9, C, and F; therefore, #693, #0C6, and #F0F are examples of web-safe colors.

Wow! Who knew there were so many ways to define a color? I'll bet you'll never look at a rainbow in quite the same way again. Now, let's move on to units that really measure up.

Length Units

A lot of CSS properties, such as margins, depend on length measurements in order to properly display various page elements. It probably comes as no surprise to you, then, that there are a number of ways to measure length in CSS.

All length units can be expressed as either positive or negative numbers, followed by a label—although some properties will only accept positive numbers. They are also real numbers; that is, numbers with decimal fractions, such as 10.5 or 4.561. All length units are followed by a two-letter abbreviation that represents the actual unit of length being specified, such as `in` (inches), or `pt` (points). The only exception to this rule is a length of 0 (zero), which need not always be followed by a unit.

These length units are divided into two types: *absolute units* and *relative units*.

Absolute Length Units

No vodka jokes, please. We start with absolute units because they're easiest to understand, despite the fact that they're almost unusable in web design. The five types of absolute units are as follows:

Inches (`in`)

> As you might expect, the inches one finds on a ruler in America. The fact that this unit is even in the specification, given that almost the entire world uses the metric system, is an interesting insight into the pervasiveness of American interests on the Internet—but let's not get into virtual sociopolitical theory right now.

Centimeters (`cm`)

> The centimeters that one finds on rulers the world over. There are 2.54 cm to an inch, and one centimeter equals 0.394 inches.

Millimeters (`mm`)

> You guessed it. For those Americans who are metric-challenged, there are 10 millimeters to a centimeter, so you get 25.4 mm to an inch, and 1 millimeter equals 0.0394 inches.

Points (`pt`)

> Now it gets interesting. Points are standard typographical measures, used by printers and typesetters for decades and by word-processing programs for many years. By definition, there are 72 points to an inch, since points were

defined before use of the metric system had really caught on. Therefore, the capital letters of text set to 12 points should be a sixth of an inch tall. For example, `P {font-size: 18pt;}` is equivalent to `P {font-size: 0.25in;}`.

Picas (`pc`)

Another typographical term. A pica is equivalent to 12 points, which means there are 6 picas to an inch. As above, the capital letters of text set to 1 pica should be a sixth of an inch tall. For example, `P {font-size: 1.5pc;}` would set text to be the same size as the example declarations found in the definition of points.

These units are, of course, only really useful if the browser knows all the details of the monitor on which your page is displayed, or the printer you're using to generate hard copy, or whatever other user agent you might be using.

The sorts of things that can affect the display in a web browser, for example, are the size of the monitor and the resolution to which the monitor is set. Of course, there isn't a lot that you, as the author, can do about this. You can only hope that even if the browser can't get all that information, at least the measurements will be consistent in relation to each other; that is, a setting of `1.0in` will be twice as large as `0.5in`, as shown in Figure 3-3.

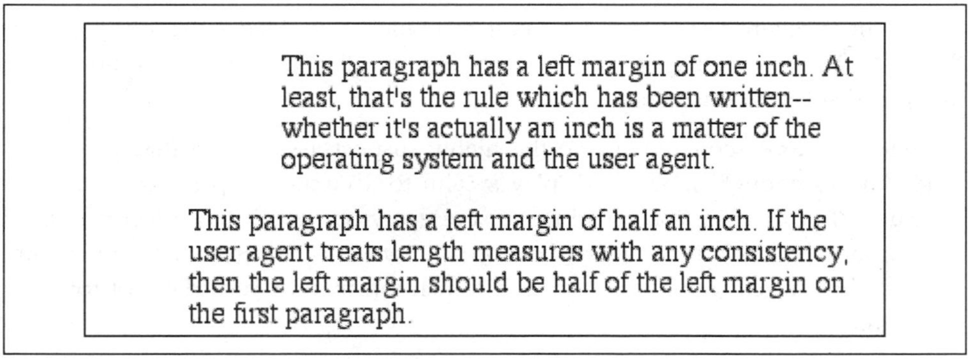

This paragraph has a left margin of one inch. At least, that's the rule which has been written-- whether it's actually an inch is a matter of the operating system and the user agent.

This paragraph has a left margin of half an inch. If the user agent treats length measures with any consistency, then the left margin should be half of the left margin on the first paragraph.

Figure 3-3. A margin of 1.0 inches (top) and 0.5 inches (bottom)

Working with absolute lengths

As a Windows user, you might be able to set your display driver to use real-world measures. Try clicking on the Start button, pointing to Settings, then clicking Control Panel, and from the Control Panel window double-click on Display. On the Display dialog box there should be a Settings tab. Click on this, and then click on the Advanced button to reveal a dialog box which may be different on each PC. You should see a section labeled Font Size, in which case select Other, and then hold a ruler up to the screen and move the slider until the two match. Finally click OK several times and you're set!

If you're a Macintosh user, there isn't a place to set this information, but that's all right—the Mac OS has already made an assumption about the relationship between on-screen pixels and absolute measures, by declaring your monitor to have 72 pixels to the inch. This assumption is totally wrong, but it's built into the operating system, and therefore pretty much unavoidable, at least for now. (With any luck, future browsers will include a preference setting for defining your own pixel-per-inch value, thus circumventing any OS-imposed limitations.)

Therefore, on many Macintosh-based web browsers, such as Netscape 4.x, and Internet Explorer 3.x and 4.x, any point value will be equivalent to the same length in pixels: 24pt text will be 24 pixels tall, and 8pt text will be 8 pixels tall. This is, unfortunately, just slightly too small to be legible, despite the fact it looks pretty good on a Windows-based browser. Figure 3-4 illustrates the problem.

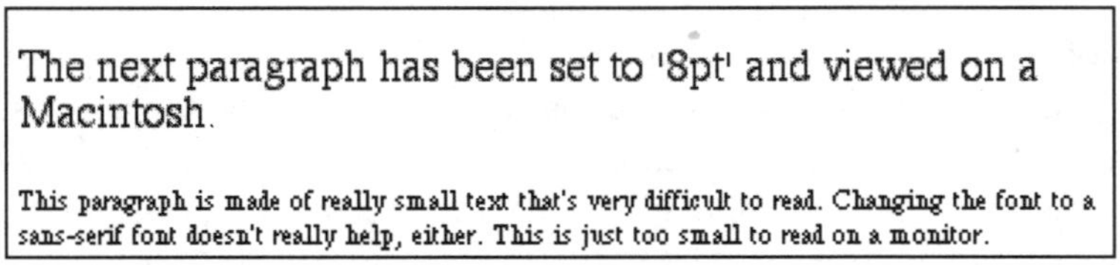

Figure 3-4. Macintosh displays tend to be illegible at small point sizes

This is an excellent example of why points should be avoided when designing for the web. Ems, percentages, and even pixels are all preferable to points where browser display is concerned.

Despite all we've seen, let's make the highly suspect assumption that your computer knows enough about its display system to accurately reproduce real-world measures. In that case, you could make sure every paragraph has a top margin of half an inch by declaring P {margin-top: 0.5in;}. No matter what the circumstances, then, a paragraph will have a half-inch top margin, regardless of font size or anything else.

Absolute units are much more useful in defining style sheets for printed documents, where measuring things in terms of inches, points, and picas is much more common. As we've seen, attempting to use absolute measures in web design is fraught with peril at best, so let's turn to some more useful units of measure.

Relative Length Units

Far from being Einsteinian in nature, relative units are so called because they are measured in relation to other things. The actual (or absolute) distance they measure can change due to factors beyond their control, such as screen resolution, the width of the viewing area, the user's preference settings, and a whole host of other things. In addition, for some relative units, their size is almost always relative to the element that uses them and will thus change from element to element.

There are three relative length units: em, ex, and px. The first two stand for "em-height" and "x-height," which are common typographical measurements; however, in CSS, they have meanings you might not expect if you are familiar with typography. The last type of length is px, which stands for "pixels." A pixel is one of the dots you can see on your computer's monitor if you look closely enough. This value is defined to be relative because it depends on the resolution of the display device, a subject that we'll discuss at length.

em and ex units

First, let us consider em and ex. In CSS, one "em" is the value of font-size for a given font, so if the font-size of an element is 14 points, then for that element, one "em" is the same as 14 points. In other words, whatever size you set the font's size to be, that's the value of one em for that element. In relation to a paragraph of 18-point text, the length of an em is 18 points.

Obviously, this value can change from element to element. For example, given an H1 whose font is 24 pixels in size, an H2 element whose font is 18 pixels in size, and a paragraph whose font is 12 pixels, we get what's shown in Figure 3-5:

```
H1 {font-size: 24px;}
H2 {font-size: 18px;}
P {font-size: 12px;}
H1, H2, P {margin-left: 1em;}

<H1>Left margin = 24 pixels</H1>
<H2>Left margin = 18 pixels</H1>
<P>Left margin = 12 pixels</P>
```

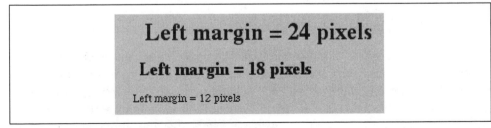

Figure 3-5. Margins change according to point size

The only exception to this rule is setting the size of the font, in which case the value of em is relative to the parent element (this is shown in Figure 3-6):

```
SMALL {font-size: 0.8em;}

<P>Although this text is the default size for the user agent, the
<SMALL>small-text element</SMALL> within the paragraph has a font
size which is 80% the rest of the text in the paragraph.</P>
```

Although this text is the default size for the user agent,
the small-text element within the paragraph has a font size
which is 80% the rest of the text in the paragraph.

Figure 3-6. Font size set in ems is relative to the parent element

ex, on the other hand, refers to the height of a lowercase *x* in the font being used.
Therefore, if you have two paragraphs of text in which the text is 24 points in size,
but each paragraph uses a different font, then the value of ex could be different
for each paragraph. This is because different fonts have different heights for *x*, as
we see in Figure 3-7.

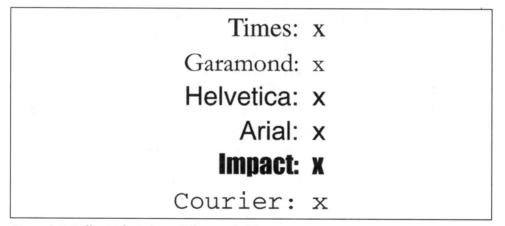

Figure 3-7. Different fonts have different x-heights

Even though the examples use 24-point text, and therefore each have an em of 24
points, the ex for each is different.

Practical issues with em and ex

This is all difficult enough, but just to make things more so, this is all what's supposed to happen in theory. In practice, however, many user agents get their value
for ex by taking the value of em and dividing it in half. Why? Well, apparently
most fonts don't have the value of their x-height built in, and it's a difficult thing to
compute. Since most fonts have lowercase letters that are about half as tall as
uppercase letters, it's a convenient fiction to assume that 1ex is equivalent to
0.5em. It is hoped that, as time goes on, user agents will start using real values for
ex, and the half-em shortcut will fade into the past.

Pixel lengths

Now to pixels, where the situation gets *really* confusing. On the face of things,
pixels really should be very straightforward. After all, if you look at a monitor

closely enough, you can see that it's broken up into a grid of tiny little boxes. Each box is a pixel. However, how many of those boxes equal an inch? If the monitor is set to be 1,024 pixels wide by 768 pixels tall, and the monitor's screen is exactly 14.22 inches wide by 10.67 inches tall, and the display area exactly fills the monitor, then each pixel will be 1/72 of an inch wide and tall. As you might guess, this is a very, very rare occurrence, especially since it's tough to find a monitor with exactly those dimensions. So it turns out that on most monitors, the actual number of pixels per inch (ppi) is higher than 72—sometimes much higher, up to 120 ppi and beyond.

To make things even more confusing, the CSS specification recommends a "reference pixel" which works out to roughly 90 ppi—a measure very few (if any) operating systems actually use. While the specification assumes that `90px` should equal `1in`, nothing else really does, so that doesn't help. In general, if you declare something like `font-size: 18px`, then you're leaving it up to the user agent to decide how big a pixel really is. A web browser will almost certainly use actual pixels on your monitor—after all, they're already there—but with other display devices, like printers, the situation gets a little uncertain.

 One example of problems with pixel measurements can be found in an early CSS1 implementation. In Internet Explorer 3.x, when a document is printed, IE3 assumes that `18px` is the same as 18 dots, which works out to be 18/300, or 6/100, of an inch—or, if you prefer, `.06in`. That's pretty small text!

On the other hand, pixel measurements are perfect for expressing the size of images, which are already a certain number of pixels tall and wide. In fact, the only time you would want to use other units of measure to express the size of images is if you want them scale along with the size of the text. This is an admirable and occasionally useful approach, and one which would really make sense if you were using vector-based images instead of pixel-based images. (With the adoption of Scalable Vector Graphics, this could actually become a reality.)

What to do?

Given all the issues involved, the best measures to use are probably the relative measures, most especially `em`, and also `px` when appropriate. Since `ex` is at present basically a fractional measure of `em`, it's not all that useful for the time being. If user agents are ever able to support real x-height measures, then `ex` might come into its own.

With that, we close out our discussion of length measurements. The rest of the chapter is pretty straightforward and not nearly so pessimistic.

Percentage Values

Compared to length units, percentage units are almost laughably simple. They're pretty much exactly what you'd expect—a positive or negative number, followed by a percent sign (%). For example:

```
H1 {font-size: 18pt;}
H1.tall {line-height: 150%;}
```

This sets the `line-height` of all H1 elements with a class of `tall` to be half again as large as normal, as we see in Figure 3-8.

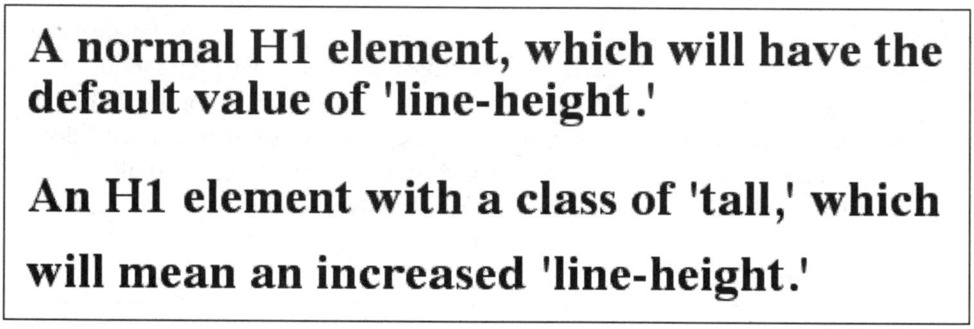

A normal H1 element, which will have the default value of 'line-height.'

An H1 element with a class of 'tall,' which will mean an increased 'line-height.'

Figure 3-8. Line height of 100% (top) and 150% (bottom)

Percentage values are always computed relative to another value—usually a length unit. In this case, the `line-height` is exactly 27 points (`18pt` times 1.5). This is the same as setting the `line-height` to `1.5em`, although neither method is particularly recommended over the other.

Percentages can, in general, be either positive or negative. However, there are properties that accept percentage values, but will not permit negative values (of any kind, including percentages). These will be mentioned as the properties are covered in subsequent chapters.

URLs

If you've written web pages, then you're familiar with URLs. URLs aren't often used in style sheets, but if you do need to refer to one—as in the `@import` statement, which is used when importing an external style sheet—then the general format is:

```
url(http://server/pathname)
```

This example defines an absolute URL. By absolute, we mean a URL that will work no matter what page it's found in, because it defines an absolute location in web space. Let's say that we have a server called *www.waffles.org*. On that server, there is a directory called *pix*, and in this directory is an image *waffle22.gif*. In this case, the absolute URL of that image would be *http://www.waffles.org/pix/waffle22.gif*. This URL is valid no matter where it is found, whether the page is on the server *www.waffles.org* or *web.pancakes.com*.

The other type of URL is a relative URL, so named because this type of URL specifies a location that is relative to the document that uses it. If you're referring to a relative location, such as a file in the same directory as your web page, then the general format is:

```
url(pathname)
```

This only works if the image is on the same server as the page that contains the URL. For argument's sake, we'll assume that we have a web page located at *http://www.waffles.org/syrup.html* and that we want the image *waffle.gif* to appear on this page. In that case, the relative URL could be *pix/waffle22.gif*.

This works because the web browser knows that it should take the same place it found the web document and add the relative URL to it. In this case, the server name *http://www.waffles.org/* added to the pathname *pix/waffles22.gif* equals *http://www.waffles.org/pix/waffle22.gif*.

Here are two more examples:

```
@import url(http://css1.style.org/example.css);
```

```
BODY {background-image: url(hatch.gif);}
```

It doesn't really matter whether you use absolute or relative URLs, so long as they define valid locations. You can use whichever is easier for you and your project.

Another thing you need to watch out for is that relative URLs are relative to the style sheet, not the HTML document. For example, you may have an external style sheet that imports another style sheet. If you use a relative URL to import the second style sheet, then it has to be relative to the first style sheet. As an example, consider an HTML document at *http://www.waffles.org/toppings/tips.html*, which has a LINK to the style sheet *http://www.waffles.org/styles/basic.css*:

```
<LINK REL="stylesheet" TYPE="text/css"
    HREF="http://www.waffles.org/styles/basic.css">
```

Inside the file *basic.css* is an @import statement referring to another style sheet:

```
@import url(special/toppings.css);
```

This @import will load the file *http://www.waffles.org/styles/special/toppings.css*, not *http://www.waffles.org/toppings/special/toppings.css*. If you have a style sheet at the latter location, then the @import in *basic.css* should read:

```
@import url(http://www.waffles.org/toppings/special/toppings.css);
```

In other words, use an absolute URL.

This might be a good idea in any case. As it happens, Navigator 4 interprets relative URLs in relation to the HTML document, not the style sheet. Yes, this is wrong, but that's how Navigator 4 does things. Therefore, it's generally easiest if you make all of your URLs absolute, since Navigator does at least handle those correctly.

Note that there cannot be a space between the `url` and the opening parenthesis. Thus:

```
BODY {background: url(http://www.pix.web/picture1.jpg);}      /* correct */
BODY {background: url (images/picture2.jpg);}                 /* INCORRECT */
```

If the space is included, the entire rule will be invalidated, and therefore ignored.

CSS2 Units

In addition to what we've covered, CSS2 adds a small number of new units, almost all of which are concerned with aural style sheets (employed by those browsers that are capable of speech). We'll briefly cover them here:

Angle values

Used to define the position from which a given sound should seem to originate. There are three type of angles: degrees (`deg`), grads (`grad`), and radians (`rad`). For example, a right angle could be declared as `90deg`, `100grad`, or `1.57rad`; in each case, the values are translated into degrees in the range 0 through 360. This is also true of negative values, which are allowed. The measure `-90deg` is the same as `270deg`.

Time values

Used to specify delays between speaking elements, these values can be expressed as either milliseconds (`ms`) or seconds (`s`). Thus, `100ms` and `0.1s` are equivalent. Time values may not be negative.

Frequency values

Used to declare a given frequency for the sounds that speaking browsers can produce. Frequency values can be expressed as hertz (`Hz`) or megahertz (`mHz`) and cannot be negative. The values labels are case-insensitive, so `10mHz` and `10mhz` are equivalent.

In addition to these values, there is also an old friend with a new name. A *URI* is a *Uniform Resource Identifier*, which is sort of another name for a Uniform Resource Locator (URL). The difference is, for now, mostly semantic, but many authors are beginning to adopt the convention of referring to online addresses as URIs, not URLs. The specification still requires that URIs be declared with the form `url(...)`, though, so it's hard to know exactly what the point was of including a section in CSS2 about how CSS2 uses URIs instead of URLs.

Summary

Units and values cover a wide spectrum of areas, from length units to color units to the location of files (such as images). For the most part, units are the one area that user agents get almost totally correct; it's those few little bugs and quirks that get you, though. Interpreting relative URLs incorrectly, for example, has bedeviled many authors, and leads to an over-reliance on absolute URLs. Colors are another area where user agents almost always do well, except for a few little quirks here and there. The vagaries of length units, however, far from being bugs, are an interesting problem for any author to tackle.

These units all have their advantages and drawbacks, depending on the circumstance in which they're used. We've already seen some of these, and the nuances of such circumstances will be discussed in the rest of the book, beginning with the CSS properties that describe ways to alter the way text is displayed.

4

Text Properties

While your web design efforts may be largely focused on picking the right colors and getting the coolest look for your pages, when it comes right down to it, you'll probably spend most of your time worrying about where text will go and how it will look. This concern gave rise to HTML tags such as <FONT> and <CENTER>, which give you some measure of control over the appearance and placement of text.

Because of this fact, much of CSS is concerned with properties that affect text in one way or another. In CSS1, the properties are split up into two sections: "Text Properties" and "Font Properties." This chapter is devoted to explaining the former. We'll tackle fonts in Chapter 5, *Fonts*—they're quite complicated in their own way and so deserve a chapter all their own.

Manipulating Text

You may well wonder what the difference is between text and fonts. Simply put, text is the content. The font used to display it is just one more way of altering the appearance of the text. Before we get into fonts, though, there are some simpler ways to affect the appearance of your text. Besides, some of the things we discuss here will be important when we discuss the font properties, so it makes more sense to discuss the text properties first.

With the text properties, you can affect the position of text in relation to the rest of the line, and do things like superscripting, underlining, and changing the capitalization. You can even simulate, to a limited degree, the use of the Tab key on a typewriter.

Indentation and Horizontal Alignment

It's best to start with a discussion of how you can affect the horizontal positioning of text within a line. This is not the same as actual positioning, which is done with respect to the page itself. Think of these properties as ways to affect how the lines of text are laid out, as you might do when creating a newsletter or writing a report.

Indenting text

One of the most sought-after effects in text formatting on the Web is the ability to indent the first line of a paragraph. (Close behind that is the desire to eliminate the "blank line" between paragraphs, which is discussed in Chapter 7, *Boxes and Borders*). Some sites solve this by placing a small transparent image before the first letter in a paragraph, thus shoving the text over, and others use the utterly non-standard SPACER tag to get a similar effect. There is a better way, thanks to CSS.

---

text-indent

Values	<length> | <percentage>
Initial value	0
Inherited	yes
Applies to	block-level elements

Note: Percentage values refer to parent element's width.

Using text-indent, any element can have its first line indented by a given length—even if that length is negative. The most common use for this property, of course, is to indent the first line of paragraphs:

```
P {text-indent: 0.25in;}
```

This rule will cause the first line of any paragraph to be indented a quarter-inch, as shown in Figure 4-1.

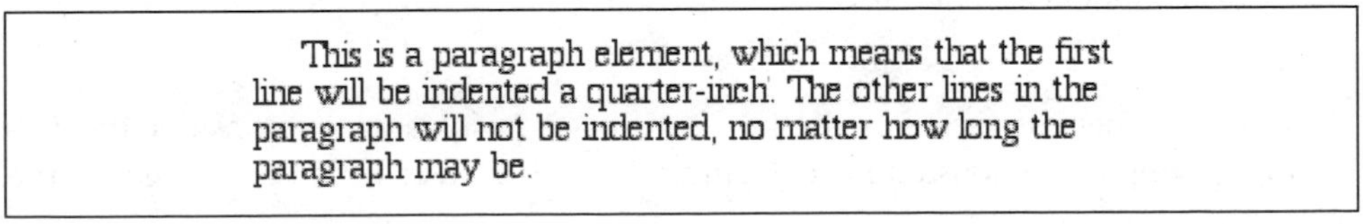

> This is a paragraph element, which means that the first line will be indented a quarter-inch. The other lines in the paragraph will not be indented, no matter how long the paragraph may be.

Figure 4-1. Text indenting

In general, `text-indent` can be applied to any block-level element, such as PRE, H1, or BLOCKQUOTE. You can't apply it to inline elements, such as STRONG or A, nor can you use it on replaced elements such as images—which makes sense, of course. However, if you have an image within the first line of a block-level element like a paragraph, it will be shifted over with the rest of the text, as shown in Figure 4-2.

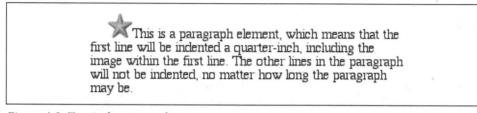

Figure 4-2. Text indenting and images

It's possible to set negative values for `text-indent`, which can be used in a number of interesting ways. The most common is known as a "hanging indent," where the first line hangs out to the left of the rest of the element, as shown in Figure 4-3:

```
P {text-indent: -4em;}
```

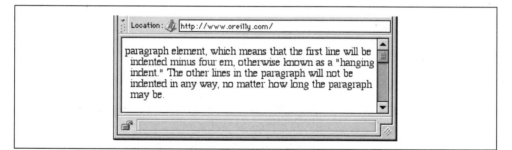

Figure 4-3. Negative text indenting

As you can see in Figure 4-3, there is an inherent danger in setting a negative value for `text-indent`: the first three words ("This is a") have been chopped off by the left edge of the browser window. In order to avoid such display problems, it is generally advisable to use a margin or some padding that will accommodate the negative indentation, as shown in Figure 4-4:

```
P {text-indent: -4em; padding-left: 4em;}
```

Negative indents can occasionally be used to one's advantage. Consider the following example, demonstrated in Figure 4-5, which adds a floated image to the mix:

```
P.hang {text-indent: -30px;}
```

```
<P CLASS="hang"><IMG SRC="floater.gif" WIDTH="30px" HEIGHT="60px"
ALIGN="left" ALT="Floated">This paragraph has a negatively indented first
line, which overlaps the floated image which precedes the text.  Subsequent
lines do not overlap the image, since they are not indented in any way.</P>
```

> This is a paragraph element, which means that the first line
> will be indented minus four em, otherwise
> known as a "hanging indent." The other lines in
> the paragraph will not be indented in any way,
> no matter how long the paragraph may be.

Figure 4-4. Floated images and negative text-indenting

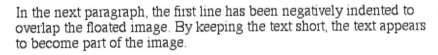

> This paragraph has a negatively-indented first line,
> which overlaps the floated image which
> precedes the text. Subsequent lines do not
> overlap the image, since they are not indented
> in any way.

Figure 4-5. Accounting for negative text-indenting

Many interesting designs can be achieved using this simple technique. Figure 4-6 shows one example, where the first line of text has been indented –40px.

In the next paragraph, the first line has been negatively indented to overlap the floated image. By keeping the text short, the text appears to become part of the image.

Figure 4-6. Negative indents and floating images

Any unit of length may be used with `text-indent`. In addition, percentage values are allowed. In this case, the percentage refers to the width of the parent element being indented. Thus, if you set the indent value to `5%`, the first line of an affected element will be indented by 5% of the parent element's width, as shown in Figure 4-7:

```
DIV {width: 400px;}
P {text-indent: 5%;}
```

```
<P>This paragraph is contained inside a DIV which is 400px wide, so the
first line of the paragraph is indented 20px (400 * 5% = 20).  This is because
percentages are computed with respect to the width of the parent element.</P>
```

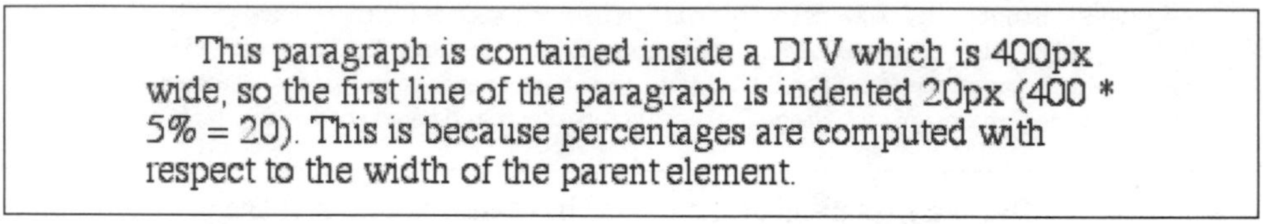

> This paragraph is contained inside a DIV which is 400px wide, so the first line of the paragraph is indented 20px (400 * 5% = 20). This is because percentages are computed with respect to the width of the parent element.

Figure 4-7. Text-indenting with percentages

Note that this indentation will only apply to the first line of an element, even if you insert line breaks. Thus, as Figure 4-8 shows:

```
DIV {width: 400px;}
P {text-indent: 5%;}


<DIV>
<P>This paragraph is contained inside a DIV which is 400px wide, so the
first line of the paragraph is indented 20px (400 * 5% = 20).  Subsequent
lines within the same element are not indented,<BR>
even if they follow a<BR>
line-break.</P>
<P>Once again, the first line of this paragraph is indented by 20px,
but other lines in the same element are not.</P>
</DIV>
```

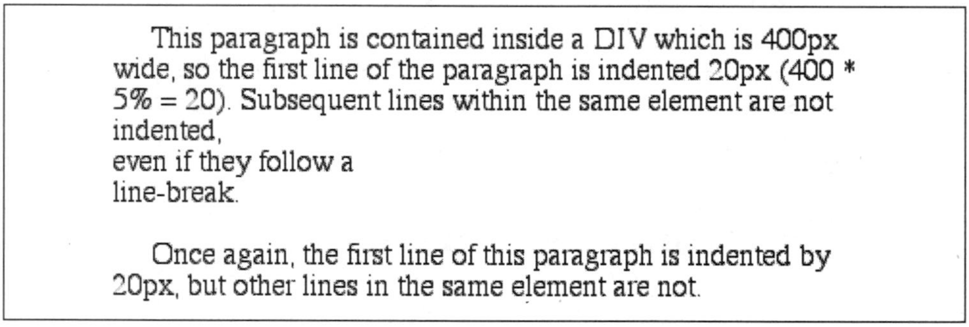

> This paragraph is contained inside a DIV which is 400px wide, so the first line of the paragraph is indented 20px (400 * 5% = 20). Subsequent lines within the same element are not indented,
> even if they follow a
> line-break.
>
> Once again, the first line of this paragraph is indented by 20px, but other lines in the same element are not.

Figure 4-8. Text-indenting and line breaks

The interesting part about `text-indent` is that it's inherited, but what's inherited is the computed value, not the declared value. Take the following markup:

```
BODY {width: 500px;}
DIV {width: 500px; text-indent: 10%;}
P {width: 200px;}


<DIV>
This first line of the DIV is indented by 50 pixels.
<P>This paragraph is 200px wide, and the first line of the paragraph
is indented 50px.  This is because computed values for 'text-indent'
are inherited, instead of the declared values.</P>
</DIV>
```

Even though the paragraph is only 200 pixels wide, its first line is indented by 50 pixels (as Figure 4-9 shows), which is the inherited value for `text-indent`.

> This first line of the DIV is indented by 50 pixels, as we can see in the first line of this document. It is indented this far because the BODY is 500px wide, and 50 is 10% of 500.
>
> This paragraph is 200px wide, and the first line of the paragraph is indented 50px. This is because the computed values for 'text-indent' are inherited, instead of the declared values.

Figure 4-9. Inherited text-indenting

Aligning text

Even more basic than `text-indent` is the property `text-align`, which affects how lines of text in an element are aligned with respect to one another. There are four values; the first three are pretty simple, but the fourth has a few complexities.

text-align

Values	`left` | `center` | `right` | `justify`
Initial value	UA specific
Inherited	yes
Applies to	block-level elements

The fastest way to understand how these values work is to examine Figure 4-10.

> This paragraph is set to `text-align: left`, which causes the text within the element to line up along the left margin.
>
> This paragraph is set to `text-align: center`, which centers the text within the element.
>
> This paragraph is set to `text-align: right`, which causes the the text within the element to line up along the right margin.
>
> This paragraph is set to `text-align: justify`, which causes the the text within the element to line up along the both margins. This can have some unforeseen effects in terms of how the words and letters are distributed on each line.

Figure 4-10. Behaviors of the text-align property

`text-align` is another property that only applies to block-level elements such as paragraphs. It isn't possible to center an anchor within its line without aligning the rest of the line (nor would you really want to).

The rule `text-align: center` can be used to replace the operation of the CENTER tag, as shown in Figure 4-11:

```
H1 {text-align: center;}
```

A Centered H1 Element

This is a paragraph without any alignment styles applied to it. It should therefore default to a left justification, since this document uses the English language. Other languages may have other default values for text-align.

Figure 4-11. Centering text with the text-align property

You can also cause the centering of elements that have both text and images within them—again, it will act just like the CENTER tag, as Figure 4-12 and the following markup show:

```
DIV.first {text-align: center;}


<H1>An Un-centered H1 Element</H1>
<DIV CLASS="first">
<P>
This is a paragraph without any alignment styles applied to it.  However, it is
contained within a DIV element which has alignment set, and this alignment will
inherit into the paragraph.  This will also affect any images which appear within
the DIV, such as this one <IMG SRC="star.gif"> or the next one.
</P>
<IMG SRC="floater.gif">
</DIV>
```

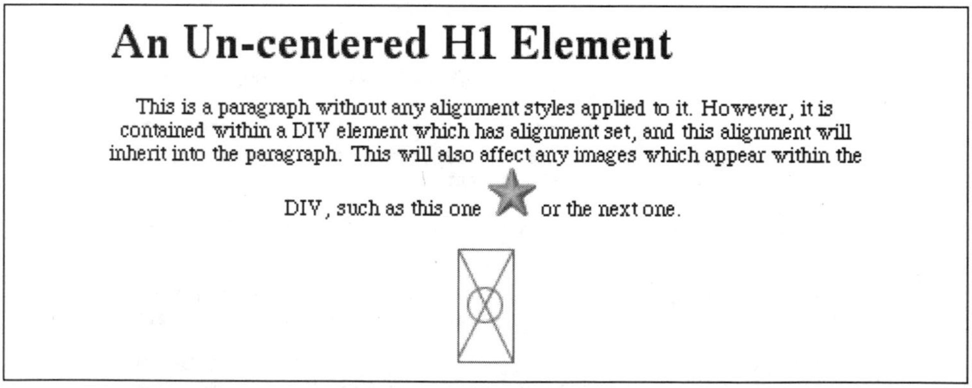

An Un-centered H1 Element

This is a paragraph without any alignment styles applied to it. However, it is contained within a DIV element which has alignment set, and this alignment will inherit into the paragraph. This will also affect any images which appear within the

DIV, such as this one ★ or the next one.

Figure 4-12. Centering text and inline images with the text-align property

However, if you want to center an image all by itself, `text-align` is *not* the correct way to go about it. Given the following markup, you'll get the result in Figure 4-13:

```
IMG {text-align: center;}
```

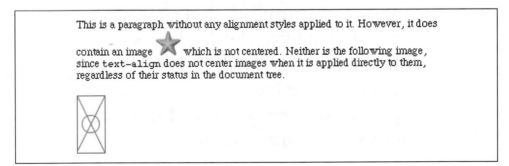

Figure 4-13. *The text-align property and block-level images*

The basic reason the image isn't centered is that it isn't a block-level element. The only way to center an image using `text-align` is to wrap a DIV around the image, and set the DIV's contents to be centered:

```
<DIV STYLE="text-align: center;">
   <IMG SRC="shiny.gif" ALT="Shiny object">
</DIV>
```

As Figure 4-14 shows, this will center the image.

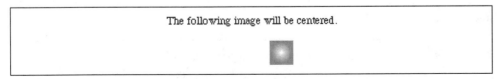

Figure 4-14. *Centering images the hard way*

For Western languages, which are read from left to right, the default value of `text-align` will be `left`, with text lining up on the left margin and having a ragged right margin (otherwise known as "left-to-right" text). Other languages, such as Hebrew and Arabic, will default to `right` instead, since these languages are written right-to-left. `center` has the expected effect, in that it causes each line of text to be centered within the element.

As for `justify`, there are a few issues to consider. As Figure 4-15 shows, justified text is formatted such that the ends of each line of text are placed at the inner edge of the parent element. This is accomplished by changing the spacing between words and letters so that each line is precisely the same length. This is an effect common to the print world (such as in this book), but under CSS, some extra considerations come into play.

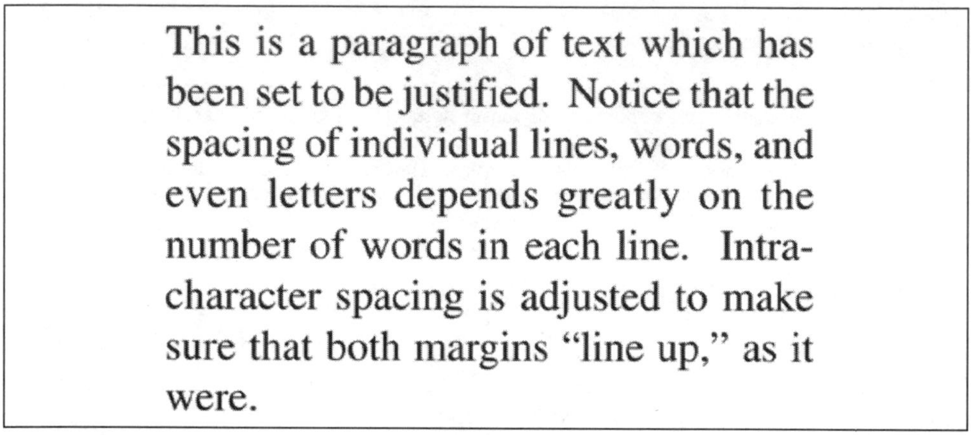

This is a paragraph of text which has been set to be justified. Notice that the spacing of individual lines, words, and even letters depends greatly on the number of words in each line. Intra-character spacing is adjusted to make sure that both margins "line up," as it were.

Figure 4-15. Justified text

CSS does not specify how justified text should be "stretched out" to fill the space between the left and right edges of the parent, so some user agents might add extra space only between words, while others might distribute the extra space between letters. It's also possible that some user agents will reduce space on some lines, thus shmushing text together a bit more than usual. All of these various choices will affect the appearance of an element, and possibly even change its height, depending on how many lines result from the justification choices the user agent makes (see Figure 4-16).

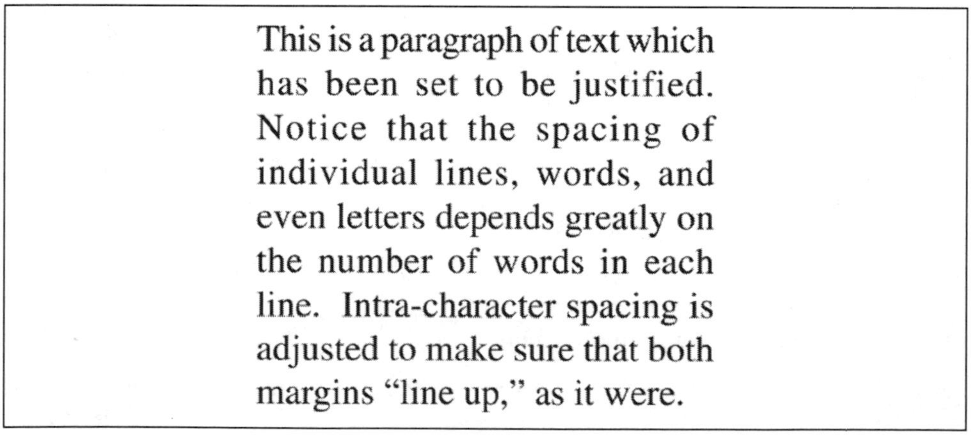

This is a paragraph of text which has been set to be justified. Notice that the spacing of individual lines, words, and even letters depends greatly on the number of words in each line. Intra-character spacing is adjusted to make sure that both margins "line up," as it were.

Figure 4-16. Justification choices

Another problem is that CSS doesn't say anything about how hyphenation should be handled. Most justified text uses hyphenation to break long words across two lines, thus reducing the space between words and improving the appearance of lines (see Figure 4-17).

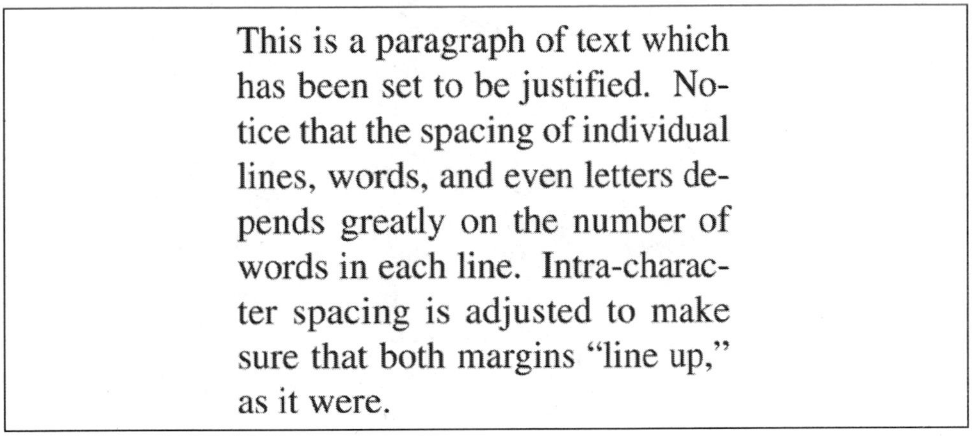

This is a paragraph of text which has been set to be justified. Notice that the spacing of individual lines, words, and even letters depends greatly on the number of words in each line. Intra-character spacing is adjusted to make sure that both margins "line up," as it were.

Figure 4-17. Justification with hyphenation

The fact that hyphenation is not described in CSS has more to do with the fact that different languages have different hyphenation rules. Rather than try to concoct a set of rules that would most likely be incomplete, the specification simply avoids the problem. In addition, this allows user agents to employ their own hyphenation rules, and improve them over time without being hindered by anything in the CSS specification.

Since there is no hyphenation in CSS, user agents are unlikely to be able to perform any automatic hyphenation. Thus, justified text will very likely be less attractive under CSS than it might be in print, especially when elements become so narrow that only a few words can fit on each line, as shown in Figure 4-18. You can still justify text, of course, but be aware of the drawbacks.

While almost every browser that supports CSS will handle most values of `text-align`, they often fall down when handling `justify`. Navigator 4 does support `justify`, but it's fairly buggy—it most often breaks down within tables. Internet Explorer 4.x does not support `justify`, while IE5 does, and Opera 3.6 supports it as well.

This is a
paragraph of
text which has
been set to be
j u s t i f i e d .
Notice that the
spacing   of
individual lines,
words, and even
letters depends
greatly on the
number   of
words in each
line.   Intra-
c h a r a c t e r
spacing   is
adjusted   to
make sure that
both   margins
"line up," as it
were.

Figure 4-18. Justification without hyphenation in narrow circumstances

Handling whitespace

For a change of pace, let's talk about the property `white-space`, which can greatly impact how text is actually displayed.

white-space

Values	`pre` | `nowrap` | `normal`
Initial value	`normal`
Inherited	`no`
Applies to	block-level elements

Using this property, you can affect how browser treats the whitespace between words and lines of text. To a certain extent, HTML already does this: it collapses any whitespace down to a single space. Thus, the following markup would be rendered as shown in Figure 4-19, with only one space between each word:

```
<P>This     paragraph   has      many
    spaces          in it.</P>
```

```
                This paragraph has many spaces in it.
```

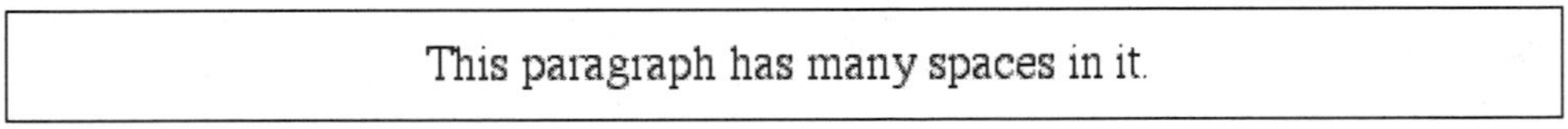

Figure 4-19. Displaying a paragraph with many spaces

You can explicitly set this behavior with the following declaration:

```
P {white-space: normal;}
```

This rule will tell the browser that it should do as browsers have always done, and discard extra whitespace. Any extra spaces and carriage returns are completely ignored by the browser.

Should you set **white-space** to **pre**, however, the whitespace in affected elements will be treated as though the elements were **PRE** elements, in that whitespace would not be ignored, as shown in Figure 4-20:

```
P {white-space: pre;}
```

```
<P>This     paragraph   has      many
    spaces          in it.</P>
```

```
            This   paragraph  has    many
              spaces      in it.
```

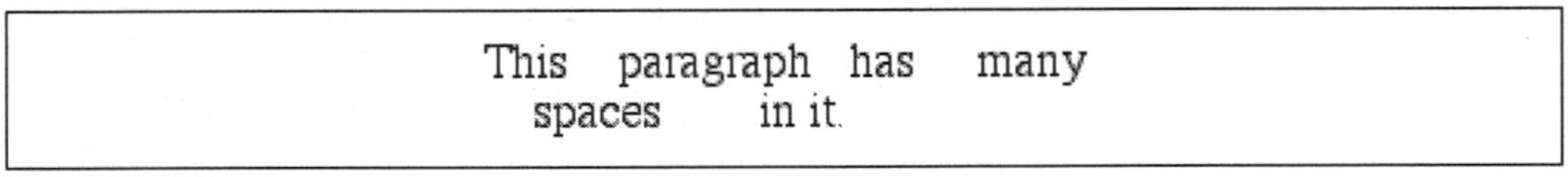

Figure 4-20. Honoring the spaces in markup

With a **white-space** value of **pre**, the browser will pay attention to extra spaces and even carriage returns. In this respect, and in this respect alone, any element can be made to act like a **PRE** element.

On the other side of the coin is **nowrap**, which prevents text from wrapping within a block-level element, except through the use of **
** elements. This is rather similar to setting a table cell not to wrap through **<TD NOWRAP>**, except that **white-space** value can be applied to any block-level element. Thus you can get effects as shown in Figure 4-21:

```
<P STYLE="white-space: nowrap;">This paragraph is not allowed to wrap,
which means that the only way to end a line is to insert a line-break
element.  If no such element is inserted, then the line will go forever,
forcing the user to scroll horizontally to read whatever can't be
initially displayed <BR>in the browser window.</P>
```

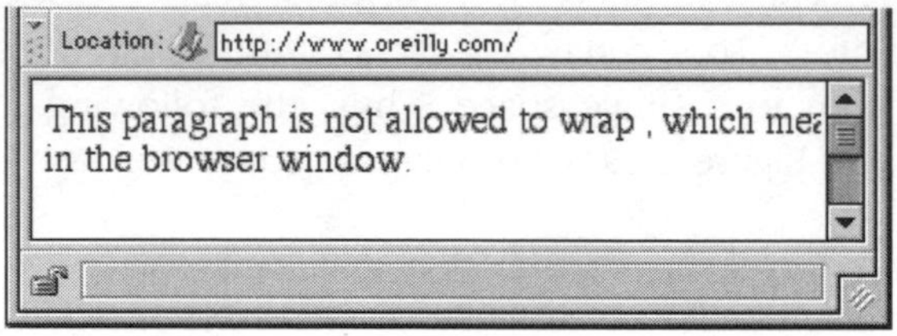

Figure 4-21. Suppressing text-wrapping with the white-space property

In fact, you can use `white-space` to replace the `nowrap` attribute on table cells, as demonstrated in Figure 4-22:

```
TD {white-space: nowrap;}

<TABLE><TR>
<TD>The contents of this cell are not wrapped.</TD>
<TD>Neither are the contents of this cell.</TD>
<TD>Nor this one, or any after it, or any other cell in this table.</TD>
<TD>CSS prevents any wrapping from happening.</TD>
</TR></TABLE>
```

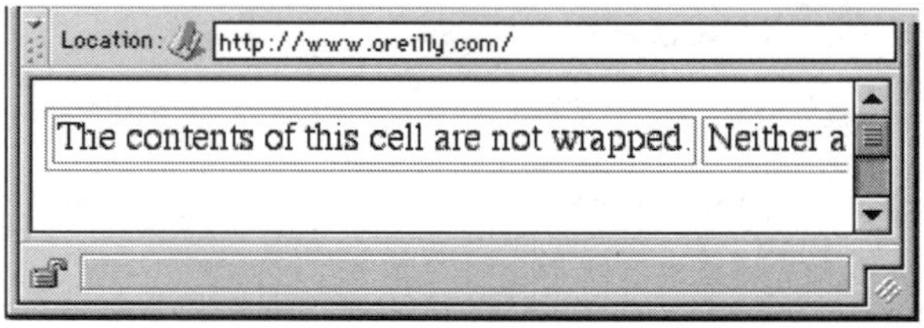

Figure 4-22. Using the white-space: nowrap property to suppress wrapping in table cells.

Although `white-space` may seem like an insanely useful property, as of this writing, it isn't supported by anything except IE5 for Macintosh and preview builds of Netscape 6. Not even the ability to use `nowrap` for table cells is available in other browsers, despite the fact that it would seem to be a very simple behavior to support.

The Height of Lines

As opposed to the size of a font, which will be discussed in Chapter 5, `line-height` refers to the distance between the baselines of lines of text—sort of. In fact, this property determines the amount by which the height of each element's line box is increased or decreased. In the simplest cases, it's a way of increasing (or decreasing) the vertical space between lines of text, but this is a misleadingly simple way of looking at how `line-height` works. If you're familiar with desktop publishing packages, then `line-height` controls the *leading*, which is the extra space between lines of text above and beyond the font's size. The difference between the value of `line-height` and the size of the font is the leading.

---

line-height

Values	<length>	<percentage>	<number>	`normal`
Initial value	`normal`
Inherited	yes
Applies to	all elements

Note: Percentage values are relative to the font size of the element.

In technical terms, every element in a line generates a *content area*, which is determined by the size of the font. This content area also generates an *inline box* which is, in the absence of any other factors, exactly equal to the content area. However, the leading generated by `line-height` can increase or decrease the height of the inline box. This is done by dividing the leading in half and applying each half-leading to the top and bottom of the content area. The result is the inline box. For example, if the content area is 14 points tall, and the `line-height` is set to 18 points, then the difference (4 points) is divided in half, and each half applied to the top and bottom of the inline box to arrive at an inline box which is 18 points tall. This sounds like a roundabout way to describe how line height works, but rest assured that there are excellent reasons for the description. See Chapter 8, *Visual Formatting*, for a detailed explanation of the inline formatting model.

If you use the default value of **normal**, the amount of vertical space between lines will be the user agent's default. This is generally somewhere between 1.0 and 1.2 times the size of the font, but this can vary by user agent.

Allowed lengths other than **em** and **ex** are simple length measures (e.g., `0.125in`). The usual caveats apply here; even if you use a valid length measure like `4cm`, the browser (or the operating system) may have an incorrect metric for real-world measures. Thus, when you display your document on a monitor, a ruler might reveal that the line height was not exactly four centimeters. For more details, see Chapter 3, *Units and Values*.

Percentages, as well as **em** and **ex**, are calculated with respect to the element's `font-size`. Thus, this markup is relatively straightforward, as Figure 4-23 shows:

```
BODY {line-height: 14pt; font-size: 13pt;}
P.one {line-height: 1.2em;}
```

```
P.two {font-size: 10pt; line-height: 150%;}
P.three {line-height: 0.33in;}

<P>This paragraph inherits a 'line-height' of 14pt from the BODY, as well as
a 'font-size' of 13pt.</P>
<P CLASS="one">This paragraph has a 'line-height' of 16.8pt (14 * 1.2), so
it will have slightly more line-height than usual.</P>
<P CLASS="two">This paragraph has a 'line-height' of 15pt (10 * 150%), so
it will have slightly more line-height than usual.</P>
<P CLASS="three">This paragraph has a 'line-height' of 0.33in, so it will have
slightly more line-height than usual.</P>
```

> This paragraph inherits a 'line-height' of 14pt from the BODY, as well as a 'font-size' of 13pt.
>
> This paragraph has a 'line-height' of 16.8pt (14 * 1.2), so it will have slightly more line-height than usual.
>
> This paragraph has a 'line-height' of 15pt (10 * 150%), so it will have slightly more line-height than usual.
>
> This paragraph has a 'line-height' of 0.33in, so it will have
>
> slightly more line-height than usual.

Figure 4-23. Simple calculations with the line-height property

However, things get less predictable once the `line-height` is inherited from one block-level element to another. The computed `line-height` values are inherited no matter what `font-size` might be set for a child element. This can be something of a problem, as you can see in Figure 4-24:

```
BODY {font-size: 10pt;}
DIV {line-height: 12pt;}
P {font-size: 18pt;}

<DIV>
<P>This paragraph's 'font-size' is 18pt, but the inherited 'line-height'
is only 12pt.  This may cause the lines of text to overlap each other by
a small amount.</P>
</DIV>
```

Figure 4-24. Small line height, large font size, slight problem

There are two solutions. One is to set the `line-height` explicitly for every element, but this is not a very practical approach, given that you may have a number of elements that need such properties. The other possibility is to set a plain number instead, which actually sets a scaling factor:

```
BODY {font-size: 10pt;}
DIV {line-height: 1.5;}
P {font-size: 18pt;}
```

When a number is used, the scaling factor is inherited instead of a computed value. This factor is applied to the element and all of its child elements, so that each element has a `line-height` calculated with respect to its own `font-size`, as demonstrated in Figure 4-25:

```
BODY {font-size: 10pt;}
DIV {line-height: 1.5;}
P {font-size: 18pt;}

<DIV>
<P>This paragraph's 'font-size' is 18pt, and since the 'line-height'
set for the parent DIV is 1.5, the 'line-height' for this paragraph
is 27pt (18 * 1.5).</P>
</DIV>
```

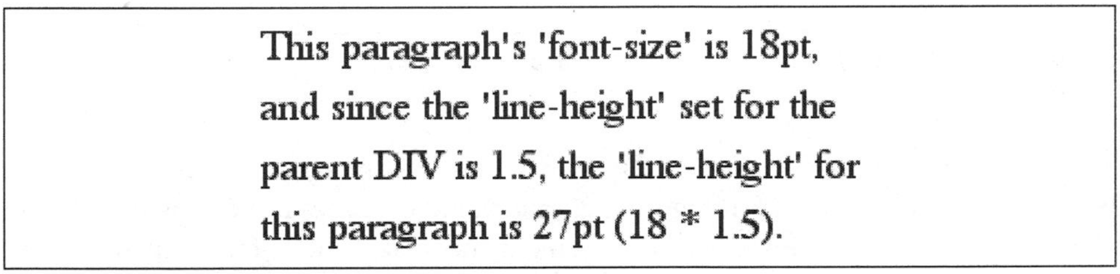

This paragraph's 'font-size' is 18pt, and since the 'line-height' set for the parent DIV is 1.5, the 'line-height' for this paragraph is 27pt (18 * 1.5).

Figure 4-25. Using line-height factors to overcome inheritance problems

As I said previously, although it seems like `line-height` distributes extra space both above and below each line of text, it actually adds (or subtracts) a certain amount from the top and bottom of an inline element. This leads to some odd cases when a line has elements with different font sizes, but for the moment, let's stick to a simple case. Assume that the default `font-size` of a paragraph is `12pt` and consider the following:

```
P {line-height: 16pt;}
```

Since the "inherent" line height of 12-point text is 12 points, the preceding rule means that there will be an extra 4 points of space around each line of text in the paragraph. This extra amount is divided in two, with half going above each line, and the other half below. While there is a distance of 16 points between the lines, this is an indirect result of how the extra space is apportioned.

Now let's look at a slightly more complex case. Take the following example:

```
BODY {font-size: 10pt;}
P {font-size: 18pt; line-height: 23pt;}
BIG {font-size: 250%;}

<P>This paragraph's 'font-size' is 18pt, and the 'line-height' for this
paragraph is 23pt. However, a <BIG>larger element</BIG> within the
paragraph does not cause the value of 'line-height' to change, which can
lead to some interesting effects.</P>
```

The result shown in Figure 4-26 may look like a browser bug, but it isn't. It's exactly how the example markup should be displayed.

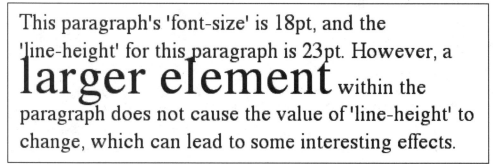

Figure 4-26. Possible behavior with the line-height property and inline elements of different sizes

This is by no means the only oddity which arises from using line-height. As backwards as it may seem, in Figure 4-27, the value of line-height is exactly the same for each and every line in the element, no matter how far apart they may actually appear to be. This fact will come up again in the next section, "Vertical Alignment."

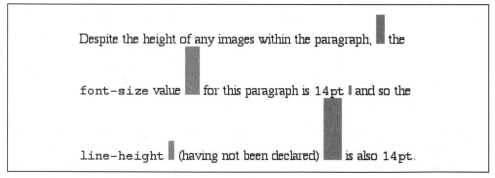

Figure 4-27. Tall images don't change line height

Again, the actual value for line-height in Figure 4-27 is the same for every line.

You can take advantage of the fact that `line-height` can be set for any element, including inline elements. Let's return to our previous example and make one small change by adding a `line-height` to the styles for the BIG element. This will have the result shown in Figure 4-28:

```
BODY {font-size: 10pt;}
P {font-size: 18pt; line-height: 27pt;}
BIG {font-size: 250%; line-height: 1em;}

<P>This paragraph's 'font-size' is 18pt, and the 'line-height' for this
paragraph is 27pt. A <BIG>larger element</BIG> within the paragraph does
not cause the line's height to change, but setting its 'line-height' does,
which leads to some interesting effects.</P>
```

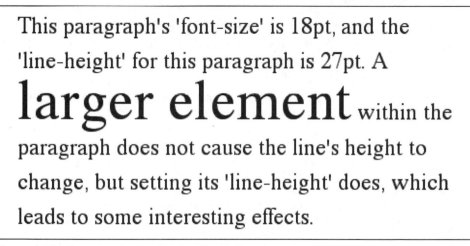

Figure 4-28. Changing the line-height of an inline element

Setting a `line-height` of `1em` for the BIG element will actually cause its `line-height` to be the same size as the BIG text itself. This has the same effect the images did: it opens up the entire line of text enough to clearly display the elements within it. In this case, the effect is due to the increased `line-height` of the inline element BIG, as opposed to the intrinsic size of an image, but the effect is largely the same.

The reasons why all of this happens are actually rather complex. For more details, please refer to the discussion of the inline formatting model found in Chapter 8.

Real-world issues

As we saw in the preceding section, a scaling factor is the best way to avoid the kinds of inheritance problems you encounter with length measures for `line-height`. It would therefore seem that using a number is always preferred. Alas, this is not necessarily so. Internet Explorer 3 will interpret a scaling factor as a pixel value, so you get something like what's shown in Figure 4-29.

Figure 4-29. Internet Explorer 3 and line-height factors mean big trouble

According to the CSS specification, user agents are free to set whatever value they think best for the default keyword **normal**, but the suggested range is 1.0 to 1.2, depending on what works best for the display medium and the font in use. Most browsers seem to use something in the vicinity of 1.2, but of course that could change with a new browser, or even a new version of an old browser.

Vertical Alignment

The odds are that you're already, to a certain extent, familiar with the concept of vertical alignment of text. If you've ever used the elements **SUP** and **SUB** (the superscript and subscript elements) or used an image with markup along the lines of **<IMG SRC="foo.gif" ALIGN="texttop">**, then you've done some rudimentary vertical alignment. The CSS property **vertical-align** permits all of the alignment you used to do on inline elements, and more besides.

There is one thing to remember: **vertical-align** is *not* meant to affect the alignment of content in table cells, or within a block-level element. Under CSS1, there is no provision for duplicating markup such as **<TD valign="top">**. (This changes under CSS2; see the section "Tables" in Chapter 10, *CSS2: A Look Ahead*, for more details.)

So, let's see what can be done with **vertical-align**. This property applies only to inline elements, although that includes replaced elements such as images and form inputs, and it is not inherited.

vertical-align

Values	baseline | sub | super | bottom | text-bottom | middle | top | text-top | <percentage>
Initial value	baseline
Inherited	no
Applies to	inline elements

Note: Percentage values refer to the line-height of the element.

`vertical-align` accepts any one of eight keywords, or a percentage value, but never both. The keywords are a mix of the familiar and unfamiliar: `baseline` (the default value), `sub`, `super`, `bottom`, `text-bottom`, `middle`, `top`, and `text-top`. We'll examine how each works in turn.

Baseline alignment

`vertical-align: baseline` forces an element to align its baseline with the baseline of its parent, which is pretty much what browsers already do anyway. For example, this markup results in Figure 4-30:

```
B {vertical-align: baseline;}

<P>The baseline of the <B>boldfaced text</B> is aligned with the baseline
of this paragraph.</P>
```

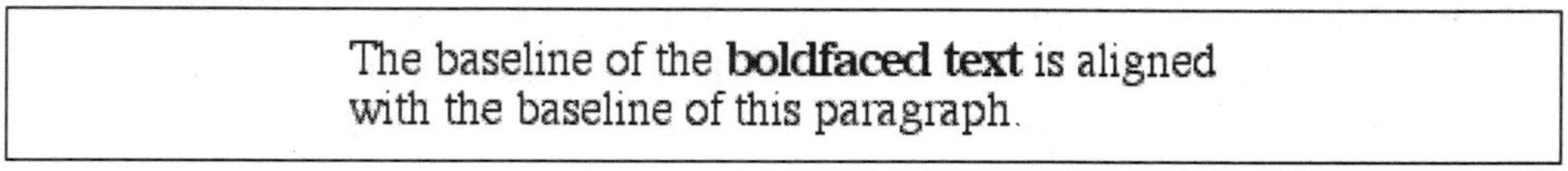

The baseline of the **boldfaced text** is aligned
with the baseline of this paragraph.

Figure 4-30. Baseline alignment

In examining Figure 4-30, you'll see that it doesn't look any different than you would expect. It shouldn't.

If a vertically aligned element doesn't have a baseline—that is, if it's an image, a form input, or another replaced element—then the bottom of the element is aligned with the baseline of its parent, as Figure 4-31 shows:

```
IMG {vertical-align: baseline;}

<P>The image found in this paragraph <IMG SRC="dot.gif" ALT="a dot"> has its
bottom edge aligned with the baseline of the paragraph.</P>
```

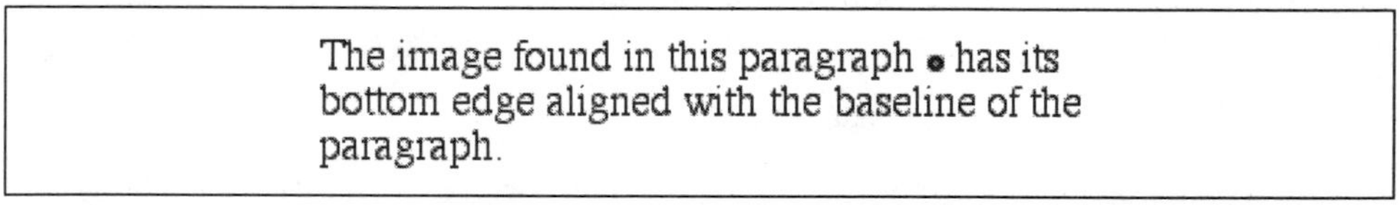

The image found in this paragraph ● has its
bottom edge aligned with the baseline of the
paragraph.

Figure 4-31. Baseline alignment of an image

Superscripting and subscripting

The declaration `vertical-align: sub` causes the element to be "subscripted." In general, this means that the element's baseline (or bottom, if it's a replaced element) is lowered with respect to its parent's baseline. However, the distance it is lowered is not defined in the specification, so it may vary from one user agent to another. Note that `sub` does *not* imply a change in the element's font size, so it should not cause subscripted text to become smaller (or larger). Instead, any text in the subscripted element should be, by default, the same size as text in the parent element, as shown in Figure 4-32:

```
SUB {vertical-align: sub;}

<P>This paragraph contains <SUB>subscripted</SUB> text.</P>
```

> This paragraph contains subscripted text.

Figure 4-32. Subscript alignment

Of course, you could make the text smaller by using `font-size`, but you have to do it yourself.

`super` acts in a fashion similar to `sub`, but in this case, the element's baseline (or bottom of a replaced element) is raised with respect to the parent's baseline. Again, the distance the text will be raised is dependent on the user agent, and there is no implied change in the size of the font. This is demonstrated in Figure 4-33:

```
SUP {vertical-align: super;}

<P>This paragraph contains <SUP>superscripted</SUP> text.</P>
```

> This paragraph contains superscripted text.

Figure 4-33. Superscript alignment

Bottom feeding

`vertical-align: bottom` sounds pretty simple: it aligns the bottom of the element's inline box with the bottom of the line box. For example, this markup results in Figure 4-34:

```
IMG.feeder {vertical-align: bottom;}

<P>This paragraph contains first a single fairly <IMG SRC="tall.gif" align="middle"
ALT="tall image"> which is tall, and then an image <IMG SRC="short.gif"
CLASS="feeder" ALT="short image"> which is not tall.</P>
```

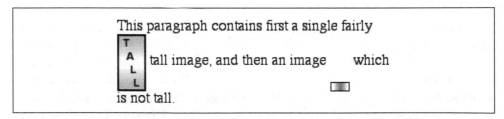

Figure 4-34. Bottom alignment

As you can see from Figure 4-34, the second line of the paragraph contains two images, and their bottom edges are aligned with each other. (The first image has been set to a middle alignment using the HTML attribute `align`. We'll look into ways of achieving a similar effect with CSS a little later in this chapter.)

`vertical-align: text-bottom` refers to the bottom of the text in the line. Replaced elements, or indeed nontext elements of any kind, are ignored for the purposes of this value. Instead, a "default" text box is considered. This default box is derived from the `font-size` of the parent element. The bottom of the aligned element's inline box is then aligned with the bottom of default text box. Thus, given the following markup, we get a situation such as that shown in Figure 4-35:

```
IMG.tbot {vertical-align: text-bottom;}

<P>Here: a <IMG SRC="tall.gif" ALIGN="middle"
ALT="tall image"> tall image, and then a <IMG SRC="short.gif"
CLASS="tbot" ALT="short image"> short image.</P>
```

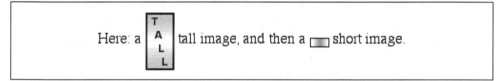

Figure 4-35. Text-bottom alignment

Getting on top

Employing `vertical-align: top` has pretty much the opposite effect of `bottom`. Likewise, `vertical-align: text-top` is the reverse of `text-bottom`. Figure 4-36 shows how the following markup would be rendered:

```
IMG.up {vertical-align: top;}
IMG.textup {vertical-align: text-top;}

<P>Here: a <IMG SRC="tall.gif" ALIGN="middle"
ALT="tall image"> tall image, and then a <IMG SRC="short.gif"
CLASS="up" ALT="short image"> short image.</P>
<P> Here: a <IMG SRC="tall.gif" CLASS="textup"
ALT="tall image"> tall image, and then a <IMG SRC="short.gif"
CLASS="textup" ALT="short image"> short image.</P>
```

Of course, the exact position of that alignment will depend on what elements are in the line and how tall they are.

In the middle

Then there is `vertical-align: middle`. This value is usually applied to images, since it causes the vertical midpoint of the element to be aligned with the "middle"

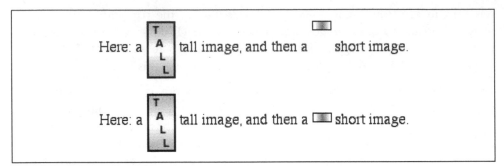

Figure 4-36. Aligning with the top and text-top of a line

of the line. The middle of the line is defined to be the point which is one-half **ex** above the baseline, where the value of **ex** is derived from the **font-size** of the parent element. An example is shown in Figure 4-37:

```
IMG {vertical-align: middle;}
```

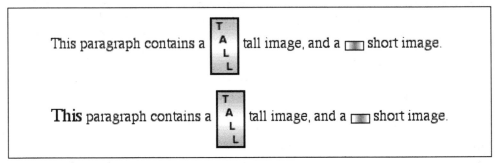

Figure 4-37. Middle alignment

In practice, since most user agents treat **1ex** as one-half em, **middle** will cause the vertical midpoint of an element to be aligned with a point one-quarter em above the parent's baseline. Figure 4-38 shows this in more detail.

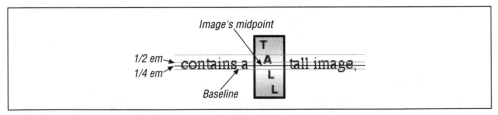

Figure 4-38. Precise detail of middle alignment

This is pretty close to simulating **<IMG ALIGN="middle">**, as you can see, and you'd probably think that percentages would get even closer.

Percentages

As it turns out, no, percentages don't let you simulate `ALIGN="middle"` for images. Instead, setting a percentage value for `vertical-align` causes the baseline (or bottom of a replaced element) of the element to be raised or lowered by the amount declared, with respect to the parent's baseline. The percentage you specify is calculated as a percentage of the value for `line-height`. Positive percentage values cause the element to be raised, and negative values cause it to be lowered. This can cause elements to be raised or lowered such that they appear to be placed in adjacent lines, as shown in Figure 4-39, so you should take care when using percentage values:

```
B {vertical-align: 100%;}

<P>This paragraph contains some <B>boldfaced</B> text, which is raised
up 100%.  This makes it look as though it's on a preceding line.</P>
```

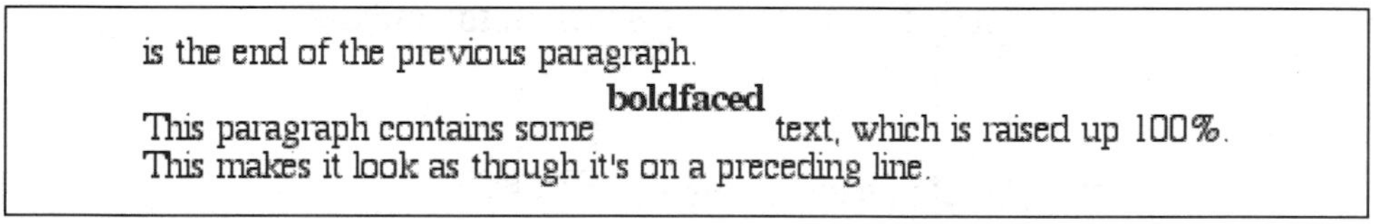

Figure 4-39. Vertical alignment with percentages

However, it's important to realize that the vertically aligned text is not part of another line. It just appears that way when there isn't any other text around. Consider Figure 4-40, in which some vertically aligned text appears in the middle of a paragraph.

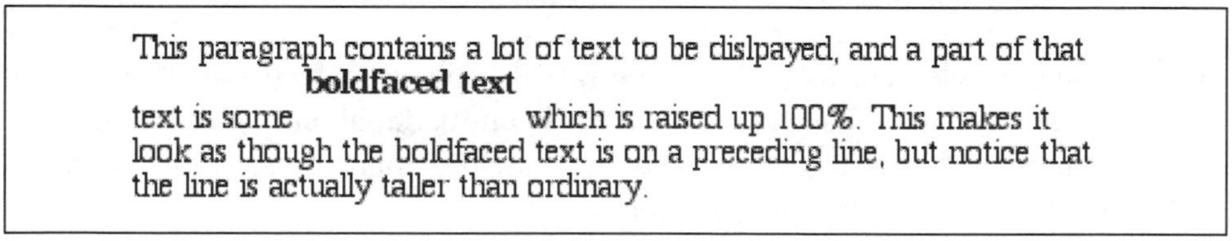

Figure 4-40. Percentage alignments can affect the height of a line

Of course, this sort of thing can lead to some fun visual effects, as we see in Figure 4-41:

```
SUB {vertical-align: -100%;}
SUP {vertical-align: 100%;}

<P>We can either <SUP>soar to new heights</SUP> or, instead,
<SUB>sink into despair...</SUB></P>
```

Since percentage values are meant to be percentages of the `line-height`, what happens when a particularly tall image within a line causes the line's apparent height to increase?

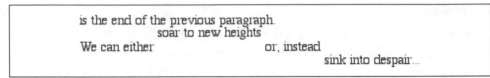

Figure 4-41. Percentages and fun effects

If you'll recall from before, the answer is that an image, no matter how tall it is, doesn't actually cause the `line-height` to increase. What is increased is the height of the line box. Therefore, if a line's height is `14px`, and an element within that line is vertically aligned to 50%, and within that same line, there is an image 50 pixels tall, you get the result shown in Figure 4-42:

```
SUP {vertical-align: 50%;}
```

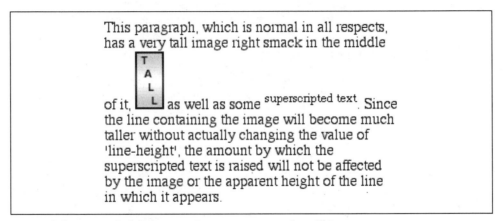

Figure 4-42. Vertical alignment with a percentage and a tall image

The 50%-aligned element has its baseline raised 7 pixels (which is half of `14px`), *not* 25 pixels. Also note that the line-box has been made tall enough to accommodate the image. This is actually consistent with the inline box model, because replaced elements have this kind of effect.

We can see the operation of vertical alignment more clearly if we have two images, one of which is vertically aligned with a percentage value. The results, shown in Figure 4-43, are dependent on the `line-height`, which we'll explicitly declare to be `14px`:

```
P {line-height: 14px;}
IMG.up {vertical-align: 50%;}

<P>Some <IMG SRC="tall.gif" alt="tall image">
<IMG SRC="short.gif" CLASS="up" ALT="short image"> text.</P>
```

The bottom (or baseline) of the smaller image is raised by one-half (50%) of the `line-height`, or 7 pixels. If we had set the alignment for `IMG.up` to be -50%, then the shorter image would have been lowered by 7 pixels.

Figure 4-43. Vertical alignment with percentage and two images

Combined alignment

As we've already seen, the way a given line of text is displayed will depend greatly on the vertical alignments of the various elements within that line. However, this fact deserves to be emphasized again, due to its importance. Assume, for example, that a line contains an image which has been middle-aligned, and an inline text element which has been bottom-aligned. This would result in the situation shown in Figure 4-44:

```
IMG {vertical-align: middle;}
SUB {vertical-align: bottom;}
```

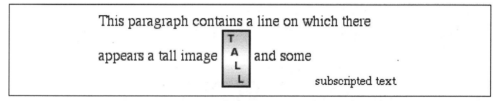

Figure 4-44. Combining vertical alignments

If we change the text element so that it's `text-bottom`-aligned, though, the situation changes quite radically, as Figure 4-45 shows:

```
IMG {vertical-align: middle;}
SUB {vertical-align: text-bottom;}
```

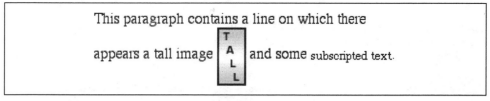

Figure 4-45. Combining vertical alignments in a different way

Word Spacing and Letterspacing

The concepts here are fairly simple: word and letterspacing are ways of inserting or reducing space between either words or letters. As usual, though, there are some nonintuitive issues to consider with these properties; first, let's talk about the spaces between words.

Word spacing

---

word-spacing

Values	<length> | normal
Initial value	normal
Inherited	yes
Applies to	all elements

The word-spacing property will accept a length that is either positive or negative. This value is *added* to the usual space between words, which perhaps isn't quite what you might expect. In effect, word-spacing is used as a *modifier* to interword spacing. Therefore, the default value of normal is the same as setting a value of zero (0), as shown in Figure 4-46:

```
P.base {word-spacing: normal;}
P.norm {word-spacing: 0;}
```

> This paragraph has ordinary word-spacing, which is to say that it appears no different than an unstyled paragraph.
>
> This paragraph also features ordinary word-spacing, which is to say that it appears no different than an unstyled paragraph.

Figure 4-46. Two ways to achieve ordinary word spacing

Therefore, if we supply a positive length value, then the space between words will increase, as demonstrated in Figure 4-47:

```
P {word-spacing: 0.2em;}
```

```
<P>The spaces between words in paragraphs will be increased by 0.2em.</P>
```

> The spaces between words in paragraphs will be increased by 0.2em.

Figure 4-47. Increasing the space between words

By setting a negative value for `word-spacing`, words can be brought closer together. This has an effect like that shown in Figure 4-48:

```
P {word-spacing: -0.4em;}
```

```
<P>The spaces between words in paragraphs will be decreased by 0.4em.</P>
```

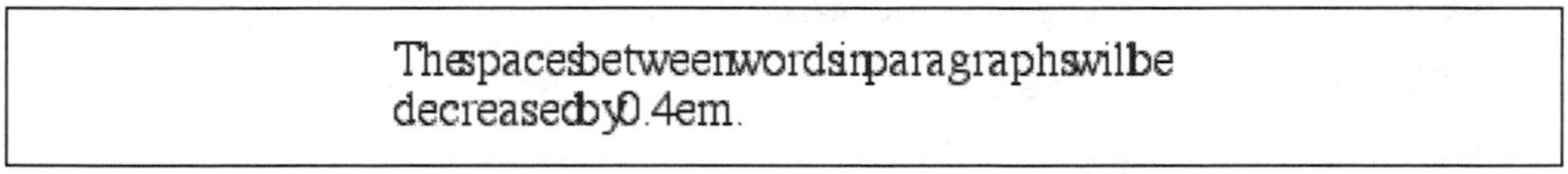

> Thespacesbetweenwordsinparagraphswillbe
> decreasedby0.4em.

Figure 4-48. Decreasing the space between words

So far, we've left out a precise definition of what a "word" really is. In the simplest CSS terms, a "word" is any string of non-whitespace characters that is surrounded by whitespace of some kind. This definition has no real semantic significance—it is merely assumed that an author will write a document such that each word is surrounded by one or more whitespace characters. Obviously, a CSS-aware user agent cannot be expected to decide what is a valid word in a given language and what isn't.

This also means that any languages that employ pictographs, or other non-Roman writing styles, will probably not be able to take advantage of this property. Furthermore, this definition of "word" is not something user agents are required to follow; it merely represents the most basic way of defining a word. User agents may employ more sophisticated ways of deciding what a word is or isn't.

It is, of course, possible to create very unreadable documents with this property, as Figure 4-49 makes clear:

```
P {word-spacing: 1in;}
```

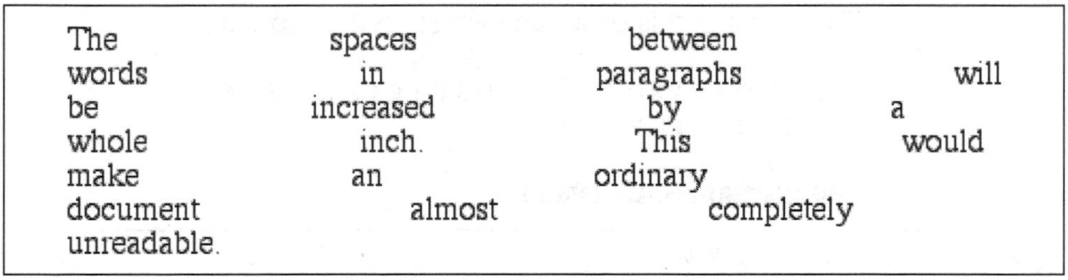

> The   spaces   between
> words   in   paragraphs   will
> be   increased   by   a
> whole   inch.   This   would
> make   an   ordinary
> document   almost   completely
> unreadable.

Figure 4-49. Really wide word spacing

Letterspacing

---

letter-spacing

Values	\<length\> | normal
Initial value	normal
Inherited	yes
Applies to	all elements

Many of the same issues with `word-spacing` return for `letter-spacing`. The only real difference between this property and `word-spacing` is that `letter-spacing` is a modifier of the usual amount of space between characters, or letters.

Once again, the permitted values are any length value and the default keyword `normal` (which is functionally the same as `letter-spacing: 0`). Any length value will increase or decrease the space between letters by the amount declared. Figure 4-50 shows the results of the following markup:

```
P {letter-spacing: 0;}    /*  identical to 'normal'  */
P.spacious {letter-spacing: 0.25em;}
P.tight {letter-spacing: -0.25em;}

<P>The letters in this paragraph are spaced as normal.</P>
<P CLASS="spacious">The letters in this paragraph are spread out a bit.</P>
<P CLASS="tight">The letters in this paragraph are smooshed together a bit.</P>
```

The letters in this paragraph are spaced as normal.

The letters in this paragraph are
spread out a bit.

Tehlsinspegphæsnroheltglerathi

Figure 4-50. Various kinds of letterspacing

One interesting use for `letter-spacing` is to increase emphasis, which is a technique that was common in past centuries. Thus, you might declare the following to get an effect like that shown in Figure 4-51:

```
STRONG {letter-spacing: 0.2em;}

<P>This paragraph contains <STRONG>strongly emphasized text</STRONG>
which is spread out for extra emphasis.</P>
```

This paragraph contains **strongly emphasized text** which is spread out for extra emphasis.

Figure 4-51. Using letterspacing to increase emphasis

Spacing, alignment, and font size

Both `word-spacing` and `letter-spacing` can be influenced by the value of `text-align`. If an element is set to be justified, then the spaces between letters and words may be altered to permit full justification, which may in turn alter the spacing declared by the author with `word-spacing` or `letter-spacing`. The CSS specification does not specify how the spacing should be calculated in such a case, so user agents are free to do whatever their programmers thought best.

Furthermore, as usual, the computed value of an element is inherited by any child elements. Unlike `line-height`, there is no way to define a scaling factor for `word-spacing` or `letter-spacing` to be inherited in place of the computed value. Thus we have problems such as those shown in Figure 4-52:

```
P {letter-spacing: 0.25em;}
SMALL {font-size: 50%;}

<P>This spacious paragraph features <SMALL>tiny text which is just
as spacious</SMALL>, even though the author probably wanted the
spacing to be in proportion to the size of the text.</P>
```

This spacious paragraph features tiny text which is just as spacious, even though the author probably wanted the spacing to be in proportion to the size of the text.

Figure 4-52. Inherited letterspacing

The only way to get an effect where the letterspacing is in proportion to the size of the text is to set it explicitly, with the result shown in Figure 4-53:

```
P {letter-spacing: 0.25em;}
SMALL {font-size: 50%; letter-spacing: 0.25em;}

<P>This spacious paragraph features <SMALL>tiny text which is
proportionally spacious</SMALL>, which is what the author
probably wanted.</P>
```

> ## This spacious paragraph features
> tiny text which is proportionally spacious ,
> ## which is what the author probably
> ## wanted .

Figure 4-53. Overcoming inherited letterspacing

Text Transformation

Now we turn to ways to fiddle with the capitalization of text. This is done with the property `text-transform`.

---

text-transform

Values	uppercase | lowercase | capitalize | none
Initial value	none
Inherited	yes
Applies to	all elements

The default value **none** will simply leave the text alone and use whatever capitalization exists in the source document. **uppercase** and **lowercase** cause the text to be converted into all upper- or lowercase characters, as their names would indicate. Finally, **capitalize** causes the first letter of each word to be capitalized and leaves the rest of the characters in each word alone. (Note that for the purposes of this property, a "word" is the same as discussed in the section on **word-spacing**.)

Figure 4-54 shows each of these settings in a variety of ways:

```
STRONG {text-transform: uppercase;}
H1, H2, H3 {text-transform: capitalize;}
P.cummings {text-transform: lowercase;}
P.raw {text-transform: none;}

<H1>The heading-one at the beginninG</H1>
<P>
By default, text is displayed in the capitalization it has in the source
document, but <STRONG>it is possible to change this</STRONG> using
the property 'text-transform'.
</P>
<P CLASS="cummings">
For example, one could Create TEXT such as might have been Written by
the late Poet E.E.Cummings.
</P>
<P CLASS="raw">
```

```
If you feel the need to Explicitly Declare the transformation of text,
that can be done as well.
</P>
```

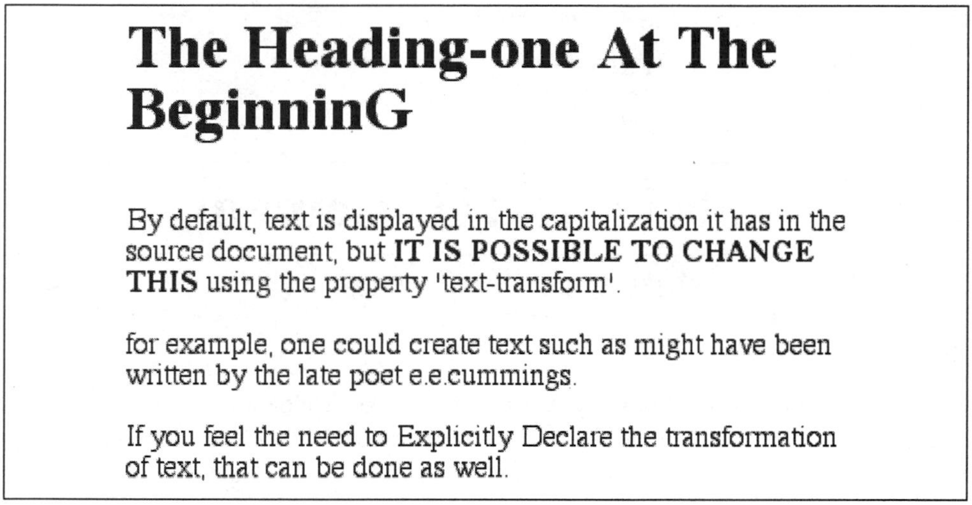

The Heading-one At The BeginninG

By default, text is displayed in the capitalization it has in the source document, but **IT IS POSSIBLE TO CHANGE THIS** using the property 'text-transform'.

for example, one could create text such as might have been written by the late poet e.e.cummings.

If you feel the need to Explicitly Declare the transformation of text, that can be done as well.

Figure 4-54. Various kinds of text transformation

Note that different user agents may have different ways of deciding where words begin, and thus which letters should be capitalized. As an example, the text "heading-one" in the `H1` element, shown in Figure 4-54, could be rendered in one of two ways: "Heading-one" or "Heading-One." CSS does not say which is correct, so either one is possible.

Also note that the last letter in the H1 element in Figure 4-54 is still in uppercase. This is correct: when applying a `text-transform` of `capitalize`, CSS only requires that user agents make sure that the first letter of each word is capitalized. They don't have to do anything to the rest of the word.

As a property, `text-transform` may not seem like it does very much. In fact, it's very useful if you suddenly decide that you want all of your `H1` elements to be all capitals. Instead of having to actually change the content of all your `H1` elements, you can just use `text-transform` to make the change for you:

```
H1 {text-transform: uppercase;}

<H1>This is an H1 element</H1>
```

As you can see from Figure 4-55, the text is now all capitals.

THIS IS AN H1 ELEMENT

Figure 4-55. Transforming an H1 element

The advantages are twofold. First, all you have to do is write a single rule to make this change, rather than having to make changes to the H1 itself. Second, if you decide later to switch from all capitals to capitalizing the first letter of each word, the change is even easier, as Figure 4-56 shows:

```
H1 {text-transform: capitalize;}

<H1>This is an H1 element</H1>
```

This Is An H1 Element

Figure 4-56. Transforming an H1 element in a different way.

Text Decoration

Finally, we come to `text-decoration`, which is a fascinating property that carries along a whole truckload of oddities and inconsistencies in browsers. First, however, let's talk about how it should work in theory.

---

text-decoration

Values	none | [underline || overline || line-through || blink]
Initial value	none
Inherited	no
Applies to	all elements

As you might expect, `underline` causes an element to be underlined, just like the U element in HTML. `overline` is the flip side; a line is drawn across the top of the text in an overlined element. The value `line-through` draws a line straight through the middle of the text, which also known as "strikethrough" text and is equivalent to the S and STRIKE elements in HTML. And, of course, `blink` causes the text to blink on and off, just like the BLINK tag supported by Netscape. Figure 4-57 shows examples of each of these values:

```
P.emph {text-decoration: underline;}
P.topper {text-decoration: overline;}
P.old {text-decoration: line-through;}
P.annoy {text-decoration: blink;}
P.plain {text-decoration: none;}
```

The text of this paragraph, which has a class of 'emph', is underlined.

The text of this paragraph, which has a class of 'topper', is overlined.

~~The text of this paragraph, which has a class of 'old', is stricken (line-through).~~

The text of this paragraph, which has a class of 'annoy', is blinking (trust us).

The text of this paragraph, which has a class of 'plain', has no decoration of any kind.

Figure 4-57. Various kinds of text decoration

It's impossible to show the effect of `blink` in print, of course, but it's easy enough to imagine. User agents are not required to support `blink`, incidentally, and only Navigator 4.x actually supports it as of this writing.

As the last part of Figure 4-57 shows, the value **none** turns off any decoration which might otherwise have been applied to an element. This is usually the default appearance for text, but not always. For example, links are usually underlined by default. If you wished to suppress the underlining of hyperlinks, a CSS rule to do so would be:

```
A:link {text-decoration: none;}
```

The text in Figure 4-58 contains three hyperlinks: the three list items. Since we explicitly turned off link underlining, the only visual difference between the anchors and normal text is the color.

Any hyperlinks which may appear in this document will not be underlined. Here are three examples:

- World Wide Web Consortium Web site
- Web Review's Style Sheets Reference Guide
- CSS Pointers Group

Figure 4-58. Suppressing the underlining of hyperlinks

Although I personally don't have a problem with it, many users have a tendency to get violently annoyed when they realize you've turned off link underlining. Obviously, it's a matter of opinion, so let your own tastes be your guide—but remember that if your link colors aren't sufficiently different from normal text, visually impaired users may have a really hard time finding hyperlinks in your documents.

It is also possible to combine decorations in a single rule. For example, assume that you wish to have all hyperlinks be both underlined and overlined. The needed rule for such an effect is:

```
A:link, A:visited {text-decoration: underline overline;}
```

This effectively makes `text-decoration` a shorthand element. You have to be careful in this case, because if you have two different decorations matched to the same element, the value of the rule that wins out will completely replace the value of the loser. Consider:

```
H2.stricken {text-decoration: line-through;}
H2 {text-decoration: underline overline;}
```

Given these rules, any H2 element with a class of `stricken` will have only a line-through decoration. The underline and overline decorations are lost, since short-hand values replace one another, instead of accumulating.

Weird decorations

Now, let's get into the many strange things about `text-decoration`. First off is the fact that `text-decoration` is *not* inherited. This implies a requirement that any decoration lines drawn with the text—either under, over, or through it—should be the same color as the parent element. This is the case even if the child elements are different colors, as depicted in Figure 4-59:

```
P {text-decoration: underline; color: black;}
B {color: gray;}

<P>This paragraph, which is black and has a black underline, also contains
<B>boldfaced text</B> which has the black underline beneath it as well.</P>
```

> This paragraph, which is black and has a black underline, also contains boldfaced text which has the black underline beneath it as well.

Figure 4-59. Color consistency in underlines

Why is this so? Because the value of `text-decoration` is not inherited, the B element has a default value of `none`. Therefore, the B element has *no* underline. Of course, there is very clearly a line under the B element, so it seems silly to say that it has no underline. Still, it doesn't. What you see under the B element is the paragraph's underline, which is effectively "spanning" the B element. This can be made more explicit by altering the styles for the boldface element thus:

```
P {text-decoration: underline; color: black;}
B {color: gray; text-decoration: none;}

<P>This paragraph, which is black and has a black underline, also contains
<B>boldfaced text</B> which has the black underline beneath it as well.</P>
```

The result is the same, since all we've done is to explicitly declare what was already the case. In other words, there is no way to "turn off" underlining (or overlining or a line-through) within an element. If a decoration has been set for an element, then all of its children will have the decoration applied visually, if not in fact.

Combined with `vertical-align`, even stranger things will happen. Figure 4-60 shows but one of these oddities. Since the SUP element has no decoration of its own, but it is elevated within an overlined element, the overline cuts through the middle of the SUP element:

```
P {text-decoration: overline; font-size: 12pt;}
SUP {vertical-align: 50%; font-size: 12pt;}
```

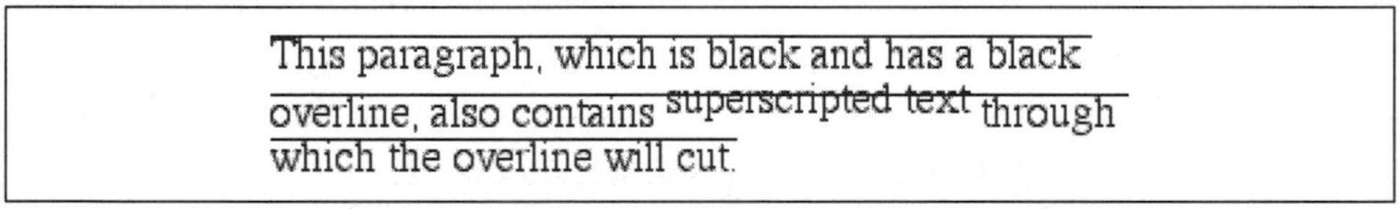

This paragraph, which is black and has a black overline, also contains superscripted text through which the overline will cut.

Figure 4-60. Correct, although strange, decorative behavior

By now, you may be despairing of ever using text decorations, thanks to all the problems they could cause. It gets worse, though (or maybe better), because so far we've been exploring the way things *should* work according to the specification. In reality, many web browsers do turn off underlining in child elements, even though they shouldn't really do so. The reason they violate the specification is simple enough: author expectations.

```
P {text-decoration: underline; color: black;}
B {color: gray; text-decoration: none;}

<P>This paragraph, which is black and has a black underline, also contains
<B>boldfaced text</B> which does not have black underline beneath it.</P>
```

As Figure 4-61 shows, a web browser switched off the underlining for the B element. Navigator, Explorer, and Opera all do this, if there is an explicit `text-decoration: none` to cause the suppression of underlining. This is, of course, what an author would tend to expect, and that's why the browsers do it.

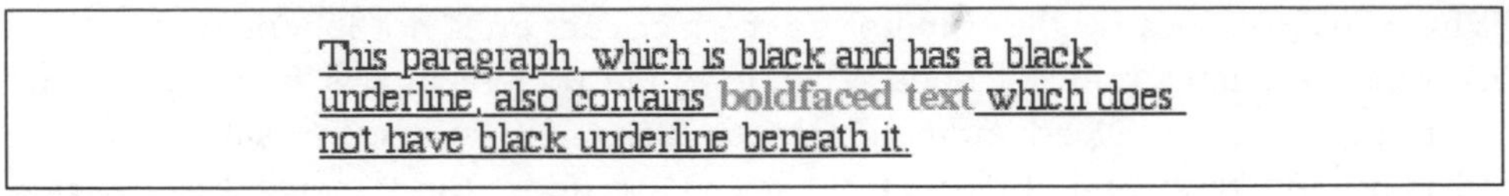

> This paragraph, which is black and has a black
> underline, also contains boldfaced text which does
> not have black underline beneath it.

Figure 4-61. How browsers really behave

The caveat here is that browsers (or any other user agents) might one day follow the specification precisely. If you depend on using none for the suppression of decorations, realize that it may come back to haunt you in the future. Then again, future versions of CSS could include a way to turn off decorations without using none in the wrong way, so maybe there's hope.

Finally, there is a way to change the color of a decoration without violating the specification. As you'll recall, setting a text decoration on an element means that the entire element should have the same color decoration, even if there are child elements of different colors. In order to match the decoration color with each element, you need to explicitly declare the decoration, as follows:

```
P {text-decoration: underline; color: black;}
B {color: gray; text-decoration: underline;}

<P>This paragraph, which is black and has a black underline, also contains
<B>boldfaced text</B> which has its own gray underline.</P>
```

In Figure 4-62, the B element is set to be gray and to have an underline. The gray underline "overwrites" the parent's black underline, and so the decoration's color matches the color of the B element.

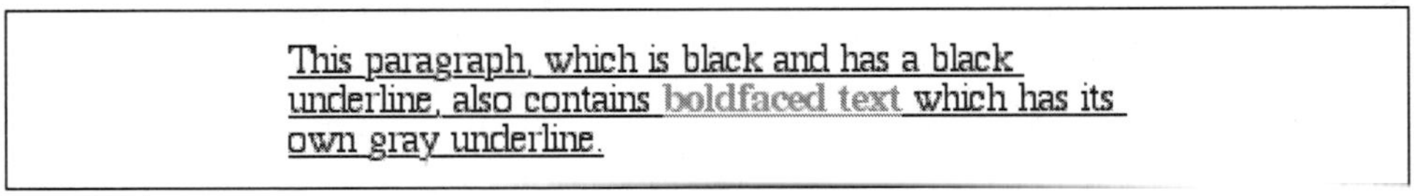

> This paragraph, which is black and has a black
> underline, also contains boldfaced text which has its
> own gray underline.

Figure 4-62. Overcoming the default behavior of underlines

Summary

Even without trying to alter the font in use, there are many ways to change the appearance of text. There are classic effects such as underlining, of course, but CSS also gives us the ability to draw lines over text or through it, change the amount of space between words and letters, indent the first line of a paragraph (or other block-level element), align text to the left or right, and much more. You can even alter the amount of space between lines of text, although this operation is unexpectedly complicated and covered in detail in Chapter 8.

These behaviors are all relatively well supported, or else not supported at all. Full justification of text is one of the big ones that is not well supported, and most user agents released during the twentieth century exhibited bugs in the text decoration and vertical alignment, as well as line height calculations. On the other hand, word and letterspacing almost always work correctly when they're supported, and text indentation has experienced only a few very small bugs. The same is true of the ability to alter capitalization, which is usually supported correctly.

Of course, the other thing authors generally want to do with text is change which font is being used, as well as change its size, weight, and other aspects of the font. We'll see how this happens in the next chapter.

5

Fonts

As the authors of the specification clearly recognized, font selection will be a popular feature of CSS. After all, how many pages are littered with dozens, or even hundreds, of `<FONT face="...">` tags? In fact, the beginning of the "Font Properties" section of CSS1 begins with the sentence, "Setting font properties will be among the most common uses of style sheets."

The truth is that, for now, there isn't a way to ensure consistent font use on the Web, because there isn't a uniform way of describing fonts and variants of fonts. For example, the fonts Times, Times New Roman, and TimesNR may be similar or the same, but how would a user agent know that? An author might specify TimesNR in a document, but what happens when a user without that particular font installed views the document? Even if Times New Roman is installed, the user agent cannot know that the two are effectively interchangeable. And if you're hoping to force a certain font on a reader, forget it. Although CSS2 has facilities for downloadable fonts, these are not well implemented, and a reader could always refuse to download fonts for performance reasons. CSS does *not* provide ultimate control over fonts, any more than does a word processor: when a Microsoft Office document you have created is loaded on someone else's machine, its display will depend on that person's installed fonts. If they don't have the same fonts you do, then the document will look different. The same is true of documents designed using CSS.

The font naming problem extends much further than trying to match font names and becomes especially confusing in the realm of font variants, such as bold or italic text. Most people know what italic text looks like, but how is it different from slanted text? Yes, there are differences, but most people would be hard put to describe them. These are not the only terms used to refer to such text, of course; there are also the terms *oblique, incline* (or *inclined*), *cursive,* and *kursiv,* among others. Thus, one font may have a variant called something like *Times Italic*, whereas another uses something like *Garamond Oblique*. Although the two may be effectively equivalent as the "italic form" of each font, they are labeled quite differently. Similarly, the font variant terms *Bold*, *Black*, and *Heavy* may or may not mean the same thing.

CSS1 attempts to provide some resolution mechanisms for all these questions, although it cannot provide a complete solution. The most complicated parts of font handling in CSS1 are font family matching and font weight matching, with font size calculations running a close third. The font aspects addressed by CSS1 are font styles, such as italic, and font variants such as small caps; these are much more straightforward, relatively speaking. These features are all brought together in a single property, `font`, which we'll discuss at the end of this section. First, let's discuss font families, since they're the most basic step in choosing the right font for your document.

Font Families

Although there are, as was discussed earlier, a number of ways to label what is effectively the same font, CSS1 makes a valiant attempt to help user agents sort out the mess. After all, what we think of as a "font" may be composed of a large number of variations to describe boldfacing, italic text, and so forth. As an example, you're probably familiar with the font Times. However, Times is actually a combination of many variants, including TimesRegular, TimesBold, TimesItalic, Times-Oblique, TimesBoldItalic, TimesBoldOblique, and so on. Each of these variants of Times is an actual *font face*, but Times, as we usually think of it, is a combination of all these variant faces. In other words, Times is actually a *font family*, not just a single font, even though most of us think about fonts as being single entities.

In addition to each specific font family such as Times, Verdana, Helvetica, or Arial, CSS defines five generic font families:

Serif fonts
> Fonts that are proportional and have serifs. A font is proportional if all characters in the font have a different widths due to their various sizes. Thus, a lowercase *i* and a lowercase *m* are of different widths. (This book's default font is proportional, for example.) Serifs are the decorations on the ends of strokes within each character, such as little lines at the top and bottom of a lowercase *l* or at the bottom of each leg of an uppercase *A*. Examples of serif fonts are Times, Garamond, and New Century Schoolbook.

Sans serif fonts
> Fonts that are proportional but do not have serifs. Examples of sans serif fonts are Helvetica, Geneva, Verdana, Arial, and Univers.

Monospace fonts

Fonts that are not proportional. These generally are used to emulate typewritten text or the output from an old dot-matrix printer or an even older video display terminal. In these fonts, each character is exactly the same width as all the others, so that a lowercase *i* is the same width as a lowercase *m*. These fonts may or may not have serifs. If a font has uniform character widths, it is classified as monospace, regardless of the presence of serifs. Examples of monospace fonts are Courier and Andale Mono.

Cursive fonts

Fonts that attempt to emulate human handwriting. Usually, these fonts are composed largely of curves and have stroke decorations that exceed those found in serif fonts. For example, an uppercase *A* might have a small curl at the bottom of its left leg. Examples of cursive fonts are Zapf Chancery, Author, and Comic Sans.

Fantasy fonts

Fonts that are not really defined by any single characteristic other than their inability to be easily classified in one of the other families. A few such fonts are Western and Klingon.

In theory, every font family a user could install will fall into one of these generic families. In practice, this may not be the case, but the exceptions (if any) are likely to be few and far between.

Using Generic Font Families

Any of these families can be employed in a document by using the property `font-family`.

---

font-family

Values	[[<family-name> | <generic-family>],]* [<family-name> | <generic-family>]
Initial value	UA specific
Inherited	yes
Applies to	all elements

If you wish for a document to use a sans serif font, but you do not particularly care which, then the appropriate declaration would be this:

```
BODY {font-family: sans-serif;}
```

This will cause the user agent to pick a sans serif font family such as Helvetica and apply it to the BODY element. Thanks to inheritance, this will apply that font choice to the entire document (unless a more specific selector overrides it, of course). The result is something like what's shown in Figure 5-1.

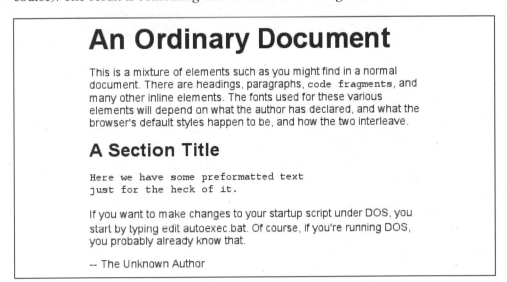

Figure 5-1. Using a sans serif font

Using nothing more than these generic families, an author can create a fairly sophisticated style sheet. Take the following rule set, which is illustrated in Figure 5-2:

```
BODY {font-family: serif;}
H1, H2, H3, H4 {font-family: sans-serif;}
CODE, PRE, TT, SPAN.input {font-family: monospace;}
P.signature {font-family: cursive;}
```

Thus, most of the document will be in a serif font such as Times, including all paragraphs save those that have a class of signature, which will instead be rendered in a cursive font such as Author. Headings 1 through 4 will be in a sans serif font like Helvetica, while the elements CODE, PRE, TT, and SPAN.input will be in a monospace font like Courier—which, as it happens, is how the first three of those elements are usually presented.

Specifying Actual Font Names

An author may, on the other hand, have more specific preferences about which font is used in the display of an element. In a similar vein, a user may want to create a user style sheet that defines the exact fonts used in the display of all documents. In either case, font-family is still the property to use.

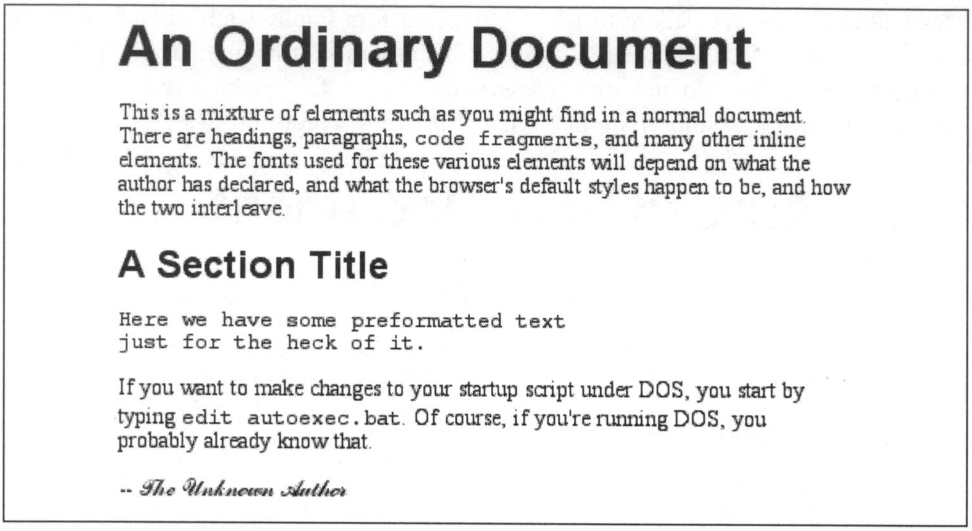

An Ordinary Document

This is a mixture of elements such as you might find in a normal document.
There are headings, paragraphs, `code fragments`, and many other inline
elements. The fonts used for these various elements will depend on what the
author has declared, and what the browser's default styles happen to be, and how
the two interleave.

A Section Title

```
Here we have some preformatted text
just for the heck of it.
```

If you want to make changes to your startup script under DOS, you start by
typing `edit autoexec.bat`. Of course, if you're running DOS, you
probably already know that.

-- *The Unknown Author*

Figure 5-2. Various font families

Assume for the moment that all H1s should use Garamond as their font. The simplest rule for this would be the following:

```
H1 {font-family: Garamond;}
```

This will cause a user agent displaying the document to use Garamond for all H1s,
as shown in Figure 5-3.

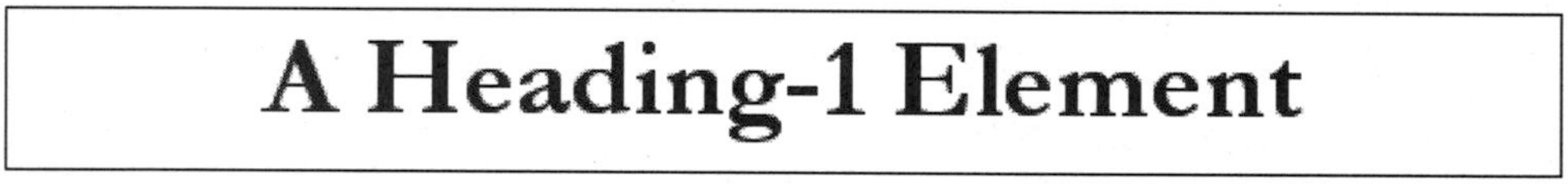

A Heading-1 Element

Figure 5-3. An H1 element using Garamond

Assuming, that is, the user agent has Garamond available for use. What if, for
whatever reason, it doesn't? In that case, the user agent will be unable to use the
rule at all. It won't ignore the rule, but if it can't find a font called "Garamond,"
then it won't be able to do anything with the rule.

All is not lost, however. By combining specific font names with generic font families, documents will come out at least close to the author's intentions. To continue
the previous example, the following markup tells a user agent to use Garamond, if
it's available, but if not, then to use another serif font:

```
H1 {font-family: Garamond, serif;}
```

If a reader doesn't have Garamond installed but does have Times, the user agent
might use Times for H1 elements, as Figure 5-4 depicts. Even though this isn't an
exact match, it's probably close enough.

A Heading-1 Element

Figure 5-4. An H1 element using a browser-selected serif font

For this reason, authors are very strongly encouraged to always provide a generic family as part of any `font-family` rule. By doing so, you let user agents that can't provide an exact font match use their fallback mechanisms to pick an alternative.

This is especially helpful since, in a cross-platform environment, there is no way to know who has which fonts installed. Sure, every Windows machine in the world may have Arial and Times New Roman installed, but many Macintoshes do not, and the same is probably true of Unix machines. Conversely, while Chicago and Charcoal are common to all recent Macintoshes, it's unlikely that Windows and Unix users will have either font installed, and even less likely that they'll have both. Therefore, declarations involving these fonts, and any others, should always end with a generic font family:

```
H1 {font-family: Arial, sans-serif;}
H2 {font-family: Charcoal, sans-serif;}
P {font-family: TimesNR, serif;}
ADDRESS {font-family: Chicago, sans-serif;}
```

Again, this isn't required, but it is a very good idea.

If you're familiar with fonts, you might have a number of similar fonts in mind for use in displaying a given element. Let's say that you want all paragraphs in a document to be displayed using Times, but you would also accept TimesNR, Garamond, New Century Schoolbook, and New York (all of which are serif fonts). First, decide the order of preference for these fonts, and then string them together with commas like this:

```
P {font-family: Times, TimesNR, 'New Century Schoolbook', Garamond,
    'New York', serif;}
```

Based on this list, a user agent will look for the fonts in the order they're listed. If none of the listed fonts are available, then it will simply pick a serif font that is available.

Using Quotation Marks

You may have noticed the presence of single quotation marks in the previous example, which we haven't seen before. Quotation marks are needed in a `font-family` declaration only if a font name has one or more spaces in it, such as "New York," or if the font name includes symbols such as # or $. In both cases, the entire font name needs to be enclosed in quotation marks to keep the user agent from getting confused about what the name really is. (You might think the commas would suffice for this, but no.) Thus, a font called Karrank% would need to be quoted:

```
H2 {Wedgie, 'Karrank%', Klingon, fantasy;}
```

If you leave off the quotation marks, the odds are high that user agents will ignore that particular font name altogether, although they'll still process the rest of the rule. Font names that use a single word, like Garamond, need not be quoted, and generic family names ("serif," "monospace," and the like) should *never* be quoted. If you quote a generic name, then the user agent will assume you are asking for a specific font with that name (for example, "serif"), not a generic family.

As for which quotation marks to use, both single and double quotation marks are acceptable. However, if you place a `font-family` rule in a `STYLE` attribute, you'll need to use whichever quotes you didn't use for the attribute itself. Thus, if you use double quotation marks to enclose the font-family rule, then within the rule you'll have to use single quotes. If you used double quotes in such a circumstance, they would interfere with the attribute syntax, as you can see from Figure 5-5:

```
P {font-family: sans-serif;}   /* sets paragraphs to sans-serif by default */

<!-- the next example is correct (uses single-quotes) -->
<P STYLE="font-family: 'New Century Schoolbook', Times, serif;">...</P>

<!-- the next example is NOT correct (uses double-quotes) -->
<P STYLE="font-family: "New Century Schoolbook", Times, serif;">...</P>
```

Greetings! This paragraph is supposed to use either 'New Century Schoolbook', Times, or an alternate serif font for its display.

Greetings! This paragraph is also supposed to use either 'New Century Schoolbook', Times, or an alternate serif font for its display.

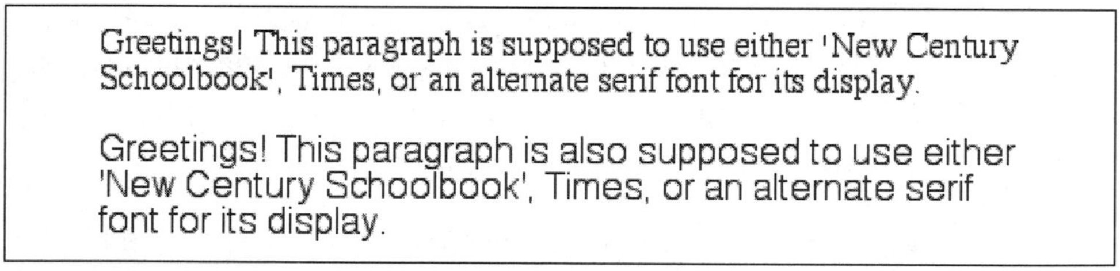

Figure 5-5. The perils of incorrect quotation marks

Good Practices

Returning to the subject of providing alternate fonts: generally, such lists are comprised of fonts from the same generic family, but this need not be the case. Instead of listing all serif fonts or all sans serif fonts or all cursive fonts, you can mix them up as much as you like. The only restriction is that you can provide only a single generic family at the end of the `font-family` declaration:

```
P.signature {Author99, ScriptTM, serif;}
```

Here, the author has said that if neither Author99 nor ScriptTM are available for use, then the user agent should use any serif font. Why not specify `cursive` for the generic font family? Let's extend the example a little further:

```
P {font-family: Verdana, sans-serif;}
P.signature {font-family: Author99, ScriptTM, cursive;}
```

Assume that these styles are applied to a document and that the document is viewed by someone who has neither of the two listed "signature" fonts available and who further has no cursive fonts available. In such a circumstance, the entire rule must be ignored by the user agent, and the element `<P CLASS="signature">` will be displayed in Verdana, or another sans serif font if Verdana is not available, as shown in Figure 5-6.

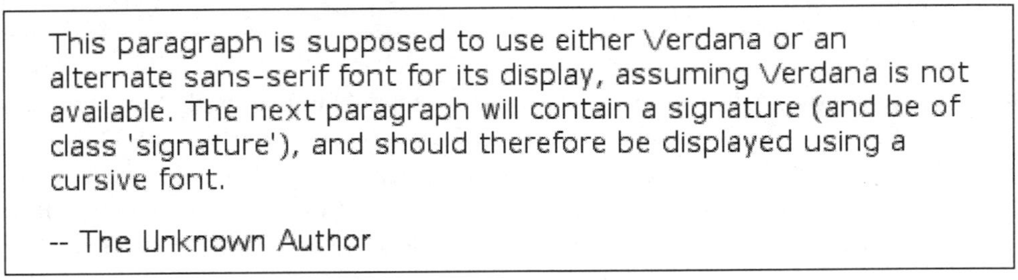

This paragraph is supposed to use either Verdana or an alternate sans-serif font for its display, assuming Verdana is not available. The next paragraph will contain a signature (and be of class 'signature'), and should therefore be displayed using a cursive font.

-- The Unknown Author

Figure 5-6. The result of having no cursive fonts installed

This happens because the element is a paragraph, and since its rule cannot be used, the more generic rule `P {font-family: Verdana, sans-serif;}` applies. In order to avoid this, a better set of rules would be as follows:

```
P {font-family: Verdana, sans-serif;}
P.signature {font-family: Author99, ScriptTM, serif;}
```

This way, the "signature" paragraph is more likely to be in a font different than the rest of the document, as shown in Figure 5-7.

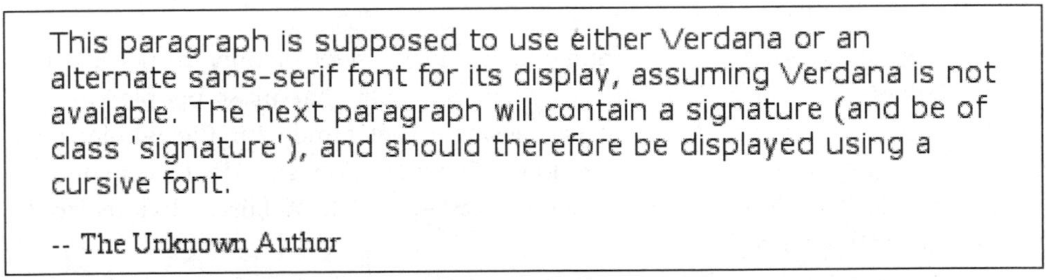

This paragraph is supposed to use either Verdana or an alternate sans-serif font for its display, assuming Verdana is not available. The next paragraph will contain a signature (and be of class 'signature'), and should therefore be displayed using a cursive font.

-- The Unknown Author

Figure 5-7. Planning for the absence of cursive fonts

All of this fun font-matching stuff crops up again in another realm: selecting the weight of a given font.

Font Weights

---

font-weight

Values	normal | bold | bolder | lighter | 100 | 200 | 300 | 400 | 500 | 600 | 700 | 800 | 900
Initial value	normal
Inherited	yes
Applies to	all elements

Even though you may not realize it, you're already familiar with font weights: boldfaced text is a very common example of an increased font weight. Generally speaking, the darker and "more bold" a font appears, the heavier it is said to be. There are a great many ways to label the heaviness of fonts. For example, the font family known as Zurich has a number of variants such as Zurich Bold, Zurich Black, Zurich UltraBlack, Zurich Light, and Zurich Regular. Each of these uses the same basic font, but each has a different weight.

So let's say that you want to use Zurich for a document, but you'd like to make use of all those different heaviness levels. You could refer to them directly through the `font-family` property, but you really shouldn't have to do that. Besides, it's no fun having to write a style sheet such as this:

```
H1 {font-family: 'Zurich UltraBlack', sans-serif;}
H2 {font-family: 'Zurich Black', sans-serif;}
H3 {font-family: 'Zurich Bold', sans-serif;}
H4, P {font-family: Zurich, sans-serif;}
SMALL {font-family: 'Zurich Light', sans-serif;}
```

Besides the obvious tedium of writing such a style sheet, it only works if everyone has these fonts installed, and it's pretty safe bet that most people don't. It would make far more sense to specify a single font family for the whole document and then assign weights to various elements. You can do this, in theory, using the various values for the property `font-weight`. A fairly obvious `font-weight` declaration is this:

```
B {font-weight: bold;}
```

This says, simply, that the B element should be displayed using a boldface font; or, to put it another way, a font that is heavier than is normal for the document, as shown in Figure 5-8. This is what we're used to, of course, since B does cause text to be boldfaced.

Within this paragraph we find a 'B' element,
which will contain **boldfaced text**, as expected.

Figure 5-8. Making the B tag bold

However, what's really happening is that a heavier variant of the font is used for displaying a B element. Thus, if you have a paragraph displayed using Times, and part of it is boldfaced, then there are really two variants of the same font in use: Times and TimesBold. The regular text is displayed using Times, and the bold-faced text uses TimesBold.

How Weights Work

In order to understand how a user agent determines the heaviness, or weight, of a given font variant, not to mention how weight is inherited, it's easiest to start by talking about the keywords 100 through 900. These number keywords were defined to map to a relatively common feature of font design in which a font is given nine levels of weight. OpenType, for example, employs a numeric scale with nine values. If a font has these levels built in, then the numbers are mapped directly to the predefined levels, with 100 as the lightest variant of the font, and 900 as the heaviest.

In fact, there is no intrinsic weight in these numbers. The CSS specification says only that each number corresponds to a weight at least as heavy as the number that precedes it. Thus, 100, 200, 300, and 400 might all map to the same relatively lightweight variant, while 500 and 600 could correspond to the same heavier font variant, and 700, 800, and 900 could all produce the same very heavy font variant. As long as no keyword corresponds to a variant that is lighter than the variant assigned to the previous keyword, then everything will be all right.

As it happens, these numbers are defined to be equivalent to certain common variant names, not to mention other values for font-weight. 400 is defined to be equivalent to normal, and 700 corresponds to bold. The other numbers do not match up with any other values for font-weight, but they can correspond to common variant names. If there is a font variant labeled something such as "Normal," "Regular," "Roman," or "Book," then it is assigned to the number 400 and any variant with the label "Medium" is assigned to 500. However, if a variant labeled "Medium" is the only variant available, it is *not* assigned to 500.

A user agent has to do even more work if there are less than nine weights in a given font family. In this case, it has to fill in the gaps in a predetermined way:

- If the value 500 is unassigned, it is given the same font weight as that assigned to 400.

- If 300 is unassigned, it is given the next variant lighter than 400. If no lighter variant is available, 300 is assigned the same variant as 400. In this case, it will usually be "Normal" or "Medium." This method is also used for 200 and 100.

- If 600 is unassigned, it is given the next variant darker than 400. If no darker variant is available, 600 is assigned the same variant as 500. This method is also used for 700, 800, and 900.

In order to understand this more clearly, let's look at three examples of font-weight assignment. In the first, assume that the font family Karrank% is an Open-Type font and so already has nine weights already defined. In this case, the numbers are assigned to each level, and the keywords `normal` and `bold` are assigned to the numbers 400 and 700, respectively.

In our second example, we consider the font family Zurich, which was discussed near the beginning of this section. Hypothetically, its variants might be assigned values for `font-weight` as shown in Table 5-1.

Table 5-1. Hypothetical Weight Assignments for a Specific Font

Font Face	Assigned Keyword	Assigned Number(s)
Zurich Light		100, 200, 300
Zurich Regular	normal	400
Zurich Medium		500
Zurich Bold	bold	600, 700
Zurich Black		800
Zurich UltraBlack		900

The first three number values are assigned to the lightest weight. The Regular face gets the keywords 400 and `normal`, as expected. Since there is a Medium font, it's assigned to the number 500. There is nothing to assign to 600, so it's mapped to the Bold font face, which is also the variant to which 700 and `bold` are assigned. Finally, 800 and 900 are assigned to the Black and UltraBlack variants. Note that this last would only happen if those faces had the top two weight levels already assigned. Otherwise, the user agent might ignore them, and assign 800 and 900 to the Bold face instead, or it might assign them both to one or the other of the Black variants.

Finally, let's consider a stripped-down version of Times, in which there are only two weight variants, TimesRegular and TimesBold, as shown in Table 5-2.

Table 5-2. Hypothetical Weight Assignments for Times

Font Face	Assigned Keyword	Assigned Number(s)
TimesRegular	normal	100, 200, 300, 400, 500
TimesBold	bold	600, 700, 800, 900

The assignment of the keywords `normal` and `bold` is straightforward enough, of course. As for the numbers, 100 through 300 are assigned to the Regular face because there isn't a lighter face available. 400 goes to Regular as expected, but what about 500? It is assigned to the Regular (or `normal`) face because there isn't a Medium face available; thus, it is assigned the same as 400. As for the rest, 700 goes with `bold` as always, while 800 and 900, lacking a heavier face, are assigned to the Bold font face. Finally, 600 is assigned to the next-heavier face, which is, of course, the Bold face.

`font-weight` is inherited, so if you set a paragraph to be `bold`, then all of its children will inherit that boldness, as we see in Figure 5-9.

```
P.one {font-weight: bold;}
```

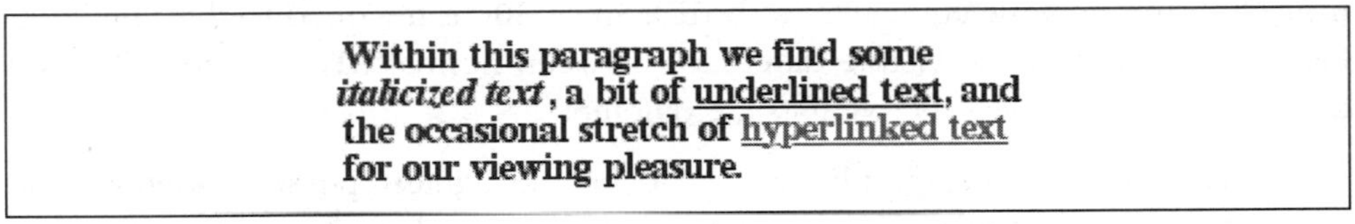

> **Within this paragraph we find some**
> ***italicized text*, a bit of <u>underlined text</u>, and**
> **the occasional stretch of <u>hyperlinked text</u>**
> **for our viewing pleasure.**

Figure 5-9. Inherited font weight

This isn't unusual, but the situation gets interesting when you use the last two values we have to discuss: `bolder` and `lighter`. In general terms, these keywords have the effect you'd anticipate: they make text more or less bold with comparison to its parent's font weight. Let's consider `bolder` first.

Getting Bolder

If you set an element to have a weight of `bolder`, then the user agent first must determine what `font-weight` was inherited from the parent element. It then selects the lowest number which corresponds to a font weight darker than what was inherited. If none is available, then the user agent sets the element's font weight to the next numerical value, unless the value is already 900, in which case the weight remains at 900. Thus, you might encounter the following situations, illustrated in Figure 5-10:

```
P {font-weight: normal;}
P EM {font-weight: bolder;}  /* results in 'bold' text, evaluates to '700' */

H1 {font-weight: bold;}
H1 B {font-weight: bolder;}  /* if no bolder face exists, evaluates to '800' */

P {font-weight: 100;} /* assume 'Light' face exists ; see explanation */
P STRONG {font-weight: bolder;} /* results in 'normal' text, weight '400' */
```

In the first example, the user agent moves up the weight ladder from `normal` to `bold`; in numeric terms, this is a jump from 400 to 700. In the second example, H1 text is already set to `bold`. If there is no bolder face available, then the user

Within this paragraph we find some *emphasized text.*

This H1 contains bold text

Meanwhile, this paragraph has some strong text but it shouldn't look much different, at least in terms of font weight.

Figure 5-10. Text trying to be more bold

agent sets the weight of B text within an H1 to 800, since that is the next step up from 700 (the numeric equivalent to bold). Since 800 is assigned to the same font face as 700, there is no visible difference between normal H1 text and boldfaced H1 text, but nonetheless the weights are different.

In the last example, paragraphs are set to be the lightest possible font weight, which we assume exists as a Light variant. Furthermore, the other faces in this font family are Regular and Bold. Any EM text within a paragraph will evaluate to normal, since that is the next-heaviest face within the font family. However, what if the only faces in the font are Regular and Bold? In that case, the declarations would evaluate like this:

```
/*   assume only two faces for this example: 'Regular' and 'Bold'   */
P {font-weight: 100;}   /* looks the same as 'normal' text */
P SPAN {font-weight: bolder;}   /* maps to '700' */
```

As we can see, the weight 100 is assigned to the normal font face, but the value of font-weight is still 100. Thus, the SPAN text (which is set to be bolder) will inherit the value of 100 and then evaluate to the next-heaviest face, which is the Bold face and which has a numerical weight of 700. Figure 5-11 shows us the visual result of all this.

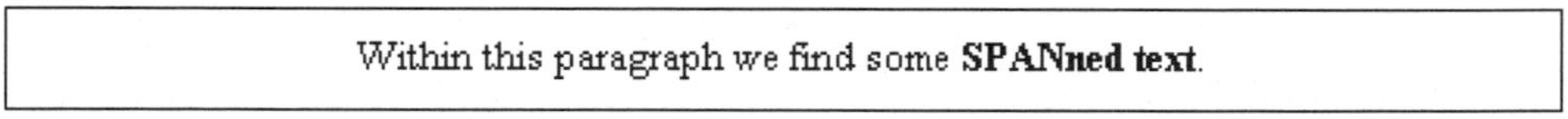

Within this paragraph we find some **SPANned text.**

Figure 5-11. Greater weight will usually confer visual boldness

Let's take this all one step further, and add two more rules, plus some markup, to illustrate how all this works (see Figure 5-12 for the results):

```
/*   assume only two faces for this example: 'Regular' and 'Bold'   */
P {font-weight: 100;}   /* looks the same as 'normal' text */
P SPAN {font-weight: 400;}   /* so does this */
STRONG {font-weight: bolder;}   /* bolder than its parent */
STRONG B {font-weight: bolder;}   /* bolder still */
```

```
<P>
This paragraph contains elements of increasing weight: there is an
<SPAN>SPAN element which contains a <STRONG>strongly emphasized
element, and that contains a <B>boldface element</B></STRONG></SPAN>.
</P>
```

> This paragraph contains elements of increasing weight: there
> is an SPAN element which contains a **strongly emphasized**
> **element, and that contains a boldface element**.

Figure 5-12. Moving up the weight scale

In the last two nested elements, the computed value of `font-weight` is increased because of the liberal use of the keyword `bolder`. If we were to replace the text in the paragraph with numbers representing the `font-weight` of each element, we would get the results in Figure 5-13:

```
<P>
100 <SPAN> 400 <STRONG> 700 <B> 800 </B></STRONG></SPAN>.
</P>
```

> 100 400 **700 800** .

Figure 5-13. Changing weight, with the numbers to illustrate it

The first two weight increases are large because they represent jumps from 100 to 400, and from 400 to `bold` (700). From 700, there is no heavier face, so the user agent simply moves the value of `font-weight` one notch up the numeric scale (800). Furthermore, if we were to insert a `STRONG` element into the B element, it would come out like Figure 5-14:

```
<P>
100 <SPAN> 400 <STRONG> 700 <B> 800 <STRONG> 900
</STRONG></B></STRONG></SPAN>.
</P>
```

> 100 400 **700 800 900** .

Figure 5-14. Weight numbers, again

If there were yet another B element inserted into the innermost `STRONG` element, its weight would also be 900, since `font-weight` can never be higher than 900. Assuming, as we have, that there are only two font faces available, then the text would appear to be either Regular or Bold text, as we see in Figure 5-15:

```
<P>
regular <SPAN> regular <STRONG> bold <B> bold
<STRONG> bold </STRONG></B></STRONG></SPAN>.
</P>
```

regular regular **bold bold bold** .

Figure 5-15. Visual weight, with descriptors

Lightening Weights

As you might expect, `lighter` works in just the same way, except that it causes the user agent to move down the weight scale, instead of up. With a quick modification of the previous example, we can see this very clearly:

```
/*   assume only two faces for this example: 'Regular' and 'Bold'   */
P {font-weight: 900;}   /* as bold as possible, which will look 'bold' */
P SPAN {font-weight: 700;}   /* this will also be bold */
STRONG {font-weight: lighter;}   /* lighter than its parent */
B {font-weight: lighter;}   /*lighter still */

<P>
900 <SPAN> 700 <STRONG> 400 <B> 300 <STRONG> 200
</STRONG></B></STRONG></SPAN>.
</P>
<!-- ...or, to put it another way... -->
<P>
bold <SPAN> bold <STRONG> regular <B> regular
<STRONG> regular </STRONG></B></STRONG></SPAN>.
</P>
```

Ignoring the fact that this would be entirely counterintuitive, what we see in Figure 5-16 is that the main paragraph text has a weight of 900 and the SPAN a weight of 700. When the STRONG text is set to `lighter`, it evaluates to the next-lighter face, which is the regular face, or 400 (the same as `normal`) on the numeric scale. The next step down is to 300, which comes out the same as `normal` since no lighter faces exist. From there, the user agent can only reduce the weight one numeric step at a time until it reaches 100 (which it doesn't do in the example). The second paragraph shows which text will be bold, and which regular.

900 700 400 300 200 .

bold bold regular regular regular .

Figure 5-16. Making text lighter

Font Size

The methods for determining font size are both very familiar and very different.

---

font-size

Values	xx-small | x-small | small | medium | large | x-large | xx-large | smaller | larger | <length> | <percentage>
Initial value	medium
Inherited	yes

Note: Percentage elements refer to parent element's font size.

Applies to	all elements

In a fashion very similar to the font-weight keywords bolder and lighter, the property font-size has relative-size keywords called larger and smaller. Much as we saw with relative font weights, these keywords cause the computed value of font-size to move up and down a scale of absolute values, which we'll need to understand before we can explore larger and smaller. First, though, we need to explore how fonts are sized in the first place.

In fact, the relation of the font-size property to what you actually see rendered is determined by the font's designer. This relationship is set as an *em square* (some call it an em box) within the font itself. This em square, and thus the font size, doesn't have to refer to any boundaries established by the characters in a font themselves. Instead, it refers to the distance between baselines when the font is set without any extra leading (line-height in CSS). It is quite possible for fonts to have characters that are taller than the default distance between baselines. For that matter, a font might be defined such that all of its characters are smaller than its em square. Some hypothetical examples are shown in Figure 5-17.

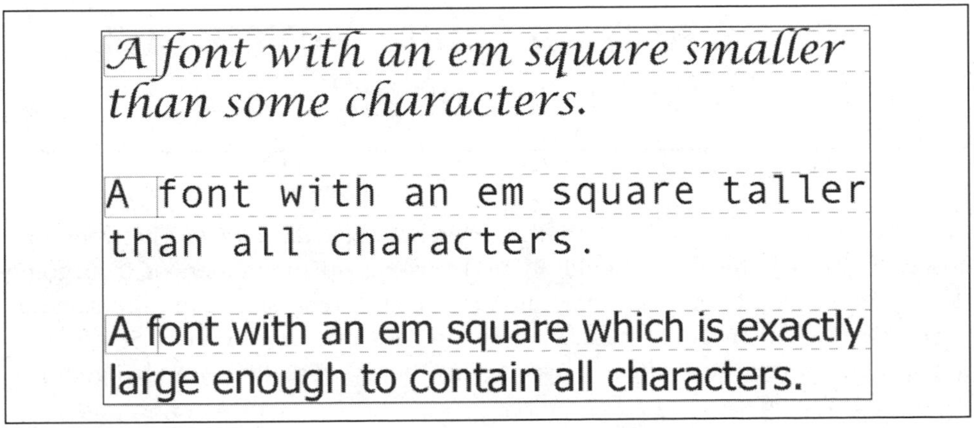

Figure 5-17. Fonts and font size

Thus, the effect of `font-size` is to provide a size for the em box of a given font. This does not guarantee that any of the actual characters which are displayed will be this size.

Absolute Sizes

Having established all that, we turn now to the absolute-size keywords. There are seven absolute-size values for `font-size`: `xx-small`, `x-small`, `small`, `medium`, `large`, `x-large`, and `xx-large`. These are not defined precisely, but are relative to each other, as Figure 5-18 demonstrates:

```
P.one {font-size: xx-small}
P.two {font-size: x-small;}
P.three {font-size: small;}
P.four {font-size: medium;}
P.five {font-size: large;}
P.six {font-size: x-large;}
P.seven {font-size: xx-large;}
```

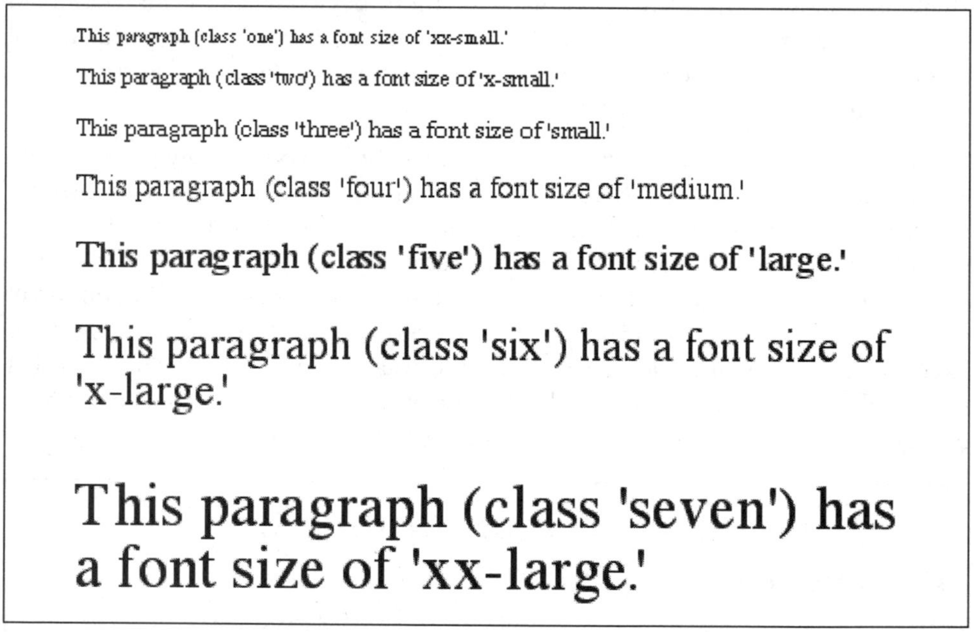

This paragraph (class 'one') has a font size of 'xx-small.'

This paragraph (class 'two') has a font size of 'x-small.'

This paragraph (class 'three') has a font size of 'small.'

This paragraph (class 'four') has a font size of 'medium.'

This paragraph (class 'five') has a font size of 'large.'

This paragraph (class 'six') has a font size of 'x-large.'

This paragraph (class 'seven') has a font size of 'xx-large.'

Figure 5-18. Absolute font sizes

According to the CSS1 specification, the difference (or *scaling factor*) between one absolute size and the next should about 1.5 going up the ladder, or 0.66 going down. Thus, if `medium` is the same as `10px`, then `large` should be the same as `15px`. On the other hand, the scaling factor does not have to be 1.5; not only might it be different for different user agents, but it's already been changed to a factor of `1.2` by CSS2.

Working from the assumption that `medium` equals `12px`, for different scaling factors, we get the absolute sizes shown in Table 5-3. (The values are approximations, of course.)

Table 5-3. Scaling Factors Translated to Points

Keyword	Scaling: 1.5	Scaling: 1.3	Scaling: 1.2
`xx-small`	4px	5px	6px
`x-small`	6px	7px	8px
`small`	8px	9px	10px
`medium`	12px	12px	12px
`large`	18px	16px	14px
`x-large`	27px	21px	17px
`xx-large`	42px	27px	20px

In general, these sizes are precomputed by browsers and do not change once they have been computed. Thus, if a browser considers `x-large` to be `27px`, then it will be that size no matter what happens. This is a shame, because it would make far more sense (and be more in line with the aims of CSS) to have the absolute sizes recomputed whenever users change their browser preferences.

Further complicating the situation is the fact that different user agents can assign the "default" font size to different absolute keywords. Take the Version 4 browsers as an example: Navigator makes `medium` the same size as unstyled text, whereas Internet Explorer assumes that `small` text is equivalent in size to unstyled text. Despite the fact that the default value for `font-style` is supposed to be `medium`, Internet Explorer's behavior isn't quite so wrongheaded as it might first appear.[*]

Relative Sizes

Compared to all this, the keywords `larger` and `smaller` are simple to understand: they cause the size of an element to be shifted up or down the absolute-size scale, relative to their parent element, using the same scaling factor employed to calculate absolute sizes. In other words, if the browser used a scaling factor of 1.2

---

[*] Note that there are seven absolute-size keywords, just as there are seven FONT sizes (e.g., <FONT SIZE="5">). Since the typical default font size has historically been 3, it makes some sense that the third value on the CSS absolute-size keyword list would be used to indicate a default font size. Since the third keyword turns out to be `small`, you get Explorer's behavior. Technically, Microsoft has included this default style: BODY {font-size: small;}. The only way to override it is to explicitly declare a value of `medium`, but then the document's font size would be different in Internet Explorer than in Navigator.

for absolute sizes, then it should use the same factor when applying relative-size keywords. Thus:

```
P {font-size: medium;}
STRONG, EM {font-size: larger;}

<P>This paragraph element contain <STRONG>a strong-emphasis element
which itself contains <EM>an emphasis element that also contains
<STRONG>a strong element.</STRONG></EM></STRONG></P>

<P> medium <STRONG>large <EM> x-large
<STRONG>xx-large</STRONG></EM></STRONG></P>
```

Thanks to the way `font-size` operates, the sizes get larger (or smaller) as shown in Figure 5-19.

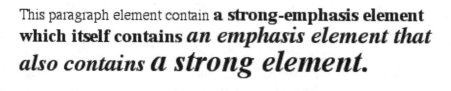

Figure 5-19. Relative font sizing

Unlike the relative values for weight, the relative-size values are not necessarily constrained to the limits of the absolute-size range. Thus, a font's size can be pushed beyond the values for `xx-small` and `xx-large`. For example:

```
H1 {font-size: xx-large;}
EM {font-size: larger;}

<H1>A Heading with <EM>Emphasis</EM> added</H1>
<P>This paragraph has some <EM>emphasis</EM> as well.</P>

<H1> xx-large <EM> xx-large </EM> xx-large </H1>
<P> medium <EM>large </EM> medium </P>
```

As we can see in Figure 5-20, the emphasized text in the `H1` element is slightly larger than `xx-large`. The amount of scaling is left up to the user agent, with the recommended scaling factor of 1.2 being preferred. The `EM` text in the paragraph, of course, is shifted one slot up the absolute-size scale (`large`).

Percentages and Sizes

In a way, percentage values are very similar to the relative-size keywords in that a percentage value is always computed in terms of whatever size is inherited from an element's parent. Percentages, unlike the relative-size keywords, permit much

Figure 5-20. Relative font sizing at the edges of the absolute sizes

finer control over the computed font size. Consider the following, illustrated in Figure 5-21:

```
P {font-size: 12px;}
EM {font-size: 120%;}
STRONG {font-size: 135%;}
SMALL, .fnote {font-size: 75%;}

<P>This paragraph contains both <EM>emphasis</EM> and <STRONG>strong
emphasis</STRONG>, both of which are larger than their parent element.
The <SMALL>small text</SMALL>, on the other hand, is smaller by a quarter.</P>
<P CLASS="fnote">This is a 'footnote' and is smaller than regular text.</P>

<P> 12px <EM> 14.4px </EM> 12px <STRONG> 16.2px </STRONG>  12px
<SMALL> 9px </SMALL> 12px </P>
<P CLASS="fnote"> 9px </P>
```

> This paragraph contains both *emphasis* and **strong emphasis**, both of which are larger than their parent element. The small text, on the other hand, is smaller by a quarter.
>
> This is a 'footnote' and is smaller than regular text.
>
> 12px *14.4px* 12px **16.2px** 12px 9px 12px
>
> 9px

Figure 5-21. Throwing percentages into the mix

In this example, the exact pixel size values are shown. In practice, a web browser would very likely not round the values off to the nearest whole-number point size, such as 14px, but instead would use fractional sizes.

Incidentally, CSS defines the length value em to be equivalent to percentage values, in the sense that 1em is the same as 100%. Thus, the following would yield identical results:

```
P.one {font-size: 166%;}
P.two {font-size: 1.6em;}
```

When using em measures, the same principles apply as with percentages, such as the inheritance of computed sizes and so forth.

Font Size and Inheritance

In CSS, although font-size is inherited, it is the computed values that are inherited, not percentages, as shown in Figure 5-21. Thus, the value inherited by the STRONG element is 12px, and this value is modified by the declared value 135% to arrive at 16.2 pixels (which might be rounded off to 16 pixels).

As with the relative-size keywords, percentages are effectively cumulative. Thus, the following markup is displayed as shown in Figure 5-22:

```
P {font-size: 12px;}
EM {font-size: 120%;}
STRONG {font-size: 135%;}

<P>This paragraph contains both <EM>emphasis and <STRONG>strong
emphasis</STRONG></EM>, both of which are larger than the paragraph text. </P>

<P> 12px <EM>14.4px <STRONG>19.44px</STRONG></EM> 12px  </P>
```

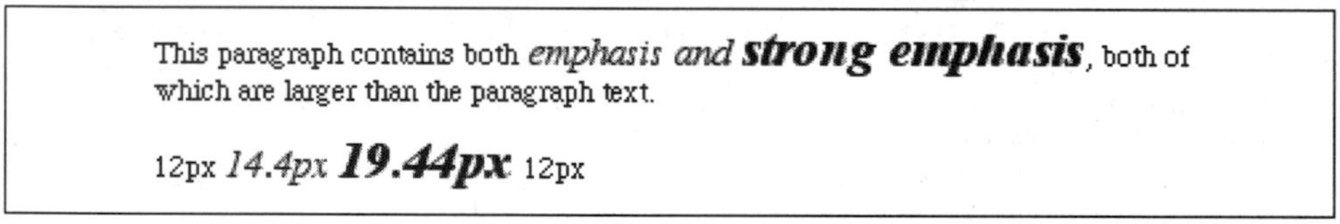

This paragraph contains both *emphasis* and **strong emphasis**, both of which are larger than the paragraph text.

12px *14.4px* **19.44px** 12px

Figure 5-22. The issues of inheritance

The size value for the STRONG element shown in Figure 5-22 is computed as follows:

12 px × 120% = 14.4 px
14.4 px × 135% = 19.44 px (possibly rounded to 19 px)

There is an alternative scenario, however, in which the final value is slightly different. In this scenario, the user agent rounds off pixel size, and these rounded values are then inherited normally by any child elements. Thus, we would have:

12 px × 120% = 14.4 px [14.4 px ≈ 14 px]
14 px × 135% = 18.9 px [18.9 px ≈ 19 px]

If one assumes that the user agent is rounding off at each step, then the end result of both this calculation and the previous one is the same: 19 pixels. However, as more and more percentages are multiplied together, the rounding errors will begin to accumulate. This shouldn't be a major problem—after all, CSS doesn't guarantee you precise control over anything—but it is still a factor to consider.

Using Length Units

The `font-size` can be set using any of the length values discussed in detail in Chapter 3, *Units and Values*. In a 72 dots-per-inch (dpi) environment, all of the following `font-size` declarations should be equivalent:

```
P.one {font-size: 36pt;}     /* assuming 72 dpi, these are all the same thing */
P.two {font-size: 3pc;}
P.three {font-size: 0.5in;}
P.four {font-size: 1.27cm;}
P.five {font-size: 12.7mm;}
```

Correct display assumes that the user agent knows how many dots per inch are used in the display medium. Different user agents make different assumptions—some based on the operating system, some based on preferences settings, and some based on the assumptions of the programmer who wrote the user agent. However, the five lines should always be the same size. So, while the result may not exactly match reality (for example, the actual size of `P.three` may not be half an inch), the measures should all be consistent to one another.

There is one more value that is potentially the same as those just discussed, and that's `36px`, which would be the same physical distance if the display medium is 72 pixels per inch (ppi). However, there are very few monitors with that setting anymore. Most are much higher, in the range of 96 dpi to 120 ppi. Despite this, many Macintosh web browsers tend to treat points (pt) and pixels (px) as though they were equivalent, so the values `14pt` and `14px` may look the same on a Macintosh. This is not the case, however, for Windows and other platforms, which is one of the primary reasons why points can be a very difficult measure to use in document design.

The variations between operating systems are a primary reason why many authors choose to use pixel values for font sizes. This approach is especially attractive when mixing text and images together on a web page, since text can (in theory) be set to the same height as graphic elements on the page by declaring `font-size: 11px;` or something similar, as illustrated by Figure 5-23.

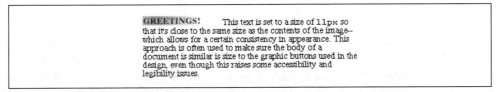

Figure 5-23. Keeping text and graphics in scale with pixel sizes

Using pixel measures is certainly one way to get "consistent" results with `font-size` (and, indeed, with any length at all), but remember what can happen when a user agent mistakenly defines "pixel" to be the same as "smallest dot." In a 300-dpi environment, that will make text nearly twenty times smaller than was likely intended. In addition, pixel-sized text will be of different physical sizes on different monitors, and under different resolutions, such that any use of px for measurements effectively prohibits the use of measurements such as in and cm within the same document. In fact, if you're designing for display in a web browser, it's generally best to avoid length units altogether. The other approaches shown in this chapter, such as keywords and percentages, are a much more robust (and user-friendly) way to go.

Styles and Variants

In comparison with everything that's gone before, this section is practically a no-brainer. The properties discussed herein are so straightforward, and the complexities so minimal, that this will probably all come as a great relief. First we'll talk about font-style, and then move on to font-variant before wrapping up the font properties.

Fonts with Style

font-style is very simple: it's used to select between normal text, italic text, and oblique text. That's it! The only complications are in recognizing the difference between italic and oblique text and knowing why browsers don't always give you a choice anyway.

<table>
<tr><td colspan="2">font-style</td></tr>
<tr><td>Values</td><td>italic | oblique | normal</td></tr>
<tr><td>Initial value</td><td>normal</td></tr>
<tr><td>Inherited</td><td>yes</td></tr>
<tr><td>Applies to</td><td>all elements</td></tr>
</table>

The default value of font-style is, as we can see, normal. This refers to "upright" text, which is probably best described as "text that is not italic or otherwise slanted." The vast majority of text in this book is upright, for instance.

That leaves only an explanation of the difference between `italic` and `oblique` text. For that, it's easiest to turn to Figure 5-24, which illustrates the differences very clearly.

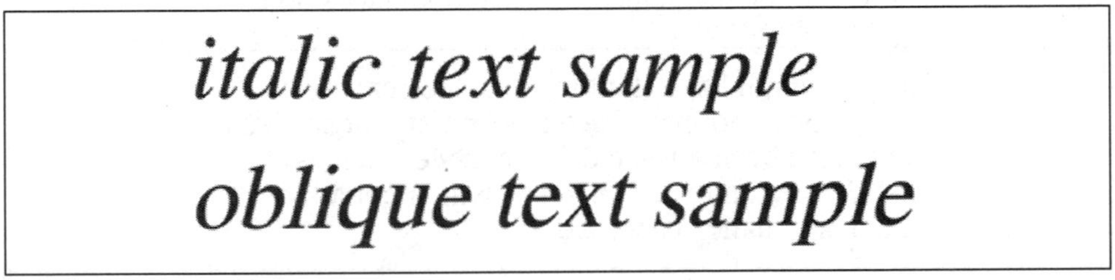

italic text sample

oblique text sample

Figure 5-24. Italic and oblique text in detail

Basically, italic text is in some way its own font, with small changes made to the structure of each letter to account for the altered appearance. This is especially true of serif fonts, where in addition to the fact that the text characters "lean," the serifs may be altered in an italic face. Oblique text, on the other hand, is simply a slanted version of the normal, upright text. Font faces with labels like Italic, Cursive, and Kursiv are usually mapped to the `italic` keyword, while `oblique` can be assigned faces with labels such as Oblique, Slanted, and Incline.

If you wanted to make sure that a document uses italic text in familiar ways, you could write a style sheet like this:

```
P {font-style: normal;}
EM, I {font-style: italic;}
```

As we can see in Figure 5-25, these styles would make paragraphs use an upright font, as usual, and cause the `EM` and `I` elements to use an italic font—again, as usual.

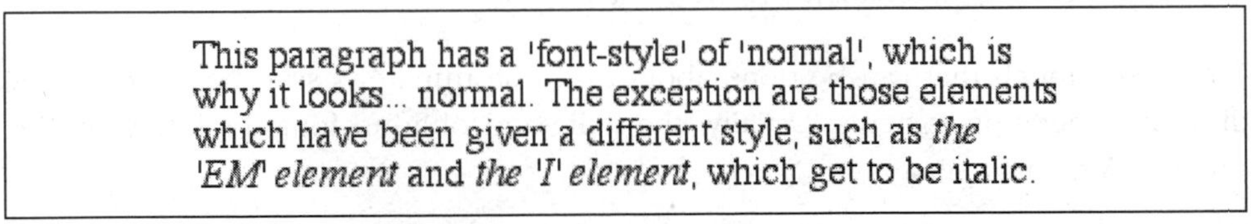

This paragraph has a 'font-style' of 'normal', which is why it looks... normal. The exception are those elements which have been given a different style, such as *the 'EM' element* and *the 'I' element*, which get to be italic.

Figure 5-25. Ordinary document behavior through CSS

On the other hand, you might decide that there should be a subtle difference between `EM` and `I`:

```
P {font-style: normal;}
EM {font-style: oblique;}
I {font-style: italic;}
```

If you look closely at Figure 5-26, you'll see there is no apparent difference between the EM and I elements. In practice, not every font is so sophisticated as to have both an italic face and an oblique face, and even fewer web browsers are sophisticated enough to tell the difference when both faces do exist.

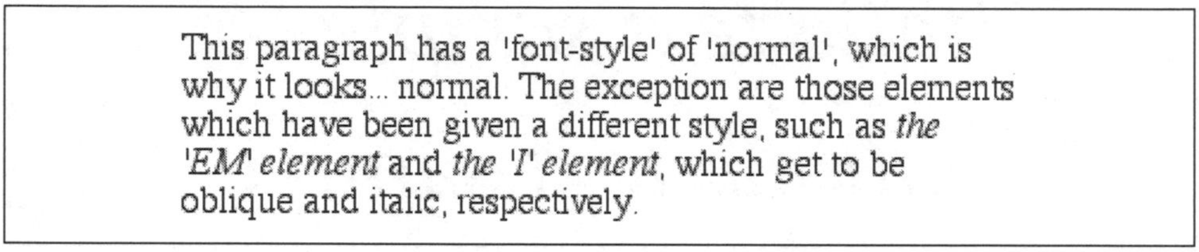

This paragraph has a 'font-style' of 'normal', which is why it looks... normal. The exception are those elements which have been given a different style, such as *the 'EM' element* and *the 'I' element*, which get to be oblique and italic, respectively.

Figure 5-26. More font styles

If either of these is the case, a few things can happen. If there is no Italic face, but there is an Oblique face, then the latter can be used for the former. If the situation is reversed—an Italic face exists, but there is no defined Oblique face—the user agent may not substitute the former for the latter, according to the CSS specification. Finally, the user agent can simply generate the oblique face by computing a slanted version of the upright font. In fact, this is what most often happens in a digital world, where it's fairly easy to slant a font using a simple computation.

Furthermore, you may find that in some operating systems, a given font that has been declared to be `italic` may switch from being italic to oblique depending on the actual size of the font. The display of Times on a Macintosh, for example, is as shown in Figure 5-27, and the only difference there is a single point in size.

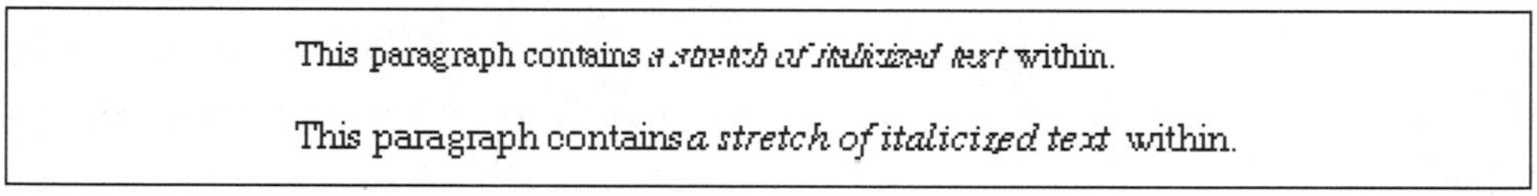

This paragraph contains *a stretch of italicized text* within.

This paragraph contains *a stretch of italicized text* within.

Figure 5-27. Same font, same style, different sizes

There isn't much that can be done about this, unfortunately, save better font handling by operating systems. Usually, the italic and oblique fonts look exactly the same in web browsers.

Still, `font-style` can be useful. For example, it is a common typographic convention that a block quote should be italicized, but that any specially emphasized text within the quote should be upright. In order to employ this effect, shown in Figure 5-28, you would use these styles:

```
BLOCKQUOTE {font-style: italic;}
BLOCKQUOTE EM, BLOCKQUOTE I {font-style: normal;}
```

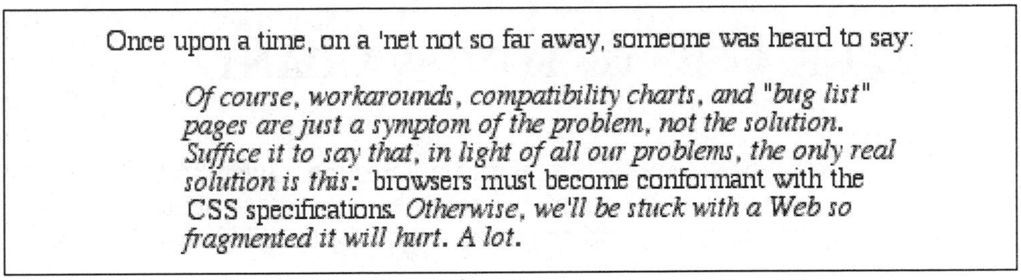

> Once upon a time, on a 'net not so far away, someone was heard to say:
>
> *Of course, workarounds, compatibility charts, and "bug list" pages are just a symptom of the problem, not the solution. Suffice it to say that, in light of all our problems, the only real solution is this:* browsers must become conformant with the CSS specifications. *Otherwise, we'll be stuck with a Web so fragmented it will hurt. A lot.*

Figure 5-28. Common typographical conventions through CSS

Font Variations

In addition to sizes and styles, fonts can also have variants. CSS offers a way to address one very common variant.

font-variant

Values	small-caps | normal
Initial value	normal
Inherited	yes
Applies to	all elements

As for `font-variant`, it has but two values: the default of `normal`, which describes ordinary text, and `small-caps`, which calls for the use of small caps text. If you aren't familiar with such an effect, IT LOOKS SOMETHING LIKE THIS. Instead of upper- and lowercase letters, a small-caps font employs uppercase letters of different sizes. Thus you might see something like the following, shown in Figure 5-29:

```
H1 {font-variant: small-caps;}
P {font-variant: normal;}

<H1>The Uses of font-variant</H1>
<P>
The property <CODE>font-variant</CODE> is very interesting...
</P>
```

As you may notice, in the display of the H1 element, there is a larger uppercase letter wherever an uppercase letter appears in the source and a small uppercase wherever there is a lowercase letter in the source. This may remind you rather strongly of `text-transform: uppercase`, with the only real difference that here,

THE USES OF FONT-VARIANT

The property font-variant is very interesting. Given how common its use is in print media and the relative ease of its implementation, it should be supported by every CSS1-aware browser.

Figure 5-29. Small caps in use

the uppercase letters are of different sizes. That's true, but the reason that small-caps is declared using a font property is that some fonts have a specific small-caps face. Thus, a font property is used to select that face.

What happens if no such face exists? There are two options provided in the specification. The first is for the user agent to create a small-caps face by scaling uppercase letters on its own. The second is simply to make all letters uppercase and the same size, exactly as if the declaration text-transform: uppercase; had been used instead, as shown in Figure 5-30. This is obviously not an ideal solution, but it is permitted.

```
H1 {font-variant: small-caps;}
```

THE USES OF FONT-VARIANT

Figure 5-30. Legal, if not optimal, rendering of small caps

Of the browsers which even recognize font-variant: small-caps (Explorer 4 and 5, and Opera 3.5), only Opera and IE5 for Macintosh do what authors would expect in the display of the text. Other versions of Explorer take the all-capitals route.

Using Shorthand: The font Property

All of these properties are very sophisticated, of course, but using them all could start to get a little tedious:

```
H1 {font-family: Verdana, Helvetica, Arial, sans-serif; font-size: 30px;
    font-weight: 900; font-style: italic; font-variant: small-caps;}
H2 {font-family: Verdana, Helvetica, Arial, sans-serif; font-size: 24px;
    font-weight: bold; font-style: italic; font-variant: normal;}
```

Some of that could be solved by grouping selectors, but wouldn't it be easier to combine everything into a single property? Enter font, which is the shorthand property for all the other font properties (and a little more besides).

---

font

Values	[<font-style> || <font-variant> || <font-weight>]? <font-size> [/ <line-height>]? <font-family>
Initial value	refer to individual properties
Inherited	yes
Applies to	all elements

Generally speaking, a font declaration can have one value from each of the other font properties. Thus the preceding example could be shortened, while having exactly the same effect as the preceding example (illustrated by Figure 5-31):

```
H1 {font: italic 900 small-caps 30px Verdana, Helvetica, Arial, sans-serif;}
H2 {font: bold normal italic 24px Verdana, Helvetica, Arial, sans-serif;}
```

THIS IS A HEADING-1 ELEMENT

This is a Heading-2 element

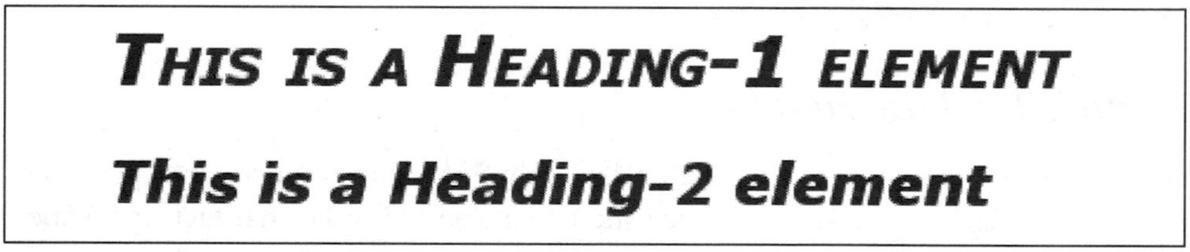

Figure 5-31. Typical font rules

I say that the styles "could be" shortened in this way because there are a few other possibilities, thanks to the relatively loose way in which font can be written. If you look closely at the preceding example, you'll see that the first three values don't occur in the same order. In the H1 rule, the first three values are the values for font-style, font-weight, and font-variant, in that order, whereas in the second, they're ordered font-weight, font-variant, and font-style. There is nothing wrong here, because these three can be written in any order. Furthermore, if any of them has a value of normal, that can be left out altogether.

```
H1 {font: italic 900 small-caps 30px Verdana, Helvetica, Arial, sans-serif;}
H2 {font: bold italic 24px Verdana, Helvetica, Arial, sans-serif;}
```

In this example, the value of normal was left out of the H2 rule, but the effect is exactly the same as in Figure 5-31.

It's important to realize, however, that this free-for-all situation only applies to the first three values of `font`. The last two are much more strict in their behavior. Not only must `font-size` and `font-family` appear in that order as the last two values in the declaration, but both must always be present in a `font` declaration. Period, end of story. If either is left out, then the entire rule will be invalid, and very likely ignored completely by a user agent. Thus the following rules will get you the result shown in Figure 5-32:

```
H1 {font: normal normal italic 30px sans-serif;}    /* no problem here */
H2 {font: 1.5em sans-serif;}    /* also fine; omitted values set to 'normal' */
H3 {font: sans-serif;}    /* INVALID--no 'font-size' provided */
H4 {font: light 24pt;}    /* INVALID--no 'font-family' provided */
```

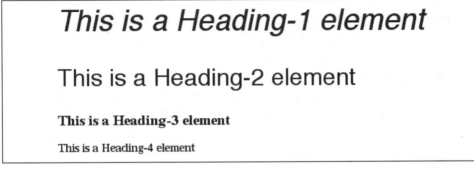

Figure 5-32. The necessity of both size and family

Adding the Line Height

So far, we've treated `font` as though it has only five values, which isn't quite true. It is also possible to set the `line-height` using `font`, despite that fact that `line-height` is a text property, not a font property. It's done as a sort of addition to the `font-size` value, separated from it by a forward slash (`/`):

```
H2 {font: bold italic 200%/1.2 Verdana, Helvetica, Arial, sans-serif;}
```

This rule, demonstrated in Figure 5-33, sets all H2 elements to be bold and italic, using the face for one of the sans serif font families, plus it sets the `font-size` to 24px and the `line-height` to 30px.

This is a Heading-2 element which has had a 'font-size' of '200%' and 'line-height' of '1.2' set for it.

Figure 5-33. Adding line height to the mix

This addition of a value for `line-height` is entirely optional, just as the first three `font` values are, and need only be present if it is needed for some reason. Remember, however, that the `font-size` always comes before `line-height`, never after, and the two are separated by a slash.

This may seem repetitive, but it's one of the most common errors by CSS authors, so I can't say it enough times: the required values for `font` are `font-size` and `font-family`, in that order. Everything else is strictly optional.

Font Matching

As we've seen, CSS allows for the matching of font families, weights, and variants. This is done through font matching, which is a vaguely complicated procedure. Understanding it is important for authors who wish to help user agents make good font selections when displaying their documents. I left it for the end of this chapter because it's not really necessary to understand how the font properties work, and some people will probably want to skip this part and go on to Chapter 6, *Colors and Backgrounds*. If you're still interested, here's how font matching works.

In the first step of font matching, the user agent creates, or otherwise accesses, a database of font properties. This database lists the various CSS1 properties of all the fonts to which the UA has access. Typically, this will be all fonts installed on the machine, although there could be others (for example, the UA could have its own built-in fonts). If the UA encounters two identical fonts, it will simply ignore one of them.

Second, the UA takes apart an element to determine which font properties have been applied, and constructs a list of font properties necessary for the display of that element. Based on that list, the UA makes an initial choice of a font family to use in displaying the element. If there is a complete match, then the UA can use that font. Otherwise, it needs to do a little more work.

Third, if there was no font match in step two, the UA looks for alternate fonts within the same font family. If it finds any, then it repeats step two for that font.

Fourth, assuming a generic match has been found, but it doesn't contain everything needed to display a given element—the font is missing the copyright symbol, for instance—then the UA goes back to step three, which entails a search for another alternate font and another trip through step two.

Finally, if no match has been made and all alternate fonts have been tried, the UA selects the default font for the given generic font family and does the best it can to display the element correctly.

As you can see, step two gets visited a lot in this process. It can be broken down into more precise steps:

1. A font is first matched against the `font-style`. The keyword `italic` is matched by any font which is labeled as either "italic" or "oblique." If neither is available, then the match fails.

2. The next match attempt is on `font-variant`. Any font which is not labeled "small-caps" is assumed to be `normal`. A font can be matched to `small-caps` by any font which is labeled as "small-caps," by any font which allows the synthesis of a small-caps style, or by any font where lowercase letters are replaced by uppercase letters.

3. The next match is to `font-weight`, which can never fail, thanks to the way `font-weight` is handled under CSS1.

4. Finally, `font-size` is tackled. This must be matched within a certain tolerance, but the tolerance is left to the user agent to define. Thus, one user agent might allow matching within a 20% margin of error, whereas another might allow only 10% differences between the size specified and the size that is actually used.

The whole process is long and tedious, but it helps to understand how user agents pick the fonts they do. For example, you might specify the use of Times or any other serif font in a document, to get what's shown in Figure 5-34.

```
BODY {font-family: Times, serif;}
```

This is a document

Always one for stating the obvious, this document will now go on to mention that this element is a paragraph, and the following structure will be a table.

This is the first table cell.	This is the second table cell.	Look! The Third Cell!

Figure 5-34. The end result of font matching

For each element, the user agent should examine the characters in that element and determine whether Times can provide characters to match. In most cases, it can do so with no problem. Assume, however, that a Chinese character has been placed in the middle of a paragraph. Times has nothing that can match this character, so the user agent has to either work around the character or look for another font that can fulfill the needs of displaying that element. Of course, any Western font is highly unlikely to contain Chinese characters, but should one exist (let's call it AsiaTimes), the user agent could use it in the display of that one element—or simply for the single character. Thus, the whole paragraph might be displayed using AsiaTimes, or everything in the paragraph might be in Times except for the single Chinese character, which is displayed in AsiaTimes.

Summary

Although authors cannot count on a specific font being used in a document, they can very easily specify generic font families to be used. This particular behavior is generally very well supported, since any user agent that didn't let authors (or even readers) assign fonts would quickly find itself out of favor.

As for the other areas of font manipulation, support varies. Changing the size of fonts usually works well, but twentieth-century implementations ranged from frustratingly simplistic to very nearly correct in this area. The frustrating part for authors, though, is usually not how font sizing is supported, but how a unit they want to use (points) can yield very different results in different media, or even different operating systems and user agents. The dangers of using points are many, and using length units for web design is generally not a good idea. Percentages, em units, and ex units are usually best for changing font sizes, since these scale very well in all common display environments.

Now that we've worked our way through altering text and fonts, let's turn to ways to style the elements that contain the text.

6

Colors and Backgrounds

Many of you will no doubt remember the first time you changed the colors of a web page. Instead of the old black text on a gray background with blue links, all of a sudden you could use any combination of colors you desired—perhaps light blue text on a black background with lime green hyperlinks. From there, you probably moved on to putting images in the background and combining background images with appropriately colored text to make some really cool-looking pages.

Eventually, though, one comes to realize that setting a single color for all of the text in a page just isn't enough. That's how `<FONT COLOR="...">` came into being. Without it, you wouldn't be able to have pages where some text is black, some red, and some white, for example.

Now, thanks to the power of CSS, you can have many, many different colors within a single page, and without using a single FONT tag. This gives authors the ability to set up pages where the main text is black with a white background, but the navigational hyperlinks along the side of the page are black on a light purple background. There are almost infinite possibilities: defining red text for warnings, using a dark purple to make boldfaced text even more obvious, setting each heading to be a different shade of green, and on and on.

Of course, this means that when you're designing a page, you need to put some thought into it first. That's generally true in any case, but with colors, it's even more so. For example, if you're going to set all hyperlinks to be yellow, will that clash with the background color in any part of your document? If you use too many colors, will the user be too overwhelmed? If you change the default hyperlink colors, will users still be able to figure out where your links are? If you set both regular text and hyperlink text to be the same color, for instance, then it will be much harder to spot links—in fact, almost impossible if the user's links aren't underlined.

Despite all these issues, the ability to change the colors of elements is something almost every author will want to use, probably quite often. Used properly, colors can really strengthen the presentation of a document. Once you've decided how you plan to use color, you have to decide how you'll apply it, since some approaches will require the use of classes as well as simple element selectors.

As an example, let's say you have a design where all H1 elements should be green, most H2 elements should be blue, and all hyperlinks should be dark red. However, in some cases H2 elements should be dark blue because they're associated with different types of information. The simplest way to handle this is to put a class of dkblue on each H2 that needs to be dark blue and declare the following:

```
H1 {color: green;}
H2 {color: blue;}
H2.dkblue {color: navy;}
A:link {color: maroon;}   /* a good dark red color */
```

Any H2 which should be dark blue would then be marked up as <H2 CLASS="dkblue">...</H2>.

It's actually better to pick class names that are descriptive of the type of information contained within, not of the visual effect you're trying to achieve at the moment. For example, let's say that we want the dark blue color to be applied to all H2 elements that are subsection headings. It would be much better to pick a class name like subsec or even sub-section. Both of these names have the advantage of actually meaning something—and, furthermore, of being independent of any presentational concepts. After all, you might decide later to make all subsection titles dark red instead of dark blue, and the statement H2.dkblue {color: maroon;} is a little silly.

From this simple example, we draw the general lesson that when you're planning to use styles, it's generally to your advantage to plan ahead and use all of the tools you can. To take the preceding example a little further, suppose that a navigational bar is added to the page. Within this bar, hyperlinks should be yellow, not dark red. If the bar is marked with an ID of navbar, then you need only add this rule:

```
#navbar A:link {color: yellow;}
```

This will change the color of hyperlinks within the navigation bar without affecting other hyperlinks throughout the document.

Colors

There is really only one type of color in CSS, and that's plain, solid color. If you set the background of a page to be `red`, then the entire background will be the same shade of red. This is no different than what's been possible in HTML up until now, of course. When you declare `<BODY LINK="blue" VLINK="blue">`, you probably expect that all hyperlinks will be the same shade of blue, no matter where they are in the document.

Well, don't change that thinking when you're using CSS. If you use CSS to set the color of all hyperlinks (both visited and unvisited) to be `blue`, then that's what they'll be. In the same way, if you use styles to set the background of a page to be `green`, then the entire page background will be the same shade of green throughout the entire document. If you set the background of H1 elements to be `navy`, then the whole background of every H1 will be the same dark blue color.

In CSS, you can set both the foreground and background colors of any element, from the `BODY` down to the underline and italics tags, and almost everything in between—list items, entire lists, headings, hyperlinks, table cells, form elements, and even (in a limited fashion) images. In order to understand how this works, though, it's important to understand what's in the foreground of an element and what isn't.

What's the foreground of an element? Generally speaking, it's the text of an element, although that isn't the whole story: the borders around an element are also considered to be part of its foreground. Thus, there are two ways to directly affect the foreground color of an element: by using the `color` property and by setting the border colors using one of a number of border properties. Primarily there is the `border-color` property, as well as shorthand properties such as `border-top`, `border-right`, `border-bottom`, `border-left`, and `border`.

The background of an element is all of the space behind the foreground, out to the edge of the borders; thus, the content box and the padding are all part of an element's background. There are two ways to set the background color: the `background-color` and `background` properties.

Foreground Colors

The easiest way to set the foreground color of an element is with the property `color`.

---

color

Values	<color>
Initial value	UA specific
Inherited	yes
Applies to	all elements

This property accepts as a value any valid color, as discussed in Chapter 3, *Units and Values*, such as `#FFCC00` or `rgb(100%,80%,0%)`. It has the effect of setting the color of the text in the element, as shown in Figure 6-1:

```
<P STYLE="color: gray;">This paragraph has a gray foreground.</P>
<P>This paragraph has the default foreground.</P>
```

> This paragraph has a gray foreground.
>
> This paragraph has the default foreground.

Figure 6-1. Declared color versus default color

 In Figure 6-1, the default foreground color is black. That doesn't have to be the case, since users might have set their browsers (or other user agents) to use different foreground (text) colors. If the default text were set to green, the second paragraph in the preceding example would be green, not black—but the first paragraph would still be gray.

You need not restrict yourself to such simple operations, of course. There are plenty of ways to use color. You might have some paragraphs that contain text warning the user of a potential problem. In order to make this text stand out more than usual, you might decide to color it red. All that's needed is a class of **warn** on each paragraph that contains warning text (`<P CLASS="warn">`) and the following rule:

```
P.warn {color: red;}
```

In the same document, you decide that any links within a warning paragraph should be green. Thus:

```
P.warn {color: red;}
P.warn A:link {color: green;}
```

Then you change your mind, deciding that warning text should be gray and that links in such text should be silver. The preceding rules need only be changed to reflect the new values:

```
P.warn {color: gray;}
P.warn A:link {color: silver;}
```

Another use for color is to draw attention to certain types of text. For example, boldfaced text is already fairly obvious, but you could give it a different color to make it stand out even further:

```
B {color: maroon;}
```

Then you decide that you want all table cells with a class of `highlight` to contain yellow text:

```
TD.highlight {color: yellow;}
```

This sets the foreground color of all elements within any table cell with a class of `highlight` to be yellow, as shown in Figure 6-2:

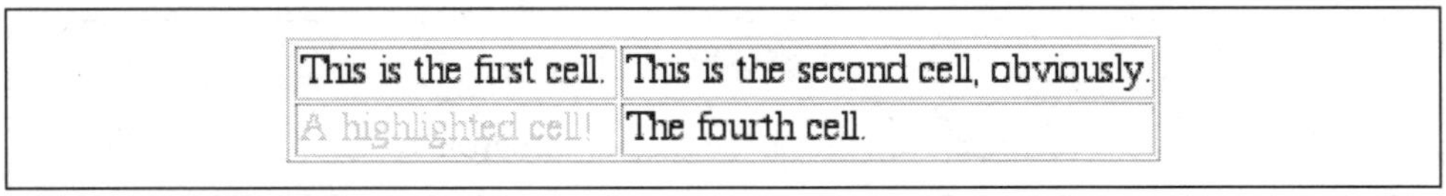

Figure 6-2. Highlighting a table cell's contents

BODY attributes

There are many uses for `color`, of course, the most basic of which is to replace the `BODY` attributes `TEXT`, `LINK`, `ALINK`, and `VLINK`. In conjunction with the anchor pseudo-classes, `color` can replace these `BODY` attributes outright. The first line in the following example can be rewritten with the subsequent CSS, and either will have the result depicted in Figure 6-3:

```
<BODY TEXT="black" LINK="#808080" ALINK="silver" VLINK="#333333">

BODY {color: black;}      /* replacement CSS */
A:link {color: #808080;}
A:active {color: silver;}
A:visited {color: #333333;}
```

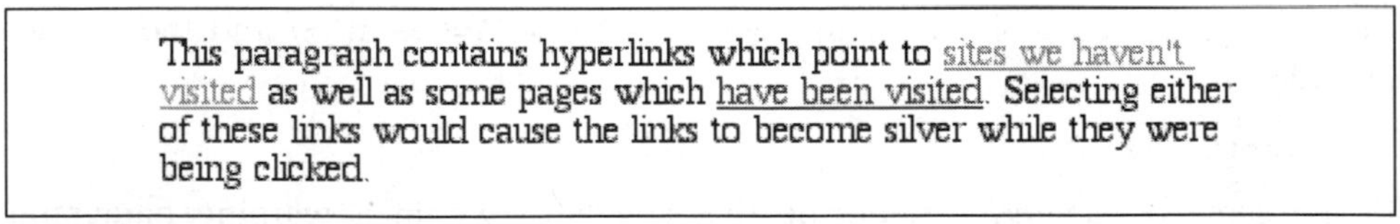

Figure 6-3. Replacing BODY attributes with CSS

While this may seem like a lot of extra typing, consider that using the old method of `BODY` attributes, you could only make changes at the document level. For example, if you wanted some links to be medium gray and others a relatively dark gray, you couldn't do that with the BODY attributes. Instead, you'd have to use <FONT COLOR="#666666"> on every single anchor that needed to be relatively dark. Not so with CSS; all you need to do is add a class to all anchors that need to be this shade of gray and modify your styles accordingly, with the result seen in Figure 6-4:

```
BODY {color: black;}
A:link {color: #808080;}      /* medium gray */
A.external:link  {color: silver;}
A:active {color: silver;}
A:visited {color: #333333;}    /* a very dark gray */
```

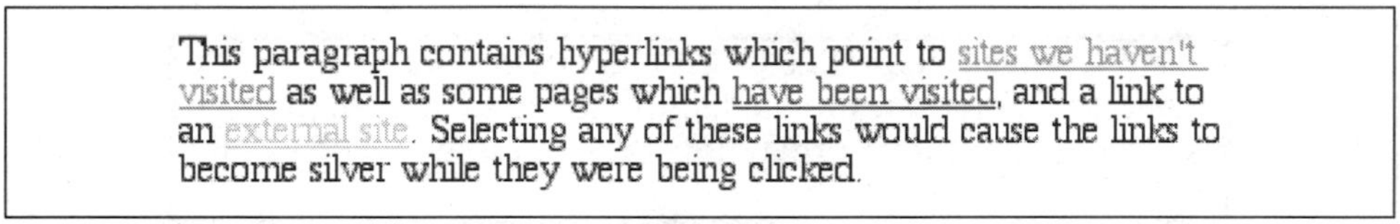

This paragraph contains hyperlinks which point to sites we haven't visited as well as some pages which have been visited, and a link to an external site. Selecting any of these links would cause the links to become silver while they were being clicked.

Figure 6-4. Changing colors of hyperlinks

This sets all anchors with the class external (<A CLASS="external" HREF="... ">) to be silver, instead of medium gray. They'll still be a dark gray once they've been visited, of course, unless you add a special rule for that as well:

```
BODY {color: black;}
A:link {color: #808080;}      /* medium gray */
A.external:link  {color: #666666;}
A:active {color: silver;}
A:visited {color: #333333;}    /* a very dark gray */
A.external:visited {color: black;}
```

This will cause all external links to be medium gray before they're visited and black once they've been visited, while all other links will be dark gray when visited and medium gray when unvisited—as Figure 6-5 makes clear.

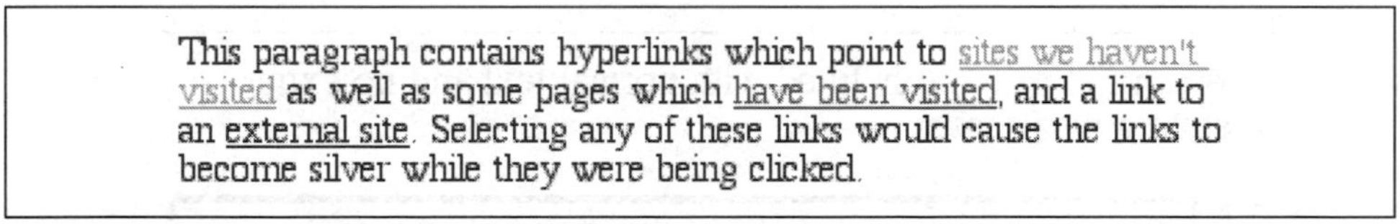

This paragraph contains hyperlinks which point to sites we haven't visited as well as some pages which have been visited, and a link to an external site. Selecting any of these links would cause the links to become silver while they were being clicked.

Figure 6-5. Setting different colors for different hyperlink classes

This sort of thing simply isn't possible with the old BODY attributes. Furthermore, if you're going to use the BODY attributes, you have to define them in each and every document. If you ever decide to change those values…well, you have a lot of files to edit, don't you? On the other hand, if you set up these colors as an external style sheet, and then link all of your pages to the style sheet, then you only have to edit one file in order to change the text colors of every last one of your pages.

Affecting borders

The value of `color` can also affect the borders around an element. Let's assume that you've declared these styles, which have the result shown in Figure 6-6:

```
P.aside {color: gray; border-style: solid;}
```

A normal paragraph, filled with normal text and no extra styling whatsoever.

This is an aside. It's set apart from the others, visually speaking, in order to draw attention to it and also emphasize its removal from the normal flow of the narrative (such as it is).

Another normal paragraph, filled with normal text and no extra styling whatsoever. Exciting, no?

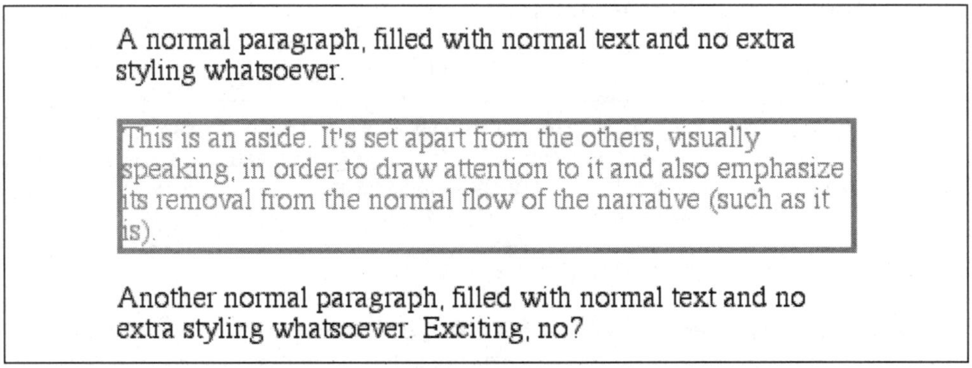

Figure 6-6. Border colors are taken from the content's color

This will result in the element `<P CLASS="aside">` having gray text and a gray medium-width solid border. That's because the foreground color is applied to the borders by default. The basic way to override that is with the property `border-color`:

```
P.aside {color: gray; border-style: solid; border-color: black;}
```

This will make the text `gray`, but the borders will be `black` in color, as we can see from Figure 6-7. Any value set for `border-color` will always override the value of `color`.

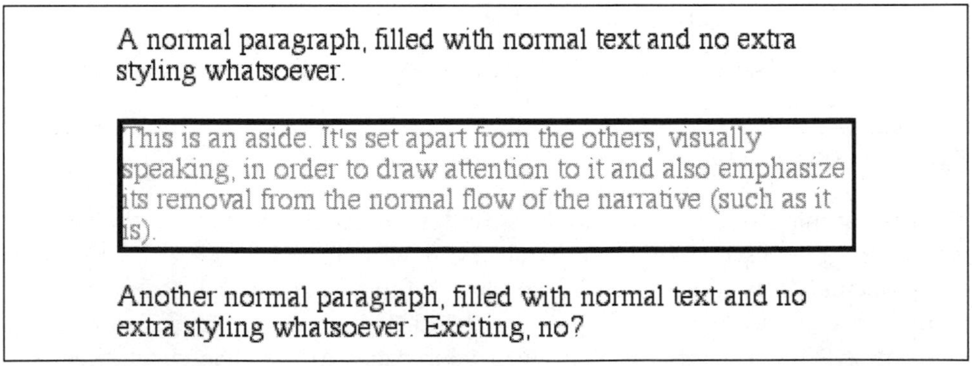

A normal paragraph, filled with normal text and no extra styling whatsoever.

This is an aside. It's set apart from the others, visually speaking, in order to draw attention to it and also emphasize its removal from the normal flow of the narrative (such as it is).

Another normal paragraph, filled with normal text and no extra styling whatsoever. Exciting, no?

Figure 6-7. Overriding the default border color

It's in the borders, incidentally, where you can have an effect on the foreground color of images. Since images are already composed of colors, you can't really affect them using `color`, but you can change the color of any border that appears around the image. This can be done using either `color` or `border-color`. Therefore, the following rules will have the same visual effect on images of class `type1` *and* `type2`, as shown in Figure 6-8:

```
IMG.type1 {color: gray; border-style: solid;}
IMG.type2 {border-color: gray; border-style: solid;}
```

Figure 6-8. Setting the border color for images

Border colors, and borders in general, are all discussed in much greater detail in the Chapter 7, *Boxes and Borders*.

Inheriting color

By this time, you may have guessed that `color` is inherited, and you're right. This makes good sense, since if you declare `P {color: maroon;}`, you probably expect that any text within that paragraph will also be maroon, even if it's emphasized or boldfaced or whatever. Of course, if you *want* such elements to be different colors, that's easy enough, as illustrated by Figure 6-9:

```
P {color: maroon;}
EM {color: #999999;}
```

> This is a paragraph which is, for the most part, utterly undistinguished-- but its *emphasized text* is quite another story altogether.

Figure 6-9. Different colors for different elements

Thanks to the inheritability of color, it's theoretically possible to set all of the ordinary text in a document to be a color such as red by declaring `BODY {color: red;}`. This should cause all text which is not otherwise styled (such as anchors, which have their own color styles) to be red. This should not affect elements such as horizontal rules (`HR`) or images. However, early versions of Explorer did inherit colors onto `HR` elements, while they didn't allow the colors to inherit onto form elements. This is more of a problem with inheritance than it is with color, but unfortunately the problem is still there. In fact, even today it's possible to find browsers that have predefined colors for things like tables, which prevent BODY colors from inheriting into table cells:

```
BODY {color: red;}
TABLE {color: black;}
```

That's because the combination of your style, and the browser's built-in styles looks like Figure 6-10.

This is a paragraph which is, for the most part, utterly undistinguished. It's red in color, as is everything else in the document-- or at least, as everything else in the document should be.

| Unfortunately, the contents of this table are black, because the browser assigns styles to the TABLE element which block inheritance of color. | This is annoying, yes, and perhaps foolish, but there it is anyway. | So remember, a good way to circumvent the problem is through selectors like BODY, TABLE, TD, TH. |

Figure 6-10. The result of combining author styles and browser styles

Since there is a `color` value defined by the browser for TABLE elements, it will take precedence over the inherited value. This is annoying and unnecessary, but it is an obstacle to be overcome. You can overcome it (usually) with selectors that list various table elements. For example, in order to get all your table content to be red along with your document's body, try this:

```
BODY, TABLE, TD, TH {color: red;}
```

This will often solve the problem. I say "often" because it doesn't always work, for reasons that are poorly understood. Navigator 4 has the most trouble getting it right, but its failures are not consistent. The best minds in CSS analysis have yet to come up with a recipe for predicting Navigator's behavior, unfortunately.

 Something else to watch out for is Navigator 4's handling of values for `color` that it doesn't recognize. If Navigator 4 encounters an unknown word (such as `invalidValue`) somehow, through mechanisms known only to itself, it actually arrives at and uses a color. It doesn't do so randomly, exactly, but the effect is practically the same. For example, `invalidValue` comes out as a dark blue, and `inherit`, which is a valid value under CSS2 but not CSS1, will come out as a really awful shade of yellow-green. This is not correct behavior, but you'll need to remember it as you write your styles.

Affecting form elements

Setting a value for `color` should (in theory, anyway) apply to form elements. As Figure 6-11 proves, declaring `SELECT` elements to have dark gray text is as simple as this:

```
SELECT {color: rgb(33%,33%,33%);}
```

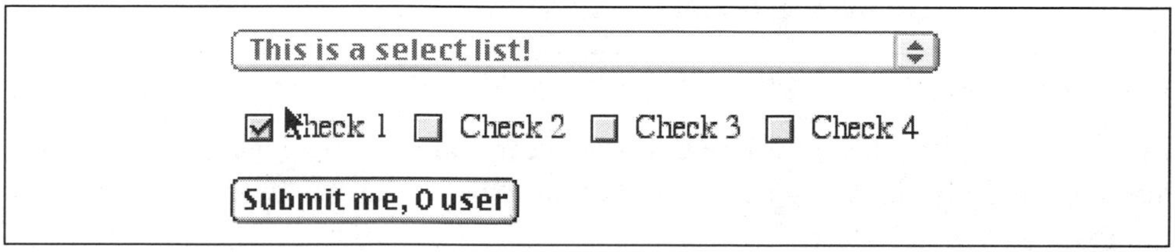

Figure 6-11. Setting color on form elements

You could also set the foreground color of `INPUT` elements, although as we can see in Figure 6-12, this would have the effect of setting that color on all inputs, from text to radio-button to checkbox inputs:

```
SELECT {color: rgb(33%,33%,33%);}
INPUT {color: gray;}
```

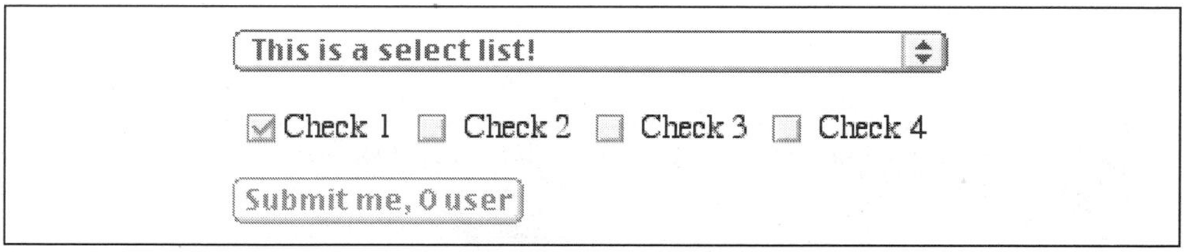

Figure 6-12. Changing form element foregrounds

Note in Figure 6-12 that the text color next to the checkboxes is still black. This is because we've only assigned styles to elements like `INPUT` and `SELECT`, not normal paragraph (or other) text.

One limitation under CSS1 is that there isn't a way to distinguish between different types of `INPUT` elements. If you need to have checkboxes be a different color than radio buttons, then you'll need to assign them classes so that you get the desired result (seen in Figure 6-13):

```
INPUT.radio {color: #666666;}
INPUT.check {color: #CCCCCC;}

<INPUT TYPE="radio" NAME="r2" VALUE="A" CLASS="radio">
<INPUT TYPE="checkbox" NAME="c3" VALUE="one" CLASS="check">
```

┌───┐
│ ┌───┐ ┌─┐ │
│ │ This is a select list!   │ │◆│ │
│ └───┘ └─┘ │
│   ☑ Check 1   ☐ Check 2   ☐ Check 3   ☐ Check 4   │
│   ◉ Radio 1: WRUW   ◯ Radio 2   ◯ Radio 3   │
│ ┌──────────────────┐   │
│ │ Submit me, 0 user │   │
│ └──────────────────┘   │
└───┘

Figure 6-13. Using classes to apply styles to different INPUT elements

In CSS2, it's a little easier to distinguish between different elements based on what attributes they have. As an example, the rules shown here will match the following two INPUT tags, respectively:

```
INPUT[type="radio"] {color: #333333;}
INPUT[type="checkbox"] {color: #666666;}

<INPUT TYPE="radio" NAME="r2" VALUE="A ">
<INPUT TYPE="checkbox" NAME="c3" VALUE="one ">
```

This allows you to dispense with the classes altogether, at least in this instance. See the Chapter 10, *CSS2: A Look Ahead*, for more details on how this kind of selector works.

 Navigator 4 does not apply colors to form elements, but setting the colors for form elements does work in Internet Explorer 4 and 5, and Opera 3.5 and later.

Background Color

In a fashion very similar to setting the foreground color, it's possible to declare a color for the background of an element. For this, you use the property `background-color`, which accepts (unsurprisingly) any valid color.

┌───┐
│   │
│ **background-color**   │
│   │
│ **Values**   <color> | transparent   │
│ **Initial value**   transparent   │
│ **Inherited**   no   │
│ **Applies to**   all elements   │
│   │
└───┘

The background is the area of the content box and the padding and is always behind the foreground of the element. Therefore, the declared background color is applied to both the element's content box and its padding, as illustrated in Figure 6-14:

```
P {background-color: gray;}
```

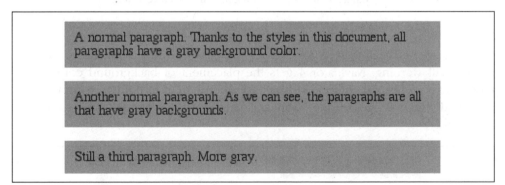

Figure 6-14. Background gray for paragraphs

If you wish the color to extend out a little bit from the text in the element, then you need only add some padding to the mix, with the result shown in Figure 6-15:

```
P {background-color: gray; padding: 10px;}
```

Figure 6-15. Backgrounds and padding

(Padding will be discussed in detail in Chapter 7.)

The background color of just about any element can be set, from BODY all the way down to inline elements such as EM and A. Even form elements should be affected by the property, although not all user agents can do this correctly. Also, **background-color** is not inherited. Its default value is **transparent**, which makes sense; if an element doesn't have a defined color, then its background should be transparent so that the background of its ancestor elements will be visible. Imagine for a moment that the default value were something else, such as **silver**. Then you would always see something along the lines of Figure 6-16. This could be quite a problem, if that's how browsers behaved! Fortunately, they don't.

A normal paragraph. Thanks to the styles in this document, all paragraphs have black text.

Another normal paragraph. The black text continues, and our joy is great to see that there is a hyperlink here in its midst.

Still a third paragraph. More black.

Figure 6-16. Nontransparent backgrounds

Most of the time, you'll have no reason to use the keyword **transparent**. On occasion, though, it can be useful. Although it's the default value, users might set their browsers to make all links have a white background. When you design your page, though, you set anchors to have a white foreground, and you don't want a background on those anchors. In order to make sure that this happens, you would declare:

```
A:link {color: white; background-color: transparent;}
```

If you left out the background color, then your white foreground would combine with the user's white background to yield totally unreadable links.

Real-world issues

That's pretty much all there is to setting a background color. Well, except for one more small warning: Navigator 4 gets the placement of background colors completely wrong. Instead of applying the background color to the entire content box and padding, the color only appears behind the text itself, as shown in Figure 6-17.

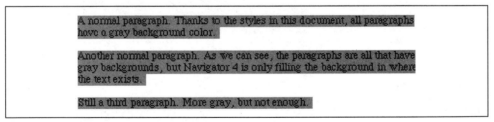

Figure 6-17. Navigator's incorrect behavior

Let me reiterate: *this is totally wrong.* However, there is a way around it, which is to set a border on the element. You can do this by setting the border the same color as the background color of your document:

```
BODY {background: silver;}
P {background-color: gray; padding: 1px; border: 0.1px solid gray;}
```

It is necessary to set a `border-style` for this technique to work. Whether you use that specific property, or simply a value of the `border` property, doesn't really matter.

Of course, by doing this, you're setting a border on the element, and that border will show up in other user agents as well. And, just to top things off, Navigator doesn't handle padding very well, so the previous example would result in a small amount of blank space between the content box and the borders. Altogether, it isn't a very pretty picture.

Special Effects

Let's return to the happier realm of how things should work. Thanks to `color` and `background-color`, you can create some nice effects. This example is shown in Figure 6-18:

```
P {color: black;}
H1 {color: white; background-color: rgb(20%,20%,20%);}
```

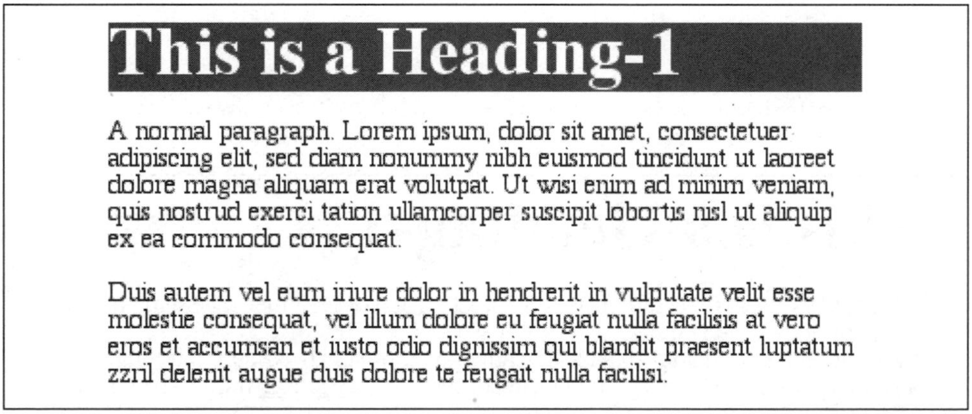

Figure 6-18. A nifty effect for H1 elements

This shows but one example of how displays can be dramatically changed with just a few styles. Of course, there are as many combinations as there are colors, but we can't exactly show them here—being stuck in grayscale as we are—however, we'll try to give you some idea of what you can do. Here are a few ideas to get you started.

This is a simple style sheet, as shown in Figure 6-19:

```
BODY {color: rgb(0%,50%,0%); background-color: #CCFFCC;}
H1, H2 {color: yellow; background-color: rgb(0,51,0);}
```

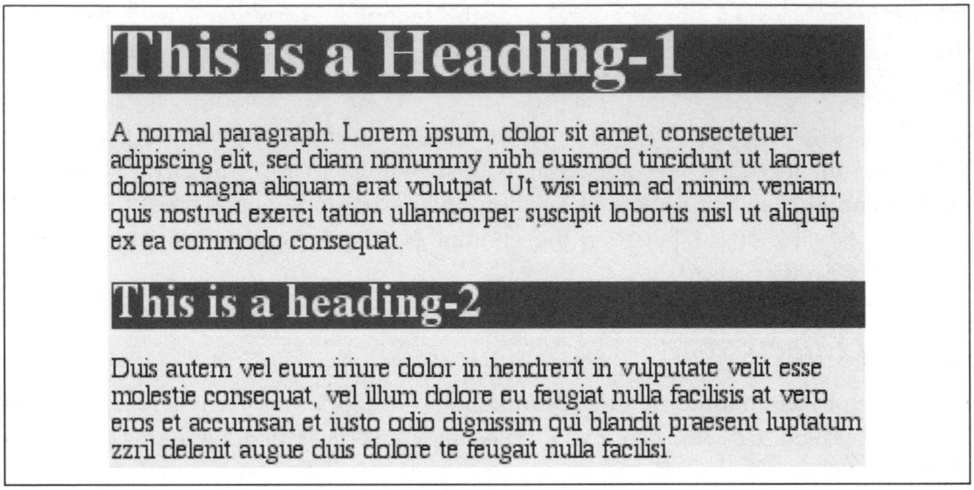

Figure 6-19. The results of a simple style sheet

This style sheet is more sophisticated (shown in Figure 6-20):

```
BODY {color: black; background-color: white;}
P {color: #333;}
PRE, CODE, TT {color: rgb(50%,50%,50%); background-color: #FFFFCC;}
A:link {color: blue; background-color: yellow;}
A:visited {color: navy; background-color: white;}
```

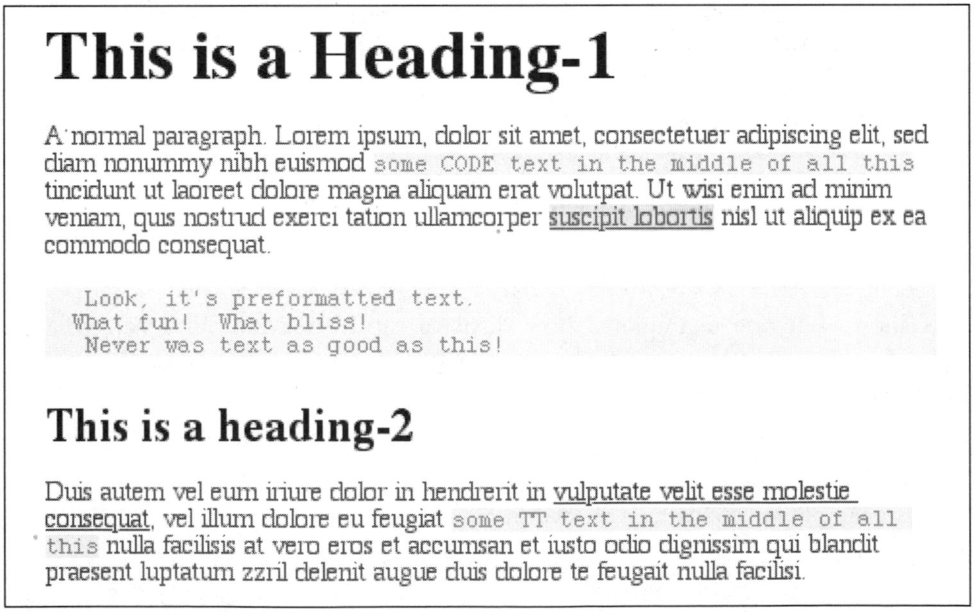

Figure 6-20. The results of a more sophisticated style sheet

This is but the tiniest beginning of what's possible, of course. By all means, try some examples of your own!

Good Practices

You may have noticed that in almost every circumstance, where we set a foreground color, we also set a background color. In general, this is a good idea. Since you don't know what styles a user may have predefined, you don't know how your styles might interact with them. Remember the example where links ended up being white on white? That's the sort of thing we want to avoid.

Let's explore this in a little more detail. Assume the following:

```
/* reader styles */
BODY {color: white; background-color: black;}

/* author styles */
BODY {color: black;}
```

Since, in this circumstance, the author's styles will outweigh the reader's styles—that's how it is under CSS1, anyway—then the new style sheet for this document will be as follows (shown in Figure 6-21):

```
/* combined styles */
BODY {color: black; background-color: black;}
```

Figure 6-21. Black on black

Not exactly readable, is it? Only the hyperlinks are visible, thanks to their default styles. That's why it's always a good idea to combine foreground and background colors in the same declaration. If it's important enough that you declare one, then it's definitely important enough to declare both.

Complex Backgrounds

Having covered the basics of foreground and background colors, we turn now to the subject of background images. In HTML, it's possible to associate an image with the background of the document by using the BODY attribute BACKGROUND:

```
<BODY BACKGROUND="bg23.gif">
```

This will cause a user agent to load the file `bg23.gif` and then "tile" it in the document background, repeating it in both the horizontal and vertical directions to fill up the entire background of the document, as shown in Figure 6-22.

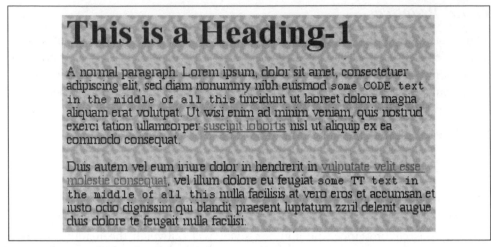

Figure 6-22. Applying a background image in HTML

This effect can be duplicated in CSS, but CSS contains a great deal more than simple tiling of background images. We'll start with the basics and then work our way up.

Background Images

In order to get an image into the background in the first place, the property `background-image` is used.

background-image

Values	<url> | none
Initial value	none
Inherited	no
Applies to	all elements

The default value of **none** means about what you'd expect: no image is placed in the background. If you want a background image, then you need only give this property a URL value:

```
BODY {background-image: url(bg23.gif);}
```

Due to the default values of other background properties, this will cause the image *bg23.gif* to be tiled in the document's background, as shown in Figure 6-22.

It's usually a good idea to specify a background color to go along with your background image. I won't do so in this section, since we're concentrating on `background-image` for the moment. We'll come back to why setting a color is a good idea later on in the chapter.

A background image can be applied to any element, whether block-level or inline. BODY is the most common element to which backgrounds are applied, of course, but there's no need to stop there. For example:

```
P.starry{background-image: url(http://www.site.web/pix/stars.gif);
   color: white;}

<P CLASS="starry">It's the end of autumn, which means the stars will be
brighter than  ever!  Join us...
```

As we can see in Figure 6-23, a background has been applied to a single paragraph and no other part of the document.

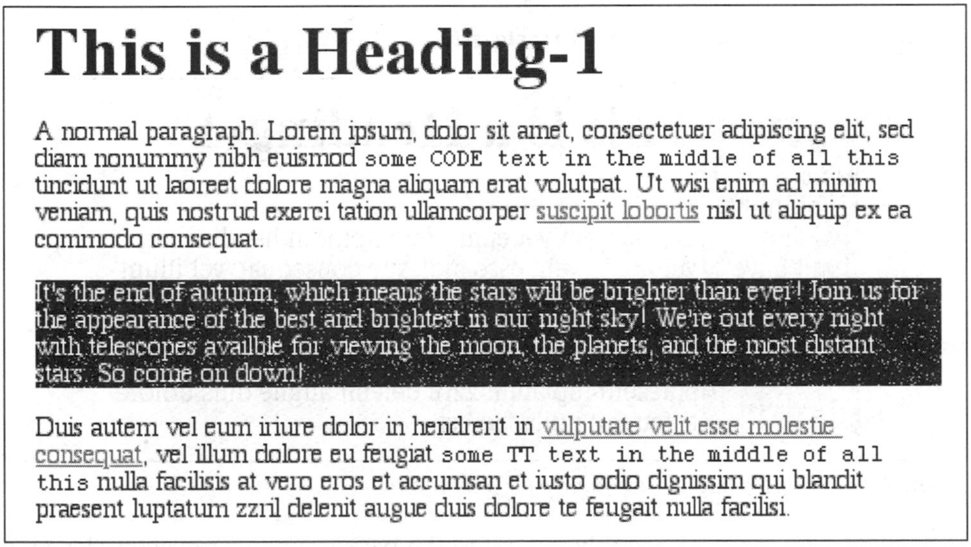

Figure 6-23. Applying a background image for a single element

This ability goes even further, allowing you to place background images on inline elements like hyperlinks, as depicted in Figure 6-24. Of course, if you want to be able to see the tiling pattern, the image will probably need to be pretty small. After all, individual letters aren't that large!

```
A.grid {background-image: url(smallgrid.gif);}

<P>This paragraph contains <A HREF="..." CLASS="grid">an anchor with a
background image</A> which is tiled only within the anchor.</P>
```

There are a number of ways to employ this technique. You might place an image in the background of STRONG elements, in order to make them stand out more.

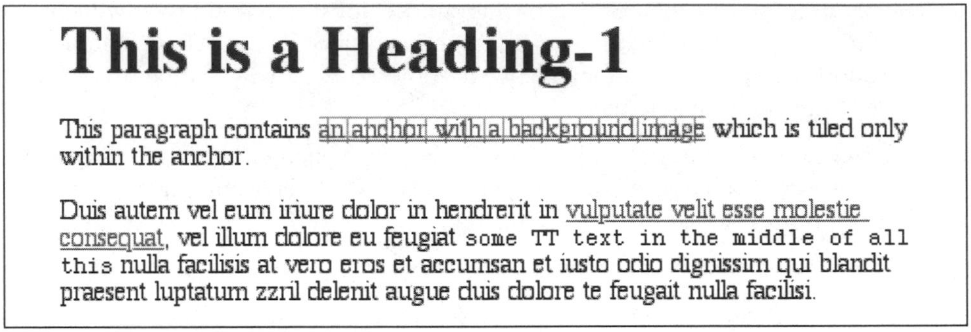

This is a Heading-1

This paragraph contains an anchor with a background image which is tiled only within the anchor.

Duis autem vel eum iriure dolor in hendrerit in vulputate velit esse molestie consequat, vel illum dolore eu feugiat some TT text in the middle of all this nulla facilisis at vero eros et accumsan et iusto odio dignissim qui blandit praesent luptatum zzril delenit augue duis dolore te feugait nulla facilisi.

Figure 6-24. A background image on an inline element

You could fill in the background of headings with a wavy pattern, or with little dots. You can even fill in the cells of tables with patterns to make them distinct from the rest of the page, as shown in Figure 6-25:

```
TD.nav {background-image: url(darkgrid.gif);}
```

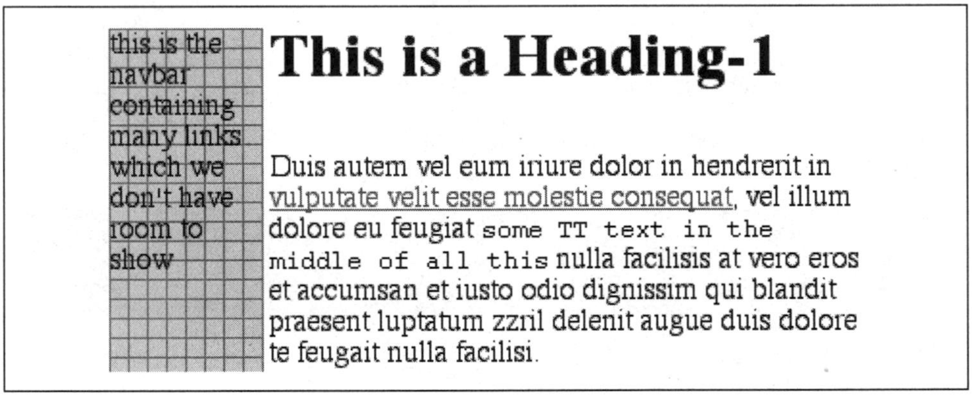

this is the navbar containing many links which we don't have room to show

This is a Heading-1

Duis autem vel eum iriure dolor in hendrerit in vulputate velit esse molestie consequat, vel illum dolore eu feugiat some TT text in the middle of all this nulla facilisis at vero eros et accumsan et iusto odio dignissim qui blandit praesent luptatum zzril delenit augue duis dolore te feugait nulla facilisi.

Figure 6-25. Setting a background image for a table cell

You could even, in theory, apply images to the background of replaced elements like TEXTAREAs and SELECT lists, although user agents aren't very good about that sort of thing yet—in fact, as of this writing, no browser will correctly place images in the backgrounds of form elements.

Just like `background-color`, `background-image` is not inherited—in fact, none of the background properties are inherited. Remember also that when specifying the URL of a background image, it falls under the usual restrictions and caveats for `url` values: a relative URL should be interpreted with respect to the style sheet, but Navigator 4.x doesn't do this correctly, so absolute URLs may be a better answer.

Good background practices

An interesting thing about images is that they're laid on top of whatever background color you may have specified. If you're completely tiling GIF, JPEG, or other opaque image types, this doesn't really make a difference, since they'll fill up the document background, leaving nowhere for the color to "peek through," so to speak. However, image formats with an alpha channel, such as PNG, can be partially or wholly transparent, and this will cause the image to be combined with the background color. In addition, if the image fails to load for some reason, the user agent will use the background color specified in place of the image. Consider how the "starry paragraph" example would look if the background image failed to load, as in Figure 6-26.

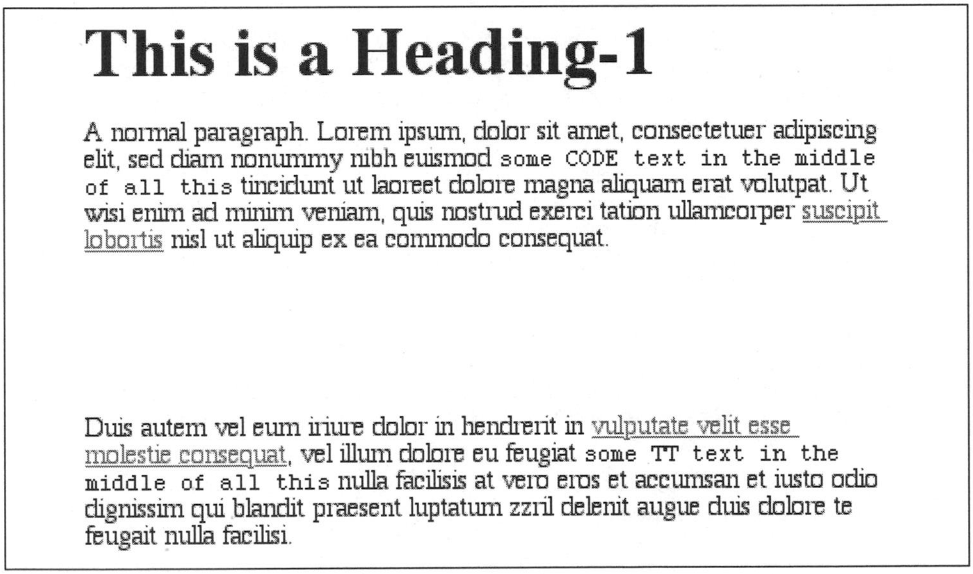

This is a Heading-1

A normal paragraph. Lorem ipsum, dolor sit amet, consectetuer adipiscing elit, sed diam nonummy nibh euismod some CODE text in the middle of all this tincidunt ut laoreet dolore magna aliquam erat volutpat. Ut wisi enim ad minim veniam, quis nostrud exerci tation ullamcorper suscipit lobortis nisl ut aliquip ex ea commodo consequat.

Duis autem vel eum iriure dolor in hendrerit in vulputate velit esse molestie consequat, vel illum dolore eu feugiat some TT text in the middle of all this nulla facilisis at vero eros et accumsan et iusto odio dignissim qui blandit praesent luptatum zzril delenit augue duis dolore te feugait nulla facilisi.

Figure 6-26. The consequences of a missing background image

Given this reason alone, it's always a good idea to specify a background color when using a background image, so that your white text will at least be visible:

```
P.starry {background-image: url(http://www.site.web/pix/stars.gif);
    background-color: black; color: white;}

<P CLASS="starry">It's the end of autumn, which means the stars will be
brighter than ever!  Join us...
```

Besides, if you have the image do something other than fully tile across the entire background of the document, then you'll need a color to cover the parts that the image doesn't. Speaking of which...

Repeats with Direction

Thus far, all we've ever been able to do in document design is repeat background images in both the horizontal and vertical directions. If we wanted some kind of "sidebar" background, it was necessary to create a very short, but incredibly wide, image to place in the background; a favorite size for these images is 10 pixels tall by 2,500 pixels wide. Most of that image is blank space, of course. Only the left 100 or so pixels contain the "sidebar" image. The rest of the image is basically wasted, as we can see in Figure 6-27.

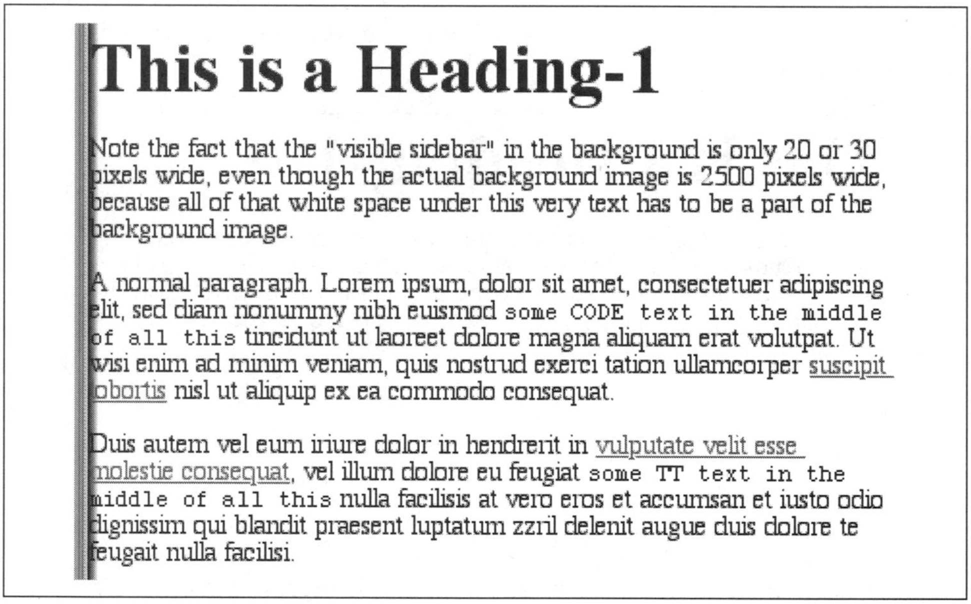

This is a Heading-1

Note the fact that the "visible sidebar" in the background is only 20 or 30 pixels wide, even though the actual background image is 2500 pixels wide, because all of that white space under this very text has to be a part of the background image.

A normal paragraph. Lorem ipsum, dolor sit amet, consectetuer adipiscing elit, sed diam nonummy nibh euismod some CODE text in the middle of all this tincidunt ut laoreet dolore magna aliquam erat volutpat. Ut wisi enim ad minim veniam, quis nostrud exerci tation ullamcorper suscipit lobortis nisl ut aliquip ex ea commodo consequat.

Duis autem vel eum iriure dolor in hendrerit in vulputate velit esse molestie consequat, vel illum dolore eu feugiat some TT text in the middle of all this nulla facilisis at vero eros et accumsan et iusto odio dignissim qui blandit praesent luptatum zzril delenit augue duis dolore te feugait nulla facilisi.

Figure 6-27. Using a really wide image for a really small effect

Wouldn't it be much nicer to just create a sidebar image which is 10 pixels tall and 100 pixels wide, with no wasted blank space, and then repeat it only in the vertical direction? This would certainly make your design job a little easier, and your users' download times a lot shorter. Enter `background-repeat`.

background-repeat

Values	repeat | repeat-x | repeat-y | no-repeat
Initial value	repeat
Inherited	no
Applies to	all elements

As you might guess, `repeat` causes the image to tile in both the horizontal and vertical directions, just as background images have always done in the past. `repeat-x` and `repeat-y` cause the image to be repeated in the horizontal or vertical directions, respectively, and `no-repeat` prevents the image from tiling in any direction.

By default, the background image will start from the top left corner of an element. (We'll see how to change this later in the chapter.) Therefore, the following rules will have the effect seen in Figure 6-28:

```
BODY {background-image: url(yinyang.gif);
    background-repeat: repeat;}
```

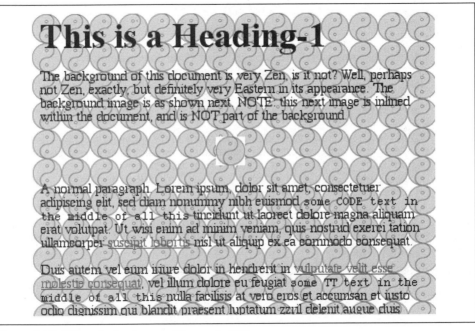

Figure 6-28. Tiling the background image in CSS

I've left out a background color in order to keep the rule short, but remember to include a background color any time you have a background image. And, of course, the effect shown in Figure 6-28 would have been the same if we'd left out the `background-repeat` property altogether, since `repeat` is its default value.

Let's assume, though, that we just want images down the left side of the document. Instead of having to create a special image with a whole lot of blank space to the right of the image, we can instead make a small change to our styles:

```
BODY {background-image: url(yinyang.gif);
    background-repeat: repeat-y;}
```

As Figure 6-29 demonstrates, the image is simply repeated along the y-axis (that is, vertically) from its starting position—in this case, the top left corner of the browser window.

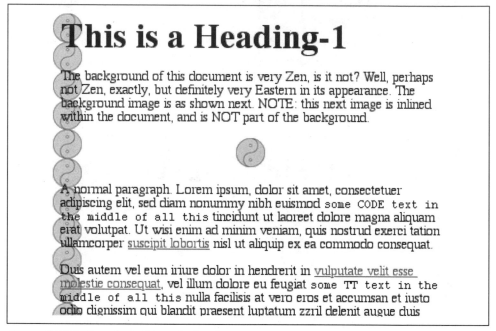

Figure 6-29. Tiling along the vertical axis

In effect, there is a repeated column in the background, and there is only one such column. Should you want two columns of symbols in this example, then the base image would have to be altered to contain side-by-side symbols, as in Figure 6-30.

The expected result occurs when we change the repeat value to be **repeat-x**:

```
BODY {background-image: url(yinyang.gif);
    background-repeat: repeat-x;}
```

Now the image is repeated along the x-axis (in other words, horizontally), as illustrated in Figure 6-31.

Finally, of course, we may wish not to repeat the background image at all. In that case, we use the last value, **no-repeat**, which is illustrated in Figure 6-32:

```
BODY {background-image: url(yinyang.gif);
    background-repeat: no-repeat;}
```

This may not seem terribly useful, given that there is only a small symbol in the top left corner of the document, but let's try it again with a much bigger symbol, as shown in Figure 6-33:

```
BODY {background-image: url(bigyinyang.gif);
    background-repeat: no-repeat;}
```

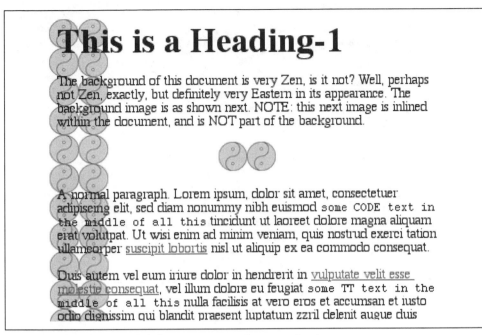

Figure 6-30. Tiling a slightly larger image on the vertical axis

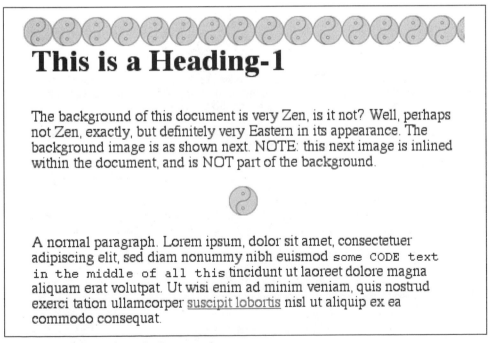

Figure 6-31. Tiling along the horizontal axis

Figure 6-32. No tiling at all

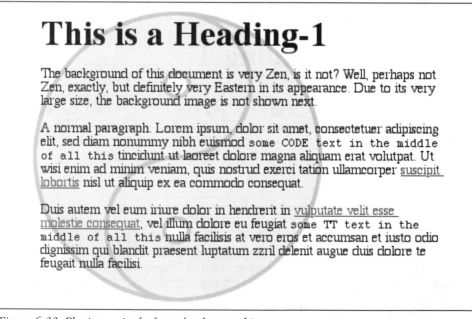

Figure 6-33. Placing a single, large background image

Real-world uses

The ability to control the repeat direction dramatically expands the range of effects possible in document design. For example, let's say you want a triple border on the left side of each H1 element in your document. You could then declare the following:

```
H1 {background-image: url(triplebor.gif); background-repeat: repeat-y;}
```

As we can see in Figure 6-34, the very small image `triplebor.gif` is repeated vertically along the left side of the heading element, resulting in an effect that isn't otherwise possible.

‖This is a Heading-1

Figure 6-34. Creating a "triple border" on H2 elements

We can take that further and decide to set a wavy border along the top of each H1 element, as illustrated in Figure 6-35. The image is colored in such a way that it blends with the background color and produces the wavy effect shown:

```
H1 {background-image: url(wavybord.gif); background-repeat: repeat-x;
    background-color: #CCCCCC;}
```

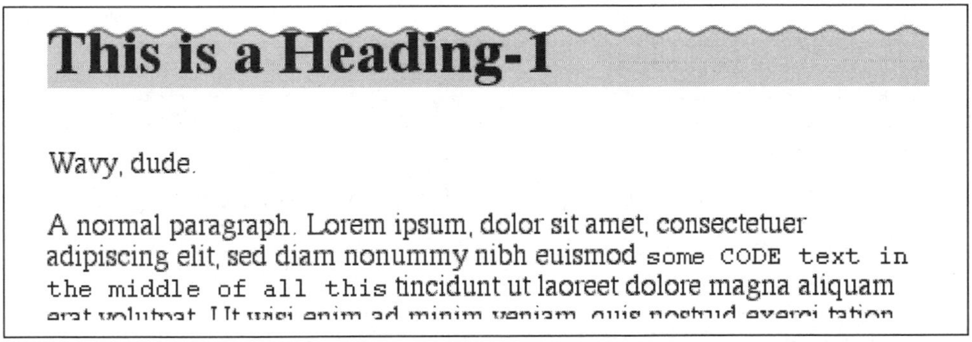

This is a Heading-1

Wavy, dude.

A normal paragraph. Lorem ipsum, dolor sit amet, consectetuer adipiscing elit, sed diam nonummy nibh euismod some CODE text in the middle of all this tincidunt ut laoreet dolore magna aliquam erat volutpat. Ut wisi enim ad minim veniam, quis nostrud exerci tation

Figure 6-35. Setting a wavy top border on H1 elements

Simply by choosing the appropriate image for the job, and employing it in some creative ways, you can set up some truly astonishing appearances. And that isn't the end of what's possible. Now that we know how to keep a background image from repeating, how about moving it around in the background?

Background Positioning

Thanks to `background-repeat`, it's possible to place a large image in the background of a document, and then keep it from repeating. Let's add to that and actually change the image's position in the background.

background-position

Values	[<percentage> | <length>]{1,2} | [top | center | bottom] || [left | center | right]
Initial value	0% 0%
Inherited	no
Applies to	block-level and replaced elements

Note: Percentage values refer to a point on both the element and the origin image (see explanation in section "Percentage Values" later in this chapter).

For example, we could center it, with the result depicted in Figure 6-36:

```
BODY {background-image: url(bigyinyang.gif);
   background-repeat: no-repeat;
   background-position: center;}
```

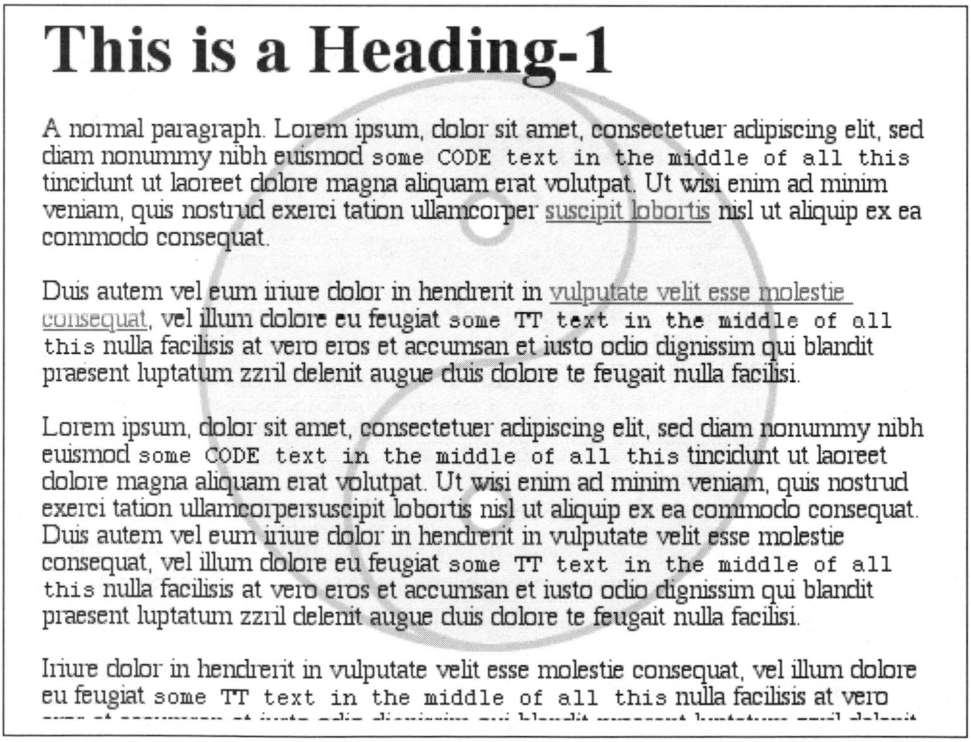

This is a Heading-1

A normal paragraph. Lorem ipsum, dolor sit amet, consectetuer adipiscing elit, sed diam nonummy nibh euismod some CODE text in the middle of all this tincidunt ut laoreet dolore magna aliquam erat volutpat. Ut wisi enim ad minim veniam, quis nostrud exerci tation ullamcorper suscipit lobortis nisl ut aliquip ex ea commodo consequat.

Duis autem vel eum iriure dolor in hendrerit in vulputate velit esse molestie consequat, vel illum dolore eu feugiat some TT text in the middle of all this nulla facilisis at vero eros et accumsan et iusto odio dignissim qui blandit praesent luptatum zzril delenit augue duis dolore te feugait nulla facilisi.

Lorem ipsum, dolor sit amet, consectetuer adipiscing elit, sed diam nonummy nibh euismod some CODE text in the middle of all this tincidunt ut laoreet dolore magna aliquam erat volutpat. Ut wisi enim ad minim veniam, quis nostrud exerci tation ullamcorpersuscipit lobortis nisl ut aliquip ex ea commodo consequat. Duis autem vel eum iriure dolor in hendrerit in vulputate velit esse molestie consequat, vel illum dolore eu feugiat some TT text in the middle of all this nulla facilisis at vero eros et accumsan et iusto odio dignissim qui blandit praesent luptatum zzril delenit augue duis dolore te feugait nulla facilisi.

Iriure dolor in hendrerit in vulputate velit esse molestie consequat, vel illum dolore eu feugiat some TT text in the middle of all this nulla facilisis at vero

Figure 6-36. Centering a single background image

This positioning is all done using `background-position`, of course, but there are a whole lot of ways to supply values for this property. First off, there are the keywords `top`, `bottom`, `left`, `right`, and `center`. Usually, these appear in pairs, but (as Figure 6-36 shows) this is not always true. Then there are length values, such as `50px` or `2cm`, and finally, percentage values. Each type of value has a slightly different effect on the placement of the background image.

Keywords

Easiest to understand are the keywords. They have the effects you'd expect from their names; for example, `top right` would cause the background image to be placed in the top right corner of the element. Let's go back to the small yin-yang symbol:

```
BODY {background-image: url(yinyang.gif);
    background-repeat: no-repeat;
    background-position: top right;}
```

Incidentally, the result, shown in Figure 6-37, would have been exactly the same had the position been declared as `right top`. When using the position keywords, they can appear in any order, so long as there are no more than two of them, one for the horizontal and the other for the vertical.

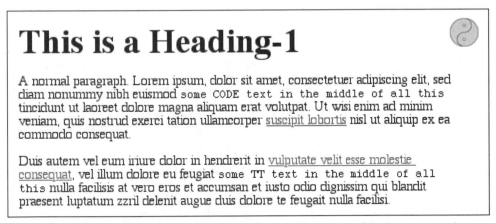

Figure 6-37. Placing the background image in the top right corner of the browser window

If only one keyword appears, then the other is assumed to be `center`. Table 6-1 shows equivalent keyword statements.

Table 6-1. Position Keyword Equivalents

Single Keyword	Equivalent To
center	center center
top	top center center top

Table 6-1. Position Keyword Equivalents (continued)

Single Keyword	Equivalent To
bottom	bottom center center bottom
right	center right right center
left	center left left center

So if you want an image to appear in the very top center of each paragraph, as in Figure 6-38, you need only declare:

```
P {background-image: url(bg23.gif);
    background-repeat: no-repeat;
    background-position: top;}
```

Figure 6-38. Putting a single background image at the top of every paragraph

Percentage values

Closely related to the keywords are percentage values, although they behave in a rather interesting way. Let's say that you want to center a background image within its element by using percentage values. That's easy enough:

```
BODY {background-image: url(bigyinyang.gif);
    background-repeat: no-repeat;
    background-position: 50% 50%;}
```

This causes the background image to be placed such that its center is aligned with the center of its parent element, as demonstrated in Figure 6-39. In other words, the percentage values apply to both the element and the background image.

In order to understand this concept, let's examine this process in closer detail. When you center a background image in an element, the point in the image which can be described as 50% 50% is lined up with the point in the element that can be described the same way. This is shown in Figure 6-40.

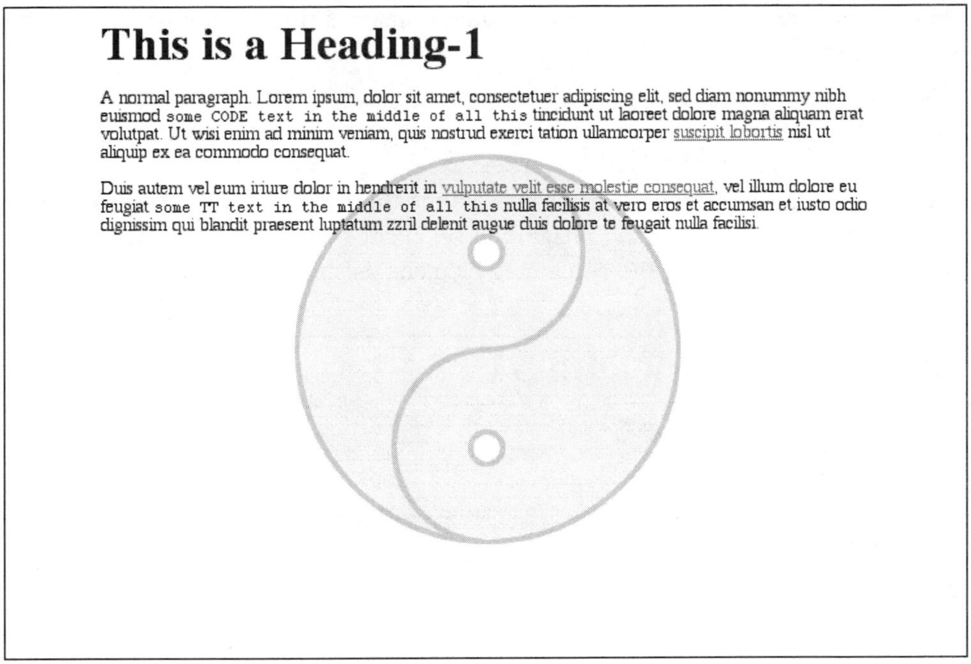

This is a Heading-1

A normal paragraph. Lorem ipsum, dolor sit amet, consectetuer adipiscing elit, sed diam nonummy nibh euismod some CODE text in the middle of all this tincidunt ut laoreet dolore magna aliquam erat volutpat. Ut wisi enim ad minim veniam, quis nostrud exerci tation ullamcorper suscipit lobortis nisl ut aliquip ex ea commodo consequat.

Duis autem vel eum iriure dolor in hendrerit in vulputate velit esse molestie consequat, vel illum dolore eu feugiat some TT text in the middle of all this nulla facilisis at vero eros et accumsan et iusto odio dignissim qui blandit praesent luptatum zzril delenit augue duis dolore te feugait nulla facilisi.

Figure 6-39. Centering the background image using percentages

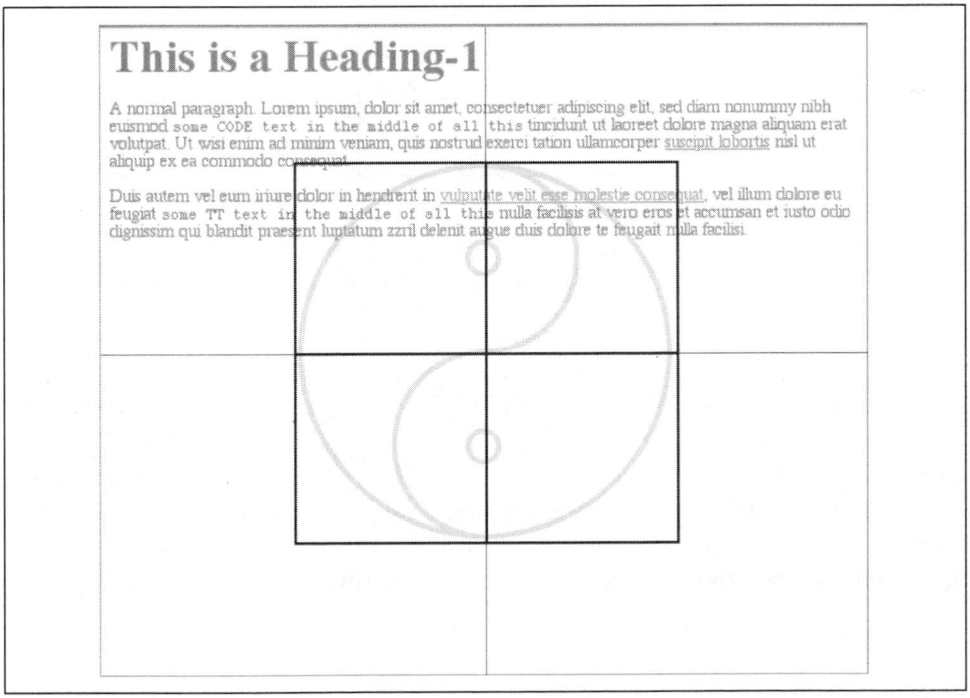

This is a Heading-1

A normal paragraph. Lorem ipsum, dolor sit amet, consectetuer adipiscing elit, sed diam nonummy nibh euismod some CODE text in the middle of all this tincidunt ut laoreet dolore magna aliquam erat volutpat. Ut wisi enim ad minim veniam, quis nostrud exerci tation ullamcorper suscipit lobortis nisl ut aliquip ex ea commodo consequat.

Duis autem vel eum iriure dolor in hendrerit in vulputate velit esse molestie consequat, vel illum dolore eu feugiat some TT text in the middle of all this nulla facilisis at vero eros et accumsan et iusto odio dignissim qui blandit praesent luptatum zzril delenit augue duis dolore te feugait nulla facilisi.

Figure 6-40. Lining up the center of the image with the center of the browser window

Thus, if you want to place a single background image a third of the way across the element and two-thirds of the way down, then your declaration would be:

```
BODY {background-image: url(bigyinyang.gif);
    background-repeat: no-repeat;
    background-position: 33% 66%;}
```

The point in the background image that is one-third across and two-thirds down from the top left corner of the image will be aligned with the point that is as far from the top left corner of the containing element, as shown in Figure 6-41.

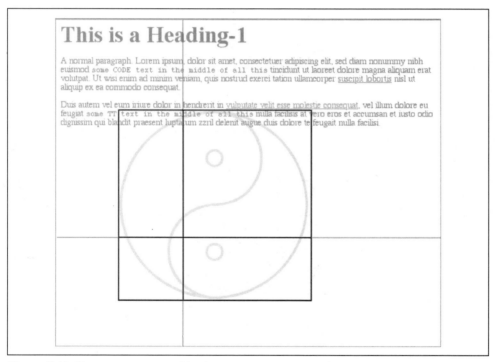

Figure 6-41. More percentage positioning

Note that with percentages the horizontal value *always* comes first. If you were to switch the percentages in the preceding example, the image would be placed two-thirds of the way across the element and one-third of the way down. It's also worth noting what happens if you only supply one value. In that case, the single value supplied is taken to be the horizontal value, and the vertical is assumed to be 50%. This is basically the same as with the keywords, where if only one keyword is given, the other is assumed to be center. Thus:

```
BODY {background-image: url(bigyinyang.gif);
    background-repeat: no-repeat;
    background-position: 33%;}
```

The background image is placed one-third of the way across the page, and half-way down it, as depicted in Figure 6-42.

This is a Heading-1

A normal paragraph. Lorem ipsum, dolor sit amet, consectetuer adipiscing elit, sed diam nonummy nibh euismod some CODE text in the middle of all this tincidunt ut laoreet dolore magna aliquam erat volutpat. Ut wisi enim ad minim veniam, quis nostrud exerci tation ullamcorper suscipit lobortis nisl ut aliquip ex ea commodo consequat.

Duis autem vel eum iriure dolor in hendrerit in vulputate velit esse molestie consequat, vel illum dolore eu feugiat some TT text in the middle of all this nulla facilisis at vero eros et accumsan et iusto odio dignissim qui blandit praesent luptatum zzril delenit augue duis dolore te feugait nulla facilisi.

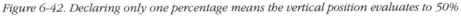

Figure 6-42. Declaring only one percentage means the vertical position evaluates to 50%

Table 6-2 gives a breakdown of keyword and percentage equivalencies.

Table 6-2. Positional Equivalents

Single Keyword	Equivalent To	Equivalent To
center	center center	50% 50%
top	top center center top	50% 0%
bottom	bottom center center bottom	50% 100%
right	center right right center	100% 50% 100%
left	center left left center	0% 50% 0%
	top left left top	0% 0%
	top right right top	0% 100%
	bottom right right bottom	100% 100%
	bottom left left bottom	0% 100%

In case you were wondering, the default values for `background-position` are
`0% 0%`, which is functionally the same as `top left`. That's why, unless you set different values for the position, background images always start tiling from the top
left corner of the containing element.

Length values

Finally, we turn to length values for positioning. When you supply lengths for the
position of the background image, they are interpreted as offsets from the top left
corner of the element. The offset point is the top left corner of the background
image; thus, if you set the values `20px 30px`, the top left corner of the background image will be 20 pixels to the right of, and 30 pixels below, the top left
corner of the containing element, as in Figure 6-43:

```
BODY {background-image: url(bg23.gif);
    background-repeat: no-repeat;
    background-position: 20px 30px;}
```

Figure 6-43. Offsetting the background image using length measures

This is, of course, different than percentage values, in the sense that the offset is
simply from one top left corner to another. In other words, the top left corner of
the background image lines up with the point specified in the `background-
position` declaration. You can combine length and percentage values, though, to
get a sort of "best of both worlds" effect. Let's say you need to have a background
image that is all the way to the right side of an element and 10 pixels down from
the top, as illustrated in Figure 6-44. As always, the horizontal value comes first:

```
BODY {background-image: url(bg23.gif);
    background-repeat: no-repeat;
    background-position: 100% 10px;}
```

You *cannot*, however, mix keywords with other values. Thus, `top 75%` is not
valid. If you use a keyword, you're stuck using only keywords, but percentages
and lengths can be mixed together.

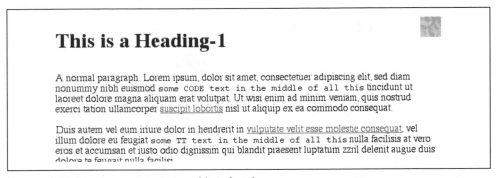

Figure 6-44. Mixing percentages and length values

Not only that, but if you're using lengths or percentages, you can give negative values, thus pushing the image out of the element, to some degree. Consider the example with the very large yin-yang symbol for a background. At one point, we centered it, but what if we only want part of it visible in the top left corner of the containing element? No problem, at least in theory. First, assume the image is 300 pixels tall by 300 pixels wide. Then, assume that only the bottom right third of it should be visible. We can get the desired effect (shown in Figure 6-45) like this:

```
BODY {background-image: url(bigyinyang.gif);
    background-repeat: no-repeat;
    background-position: -200px -200px;}
```

This is a Heading-1

A normal paragraph. Lorem ipsum, dolor sit amet, consectetuer adipiscing elit, sed diam nonummy nibh euismod some CODE text in the middle of all this tincidunt ut laoreet dolore magna aliquam erat volutpat. Ut wisi enim ad minim veniam, quis nostrud exerci tation ullamcorper suscipit lobortis nisl ut aliquip ex ea commodo consequat.

Duis autem vel eum iriure dolor in hendrerit in vulputate velit esse molestie consequat, vel illum dolore eu feugiat some TT text in the middle of all this nulla facilisis at vero eros et accumsan et iusto odio dignissim qui blandit praesent luptatum zzril delenit augue duis dolore te feugait nulla facilisi.

Lorem ipsum, dolor sit amet, consectetuer adipiscing elit, sed diam nonummy nibh euismod some CODE text in the middle of all this tincidunt ut laoreet dolore magna aliquam erat volutpat. Ut wisi enim ad minim veniam, quis nostrud exerci tation ullamcorpersuscipit lobortis nisl ut aliquip ex ea commodo consequat. Duis autem vel eum iriure dolor in hendrerit in vulputate velit esse molestie consequat, vel illum dolore eu feugiat some TT text in the middle of all this nulla facilisis at vero eros et accumsan et iusto odio dignissim qui blandit praesent luptatum zzril delenit augue duis dolore te feugait nulla facilisi.

Iriure dolor in hendrerit in vulputate velit esse molestie consequat, vel illum dolore eu feugiat

Figure 6-45. Using negative length values

Or, let's say we want a little more of it visible, as in Figure 6-46:

```
BODY {background-image: url(bigyinyang.gif);
    background-repeat: no-repeat;
    background-position: -150px -100px;}
```

This is a Heading-1

A normal paragraph. Lorem ipsum, dolor sit amet, consectetuer adipiscing elit, sed diam nonummy nibh euismod some `CODE` text in the middle of all this tincidunt ut laoreet dolore magna aliquam erat volutpat. Ut wisi enim ad minim veniam, quis nostrud exerci tation ullamcorper suscipit lobortis nisl ut aliquip ex ea commodo consequat.

Duis autem vel eum iriure dolor in hendrerit in vulputate velit esse molestie consequat, vel illum dolore eu feugiat some `TT text in the middle of all this` nulla facilisis at vero eros et accumsan et iusto odio dignissim qui blandit praesent luptatum zzril delenit augue duis dolore te feugait nulla facilisi.

Lorem ipsum, dolor sit amet, consectetuer adipiscing elit, sed diam nonummy nibh euismod some `CODE text in the middle of all this` tincidunt ut laoreet dolore magna aliquam erat volutpat. Ut wisi enim ad minim veniam, quis nostrud exerci tation ullamcorpersuscipit lobortis nisl ut aliquip ex ea commodo consequat. Duis autem vel eum iriure dolor in hendrerit in vulputate velit esse molestie consequat, vel illum dolore eu feugiat some `TT text in the middle of all this` nulla facilisis at vero eros et accumsan et iusto odio dignissim qui blandit praesent luptatum zzril delenit augue duis dolore te feugait nulla facilisi.

Iriure dolor in hendrerit in vulputate velit esse molestie consequat, vel illum dolore eu feugiat

Figure 6-46. Another set of negative lengths

Negative percentages are also possible in theory, although there are two issues involved. The first is the limitations of user agents, which may not recognize negative values for `background-position`. The other is that negative percentages are somewhat interesting to calculate. Figure 6-47 shows why.

This isn't to say that you shouldn't use negative values, of course, just that there are issues to consider. As always.

Although most CSS-aware browsers (Explorer 4.x and 5.x and Opera 3.5 and later) honor negative background positions, the effects are wildly unpredictable at best. This applies even to negative lengths, which can cause unwanted tiling, inappropriate positioning of the background images, and more. If you really need to set a single background image so that it's hanging off the page, you're probably better off producing an image that is already cut off and just putting it in the top left corner.

Throughout this section, every example has had a repeat value of `no-repeat`. The reason for this is simple: with only a single background image, it's much easier to see how positioning affects the placement of the first background image. We don't have to prevent the background image from repeating, though:

```
BODY {background-image: url(bigyinyang.gif);
    background-position: -150px -100px;}
```

Figure 6-47. Aligning negative percentage points: two scenarios

So, with the background repeating, we can see from Figure 6-48 that the tiling pattern starts with the position specified by `background-position`. This first image is known as the *origin image*, and it's very important to understanding the next section.

As it happens, the positioning of backgrounds does contradict something I said earlier. `background-position` is the only background property with restrictions, as it may only be applied to block-level and replaced elements; background image positioning cannot be done on inline elements such as hyperlinks.

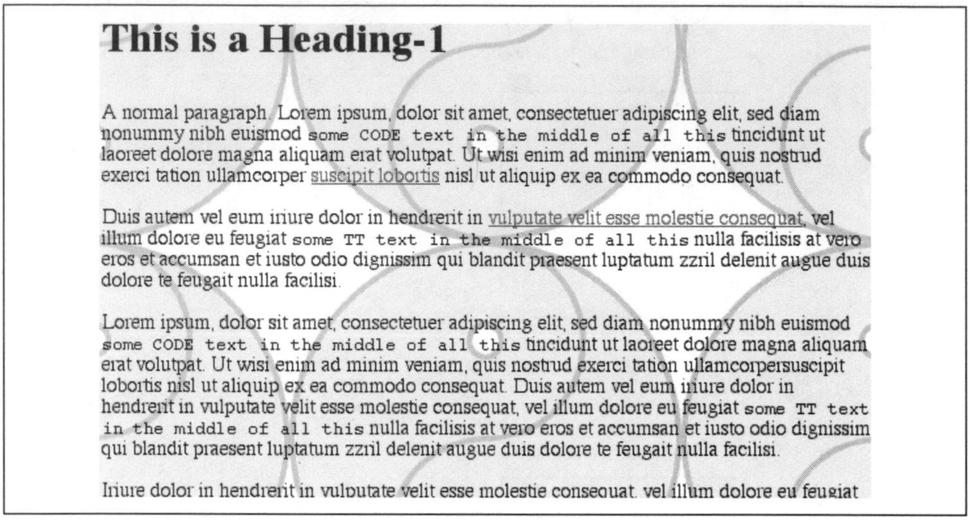

This is a Heading-1

A normal paragraph. Lorem ipsum, dolor sit amet, consectetuer adipiscing elit, sed diam nonummy nibh euismod `some CODE text in the middle of all this` tincidunt ut laoreet dolore magna aliquam erat volutpat. Ut wisi enim ad minim veniam, quis nostrud exerci tation ullamcorper suscipit lobortis nisl ut aliquip ex ea commodo consequat.

Duis autem vel eum iriure dolor in hendrerit in vulputate velit esse molestie consequat, vel illum dolore eu feugiat `some TT text in the middle of all this` nulla facilisis at vero eros et accumsan et iusto odio dignissim qui blandit praesent luptatum zzril delenit augue duis dolore te feugait nulla facilisi.

Lorem ipsum, dolor sit amet, consectetuer adipiscing elit, sed diam nonummy nibh euismod `some CODE text in the middle of all this` tincidunt ut laoreet dolore magna aliquam erat volutpat. Ut wisi enim ad minim veniam, quis nostrud exerci tation ullamcorpersuscipit lobortis nisl ut aliquip ex ea commodo consequat. Duis autem vel eum iriure dolor in hendrerit in vulputate velit esse molestie consequat, vel illum dolore eu feugiat `some TT text in the middle of all this` nulla facilisis at vero eros et accumsan et iusto odio dignissim qui blandit praesent luptatum zzril delenit augue duis dolore te feugait nulla facilisi.

Iriure dolor in hendrerit in vulputate velit esse molestie consequat, vel illum dolore eu feugiat

Figure 6-48. Use of the background-position property sets the origin of the tiling pattern

Repeats with Direction (Revisited)

In the previous section on repetition, we explored the values **`repeat-x`**, **`repeat-y`**, and **`repeat`**, and how they affect the tiling of background images. In each case, however, the tiling pattern always started from the top left corner of the containing element (e.g., `BODY`). That isn't a requirement, of course; as we've seen, the default values for **`background-position`** are `0% 0%`. So, unless you change the position of the origin image, that's where the tiling starts. Now that we know how to change the position of the origin image, we need to figure out how user agents will handle the situation.

It will be easier to show an example, and then explain it. Consider the following, which is illustrated by Figure 6-49:

```
BODY {background-image: url(bg23.gif);
   background-repeat: repeat-y;
   background-position: center;}
```

So there you have it: a stripe running through the center of the document. It may look wrong, but it isn't.

The example shown in Figure 6-49 is correct because the origin image has been placed in the center of the `BODY` element and then tiled along the y-axis *in both directions*—in other words, both up *and* down. In a similar fashion, when the repeat direction is horizontal, the background image is repeated to both the right and the left, as shown in Figure 6-50:

```
BODY {background-image: url(bg23.gif);
   background-repeat: repeat-x;
   background-position: center;}
```

Figure 6-49. Centering the origin image and repeating vertically

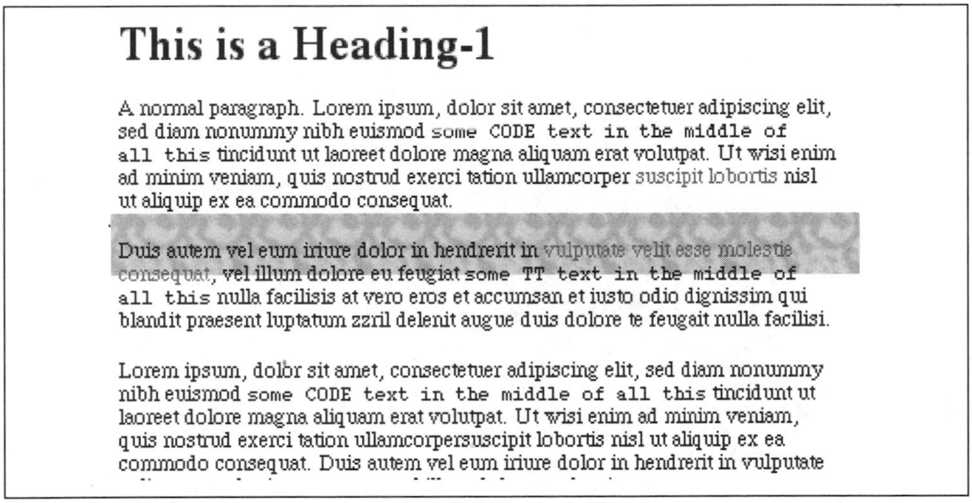

Figure 6-50. Centering with a horizontal repeat

Therefore, setting a large image in the center of the BODY and then letting it repeat will cause it to tile in all *four* directions: up, down, left, and right. The only difference `background-position` makes is in where the tiling starts. Figure 6-51 shows the difference between tiling from the center of the BODY, and from its top left corner.

Note the differences along the edges of the browser window. When the background repeats from the center, the grid is centered within the viewport, resulting

Figure 6-51. The difference between starting a repeat from top left (left) and centering it (right)

in consistent "clipping" along the edges. The variations may seem subtle, but the odds are that you'll have reason to use both approaches at some point in your design career.

In case you're wondering, there is no way to control the repeat any more than we've already discussed. There is no `repeat-left`, for example, although it could certainly be added in some future version of CSS. For now, you get full tiling, horizontal tiling, vertical tiling, or no tiling at all.

Repeating: Real-world issues

There are a few things to keep in mind when it comes to web browsers. First is that in Navigator 4 and Internet Explorer 4, tiling only happened down and to the right. If you're using Explorer 4, centering an image in the background and then tiling it would look like Figure 6-52.

This is a Heading-1

A normal paragraph. Lorem ipsum, dolor sit amet, consectetuer adipiscing elit, sed diam nonummy nibh euismod some CODE text in the middle of all this tincidunt ut laoreet dolore magna aliquam erat volutpat. Ut wisi enim ad minim veniam, quis nostrud exerci tation ullamcorper suscipit lobortis nisl ut aliquip ex ea commodo consequat.

Duis autem vel eum iriure dolor in hendrerit in vulputate velit esse molestie consequat, vel illum dolore eu feugiat some TT text in the middle of all this nulla facilisis at vero eros et accumsan et iusto odio dignissim qui blandit praesent luptatum zzril delenit augue duis dolore te feugait nulla facilisi.

Lorem ipsum, dolor sit amet, consectetuer adipiscing elit, sed diam nonummy nibh euismod some CODE text in the middle of all this tincidunt ut laoreet dolore magna aliquam erat volutpat. Ut wisi enim ad minim veniam, quis nostrud exerci tation ullamcorpersuscipit lobortis nisl ut aliquip ex ea commodo consequat. Duis autem vel eum iriure dolor in hendrerit in vulputate velit esse molestie

Figure 6-52. Incorrect behavior in Internet Explorer 4

Navigator 4 manages to avoid this error by not honoring background positioning at all, which means that the origin image *always* appears in the top left corner of an element under Navigator 4. Of the browsers that correctly position background images, only four managed correct repeating, as of this writing: Opera 3.6 for Windows, Internet Explorer 4.5 and 5 for Macintosh, and Internet Explorer 5 for Windows.

Getting Attached

Okay, so we can place the origin image for the background anywhere in the background of an element, and we can control (to a degree) how it tiles. As you may have already realized, setting an image to be in the center of the document may mean, given a sufficiently long document, that the background image isn't initially visible to the reader. After all, a browser only provides a window onto the document. If the document is too long to be displayed in the window, then the user can scroll back and forth through the document. The center could be two or three "screens" below the beginning of the document, or just far enough down to push much of the background image beyond the bottom of the browser window, as shown in Figure 6-53.

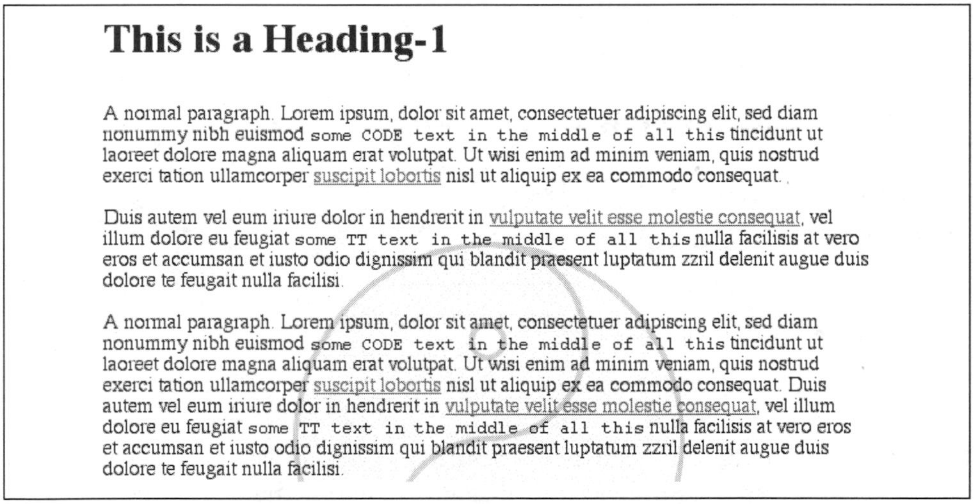

Figure 6-53. The background image appears too low to be seen fully

Furthermore, even assuming that the background image is initially visible, it always scrolls with the document. Perhaps you don't want to see what Figure 6-54 depicts:

```
BODY {background-image: url(bigyinyang.gif);
    background-repeat: no-repeat;
    background-position: center;}
```

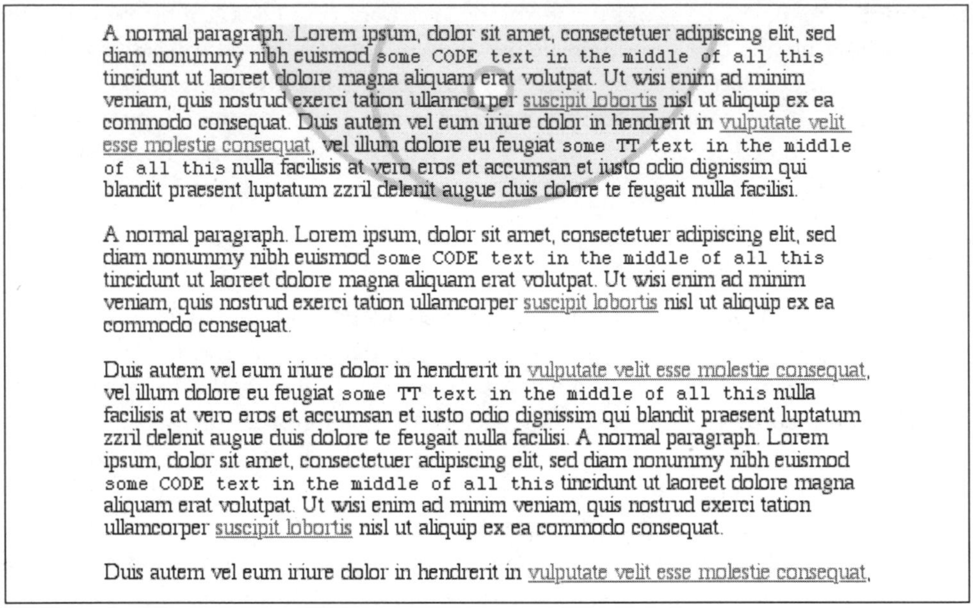

A normal paragraph. Lorem ipsum, dolor sit amet, consectetuer adipiscing elit, sed diam nonummy nibh euismod some CODE text in the middle of all this tincidunt ut laoreet dolore magna aliquam erat volutpat. Ut wisi enim ad minim veniam, quis nostrud exerci tation ullamcorper suscipit lobortis nisl ut aliquip ex ea commodo consequat. Duis autem vel eum iriure dolor in hendrerit in vulputate velit esse molestie consequat, vel illum dolore eu feugiat some TT text in the middle of all this nulla facilisis at vero eros et accumsan et iusto odio dignissim qui blandit praesent luptatum zzril delenit augue duis dolore te feugait nulla facilisi.

A normal paragraph. Lorem ipsum, dolor sit amet, consectetuer adipiscing elit, sed diam nonummy nibh euismod some CODE text in the middle of all this tincidunt ut laoreet dolore magna aliquam erat volutpat. Ut wisi enim ad minim veniam, quis nostrud exerci tation ullamcorper suscipit lobortis nisl ut aliquip ex ea commodo consequat.

Duis autem vel eum iriure dolor in hendrerit in vulputate velit esse molestie consequat, vel illum dolore eu feugiat some TT text in the middle of all this nulla facilisis at vero eros et accumsan et iusto odio dignissim qui blandit praesent luptatum zzril delenit augue duis dolore te feugait nulla facilisi. A normal paragraph. Lorem ipsum, dolor sit amet, consectetuer adipiscing elit, sed diam nonummy nibh euismod some CODE text in the middle of all this tincidunt ut laoreet dolore magna aliquam erat volutpat. Ut wisi enim ad minim veniam, quis nostrud exerci tation ullamcorper suscipit lobortis nisl ut aliquip ex ea commodo consequat.

Duis autem vel eum iriure dolor in hendrerit in vulputate velit esse molestie consequat,

Figure 6-54. Scrolling the background image out of view

Never fear: there is a way to prevent this scrolling.

background-attachment

Values	scroll | fixed
Initial value	scroll
Inherited	no
Applies to	all elements

Using the property `background-attachment`, you can declare the background to be `fixed` with respect to the viewing area and therefore immune to the effects of scrolling:

```
BODY {background-image: url(bigyinyang.gif);
    background-repeat: no-repeat;
    background-position: center;
    background-attachment: fixed;}
```

Doing this has two immediate effects, as we can see from Figure 6-55. The first is that the background does not scroll along with the document. The second is that the position of the image is determined by the viewing area, not the document size.

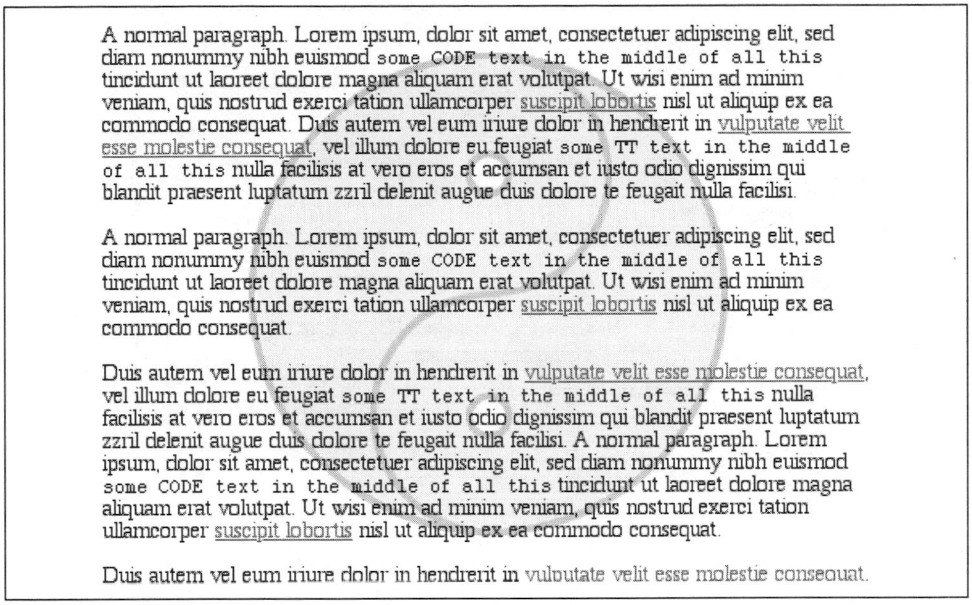

A normal paragraph. Lorem ipsum, dolor sit amet, consectetuer adipiscing elit, sed diam nonummy nibh euismod some CODE text in the middle of all this tincidunt ut laoreet dolore magna aliquam erat volutpat. Ut wisi enim ad minim veniam, quis nostrud exerci tation ullamcorper suscipit lobortis nisl ut aliquip ex ea commodo consequat. Duis autem vel eum iriure dolor in hendrerit in vulputate velit esse molestie consequat, vel illum dolore eu feugiat some TT text in the middle of all this nulla facilisis at vero eros et accumsan et iusto odio dignissim qui blandit praesent luptatum zzril delenit augue duis dolore te feugait nulla facilisi.

A normal paragraph. Lorem ipsum, dolor sit amet, consectetuer adipiscing elit, sed diam nonummy nibh euismod some CODE text in the middle of all this tincidunt ut laoreet dolore magna aliquam erat volutpat. Ut wisi enim ad minim veniam, quis nostrud exerci tation ullamcorper suscipit lobortis nisl ut aliquip ex ea commodo consequat.

Duis autem vel eum iriure dolor in hendrerit in vulputate velit esse molestie consequat, vel illum dolore eu feugiat some TT text in the middle of all this nulla facilisis at vero eros et accumsan et iusto odio dignissim qui blandit praesent luptatum zzril delenit augue duis dolore te feugait nulla facilisi. A normal paragraph. Lorem ipsum, dolor sit amet, consectetuer adipiscing elit, sed diam nonummy nibh euismod some CODE text in the middle of all this tincidunt ut laoreet dolore magna aliquam erat volutpat. Ut wisi enim ad minim veniam, quis nostrud exerci tation ullamcorper suscipit lobortis nisl ut aliquip ex ea commodo consequat.

Duis autem vel eum iriure dolor in hendrerit in vulputate velit esse molestie consequat.

Figure 6-55. Nailing the background in place

When printed, of course, the two are the same, since the display area (the paper) is the same as the document size, at least for that page. In a web browser, though, the viewing area can change as the user resizes the browser's window. This will cause the background's origin image to shift as the window changes size. Figure 6-56 depicts several views of the same document. So in a certain sense the image isn't fixed in place, but it will remain fixed so long as the viewing area isn't resized.

There is only one other value for `background-attachment`, and that's the default value `scroll`. As you'd expect, this causes the background to scroll along with the rest of the document when viewed in a web browser, and it doesn't necessarily change the origin image's position as the window is resized. If the document width is fixed (perhaps by assigning an explicit width to the BODY element), then resizing the viewing area won't affect the placement of the origin image.

Interesting effects

In technical terms, when a background image has been set to be `fixed`, it is positioned with respect to the viewing area, not the element that contains it. However, the background will only be visible within its containing element. This leads to a rather interesting consequence.

Let's say we have a document with a tiled background that actually looks like it's tiled and an H1 element with the same pattern, only in a different color. Both the

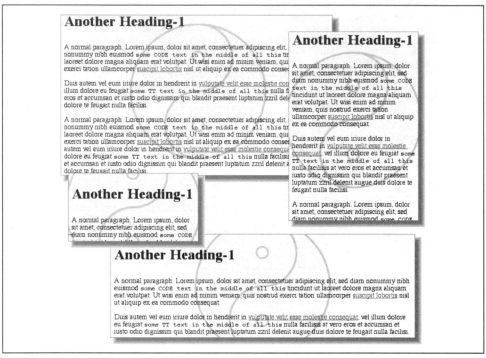

Figure 6-56. Centering still holds, even if the image is "fixed"

BODY and H1 elements are set to have **fixed** backgrounds, resulting in something like Figure 6-57:

```
BODY {background-image: url(tile1.gif);  background-repeat: repeat;
   background-attachment: fixed;}
H1 {background-image: url(tile2.gif);  background-repeat: repeat;
   background-attachment: fixed;}
```

How is this perfect alignment possible? Remember, when a background is **fixed**, the origin element is positioned with respect to the canvas. Thus, both background patterns begin tiling from the top left corner of the document, not the individual elements. For the BODY, we can see the entire repeat pattern. For the H1, however, the only place we can see its background is in the padding and content of the H1 itself. Since both background images are the same size, and they have precisely the same origin position, they appear to "line up" as shown in Figure 6-57.

There's a downside: as of this writing, web browsers don't get this fixed alignment right, so this example was just an interesting theoretical exercise.

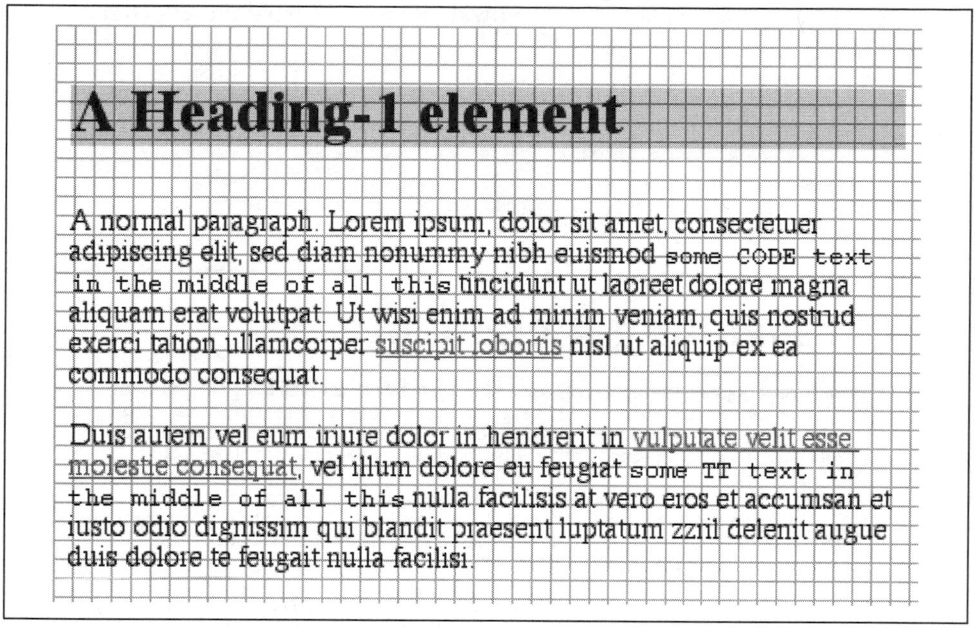

Figure 6-57. Perfect alignment of backgrounds

Bringing It All Together

Just like with the font properties, the background properties can all be brought together in a single shorthand property: `background`. This property can take a single value from each of the other background properties, in literally any order.

background

Values	<background-color> || <background-image> || <background-repeat> || <background-attachment> || <background-position>
Initial value	refer to individual properties
Inherited	no
Applies to	all elements

Note: Percentage values are allowed for <background-position>.

Thus the following statements are all equivalent and will have the effect shown in Figure 6-58:

```
BODY {background-color: white; background-image: url(yinyang.gif);
    background-position: top left; background-repeat: repeat-y;
    background-attachment: fixed;}
BODY {background: white url(yinyang.gif) top left repeat-y fixed;}
BODY {background: fixed url(yinyang.gif) white top left repeat-y;}
BODY {background: url(yinyang.gif) white repeat-y fixed top left;}
```

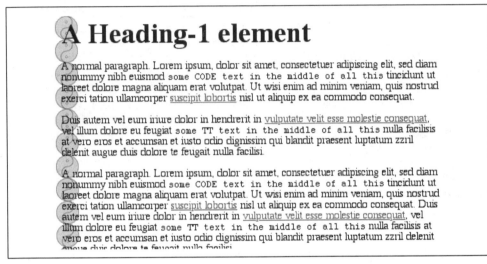

Figure 6-58. Using shorthand

Actually, there is one slight restriction to how the values are ordered in **background**, which is that if you have two values for **background-position**, they must appear together, horizontal first, then vertical. That probably isn't a surprise, but it is important to remember.

As is the case for shorthand properties, if you leave out any values, the defaults for the relevant properties are filled in automatically. Thus, the following two are equivalent:

```
BODY {background: white url(yinyang.gif;}
BODY {background: white url(yinyang.gif) top left repeat scroll;}
```

What's even better, there are no required values for **background**—as long as you have at least one value present, you can omit all the rest. Therefore, it's possible to set just the background color using the shorthand property, which is a very common practice:

```
BODY {background: white;}
```

This is perfectly legal, and in some ways preferred, given the reduced number of keystrokes. In addition, it has the effect of setting all of the other background properties to their defaults, which means that **background-image** will be set to none. This helps ensure readability by preventing other rules (in, for example, the reader style sheet) from setting an image in the background.

Any of the following rules are also legal, as illustrated by Figure 6-59:

```
H1 {background: silver;}
H2 {background: url(h2bg.gif);}
P {background: url(parabg.gif);}
P.type1 {background: repeat-x left center;} /* BG from previous rule is lost */
P.type2 {background: center;}  /* same BG loss applies here as well */
```

A Heading-1 element

A normal paragraph. Lorem ipsum, dolor sit amet, consectetuer adipiscing elit, sed diam nonummy nibh euismod some CODE text in the middle of all this tincidunt ut laoreet dolore magna aliquam erat volutpat. Ut wisi enim ad minim veniam, quis nostrud exerci tation ullamcorper suscipit lobortis nisl ut aliquip ex ea commodo consequat.

Duis autem vel eum iriure dolor in hendrerit in vulputate velit esse molestie consequat, vel illum dolore eu feugiat some TT text in the middle of all this nulla facilisis at vero eros et accumsan et iusto odio dignissim qui blandit praesent luptatum zzril delenit augue duis dolore te feugait nulla facilisi.

Hey, it's an H2 element!

A normal paragraph. Lorem ipsum, dolor sit amet, consectetuer adipiscing elit, sed diam nonummy nibh euismod some CODE text in the middle of all this tincidunt ut laoreet dolore magna aliquam erat volutpat. Ut wisi enim ad minim veniam, quis nostrud exerci tation ullamcorper suscipit lobortis nisl ut aliquip ex ea commodo consequat. Duis autem vel eum iriure dolor in hendrerit in vulputate velit esse molestie consequat, vel illum dolore eu feugiat some TT text in the middle of all this nulla facilisis at vero eros et accumsan et iusto odio dignissim qui blandit praesent luptatum zzril delenit augue duis dolore te feugait nulla facilisi.

Figure 6-59. Applying many backgrounds to one document

Note the absence of an image on two of the paragraphs. This is because the styles for **type1** and **type2** paragraphs do not include the URL of a background image.

In older browsers, such as the early version of Navigator 4, the background property was supported while many of the individual properties, such as background-color, were not. Therefore, it generally makes sense to use background whenever possible and to avoid the more specific properties when you can.

Summary

Setting colors and backgrounds on elements gives authors a great deal of power in CSS. The advantage of CSS over traditional methods is that colors and backgrounds can be applied to any element in a document—not just table cells, for example, or anything enclosed in a `FONT` tag. Despite a few bugs in some implementations, like Navigator 4's reluctance to apply a background to the entire content area of an element, these are very widely used properties. Their popularity isn't too hard to understand, either, since color is one easy way to distinguish the look of one page from another.

CSS allows for a great deal more in the way of element styling, however: borders that can be placed on any element, extra margins and padding, and even a way to "float" elements other than images. These are all covered in the next chapter.

7

Boxes and Borders

Most web designers are familiar with the limitations of HTML as a page layout language, even if they're not quite aware of it. Think about your page designs for a moment. How many of them depend on tables to get everything where it's supposed to go? If you're like the vast majority of web designers, all of your pages use tables. This is because tables can be used to create sidebars, of course, and to set up a complicated structure for an entire page's appearance, but also to do simpler things, like put text in a colored box with a border.

On the face of it, though, this latter effect is a little simple to be requiring a table. If all that's needed is a paragraph that has a red border and a yellow background, why should you have to wrap a single-cell table around the paragraph just to get that effect? Wouldn't it be much easier to simply say that the paragraph itself should have the border and background, and forget about all that table markup?

Thankfully, the authors of CSS felt the same way, so they devoted a great deal of attention to including the ability to define borders for darned near everything a web page can contain. Paragraphs, headings, DIVs, anchors, images, and more can be assigned borders of various types. These borders can be used to set an element apart from others, or accentuate its appearance, or to mark certain kinds of data as having been changed, or to do any number of other things.

In addition to borders, it's also possible to define regions around an element that control how the border is placed in relation to the content and how close other elements can get. Between the content of an element and its border, we find the *padding* of an element, and beyond the border, the *margins*. These properties affect how the entire document is laid out, of course, but more importantly, they very deeply affect the appearance of a given element. This is the foundation of much of the formatting model of CSS, and in order to understand it, we need to examine how an element is constructed.

Basic Element Boxes

Thanks to CSS, all document elements generate a rectangular box. This is called the *element box*. This box describes the amount of space that an element and its properties occupy in the layout of the document, and each box can therefore influence the position and size of other element boxes. For example, if the first element box in the document is an inch tall, then the next box will begin an inch below the top of the document. If the first element box is somehow altered in such a way as to make it be two inches tall, then every following element box will be shifted downward two inches, and the second element box will begin two inches below the top of the document.

As we can infer from Figure 7-1, the entirety of an HTML document is composed of a number of rectangular boxes that are distributed such that they don't overlap each other. Also, within certain constraints, these boxes take up as little space as possible, while still maintaining a sufficient separation to make clear which content belongs to which element.

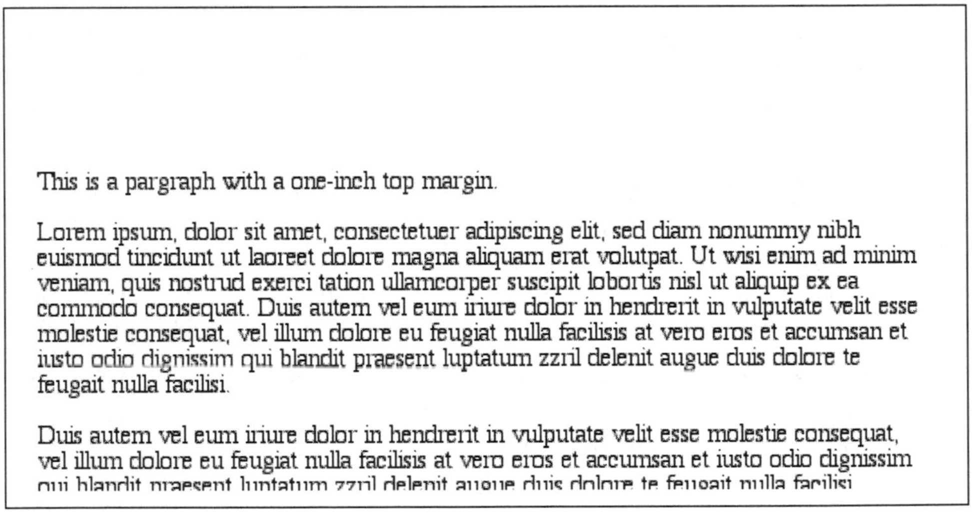

This is a pargraph with a one-inch top margin.

Lorem ipsum, dolor sit amet, consectetuer adipiscing elit, sed diam nonummy nibh euismod tincidunt ut laoreet dolore magna aliquam erat volutpat. Ut wisi enim ad minim veniam, quis nostrud exerci tation ullamcorper suscipit lobortis nisl ut aliquip ex ea commodo consequat. Duis autem vel eum iriure dolor in hendrerit in vulputate velit esse molestie consequat, vel illum dolore eu feugiat nulla facilisis at vero eros et accumsan et iusto odio dignissim qui blandit praesent luptatum zzril delenit augue duis dolore te feugait nulla facilisi.

Duis autem vel eum iriure dolor in hendrerit in vulputate velit esse molestie consequat, vel illum dolore eu feugiat nulla facilisis at vero eros et accumsan et iusto odio dignissim qui blandit praesent luntatum zzril delenit augue duis dolore te feugait nulla facilisi

Figure 7-1. How one element affects all elements

For the first time, however, it is possible for authors to influence the separation between text elements in a fundamental way—even to the point of causing elements to overlap each other! The margins and padding of the element boxes are the keys to this new power.

In order to fully understand how margins, padding, and borders are handled, you must clearly understand a number of boundaries and areas. They are shown in detail in Figure 7-2.

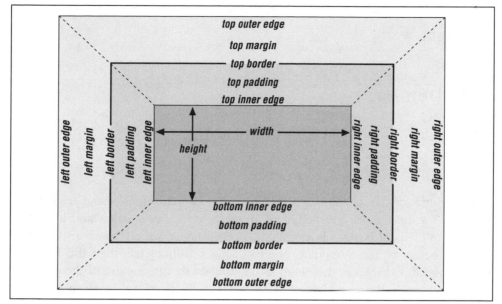

Figure 7-2. The CSS box model

In general, the `width` of an element is defined to be the distance from the left inner edge to the right inner edge, and the `height` is the distance from the inner top to the inner bottom. Not coincidentally, these are both properties that can be applied to an element.

width

Values	\<length>	\<percentage>	auto
Initial value	auto
Inherited	no
Applies to	block-level and replaced elements

Note: Percentage values refer to the width of the parent element.

The counterpart to `width` is `height`.

---

height

Values	<length> | auto
Initial value	auto
Inherited	no
Applies to	block-level and replaced elements

In the course of this chapter, we will make two assumptions about `width` and `height`. The first is that the height of an element is always calculated automatically. If an element is eight lines long, and each line is an eighth of an inch tall, then the height of the element is one inch. If it's 10 lines tall, then the height is 1.25 inches; in either case, the height is determined by the content of the element, not the author. In the next chapter, we'll see that this need not be so, but for this chapter, we assume that height is only determined by the way an element is displayed.

The second assumption is that the width of an element is just as wide as it needs to be. Under CSS, all element boxes are as wide as the content area of their parent element. Thus, if the content area of a `DIV` is two inches wide, then the overall element box of any paragraph within that `DIV` will be two inches wide as well. Figure 7-3 shows this in more detail.

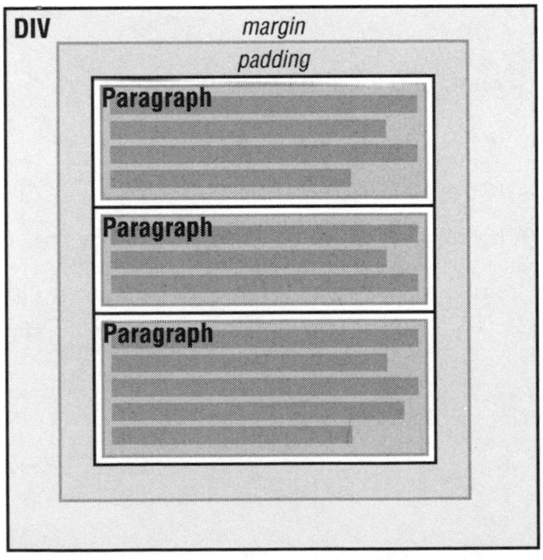

Figure 7-3. Element widths depend on the width of the parent element

Under many circumstances, the width of the margins, padding, and border of an element will all total zero, so the width of the element equals the content area of its parent. If there are margins or padding, for example, these are added to the element's width in order to equal the width of the parent element's content area. In any case, in this chapter, we always assume that the width of the element is as wide as it needs to be to equal its parent's content width.

Margins or Padding?

There are three ways to generate extra space around elements. The first is to add only padding to an element; second, to add only margins; and third, to add a combination of padding and margins. Under certain circumstances, it doesn't really matter which you pick. If an element has a background, however, then it does matter which of the three options you choose. That's because the background will extend into the padding, but not the margin. Thus, the amount of padding and margin you assign to a given element will influence where the background of the element will end.

If you set background colors for the elements involved, as illustrated in Figure 7-4, the difference becomes a little more clear. The elements with padding have extra background, as it were, whereas those with margins do not.

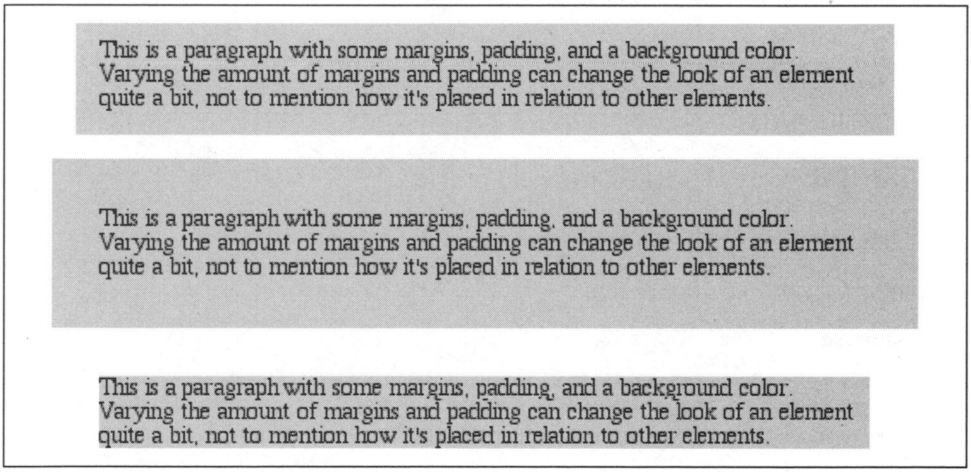

Figure 7-4. Paragraphs with different margins and padding, with backgrounds to illustrate the differences

In the end, deciding how to set margins and padding is up to the designer, who has to balance the various possibilities against the intended effect and pick the best alternative. In order to be able to make these choices, of course, it helps to know what properties can be used.

Margins

The most basic things you can add to an element are margins. These create extra blank space around an element. "Blank space" generally refers to the area in which other elements cannot also exist and in which the parent element's background is visible. For example, look at Figure 7-5, which shows the difference between two paragraphs without any margins, and the same two paragraphs with some margins.

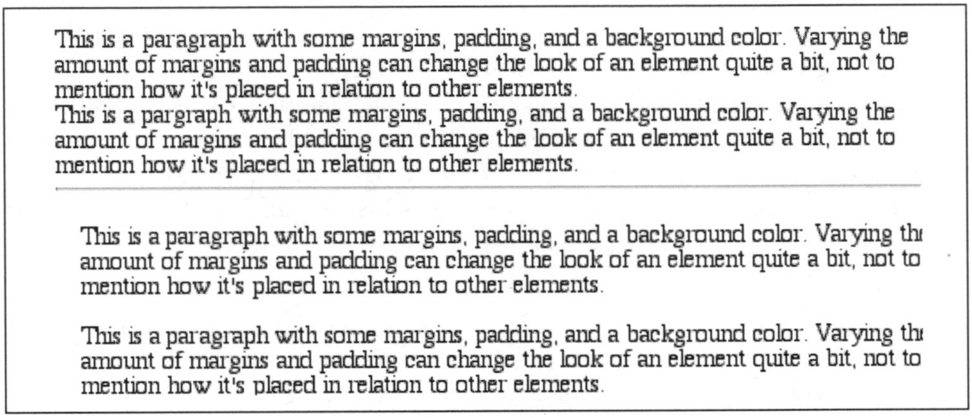

This is a paragraph with some margins, padding, and a background color. Varying the amount of margins and padding can change the look of an element quite a bit, not to mention how it's placed in relation to other elements.
This is a pargraph with some margins, padding, and a background color. Varying the amount of margins and padding can change the look of an element quite a bit, not to mention how it's placed in relation to other elements.

This is a paragraph with some margins, padding, and a background color. Varying the amount of margins and padding can change the look of an element quite a bit, not to mention how it's placed in relation to other elements.

This is a paragraph with some margins, padding, and a background color. Varying the amount of margins and padding can change the look of an element quite a bit, not to mention how it's placed in relation to other elements.

Figure 7-5. Paragraphs with, and without, margins

The simplest way to set a margin is by using the property `margin`.

margin

Values	[<length>	<percentage>	auto]{1,4}
Initial value	not defined
Inherited	no
Applies to	all elements

Note: Percentage values refer to width of the parent element.

Suppose we wish to set a quarter-inch margin on H1 elements, as illustrated in Figure 7-6. (A background color has been added in order to be able to see the edges of the content area.) For example:

```
H1 {margin: 0.25in; background-color: silver;}
```

This is an H1 element

This is a normal, unstyled paragraph. Lorem ipsum, dolor sit amet, consectetuer adipiscing elit, sed diam nonummy nibh euismod tincidunt ut laoreet dolore magna aliquam erat volutpat. Ut wisi enim ad minim veniam, quis nostrud exerci tation ullamcorper suscipit lobortis nisl ut aliquip ex ea commodo consequat.

Figure 7-6. Setting a margin for H1 elements

This sets a quarter-inch of blank space on each side of an H1 element. In Figure 7-6, this is represented using dashed lines which are included for illustrative purposes. These lines would not actually appear in a web browser.

`margin` can accept any length measure, whether in pixels, inches, millimeters, or ems. However, the default value for `margin` is effectively 0 (zero), which means that if you don't declare a value, then by default, there won't be a margin.

In practice, browsers come with pre-assigned styles for many elements, and margins are no exception. For example, in CSS-enabled browsers, the "blank line" above and below each paragraph element is generated using margins. Therefore, if you don't declare margins for the P element, the browser may apply some margins on its own—which is to say that just because you don't declare margins for an element doesn't mean that there won't be any.

You can also declare a margin to be `auto`. For now, assume that `auto` will get you an automatically calculated value, which is usually, but not quite always, zero. (Fortunately, the circumstances under which `auto` becomes something other than zero are very well-defined, and are discussed in detail in the next chapter.)

Finally, it's possible to set a percentage value for `margin`. The details of this type of value will be discussed in a later section.

Length Values and Margins

As stated before, any length value can be used in setting the margins of an element. If we want a 10-pixel whitespace around paragraph elements, that's simple enough. The following markup creates a normal paragraph and one that has a ten-pixel margin applied to it, shown in Figure 7-7:

```
P {background-color: silver;}
P.one {margin: 10px;}
```

This is a normal, unstyled pargraph. Lorem ipsum, dolor sit amet, consectetuer adipiscing elit, sed diam nonummy nibh euismod tincidunt ut laoreet dolore magna aliquam erat volutpat.

This is a pargraph with a class of 'one'. Lorem ipsum, dolor sit amet, consectetuer adipiscing elit, sed diam nonummy nibh euismod tincidunt ut laoreet dolore magna aliquam erat volutpat.

Figure 7-7. Comparative paragraphs

(Again, the background color helps show the content area, and the dashed lines are for illustrative purposes only.) As Figure 7-7 demonstrates, 10 pixels of space are added to each side of the content area. This is somewhat similar to using the HSPACE and VSPACE attributes in HTML. In fact, you can use `margin` to set extra space around an image. Let's say you want 1 em of space surrounding all images:

```
IMG {margin: 1em;}
```

That's all it takes.

There may be times where you want a different amount of space on each side of an element. That's simple as well. If we want all H1 elements to have a top margin of 10 pixels, a right margin of 20 pixels, a bottom margin of 15 pixels, and a left margin of 5 pixels, here's all we need:

```
H1 {margin: 10px 20px 15px 5px; background-color: silver;}
```

As Figure 7-8 reveals, we have what we wanted. The order of the values is obviously important, and follows this pattern:

```
margin: top right bottom left
```

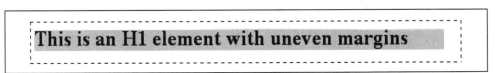

This is an H1 element with uneven margins

Figure 7-8. Uneven margins

A good way to remember this pattern is to keep in mind that the four values go clockwise around the element, starting from the top. The values are *always* applied in this order, so in order to get the effect you want, you have to arrange the values correctly.

An easy way to remember the order in which sides have to be declared, other than thinking of it as being clockwise from the top, is to keep in mind that getting the sides in the correct order helps you avoid "trouble"—that is, TRBL, for "Top Right Bottom Left."

It's also possible to mix up the types of length value you use. You aren't restricted to using a single length type in a given rule, as shown here:

```
H2 {margin: 14px 5em 0.1in 3ex;}   /* value variety! */
```

Figure 7-9 shows us, with a little extra annotation, the results of this declaration.

This is an H2 element with uneven margins of mixed values

Figure 7-9. Mixed-value margins

Percentages and Margins

As stated earlier, it's possible to set percentage values for the margins of an element. Percentages are computed in relation to the width of the parent element, so they change if the parent element's width changes in some way. For example, assume the following, shown in Figure 7-10:

```
P {margin: 10%;}

<DIV STYLE="width: 200px;">
<P>This paragraph is contained within a DIV which has a width of 200 pixels,
so its margin will be 10% of the width of the paragraph's parent (the DIV).
Given the declared width of 200 pixels, the margin will be 20 pixels on
all sides.</P>
</DIV>
<DIV STYLE="width: 100px;">
<P>This paragraph is contained within a DIV with a width of 100 pixels,
so its margin will still be 10% of the width of the paragraph's parent.
There will, therefore, be half as much margin on this paragraph as that
on the first paragraph.</P></DIV>
```

While this is interesting enough, consider the case of elements without a declared `width`, whose overall width (including margins) is therefore dependent on the `width` of the parent element.

```
P {margin: 10%}
```

Figure 7-11 shows how the margin of a paragraph changes as it's viewed in browsers windows of two different sizes.

As you can imagine, this leads to the possibility of "fluid" pages, where the margins and padding of elements enlarge or reduce to match the actual size of the display canvas. In theory, as the user changes the width of a browser window, the margins and padding will expand or shrink dynamically—but not every browser supports this sort of behavior. Still, using percentages for `margin` and `padding` may be the best way to set styles that will hold up in more than one media; for example, documents that will look good on a monitor as well as a printout.

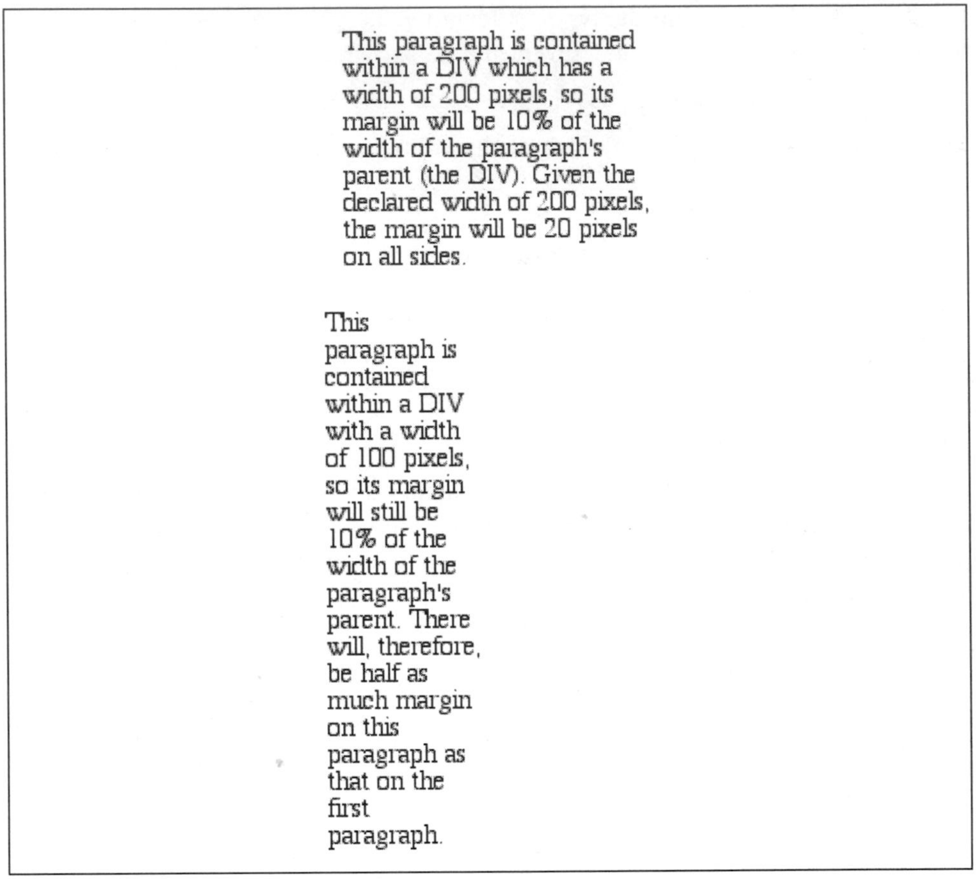

This paragraph is contained within a DIV which has a width of 200 pixels, so its margin will be 10% of the width of the paragraph's parent (the DIV). Given the declared width of 200 pixels, the margin will be 20 pixels on all sides.

This paragraph is contained within a DIV with a width of 100 pixels, so its margin will still be 10% of the width of the paragraph's parent. There will, therefore, be half as much margin on this paragraph as that on the first paragraph.

Figure 7-10. Parent widths and percentages

It's also possible to mix percentages with length values. Thus, to set H1 elements to have top and bottom margins of one-half em and side margins that are 10% of the width of the browser window, you can declare the following, shown in Figure 7-12:

```
H1 {margin: 0.5em 10% 0.5em 10%;}
```

Here, although the top and bottom margins will stay constant in any situation, the side margins will change based on the width of the browser window. This of course assumes that all H1 elements are the child of the BODY element and that BODY is as wide as the browser window. More properly stated, the side margins of H1 elements will be 10% of the width of the H1's parent element.

Let's revisit that example for a moment:

```
H1 {margin: 0.5em 10% 0.5em 10%;}
```

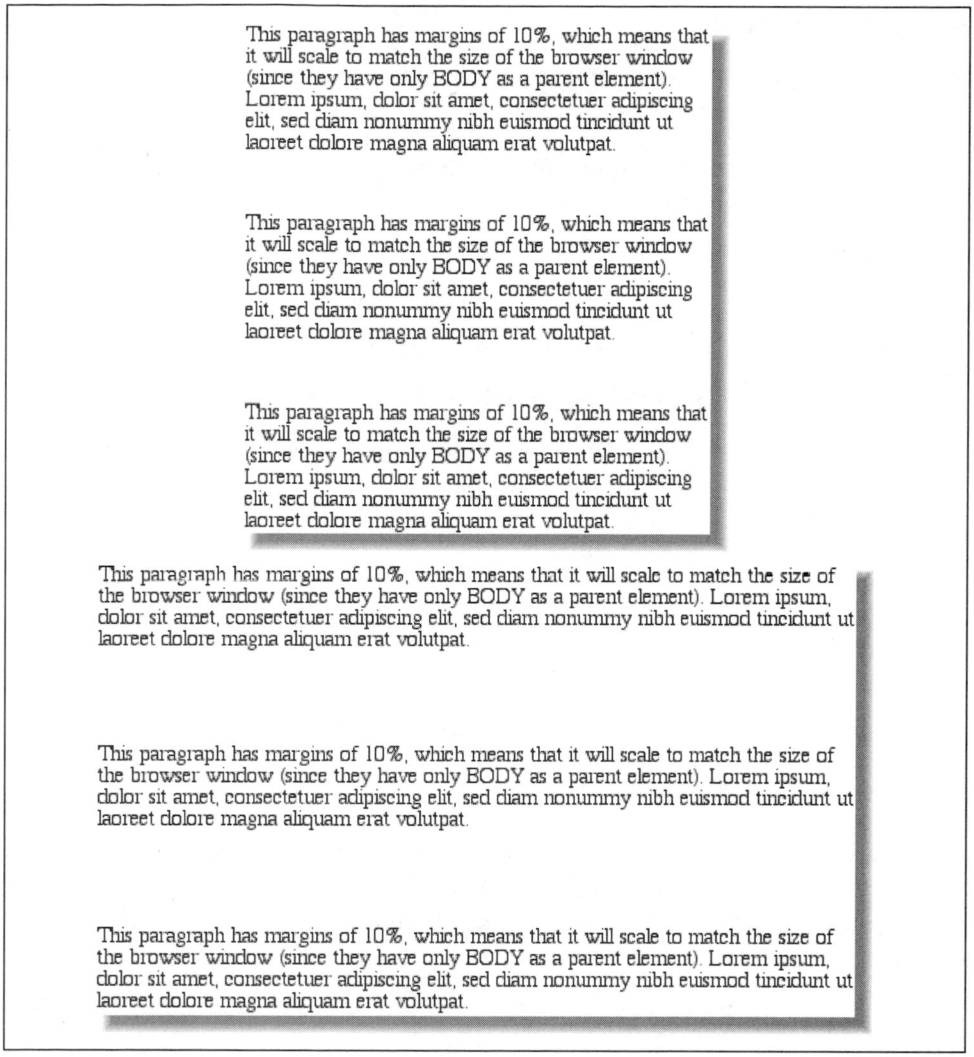

> This paragraph has margins of 10%, which means that it will scale to match the size of the browser window (since they have only BODY as a parent element). Lorem ipsum, dolor sit amet, consectetuer adipiscing elit, sed diam nonummy nibh euismod tincidunt ut laoreet dolore magna aliquam erat volutpat.
>
> This paragraph has margins of 10%, which means that it will scale to match the size of the browser window (since they have only BODY as a parent element). Lorem ipsum, dolor sit amet, consectetuer adipiscing elit, sed diam nonummy nibh euismod tincidunt ut laoreet dolore magna aliquam erat volutpat.
>
> This paragraph has margins of 10%, which means that it will scale to match the size of the browser window (since they have only BODY as a parent element). Lorem ipsum, dolor sit amet, consectetuer adipiscing elit, sed diam nonummy nibh euismod tincidunt ut laoreet dolore magna aliquam erat volutpat.

This paragraph has margins of 10%, which means that it will scale to match the size of the browser window (since they have only BODY as a parent element). Lorem ipsum, dolor sit amet, consectetuer adipiscing elit, sed diam nonummy nibh euismod tincidunt ut laoreet dolore magna aliquam erat volutpat.

This paragraph has margins of 10%, which means that it will scale to match the size of the browser window (since they have only BODY as a parent element). Lorem ipsum, dolor sit amet, consectetuer adipiscing elit, sed diam nonummy nibh euismod tincidunt ut laoreet dolore magna aliquam erat volutpat.

This paragraph has margins of 10%, which means that it will scale to match the size of the browser window (since they have only BODY as a parent element). Lorem ipsum, dolor sit amet, consectetuer adipiscing elit, sed diam nonummy nibh euismod tincidunt ut laoreet dolore magna aliquam erat volutpat.

Figure 7-11. Percentage margins and changing environments

This is an H1 element

This paragraph has no styles. Lorem ipsum, dolor sit amet, consectetuer adipiscing elit, sed diam nonummy nibh euismod tincidunt ut laoreet dolore magna aliquam erat volutpat.

Figure 7-12. Mixed margins

Seems a little redundant, doesn't it? After all, you have to type in the same pair of values twice. Fortunately, CSS offers an easy way to avoid this.

Replicating Values

Sometimes, the values you're entering for `margin` get a little repetitive:

```
P {margin: 0.25em 1em 0.25em 1em;}
```

You don't have to keep typing in pairs of numbers like this, though. Instead of the preceding markup, try this:

```
P {margin: 0.25em 1em;}
```

These two values are enough to take the place of four. But how?

CSS defines a few steps to accommodate fewer than four values for `margin`:

- If the value for *left* is missing, use the value provided for *right.*
- If the value for *bottom* is missing, use the value provided for *top.*
- If the value for *right* is missing, use the value provided for *top.*

If you prefer a more visual approach, take a look at the diagram shown in Figure 7-13.

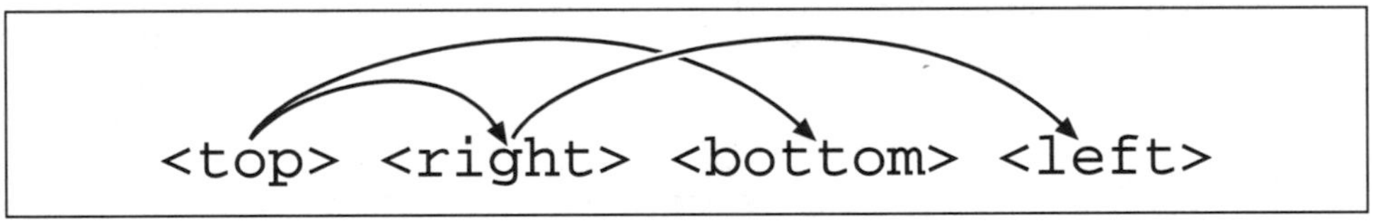

Figure 7-13. Value replication pattern

In other words, if there are three values given for `margin`, the fourth (*left*) is copied from the second (*right*). If there are two values given, the fourth is copied from the second, and the third (*bottom*) from the first (*top*). Finally, if there is only one value given, then it's copied to all the others.

This simple mechanism allows authors to supply only as many values as necessary, as shown here:

```
H1 {margin: 0.25em 0 0.5em;} /* same as '0.25em 0 0.5em 0' */
H2 {margin: 0.15em 0.2em;}   /* same as '0.15em 0.2em 0.15em 0.2em' */
P {margin: 0.5em 10px;}   /* same as '0.5em 10px 0.5em 10px' */
P.close {margin: 0.1em;}   /* same as '0.1em 0.1em 0.1em 0.1em' */
```

The only drawback to this ability is a small one, but you're bound to run into it eventually. Suppose you want to set the top and left margins for H1 elements to be 10 pixels, and the bottom and right margins to be 20 pixels. In that case, you have to write the following:

```
H1 {margin: 10px 20px 20px 10px;} /* can't be any shorter */
```

Unfortunately, there is no way to cut down on the number of values needed in such a circumstance.

Let's take another example: one where we want all of the margins to be auto—except for the left margin, which should be 3em:

```
H2 {margin: auto auto auto 3em;}
```

Again, we got the effect we wanted. The problem is all that typing of auto gets a little tedious. After all, all we want to do is affect the margin on one side of the element as shown in Figure 7-14, which leads us to the next topic.

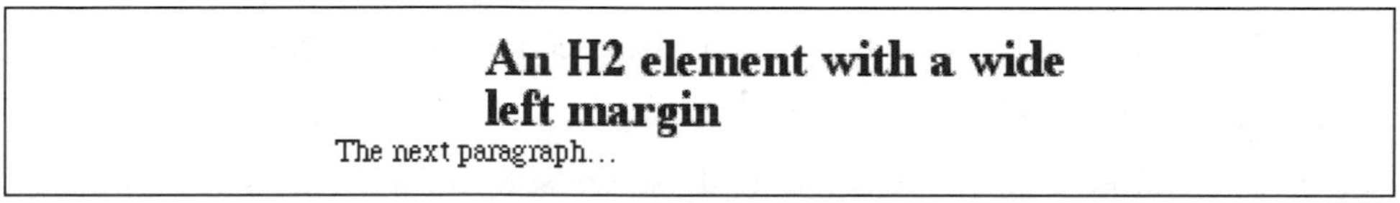

**An H2 element with a wide
left margin**
The next paragraph...

Figure 7-14. Setting a new value for just the left margin

Single-Side Margin Properties

Fortunately, there's a way to assign a value to the margin on a single side of an element. Let's say we only want to set the left margin of H2 elements to be 3em. Instead of all the typing required with **margin**, we could take this approach:

```
H2 {margin-left: 3em;}
```

margin-left is one of four properties devoted to setting the margins on each of the four sides of an element box. Their names should come as little surprise.

margin-top, margin-right, margin-bottom, margin-left

Values	<length> | <percentage> | auto
Initial value	0
Inherited	no
Applies to	all elements

Note: Percentage values refer to the width of the parent element.

Using any one of these properties allows you to set a margin on that side only, without directly affecting any of the other margins.

It's possible to use more than one of these single-side properties in a single rule; for example:

```
H2 {margin-left: 3em; margin-bottom: 2em; margin-right: 0; margin-top: 0;}
```

As we see in Figure 7-15, the margins were set as we wanted them.

An H2 element with wide left and bottom margins

The next paragraph...

Figure 7-15. More than one single-side margin

However, in this case, it might have been easier to use `margin` after all:

```
H2 {margin: 0 0 2em 3em;}
```

The results will be exactly the same as those we saw before, only with a little bit less typing. In general, once you're trying to set margins for more than one side, it's almost easier to simply use `margin`. From the standpoint of your document's display, however, it doesn't really matter which approach you use, so feel free to choose whichever is easier for you.

Collapsing Margins

There is one interesting aspect of applying margins to block-level elements: the collapsing of adjacent vertical margins. This comes into play when an element with margins immediately follows another such element in the document's layout.

A perfect example is an unordered list, in which the list items follow one another. Assume that the following is declared for a list that contains five list items:

```
LI {margin-top: 10px; margin-bottom: 15px;}
```

Thus, each list item has a 10-pixel top margin and a 15-pixel bottom margin. However, when the list is rendered, the distance between adjacent list items is 15 pixels, not 25. This is because along the vertical axis, adjacent margins are said to be collapsed. In other words, the smaller of the two margins is eliminated in favor of the larger. Figure 7-16 shows the difference between collapsed and uncollapsed margins.

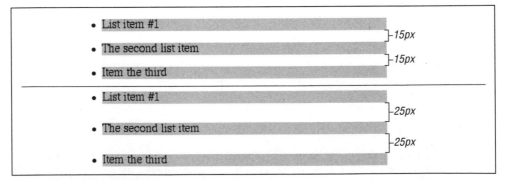

Figure 7-16. Collapsed versus uncollapsed margins

Correctly implemented user agents will collapse the vertically adjacent margins, as shown in the first list in Figure 7-16, where there are 15-pixel spaces between each list item. The second list shows what would happen if the user agent didn't collapse margins, resulting in 25-pixel spaces between list items.

Another word to use, if you don't like "collapse," is "overlap." Although the margins are not really overlapping, you can visualize what's happening using the following analogy. Imagine that each element, such as a paragraph, is a small piece of paper with the content of the element written on it. Around each piece of paper is some amount of clear plastic; this plastic represents the margins. The first piece of paper (say an H1 piece) is laid down on the canvas (browser window). The second (a paragraph) is laid below it and then slid up until the edge of one of the piece's plastic touches the edge of the other's content. If the first piece of paper has half an inch of plastic along its bottom edge, and the second has a third of an inch along its top, then when they slide together, the first piece's plastic will touch the top edge of the second piece of paper. The two are now done being placed on the canvas, and the plastic attached to the pieces is overlapping.

This is also occurs where multiple margins meet, such as at the end of a list. Adding to the earlier example, let us assume the following rules:

```
UL {margin-bottom: 10px;}
LI {margin-top: 10px; margin-bottom: 20px;}
H1 {margin-top: 28px;}
```

Therefore, the last item in the list has a bottom margin of 20 pixels, the bottom margin of the UL is 10 pixels, and the top margin of a succeeding H1 is 28 pixels. Given all this, once the margins have been collapsed (or, if you prefer, overlapped), the distance between the end of the LI and the beginning of the H1 is 28 pixels, as shown in Figure 7-17.

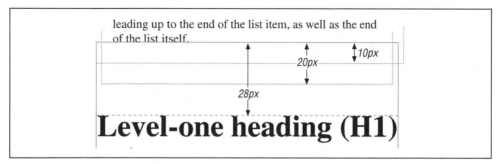

Figure 7-17. Collapsing in detail

This collapsing behavior only applies to margins. Padding and borders, where they exist, are never collapsed by anything.

Negative Margin Values

There's another side to margins: the negative side. That's right, it's possible to set negative values for margins. This will have some interesting effects, assuming that a user agent supports negative margins at all.

> User agents are not, according to the CSS1 specification, required to fully support negative margins, using the phrase, "A negative value is allowed, but there may be implementation-specific limits." In the world of web browsers, though Navigator 4.x, Explorer 4.x/5.x, and Opera 3.x do permit negative margins:

Negative margins have an impact on vertical formatting, affecting how margins are collapsed. If there are negative vertical margins, then the browser should take the absolute maximum of the negative margins and subtract that from the maximum of any positive margins.

In the case where there are only two margins to be collapsed, one positive and the other negative, the situation is handled in a fairly simple manner. The absolute value of the negative margin is subtracted from the positive margin—or, to put it another way, the negative is added to the positive—and the resulting value is the distance between the elements.

To see what this means, let's start with a paragraph that has a negative top margin and no margins on its other sides—this will keep the example simple. In addition, we'll make the paragraph bold, so that it's easier to distinguish from its neighbors:

```
<P STYLE="margin: -1.75em 0 0 0; font-weight: bold;">
This paragraph has a negative top margin...
</P>
```

We can see in Figure 7-18 that the paragraph has been pulled up so far that it's practically overlapping the end of the previous paragraph. This is the expected effect.

In a like manner, setting a negative value on the other sides will pull them beyond their normal limits:

```
<P STYLE="margin: -2em; font-weight: bold;">...
```

As Figure 7-19 makes abundantly clear, the paragraph has spilled beyond the edges of the browser window and has not only pulled up far enough to overlap the end of the previous paragraph, but has also pulled the following paragraph up to overlap its last line.

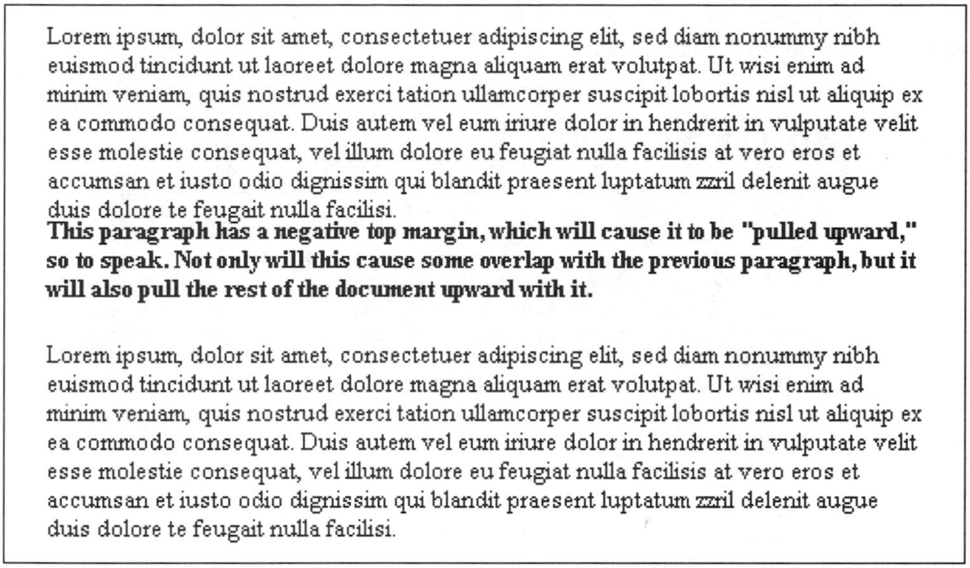

Lorem ipsum, dolor sit amet, consectetuer adipiscing elit, sed diam nonummy nibh euismod tincidunt ut laoreet dolore magna aliquam erat volutpat. Ut wisi enim ad minim veniam, quis nostrud exerci tation ullamcorper suscipit lobortis nisl ut aliquip ex ea commodo consequat. Duis autem vel eum iriure dolor in hendrerit in vulputate velit esse molestie consequat, vel illum dolore eu feugiat nulla facilisis at vero eros et accumsan et iusto odio dignissim qui blandit praesent luptatum zzril delenit augue duis dolore te feugait nulla facilisi.
This paragraph has a negative top margin, which will cause it to be "pulled upward," so to speak. Not only will this cause some overlap with the previous paragraph, but it will also pull the rest of the document upward with it.

Lorem ipsum, dolor sit amet, consectetuer adipiscing elit, sed diam nonummy nibh euismod tincidunt ut laoreet dolore magna aliquam erat volutpat. Ut wisi enim ad minim veniam, quis nostrud exerci tation ullamcorper suscipit lobortis nisl ut aliquip ex ea commodo consequat. Duis autem vel eum iriure dolor in hendrerit in vulputate velit esse molestie consequat, vel illum dolore eu feugiat nulla facilisis at vero eros et accumsan et iusto odio dignissim qui blandit praesent luptatum zzril delenit augue duis dolore te feugait nulla facilisi.

Figure 7-18. Negative top margin

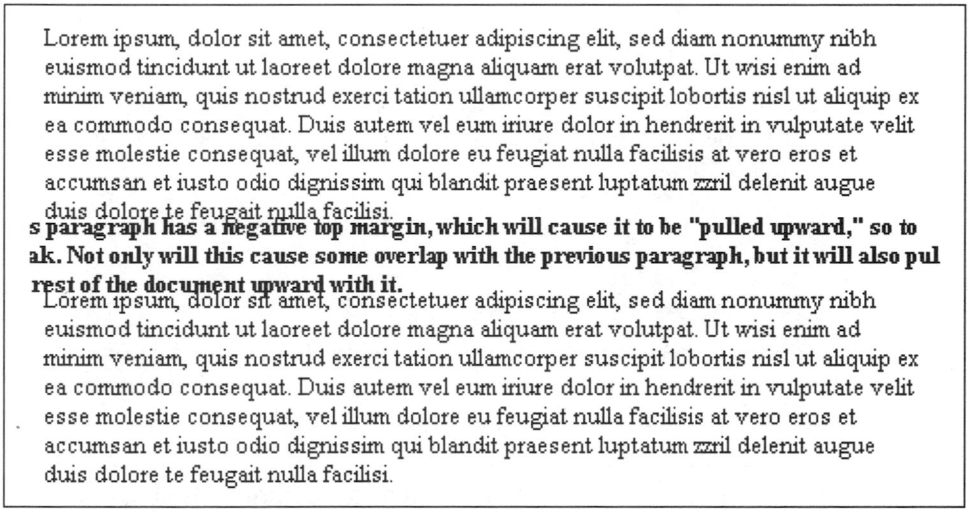

Lorem ipsum, dolor sit amet, consectetuer adipiscing elit, sed diam nonummy nibh euismod tincidunt ut laoreet dolore magna aliquam erat volutpat. Ut wisi enim ad minim veniam, quis nostrud exerci tation ullamcorper suscipit lobortis nisl ut aliquip ex ea commodo consequat. Duis autem vel eum iriure dolor in hendrerit in vulputate velit esse molestie consequat, vel illum dolore eu feugiat nulla facilisis at vero eros et accumsan et iusto odio dignissim qui blandit praesent luptatum zzril delenit augue duis dolore te feugait nulla facilisi.
s paragraph has a negative top margin, which will cause it to be "pulled upward," so to ak. Not only will this cause some overlap with the previous paragraph, but it will also pul rest of the document upward with it.
Lorem ipsum, dolor sit amet, consectetuer adipiscing elit, sed diam nonummy nibh euismod tincidunt ut laoreet dolore magna aliquam erat volutpat. Ut wisi enim ad minim veniam, quis nostrud exerci tation ullamcorper suscipit lobortis nisl ut aliquip ex ea commodo consequat. Duis autem vel eum iriure dolor in hendrerit in vulputate velit esse molestie consequat, vel illum dolore eu feugiat nulla facilisis at vero eros et accumsan et iusto odio dignissim qui blandit praesent luptatum zzril delenit augue duis dolore te feugait nulla facilisi.

Figure 7-19. Negative margin

Negative percentages are also permitted. These will behave like any negative length value, with the obvious difference that the amount of negativity will depend on the width of the parent element. Thus:

```
P {margin: -10%;}
```

Figure 7-20 illustrates the consequences of such a rule, where the amount by which paragraphs overlap each other and spill beyond the browser window is entirely dependent on the width of the window itself—and the wider the window, the worse the situation becomes.

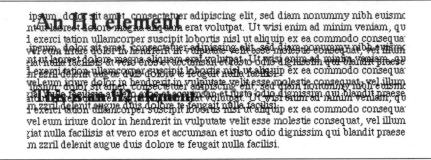

Figure 7-20. The dangers of document-wide negative-margin rules

Using negative margins with block-level elements such as these can quite obviously be dangerous and is rarely worth the trouble—but it can also be rewarding. It takes a good deal of practice, and many mistakes, to learn to tell the difference between the two.

Margins and Inline Elements

So far, we've only talked about how margins apply to block-level elements like paragraphs and headers. Margins can also be applied to inline elements, although the effects are a little different.

Let's say that you want to set top and bottom margins on boldfaced text. You declare:

```
B {margin-top: 25px; margin-bottom: 50px;}
```

This is allowed in the specification, but it will have absolutely no effect on the line height, and since margins are effectively transparent, this will have no visual effect whatsoever—as you can see for yourself in Figure 7-21.

> This paragraph contains a small amount of **boldfaced text** to which a margin has been applied.

Figure 7-21. Margins on an inline element

This happens because margins on inline elements don't change the line height of an element. (In fact, the only properties that can change the distance between lines containing only text are `line-height`, `font-size`, and `vertical-align`.)

However, all of this is true only for the top and bottom sides of inline elements; the left and right sides are a different story altogether. We'll start by considering the simple case of a small inline element within a single line, as depicted in Figure 7-22.

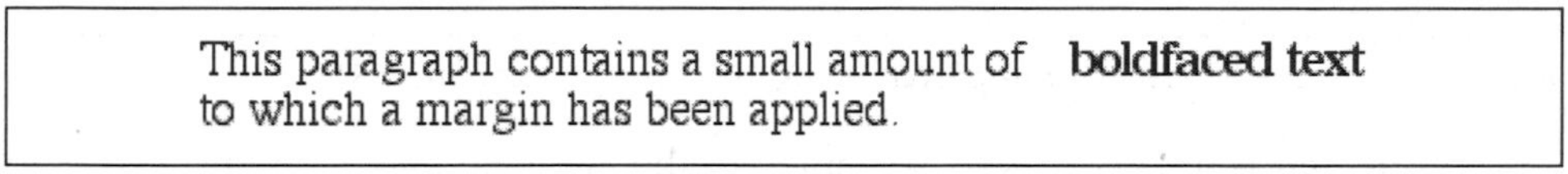

> This paragraph contains a small amount of **boldfaced text** to which a margin has been applied.

Figure 7-22. A single-line inline element with a left margin

Here, if we set values for the left or right margin, they will be visible, as Figure 7-23 makes obvious:

```
B {margin-left: 10px; background: silver;}
```

> This paragraph contains a small amount of **boldfaced text** to which a margin has been applied.

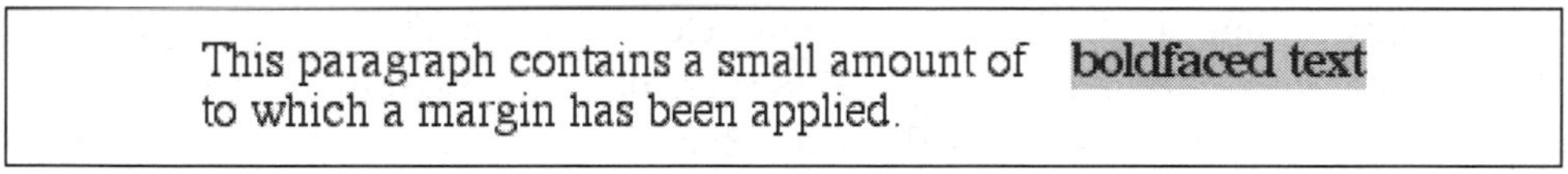

Figure 7-23. An inline element with a left margin

Note the extra space between the end of the word just before the inline element, and the edge of the inline element's background. This can end up on both ends of the inline if we wish:

```
B {margin: 10px; background: silver;}
```

As expected, Figure 7-24 shows a little extra space on the right and left sides of the inline element, and no extra space above or below it.

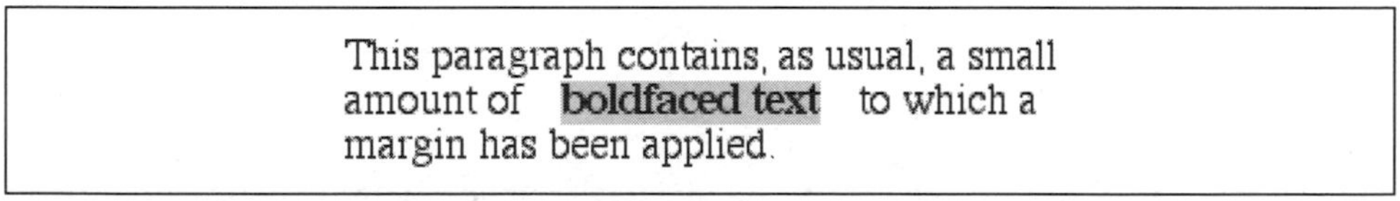

> This paragraph contains, as usual, a small amount of **boldfaced text** to which a margin has been applied.

Figure 7-24. An inline element with a 10-pixel margin

This all seems simple enough, but when the boldfaced text stretches across multiple lines, the situation becomes a little odd. First, realize that the margins set for inline elements are not applied at the point where line-breaking occurs. This line-breaking happens in the course of wrapping text so that it fits inside the browser's window, for example, or inside a parent element. The only effect margins have on line-breaking is that, by causing extra space to appear within the line, they can move content over. This may cause a line to break at a different spot than it ordinarily would have.

Turn to Figure 7-25 to see what happens when an inline element with a margin is displayed across multiple lines:

```
B {margin: 10px; background: silver;}
```

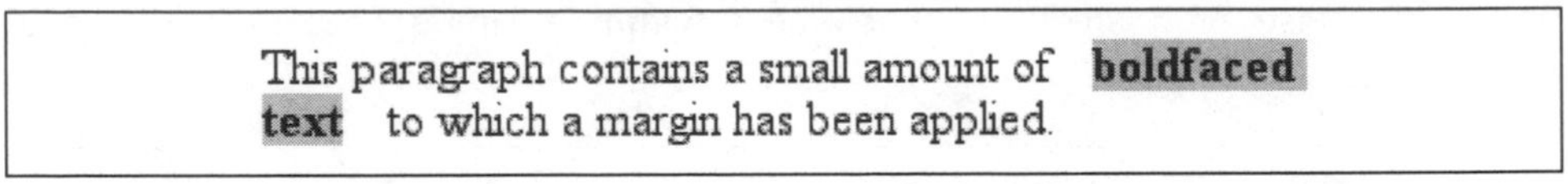

> This paragraph contains a small amount of **boldfaced** **text** to which a margin has been applied.

Figure 7-25. An inline element displayed across two lines of text with a 10-pixel margin

The left margin is applied to the beginning of the element, and the right margin to the end of it. Margins are *not* applied to the right and left side of each line. Also, you can see that if not for the margins, the line may have broken after "text" instead of after "boldfaced." This is the only real way in which margins affect line-breaking.

To understand why, let's go back to the paper-and-plastic analogy employed in the previous section. Think of an inline element as a strip of paper with marginal plastic surrounding it. Displaying the inline element on multiple lines is like cutting up the strip into smaller strips. However, no extra plastic is added to each smaller strip. The only plastic used is that which was on the strip to begin with, so it only appears at the beginning and end of the inline element.

Margins: Known Issues

As useful as margins are, a number of problems can arise with their use—enough, in fact, that they warrant their own section, instead of just a small warning box.

The first is that Navigator 4.x generally *adds* margin rules to its built-in margins, instead of replacing the built-in values. For example, let's say you want to eliminate the space between H1 elements and paragraphs. Here's the simplest case for doing so:

```
H1 {margin-bottom: 0;}
P {margin-top: 0;}
```

This is, after all, one correct way to eliminate the space between succeeding elements. Navigator 4.x, however, will display the elements with the usual blank line between them, as you can see in Figure 7-26. This is because it's adding the zero values to its own default margins.

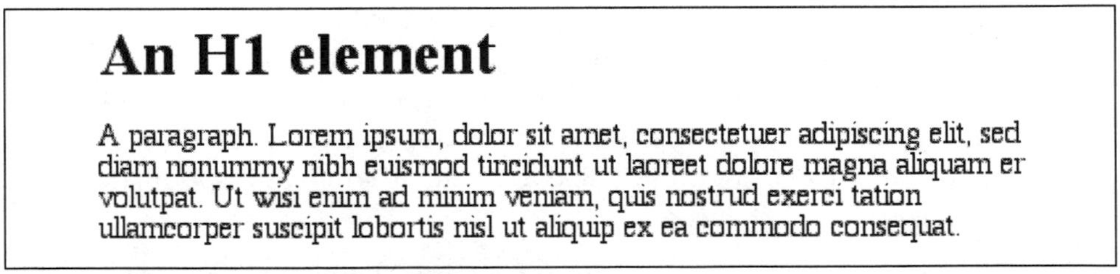

An H1 element

A paragraph. Lorem ipsum, dolor sit amet, consectetuer adipiscing elit, sed diam nonummy nibh euismod tincidunt ut laoreet dolore magna aliquam er volutpat. Ut wisi enim ad minim veniam, quis nostrud exerci tation ullamcorper suscipit lobortis nisl ut aliquip ex ea commodo consequat.

Figure 7-26. Navigator 4.x and margins

If you want to overcome this space, you can always use negative margins. Here's one possible declaration:

```
H1 {margin-bottom: 0;}
P {margin-top: -1em;}
```

The problem with this solution arises when the document is viewed in Internet Explorer, which will display what's shown in Figure 7-27. The overlapping text is not a mistake on Explorer's part—it's doing exactly as you specified. Basically, there isn't an easy way to circumvent this problem, although two possible approaches are detailed in Chapter 11, *CSS in Action*.

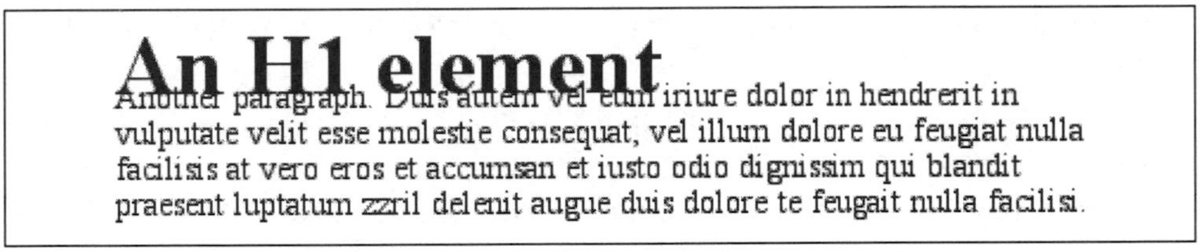

Figure 7-27. Overlapping text in Explorer

It gets worse, unfortunately. If you apply margins to inline elements, as was discussed previously, you'll get results from Navigator 4.x like those shown in Figure 7-28.

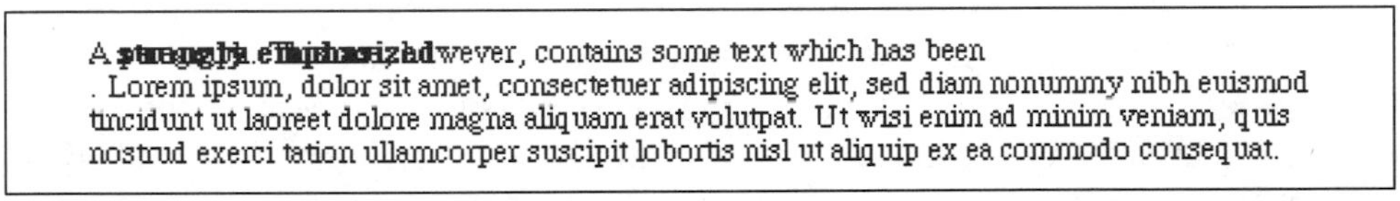

Figure 7-28. Margins, inline elements, and Navigator 4.x

The style used to generate Figure 7-28 was as follows:

```
STRONG {margin-left: 10px;}
```

Instead of adding ten pixels of blank space to the beginning of the STRONG element, Navigator assumes that the margin refers to the left edge of the browser window, and places the STRONG element accordingly This is utterly, completely wrong. (There are those who speculate that Navigator turns the inline element into a block-level element, but its placement implies that things may be otherwise. It's difficult to be sure.) Unfortunately, the fact that this happens means that the use of margins on inline elements is a risky proposition, and not one to be undertaken lightly.

Borders

The border of an element is simply a line (sometimes more than one) that surrounds the content and padding of an element. Thus, the background of the element will stop at the outer edge of the border, since the background does not extend into the margins, and the border is just inside the margin. The CSS specification strongly implies that the background extends to the outside edge of the border, since it talks about the borders being drawn "on top of the background of the element," but not all browsers seem to agree. This is important because some borders are "intermittent"—for example, dotted and dashed styles—and the element's background should appear in the spaces between the visible portions of the border.

Every border has three aspects: its width, or thickness; its style, or appearance; and its color. The default value for the width of a border is `medium`, which is not explicitly defined but usually works out to be two or three pixels. Despite this, the reason you don't usually see borders is that the default style is `none`, which prevents them from existing. If a border has no style, then it may as well not exist, so it doesn't. The absence of a border style also resets the width, but we'll get to that in a little while.

Finally, the default border color is the foreground color of the element itself. If no color has been declared for the border, then it will be the same color as the text of the element. If, on the other hand, an element has no text—let's say a table which contains only images—then thanks to the fact that color is inherited, the border color for that table would be the text color of its parent element. This is likely to be BODY, DIV, or another TABLE. Thus, if an image has a border, and the BODY is its parent, given this rule:

```
BODY {color: purple;}
```

then, by default, the border around the image will be purple. Of course, to get that border to appear, you have to do a little work first.

Borders with Style

We'll talk about the border's style first because it is the most important part of a border. It's most important not because it controls the appearance of the border, although it does do that, but because without a style there would be no border at all.

border-style

Values	none | dotted | dashed | solid | double | groove | ridge | inset | outset
Initial value	none
Inherited	no
Applies to	all elements

Note: Support for only solid is required for CSS1 compliance.

There are nine distinct styles for the property border-style defined in CSS1, including the default value of none. They are demonstrated in Figure 7-29.

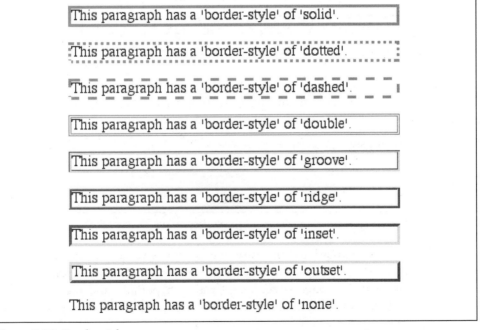

Figure 7-29. Border styles

The most interesting border style is `double`. It's defined such that the width of the two lines, plus the width of the space between them, is equal to the value of `border-width` (discussed in the next section). However, the specification doesn't say whether one of the lines should be thicker than the other, or if they should be the same width, or if the space should be thicker or thinner than the lines. All of these things are left up to the user agent to decide.

All of the borders shown in Figure 7-29 are based on a color of `gray`, which makes all of the effects easier to see. The look of a border style is always based in some way on the color of the border, although the exact method may vary between user agents. For example, Figure 7-30 illustrates two different ways of rendering an `inset` border.

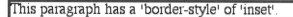

Figure 7-30. Two valid ways of rendering inset

So let's assume that you want to define a border style for images that are inside a hyperlink. You might make them outset, so they have a "raised button" look, as depicted in Figure 7-31:

```
A:link IMG {border-style: outset;}
```

Figure 7-31. Applying an outset border to a hyperlinked image

Again, the color of the border is based on the element's value for `color`, which in this circumstance is likely to be blue (although we can't show that in print). This is due to the fact that the image is contained with a hyperlink, and the foreground color of hyperlinks is usually `blue`. If we so desired, we could change that color to be `silver`, like this:

```
A:link IMG {border-style: outset; color: silver;}
```

As Figure 7-32 shows, the border is now based on the light gray `silver`, since that's now the foreground color of the image—even though the image doesn't actually use that color, it's still passed on to the border. We'll talk about another way to change border colors in a later section.

Figure 7-32. Changing the color of the border

Multiple styles

It's also possible to define more than one style for a given border. For example:

```
P.aside {border-style: solid dashed dotted solid;}
```

The result, shown in Figure 7-33, is a paragraph with a solid top border, a dashed right border, a dotted bottom border, and a solid left border.

A normal paragraph. Lorem ipsum, dolor sit amet, consectetuer adipiscing elit, sed diam nonummy nibh euismod tincidunt ut laoreet dolore magna aliquam erat volutpat.

Just as an aside, it's possible to set different border styles on the same element.

Another normal paragraph. Ut wisi enim ad minim veniam, quis nostrud exerci tation ullamcorper suscipit lobortis nisl ut aliquip ex ea commodo consequat.

Figure 7-33. Multiple border styles on a single element

Again we see the top-right-bottom-left order of values. This is just like the ability to set different margins with multiple values. All the same rules about value replication apply to border styles, just as they did with margins and padding. Thus, the following two statements would have the same effect, as depicted in Figure 7-34:

```
P.new1 {border-style: solid dashed none;}
P.new2 {border-style: solid dashed none dashed;}
```

A paragraph of class 'new1'. Lorem ipsum, dolor sit amet, consectetuer adipiscing elit, sed diam nonummy nibh euismod tincidunt ut laoreet dolore magna aliquam erat volutpat.

A paragraph of class 'new2'. Note the similarities in the borders. Ut wisi enim ad minim veniam, quis nostrud exerci tation ullamcorper suscipit lobortis nisl ut aliquip ex ea commodo consequat.

Figure 7-34. Equivalent style rules

In case you're wondering, under CSS1, there is no way to directly set the style for only a single side using something like `border-top-style`, since no such property exists in CSS1 (although that property, and others like it, were introduced in CSS2). You can, however, sneak around this limitation by declaring the style for a given border using one of the shorthand properties we'll discuss later in the chapter.

Falling back on solid

There is one interesting thing about CSS that can make life difficult for authors. According to CSS1, a user agent is allowed to interpret any value of `border-style` (besides `none`) as `solid`. Because of this allowance, a user agent that is technically CSS1-compliant could display the following as all solid:

```
P.new3 {border-style: ridge dashed double;}
```

The result shown in Figure 7-35 wouldn't be what the author had in mind, of course, but it's technically correct. So long as `none` and `solid` are supported, and any other legal values are interpreted as `solid`, that's enough to be CSS1-compliant. Accordingly, even though Navigator 4.x fails to render `dashed` and `dotted` borders, since it does render them as `solid`, it's not behaving badly.

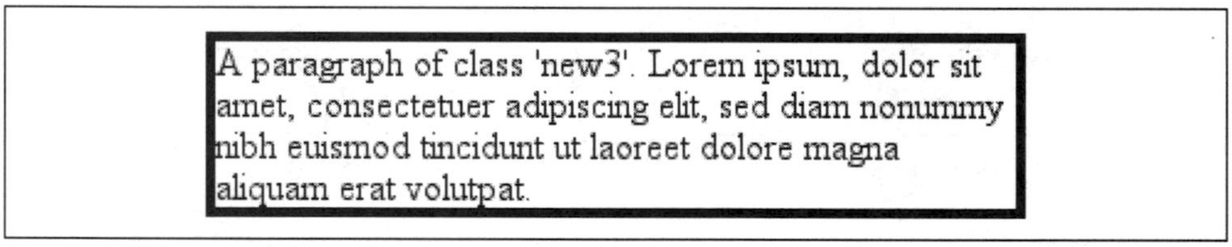

A paragraph of class 'new3'. Lorem ipsum, dolor sit amet, consectetuer adipiscing elit, sed diam nonummy nibh euismod tincidunt ut laoreet dolore magna aliquam erat volutpat.

Figure 7-35. Using solid to stand in for unrecognized border styles

You may have noticed that all of the examples in this section had borders of exactly the same width. That's because we didn't define a width, so it defaulted to a certain value. Next, we'll find out about that default, and much more.

Border Widths

Once you've assigned a style, the next step in customizing a border is to give it some width. This is done with the property `border-width`. You can also use one of the cousin properties: `border-top-width`, `border-right-width`, `border-button-width`, and `border-left-width`.

Each of these is used to set the width on a specific border side, of course, just as with the margin properties.

border-width

Values	[thin	medium	thick	<length>]{1,4}
Initial value	not defined for shorthand properties
Inherited	no
Applies to	all elements

border-top-width, border-right-width, border-bottom-width, border-left-width

Values	thin	medium	thick	<length>
Initial value	medium
Inherited	no
Applies to	all elements

There are four ways to assign a width to a border: you can give it a length value such as 4px or 0.1em or use one of three keywords. These keywords are thin, medium (the default value), and thick. These keywords don't necessarily correspond to any particular width but are simply defined in relation to one another. According to the specification, thick is always wider than medium, which is in turn always wider than thin.

However, the exact widths are not defined, so one user agent could set them to be equivalent to 5px, 3px, and 2px, while another sets them to be 3px, 2px, and 1px. Whatever width the user agent uses for each keyword, it will be the same throughout the document, regardless of the circumstances. If medium is the same as 2px, then a medium-width border will always be two pixels wide, whether the border surrounds an H1 or a P element. Figure 7-36 illustrates one way to handle these three keywords, as well as how they relate to each other and to the content they surround.

Let's suppose a paragraph has margins, a background color, and a border style set as shown in Figure 7-37:

```
P {margin: 5px; background-color: silver; border-style: solid;}
```

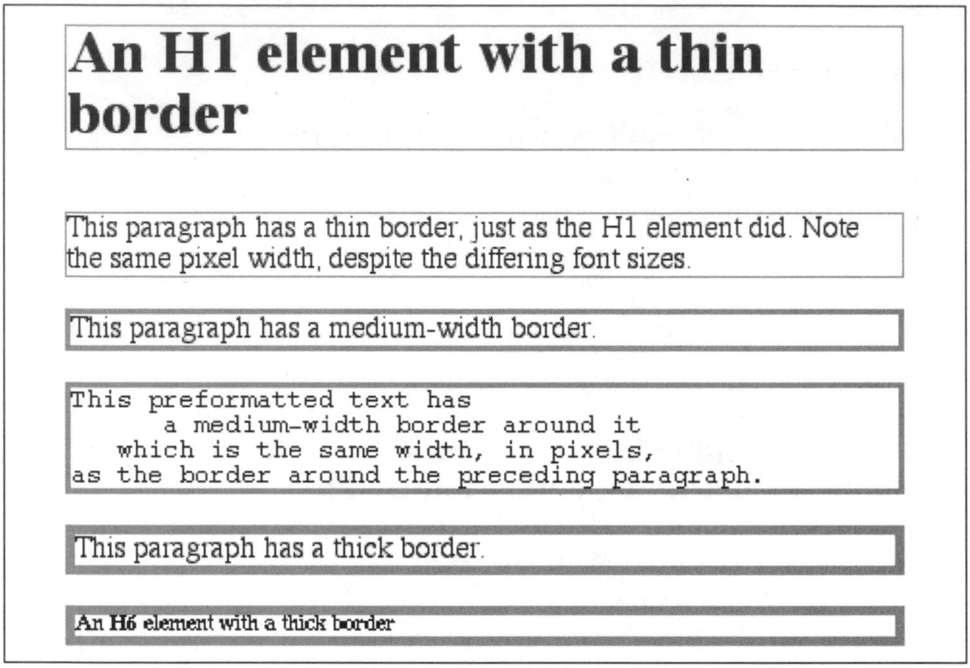

An H1 element with a thin border

This paragraph has a thin border, just as the H1 element did. Note the same pixel width, despite the differing font sizes.

This paragraph has a medium-width border.

```
This preformatted text has
        a medium-width border around it
    which is the same width, in pixels,
as the border around the preceding paragraph.
```

This paragraph has a thick border.

An H6 element with a thick border

Figure 7-36. The relation of border-width keywords to each other

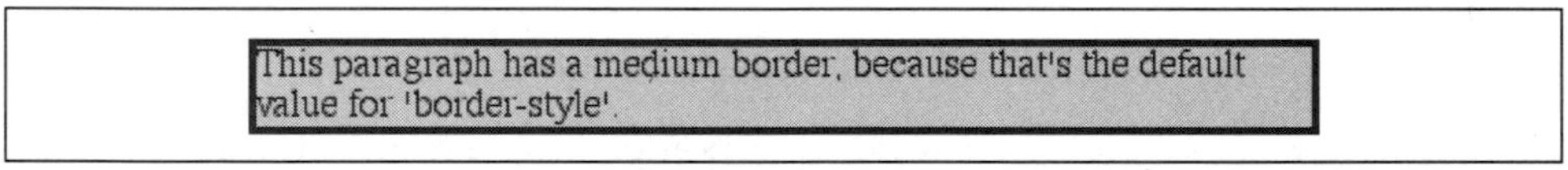

This paragraph has a medium border, because that's the default value for 'border-style'.

Figure 7-37. Margins, backgrounds, and borders

The border's width is, by default, `medium`, as we can see in Figure 7-37. We can change that to the result in Figure 7-38 as follows:

```
P {margin: 5px; background-color: silver;
   border-style: solid; border-width: thick;}
```

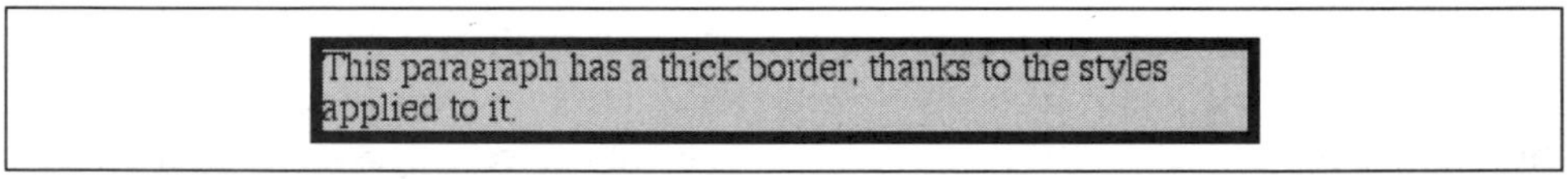

This paragraph has a thick border, thanks to the styles applied to it.

Figure 7-38. Changing the width of the border

This can be taken to fairly ridiculous extremes, such as setting 20-pixel borders as depicted in Figure 7-39:

```
P {margin: 5px; background-color: silver;
   border-style: solid; border-width: 20px;}
```

This is all as expected: the style and width combine to create a border whose color is based on the foreground color of the element.

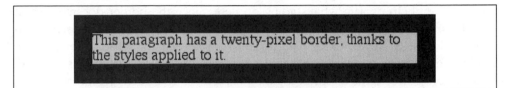

Figure 7-39. Inflating the border width to unhealthy levels

It's also possible to set widths for individual sides. This is done in two familiar ways. The first is to use any of the specific properties mentioned at the beginning of the section, such as `border-bottom-width`. The other way is to use value replication in `border-width`. These are both illustrated in Figure 7-40.

```
H1 {border-style: none none dotted; border-bottom-width: thin;}
P {border-style: solid; border-width: 15px 2px 7px 4px;}
```

An H1 element with
variable-width borders

This paragraph has a variable-width border, thanks to the styles applied to it. This can be used in a variety of ways to create interesting effects.

Figure 7-40. Value replication and uneven border widths

No border at all

So far, we've only talked about what happens when you're using a visible border style such as `solid` or `outset`. Things start to get interesting, though, when the border style is set to be `none`:

```
P {margin: 5px; border-style: none; border-width: 20px;}
```

As we can see in Figure 7-41, despite the fact that the border's width was set to be `20px`, when the style is set to `none`, not only does the border's style go away, so does its width! Why?

This paragraph has a border which, although it's defined to be twenty pixels wide, actually doesn't exist at all!

Figure 7-41. The incredible disappearing border

If you'll remember, the terminology used in the previous section was that a border with a style of `none` does not exist. Those words were picked carefully because they help explain what's going on here. Since the border doesn't exist, it can't have any width, so the width is automatically set to 0 (zero). This may seem completely backward, but it actually makes a great deal of sense. After all, if a drinking glass is empty, you can't really describe it as being half-full of nothing. You can only discuss the depth of a glass's contents if it has actual contents. In the same way, talking about the width of a border only makes sense in the context of borders that have some existence.

This is important to bear in mind because a common mistake is to forget to declare a border style. This leads to all kinds of author frustration because at first glance, the styles appear correct. The result, though, is a paragraph with no border:

```
P {margin: 5px; border-width: 20px;}
```

Since the default value of **border-style** is **none**, failure to declare a style is exactly the same as declaring **border-style: none**. Therefore, if you want a border to appear, you need to pick a style and declare it.

Border Colors

Compared to the other aspects of borders, setting the color is pretty easy. In CSS1, there is the single property **border-color**, which can accept up to four color values at one time.

---

border-color

Values	<color>{1,4}
Initial value	the value of <color> for the element
Inherited	no
Applies to	all elements

If there are less than four values, value replication takes effect. So if you want H1 elements to have thin, black top and bottom borders with thick, gray side borders, and medium, gray borders around P elements, this will suffice, as we can see in Figure 7-42:

```
H1 {border-style: solid; border-width: thin thick; border-color: black gray;}
P {border-style: solid; border-color: gray;}
```

By default, a single color value will be applied to all four sides, as with the paragraph in the previous example. On the other hand, if you supply four color val-

An H1 element with variable borders

This paragraph has a solid gray medium border, thanks to the styles applied to it. (The width of 'medium' is inferred from the default value for 'border-width', which is not declared for this element.)

Figure 7-42. Borders have many aspects

ues, you can get a different color on each side. Any type of color value can be used, from named colors to hexadecimal and RGB values.

```
P {border-style: solid; border-width: thick;
   border-color: black rgb(25%,25%,25%) #808080 silver;}
```

Figure 7-43 shows us varying shades of gray for borders. Thanks to the grayscale nature of this book, I've been sticking mostly to shades of gray, but any color could be used. If you wanted an H1 with a red, green, blue, and yellow border, it's this easy:

```
H1 {border-style: solid; border-color: red green blue yellow;}
```

This paragraph has a solid thick border of various colors (okay, shades of gray), thanks to the styles applied to it.

Figure 7-43. One border, many colors

As previously discussed, if no colors are defined, then the default color is the foreground color of the element. Thus, the following declaration will be displayed as shown in Figure 7-44:

```
P.shade1 {border-style: solid; border-width: thick; color: gray;}
P.shade2 {border-style: solid; border-width: thick; color: gray;
   border-color: black;}
```

This paragraph has a solid gray thick border.

This paragraph has a solid black thick border.

Figure 7-44. Border colors based on the element's foreground (top) and the value of the border-color property (bottom)

The result is that the first paragraph has a gray border, having taken the value `gray` from the foreground color of the paragraph itself. The second paragraph, on the other hand, has a black border because that color was explicitly assigned using `border-color`.

Shorthand Border Properties

While it's nice to have shorthand properties like `border-color` and `border-style`, they aren't always a whole lot of help. For example, you might want to set all `H1` elements to have a thick, gray, solid border, but only along the bottom. There are two ways to accomplish this:

```
H1 {border-bottom-width: thick;    /* option #1 */
   border-style: none none solid;
   border-color: gray;}
H1 {border-width: 0 0 thick;       /* option #2 */
   border-style: none none solid;
   border-color: gray;}
```

Neither is really convenient, given all the typing involved. Fortunately, a better solution is available:

```
H1 {border-bottom: thick solid gray;}
```

This will apply the values to the bottom border alone, as shown in Figure 7-45, leaving the others to their defaults. Since the default border style is **none**, no borders appear on the other three sides of the element.

An H1 element, with a bottom border

Figure 7-45. Shorthand properties make styles easier

As you may have guessed, there are a total of four such shorthand properties.

border-top, border-right, border-bottom, border-left

Values	<border-width> || <border-style> || <color>
Initial value	refer to individual properties
Inherited	no
Applies to	all elements

It's possible to use these properties to create some complex borders, such as those shown in Figure 7-46:

```
H1 {border-left: 3px solid gray;
    border-right: black 0.25em dotted;
    border-top: thick silver inset;
    border-bottom: double rgb(33%,33%,33%) 10px;}
```

Figure 7-46. Very complex borders

As you can see, the order of the actual values doesn't really matter. The following three rules will yield exactly the same border, as illustrated in Figure 7-47:

```
H1 {border-bottom: 3px solid gray;}
H2 {border-bottom: solid gray 3px;}
H3 {border-bottom: 3px gray solid;}
```

An H1 element with a gray border

An H2 element with a gray border

An H3 element with a gray border

Figure 7-47. Getting the same result in three different ways

You can also leave out some values and have their defaults kick in, like this:

```
H3 {color: gray; border-bottom: 3px solid;}
```

Since no border color is declared, the default value (the element's foreground) is applied instead, as we can see in Figure 7-48. Just remember that if you leave out a border style, the default value of **none** will prevent your border from appearing at all.

An H3 element with a gray border

Figure 7-48. Letting default values fill in the gaps

By contrast, if you set only a style, you will still get a border. For example, let's say you simply want a border style of `dashed` for the top of an element and are willing to let the width default to `medium` and the color to be inherited from the element itself. All you need in such a case is the following:

```
P.roof {border-top: dashed;}
```

Another thing to note is that since each of these "border-side" properties applies only to a specific side, there isn't any possibility of value replication—it wouldn't make any sense. There can only be one of each type of value: that is, only one width value, only one color value, and only one border style. So don't try to declare more than one value type:

```
H3 {border: thin thick solid purple;}  /* two width values--WRONG */
```

In such a case, the entire statement will be invalid and should be ignored altogether.

Finally, you need to take the usual precautions with shorthand properties: if you omit a value, the default will be filled in automatically. This can have unintended effects. Consider the following:

```
H4 {border-style: dashed solid double;}
H4 {border: medium green;}
```

This will result in **H4** elements having no border at all, because the lack of a border-style in the second rule means that the default value of **none** will be used. As we've seen, that will turn the border off altogether.

Setting borders as quickly as possible

With all of this shorthand stuff, you're probably starting to suspect that it goes even further, and you're right. We finally come to the shortest shorthand border property of all: `border`.

---

border

Values	<border-width> || <border-style> || <color>
Initial value	refer to individual properties
Inherited	no
Applies to	all elements

This property has the advantage of being very compact, although that brevity introduces a few limitations. Before we worry about that, let's see how **border** is used. If you want all H1 elements to have a thick, silver border, it's very simple. This declaration would be displayed as shown in Figure 7-49:

```
H1 {border: thick silver solid;}
```

Figure 7-49. A really short border declaration

The values are applied to all four sides. This is certainly preferable to the next-best alternative, which would be:

```
H1 {border-top: thick silver solid;
   border-bottom: thick silver solid;
   border-right: thick silver solid;
   border-left: thick silver solid;}   /* same as previous markup */
```

The drawback with `border` is that you can only define "global" styles, widths, and colors. In other words, the values you supply for `border` will apply to all four sides equally. If you want the borders to be different for a single element, you'll need to use some of the other border properties. Of course, it's possible to turn the cascade to your advantage:

```
H1 {border: thick silver solid;
   border-left-width: 20px;}
```

The second rule overrides the width value for the left border assigned by the first rule, thus replacing `thick` with `20px`, as we see in Figure 7-50.

An H1 element with a silver border

Figure 7-50. Using the cascade to one's advantage

Borders and Inline Elements

A lot of this story will sound pretty familiar because it's largely the same as what we discussed with margins and inline elements.

In the first place, no matter how thick you make your borders on inline elements, the line-height of the element won't change. Let's set top and bottom borders on boldfaced text:

```
B {border-top: 10px solid gray; border-bottom: 5px solid silver;}
```

Once more, this is allowed in the specification, but it will have absolutely no effect on the line height. However, since borders are visible, they'll be drawn—as you can see for yourself in Figure 7-51.

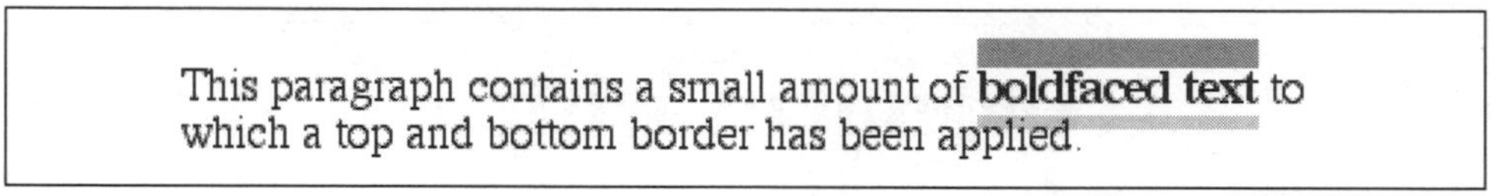

> This paragraph contains a small amount of **boldfaced text** to which a top and bottom border has been applied.

Figure 7-51. Borders on inline elements

The borders have to go somewhere. This is where they went.

Again, all of this is only true for the top and bottom sides of inline elements; the left and right sides are a different story. We'll start by considering the simple case of a small inline element within a single line, as depicted in Figure 7-52.

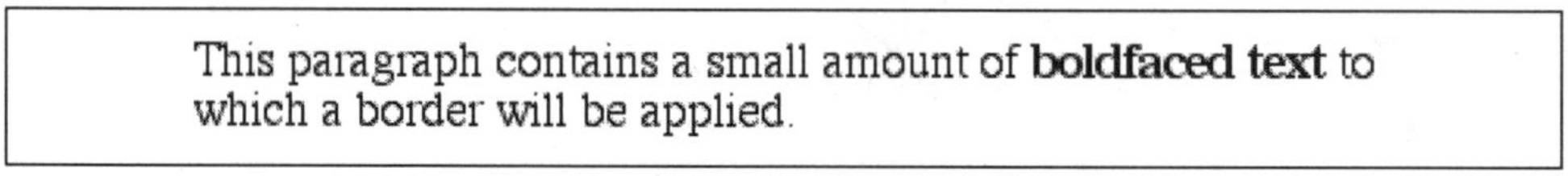

> This paragraph contains a small amount of **boldfaced text** to which a border will be applied.

Figure 7-52. An inline element

Here, if we set values for the left or right border, not only will they be visible, but they'll displace the text around them, as we see in Figure 7-53:

```
B {border-left: 10px double gray; background: silver;}
```

> This paragraph contains a small amount of **boldfaced text** to which a border will be applied.

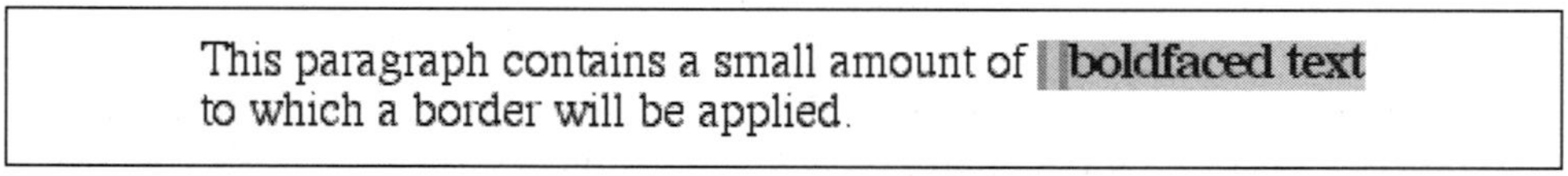

Figure 7-53. An inline element with a left border

As expected, Figure 7-53 shows a little extra space on the left side of the inline element and no extra space above or below it.

With borders, just as with margins, the browser's calculations for line-breaking are not directly affected by any box properties set for inline elements. The only effect is that the space taken up by the borders may shift portions of the line over a bit, which may in turn change which word is at the end of the line. Turn to Figure 7-54 to see what happens when an inline element with a border is displayed across multiple lines:

```
B {border: 3px solid gray; background: silver;}
```

In Figure 7-54, the left border is applied to the beginning of the element, and the right border to the end of it. Borders are *not necessarily* applied in this fashion; they can also be applied to the right and left side of each line in the element, if

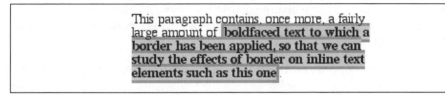

Figure 7-54. An inline element with a border displayed across multiple lines of text

the situation seems to demand it. For example, a grooved border might look better enclosed on each line end, as shown in Figure 7-55.

Figure 7-55. An inline element with a border displayed across multiple lines of text, with the border boxes closed

It's also acceptable for the lines to be "open" as shown in Figure 7-54.

 Borders cannot be applied to inline elements in Navigator 4.x or Explorer 4.x/5.x. Only Opera 3.x draws borders around inline elements, and it only caps the beginning and end of the element. This is in agreement with the CSS specification, although this is not discussed here (see Chapter 8, *Visual Formatting*, for more details).

Borders: Known Issues

Of course, there are a few problems with using borders. The most distressing is the fact that Navigator 4.x won't draw a border around the content area of a block-level element but instead inserts some space between the content and the border. There doesn't seem to be any way to override this behavior.

Despite its limitations, **border** is obviously a very useful property. It can even be used to work around what seems like a completely unrelated bug in Netscape Navigator 4.x. If you assign a background color to an element and then view it in Navigator 4.x, the color will only appear behind the letters in the text and not cover the entire content area and padding. You can get around this by declaring:

```
border {0.1px solid none;}
```

Despite the fact that no border will appear, and this shouldn't have anything to do with background colors, this will cause Navigator 4.x to fill in the background of the content area with the assigned color.

Speaking of Navigator, it is extremely dangerous to set borders—or any other box properties—on inline elements. This is as true for borders as it is for margins, and for much the same reasons.

Padding

Between the borders and the content area, we find the *padding* of the element box. It will come as no surprise that the simplest property used to affect this area is called `padding`.

padding	
Values	[<length> | <percentage>]{1,4}
Initial value	0
Inherited	no
Applies to	all elements

Note: Percentage values refer to the width of the parent element.

As you can see, this property accepts any length value or a percentage. That's all. So if you want all **H1** elements to have 10 pixels of padding on all sides, it's this easy, as the result shown in Figure 7-56 makes clear:

```
H1 {padding: 10px; background-color: silver;}
```

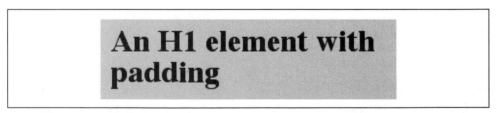

Figure 7-56. Padding applied to an H1 element

On the other hand, we might want **H1** elements to have uneven padding and H2 elements to have regular padding, as shown in Figure 7-57:

```
H1 {padding: 10px 0.25em 3ex 3cm;} /* uneven padding */
H2 {padding: 0.5em 2em;} /* values replicate to the bottom and left sides */
```

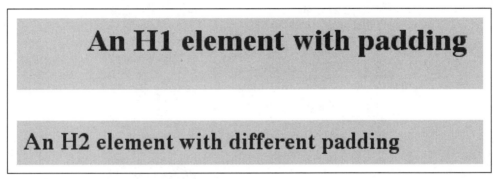

Figure 7-57. Uneven padding

It's a little tough to see the padding, though, so let's add a background color, as shown in Figure 7-58:

```
H1 {padding: 10px 0.25em 3ex 3cm; background: silver;}
H2 {padding: 0.5em 2em; background: silver;}
```

Figure 7-58. Uneven padding with background colors

As Figure 7-58 demonstrates, the background of an element extends into the padding. As we discussed before, it also extends to the outer edge of the border, but the background has to go through the padding before it even gets to the border.

The default value of `padding` is 0 (zero), and padding values cannot be negative.

 Opera 3.5 allows negative padding values, but this was fixed in Opera 3.6. The other browsers don't allow negative padding lengths.

Percentage Values and Padding

As stated earlier, it's possible to set percentage values for the padding of an element. Percentages are computed in relation to the width of the parent element, so they can change if the parent element's width changes in some way. For example, assume the following, which is illustrated in Figure 7-59:

```
P {padding: 10%; background-color: silver;}

<DIV STYLE="width: 200px;">
<P>This paragraph is contained within a DIV which has a width of 200 pixels,
so its padding will be 10% of the width of the paragraph's parent element.
Given the declared width of 200 pixels, the padding will be 20 pixels on
all sides.</P>
</DIV>
<DIV STYLE="width: 100px;">
<P>This paragraph is contained within a DIV with a width of 100 pixels,
so its padding will still be 10% of the width of the paragraph's parent.
There will, therefore, be half as much padding on this paragraph as that
on the first paragraph.</P>
```

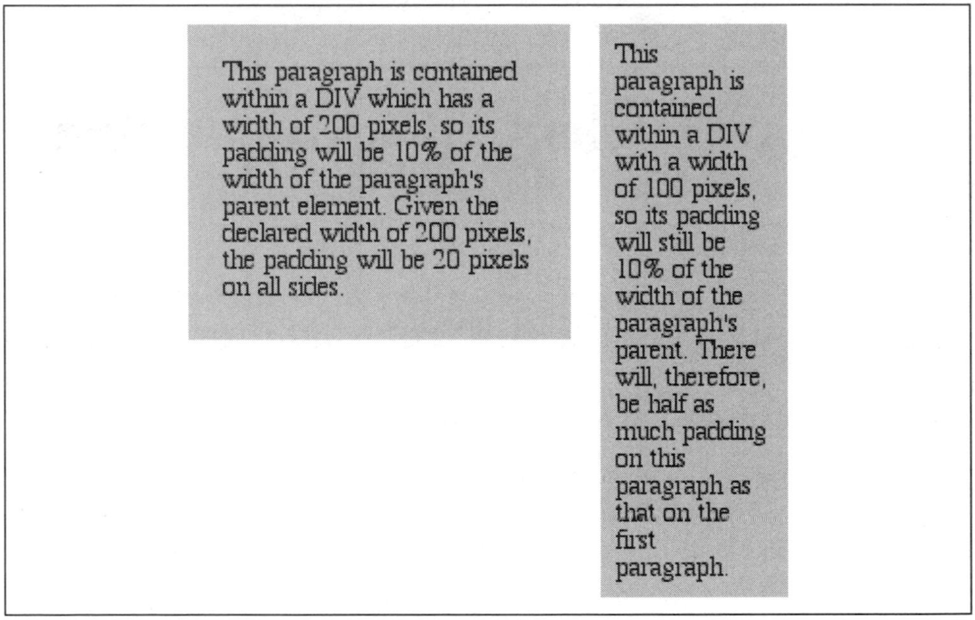

Figure 7-59. Padding, percentages, and the widths of parent

We've seen this before, of course—in the section "Margins," in case you don't remember—but it's worth reviewing again, just to see how it operates.

Single-Side Padding

You guessed it: there are properties that let you set the padding on a single side of the box, without affecting the other sides.

padding-top, padding-right, padding-bottom, padding-left

Values	<length>	<percentage>
Initial value	0
Inherited	no
Applies to	all elements

Note: Percentage values refer to the width of the parent element.

These properties operate as you'd expect by now. For example, the following two rules will give the same amount of padding:

```
H1 {padding: 0 0 0 0.25in;}
H2 {padding-left: 0.25in;}
```

Padding and Inline Elements

There is one major difference between margins and padding when it comes to inline elements. Let's turn things around and talk about left and right padding first off. Here, if we set values for the left or right padding, they will be visible, as Figure 7-60 makes apparent.

```
B {padding-left: 10px; padding-right: 10px; background: silver;}
```

> This paragraph contains a small amount of **boldfaced text** to which padding (and a background color) has been applied.

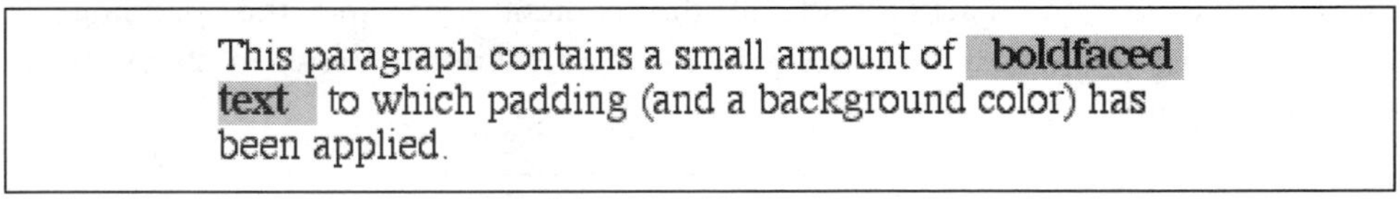

Figure 7-60. Padding on an inline element

Note the extra background space that appears on either end of the boldfaced text. There's your padding.

This all seems familiar enough, even when the boldfaced text stretches across multiple lines. Turn to Figure 7-61 to see what happens with padding set on an inline element displayed across multiple lines:

```
B {padding: 10px; background: silver;}
```

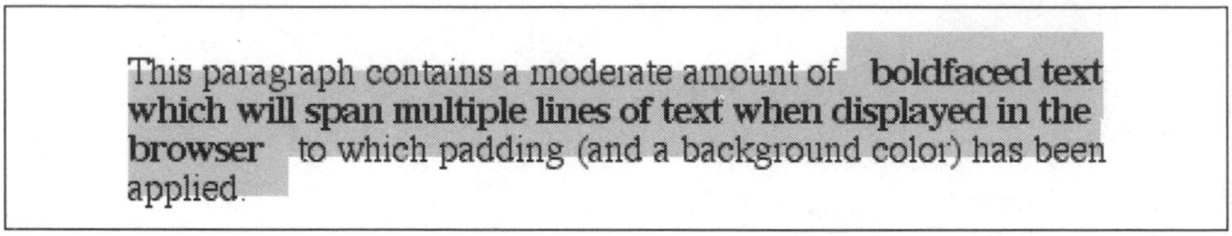

This paragraph contains a moderate amount of **boldfaced text which will span multiple lines of text when displayed in the browser** to which padding (and a background color) has been applied.

Figure 7-61. Padding on an inline element that spans multiple lines

As with margins, the left padding is applied to the beginning of the element, and the right padding to the end of it; padding is *not* applied to the right and left side of each line.

Now let's talk about top and bottom padding. In theory, an inline element with a background color and padding could have the background extend above and below the element. Figure 7-61 gives us some idea of what that might look like. The line height isn't changed, of course, but since padding does extend the background, it should be visible, right?

Here's where the famous phrase returns: "there may be implementation-specific limits." User agents aren't required to support this type of effect.

Padding: Known Issues

In the first place, padding and Navigator 4.x just plain don't get along. The main problem is that you can set padding on an element with a background color, but the background won't extend into the padding unless you get very sneaky. You need to add a border, as was discussed earlier in "Margins: Known Issues." Therefore, if you have a background color, some padding, and a border set for an element, you'll see the background fill the content area and the padding as requested, but a transparent space will incorrectly appear between the two, as shown in Figure 7-62.

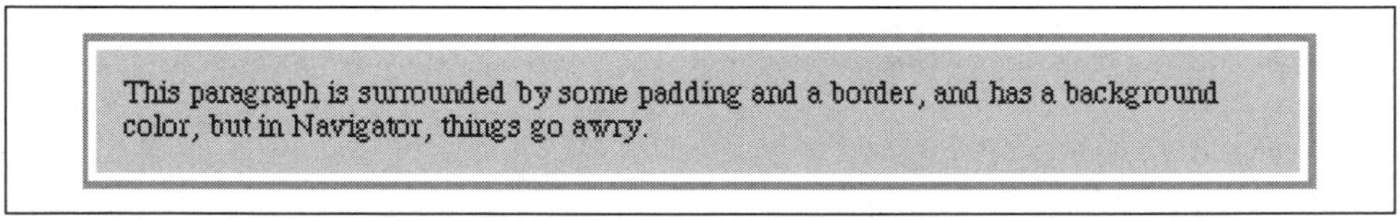

This paragraph is surrounded by some padding and a border, and has a background color, but in Navigator, things go awry.

Figure 7-62. Padding problems in Navigator 4

This may be an interesting effect, but it isn't permissible under the CSS specification, and no other browser will do the same thing, so it's best to avoid this altogether.

Even worse, if you try applying padding to inline elements in Navigator 4.x, you get a huge mess. The same sorts of things that happen when you apply margins to inline elements will happen if you apply padding, so it is wise to avoid setting margins, borders, or padding on inline elements.

Opera 3.5 incorrectly permits negative values for `padding`, but version 3.6 does not suffer from this problem. Internet Explorer 4.x will not apply padding to inline elements at all—which is probably just as well.

Floating and Clearing

You are almost certainly acquainted with the concept of floated elements. Ever since Netscape 1.0, it has been possible to float images by declaring, for instance, `<IMG SRC="b5.gif" align="right">`. This causes an image to float to the right, and allows other content (text or other images) to "flow around" the image. In the past, this was only possible with images and, in some browsers, tables. CSS, on the other hand, allows any element to float, from images to paragraphs to lists. In CSS, this behavior is accomplished using the property `float`.

---

float

Values	`left` | `right` | `none`
Initial value	`none`
Inherited	`no`
Applies to	all elements

For example, to float an image to the right, you could use this markup:

```
<IMG SRC="b5.gif" style="float: right;" alt="section b5">
```

As Figure 7-63 makes clear, the image "floats" to the right side of the browser window. This is just what we expect. However, some interesting issues are raised in the course of floating elements in CSS.

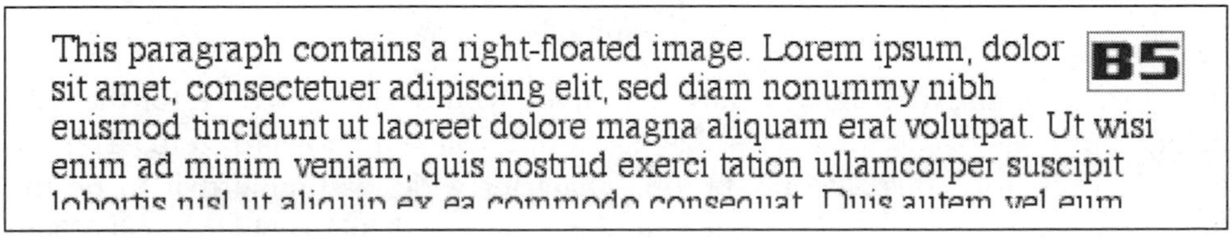

Figure 7-63. A floating image

Floated Elements

There are a few things to keep in mind with regard to floating elements. In the first place, a floated element is in some respects removed from the normal flow of the document, although it still affects the layout. In a manner utterly unique to CSS, floated elements exist almost on their own plane, yet they still have major influence over the rest of the document.

Of course, when an element is floated, other content "flows around" it. This is familiar behavior with floated images, but the same is true if you float a paragraph, for example. In Figure 7-64, we can see this effect (a margin has been added to make the situation more clear):

```
P.aside {float: left; width: 5em; margin: 1em;}
```

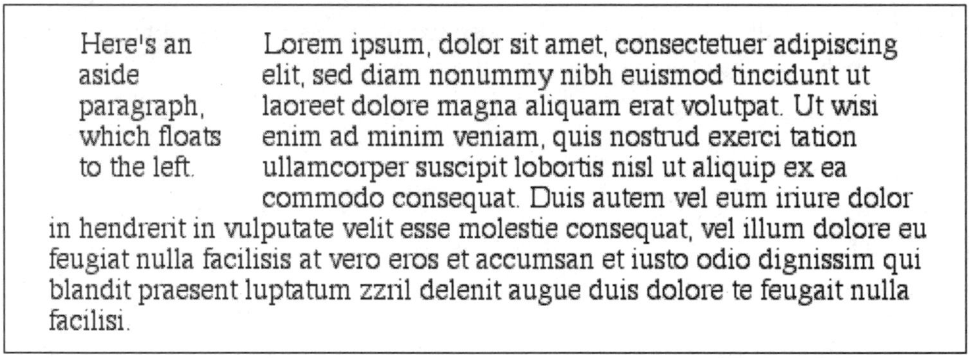

Here's an aside paragraph, which floats to the left.
Lorem ipsum, dolor sit amet, consectetuer adipiscing elit, sed diam nonummy nibh euismod tincidunt ut laoreet dolore magna aliquam erat volutpat. Ut wisi enim ad minim veniam, quis nostrud exerci tation ullamcorper suscipit lobortis nisl ut aliquip ex ea commodo consequat. Duis autem vel eum iriure dolor in hendrerit in vulputate velit esse molestie consequat, vel illum dolore eu feugiat nulla facilisis at vero eros et accumsan et iusto odio dignissim qui blandit praesent luptatum zzril delenit augue duis dolore te feugait nulla facilisi.

Figure 7-64. A floating paragraph

One of the first interesting things to notice about floated elements is that margins around floated elements do not collapse. If you float an image with 20-pixel margins, there will be at least 20 pixels of space around that image. If other elements adjacent to the image—and that means adjacent horizontally *and* vertically— also have margins, those margins will not collapse with the margins on the floated image, as we can see in Figure 7-65:

```
P IMG {float: right; margin: 20px;}
```

(To resurrect the old paper-and-plastic analogy, the plastic margins around an image *never* overlap the plastic surrounding other elements.)

If you do float a text element, realize that unless you declare a `width` for that element, the CSS specification says that its width will tend toward zero. Thus, a floated paragraph could literally be one character wide, assuming that to be the browser's minimum value for `width`. In order to avoid this problem, make sure that you declare a width for your floated elements. Otherwise, you could get something like Figure 7-66.

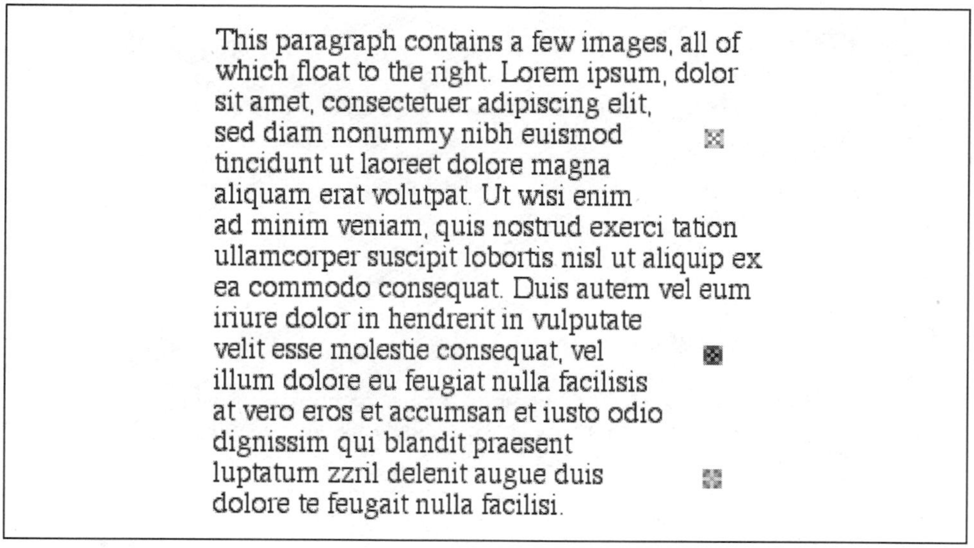

> This paragraph contains a few images, all of which float to the right. Lorem ipsum, dolor sit amet, consectetuer adipiscing elit, sed diam nonummy nibh euismod tincidunt ut laoreet dolore magna aliquam erat volutpat. Ut wisi enim ad minim veniam, quis nostrud exerci tation ullamcorper suscipit lobortis nisl ut aliquip ex ea commodo consequat. Duis autem vel eum iriure dolor in hendrerit in vulputate velit esse molestie consequat, vel illum dolore eu feugiat nulla facilisis at vero eros et accumsan et iusto odio dignissim qui blandit praesent luptatum zzril delenit augue duis dolore te feugait nulla facilisi.

Figure 7-65. Floating images with margins

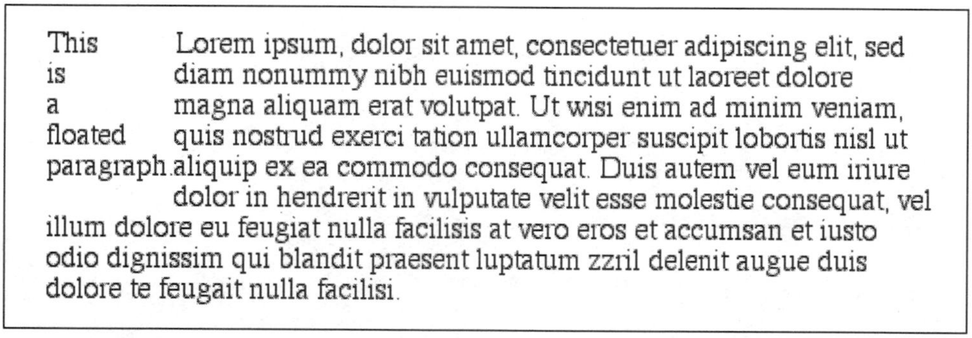

> This is a floated paragraph. Lorem ipsum, dolor sit amet, consectetuer adipiscing elit, sed diam nonummy nibh euismod tincidunt ut laoreet dolore magna aliquam erat volutpat. Ut wisi enim ad minim veniam, quis nostrud exerci tation ullamcorper suscipit lobortis nisl ut aliquip ex ea commodo consequat. Duis autem vel eum iriure dolor in hendrerit in vulputate velit esse molestie consequat, vel illum dolore eu feugiat nulla facilisis at vero eros et accumsan et iusto odio dignissim qui blandit praesent luptatum zzril delenit augue duis dolore te feugait nulla facilisi.

Figure 7-66. Floated text without an explicit width

Backgrounds and floats

There are many other interesting effects associated with floating elements. Take the example of a short document, composed of no more than a few paragraphs and H3 elements, where the first paragraph contains a floated image. Further, this floated image has a right margin of five pixels (5px). You would expect the document to be rendered very much as shown in Figure 7-67.

Nothing unusual there, of course, but look what happens when we set the first paragraph to have a background, as has been done in Figure 7-68.

There is nothing different about the second example, except for the visible background. As you can see, the floated image sticks out of the bottom of its parent element. Of course, it did so in the first example, but it was less obvious there because we couldn't see the background then. There is nothing forbidden about this behavior.

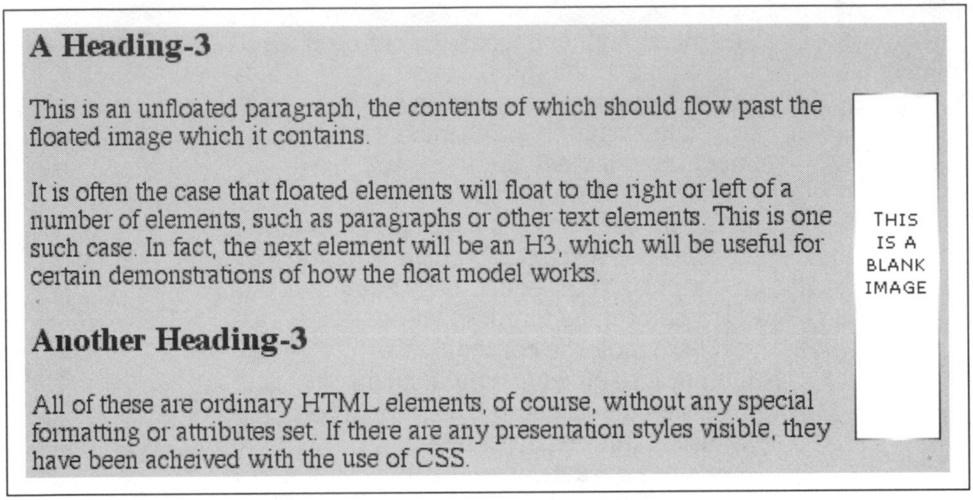

A Heading-3

This is an unfloated paragraph, the contents of which should flow past the floated image which it contains.

It is often the case that floated elements will float to the right or left of a number of elements, such as paragraphs or other text elements. This is one such case. In fact, the next element will be an H3, which will be useful for certain demonstrations of how the float model works.

Another Heading-3

All of these are ordinary HTML elements, of course, without any special formatting or attributes set. If there are any presentation styles visible, they have been acheived with the use of CSS.

THIS
IS A
BLANK
IMAGE

Figure 7-67. Floating an image

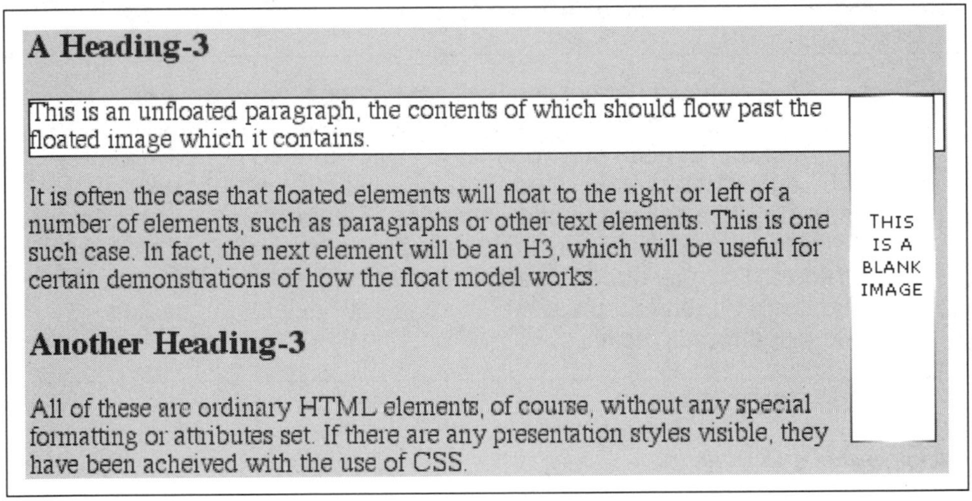

A Heading-3

This is an unfloated paragraph, the contents of which should flow past the floated image which it contains.

It is often the case that floated elements will float to the right or left of a number of elements, such as paragraphs or other text elements. This is one such case. In fact, the next element will be an H3, which will be useful for certain demonstrations of how the float model works.

Another Heading-3

All of these are ordinary HTML elements, of course, without any special formatting or attributes set. If there are any presentation styles visible, they have been acheived with the use of CSS.

THIS
IS A
BLANK
IMAGE

Figure 7-68. Floating images and element backgrounds

 In practice, some browsers may not do this correctly. Instead, they will increase the height of a parent element so that the floated element is contained within it, even though this results in a great deal of extra blank space within the parent element.

Then there is the question of what happens to elements that flow past a floated element but have visible backgrounds. Let's take the preceding example and change it so that the second H3 element has a visible background and border, as has been done in Figure 7-69.

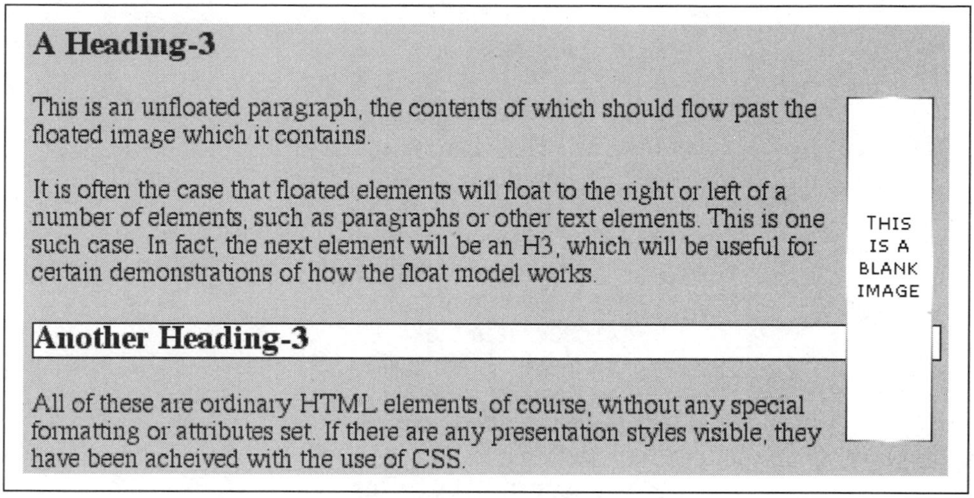

Figure 7-69. More floating images and element backgrounds

Yes, the figure is correct: the content of the H3 flows past the image, and the background "slides under" the image, so to speak. This is, in its way, no different than the example in which the paragraph that contained the floated image had a visible background.

Negative margins and floating

Negativity, of course, always complicates the situation. Let's consider an image that is floated to the left and has left and top margins of -15px. This image is placed inside a DIV that has no padding, borders, or margins. The result will be as shown in Figure 7-70.

The math in this situation works out something like this: assume the top inner edge of the DIV is at the pixel position 100. The browser, in order to figure out where the top inner edge of the floated element should be will do this: 100px + (-15px) margin + 0 padding = 85px. Thus the top inner edge of the floated element should be at pixel position 85.

A similar line of reasoning explains how the left inner edge of the floated element can be placed to the left of the left inner edge of its parent. This ability can be used for interesting effects like hanging floated images, but only if the browser honors negative margins on floated elements. If it does, the result will be something like that shown in Figure 7-71.

There is one important question here, which is this: what happens to the document display when an element is floated out of its parent element by using negative margins? For example, an image could be floated so far up that it intrudes into a paragraph that has already been displayed by the user agent.

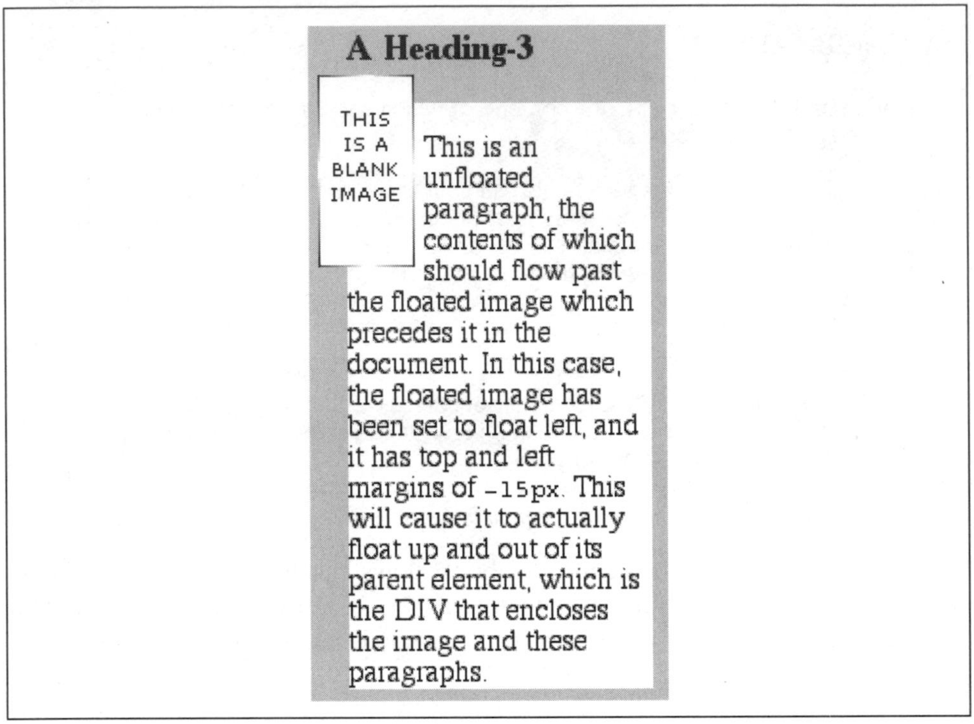

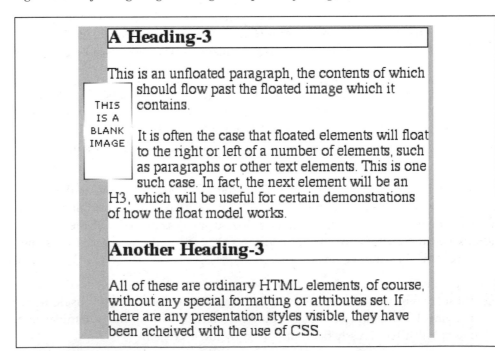

Figure 7-70. A floating image with negative top and left margins

Figure 7-71. Hanging float

In this case, it's up to the user agent, but the CSS specifications explicitly state that user agents are not required to reflow previous content to accommodate things that happen later in the document. In other words, if an image is floated up into a previous paragraph, it may simply overwrite whatever was already there. On the other hand, the user agent may handle the situation by flowing content around the float, even though doing so isn't required behavior. Either way, it's probably a bad idea to count on a particular behavior, which makes the utility of negative margins on floats rather limited. Hanging floats are probably fairly safe, but trying to push an element upward on the page is generally a bad idea.

There is one other case where a floated element can run outside of its parent element, and that's when the floated element is wider than its parent. In that case, the floated element will simply overrun either the right or left inner edge in its best attempt to display itself correctly, depending on which way it was floated. In such a case, you get the result shown in Figure 7-72.

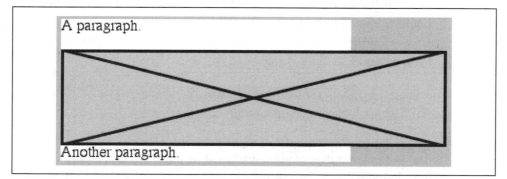

Figure 7-72. Floating an image wider than its parent element

Here, a left-floated image is wider than its parent, so its right edge overruns the right edge of the parent element. Had the image been floated to the right, then it would have overrun the left side of the parent element instead.

No floating at all

There is one other value for `float` besides `left` and `right`. `float: none` is used to prevent an element from floating at all. This might seem a little silly, since the easiest way to keep an element from floating is to simply avoid declaring a float, right? Well, first of all, the default value of `float` is `none`. In other words, the value has to exist in order for normal, nonfloating behavior to be possible; without it, all elements would float in one way or another.

Second, it's possible that you might want to override a certain style from an imported style sheet. Imagine that you're using a server-wide style sheet that floats images. On one particular page, you don't want those images to float. Rather than writing a whole new style sheet, you could simply place `IMG {float: none;}` in your document's embedded style sheet. Beyond this type of circumstance, though, there really isn't much call to use `float: none` in your HTML documents.

Clear

Well, we talked about a lot of floating behavior, so there's only one more thing to discuss. You won't always want your content to flow past a floated element—in some cases, you'll specifically want to prevent it.

If you have a document that is grouped into sections, you might not want the floated elements from one section hanging down into the next. In that case, you'd want to set the first element of each section to prohibit floating elements from appearing next to it. If it might otherwise be placed next to a floated element, it will be pushed down until it appears below the floated image, and all subsequent content will appear after that, as shown in Figure 7-73.

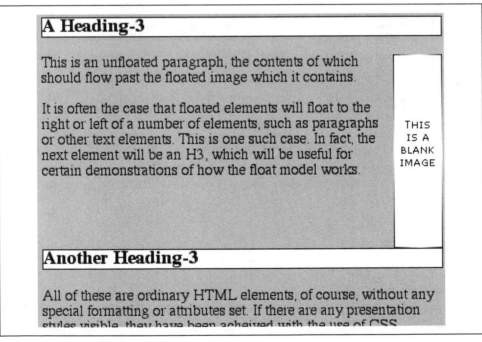

Figure 7-73. Displaying an element in the clear

This is done with `clear`.

---

clear

Values	left | right | both | none
Initial value	none
Inherited	no
Applies to	all elements

For example, to make sure all H2 elements are not placed to the right of left-floated elements, then you would declare H2 {clear: left;}. This can be translated as "make sure that the left side of an H2 is clear of floating images" and is a replacement for the HTML construct <BR clear="left">. Figure 7-74 shows the following declaration, which uses clear to prevent H2 elements from flowing past floated elements to the left side:

```
H2 {clear: left;}
```

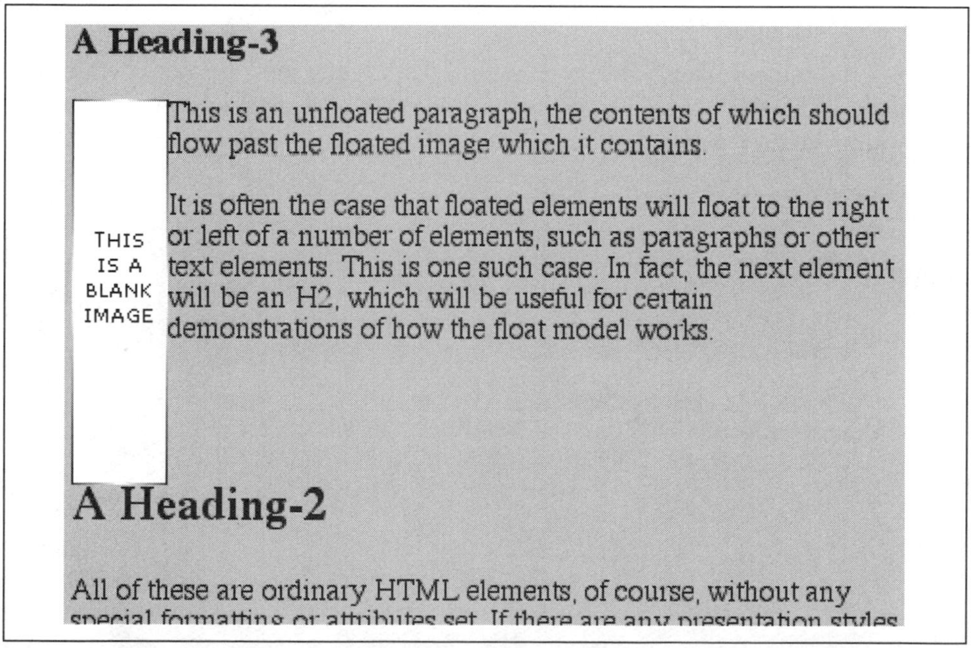

A Heading-3

This is an unfloated paragraph, the contents of which should flow past the floated image which it contains.

> THIS IS A BLANK IMAGE

It is often the case that floated elements will float to the right or left of a number of elements, such as paragraphs or other text elements. This is one such case. In fact, the next element will be an H2, which will be useful for certain demonstrations of how the float model works.

A Heading-2

All of these are ordinary HTML elements, of course, without any special formatting or attributes set. If there are any presentation styles

Figure 7-74. Clear to the left

However, this will allow floated elements to appear on the right side of H2 elements, as shown in Figure 7-75.

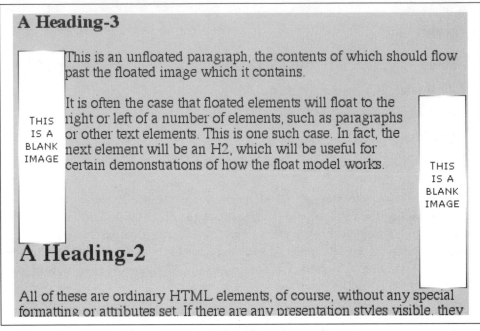

Figure 7-75. Clear to the left, but not the right

To avoid this sort of thing, and to make sure that H2 elements do not coexist on a line with any floated elements, we use the value both. This value prevents coexistence with floated elements on both sides of the element, as shown in Figure 7-76:

```
H2 {clear: both;}
```

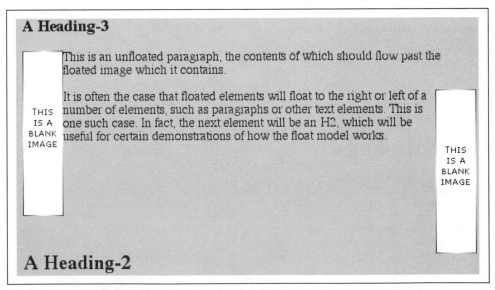

Figure 7-76. Clear on both sides

If, on the other hand, we're only worried about H2 elements flowing past floated elements to their right, then we'd use H2 {clear: right;}, with the result shown in Figure 7-77.

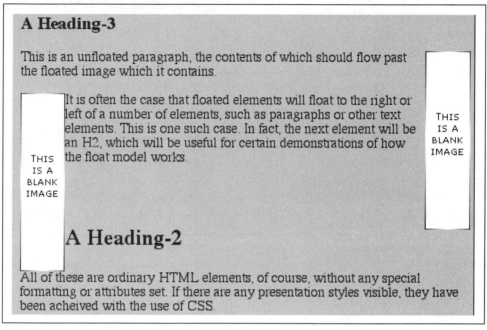

Figure 7-77. Clear to the right

Finally, there's clear: none, which allows elements to float to either side of an element. As with float: none, this value mostly exists to allow for normal document behavior, in which elements will permit floated elements to both sides. none can be used to override other styles, of course, as shown in Figure 7-78. Despite the document-wide rule that H2 elements will not permit floated elements to either side, one H2 in particular has been set so that it does permit floated elements on either side:

```
H2 {clear: both;}
```

```
<H2 STYLE="clear: none;">Not Cleared!</H2>
```

clear works by increasing the top margin of an element so that it ends up below a floated element, so any margin width set for the top of a cleared element should be effectively ignored. That is, instead of being 1.5em, for example, it could be increased to 10em, or 25px, or 7.133in, or however much is needed to move the element down far enough so that the content area is below the bottom edge of a floated element.

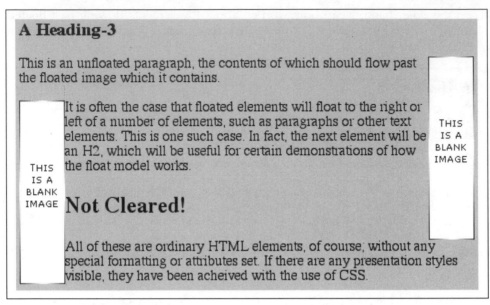

Figure 7-78. Not clear at all

Lists

There are a total of three properties that can affect the display of a list item under CSS1—CSS2 adds a few more, all of which are mentioned in Chapter 10, *CSS2: A Look Ahead*—and one shorthand property to tie them all together. These properties are used to affect the type of bullet used in a list, to replace the bullet with an image, and to affect where the bullet or image appears in relation to the text of the list item.

Just in case you're unfamiliar with the concept of a "bullet," it's the little decoration to the side of a list item, as depicted in Figure 7-79.

- This list item, and
- all other items in an
- unordered list are
- preceded by a "bullet."

Figure 7-79. Bullets

In an unordered list, these will be little symbols, but in an ordered list, the bullet could be a letter or number.

Types of Lists

This part will probably seem very familiar to those of you who have been fiddling with lists in HTML. In order to change the type of counter or bullet used for a list's items, you would use the `list-style-type`.

---

list-style-type

Values	`disc` | `circle` | `square` | `decimal` | `upper-alpha` | `lower-alpha` | `upper-roman` | `lower-roman` | `none`
Initial value	`disc`
Inherited	yes
Applies to	list-item elements

The meaning of these values is shown in Table 7-1.

Table 7-1. Values of the list-style-type property and their results

Keyword	Effect
`disc`	use a disc (usually a filled circle) for list item bullets
`circle`	use a circle (usually open) for bullets
`square`	use a square (filled or open) for bullets
`decimal`	1, 2, 3, 4, 5, ...
`upper-alpha`	A, B, C, D, E, ...
`lower-alpha`	a, b, c, d, e, ...
`upper-roman`	I, II, III, IV, V, ...
`lower-roman`	i, ii, iii, iv, v, ...
`none`	use no bullet

These properties can only be applied to any element that has a `display` of `list-item`, of course, but CSS doesn't distinguish between ordered and unordered list items. Thus, you might be able to set an ordered list to use discs instead of numbers. In fact, the default value of `list-style-type` is `disc`, so you might theorize that without explicit declarations to the contrary, all lists (ordered or unordered) will use discs as the bullet for each item. In fact, that's up to the user agent to decide. Even if the user agent doesn't have a predefined rule such as `OL {list-style-type: decimal;}`, it may prohibit ordered bullets from being applied to unordered lists, and vice versa. You can't count on this, of course, so be careful.

If you wish to suppress the display of bullets altogether, then **none** is the value you seek. **none** will cause the user agent to refrain from putting anything where the bullet would ordinarily be, although it does not interrupt the counting in ordered lists. Thus, the following markup would have the result shown in Figure 7-80:

```
OL LI {list-style-type: decimal;}
LI.off {list-style-type: none;}

<OL>
<LI>Item the first
<LI CLASS="off">Item the second
<LI>Item the third
<LI CLASS="off">Item the fourth
<LI>Item the fifth
</OL>
```

> 1. Item the first
>   Item the second
> 3. Item the third
>   Item the fourth
> 5. Item the fifth

Figure 7-80. Switching off list-item markers

`list-style-type` is inherited, so if you want to have different styles of bullet in nested lists, you'll need to define them individually. You may also have to explicitly declare styles for nested lists because the user agent's style sheet may already have defined such styles. Assume that a UA has the following styles defined:

```
UL {list-style-type: disc;}
UL UL {list-style-type: circle;}
UL UL UL {list-style-type: square;}
```

If this is so, and it's likely that it will be, you will have to declare your own styles to overcome the UA's styles. Inheritance won't be enough in such a case.

List Item Images

Sometimes, of course, a pregenerated bullet just won't do. Instead, you feel the need to use an image for each bullet. In the past, the only way to achieve this sort of effect was to fake it. Now all you need is a **list-style-image** declaration.

list-style-image

Values	\<url\> | none
Initial value	none
Inherited	yes
Applies to	list-item elements

Here's how it works:

```
UL LI {list-style-image: url(ohio.gif);}
```

Yes, that's really all there is to it. One simple `url` value, and you're putting images in for bullets, as you can see in Figure 7-81.

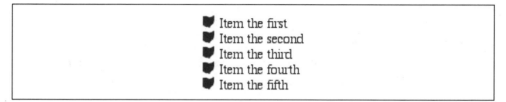

Figure 7-81. Using images as bullets

Of course, you should exercise care in the images you use, as this example makes painfully clear (shown in Figure 7-82):

```
UL LI {list-style-image: url(big-ohio.gif);}
```

Figure 7-82. Using really big images as bullets

You should usually provide a fallback for the bullet type. Do this just in case your image doesn't load, or gets corrupted, or is in a format that some user agents might not be able to display (as is the case in Figure 7-83). Therefore, you should always define a backup `list-style-type` for the list:

```
UL LI {list-style-image: url(ohio.bmp); list-style-type: square;}
```

- Item the first
- Item the second
- Item the third
- Item the fourth
- Item the fifth

Figure 7-83. Providing fallbacks for unusable images

The other thing you can do with `list-style-image` is set it to the default value of **none**. This is good practice because `list-style-image` is inherited—so any nested lists will pick up the image as the bullet, unless you prevent this from happening:

```
UL {list-style-image: url(ohio.gif); list-style-type: square;}
UL UL {list-style-image: none;}
```

Since the nested list inherits the item type **square** but has been set to use no image for its bullets, squares are used for the bullets in the nested list, as shown in Figure 7-84.

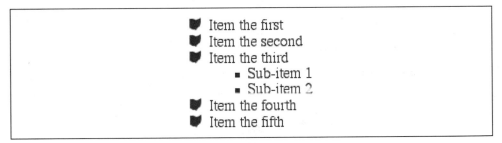

Figure 7-84. Switching off image bullets in sublists

 Remember that this may not be true in the real world: a user agent may have already defined a `list-style-type` for UL UL, so the value of **square** won't be inherited after all. Your browser may vary.

In the case of ordered lists, CSS2 goes a great deal further than CSS1 to provide control over the ordering. For example, there is no way in CSS1 to automatically create subsection counters such as "2.1" or "7.1.3." This can, however, be done under CSS2 and is briefly discussed in Chapter 10.

List Item Positions

There is one other thing you can do to influence the appearance of list items under CSS1, and that's change the position of the bullet itself, in relation to the content of the list item. This is accomplished with `list-style-position`.

---

list-style-position

Values	`inside` | `outside`
Initial value	`outside`
Inherited	yes
Applies to	list-item elements

If a bullet's position is set to `outside`, it will appear the way list items always have on the Web, as you can see in Figure 7-85:

```
LI {list-style-position: outside;}
```

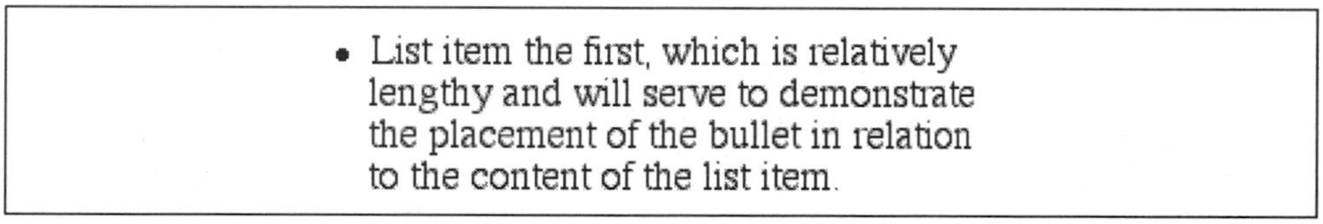

• List item the first, which is relatively
  lengthy and will serve to demonstrate
  the placement of the bullet in relation
  to the content of the list item.

Figure 7-85. Placing the bullets outside list items

Should you desire a slightly different appearance, though, you can pull the bullet in toward the content by setting the value to be `inside`:

```
LI.first {list-style-position: inside;}
```

This causes the bullet to be placed "inside" the list item's content. The exact way this happens is undefined, but Figure 7-86 shows one possibility.

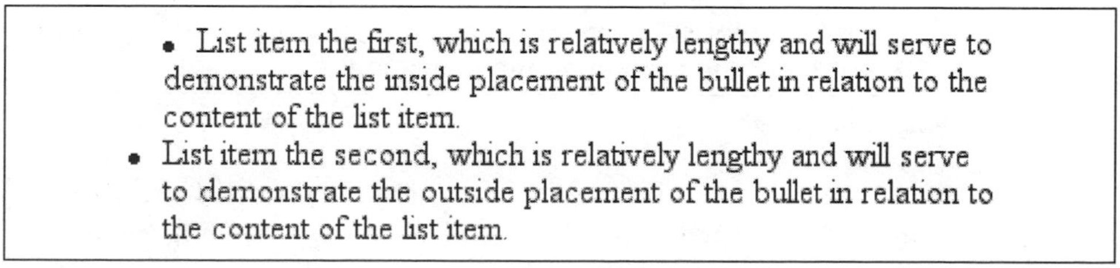

• List item the first, which is relatively lengthy and will serve to
  demonstrate the inside placement of the bullet in relation to the
  content of the list item.
• List item the second, which is relatively lengthy and will serve
  to demonstrate the outside placement of the bullet in relation to
  the content of the list item.

Figure 7-86. Placing the bullets inside and outside list items

CSS2, by the way, provides a good deal more control over the positioning of the bullets (called "markers" in CSS2); again, this is discussed in Chapter 10.

List Styles In Shorthand

For brevity's sake, you can combine the three list-style properties into a convenient single property: `list-style`.

---

list-style

Values	<list-style-type> || <list-style-image> || <list-style-position>
Initial value	refer to individual properties
Inherited	yes
Applies to	list-item elements

For example:

```
LI {list-style: url(sm-ohio.gif) square inside;}
```

As we can see in Figure 7-87, all three values are applied to the list items.

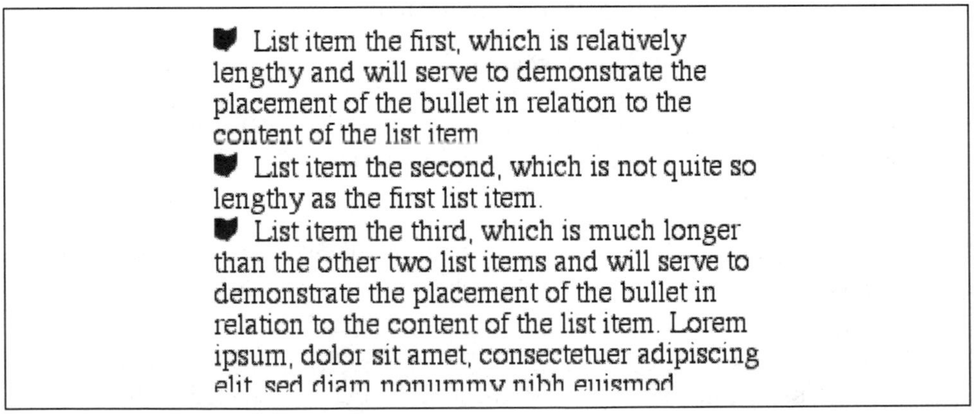

> ♥ List item the first, which is relatively lengthy and will serve to demonstrate the placement of the bullet in relation to the content of the list item
> ♥ List item the second, which is not quite so lengthy as the first list item.
> ♥ List item the third, which is much longer than the other two list items and will serve to demonstrate the placement of the bullet in relation to the content of the list item. Lorem ipsum, dolor sit amet, consectetuer adipiscing elit sed diam nonummy nibh euismod

Figure 7-87. Bringing it all together

The values for `list-style` can be listed in any order, and any of them can be omitted. As long as one is present, the rest will fill in their default values. For instance, the following two rules will have the same visual effect:

```
LI.norm {list-style: url(img42.gif);}
LI.odd {list-style: url(img42.gif) disc outside;} /* the same thing */
```

They will also override any previous rules in the same way. Take the following markup:

```
LI {list-style-type: square;}
LI.norm {list-style: url(img42.gif);}
```

No list item with a **CLASS** of **norm** will ever use a square. This is because the implied `list-style-type` value of `disc` for the rule **LI.norm** will override the previously declared value of **square**.

Summary

The ability to apply margins, borders, and padding to any element is one of the things that sets CSS so far above traditional Web markup. In the past, enclosing a heading in a colored, bordered box meant wrapping the heading in a table, which is a really bloated and awful way to create so simple an effect. It is this sort of power that makes CSS so compelling.

Unfortunately, this is also one of the areas where CSS support failed us in early implementations. Explorer 3 and Navigator 4 both had poor implementations of the box properties, although Navigator 4's bugs are almost legendary and are certainly close to being epic in nature. As the year 2000 dawned, however, the situation was rapidly improving, thanks to Explorer 4 and 5, and Opera 3.6 (and later).

List styles, on the other hand, were fairly well supported from the very beginning of CSS implementations. The ability to set images for bullets was missing from many early user agents, but support for the various kinds of counting schemes has long been evident.

Although this chapter attempted to provide a clear view of how the box properties work, there are many nuances and details to the CSS formatting model. Including all of them would have dramatically slowed down the progress of the chapter. Instead, these are all covered in the next chapter, which is largely theoretical in nature but which provides a comprehensive explanation of the workings of the CSS formatting model.

8

Visual Formatting

In the previous chapter, we covered a great deal of information on how CSS handles the visual formatting of a document. However, we did this in a mostly practical fashion: lots of explanation about how things work, with only a little lip service paid to the questions of why. In this chapter, we turn to the theoretical side of visual rendering, with only occasional references to the practical.

You may wonder why it's necessary to spend an entire chapter on the theoretical underpinnings of visual rendering in CSS. The main reason is to cover all the bases. I attempted to provide as many and varied examples as possible in the previous chapters, but with a model as open and powerful as that contained within CSS, no book could hope to cover every possible way of combining properties and effects. Every reader of this book will obviously go on to discover new ways of using CSS for their own document effects.

In the course of so doing, you may encounter what seems like strange behavior on the part of user agents. With a thorough grasp of how the visual rendering model works in CSS, you'll be able to determine whether the behavior is a correct (if unexpected) consequence of the rendering engine CSS defines or whether you've stumbled across a bug that needs to be reported. (See Appendix A, *CSS Resources*, for details on how to report problems with rendering engines.)

Basic Boxes

In the rendering of elements, CSS assumes that every element generates one or more rectangular boxes, called *element boxes*. (Future versions of the specification may allow for nonrectangular boxes, but for now everything is rectangular.) Each element box consists of a *content area* at its core. This content area is surrounded by optional amounts of padding, borders, and margins. These are considered optional because all could be set to a width of zero, effectively removing them from the element box. An example content area is shown in Figure 8-1, along with the surrounding regions of padding, border, and margins.

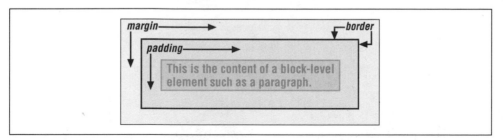

Figure 8-1. The content area and its surroundings

Each of the margins, borders, and padding can be set using various properties, such as `margin-left` or `border-bottom`. The content's background (for example, a color or tiled image) is also applied to the padding, while the margins are always transparent, allowing the background of any parent elements to be visible. In effect, the margins simulate the `HSPACE` and `VSPACE` attributes of images, although in a much more sophisticated fashion. Padding cannot be set to a negative value, but margins can. The effects of negative margins are explored later in this chapter.

The borders, on the other hand, have their own rules. Borders are generated using defined styles, such as `solid` or `inset`, and their color can be set using the `border-color` property. If no color is set, then the color of the border is based on the foreground color of the element's content. For example, if the text of a paragraph is white, then any borders around that paragraph will be white, unless a different border color is explicitly declared by the author. If a border style has "gaps" of some type, then the element's background is visible through those gaps; in other words, the border has the same background as the content and padding. Finally, the width of a border can never be negative.

There are differences in how different types of elements are formatted, however. Block-level elements are not treated in the same way that inline elements are, for example, and floated elements introduce a whole new level of complexity. Let's examine each type of element in turn.

Block-Level Elements

Block-level elements—such as paragraphs, H1s, lists, and list elements—behave in interesting ways, sometimes predictable, sometimes surprising. There are differences in the handling of element placement along the horizontal and vertical axes, for example. In order to fully understand how block-level elements are handled, you must clearly understand a number of boundaries and areas. They are shown in detail in Figure 8-2.

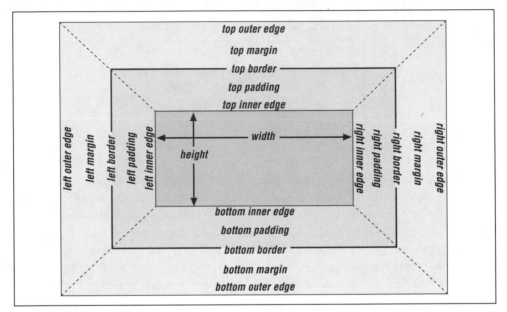

Figure 8-2. The complete box model

In general, the `width` of an element is defined to be the distance from the left inner edge to the right inner edge, and the `height` is the distance from the inner top to the inner bottom. These are both, not coincidentally, properties that can be applied to an element.

The various widths, heights, padding, margins, and borders all combine to determine how a document is laid out. In most cases, the height and width are automatically determined by the browser, based on the available display region and other factors. Under CSS, of course, you can assert more direct control over the way elements are sized and displayed. There are different effects to consider for horizontal and vertical layout, so we'll tackle them separately.

Vertical Formatting

Vertical formatting is much easier to cover, so let's do that first. A good deal of this was covered in the previous chapter, so we'll revisit the high points and delve into some trivia before moving on to the much more complex subject of horizontal formatting.

Height

In general, the height of an element is determined by its content. This can be affected by its width, of course; the skinnier a paragraph becomes, for example, the taller it has to be in order to contain all of the textual (and other) content.

In CSS, it is possible to set an explicit height on any block-level element. If this is done, the resulting behavior is somewhat uncertain. Assume that the specified height is greater than that needed to display the content:

```
<P STYLE="height: 10em;">
```

In this case, then the extra height is treated somewhat like extra padding, as depicted in Figure 8-3.

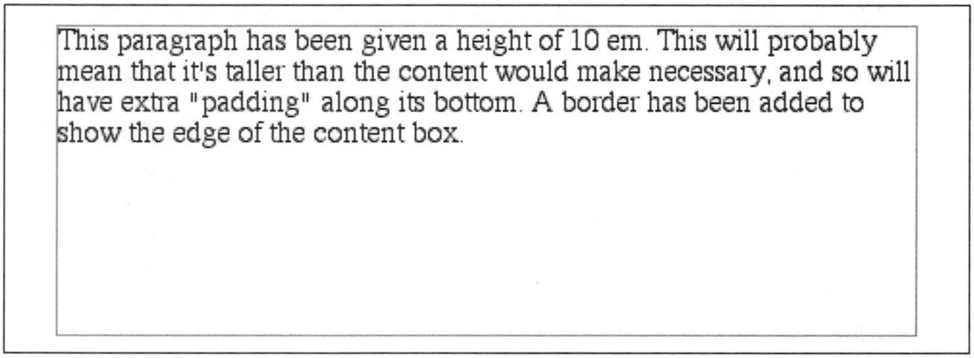

This paragraph has been given a height of 10 em. This will probably mean that it's taller than the content would make necessary, and so will have extra "padding" along its bottom. A border has been added to show the edge of the content box.

Figure 8-3. Setting the height property for block-level elements

If, on the other hand, the `height` is *less* than that needed to display the content:

```
<P STYLE="height: 3em;">
```

then the browser is supposed to provide a way to see all content without increasing the height. This could possibly mean adding a scrollbar to the element, as shown in Figure 8-4.

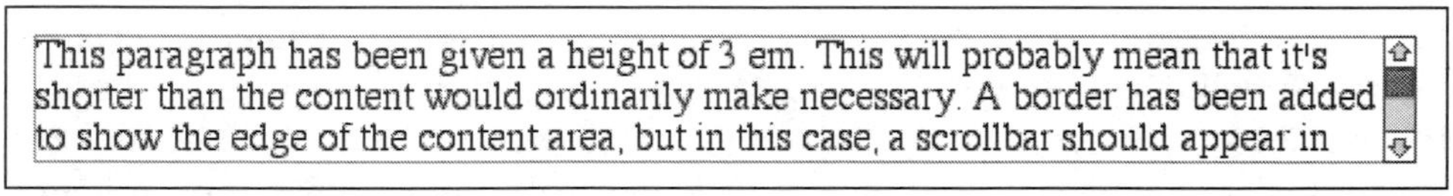

This paragraph has been given a height of 3 em. This will probably mean that it's shorter than the content would ordinarily make necessary. A border has been added to show the edge of the content area, but in this case, a scrollbar should appear in

Figure 8-4. One way to handle a short height on a tall element

In practice, most browsers will not do this. They will instead simply increase the height of the element, as though the value of `height` had been set to `auto`. This is permitted under CSS1, which states that browsers can ignore any value of `height` other than `auto` if an element is not a replaced element such as an image.

Under CSS2, it is possible to set up a situation where scrollbars would be applied to an element such as a paragraph.

It's also possible to set the top and bottom margins of a block-level element to be `auto`. If either of these properties is set to `auto`, it is reset to 0 (zero), effectively removing any top or bottom margin from the element box, as shown in Figure 8-5. The lack of any space between the borders of each paragraph is a result of `auto` being reinterpreted as zero:

```
P {margin-top: auto; margin-bottom: auto;}
```

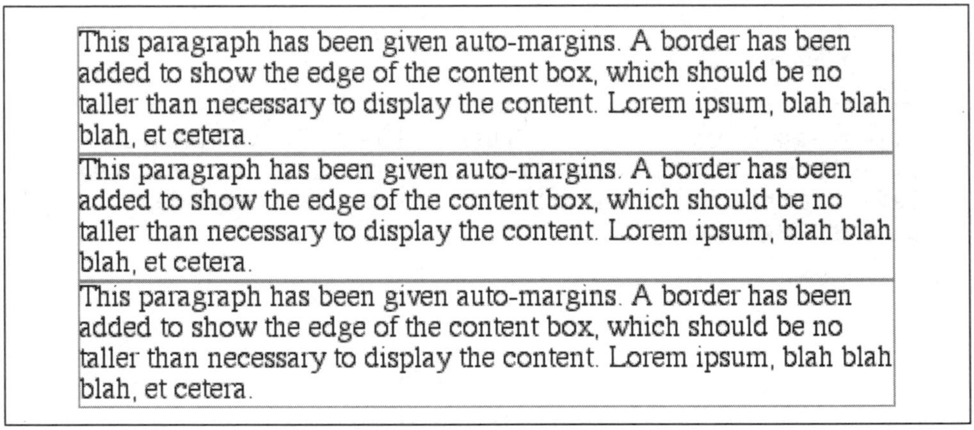

This paragraph has been given auto-margins. A border has been added to show the edge of the content box, which should be no taller than necessary to display the content. Lorem ipsum, blah blah blah, et cetera.

This paragraph has been given auto-margins. A border has been added to show the edge of the content box, which should be no taller than necessary to display the content. Lorem ipsum, blah blah blah, et cetera.

This paragraph has been given auto-margins. A border has been added to show the edge of the content box, which should be no taller than necessary to display the content. Lorem ipsum, blah blah blah, et cetera.

Figure 8-5. Automatically setting margins to zero

Collapsing vertical margins

There is one other important aspect of vertical formatting, which is the collapsing of adjacent margins. This comes into play when an element with declared margins immediately follows another such element in the document's layout. This was discussed in the previous chapter, using this example:

```
LI {margin-top: 10px; margin-bottom: 20px;}
```

Padding and borders, where they exist, are never collapsed. If neither is declared, then both will default to 0 (zero). This assumes that no style is set for the border. If a border style is set, then the value of `border-width` defaults to `medium`, not zero. The exact width of `medium` will depend on the user agent's programming, but a common value is 2 or 3 pixels.

Horizontal Formatting

In contrast to vertical formatting, horizontal formatting can get a little complicated. Fortunately, it starts out simply enough; it's only when you start putting things together that the situation becomes difficult.

First off, the simplest rule is this: unlike vertical margins, horizontal margins are not collapsed. If you somehow manage to have two block-level elements next to each other, and each has a margin, the margins will not collapse. The easiest way to illustrate this principle is to set margins on two images and then have them appear on the same line, as they do in Figure 8-6:

```
<IMG SRC="test1.gif" STYLE="margin: 5px;" ALT="first test">
<IMG SRC="test2.gif" STYLE="margin: 5px;" ALT="second test">
```

(Note that the images in Figure 8-6 are actually inline elements, but they effectively demonstrate that horizontally adjacent margins do not collapse.)

Figure 8-6. Horizontal margins don't collapse

Almost as simple is this: the sum of the horizontal components of a nonfloated block-level element box always equals the `width` of the parent. Take two paragraphs within a `DIV`, for example, whose margins have been set to be `1em`. The content width (in other words, the value of `width`) of the paragraph, plus its left and right padding, borders, and margins, always add up to the `width` of the `DIV`'s content, as illustrated in Figure 8-7.

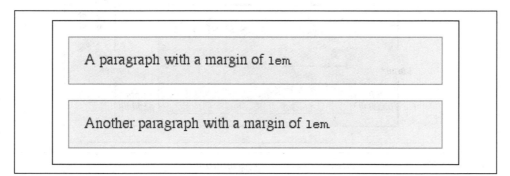

Figure 8-7. Element boxes are as wide as the width of their parent element

Thus, if the `width` of the `DIV` is `30em`, then the sum total of the content width, padding, borders, and margins of each paragraph will be `30em`. In Figure 8-7, the "blank" space around the paragraphs is actually their margins. (If the `DIV` had any padding, there would be even more blank space, but that wasn't the case here.)

In a similar fashion, the overall width of a list item's element box is equal to the content width of the list element that contains it. As you can see in Figure 8-8, the margins of a parent element can influence the layout of a child element.

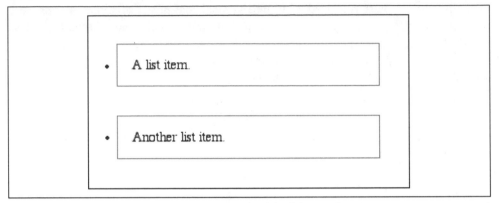

Figure 8-8. List items' overall width equals the width of the UL element

Horizontal properties

There are a number of properties relating to the layout of boxes. These are known as the "seven properties" of horizontal formatting: (from the left) `margin-left`, `border-left`, `padding-left`, `width`, `padding-right`, `border-right`, and `margin-right`. These are illustrated in Figure 8-9. The values of these seven properties must equal the value of `width` for an element's parent.

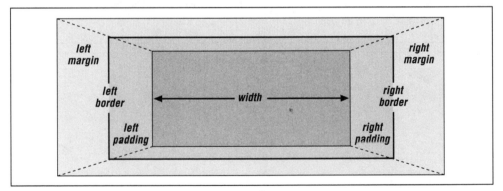

Figure 8-9. The "seven properties" of horizontal formatting

Only three of these seven properties can be set to `auto`: the `width` of the element's content, and the left and right margins. The left and right padding and borders must be set to specific values, or else they default to a width of zero (again, assuming no `border-style` is declared; if one has been set, then the width of the borders is set to be the vaguely defined value `medium`). Figure 8-10 provides a handy illustration for remembering which parts of the box can take a value of `auto`, and which cannot.

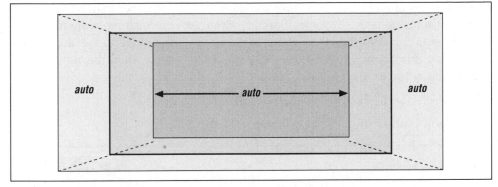

Figure 8-10. Horizontal properties that can be set to auto

`width` must be set to either `auto` or a non-negative value of some type. CSS also allows browsers to set a minimum value for `width`, below which a block-level element's `width` cannot drop. The value of this minimum can vary between browsers, as it is not defined in the specification.

Using auto

If only one of `width`, `margin-left`, or `margin-right` is set to a value of `auto`, while the others are given specific values, then the property set to be `auto` will evaluate to whatever length is required to make the element box's width equal the parent element's `width`. Thus, if the sum of the seven properties must equal 400 pixels, and no padding or borders are set, and the right margin and width are set to `100px` while the left margin is set to `auto`, then the left margin will be 200 pixels wide:

```
P {margin-left: auto; margin-right: 100px; width: 100px;}
```

The results are shown in Figure 8-11.

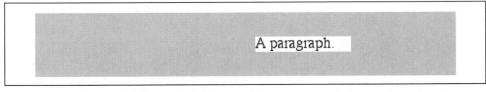

Figure 8-11. Automatic left margin

In a sense, `auto` can be used to say, "make up the difference between everything else and the required total." However, what if all three of these properties are set to `100px`, and none of them to `auto`?

In the case where all three properties are set to something other than `auto`—or, to borrow a term from the CSS specification, when these formatting properties have been over-constrained—then `margin-right` is *always* forced to be `auto`. This means that if both margins and the width are set to 100px, then the right margin will be set by the user agent to `auto`:

```
P {margin-left: 100px; margin-right: 100px; width: 100px;}
```

It will then evaluate to 200px, as shown in Figure 8-12.

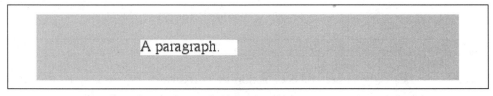

Figure 8-12. Overriding the margin-right setting

 Note that `margin-right` is forced to be `auto` only for left-to-right languages such as English. In right-to-left languages, everything gets flipped around, so `margin-left` is forced to be `auto`, not `margin-right`. This is not so much an issue under CSS1 as it is in CSS2, which introduces properties related to writing direction.

If both margins are set explicitly, and `width` is `auto`, then the value of `width` will be set to be whatever is needed to reach the required total (that is, the content width of the parent element). The following markup is displayed as shown in Figure 8-13:

```
P {margin-left: 100px; margin-right: 100px; width: auto;}
```

Figure 8-13. Automatic width

This is the most common case, in fact, since it is equivalent to setting the margins and not declaring anything for the `width`. The result of this markup is exactly the same as that shown in Figure 8-13:

```
P {margin-left: 100px; margin-right: 100px;} /* same as before */
```

In practice, only browsers released in early 1999 or later correctly handle `auto`, and not even all of them get it right. Those that do not handle `auto` margins correctly will behave in inconsistent ways, but the safest bet is to assume that they will set both margins to zero. The browsers that do get this right are Internet Explorer 4.5 and 5 for Macintosh, and Opera 3.6.

More than one auto

Now let us consider the cases where two of these three properties are set to `auto`. If both the margins are set to `auto`, then they are set to equal lengths, thus centering the element within its parent, as you can see from Figure 8-14:

```
P {width: 100px; margin-left: auto; margin-right: auto;}
```

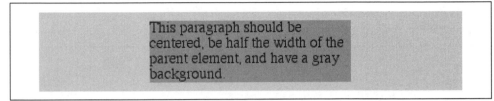

A paragraph.

Figure 8-14. Setting an explicit width

This is the correct way to center block-level elements, as a matter of fact. `text-align` is supposed to apply to only the inline content of a block-level element, so setting an element to have a `text-align` of `center` shouldn't center it. Instead, you should declare:

```
P {margin-left: auto; margin-right: auto; width: 50%;}
```

This will center all paragraphs within their parent elements, as shown in Figure 8-15.

This paragraph should be centered, be half the width of the parent element, and have a gray background.

Figure 8-15. Centering an element with automatic margins

As of this writing, only Internet Explorer 4.5 and 5 for the Macintosh and Opera 3.6 will center elements using `auto` margins.

The other possibility is when one of the margins and the width are set to be `auto`. In this case, then the margin set to be `auto` is reduced to zero:

```
P {width: auto; margin-left: auto; margin-right: 100px;}
```

The `width` is then set to the value necessary to reach the required total, as demonstrated in Figure 8-16.

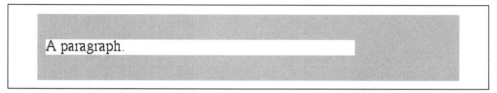

Figure 8-16. Setting an explicit right margin

Finally, what happens when all three properties are set to `auto`? The answer is simple: both margins are set to zero, and the `width` is made as wide as possible. This result is the same as the default situation when there are no values explicitly declared for margins or the width. In such a case, the margins default to zero (0) and the width defaults to `auto`. This is illustrated in Figure 8-17.

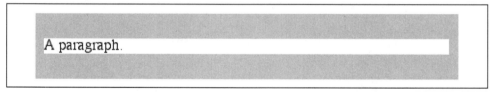

Figure 8-17. Everything set to auto

Note that since horizontal margins do not collapse, the padding, borders, and margin of a parent element can affect its children. This is an indirect effect, of course, in that the margins (and so on) of an element can induce an offset for child elements. Vertical margins are still collapsed, as shown in Figure 8-18:

```
DIV {margin: 20px; padding: 20px;}
P {margin: 10px; padding: 10px;}
```

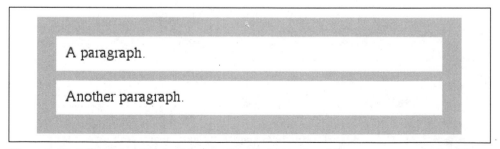

Figure 8-18. Offset is implicit in the parent's margins and padding

Negative margins

So far, this probably all seems rather straightforward, and you may be wondering why I said things could be complicated. As it turns out, the complication is that margins can have negative values.

You'll remember that I said the second-simplest rule of horizontal formatting was this: the total of the seven horizontal properties always equals the `width` of the parent element. At first glance, this can be interpreted to mean that an element can never be wider than its parent's content area—and as long as all properties are zero or greater, that's quite true. However, consider the following, depicted in Figure 8-19:

```
DIV {width: 400px; border: 3px solid black}
P.wide {margin-left: 10px; width: auto; margin-right: -50px;
  border: 1px solid gray;}
```

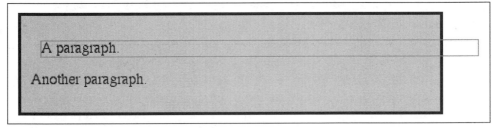

Figure 8-19. Wider children through negative margins

Yes, the child element is wider than its parent! This is mathematically correct: 10 pixels + 0 + 0 + 450 pixels + 0 + 0 − 50 pixels = 410 pixels. Even though this leads to a child element sticking out of its parent, technically the specification hasn't been violated, because the values of the seven properties add up to the required total. It's a semantic dodge, but it's valid behavior.

Let's consider another example, illustrated in Figure 8-20, where the left margin is set to be negative:

```
DIV {width: 400px; border: 1px solid black;}
P.wide {margin-left: -50px; width: auto; margin-right: 10px;
  border: 3px solid gray;}
```

In this case, not only does the paragraph spill beyond the borders of the DIV, but also beyond the edge of the browser window itself!

 Remember that padding, borders, and content widths can never be negative. Only margins can be less than zero.

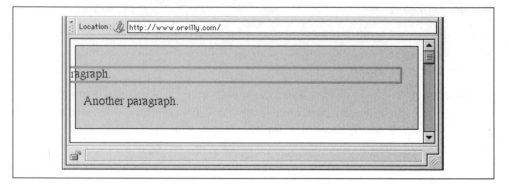

Figure 8-20. Setting a negative left margin

Negative margins have an impact on vertical formatting as well, affecting how margins are collapsed. If there are negative vertical margins, then the browser should take the absolute maximum of the negative margins and subtract that from the maximum of any positive margins.

In the case where there are only two margins to be collapsed, one positive and the other negative, the situation is handled in a fairly simple manner. The absolute value of the negative margin is subtracted from the positive margin—or, to put it another way, the negative is added to the positive—and the resulting value is the distance between the elements. Figure 8-21 provides two concrete examples.

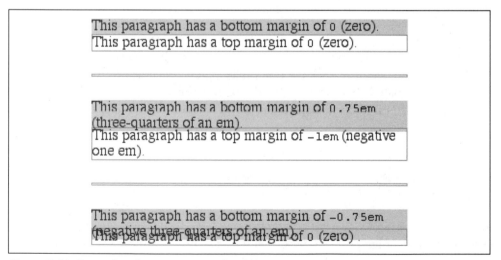

Figure 8-21. Examples of negative vertical margins

You'll notice the "pulling" effect of negative top and bottom margins. This is really no different from the way in which negative horizontal margins cause an element to push outside of its parent. Consider:

```
DIV {width: 400px; border: 1px solid black;}
P.neg {margin-top: -50px; width: auto; margin-right: 10px;
  margin-left: 10px; border: 3px solid gray;}

<DIV STYLE="width: 420px; background-color: silver;
   padding: 10px; margin-top: 75px;">
<P CLASSS="neg">
A paragraph.
</P>
</DIV>
```

As we can see from Figure 8-22, the paragraph has simply been pulled upward by its negative top margin, such that it's outside the parent DIV!

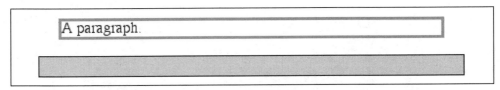

Figure 8-22. The effects of a negative top margin

With a negative bottom margin, though, it looks as though everything following the paragraph has been pulled upward. Compare the following markup to the situation shown in Figure 8-23:

```
DIV {border: 1px solid black;}
P.neg {margin-bottom: -50px; width: auto; margin-right: 10px;
  margin-left: 10px; border: 3px solid gray;}

<DIV STYLE="width: 420px; background-color: silver;
   padding: 10px; margin-top: 75px;">
<P CLASS="neg">
A paragraph.
</P>
</DIV>
<P>
The next paragraph.
</P>
```

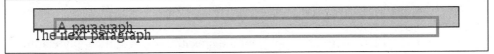

Figure 8-23. The effects of a negative bottom margin

What's really happening in Figure 8-23 is that the elements following the DIV are placed according to the location of the bottom of the DIV. As we can see, the end of the DIV is actually above the visual bottom of its child paragraph. The next element after the DIV is the appropriate distance from the bottom of the DIV. The fact that it overlaps the paragraph doesn't matter, at least not technically.

Now let's consider an example where the margins of a list item, an unordered list, and a heading are all collapsed. In this case, the unordered list and heading will be set to have negative margins:

```
LI {margin-bottom: 20px;}
UL {margin-bottom: -15px;}
H1 {margin-top: -18px;}
```

The larger of the two negative margins (–18px) is added to the largest positive margin (20px), yielding (20px–18px = 2px). Thus, there are only two pixels between the bottom of the list item's content and the top of the paragraph's content. This is what we see in Figure 8-24.

Figure 8-24. Collapsing margins and negative margins, in detail

There is one area of unresolved behavior, which is this: if elements overlap each other due to negative margins, which elements are "on top?" You'll note that few of the examples in this section use background colors for all elements. That's because if they did, content might get overwritten by the background color of a following element. The CSS specification does not say what should happen when elements overlap in this manner; instead, it's left up to implementors to decide.

It has been argued that all foreground content is always shown "in front of" all background content, and the behavior of floated elements seems to support this interpretation. On the other hand, the CSS2 property z-index makes this reasoning more complicated. As of this writing, implementations have not yet advanced sufficiently to test this out, and the CSS2 description of z-index doesn't really shed any light on this subject.

Ultimately, if you use negative margins, you may not get the same results from all browsers. Since no one can clearly say which is right, none of them can really be considered to be buggy—at least, not until the specification is sufficiently clarified.

List Items

Speaking of list items, they have a few special rules in addition to everything discussed so far. List items are typically preceded by a marker, such as a small dot or a number. This marker isn't actually part of the list-item's content area, so you get effects like those illustrated in Figure 8-25.

> • A list item.
> • Another list item.

Figure 8-25. The content of list items

In CSS1, very little is said about the placement and effects of this marker with regard to the layout of a document. CSS2 introduces properties specifically designed to address this issue, such as `marker-offset`. Since this property and its cousins are not widely supported at the time of this writing, we will not spend time on it here. There is a brief discussion of the marker properties in Chapter 10, *CSS2: A Look Ahead.*

Block-Level Replaced Elements

Block-level replaced elements are also subject to a few differences in how formatting is handled. The most important is that replaced elements are assumed to have an intrinsic height and width; for example, an image will be a certain number of pixels high and wide. Given this, if either `height` or `width` are set to `auto` for a replaced element, then the value will always evaluate to the intrinsic height or width of the element. Thus, if an image is 150 pixels wide, and its `width` property is set to the value `auto`, then its `width` will evaluate to `150px`, as shown in Figure 8-26:

```
IMG {display: block; width: auto;}
```

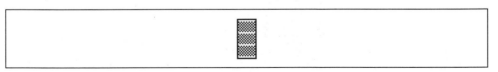

Figure 8-26. Replaced elements with auto width are rendered using their intrinsic size

Replaced elements can have their `height` and `width` set to a value other than `auto` or their intrinsic dimensions. This is most commonly used to "scale" images, either up or down. Thus, if an image is 150 pixels wide and its `width` is set to 75px, then the image will be displayed half as wide as it would ordinarily appear. In most browsers, the height will be scaled to match, unless it has been explicitly set to a certain value. Figure 8-27 shows a few possibilities.

It's also possible to scale an image (or other replaced element) using `height`:

```
<IMG SRC="test.gif" STYLE="display: block;" ALT="test image">
<IMG SRC="test.gif" STYLE="display: block; height: 50px;" ALT="test image">
<IMG SRC="test.gif" STYLE="display: block; height: 200px;" ALT="test image">
```

This is exactly the same as using the `HEIGHT` attribute on the `IMG` tag in HTML. If an image is 100 pixels tall, then by default its height will be `100px`. If you specify

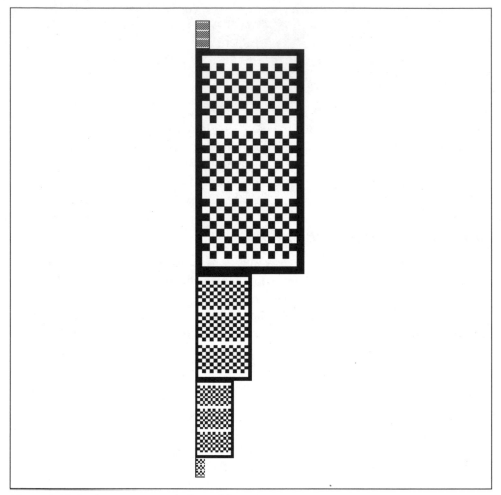

Figure 8-27. Scaling images with the width property

another value, then the image will be scaled appropriately, as illustrated in Figure 8-28.

In almost all other ways, block-level replaced elements behave the same as block-level elements when it comes to formatting: vertical margins are collapsed while horizontal margins are not, and the borders and padding default to zero unless explicitly declared otherwise. Remember, however, that not all replaced elements are images. Most form elements are replaced, for example.

In general, all replaced elements (block-level or otherwise) can be scaled using `height` and `width`. In most other ways, inline replaced elements are handled very differently, as we'll see later in this chapter.

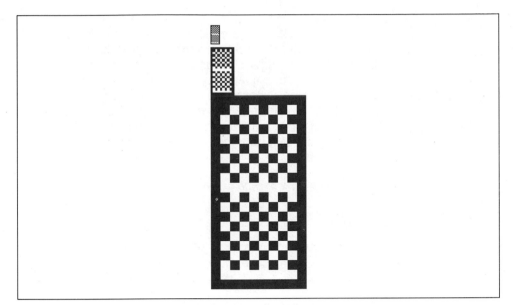

Figure 8-28. Scaling images with the height property

Floated Elements

As we saw in the previous chapter, CSS allows any element to be floated, from images to paragraphs to lists. This is not without a price: floated elements introduce their own set of strangeness. As was discussed, floated elements have an unusual place in determining the flow of the document. For example, the boxes generated by other elements are drawn as though floated elements don't exist, but the content of those elements is rendered while taking the float's presence into account. This in turn influences the generation of element boxes, which means that floats indirectly do affect these boxes.

Some particulars can help explain some of this behavior. An element that has been floated becomes a block-level element, regardless of its previous status. Thus, if an image (which is ordinarily treated as an inline element) is floated, it becomes a block-level element. This block-level status helps explain why when an element is floated, other content flows around it.

Remember that if you float a text element, its width will tend toward zero. This is exactly the opposite of the normal horizontal rules, where `width` is increased until the seven properties equal the parent's `width`. A floated element's width will default to `auto`, which then defaults to zero, which is then increased to the browser's minimum allowed width. Thus, a floated paragraph could literally be one character wide—assuming that to be the browser's minimum value for `width`. In practice, it's more likely that the browser will make the floated element as narrow as the longest word in the element, as shown in Figure 8-29.

This   Lorem ipsum, dolor sit amet, consectetuer adipiscing elit, sed
is   diam nonummy nibh euismod tincidunt ut laoreet dolore
a   magna aliquam erat volutpat. Ut wisi enim ad minim veniam,
floated   quis nostrud exerci tation ullamcorper suscipit lobortis nisl ut
paragraph. aliquip ex ea commodo consequat. Duis autem vel eum iriure
           dolor in hendrerit in vulputate velit esse molestie consequat, vel
illum dolore eu feugiat nulla facilisis at vero eros et accumsan et iusto
odio dignissim qui blandit praesent luptatum zzril delenit augue duis
dolore te feugait nulla facilisi.

Figure 8-29. Floated elements tend toward a width of zero

Floating: The Details

A series of specific rules govern the placement of a floated element. They are vaguely similar to those that govern the evaluation of margins and widths and have the same initial appearance of common sense. They are as follows:

1. The left (or right) outer edge of a floated element may not be to the left (or right) of the inner edge of its parent element.

Straightforward enough. The furthest to the left the outer left edge of a left-floated element may go is the inner left edge of its parent element; similarly, the furthest right a right-floated element may go is its parent's inner right edge, as shown in Figure 8-30. (In this and subsequent figures, the circled numbers show the position where the markup element actually appears in relation to the source, and the numbered box shows the position and size of the floated visible element.)

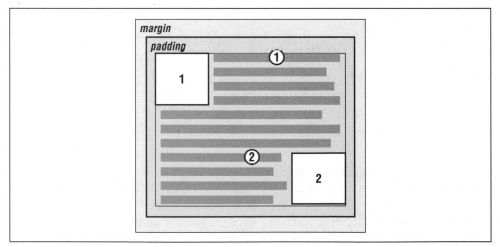

Figure 8-30. Floating to the left (1) or right (2)

2. The left (or right) outer edge of a floated element must be to the right (or left) of the right (left) outer edge of a left-floating (or right-floating) element that occurs earlier in the document's source, unless the top of the latter element is below the bottom of the former.

This rule prevents floated elements from overwriting each other. If an element is floated to the left, and there is already a floated element there due to its earlier position in the document source, then the latter element is placed against the outer right edge of the previously floated element. If, however, a floated element's top is below the bottom of all earlier floated images, then it can float all the way to the inner left edge of the parent. Some examples of this are shown in Figure 8-31.

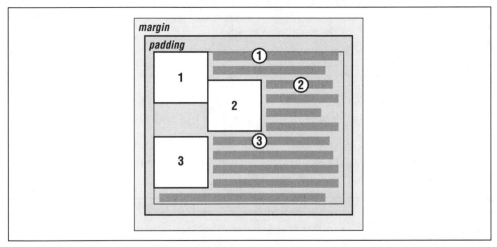

Figure 8-31. Keeping floats from overlapping

The advantage of this rule is that, since you don't have to worry about one floated element obscuring another, you can be assured that all of your floated content will be visible. This makes floating a fairly safe thing to do. The situation is markedly different when using positioning, where it is very easy to cause elements to overwrite one another.

3. The right outer edge of a left-floating element may not be to the right of the left outer edge of any right-floating element to its right. The left outer edge of a right-floating element may not be to the left of the right outer edge of any left-floating element to its left.

This rule also prevents floated elements from overlapping each other. Let's say you have a BODY that is 500 pixels wide, and its sole content is two images that are 300 pixels wide. The first is floated to the left, and the second to the right. This rule prevents the second image from overlapping the first by 100 pixels. Instead, the second image is forced down until its top is below the bottom of the left-floated image, as depicted in Figure 8-32.

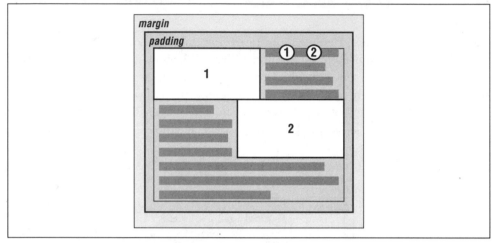

Figure 8-32. More overlap prevention

4. A floating element's top may not be higher than the inner top of its parent.

Another simple rule. This one keeps floating elements from floating all the way to the top of the document. The correct behavior is illustrated in Figure 8-33.

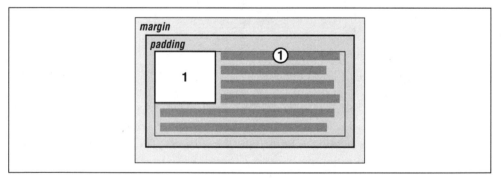

Figure 8-33. Unlike balloons, floated elements can't float upward

5. A floating element's top may not be higher than the top of any earlier floating or block-level element.

Similar to rule 4, this keeps a floated element from floating all the way to the top of its parent element. Thus, if a DIV's first child element is a paragraph, followed by a floated image and then another paragraph, the top of the floated image can't be any higher than the top of the paragraph that precedes it. It is also impossible for a floated element's top to be any higher than the top of a floated element that occurs earlier. Figure 8-34 is an example of this.

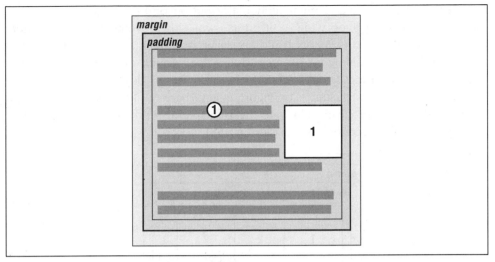

Figure 8-34. Keeping floats below their predecessors

6. A floating element's top may not be higher than the top of any line box with content that precedes the floating element.

Similar to rules 4 and 5, this further limits the upward floating of an element by preventing it from being above the top of a line containing content that precedes the floated element. Let's say that, right in the middle of a paragraph, there is a floated image. The highest the top of that image may be placed is the top of the line box from which the image originates. As you can see in Figure 8-35, this keeps images from floating too far upward.

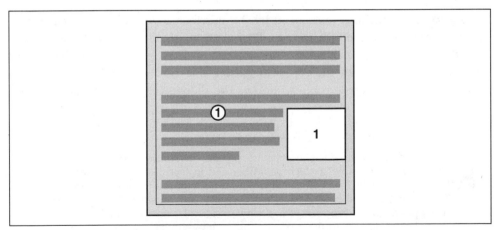

Figure 8-35. Keeping floats level with their context

7. A left (or right) floating element that has another floating element to its left (or right) may not have its right outer edge to the right (or left) of its containing block's right (or left) edge.

In other words, a floating element cannot stick out beyond the edge of its containing element, unless it's too wide to fit on its own. This prevents a situation where a succession of floated elements could appear in a horizontal line and far exceed the edges of the containing block. Instead, if a float would stick out of its containing block by appearing next to another one, it is floated down to a point below any previous floats, as illustrated by Figure 8-36 (where the floats start on the next line in order to more clearly illustrate the principle at work here). This rule first appeared in CSS2, to correct its omission in CSS1.

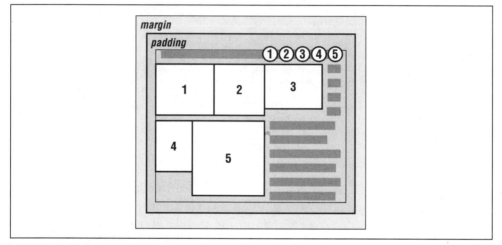

Figure 8-36. If there isn't room, floats get pushed to a new line

8. A floating element must be placed as high as possible.

Subject to the restrictions introduced by the previous seven rules, of course. Historically, browsers aligned the top of a floated element with the top of the line box after the one in which the image's tag appears. Rule 8, however, implies that its top should be even with the top of the same line box as that in which its tag appears, assuming there is room to do so. The theoretically correct behaviors are shown in Figure 8-37.

Unfortunately, since there is no precise definition meaning for "as high as possible" (which could be, and in fact has been, argued to mean "as high as conveniently possible"), you cannot rely on consistent behavior even among browsers that are considered CSS1-compliant. Most browsers will follow historical practice and float the image down into the next line, but a few—Opera 3.6, for one—will float the image into the current line if it has room to do so.

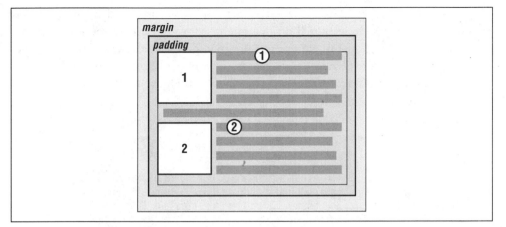

Figure 8-37. Given the other constraints, go as high as possible

9. A left-floating element must be put as far to the left as possible, a right-floating element as far to the right as possible. A higher position is preferred to one that is further to the right or left.

Again, this rule is subject to restrictions introduced in the preceding rules. There are similar caveats here as in Rule 8, although they are not quite so fuzzy. As you can see from Figure 8-38, it is pretty easy to tell when an element has gone as far as possible to the right or left.

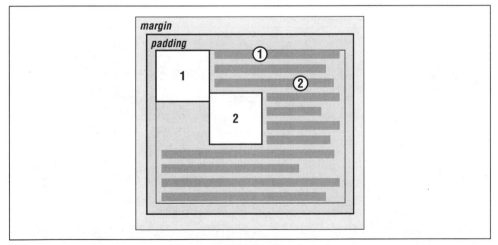

Figure 8-38. Get as far to the left (or right) as possible

Applied Behavior

There are a number of interesting consequences of the above rules, both because of what they say and what they don't say. The first thing to discuss is what happens when the floated element is taller than its parent element.

This happens quite often, as a matter of fact, and was discussed in the previous chapter. Take the example of a short document, composed of no more than a few paragraphs and H3 elements, where the first paragraph contains a floated image. Further, this floated image has a right margin of 5 pixels (5px). You would expect the document to be rendered very much as shown in Figure 8-39.

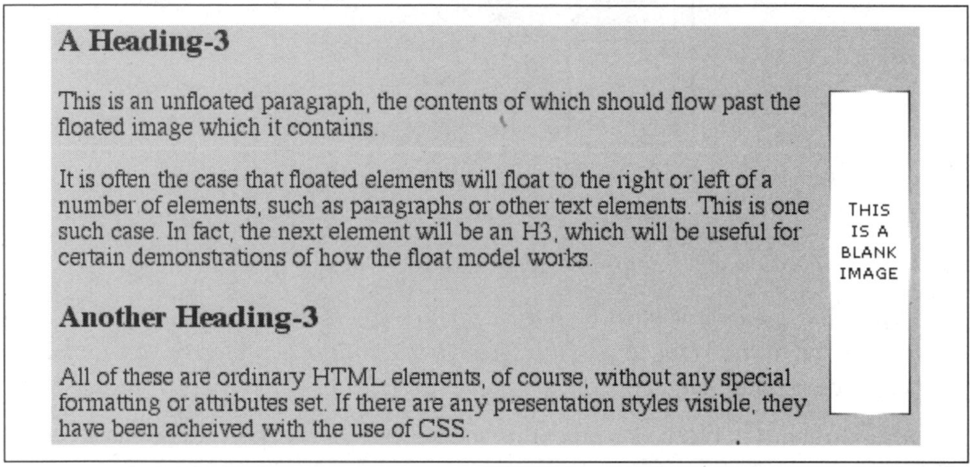

Figure 8-39. Expected floating behavior

Nothing unusual there, of course, but Figure 8-40 shows what happens when we set the first paragraph to have a background.

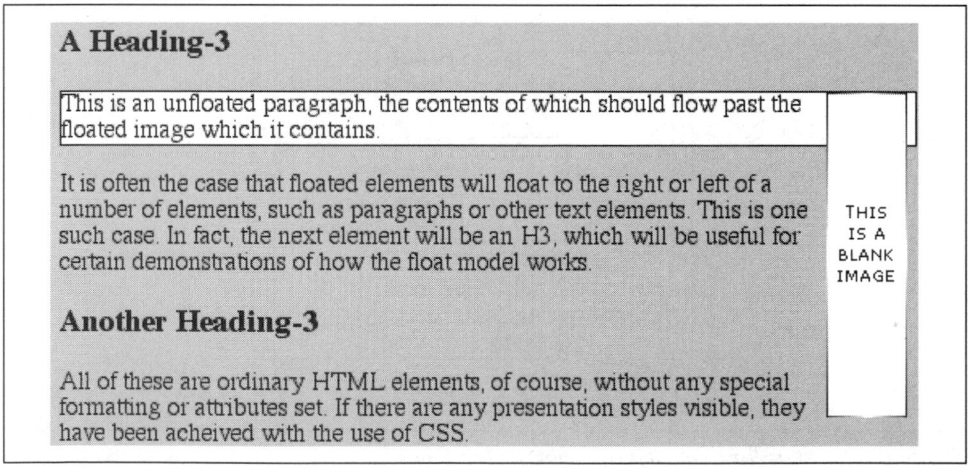

Figure 8-40. Backgrounds and floated elements

There is nothing different about the second example, except for the visible background. As you can see, the floated image sticks out of the bottom of its parent element. Of course, it did so in the first example, but it was less obvious there, because we couldn't see the background. There is nothing forbidden about this behavior. The floating rules we discussed earlier only address the left, right, and top edges of floats and their parents. The deliberate omission of bottom edges permits the behavior in Figure 8-40.

 In practice, some browsers do not do this correctly. Instead, they will increase the height of a parent element so that the floated element is contained within it, even though this results in a great deal of extra blank space within the parent element.

A related topic is the subject of backgrounds and their relationship to floated elements that occur earlier in the document, which was also discussed in the previous chapter, as has been illustrated in Figure 8-41.

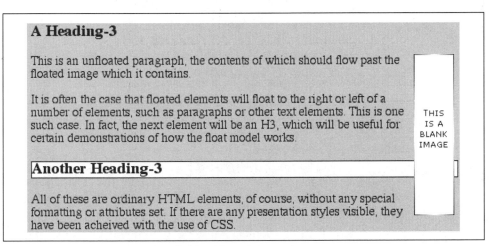

Figure 8-41. Backgrounds "slide under" floated elements

Because the floated element is both within and without the flow, this sort of thing is bound to happen. What's going on? Well, the content of the paragraphs is being "displaced" by the floated element. However, each paragraph's element width is still as wide as its parent element. Therefore, its content area spans the width of the parent, and so does the background. The actual content doesn't flow all the way across its own content area in order to avoid being obscured behind the floating element.

Negative margins

As was discussed in the previous chapter, negative margins can cause floated elements to move outside of their parent elements. This seems to be in direct contradiction to the rules explained earlier, but it isn't. In the same way that elements can appear to be wider than their parents through negative margins, floated elements can appear to protrude out of their parents.

Let's consider once again a floated image which is floated to the left, and which has left and top margins of -15px. This image is placed inside a DIV which has no padding, borders, or margins. The result will be as shown in Figure 8-42.

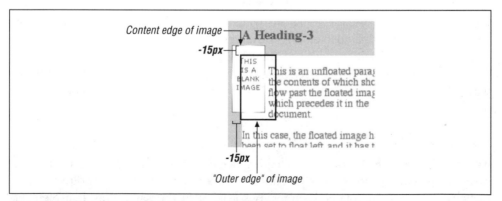

A Heading-3

THIS IS A BLANK IMAGE

This is an unfloated paragraph, the contents of which should flow past the floated image which precedes it in the document.

In this case, the floated image has been set to float left, and it has top and left margins of -15px. This will cause it to actually float up and out of its parent element, which is the DIV that encloses the image and these paragraphs.

Figure 8-42. Floating with negative margins

Contrary to appearances, this does not technically violate the restrictions on floated elements being placed outside their parent elements. Here's the technicality that permits this behavior: a close reading of the rules listed earlier will show that the outer edges of a floating element must be within the element's parent. However, negative margins can place the floated element's content such that it effectively overlaps its own outer edge, as detailed in Figure 8-43.

Content edge of image — A Heading-3

-15px —

THIS IS A BLANK IMAGE

This is an unfloated parag the contents of which shc flow past the floated imag which precedes it in the document.

In this case, the floated image h been set to float left, and it has t

-15px

"Outer edge" of image

Figure 8-43. The details of floating up and left with negative margins

The math in this situation works out something like this: assume the top inner edge of the DIV is at the pixel position 100. The browser, in order to figure out where the top inner edge of the floated element should be will do this: `100px + (-15px) margin + 0 padding = 85px`. Thus the top inner edge of the floated element should be at pixel position 85; even though this is higher than the top inner edge of the float's parent element, the math works out such that the specification isn't violated. A similar line of reasoning explains how the left inner edge of the floated element can be placed to the left of the left inner edge of its parent.

Many of you may have an overwhelming desire to cry "Foul!" right about now. Personally, I don't blame you. It seems completely wrong to allow the top inner edge to be higher than the top outer edge, for example, but with a negative top margin, that's exactly what you get—just as negative margins on normal, non-floated elements can make them wider than their parents. The same is true on all four sides of a floated element's box: set the margins to be negative, and the content can overrun the outer edge without technically violating the specification.

There is one important question here, which is this: what happens to the document display when an element is floated out of its parent element by using negative margins? For example, an image could be floated so far up that it intrudes into a paragraph that has already been displayed by the user agent. In this case, it's up to the user agent to decide whether or not the document should be reflowed. The CSS specifications explicitly state that user agents are not required to reflow previous content to accommodate things which happen later in the document. In other words, if an image is floated up into a previous paragraph, it may simply overwrite whatever was already there. On the other hand, the user agent may handle the situation by flowing content around the float, even though doing so isn't required behavior. Either way, it's probably a bad idea to count on a particular behavior, which makes the utility of negative margins on floats somewhat limited. Hanging floats are probably fairly safe, but trying to push an element upward on the page is a generally bad idea.

There is one other way for a floated element to exceed its parent's inner left and right edges, and that's when the floated element is wider than its parent. In that case, the floated element will simply overrun the right or left inner edge—depending on which way the element is floated—in its best attempt to display itself correctly. This will lead to a result like that shown in Figure 8-44.

Figure 8-44. Floating an element that is wider than its parent

Inline Elements

Any visible element that is not a block-level element (either directly, or by implication, as with floated elements) is an inline element. Setting box properties for inline elements gets into even more interesting territory than we've already covered. Some good examples of inline elements are the EM tag and the A tag, both of which are nonreplaced elements, and images, which are replaced elements.

 Note that none of this applies to table elements. CSS2 introduces new properties and behaviors for handling tables and table content, and these new features behave in ways fairly distinct from either block-level or inline formatting. See Chapter 10 for an overview.

Line Layout

First, we need to understand how inline content is laid out. It isn't as simple and straightforward as block-level elements, which just generate boxes and usually don't let anything coexist next to them. That's all well and good, of course (even if it does ignore floats), but look inside a block-level element such as a paragraph. There are all these lines of text, and we may well ask, "How did they get there? What controls their arrangement? How can I affect that?"

In order to understand how lines are generated, let's first consider the case of an element containing one very long line of text, as shown in Figure 8-45. Note that we've put a border around the line; this has been accomplished by wrapping the entire line in a SPAN element, and assigning it a border style:

```
SPAN {border: 1px dashed black;}
```

This is text content within a SPAN which is inside a containing element (a paragraph, in this case). The border shows the bounds of the

Figure 8-45. A single-line inline element

This is the simplest case of an inline element contained by a block-level element, no different in its way than a paragraph with two words in it. The only differences are that in Figure 8-45, we have a few dozen words and that most paragraphs don't contain an explicit inline element such as SPAN.

In order to get from this simplified state to something more familiar, all we have to do is determine how wide the element should be, and then break up the line so that the resulting pieces will fit into the width of the element. Thus we arrive at the state shown in Figure 8-46.

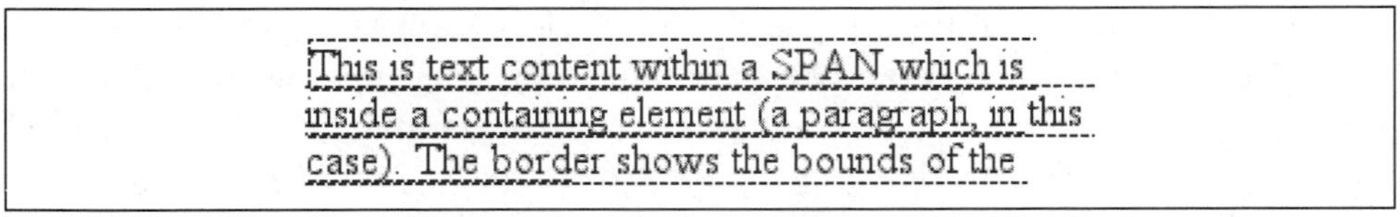

Figure 8-46. A multiple-line inline element

Basically, nothing's changed. All we did was take the single line and break it into pieces, and then stack those pieces on top of each other. Piece of cake.

In Figure 8-46, the borders for each line of text also happen to coincide with the top and bottom of each line box. This is only true because no padding or line height has been set for the inline text, but for the moment, let's use the visual cue for reference. Also, notice that the borders actually overlap each other slightly: for example, the bottom border of the first line is just below the top border of the second line. This is because the border is actually drawn on the next pixel (assuming we're using a monitor) to the *outside* of each line box. Since the line boxes are touching each other, their borders will overlap as shown in Figure 8-46.

If we alter the SPAN styles to have a background color, the actual placement of the line boxes becomes quite clear, as we can see in Figure 8-47.

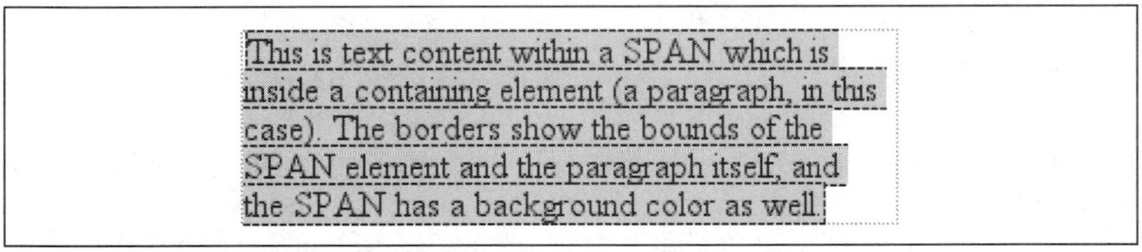

Figure 8-47. The full extent of each line box

Here we see that not every line reaches to the right edge of the paragraph's content area, which has been denoted with a dotted gray border. The end of each line box is determined by the content of the line box. For comparison, let's try the same thing, but this time right-justify the paragraph, as shown in Figure 8-48.

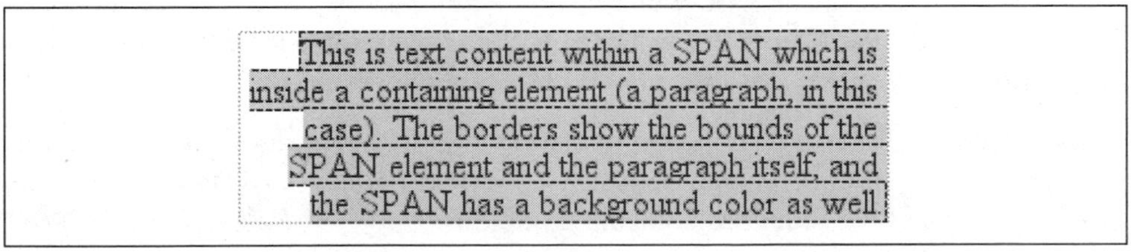

Figure 8-48. Line-box layout with right justification

Again, all we have here are the pieces of a single line of text which have been
stacked on top of one another with their right sides lined up with each other. If
we had set the paragraph to have a `text-align` of `center`, then the centers of
the line boxes would have lined up, and if it were set to `justify`, then each line
box would be forced to be as wide as the paragraph's content area. The difference is made up in letter- and word-spacing, as we see in Figure 8-49.

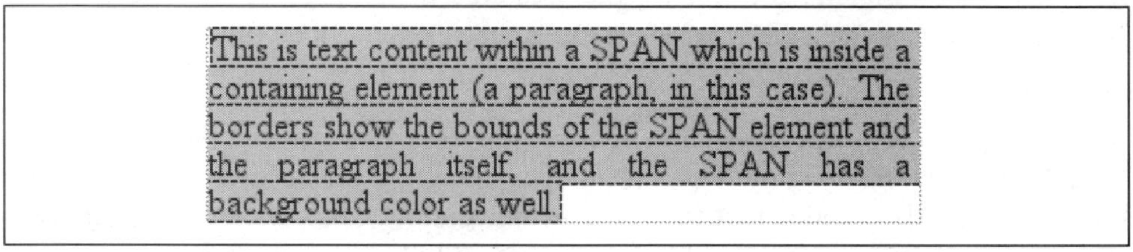

Figure 8-49. Line-box layout with full justification

That pretty well covers how line boxes are generated, at least in the simplest cases.
As we're about to see, however, the inline formatting model is not exactly simple.

Inline Formatting

As we saw in Chapter 4, *Text Properties*, all elements have a `line-height`. This
fact has a great deal to do with how inline elements are displayed, and it needs to
be covered in detail before we move on.

First, let's establish how the height of a line is determined. A line's height (or the
height of the *line box*) is determined by the height of its constituent elements and
other content (such as text). It's important to understand that `line-height` really
only applies to inline elements and other inline content and not to block-level elements. We can set a `line-height` value for a block-level element, but the only
way this will have any visual impact is by being applied to inline content within
that block-level element. Consider the following paragraph, for example:

```
<P STYLE="line-height: 0.25em;"></P>
```

Without content, the paragraph won't have anything to display, so it will not. The
fact that this paragraph has a `line-height` of any value—be it `0.25em` or `25in`—
makes no difference without inline content to take advantage of it.

In a certain sense, then, each line of text contained within a block-level element is
its own inline element, even though it isn't surrounded by any tags. If you like,
picture a fictional tag sequence something like this:

```
<P>
<LINE>This is a paragraph with a number of</LINE>
<LINE>lines of text which make up the</LINE>
<LINE>contents.</LINE>
</P>
```

Even though the LINE tags don't exist, the situation is the same as if they did. Each line of text inherits styles from the paragraph, so they may as well be contained within tags such as these. Therefore, the only reason we create line-height rules for block-level elements is so that we don't have to explicitly declare a line-height for all its inline elements, fictional or otherwise.

The fictional LINE element actually clarifies the behavior that results from setting line-height on a block-level element. According to the CSS specification, declaring line-height on a block-level element sets a *minimum* line-box height for the content of that block-level element. Thus, declaring P.spacious {line-height: 24pt;} means that the minimum height for each line box is 24 points. Technically, the only way content will inherit this line height is if it is inherited by an inline element. Most text isn't contained by an inline element. Thus, if we pretend that each line is contained by the fictional LINE element, then the model works out very nicely.

Generating a line box

Here are the steps a user agent has to go through in order to generate a line box. First, for each inline nonreplaced element (or string of text outside of an inline element), the font-size is used to determine the initial *content-height*. Thus, if an inline element has a font-size of 15px, then the content-height starts out as 15px.

Second, all of the inline elements in a given line are aligned according to their values for vertical-align. By default, this will cause all text in the line to be aligned along their baselines, but of course different vertical-align values will have different effects. All of the elements could be top-aligned, for example. We'll return to vertical alignment later in the chapter, but for now will assume that everything is baseline-aligned.

Now the line-height comes into play. Let's assume the following case:

```
<P STYLE="font-size: 12px; line-height: 12px;">
This is text, <EM>some of which is emphasized</EM>, plus other text<BR>
which is <B STYLE="font-size: 24px;">boldfaced</B> and which is<BR>
larger than the surrounding text.
</P>
```

What we have here is a situation where some of the text has a font-size of 12px, while other text has a size of 24px. However, all of the text has a line-height of 12px, since line-height is an inherited property. What happens is that the difference between font-size and line-height is divided in half, and then applied to the top and bottom of each element's content-height to arrive at the *inline box*. Each half of the divided difference is referred to as *half-leading*.

Thus, for each bit of text where both the `font-size` and `line-height` are 12px, nothing is applied to the content-height (since 12 minus 12 equals zero, and half of nothing is nothing), and so the inline box is 12px high. For the boldfaced text, however, the difference between `font-size` and `line-height` is 12px. This is divided in half to determine the half-leading (6px), and the half-leading is subtracted from both the top and bottom of the content-height to arrive at an inline box which is, in this case, 12px high. This 12-pixel inline box is centered vertically within the content-height of the element.

So far it sounds like we've done the same thing to each bit of text. This is not quite the case. The inline boxes don't actually line up, as we can see in Figure 8-50, because the text is all baseline-aligned.

Figure 8-50. How the inline boxes (gray) influence the height of the line box

However, it is precisely the inline boxes which determine the height of the overall line box. The line box is defined to be the distance from the top of the highest inline box in the line to the bottom of the lowest inline box, as illustrated by Figure 8-51.

Figure 8-51. Stacking the line boxes together

Then the top of the line box is placed against the bottom of the line box for the preceding line. This will give us a paragraph as shown in Figure 8-52.

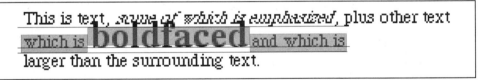

Figure 8-52. The final paragraph of stacked line boxes

As we can see, the middle line is taller than the other two, but it still isn't big enough to contain the text within it. That's because the position of the inline boxes in the line forces it to be taller than 12 pixels, but the line-box still isn't tall enough for the text to avoid overlapping other lines.

The situation can become markedly different if we change the vertical alignment of the inline boxes. Suppose that we change the boldface text to have a vertical alignment of `middle`. This would have the result shown in Figure 8-53.

This is text, *some of which is emphasized*, plus other text which is **boldfaced** and which is larger than the surrounding text.

Figure 8-53. Changing the vertical alignment of the larger text

Here, the middle of the boldfaced text's inline box has lined up with the middle of the inline boxes of the other text in the line. Because the inline boxes are all 12px tall, and their middles are all lined up, this means that the line box for this line is now only 12 pixels high, just like the others. However, it also means that the over-sized text intrudes into other lines even more than before.

Let's consider another situation where another inline element is in the same line as the boldfaced text, but its alignment is other than the baseline:

```
<P STYLE="font-size: 12px; line-height: 12px;">
This is text, <EM>some of which is emphasized</EM>, plus other text<BR>
which is <B STYLE="font-size: 24px;">boldfaced</B>
and <SPAN STYLE="vertical-align: top;">tall</SPAN> and which is<BR>
larger than the surrounding text.
</P>
```

Now we're back to our earlier example, where the middle line box is taller than the other line boxes. However, notice how the "tall" text is aligned in Figure 8-54.

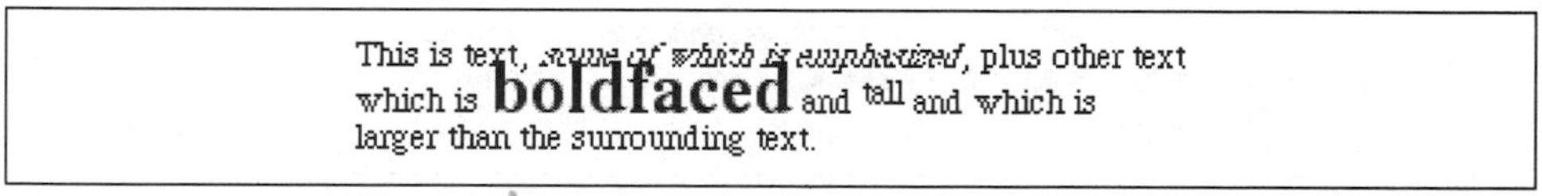

This is text, *some of which is emphasized*, plus other text which is **boldfaced** and tall and which is larger than the surrounding text.

Figure 8-54. Top-aligning text

What's happened here is that the top of the "tall" text's inline box is aligned with the top of the line box. Since the "tall" text has equal values for `font-size` and `line-height`, its content height and inline box are the same thing. However, consider this:

```
<P STYLE="font-size: 12px; line-height: 12px;">
This is text, <EM>some of which is emphasized</EM>, plus other text<BR>
which is <B STYLE="font-size: 24px;">boldfaced</B>
and <SPAN STYLE="vertical-align: top; line-height: 4px;">tall</SPAN>
and which is<BR>
larger than the surrounding text.
</P>
```

Since the `line-height` for the "tall" text is less than its `font-size`, the inline box for that element is smaller. This will change the placement of the text itself, since the top of its inline box must be aligned with the top of the line box for its line. Thus we get the result shown in Figure 8-55.

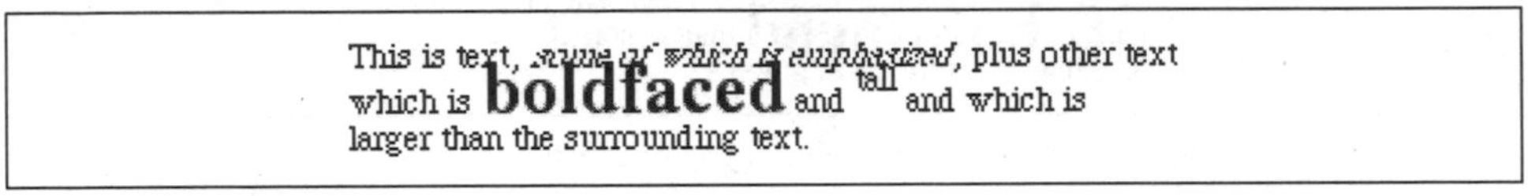

Figure 8-55. The effects of a very small inline box

On the other hand, we could set the "tall" text to have a `line-height` which is actually bigger than its font-size. For example:

```
<P STYLE="font-size: 12px; line-height: 12px;">
This is text, <EM>some of which is emphasized</EM>, plus other text<BR>
which is <B STYLE="font-size: 24px;">boldfaced</B>
and <SPAN STYLE="vertical-align: top; line-height: 18px;">tall</SPAN>
and which is<BR>
larger than the surrounding text.
</P>
```

Since we've given the "tall" text a `line-height` of 18px, the difference between `font-size` and `line-height` is 6 pixels. In this case, though, the half-leading of 3 pixels is added to the content area, not subtracted (since the `line-height` is more than the `font-size`). This will result in an inline box 18 pixels tall, and its top is aligned with the top of the line box. Thus Figure 8-56.

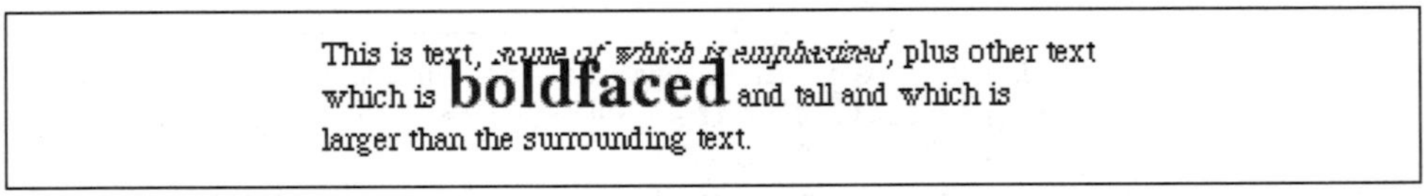

Figure 8-56. Top-aligning text with a different line height

Before we go any further, let's see what happens when we add box properties to inline elements.

Adding box properties

As we're aware from previous discussions, padding, margins, and borders may all be applied to inline nonreplaced elements, and they don't influence the `line-height` at all. If we were to apply some borders to a SPAN element without any margins or padding, we'd get results such as that shown in Figure 8-57.

The borders are placed as they are because the border edge of inline elements is controlled by the `font-size`, not the `line-height`. In other words, if a SPAN element has a `font-size` of 12pt and a `line-height` of 36pt, its content area is 12pt high, and the content area is what will be surrounded with the border.

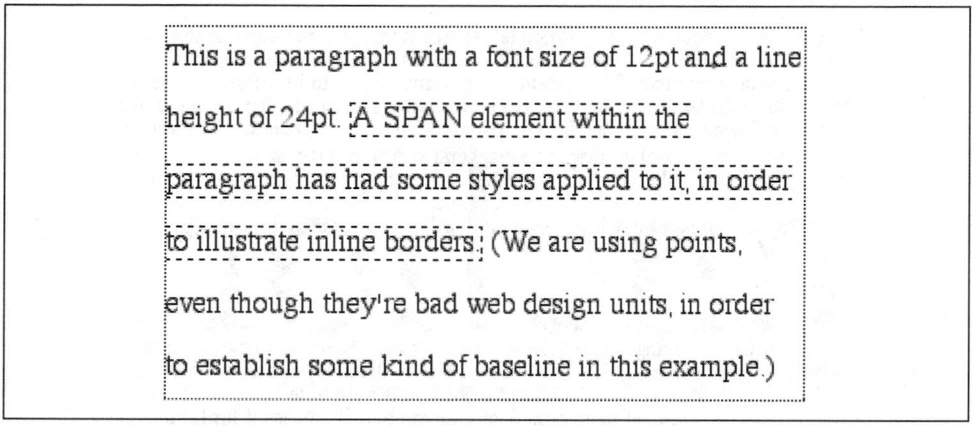

This is a paragraph with a font size of 12pt and a line height of 24pt. A SPAN element within the paragraph has had some styles applied to it, in order to illustrate inline borders. (We are using points, even though they're bad web design units, in order to establish some kind of baseline in this example.)

Figure 8-57. Inline borders and line-box layout

This behavior can be altered by assigning padding to the inline element, which will push the borders away from the text itself (shown in Figure 8-58):

```
SPAN {border: 1px dashed black; padding: 4pt;}
```

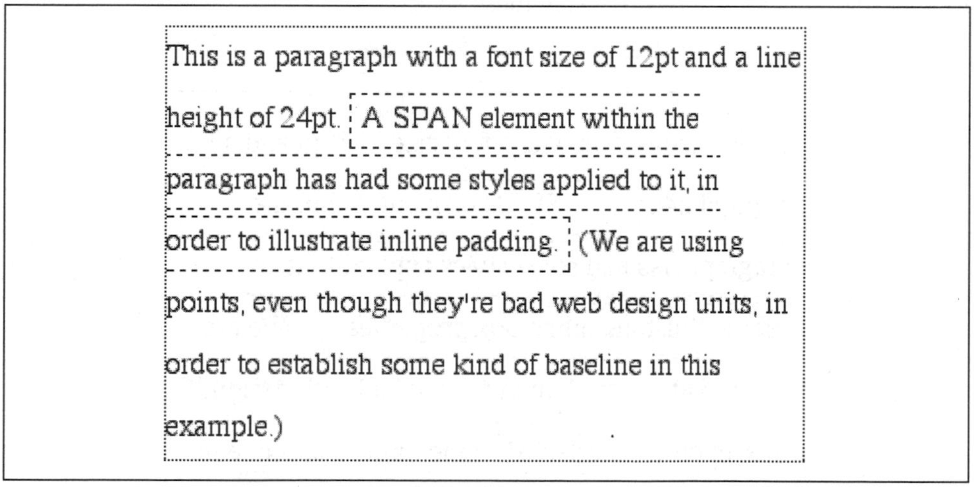

This is a paragraph with a font size of 12pt and a line height of 24pt. A SPAN element within the paragraph has had some styles applied to it, in order to illustrate inline padding. (We are using points, even though they're bad web design units, in order to establish some kind of baseline in this example.)

Figure 8-58. Inline padding and line-box layout

Note that this padding does not alter the actual shape of the content-height, and so will not affect the height of the inline box for this element. Adding borders to an inline element will not affect the way line boxes are generated, as Figure 8-59 illustrates.

One can assign margins to nonreplaced inline elements as well, but these effectively do not apply to the top and bottom of a nonreplaced inline element, and so don't affect the height of the line box. The ends of the element are another story, as we saw in Chapter 7, *Boxes and Borders*. Once again, this is because an inline

Figure 8-59. Large inline boxes can overlap many other lines

element that is displayed on multiple lines is just the same as a single-line element that has been broken into pieces. Consult Figure 8-60 for a more detailed look at this situation caused by using these styles:

```
SPAN {border: 1px dashed black; padding: 4pt; margin: 8pt;}
```

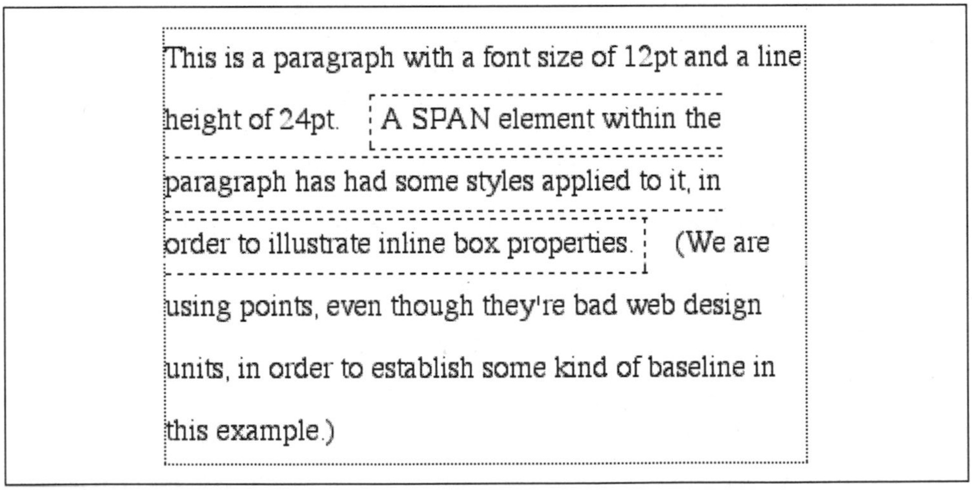

This is a paragraph with a font size of 12pt and a line height of 24pt. A SPAN element within the paragraph has had some styles applied to it, in order to illustrate inline box properties. (We are using points, even though they're bad web design units, in order to establish some kind of baseline in this example.)

Figure 8-60. Inline margins and line-box layout

Managing the Line Height of Inline Elements

In the previous section, we had a few cases where changing the `line-height` of an inline element led to the possibility of text from one line overlapping another. In each case, though, the changes were made on individual elements. So how can we affect the `line-height` of elements in a more general way, in order to keep them from overlapping?

One way to do this is to use the em unit in conjunction with an element whose `font-size` has changed. For example:

```
P {font-size: 14pt; line-height: 16pt;}
SPAN {background: gray;}
BIG {font-size: 250%; line-height: 1em; background: silver;}

...line in which</SPAN><BIG>some big text</BIG><SPAN>is found...
```

The results of this are shown in Figure 8-61. By setting a `line-height` for the BIG element, the overall height of the line box has been increased, thus providing enough room for the BIG element to be displayed without overlapping any other text and without changing the `line-height` of all lines in the paragraph. We use a value `1em` so that the `line-height` for the BIG element will be set to the same size as BIG's `font-size`—remember, `line-height` is set in relation to the `font-size` of the element itself, not the parent element.

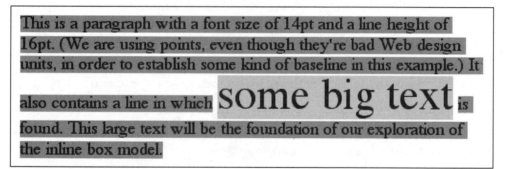

Figure 8-61. Assigning the line-height property to inline elements

It's important to keep these sorts of things in mind when you're trying to do things like add borders to an inline element. Let's say you want to put 5-pixel borders around any hyperlink:

```
A:link {border: 5px solid blue;}
```

If you don't set a large enough `line-height` to accommodate the border, it will be in danger of overwriting other lines, as shown in Figure 8-62.

One solution is to increase the `line-height` of the paragraph. This will affect every line in the entire element, not just the line in which the bordered hyperlink appears:

```
A:link {border: 5px solid blue;}
P {font-size: 14px; line-height: 24px;}
```

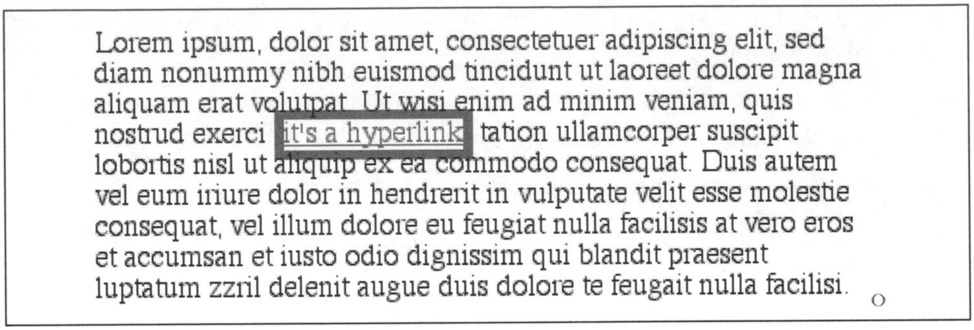

Lorem ipsum, dolor sit amet, consectetuer adipiscing elit, sed diam nonummy nibh euismod tincidunt ut laoreet dolore magna aliquam erat volutpat. Ut wisi enim ad minim veniam, quis nostrud exerci it's a hyperlink tation ullamcorper suscipit lobortis nisl ut aliquip ex ea commodo consequat. Duis autem vel eum iriure dolor in hendrerit in vulputate velit esse molestie consequat, vel illum dolore eu feugiat nulla facilisis at vero eros et accumsan et iusto odio dignissim qui blandit praesent luptatum zzril delenit augue duis dolore te feugait nulla facilisi.   O

Figure 8-62. Inline borders can be overlapped

Because there is extra space added above and below each line, the border around the hyperlink doesn't impinge on any other line, as we can see in Figure 8-63.

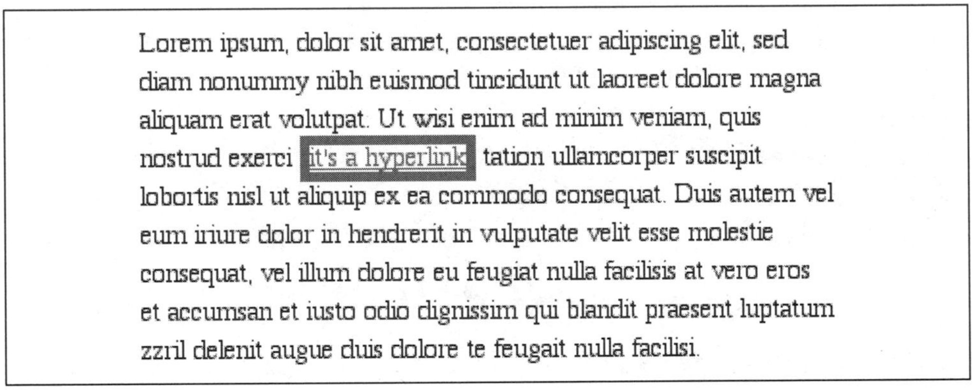

Lorem ipsum, dolor sit amet, consectetuer adipiscing elit, sed diam nonummy nibh euismod tincidunt ut laoreet dolore magna aliquam erat volutpat. Ut wisi enim ad minim veniam, quis nostrud exerci it's a hyperlink tation ullamcorper suscipit lobortis nisl ut aliquip ex ea commodo consequat. Duis autem vel eum iriure dolor in hendrerit in vulputate velit esse molestie consequat, vel illum dolore eu feugiat nulla facilisis at vero eros et accumsan et iusto odio dignissim qui blandit praesent luptatum zzril delenit augue duis dolore te feugait nulla facilisi.

Figure 8-63. Increasing line-height to leave room for inline borders

This approach works in this particular case, of course, because all of the text is the same size. Just to cover all the bases, though, it might make more sense to simply increase the `line-height` of the anchor element itself, like this:

```
A:link {border: 5px solid blue; line-height: 24px;}
P {font-size: 14px;}
```

If all the content of a line is text of the same size, then the line box is always as tall as the biggest `line-height` value contained within that line box (since this will coincide with the height of the tallest inline box in the line), so this works. Furthermore, it only affects those lines in which a hyperlink appears. However, there is yet another alternative.

Scaling the line heights

There's an even better way to set `line-height`, as it turns out, and that's to use a raw number as the value of `line-height`. This is so much better because the number is used as a scaling factor, and it is the factor that is inherited, not the computed value. Let's say you want the `line-height` of all elements in a document to be one-and-one-half times their `font-size`. You would declare:

```
BODY {line-height: 1.5;}
```

This scaling factor of `1.5` is passed down from element to element, and at each level the factor is used as a multiplier of the `font-size` of each element. Therefore, the following markup would be displayed as shown in Figure 8-64 (backgrounds added for illustrative purposes):

```
P {font-size: 12px; line-height: 1.5;}
SMALL {font-size: 66%;}
BIG {font-size: 200%;}
```

```
<P>This paragraph has a line-height of 1.5 times its font-size. In addition,
any elements within it <SMALL>such as this small element</SMALL> also have
line-heights 1.5 time their font-size... and that includes <BIG>this big
element right here</BIG>. By using a scaling factor, line-heights scale
to match the font-size of any element.</P>
```

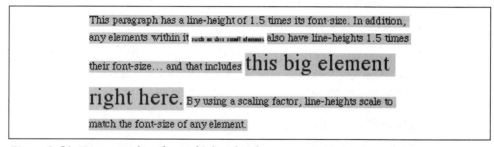

Figure 8-64. Using a scaling factor for line-height

In this example, the `line-height` for the SMALL element turns out to be `12px`, and for the BIG element, it's `36px`. These may seem excessive, but they're in keeping with the overall page design. Of course, if you don't want your BIG text to generate too much extra leading, just use these rules instead:

```
P {font-size: 12px; line-height: 1.5;}
SMALL {font-size: 66%;}
BIG {font-size: 200%; line-height: 1em;}
```

Anything this useful has to have a drawback, right? As it happens, Internet Explorer 3.x will treat scaling factors as though they were pixel units. Just try to imagine a paragraph with a `line-height` of `1.5px`. It isn't pretty.

Another solution is to set the styles such that lines are no taller than absolutely necessary to hold their content. This is where you might use a `line-height` of `1.0`. This value will multiply itself by every `font-size` to get the same value as the `font-size` of every element. Thus, for every element, the inline box will be the same as the content area.

Inline Replaced Elements

Inline replaced elements, such as images, are subject to a few crucial differences in how inline formatting is handled. This difference stems from the fact that replaced elements are still assumed to have an intrinsic height and width; for example, an image will be a certain number of pixels high and wide.

However, a replaced element with an intrinsic height can cause a line box to become taller than normal. This does *not* change the value of `line-height` for any element in the line, *including the image itself.* Instead, the line box is simply made tall enough to accommodate the replaced element, *plus* any box properties. In other words, the entirety of the replaced element—content, margins, borders, and padding—is used to define the element's inline box. The following markup gives one such example, (shown in Figure 8-65):

```
P {font-size: 12px; line-height: 18px;}
IMG {height: 30px; margin: 0; padding: 0;}
```

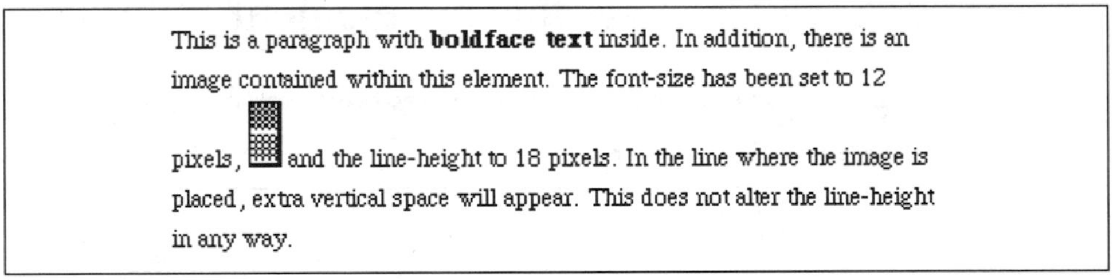

This is a paragraph with **boldface text** inside. In addition, there is an image contained within this element. The font-size has been set to 12

pixels, and the line-height to 18 pixels. In the line where the image is placed, extra vertical space will appear. This does not alter the line-height in any way.

Figure 8-65. Replaced elements don't actually increase the line height

Despite all the blank space, the effective value of `line-height` has not changed. It simply has no effect on the image's inline box, which is in this case `30px` tall.

Nonetheless, an inline replaced element still has a value for `line-height`. Why? In order to be able to correctly position the element if it's been vertically aligned. Recall that, percentage values for `vertical-align` are calculated with respect to an element's line height. Thus:

```
P {line-height: 18px;}
IMG {vertical-align: 50%;}

<P>The image in this paragraph <IMG SRC="test.gif" ALT="test image">
will be raised 9px.</P>
```

The inherited value of `line-height` is what causes the image to be raised nine pixels, instead of some other number. Without a value for `line-height`, it wouldn't be possible to perform percentage-value vertical alignments. The height of the image itself has no relevance when it comes to vertical alignment: the value of line-height is all that matters.

Adding box properties

After everything else, applying margins, borders, and padding to inline replaced elements almost seems simple.

Padding and borders are applied to replaced elements as normal; padding inserts space around the actual content (for example, a graphic) and the border surrounds the padding. What's interesting is that these two things actually do influence the height of the line box. Consider Figure 8-66.

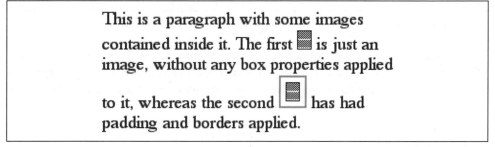

Figure 8-66. Adding padding and borders to an inline replaced element

Note that the "first" line box is tall enough to contain the image, whereas the "second" is tall enough to contain the image, its padding, and its border. This is because the totality of the replaced element (content, padding, borders) make up the inline box for the replaced element. This is what forces the line boxes to be taller in Figure 8-66.

Margins are also contained within the line box, but they have their own wrinkle. Setting a positive margin is no mystery: it will simply make the line box taller, as in Figure 8-67.

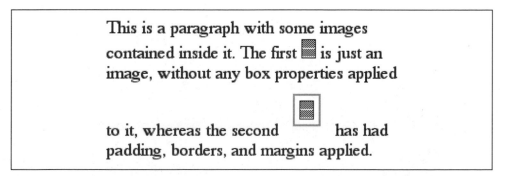

Figure 8-67. Adding padding, borders, and margins to an inline replaced element

Setting negative margins, meanwhile, has exactly the effect you might expect: it makes the line-box shorter. This is illustrated in Figure 8-68, where we can see the line above the image has been pulled down toward it.

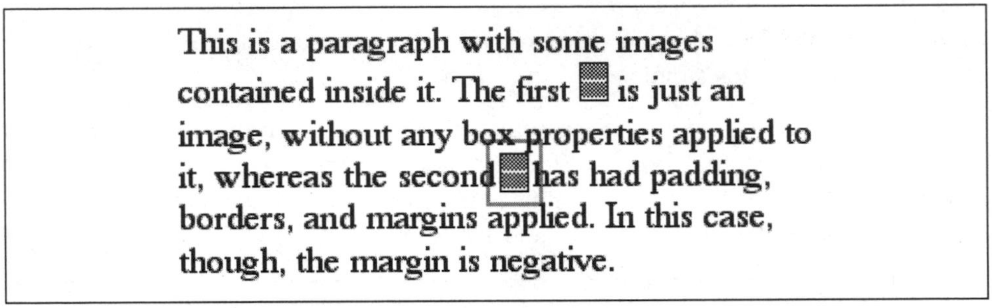

Figure 8-68. The effect of negative margins on an inline replaced element

This is quite similar to the operation of negative margins on block-level elements, of course. In this case, the negative margins are making the replaced element's inline box smaller than ordinary. This is the only way to cause inline replaced elements to bleed into other lines.

Summary

Although some aspects of the CSS formatting model may seem counterintuitive at first, they begin to make sense the more one works with them. In many cases, what seem like nonsensical or even idiotic rules turn out to exist in order to prevent bizarre or otherwise undesirable document displays.

As it happens, having a firm grasp of the visual formatting model is a good foundation for understanding how positioning works. Thus, the next chapter will cover positioning, and do so in a manner very similar to this chapter: the discussion is largely theoretical.

9

Positioning

The idea behind positioning is fairly simple. It allows you to define exactly where element boxes will appear relative to where they would ordinarily be—or relative to a parent element, or another element, or even to the browser window itself. The power of this feature is both obvious and surprising. It shouldn't be too surprising to learn that this is the part of CSS2 that user agents usually first attempt to support. Given that there were some very good positioning implementations on the horizon as the book was being completed, we felt it worthwhile to give readers a glimpse of what's coming soon—or, if you're reading this book a year or three after its publication, what can be done.

You may notice that, unlike other chapters, almost none of the figures in this chapter was generated with a web browser. This is something of a statement about the reliability and consistency of positioning implementations at the time of this writing: not one of them was solid enough to trust completely. It was actually easier to draw theoretical examples by hand than to take screenshots in web browsers and then retouch them in Photoshop.

This is also why this chapter is largely (but not entirely) free of browser warnings and caveats. Rather than drown the explanatory text in side notes, we have chosen to simply describe positioning as it is given by the CSS2 specification and leave things there. Perhaps the second edition of this book will contain more practical advice, but at this time, the only practical advice we can give is this: test your positioning code thoroughly, and be prepared for inconsistencies between positioning implementations.

General Concepts

Before delving into the specific mechanisms of positioning, we need to establish a number of concepts. These concepts actually form the foundation of CSS layout in general since every displayed element can be described in terms of its positioning. After all, any element that is placed onscreen, or printed on a piece of paper, has a position and must therefore be positioned—by the user agent, if nothing else.

The *containing block* is the context in which formatting takes place. For example, the containing block of a boldface element could be the paragraph in which it occurs, as demonstrated in Figure 9-1.

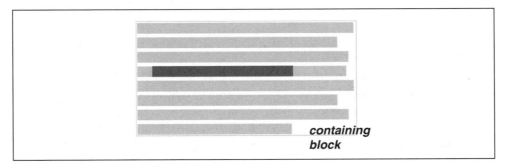

Figure 9-1. An example of a containing block

Not every element in CSS generates a containing block for its descendant elements. The rules for the establishment of a containing block are as follows:

1. The containing block of the "root element" (also called the *initial containing block*) is established by the user agent. In HTML, the root element is the HTML element, although some browsers may incorrectly use BODY.

2. For nonroot elements that are not absolutely positioned, the containing block for an element is set as the content edge of the nearest block-level ancestor. This is true even in relative positioning, although it might not seem so at first.

3. For nonroot elements that are absolutely positioned using a **position** of **absolute**, the containing block is set to the nearest ancestor (of any kind) that has a **position** other than **static**. This happens as follows:

   a. If the ancestor is block-level, the containing block is set to be that element's padding edge; in other words, the area that would be bounded by a border.

   b. If the ancestor is inline-level, the containing block is set to the content edge of the ancestor. In left-to-right languages, the top and left of the containing block are the top and left content edges of the first box in the ancestor, and the bottom and right edges are the bottom and right content edges of the last box. In right-to-left languages, the right edge of the containing block corresponds to the right content edge of the first box, and the left is taken from the last box. The top and bottom are the same.

If there is no such ancestor, then the content edge of the root element is used to establish a containing block.

The main thing to remember about the containing block is that it establishes a formatting context for all of its descendant elements. For example, if margins are declared as percentages, the percentages are calculated with respect to the containing block. This gives us rule #2, which says that the containing block is usually equivalent to the content area of an element.

Another important thing about the containing block is this: elements can be positioned outside of their containing block. This is very similar to the way in which floated elements can use negative margins to float outside of their parent's content area. It also makes it seem like the term "containing block" should really be "positioning context," but since the specification uses "containing block," so will this text. (We do try to minimize confusion. Really!)

Positioning Schemes

You can choose one of four different types of positioning by using the `position` property.

---

position

Values	`static`	`relative`	`absolute`	`fixed`	`inherit`
Initial Value	`static`
Applies to	all elements
Inherited	no

The values of `position` have the following meanings:

`static`

The element's box is generated as normal. Block-level elements generate a rectangular box that is part of the document's flow, and inline-level boxes are generated in the context of one or more line boxes that are flowed within their parent element.

relative

> The element's box is offset by some distance. Its containing block is the area that the element would occupy if it were not positioned. The element retains the shape it would have had were it not positioned, and the space that the element would ordinarily have occupied is preserved. Relative positioning is accomplished by generating the element as though it were set to static, and then simply shifting the element's box (or boxes, in the case of an inline element that crosses multiple lines). It is possible that the positioned element will overlap other content. The direction and magnitude of the offset are specified using some combination of the properties top, right, bottom, and left.

absolute

> The element's box is completely removed from the flow of the document and positioned with respect to its containing block. Whatever space the element might have occupied in the normal document flow is closed up, as though the element did not exist. The size and position of the element are defined by a combination of the properties height, width, top, right, bottom, and left, plus any margins, padding, and borders set for the element. Absolutely positioned elements can have margins, but these margins do not collapse.

fixed

> The element's box is positioned as though it were set to absolute, but its containing block is the viewport itself. In screen media such as web browsers, the element will not move within the browser window when the document is scrolled. This allows for frame-style layouts, for example. In paged media such as printouts, a fixed element will appear in the same place on every page. This potentially can be used to create running heads or footers.

inherit

> The value is inherited from the parent element. See Chapter 10, *CSS2: A Look Ahead*, for more details.

Side Offsets

Three of the positioning schemes described in the previous section—relative, absolute, and fixed—use four distinct properties to describe the offset of a positioned element's sides with respect to its containing block. These four properties, which we will refer to as the *side-offset* properties, are a big part of what makes positioning work.

top, right, bottom, left

Values	<length>	<percentage>	static-position	auto	inherit
Initial Value	auto
Applies to	positioned elements (that is, elements for which the value of position is something other than static)
Inherited	no

Note: Percentages refer to the width of the containing block (right, left) or the height of the containing block (top, bottom).

These properties describe an offset from the nearest side of the containing block (thus the term *side-offset*). For example, top describes how far the outer top edge of the positioned element should be placed from the top of its containing block. In the case of top, positive values move the top edge of the positioned element *downward*, while negative values move it *above* the top of its containing block. Similarly, left describes how far to the right (for positive values) or left (for negative values) the outer left edge of the positioned element is from the left edge of its containing block. Another way to look at it is that positive values cause inward offsets, moving the edges toward the center of the containing block, and negative values cause outward offsets.

The description of offsetting the outer edges is based on an erratum. The original CSS2 specification actually says that the content edges are offset, but it has been widely agreed that this is a serious error, and in fact, readings of other parts of the specification show that it is the outer edges that are offset.

The implication of offsetting the outer edges of a positioned element is that everything about an element—margins, borders, padding, and content—is moved in the process of positioning the element. In other words, it is possible to set margins, borders, and padding for a positioned element. These will be preserved and kept with the positioned element, and will be contained within the area defined by the side-offset properties.

There are two other side-offset property values that should be mentioned here. The first, `static-position`, causes the user agent to place the given side of a positioned element where it would have been if the element had not been positioned. For example, consider a nonpositioned element whose top edge is 3 ems from the top of its containing block. If the element is then positioned and given a `top` of `static-position`, then the top of the positioned element will be 3 ems from the top of the containing block. Later in the chapter, we'll see how this can be useful.

The other value, `auto`, allows for some even more interesting effects. It acts much the same as setting `auto` on margins, but in positioning, this can permit the creation of elements that are only as wide or tall as they need to be in order to display their content, without having to exactly specify how high or wide that will be. We'll explore this in detail later in the chapter as well.

It is important to remember that the side-offset properties define offset from the analogous side (e.g., `left` defines the offset from the left side) of the containing block, not from the upper-left corner of the containing block. That's why, for example, one way to fill up the lower-right corner of a containing block would use these values:

```
top: 50%; bottom: 0; left: 50%; right: 0;
```

In this example, the outer left edge of the positioned element is placed halfway across the containing block. This is its offset from the left edge of the containing block. The outer right edge of the positioned element, however, is not offset from the right edge of the containing block, so the two are coincident. Similar reasoning holds true for the top and bottom of the positioned element: the outer top edge is placed halfway down the containing block, but the outer bottom edge is not moved up from the bottom. This leads to what's shown in Figure 9-2.

What's depicted in Figure 9-2, and in most of the examples in this chapter, will only work if the containing block was established by an element with an explicitly defined height. This is because a line in the specification says that if the height of the containing block is not explicitly specified—say, for example, that it's dependent on the content of the element, as in a normal paragraph—then both `top` and `bottom` for any positioned element within that containing block are treated as `auto`.

In addition, even though they don't explicitly say so, the examples in this section (and the next few sections) are all based around absolute positioning. Since absolute positioning is the simplest scheme in which to demonstrate how `top`, `right`, `bottom`, and `left` work, we'll stick to that for now.

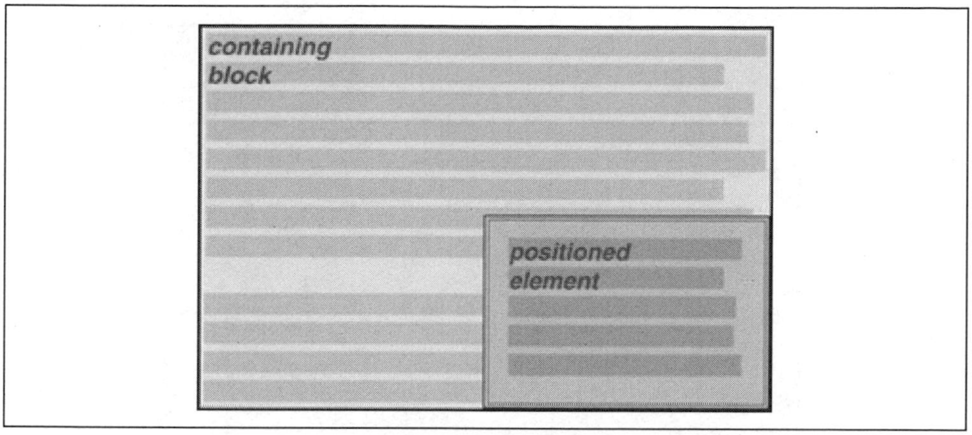

Figure 9-2. Positioning an element within its containing block

Note that the positioned element has padding, a double border, and a slightly different background color. In Figure 9-2, it has no margins, but if it did, they would create blank space between the borders and the offset edges. This would make the positioned element appear as though it did not completely fill the lower-right quarter of the containing block. In truth, it would do so, but this would not be immediately apparent to the eye. In other words, the following two sets of styles would have the same visual appearance, assuming the containing block to be 100 ems high by 100 ems wide:

```
top: 50%; bottom: 0; left: 50%; right: 0; margin: 10em;
top: 60%; bottom: 10%; left: 60%; right: 10%; margin: 0;
```

Again, the similarity would be only visual in nature.

By using negative values, it is possible to position an element outside its containing block. For example, the following values will lead to the result shown in Figure 9-3:

```
top: -5em; bottom: 50%; left: 75%; right: -3em;
```

Now let's see why leaving out `width` and `height` isn't always a bad thing in positioning, as well as how declaring them can work to your advantage.

Width and Height

There will be many cases when, having determined where you're going to position an element, you will want to go ahead and declare how wide and how high that element should be. In addition, there will likely be conditions where you'll want to limit how high or wide a positioned element gets, not to mention cases where you want the browser to go ahead and automatically calculate the width, or the height, or both.

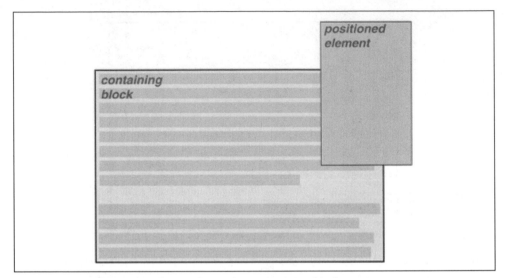

Figure 9-3. Positioning an element beyond its containing block

Setting width and height

If you want to give your positioned element a specific width, then the obvious property to turn to is `width`. Similarly, `height` will let you declare a specific height for a positioned element.

width

Values	<length> | <percentage> | auto
Initial Value	auto
Applies to	block-level and replaced elements
Inherited	no

Note: Percentage values refer to the width of the containing block.

height

Values	<length> | auto
Initial Value	auto
Applies to	block-level and replaced elements
Inherited	no

Although it is sometimes important to set the width and height of an element, this is not always necessary when positioning elements. For example, if the placement of the four sides of the element is described using `top`, `right`, `bottom`, and `left`, then the height and width of the element are determined by the placement of the sides. Assume that you want an element to fill the left half of its containing block, from top to bottom. You could use these styles, with the result depicted in Figure 9-4:

```
top: 0; bottom: 0; left: 0; right: 50%;
```

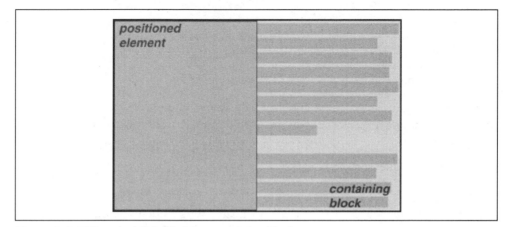

Figure 9-4. Filling the left half of the containing block

Since the default value of both `width` and `height` is `auto`, the result shown in Figure 9-4 is exactly the same as if you had used these styles:

```
top: 0; bottom: 0; left: 0; right: 50%; width: auto; height: auto;
```

Now let's say you want to position an element that is in the upper-right corner of its containing block and is one-third as wide as its containing block, but only as tall as necessary to display its content, as shown in Figure 9-5.

This is where `auto` really comes into its own. The styles needed to get the result shown in Figure 9-5 is:

```
top: 0; bottom: auto; left: auto; right: 0; width: 33%; height: auto;
```

Because `top` is set to 0, and `bottom` and `height` are set to `auto`, the user agent is free to size the element so that it's just tall enough to display its own content, and no taller. This happens thanks to the revised rules for calculating the height and width of absolutely positioned elements, which were published in an errata to the original specification.

Note that the fact that we set an explicit width helped matters. Since the user agent knew how wide the element should be, it was a trivial matter to calculate the height of the element based on its content. If width has also been set to `auto`,

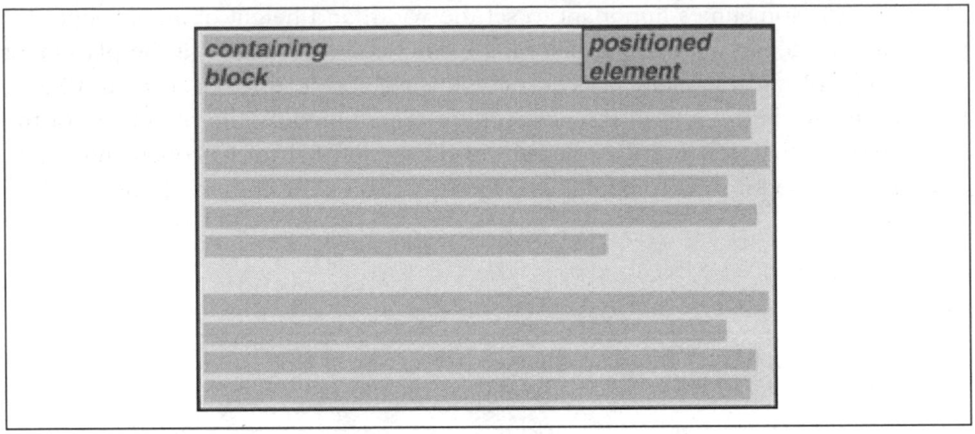

Figure 9-5. "Shrink-wrapping" a positioned element

then the user agent would have had to assign some value to it. This value is likely to vary by user agent, so it's usually better to declare a width that you like.

Of course, this is not always the case: you could set an explicit height and let the width scale to fit the content. Thus:

```
top: 0; bottom: auto; left: auto; right: 0; width: auto; height: 10em;
```

Here the element will be 10 ems tall no matter what, but its width can vary to exactly fit the content. This is sometimes called "shrink-wrapping" the content, since it mimics the act of applying shrink-wrap to a box or other product. In the same way the plastic shrink-wrap precisely hugs the contents of the package, so too does a positioned element—given the right styles, of course.

If `bottom` is set to an actual value—percentage or length—then the height of the positioned element is constrained. As a demonstration, let's set `bottom` to be a specific value, with the result shown in Figure 9-6:

```
top: 0; bottom: 10%; left: auto; right: 0; width: 33%; height: auto;
```

In this case, the `height` of the element must be 90% the height of the containing block, since 100% − 0 − 10% = 90%. This assumes, of course, that there have been no margins, borders, or padding set for the positioned element; otherwise, the effective `height` would be decreased, although the entire element (content, padding, borders, and margins) would still be 90% as tall as the containing block.

Similarly, if we specifically declare a height but leave `bottom` as `auto`, then something like Figure 9-7 will occur:

```
top: 0; bottom: auto; left: auto; right: 0; width: 33%; height: 45%;
```

In this case, the placement of the bottom of the positioned element is the same as if we'd declared `bottom: 55%`, because 100% − 0 − 45% = 55%.

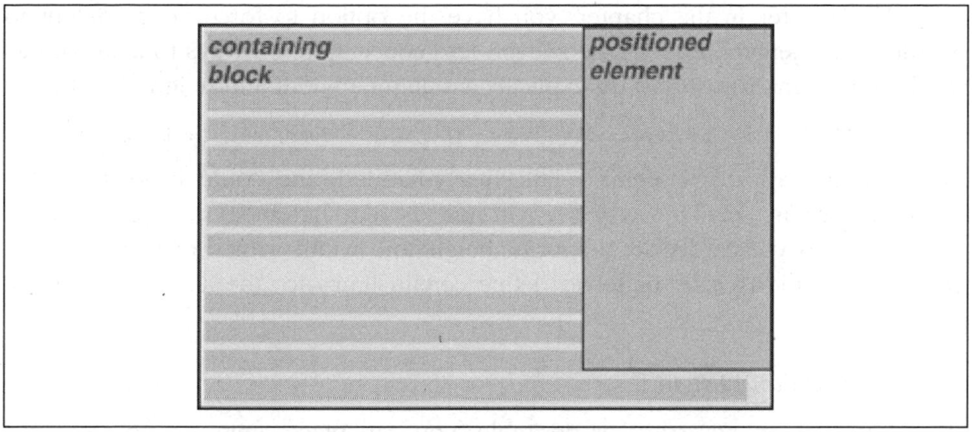

Figure 9-6. Defining a height by using an explicit bottom

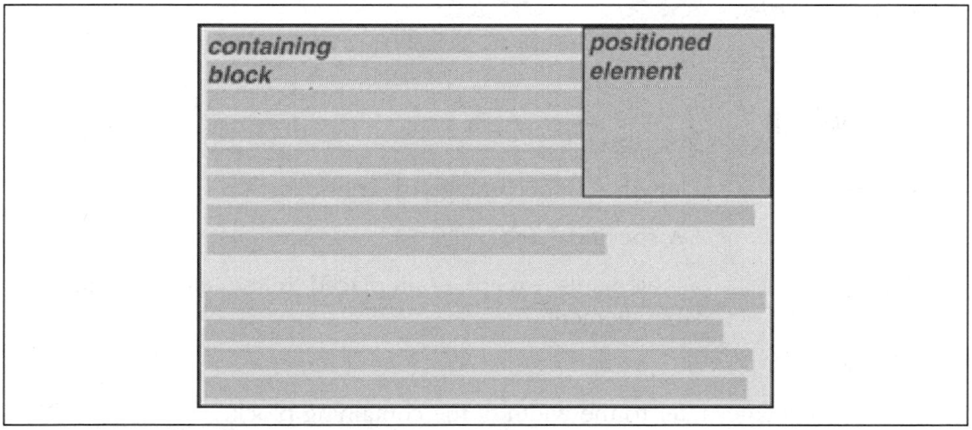

Figure 9-7. Defining a height by using an explicit height

Many of the same principles hold true for widths, of course. For example:

```
top: 100px; bottom: 200px; left: 30%; right: 10%; height: auto; width: auto;
```

Here, the width of the element is effectively 60% the width of its containing block.

As wonderful as all of this is, there arises a serious question. Suppose you have a positioned element that you don't want to be any smaller than a certain size? Consider the following styles:

```
top: 10%; bottom: 20%; left: 50%; right: 10%;
```

Thus the height is 70%, and the width 40% of the containing block's height and width. That's fine as far as it goes—but what happens if the containing block is only 50 pixels tall by 200 pixels wide? That gives you an element only 35 pixels wide by 80 pixels tall. That doesn't leave much room to show the content, but if you use `auto` for the width or height, the element might fill its entire containing block, obscuring the containing block's contents.

As we'll see later in the chapter, you have the option to force your content to overflow the element. For now, however, let's concentrate on ways to deal with its width and height. You could try explicitly assigning a width and height, like this:

```
top: 10%; bottom: 20%; left: 50%; right: 10%; width: 30em; height: 15em;
```

However, this approach seems a little heavy-handed, and could have disastrous consequences in small browsing environments like handheld devices. Furthermore, it forces you to declare a specific height and width, which gives up a lot of flexibility. Wouldn't it be better to define certain limits for the size of the height and width?

Limiting width and height

Should it become necessary or desirable, you can place limits on an element's width and height by using the following CSS2 properties, which I'll refer to as the *min-max properties.*

---

min-width

Values	<length> | <percentage> | `inherit`
Initial Value	UA specific
Applies to	all elements except nonreplaced inline elements and table elements
Inherited	no

Note: Percentages refer to the width of the containing block.

---

max-width

Values	<length> | <percentage> | `none` | `inherit`
Initial Value	UA specific
Applies to	all elements except nonreplaced inline elements and table elements
Inherited	no

Note: Percentages refer to the width of the containing block.

---

min-height

Values	<length> | <percentage> | `inherit`
Initial Value	0
Applies to	all elements except nonreplaced inline elements and table elements
Inherited	no

Note: Percentages refer to the height of the containing block.

---

max-height

Values	<length> | <percentage> | `none` | `inherit`
Initial Value	none
Applies to	all elements except nonreplaced inline elements and table elements
Inherited	no

Note: Percentages refer to the height of the containing block.

The names of these properties make them fairly self-explanatory. Here we have one possible solution for the example given in the previous section:

```
top: 10%; bottom: 20%; left: 50%; right: 10%;
  min-width: 20em; min-height: 30em;
```

Of course, this still isn't a very good solution, since it forces the element to be at least 20em wide by 30em tall. Here's a better one:

```
top: 10%; bottom: auto; left: 50%; right: 10%; height: auto; min-width: 15em;
```

Here we have a case where the element should be 40% as wide as the containing block but can never be less than 15em wide. We've also changed the `bottom` and `height` so that they're automatically determined. This will let the element be as tall as necessary to display its content, no matter how narrow it gets (never less than 15em, of course!).

We can turn this around to keep elements from getting too wide or tall by using `max-width` and `max-height`. Let's consider a situation where, for some strange reason, we want an element to have three-quarters the width of its containing block, but to stop getting wider when it hits 400 pixels. The appropriate styles are:

```
left: 0%; right: auto; width: 75%; max-width: 400px;
```

The great advantage of the min-max properties is that they let you mix units with relative safety. You can set percentage-based sizes while setting length-based limits, or vice versa.

> These min-max properties can be very useful in conjunction with floated elements as well. For example, you can allow a floated element's width to be relative to the width of its parent element (which is its containing block), while also making sure that the float's width never goes below 10em. The reverse approach is also possible:
>
> ```
> P.aside {float: left; width: 40em; max-width: 40%;}
> ```
>
> This will set the float to be 40em wide, unless that would be more than 40% the width of the containing block, in which case the float will be narrowed.

Of course, it's still possible to use these properties to keep an element from exceeding a certain size, as in this:

```
max-height: 30em; max-width: 20em;
```

The question here, though, is what happens if the content of the element doesn't all fit into the specified element size. Does it get cut off at the boundaries, or does it spill outside the positioned element? That's what the next section will explore.

Content Overflow and Clipping

Should the content of an element be too much for the element's size, it will be in danger of overflowing the element itself. There are a few alternatives in such situations, and CSS lets you select between them. It will also allow you to define a clipping region to determine the area of the element outside which these sorts of things become an issue, as well as give a way to clip off parts of an element.

Overflow

So let's say that you have, for whatever reason, an element that has been pinned to a specific size, and the content doesn't fit. You can take control of the situation with the `overflow` property.

overflow

Values	`visible` | `hidden` | `scroll` | `auto` | `inherit`
Initial Value	`visible`
Applies to	block-level and replaced elements
Inherited	no

This property only applies in one (or more) the following cases:

- When an element has negative margins.

- When a line box must be wider than its parent's content area, perhaps due to the existence of an unusually long word, nonwrapped text such as PRE text, or another circumstance where line-wrapping cannot occur.

- When a block-level box is wider than its parent's content area.

- When an element's box is taller than the height explicitly set for its parent.

- When an element has been absolutely positioned.

The default value of `visible` means that the content may be visible outside the element's box. Typically, this would lead to the content simply running outside its own element box, but not altering the shape of that box. The following styles would result in Figure 9-8:

```
DIV#sidebar {position: absolute; top: 0; left: 0; width: 25%; height: 7em;
    overflow: visible;}
```

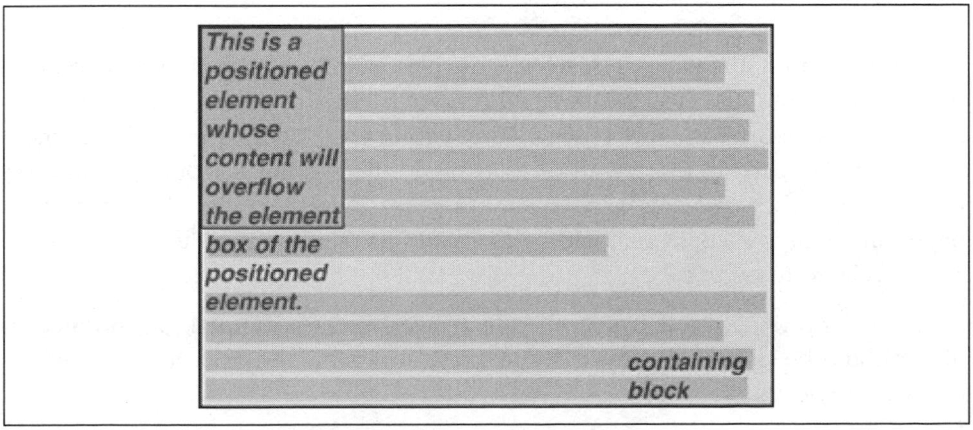

Figure 9-8. Overflowing the content area of an element

The specification does not say whether or not visible overflowed content can overlap the content of other elements, but it is reasonable to infer that this is possible. Since positioned elements can overlap other elements, it stands to reason that the content of a positioned element should be treated no differently.

If the `overflow` is set to `scroll`, the element's content is clipped—that is, cannot be seen—but some way is provided to make the extra content available to the user. In a web browser, this would mean a scrollbar (or set of them) or another method of accessing the content without altering the shape of the element itself. One possibility is depicted in Figure 9-9, which could result from the following styles:

```
DIV#sidebar {position: absolute; top: 0; left: 0; width: 15%; height: 7em;
    overflow: scroll;}
```

Figure 9-9. Invoking a scrollbar with overflow

If `scroll` is used, the panning mechanisms (e.g., scrollbars) should always be rendered. To quote the specification, "this avoids any problems with scrollbars appearing or disappearing in a dynamic environment." Thus, even if the element has sufficient space to display all of its content, the scrollbars would still appear. In addition, when printing a page or otherwise displaying the document in a paged medium, the content should be displayed as though the value of `overflow` were declared to be `visible`.

If the `overflow` is set to `hidden`, the element's content is clipped, but no mechanism should be provided to make the content accessible to the user. Consider the following styles:

```
DIV#sidebar {position: absolute; top: 0; left: 0; width: 15%; height: 7em;
    overflow: hidden;}
```

In such an instance, the clipped content would not be accessible to the user. This would lead to a situation like that illustrated by Figure 9-10.

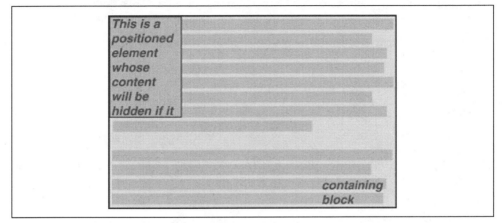

Figure 9-10. Clipping content with overflow

Finally, there is `overflow: auto`. This allows user agents to determine what behavior to use, although they are encouraged to provide a scrolling mechanism when necessary. This is a potentially useful way to use `overflow`, since user agents could interpret it to mean "provide scrollbars only when needed." (They may not, but they certainly could, and probably should.)

In the simplest case, the clipping region for any positioned element is the content area of the element itself, as depicted in Figure 9-10. However, you may wish to change the clipping area. That's what we'll do in the next section.

Overflow clipping

In situations where the content of an element overflows its element box, and `overflow` has been set such that the content should in fact be clipped, it is possible to alter the shape of the clipping region by using the property `overflow-clip`.

overflow-clip

Values	`rect(<top>, <right>, <bottom>, <left>)	auto	inherit`
Initial Value	`auto`
Applies to	block-level and replaced elements with an `overflow` value other than `visible`
Inherited	no

The default value, `auto`, means that the clipping region should have the same size and location as the element's content area. The other possibility is to define a clipping shape that is relative to the element's content area. This does not alter the shape of the content area, but instead alters the area in which content may be rendered.

> While the only clipping shape available in CSS2 is a rectangle, the specification does offer the possibility that other shapes will be included in future specifications.

This is done with the shape value `rect(`*top*`, `*right*`, `*bottom*`, `*left*`)`. We could specify no change in the clipping region like this:

```
overflow-clip: rect(0, auto, auto, 0);
```

This would be no different than declaring **overflow-clip: auto**. It's more interesting to shift the clipping area, of course. For example:

```
DIV#sidebar {position: absolute; top: 0; left: 0; width: 5em; height: 7em;
    overflow: hidden; overflow-clip: rect(0.5em, 4em, 6.5em, 1em);}
```

This sets the clipping area inward half an em from the top and bottom, and one em from the right and left. This would cause a result something like that shown in Figure 9-11, where a dashed line has been added to illustrate the edges of the clipping region. This line would not actually appear in a user agent attempting to render the document.

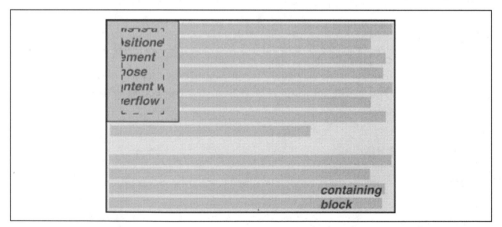

Figure 9-11. Contracting the clipping region

The syntax of **rect** is an interesting case. Technically, it can be `rect(`*top*`, `*right*`, `*bottom*`, `*left*`)`—note the commas—but the CSS2 specification contains examples both with and without commas and defines **rect** as accepting both the comma and noncomma versions. This text will stick to the comma version mostly because it makes things easier to read.

It is extremely important to note that the values for `rect(...)` are *not* side-offsets. They are, instead, distances from the upper-left corner of the element. Thus, a clipping rectangle which encloses a square 20 pixels by 20 pixels in the upper-left corner of the element would be defined as:

```
rect(0, 20px, 20px, 0)
```

The only values permitted with `rect(...)` are length values and `auto`, which is the same as "set the clipping edge to the appropriate content edge." Thus, the following two statements mean the same thing:

```
overflow-clip: rect(auto, auto, 10px, 1cm);
overflow-clip: rect(0, 0, 10px, 1cm);
```

It is possible to set negative lengths, though, which will expand the clipping area outside the element's box. If you wanted to push the clipping area up and left by a quarter-inch, it would be done with the following styles (illustrated by Figure 9-12):

```
overflow-clip: rect(-0.25in, auto, auto, -0.25in);
```

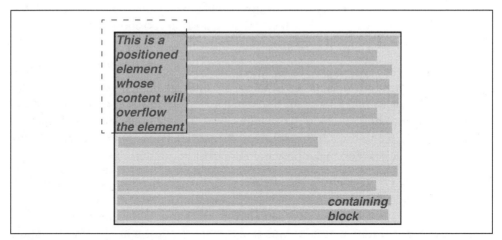

Figure 9-12. Expanding the clipping area

This doesn't do much good, as you can see. The clipping rectangle extends up and to the left, but since there isn't any content there, the visual effect is the same as if the author had declared `overflow-clip: auto`.

On the other hand, it might be okay to go beyond the bottom and right edges, but not the top or left. Figure 9-13 shows the results of these styles (and remember, the dashed lines are only for illustrative purposes):

```
DIV#sidebar {position: absolute; top: 0; left: 0; width: 5em; height: 7em;
overflow: hidden; overflow-clip: rect(0, 6em, 9em, 0);}
```

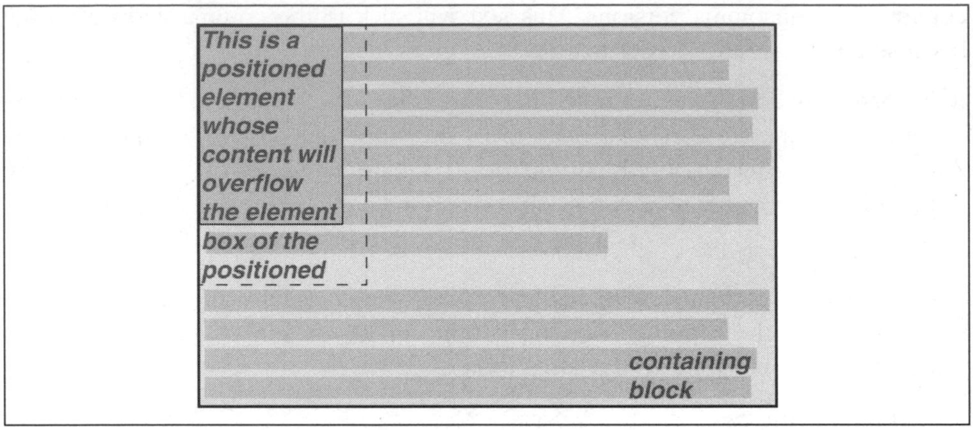

Figure 9-13. Expanding the clipping region

This extends the area in which content can be seen. However, it doesn't change the flow of the content, so the only visual effect is that more content can be seen below the element. The text does not flow out to the right, because the width of its line boxes is still constrained by the width of the positioned element. If there had been an image wider than the positioned element, or preformatted text with a long line, this might have been visible to the right of the positioned element, up to the point where the clipping rectangle ends.

The syntax of `rect(...)` is, as you may have already realized, rather unfortunate. It is based on an early draft of the positioning section, which used the top-left-offset scheme. Internet Explorer implemented this before CSS2 was made a full Recommendation, and so came into conflict with a last-minute change that made `rect(...)` use side-offsets, just like the rest of CSS2. This was done, reasonably enough, because it would make positioning consistent with itself.

By then, however, it was too late: there was an implementation in the marketplace, and rather than force Microsoft to change the browser and thus potentially cause existing pages to break, the standard was changed to reflect implementation. This means, sadly, that it is impossible to set a consistent clipping rectangle in situations where the height and width are not precisely defined. For example, there is no way to create a clipping rectangle that is 1 em larger than this element's content area:

```
position: absolute; top: 0; bottom: 50%; right: 50%; left: 0;
```

Since there is no way to know how many ems tall or wide the element will be, there is no way to make a clipping rectangle that ends 1 em to the right, or 1 em below, the content area of the element.

Further compounding the problem is that `rect(...)` only accepts length units and `auto`. The addition of percentage units as valid `rect(...)` values would go a long way toward improving things, and hopefully a future version of CSS will add this capability.

Element clipping

There is another way to clip in CSS, but this is very different from what we've just seen.

clip

Values	`rect(<top>, <right>, <bottom>, <left>)` | `auto` | `inherit`
Initial Value	`auto`
Applies to	block-level and replaced elements
Inherited	no

This property can be used to clip the element with a simple intersection operation. The area of the element contained within the `clip` rectangle is displayed, and any part of it outside that rectangle is not. In addition, the `clip` rectangle is set in relation to the outer edge of the element—not its content edge. Thus, let's say you wanted (for whatever reason) to clip the top 10 pixels of an image:

```
<IMG SRC="foo.gif" STYLE="clip: rect(10px, auto, auto, 0);">
```

The `auto` values will set the clipping rectangle's bottom to align with the bottom of the image, and the right edge to the right edge of the image. The value of 0 for `left` keeps the left edge of the clipping rectangle against the left edge of the image, but the `10px` for `top` moves the top edge of the clipping rectangle downward 10 pixels. This will cause the top 10 pixels of the image to become effectively invisible.

`clip` can be applied to any element. Thus, you could display only the top left corner of a paragraph using something like this:

```
<P STYLE="clip: rect(0, 10em, 10em, 0);">
```

This will display a square 10 ems wide by 10 ems high. This square is drawn from the top left outer corner, so any margins, borders, and padding will influence how much of the element is visible and how much is clipped out.

Element Visibility

In addition to all the clipping and overflowing, you can also control the visibility of an entire element.

visibility	
Values	`visible	hidden	collapse	inherit`
Initial Value	`inherit`
Applies to	all elements
Inherited	no

This one is pretty easy. If an element is set to have `visibility: visible`, then it is visible. Of course.

However, if an element is set to `visibility: hidden`, it is made "invisible" (to use the wording in the specification). In its invisible state, the element still affects the document's layout as though it were visible. In other words, the element is still there: you just can't see it. Note the difference between this and `display: none`. In the latter case, the element is not displayed and is removed from the document altogether so that it doesn't have any effect on document layout. Figure 9-14 shows a document in which an `EM` element has been set to be `hidden`, based on the following styles and markup:

```
EM.trans {visibility: hidden; border: 3px solid gray; background: silver;
   padding: 1em;}

<P>
This is a paragraph which should be visible. Lorem ipsum, dolor sit amet,
<EM CLASS="trans">consectetuer adipiscing elit, sed diam nonummy nibh </EM>
euismod tincidunt ut laoreet dolore magna aliquam erat volutpat.
</P>
```

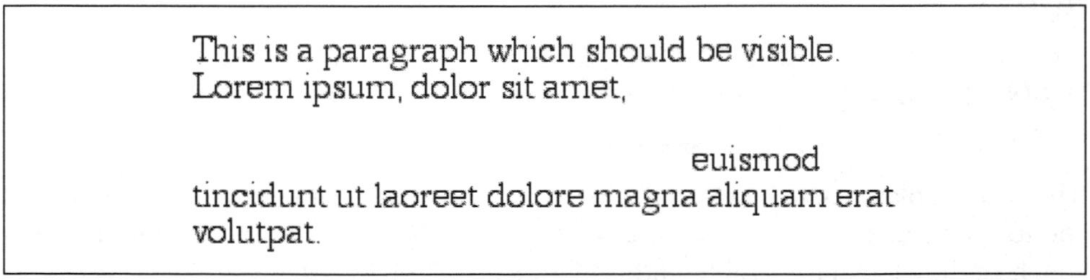

This is a paragraph which should be visible.
Lorem ipsum, dolor sit amet,

                                                    euismod
tincidunt ut laoreet dolore magna aliquam erat
volutpat.

Figure 9-14. Hiding an element

Everything visible about an element—such as content, background, and borders—will be made invisible. Note that the space is still there because the element is still part of the document's layout. We just can't see it.

Note too that it's possible to set the descendant element of a `hidden` element to be `visible`. This would cause the element to appear wherever it normally would, despite the fact that the ancestor (and possibly the siblings) is invisible. In order to do so, you would need to explicitly declare the descendant element to be `visible`, since `visibility` is inherited. Thus:

```
P.clear {visibility: hidden;}
P.clear EM {visibility: visible;}
```

As for `visbility: collapse`, this value is used in CSS table rendering, which isn't covered in this book because it wasn't well implemented as the book was being written. According to the CSS2 specification, `collapse` has the same meaning as `hidden` if it is used on nontable elements. From a semantic standpoint, this seems somewhat confusing (since `collapse` sounds like it should trigger the kind of behavior you'd see with `display: none`), but there it is nonetheless.

Relative Positioning

The simplest of the positioning schemes to understand is relative positioning. In this scheme, a positioned element is shifted by use of the side-offset properties. However, this can have some interesting consequences.

On the surface, it seems simple enough. Let's say we want to shift an image up and to the left. Figure 9-15 shows us the result of these styles:

```
IMG {position: relative; top: -20px; left: -20px;}
```

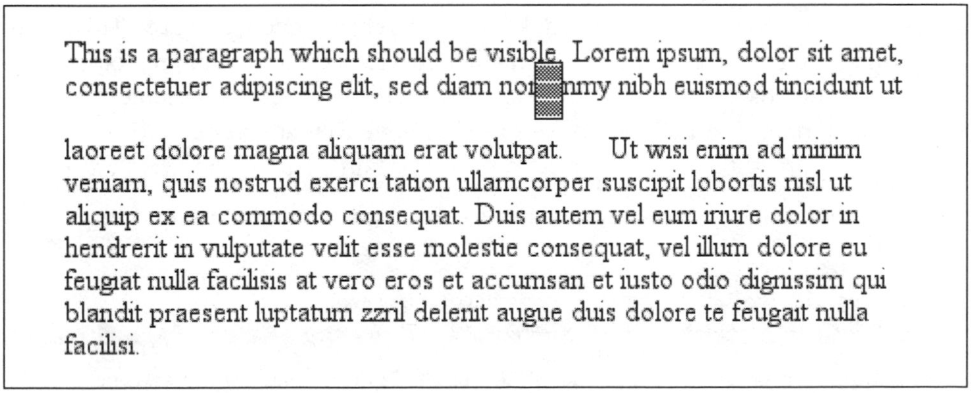

Figure 9-15. A relatively positioned element

All we've done here is offset the image's top edge 20 pixels upward and offset the left edge 20 pixels to the left. However, notice the blank space where the image was previously positioned. That space exists because when an element is relatively positioned, it's shifted from its normal place, but the space it would have occupied doesn't disappear. Consider the results of the following styles, which are depicted in Figure 9-16:

```
EM {position: relative; top: 8em; color: gray;}
```

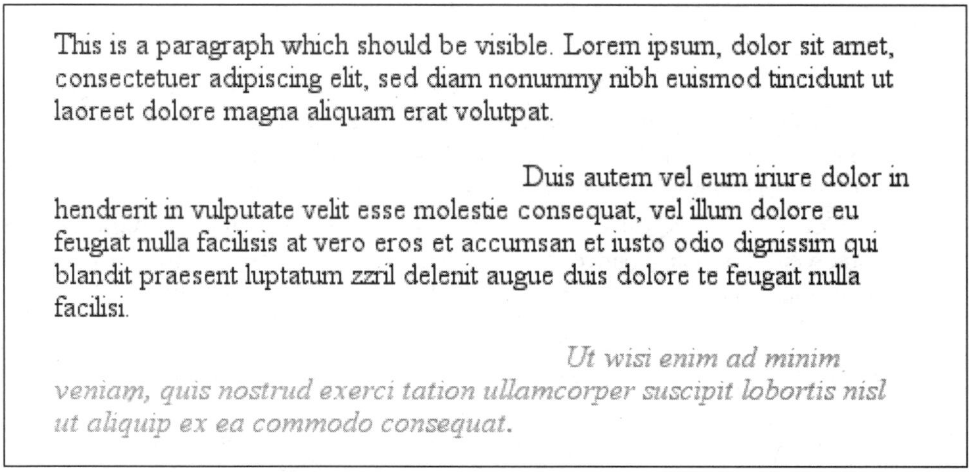

This is a paragraph which should be visible. Lorem ipsum, dolor sit amet, consectetuer adipiscing elit, sed diam nonummy nibh euismod tincidunt ut laoreet dolore magna aliquam erat volutpat.

Duis autem vel eum iriure dolor in hendrerit in vulputate velit esse molestie consequat, vel illum dolore eu feugiat nulla facilisis at vero eros et accumsan et iusto odio dignissim qui blandit praesent luptatum zzril delenit augue duis dolore te feugait nulla facilisi.

Ut wisi enim ad minim veniam, quis nostrud exerci tation ullamcorper suscipit lobortis nisl ut aliquip ex ea commodo consequat.

Figure 9-16. A relatively positioned EM element

As you can see, the paragraph has some blank space in it. That's where the **EM** element would have been, and the layout of the **EM** element in its new position exactly mirrors the space it left behind.

This works because the containing block of a relatively positioned element is the space that it would have occupied had its **position** been **static**. This is an important thing to note, since one might expect that the containing block was defined by the parent element. Instead, the relatively positioned element sets its own containing block, and then offsets itself relative to that context.

Of course, it's also possible that you can shift a relatively positioned element to overlap other content. For example, the following styles and markup will get you Figure 9-17:

```
EM {position: relative; bottom: -0.5em; color: gray;}
B {position: relative; bottom: 0.5em; color: gray;}

<P>This is a paragraph which should be visible. Lorem ipsum, dolor sit amet,
consectetuer adipiscing elit, sed diam nonummy nibh euismod tincidunt ut
laoreet dolore magna aliquam erat volutpat.
<EM>Ut wisi enim ad minim veniam, quis nostrud exerci tation ullamcorper
```

```
suscipit lobortis nisl ut aliquip ex ea commodo consequat.</EM>
Duis autem vel eum iriure dolor in hendrerit in vulputate velit esse
molestie consequat, vel illum dolore eu feugiat nulla <B>facilisis at vero
eros et accumsan et iusto odio dignissim qui blandit praesent luptatum</B>
zzril delenit augue duis dolore te feugait nulla facilisi.</P>
```

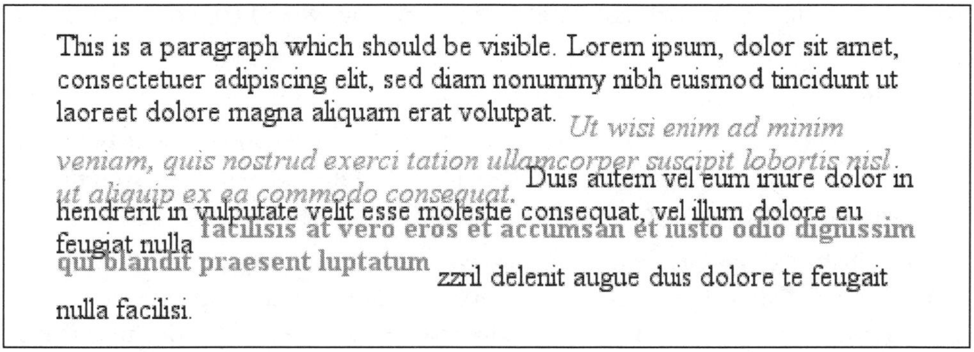

Figure 9-17. Two relatively positioned elements

When you relatively position an element, it immediately establishes a new containing block for any of its children. This containing block corresponds to the place where the element has been positioned. Thus, you can position an element relative to its parent element, which has itself been relatively positioned. Figure 9-18 shows us the results of the following styles and markup:

```
P {color: gray;}
EM {position: relative; bottom: -0.75em; color: black;}
B {position: relative; bottom: 0.5em; left: 1em; color: black;}

<P>This is a paragraph which should be visible. Lorem ipsum, dolor sit amet,
consectetuer adipiscing elit, sed diam nonummy nibh euismod tincidunt ut
laoreet dolore magna aliquam erat volutpat.
<EM>Ut wisi enim ad minim veniam, <B>quis nostrud exerci tation ullamcorper
</B> suscipit lobortis nisl ut aliquip ex ea commodo consequat.</EM>
Duis autem vel eum iriure dolor in hendrerit in vulputate velit esse
molestie consequat, vel illum dolore eu feugiat nulla facilisis at vero eros
et accumsan et iusto odio dignissim qui blandit praesent luptatum zzril
delenit augue duis dolore te feugait nulla facilisi.</P>
```

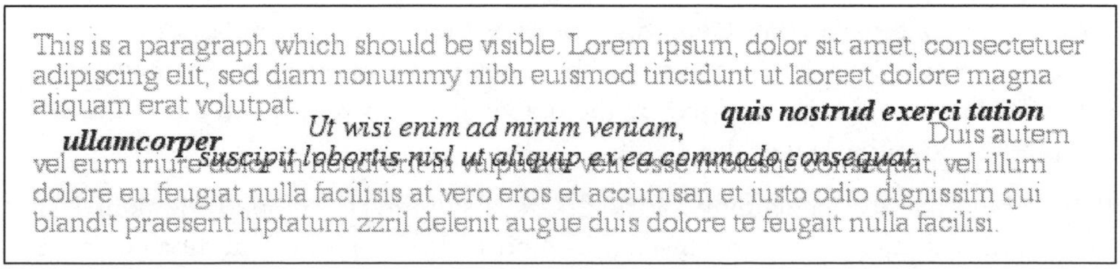

Figure 9-18. Nested relative positioning

The emphasized text has been shifted down 0.75 em from where it would have ordinarily appeared, which is to be expected. The boldface text has been moved 1 em to the right and upward half an em, but it is moved relative to the position of the emphasized text *after* it has been moved.

There is one interesting wrinkle to relative positioning: what happens when a relatively positioned element is overconstrained? For example:

```
EM {position: relative; top: 1em; bottom: 2em;}
```

Here we have values that call for two very different behaviors. If you only consider `top: 1em`, then the element should be shifted downward an em, but `bottom: 2em` clearly calls for the element to be shifted upward by 2 ems.

The original CSS2 specification does not say what should happen in this case. As of this writing, there is a published errata that states that when it comes to overconstrained relative positioning, one value would be reset to be the negative of the other. Thus, `bottom` would always equal `-top` and `right` would equal `-left`. This means that the previous example would be treated as though it had been this:

```
EM {position: relative; top: 1em; bottom: -1em;}
```

Thus the element will be shifted downward by 1 em. This proposed change also makes allowances for writing directions. It states that in relative positioning, `right` always equals `-left` in left-to-right languages, but in right-to-left languages, this is reversed: `left` would always equal `-right`.

Absolute Positioning

Since most of the examples and figures in the chapter (besides the previous section) have been examples of absolute positioning, we're already halfway to an understanding of how it works. Most of what remain are the details of what happens when absolute positioning is invoked.

When an element is positioned absolutely, it is completely removed from the document flow. It is then positioned with respect to its containing block, and its edges are placed using the side-offset properties. The positioned element does not flow around the content of other elements, nor does their content flow around the positioned element. This implies that an absolutely positioned element may overlap other elements, or be overlapped by them. (We'll see how you can affect the overlapping order at the end of the chapter.)

Remember that the containing block of an absolutely positioned element is not necessarily its parent element. In fact, it often is not, unless the author takes steps to correct this situation. Fortunately, that's easy to do. Just pick the element that you want to use as the containing block for the absolutely positioned element, and give it a **position** of **relative** with no offsets. Thus:

```
P.contain {position: relative;}
```

Consider the example in Figure 9-19. It shows two paragraphs that contain identical text. However, the first paragraph contains an inline boldface element, and the second an absolutely positioned boldface element. In the second paragraph, the styles used would be something like what is shown here:

```
P {position: relative;}    /* establish containing blocks */

<B STYLE="position: absolute; top: auto; right: 0; bottom: 0; left: auto;
    width: 8em; height: 4em;">...</B>
```

Figure 9-19. The effects of absolute positioning

For the most part, the text in both paragraphs looks fairly normal. In the second one, however, the place where the boldface element would have appeared is simply closed up, and the positioned text overlaps the some of the content. There is no way to avoid this, short of positioning the boldfaced text outside of the paragraph (by using a negative value for **right**) or by specifying a padding for the paragraph that is wide enough to accommodate the positioned element. Also, since it has a transparent background, the parent element's text shows through the positioned element. The only way to avoid this is to set a background for the positioned element.

Note that the boldface element in this case is positioned in relation to its parent element's content box, which defines its containing block. Without the relative positioning of the parent element, the containing block would be another element.

Consider a case where the element being positioned is a child of the BODY element, e.g., a paragraph or heading element. With the right styles, the containing block for the positioned element will be the entire BODY element. Thus, applying the following styles to the BODY and the fifth paragraph in a document would lead to a situation similar to that shown in Figure 9-20:

```
BODY {position: relative;}

<P STYLE="position: absolute; top: 0; right: 25%; left: 25%; bottom: auto;
    width: 50%; height: auto; background: silver;">...</P>
```

Figure 9-20. An absolutely positioned paragraph

The paragraph is now positioned at the very beginning of the document, half as wide as the document's width and overwriting the first few elements!

In addition, if the document is scrolled, the paragraph will scroll right along with it. This is because the element's containing block is the BODY element's content area, not the viewport. If you want to position elements so that they're placed relative to the viewport and don't scroll along with the rest of the document, then the next section is for you.

Before we get there, however, there are a few more things to cover. Remember that absolutely positioned boxes can have backgrounds, margins, borders, and padding; styles can be applied within them, just as with any other element. This can make them very useful for the creation of sidebars, "sticky notes," and other such effects. One example is the ability to set a "change marker" on any paragraph that has been edited. This could be done using the following styles and markup:

```
SPAN.change {position: absolute; top: 0; left: -5em; width: 4em;
   font-weight: bold;}
P {margin-left: 5em; position: relative;}

<P> Lorem ipsum, dolor sit amet, consectetuer adipiscing elit,
sed diam nonummy nibh euismod tincidunt ut <SPAN CLASS="change">***</SPAN>
laoreet dolore magna aliquam erat volutpat.</P>
```

While this does rely on inserting an extra element, the advantage is that the SPAN can be placed anywhere in the paragraph and still have the result depicted in Figure 9-21.

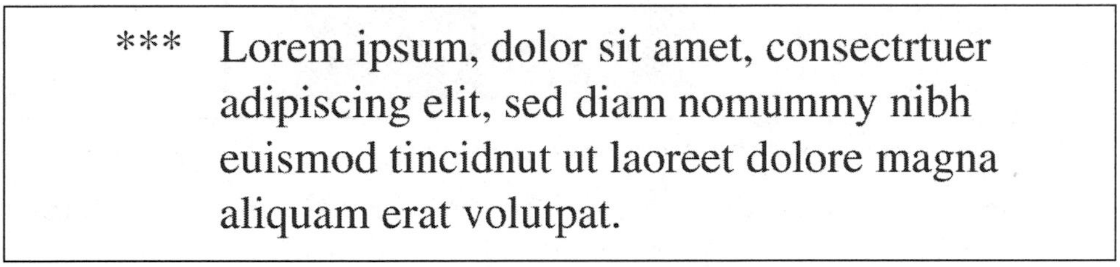

*** Lorem ipsum, dolor sit amet, consectrtuer adipiscing elit, sed diam nomummy nibh euismod tincidnut ut laoreet dolore magna aliquam erat volutpat.

Figure 9-21. Setting a "change bar" with absolute positioning

However, maybe we'd like to place the change marker next to whatever line was changed. In that case, we need to make only one small alteration to our styles, and we'll get the result shown in Figure 9-22:

```
SPAN.change {position: absolute; top: static-position; left: -5em; width: 4em;
   font-weight: bold;}
P {margin-left: 5em; position: relative;}

<P> Lorem ipsum, dolor sit amet, consectetuer adipiscing elit,
sed diam nonummy nibh euismod tincidunt ut <SPAN CLASS="change">***</SPAN>
laoreet dolore magna aliquam erat volutpat.</P>
```

Lorem ipsum, dolor sit amet, consectrtuer adipiscing elit, sed diam nomummy nibh
*** euismod tincidnut ut laoreet dolore magna aliquam erat volutpat.

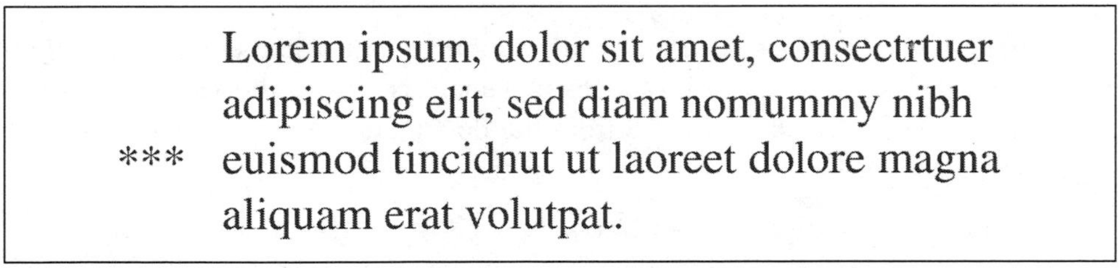

Figure 9-22. Another approach to defining a "change bar"

Remember when we mentioned static-position much earlier in the chapter? Here's one example of how it works and how it can be very useful.

Another important point is that when an element is positioned, it establishes a containing block for its descendant elements. For example, we could absolutely position an element and then absolutely position one of its children, as shown in Figure 9-23.

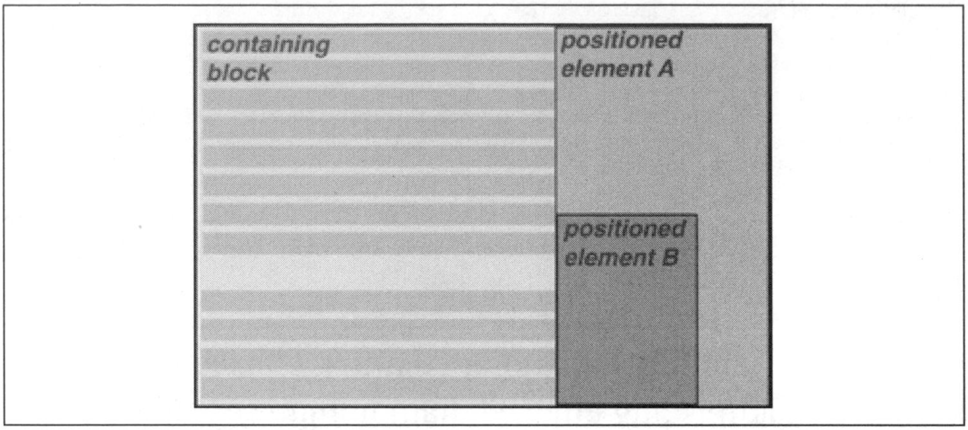

Figure 9-23. Nested absolutely positioned elements

The small box B in the lower-left corner of the element A is a child of A, which is in turn a child of a relatively positioned DIV. B was absolutely positioned, as was element A, using styles like these:

```
DIV {position: relative;}
P.A {position: absolute; top: 0; right: 0; width: 15em; height: auto;
    margin-left: auto;}
P.B {position: absolute; bottom: 0; left: 0; width: 10em; height: 50%;
    margin-top: auto;}
```

This is an important point to always keep in mind: only positioned elements establish containing blocks for their descendant elements. I know this has come up before, but it's so fundamental that it needs to be repeated.

Fixed Positioning

As implied in the previous section, fixed positioning is just like absolute positioning, except the containing block of a fixed element is always the viewport. In this case, the element is totally removed from the document's flow and does not have a position relative to any part of the document.

This can be exploited in a number of interesting ways. First off, it's possible to create frame-style interfaces using fixed positioning. Consider Figure 9-24, which shows a very common layout scheme.

This could be done using the following styles:

```
DIV#header {position: fixed; top: 0; bottom: 80%; left: 20%; right: 0;
    background: gray;}
DIV#sidebar {position: fixed; top: 0; bottom: 0; left: 0; right: 80%;
    background: silver;}
```

Figure 9-24. Emulating frames with fixed positioning

This will fix the header and sidebar to the top and side of the viewport, where they will remain regardless of how the document is scrolled. The drawback here, though, is that the rest of the document will be overlapped by the fixed elements. Therefore, the rest of the content should probably be contained in its own DIV and employ the following:

```
DIV#main {position: absolute; top: 20%; bottom: 0; left: 20%; right: 0;
    overflow: scroll; background: white;}
```

It would even be possible to create small gaps between the three positioned DIVs by adding some appropriate margins, demonstrated in Figure 9-25:

```
BODY {background: black; color: silver;}  /* colors for safety's sake */
DIV#header {position: fixed; top: 0; bottom: 80%; left: 20%; right: 0;
    background: gray; margin-bottom: 2px; color: yellow;}
DIV#sidebar {position: fixed; top: 0; bottom: 0; left: 0; right: 80%;
    background: silver; margin-right: 2px; color: maroon;}
DIV#main {position: absolute; top: 20%; bottom: 0; left: 20%; right: 0;
    overflow: scroll; background: white; color: black;}
```

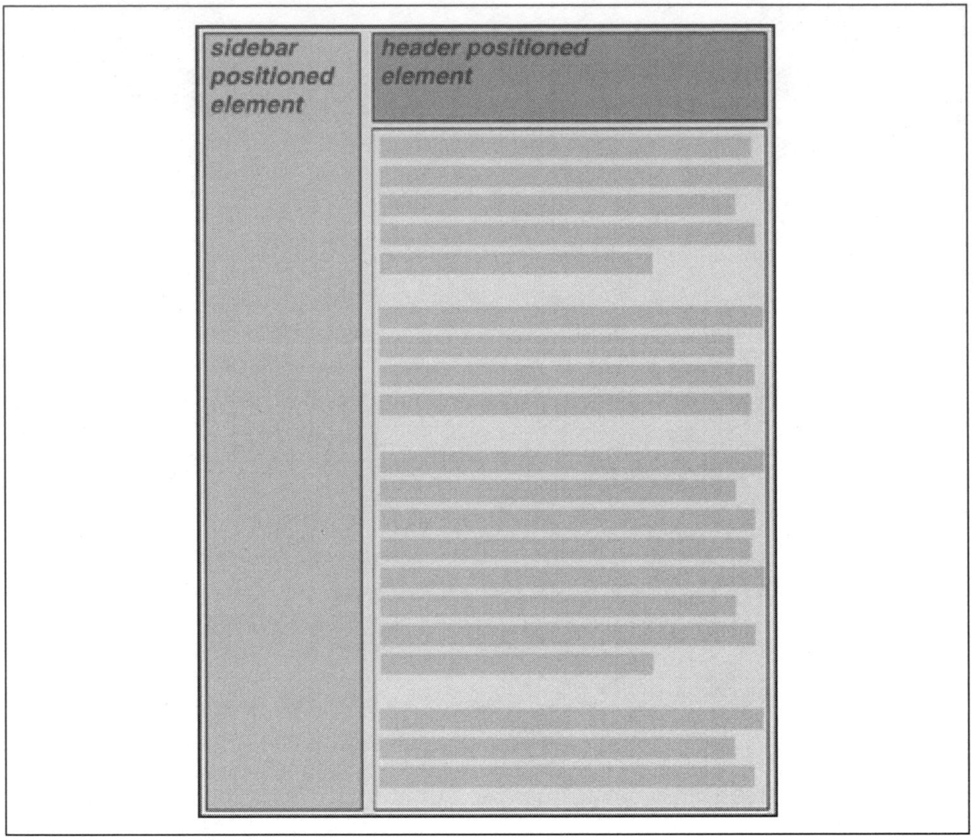

Figure 9-25. Separating the "frames"

Given such a case, a tiled image could be applied to the BODY background. This image would show through the gaps created by the margins, which could certainly be widened if the author saw fit. For that matter, if a background image was of little importance, simple borders could be applied to the DIVs instead of margins.

Stacking Positioned Elements

With all of the positioning going on, there will inevitably be a situation where two elements will try to exist in the same place, visually speaking. Obviously, one of them will have to overlap the other—but how do we control which one comes out "on top"?

This is where z-index comes in.

z-index

Values	`integer`	`auto`
Initial Value	`auto`
Applies to	positioned elements
Inherited	no

`z-index` allows the author to alter the way in which elements overlap each other It takes its name from the coordinate system in which side-to-side is the x-axis and top-to-bottom is the y-axis. In such a case, the third axis—that runs from front to back, or if you prefer, closer to further away from the user—is termed the z-axis. Thus, elements are given values along this axis and are represented using `z-index`. Figure 9-26 illustrates this system.

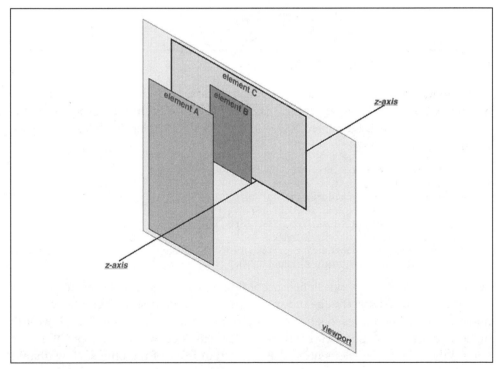

Figure 9-26. A conceptual view of z-index stacking

In this coordinate system, an element with a high `z-index` value is closer to the reader than those with lower `z-index` values. This will cause the high-value element to overlap the others, as illustrated in Figure 9-27. This is referred to as *stacking*.

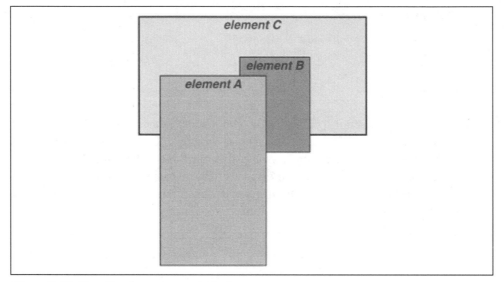

Figure 9-27. How the elements are stacked

Any integer can be used as a value for `z-index`, including negative numbers. Assigning an element a negative `z-index` will move it further away from the reader; that is, it will be moved lower in the stack. Consider the following styles, illustrated in Figure 9-28:

```
P.first {position: absolute; top: 0; left: 0;
  width: 20%; height: 10em; z-index: 6;}
P.second {position: absolute; top: 0; left: 10%;
  width: 30%; height: 5em; z-index: 2;}
P.third {position: absolute; top: 15%; left: 5%;
  width: 15%; height: 10em; z-index: -5;}
P.fourth {position: absolute; top: 10%; left: 15%;
  width: 40%; height: 10em; z-index: 0;}
```

Each of the elements is positioned according to its styles, but the usual order of stacking is altered by the `z-index` values. Assuming the paragraphs were in numeric order, then a reasonable stacking order would have been, from lowest to highest, `P.first`, `P.second`, `P.third`, `P.fourth`. This would have put `P.first` behind the other three elements and `P.fourth` in front of the others. Now, thanks to `z-index`, the stacking order is under our control.

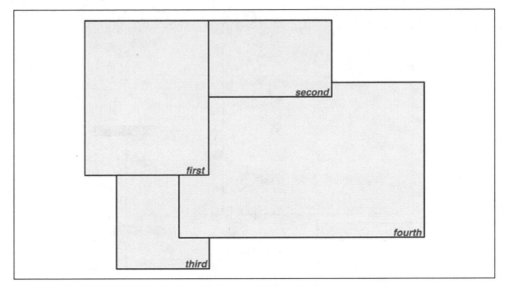

Figure 9-28. Stacked elements can overlap each other

As the previous example demonstrates, there is no particular need to have the z-index values be contiguous. You can assign any integer of any size. If you wanted to be fairly certain that an element stayed in front of everything else, you might use a rule along the lines of z-index: 100000. This would work as expected in most cases—although if you ever declared another element's z-index to be 100001 (or higher), it would appear in front.

Once you assign an element a value for z-index (other than auto), that element establishes its own local *stacking context*. This means that all of the element's descendants have their own stacking order, relative to the ancestor element. This is very similar to the way that elements establish new containing blocks. Given the following styles, you would see something like Figure 9-29:

```
P.one {position: absolute; top: 0; left: 0; width: 50%; height: 10em;
   z-index: 10;}
P.two {position: absolute; top: 30%; left: 25%; width: 50%; height: 10em;
   z-index: 7;}
P.three {position: absolute; top: 60%; left: 0; width: 50%; height: 10em;
   z-index: -1;}
P.one B {position: relative; left: 15em; top: 0; z-index: -404;}
P.two B {position: relative; left: 3em; top: -1em; z-index: 36;}
P.two EM {position: relative; top: 4em; left: 7em; z-index: -42;}
P.three B {position: relative; top: 0; left: 3em; z-index: 23;}
```

Note where the relatively positioned inline elements fall in the stacking order. Each of them is correctly positioned with respect to its parent element, of course. However, pay close attention to the children of P.two. While the B element is in

Figure 9-29. An example of positioning and z-index

front of its parent, and the **EM** is behind, both of them are in front of **P.three**!
This is because the **z-index** values of 36 and -42 are relative to **P.two**, but not
to the document in general. In a sense, **P.two** and all of its children share a
z-index of 7, while having their own mini-**z-index** within the context of **P.two**.

If you want another way to look at this, it's as though the **B** element has a
z-index of 7,36 while the **EM**'s value is 7,-42. These are merely implied conceptual values; they don't conform to anything in the specification. However, such
a system helps to illustrate how the overall stacking order is determined. Consider:

```
P.one        10
P.one B      10,-404
P.two B      7,36
P.two        7
P.two EM     7,-42
P.three B    -1,23
P.three      -1
```

This conceptual framework precisely describes the order in which these elements would be stacked. While the descendants of an element can be above or below that element in the stacking order, they are all grouped together with their ancestor.

There remains one more value to examine. The specification has this to say about the default value, `auto`:

> The stack level of the generated box in the current stacking context is the same as its parent's box. The box does not establish a new local stacking context. (CSS2: 9.9.1)

What this seems to mean is that user agents are free to use whatever stacking algorithm they already use in laying out a document. However, it can also mean that any element with `z-index: auto` can be treated as though it is set to `z-index: 0`. Unfortunately, the CSS2 specification is not entirely clear on this point, so there may be inconsistencies between different user agents.

Summary

When it comes right down to it, positioning is a very compelling technology. It's also likely to be an exercise in frustration if you're trying to get it to behave consistently in a cross-browser environment. The problem isn't so much that it won't work in some browsers: it's that it will only sort of work in a number of them, such as Navigator 4 and Internet Explorer 4 and 5. It can be great fun to play with positioning, and one day we'll be able to use it in place of tables and frames while dramatically improving accessibility and backward compatibility. As of this writing, though, it remains a great way to create design prototypes, but a tricky thing to use on a public web site.

As it happens, this sentiment may be applied to the majority of CSS2, which is given an overview in the next chapter.

10

CSS2: A Look Ahead

In the course of writing this book, I vacillated back and forth over how to handle CSS2. It's a full W3C Recommendation, of course, but so little of it has actually been implemented correctly that it seemed almost a waste of time—both mine and yours—to talk about CSS2 in detail. After all, not only would I have to fake all of the screenshots (not to mention guess at correct behavior in a few cases), but you wouldn't be able to try out anything I discussed, since browsers wouldn't recognize your CSS2 rules.

On the other hand, CSS2 can hardly be ignored. So in the end, I settled on writing a chapter that talks about CSS2 in brief, abstract detail—in other words, this chapter. The next edition of this book will almost certainly be driven by the need to add detailed information concerning CSS2, and will very likely be undertaken once the dust settles and browsers start to correctly implement major portions of CSS2.

Also realize that, of the figures shown in this chapter, the vast majority are—well—faked. There was no other way to produce most of these examples. The point of telling you this is to spare you the frustration of trying to figure out how they were produced. So, with that in mind, here's a brief taste of what CSS2 can offer.

Changes from CSS1

Only a few CSS1 properties have gained new values. These were mostly concerned with addressing issues that did not exist, or were not considered, when CSS1 was written. The one standout is a new value called `inherit`, which represents a huge change to everything—but more on that in a moment.

Additions and Changes to the display Property

The property `display` has received quite a few new values in CSS2. Now, in addition to `block`, `inline`, `line-item`, and `none`, we have `run-in`, `compact`, and `marker` (which we'll get to later), as well as a number of values specific to tables (which we'll also cover later on).

The `display` value `compact` has an effect similar to `<DL compact>` (assuming your browser supports that bit of HTML). Basically, if an element is set to `display: compact`, then it will appear in the margin of the next element, assuming there is enough room for it. Otherwise, both elements will be treated as block-level elements. Think of a "compacted" element as one that floats, but only if there is room for it to be displayed without altering the formatting of the following element, something like the illustration in Figure 10-1.

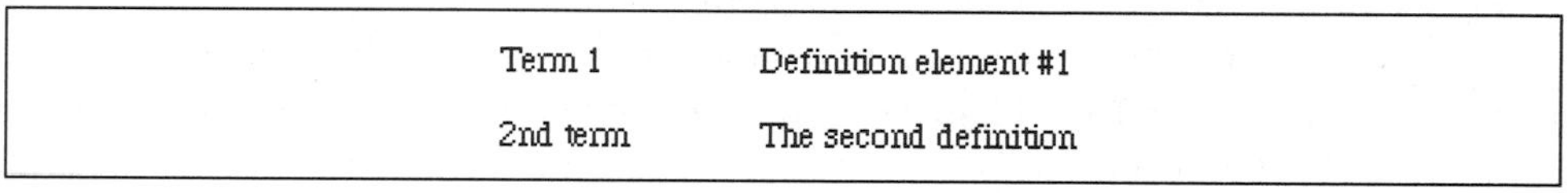

Term 1	Definition element #1
2nd term	The second definition

Figure 10-1. Compact display of a definition list

On the other hand, `run-in` has the effect of turning a block-level element into an inline element at the beginning of the following block-level element. Another way to think of it is that a block-level element set to `run-in` will be combined with the next block-level element so that the two together form a single block-level element.

Given this code:

```
<H3 STYLE="display: run-in;">A Heading.</H3>
<P>This is a paragraph of text....</P>
```

the result will look something like what's shown in Figure 10-2.

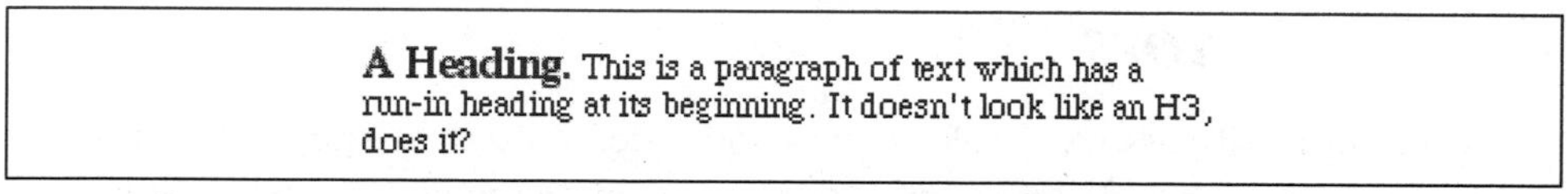

A Heading. This is a paragraph of text which has a run-in heading at its beginning. It doesn't look like an H3, does it?

Figure 10-2. A run-in heading

The `display` type `run-in` can be applied to any block-level element, not just headings. However, this rule should only work if the next element is block-level and is not floating or positioned absolutely. So, for example, if you try to set an inline anchor to `run-in`, it won't have any effect.

Another change for `display` is that its default value is `inline`, not `block`, as was defined in CSS1. The authors have termed the original default value an error, so if you don't declare a value for `display`, it is assumed to be `inline`. Of course, your browser should have its own built-in HTML styles, so don't worry about your paragraphs suddenly running together!

More Inheritance

Finally, there is one very important new feature of CSS2 that belongs in this section: the value `inherit`. If you were to ask the question, "Okay, to which properties did `inherit` get applied?" the answer would be, "Every last one of them." There is not a single property in the whole of CSS that does not accept a value of `inherit`.

`inherit` is used to explicitly declare that a given computed value should be inherited from its parent. In other words, if the `font-size` for BODY is computed to be 14 points, then the declaration P {`font-size: inherit;`} would set paragraph text to 14 points in size, as long as the paragraphs are children of the BODY element. Similarly, you could make sure that hyperlinks always have the same color as the text that surrounds them by using the simple declaration:

```
A:link, A:visited {color: inherit;}
```

The power of this change should not be underestimated. In effect, you are able to override the specificity mechanism that ordinarily takes effect. Usually, hyperlinks are (for instance) blue unless you explicitly declare them to be otherwise—and if you want differently colored links in different areas of the same page, you'd have to construct a different rule for each color.

Now, thanks to `inherit`, if it's okay to make them the same color as surrounding text, you just need one rule that will cover all circumstances. Note that I'm not saying this is a good idea, or the only thing for which `inherit` can be used. It's simply the most obvious possibility.

CSS2 Selectors

We're going to discuss CSS2 selectors in some detail because they're likely to be one of the first parts of the specification to be implemented quickly. Therefore, while you might not be able to do everything described here as soon as you read this, expect most (if not all) of this to be included in browsers released in the year 2000 or later.

Basic Selectors

First, in addition to the existing selector mechanisms like contextual selectors, we have several new selector symbols that will make it a lot easier to construct very specific, very sophisticated selections—without having to resort to sprinkling classes or IDs throughout the whole document.

Universal selector

The most powerful of the new selectors is the *universal selector*. This is specified using an asterisk (*), and it matches any element in the document. Thus, use this declaration to make sure all elements have a color of black:

```
* {color: black;}
```

When used as part of a contextual selector, the universal selector can create some interesting effects. For example, assume that you want to make gray any UL element that is at least a grandchild of the BODY. In other words, any UL that is a child of BODY would not be gray, but any other UL—whether it's child to a DIV, a list item, or a table—should be gray. This is accomplished as follows:

```
BODY * UL {color: gray;}
```

Figure 10-3 shows the result of this declaration.

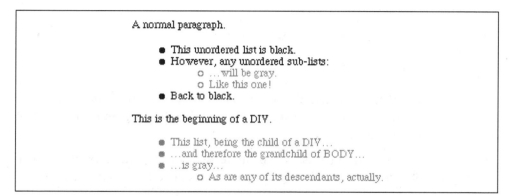

Figure 10-3. Making BODY's grandchildren (and their descendants) gray

On the other hand, perhaps you wish to make purple any element that is a descendant of DIV. This would be written:

```
DIV * {color: purple;}
```

At first glance, this seems no different than if the * were left out, instead relying on inheritance to carry the color to *all* descendants of DIV. However, there is a very real difference: the rule shown would match every DIV descendant, and therefore override the inheritance mechanism. Thus, even anchors (which are descendants of a DIV) would be made purple under the given rule, whereas simple inheritance would not be sufficient to make them purple.

While you can use the universal selector in combination with class and ID selectors, there isn't much reason to do so. The following two rules mean exactly the same thing:

```
*.apple {color: red;}
.apple {color: red;}
```

However, you should consider this: if you're concerned about older user agents that don't know about CSS2, then `*.class` (or `*#id`) is an easy way to fool them. Since both of these are examples of invalid selectors in CSS1, they should be ignored by CSS1-only parsers. If they aren't ignored, then they're likely to cause strange results. Therefore, it might be a good idea to omit the universal selector in conjunction with class and ID selectors.

Child selector

Another interesting selector is the *child selector*, which is written using a greater-than symbol (>). This is used to match elements that are direct children of other elements:

```
BODY > P {color: green;}

<BODY>
<P>This paragraph is green.</P>
<DIV>
<P>This paragraph is not green.</P>
</DIV>
<P>This paragraph is green.</P>
</BODY>
```

Only the first and third paragraphs match the rule because they are children of BODY. The second paragraph is a child of DIV, and therefore a grandchild of BODY, so it does not match the rule.

Child selectors must have at least two or more selectors separated by the > symbol. It is possible to make a child selector part of a contextual selector as well:

```
DIV OL>LI EM {color: purple;}
```

This rule matches any **EM** text that is a descendant of a list item, as long as that list item is a child of an **OL** element that is a descendant of a **DIV**. (Note also that there is no whitespace around the > symbol this time, which is legal; whitespace around this symbol is optional.) Thus:

```
<BODY>
<OL>
<LI>The EM text here is <EM>not</EM> purple.</LI>
</OL>
<DIV>
<OL>
<LI>Look, a list:
<UL>
<LI>The emphasized text here <EM>is</EM> purple.</LI>
</UL>
</LI>
</OL>
</DIV>
</BODY>
```

The purple **EM** text is purple because it's the great-grandchild of an **LI** that is the direct child of the **OL**, and the **OL** is the grandchild of the **BODY** element. The first **EM** is not matched because its grandparent **OL** is not the direct child of a **DIV**.

Even better, you can string more than one child selector together to precisely target a given type of element. Take this, for example:

```
BODY > OL > LI {color: silver;}

<BODY>
<OL>
<LI>The text here is silver.</LI>
</OL>
<DIV>
<UL>
<LI>Look, a list (and this text is not silver, by the way):
<OL>
<LI>The text here is <EM>not</EM> silver.</LI>
</OL>
</LI>
</UL>
</DIV>
</BODY>
```

Given this rule, we get results like those shown in Figure 10-4.

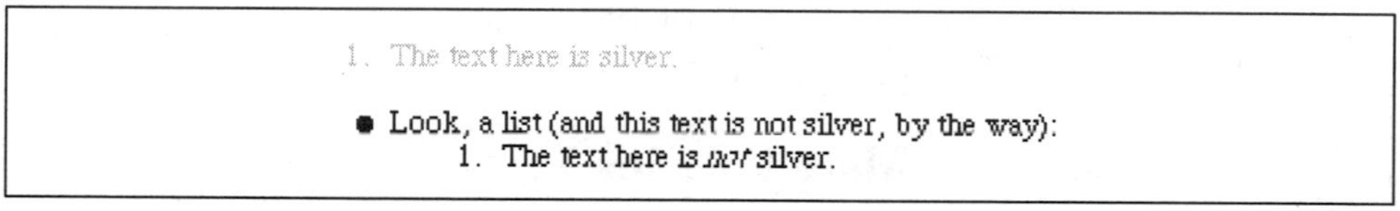

Figure 10-4. Selecting grandchildren only

The first list item in the source is silver because it's the child of an ordered list that is itself the child of a **BODY**. The second list item in the source is the child of an unordered list, so it can't match the rule. Finally, the third list item in the source is a child of an ordered list, but the **OL** element is the child of an **LI** element, so it doesn't match either.

Adjacent-sibling selector

If you thought that was interesting, consider our next subject: the *adjacent sibling* selector. This is in some ways like the child selector, but in this case, styles are applied to elements that share a parent and are next to each other in the document tree. For example:

```
H2 + P {color: silver;}

<H2>Coloring Text</H2>
<P>This paragraph is silver.</P>
<P>This paragraph is not.</P>
```

```
<H2>More Coloring Text</H2>
<UL><LI>This is not silver</LI></UL>
<P>Neither is this.</P>

<H2>More Coloring Text</H2>
This text is not silver.
<P>This paragraph is silver.</P>
<P>This paragraph is not.</P>
```

In the first set of markup, a paragraph immediately follows an H2, so it is silver. In the second, the element adjacent to the H2 is a UL, which does not match the rule, and neither does the paragraph right after that. Finally, even though there is text directly after the third H2, it isn't part of an element, so the paragraph right after the text matches the rule and is colored silver. All this is demonstrated in Figure 10-5.

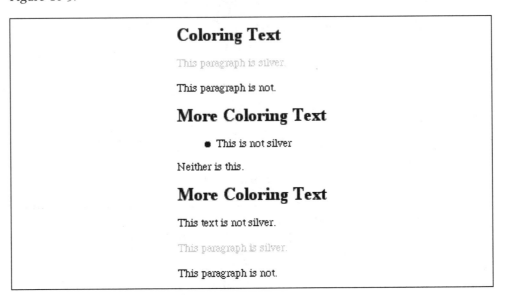

Figure 10-5. Selecting adjacent elements

If you wanted to make any element immediately following an H2 silver, then the universal selector comes into play:

```
H2 + * {color: silver;}
```

The fact that user agents ignore text between elements can actually be used to your advantage in many circumstances. Take, for example, a document design in which you want STRONG text to be gray, except when it follows EM text, in which case it should be silver:

```
STRONG {color: gray;}
EM + STRONG {color: silver;}
```

```
   <P>While the first strong element is <STRONG>gray</STRONG>, the
   <EM>second</EM> strong element is <STRONG>silver</STRONG>, because it
   follows an "EM" element.
```

The result is shown in Figure 10-6.

While the first strong element is gray, the second strong element is silver, because it follows an "EM" element.

Figure 10-6. More adjacent selections

Attribute Selectors

With the introduction of *attribute selectors*, CSS gains a great deal of flexibility, precision, and power. Attribute selectors can be matched in four ways, each of which carries its own strengths and advantages.

Attribute matching

First off, there is the ability to create a selector that matches any element with the specified attribute. For example, you can match all anchors with a NAME attribute, or all IMG elements with a BORDER attribute, or all elements that have a class of some type:

```
A[name] {color: purple;}        /* colors any NAME anchor purple */
IMG[border] {border-color: blue;}  /* sets blue border for any bordered IMG */
[class] {color: red;}           /* sets any classed element red */
```

In none of these situations does it matter what value is assigned to the attributes of each element. As long as the given attribute is present for the element, the element will match the selector shown. Thus, in the following example, the first two IMG elements shown will match the preceding rule, whereas the third will not, as illustrated by Figure 10-7:

```
IMG[border] {border-color: blue;}

<IMG SRC="one.gif" BORDER="1" ALT="image one (match)">
<IMG SRC="two.gif" BORDER="23" ALT="image two (match)">
<IMG SRC="three.gif" ALT="image three (no match)">
```

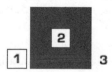

Figure 10-7. Attribute matching

Value matching

It is also possible to match attributes based on their values. Assume that you wish to style all hyperlinks as gray, except for those that point to the main page of the web site of the World Wide Web Consortium (*http://www.w3.org/*). These links should be silver instead, as shown in Figure 10-8:

```
A[href] {color: gray;}
A[href="http://www.w3.org/"] {color: silver;}
```

Figure 10-8. Matching on attribute values

Thanks to the cascade, the second rule will apply when an anchor points to the W3C web site, overriding the previous rule.

Matching single attribute values

It has been possible since HTML 3.2 to set multiple class names on a given element, such as:

```
<P CLASS="footnote example reference">
```

In CSS1 you could only refer to one of the values, using a selector like `P.example`. In CSS2, you can create a selector such that the class name must be an exact match, or you can set it up so that only one of the values has to match. `P[class="example"]` wouldn't match the preceding three-class paragraph, because the values are different (`example` isn't the same as `footnote example reference`).

On the other hand, `P[class~="example"]` *would* match `footnote example reference` because this type of selector has only to match *one* of the values in the class attribute. The only difference is the tilde character (~), but what a difference!

As an example, let's assume a document in which elements can have one or more class values of `driving`, `flying`, `nautical`, `directions`, and `title`. Thus, an element could have a class of `driving directions`, or perhaps `flying directions title`. Furthermore, we decide that while all titles should be red, anything (other than a title) relating to flying should be green and anything relating to driving should be purple. These can be declared as follows:

```
*[class~="flying"] {color: green;}
*[class~="driving"] {color: purple;}
*[class~="title"] {color: red;}
```

The tilde (~) before the equals sign is what causes these selectors to match any one of the values in the **class** attribute. Thus, the following rule would match any **IMG** element with a **class** of **figure** and an **alt** attribute that contains the word **Figure**—such as **Figure** 1, **Figure** 2, and so on:

```
IMG[class="figure"][alt~="Figure"] {margin: 5px;}

<IMG SRC="picture13.jpg" CLASS="figure" ALT="Figure 13">
```

Simulating class and ID

Using attribute selectors, you can also simulate class and ID selectors. The following pairs of rules are roughly equivalent:

```
P[class="directions"] {color: red;}
P.directions {color: red;}

DIV[ID="abc123"] {color: blue;}
DIV#abc123 {color: blue;}
```

Obviously, the latter rule in each pair is much simpler to type and edit, and you'll probably use such rules in most circumstances.

If you want an exact match, you can use an ordinary attribute selector. Thus, the following rule:

```
P[class="driving directions"] {color: green;}
```

will match this markup:

```
<P CLASS="driving directions">This is a side note (and it's green).</P>
```

If you aren't quite so concerned about exact matching, you can string class selectors together. This is a new feature of CSS2, and with this approach, you can match a **class** attribute with a value of **driving directions** in this way:

```
P.driving.directions {color: blue;}

<P CLASS="driving directions">This is a side note (and it's blue this time).
</P>
```

You could use the same selector to match the value **directions for driving**, since it contains both **driving** and **directions**—just not in that order.

Again, this probably seems a bit easier to type. So why go to all the effort of using the longer notation of attribute selectors? The reason to use attribute selectors is that the **.class** and **#ID** selectors apply only to HTML documents, or to any other document that uses a language that includes the concepts of class and ID. Other languages, such as those based on XML, might not honor these conventions, in which case you'll need to use the attribute selectors instead.

Matching hyphenated values

The last type of attribute selector is generally used for language matching, but it does have other uses. Any attribute selector using the symbols |= will match a value that begins with the specified value, given that the value is at the start of a hyphen-separated value. For example:

```
P[lang|="en"]
```

This selector will match any paragraph whose **lang** attribute has the value **en, en-US, en-UK, en-Cockney**, and so on.

In fact, this can be used to match any value with a similar format. For example, if you have images with **ALT** text of **fig-1, fig-2, fig-3**, and so on, and want to match any of them, you could use this selector:

```
IMG[alt|="fig"]
```

This is a less likely use for |=, but it's still perfectly valid. Note that the previous rule would not match the value **figure** or **config**, as neither of them starts with **fig-** or is simply **fig**. The rule would match **fig-tree**, however.

More Pseudo-Classes and Pseudo-Elements

Even though that might seem like it's more than enough, another area of expansion is in pseudo-class and pseudo-element selectors.

:hover

To begin, there is **:hover**. The basic idea is that the styles in a **:hover** rule are applied while your mouse pointer is "hovering" over an element. For example, when the pointer is positioned over a link such that clicking the mouse button would cause the browser to follow the link, the pointer is "hovering" over the link. This is in some respects similar to the somewhat famous JavaScript "rollover" trick, where images change when the pointer hovers over them. Thanks to **:hover**, you can specify a hover style very easily:

```
A:link {background: white; color: blue;}
A:hover {background: blue; color: white;}
```

These styles will cause anchors to "reverse" in color when the mouse pointer hovers over them, as illustrated in Figure 10-9.

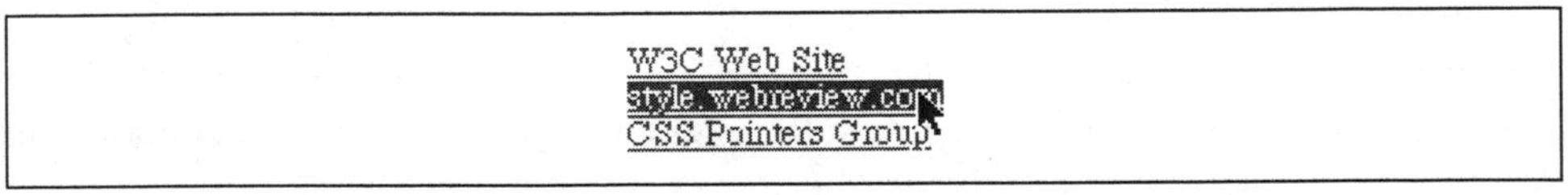

Figure 10-9. Hover styles

As a matter of fact, the rule for A:hover would be used while the pointer hovers over any anchor, not just a hyperlink. While some other pseudo-classes, like :link and :visited, are constrained to the A element in HTML, the same is not true of :hover. User agents could, in theory, allow the assignment of hover styles to any element, like this:

```
P:hover {font-weight: bold;}
```

Therefore, if you want to make sure your hover styles are applied only to your hyperlinks, you would need to use this rule:

```
A:link:hover {background: blue; color: white;}
```

The ability to combine pseudo-classes is a new feature of CSS2.

Internet Explorer 4.x and 5.x both recognize :hover on anchors only. As of this writing, no other browser will recognize :hover under any circumstances.

:focus

Similar to :hover is :focus, which is used to define styles for elements that are "in focus." A form element, for example, has "focus" when it is currently ready to accept input. Therefore, the background of INPUT elements could be set to yellow in order to highlight the currently active input:

```
INPUT:focus {background: yellow;}
```

This style would only be applied to an element as long as it was in focus. As soon as the user switched from one input to another, the styles would be removed from the former and applied to the latter. This is a welcome capability, as it reduces the need for using JavaScript to create such effects.

There are serious issues related to document reflow with :hover and :focus. Take, for example:

```
A:hover {font-size: 200%;}
```

In theory, a user agent would have to double the size of anchor text as the pointer hovers over it, which could well cause major redisplay issues. An author could cause similar problems by declaring that TEXTAREA elements should change their size when they are in focus. User agents are not required to reflow the document based on styles assigned to these pseudo-elements, although some may do so—it remains to be seen.

:lang

On a completely different note is the pseudo-class `:lang`, which is used to apply styles to elements with matching languages. Let's say you want all paragraphs in English to be black on white, and all paragraphs in French to be white on black:

```
P:lang(en) {color: black; background: white;}
P:lang(fr) {color: white; background: black;}
```

Of course, user agents aren't likely to figure out element languages on their own. Instead, they have to rely on document markup, such as the `lang` attribute in HTML:

```
<P lang="en">This paragraph is in English.</P>
<P lang="fr">Ce paragraphe est en fran&ccedil;ais.</P>
```

The results are shown in Figure 10-10.

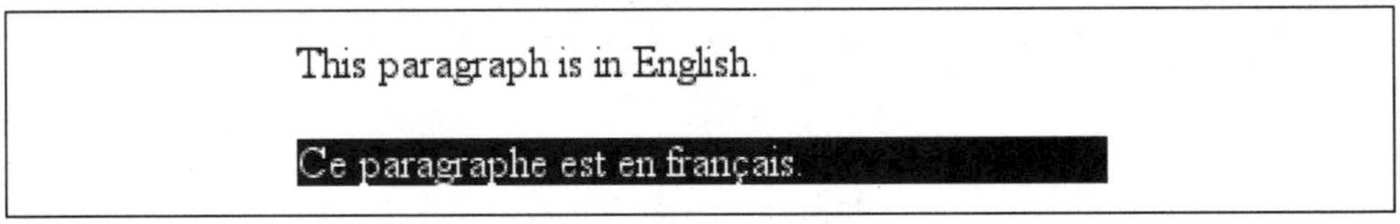

Figure 10-10. Changing styles based on language

Even if this isn't something you're likely to use often, it can still come in very handy. For example, you could define styles to apply to entire documents:

```
HTML:lang(de) {color: black; background: yellow;}
```

Thus would all HTML documents marked as German be shown as black text on a yellow background. This marking could be made with the `lang` attribute, in a **META** tag in the document's head, or even as a value in the document's HTTP headers. This is somewhat similar to the `|=` attribute selector discussed in the previous section, but it is a little more general.

:first-child

The last of the new pseudo-class selectors we'll cover here is the `:first-child` selector. This is used to match an element that is the first child of another element. For example, you might want to make the first child of every **DIV** italicized instead of normal text, as long as that first child is a paragraph (shown in Figure 10-11):

```
P {color: black;}
P:first-child {font-style: italic;}

<BODY>
<P>This paragraph should be italic.</P>
<P>This paragraph should be normal.</P>
<DIV STYLE="border: 1px dashed gray;">
```

```
This text should be normal.
<P>This paragraph should be italic.</P>
<P>This paragraph should be normal.</P>
</DIV>
<DIV STYLE="border: 1px dotted gray;">
<H2>This H2 should be normal.</H2>
<P>This paragraph should be normal.</P>
<P>This paragraph should be normal.</P>
</DIV>
</BODY>
```

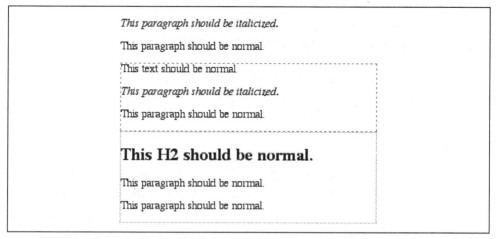

Figure 10-11. Selecting styles for certain first children

The very first paragraph is italicized because it is the first child of the BODY element. Similarly, the first paragraph in the first DIV is italicized because it is the first child of the DIV, even though text preceded it. Only structural elements count for this pseudo-class, so the text before the paragraph doesn't affect the paragraph's status as the first child. However, in the second DIV, the H2 is the first child, so it does not match the rule P:first-child. If the intent is to have the first child of any element be italicized, no matter what element that might be, then you need only leave off the element part of the selector, or use it in conjunction with the universal selector. This will yield the result shown in Figure 10-12:

```
*:first-child {font-style: italic;}
```

Now let's say we want to apply styles to elements that are part of a first child; for example, all emphasized text within a first-child paragraph should be italicized:

```
P:first-child EM {font-style: italic;}
```

Of course, this will match any first-child paragraph, no matter its parent element. Suppose instead we want a rule that applies only to paragraphs that are the first children of DIV elements. In that case, we need to use the child selector:

```
DIV > P:first-child {font-style: italic;}
```

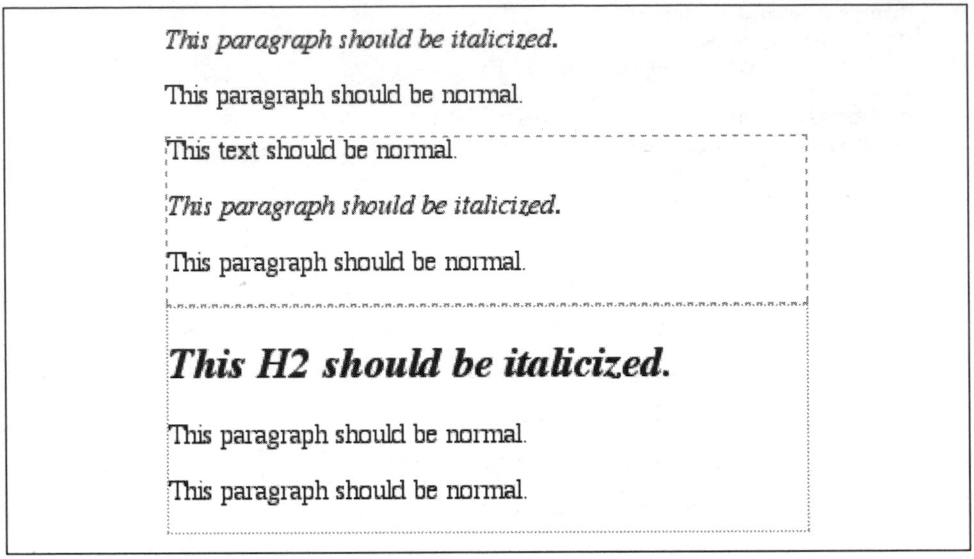

> *This paragraph should be italicized.*
>
> This paragraph should be normal.
>
> This text should be normal.
>
> *This paragraph should be italicized.*
>
> This paragraph should be normal.
>
> ## This H2 should be italicized.
>
> This paragraph should be normal.
>
> This paragraph should be normal.

Figure 10-12. Selecting any first child

This translates as, "any paragraph that is a first child, and is a child of a DIV, should be in italics." If we were to leave out the child selector as follows, though:

```
DIV P:first-child {font-style: italic;}
```

then the rule would read, "any paragraph that is a first child of any element, and is also a descendant of a DIV, should be in italics." The difference is subtle, but real.

Miscellaneous pseudo-elements and pseudo-classes

There are two other new pseudo-elements:

```
:before
:after
```

There are also three new pseudo-classes:

```
:left
:right
:first
```

The details of these pseudo-elements and pseudo-classes are discussed later in this chapter.

Fonts and Text

The font property has also picked up a few new values in CSS2:

```
caption
icon
menu
message-box
```

```
small-caption
status-bar
```

These values give the `font` property the ability to match the font family, size, weight, and so forth, according to the settings users have specified on their computers. For example, icons on a Macintosh are typically labeled using 9-point Geneva. Assuming that hasn't been changed by the user, any `font` declaration with a value of `icon` will result in 9-point Geneva for that text—as long as the page is viewed using a Macintosh:

```
SPAN.OScap {font: icon;}  /* will look like icon labels in OS */
```

On a Windows system, of course, the font would come out different, and under other window managers (like X), it would look different still. The flexibility is certainly interesting, and it allows the author to easily create pages that have an appearance familiar to the user.

New Font Properties

The font section gains two new properties in CSS2. `font-size-adjust` is intended to help browsers make sure that text will be the intended size, regardless of whether the browser can use the font specified in the style sheet. It is often a problem that authors will call for a font that is not available to the user, and when another font is substituted, it's either too big or too small to read comfortably. This new property addresses that very problem, and should be very useful for authors who want to make sure that their documents are readable no matter what font is substituted.

The other new font property is `font-stretch`, which allows you to define variable widths for the fonts you use. This is similar to setting a character width in a desktop publishing system. The property uses keywords such as `ultra-condensed`, `wider`, and `expanded`. The changes are handled in a fashion similar to font weights, where a table of condensed and expanded font faces is constructed, and the keywords are assigned to various faces. If no face exists, the user agent may try to scale a font on its own, or it may simply ignore `font-stretch` altogether. Figure 10-13 shows what a font might look like for each possible value of `font-stretch`.

text-shadow

In terms of text, there is one new property, `text-shadow`, which has the effect you'd probably expect from its name: you can define a drop shadow of a given color for text. You can even set an offset and a blur radius, which means you can get cool fuzzy shadows, or even glow effects, using this property. We should fully expect to see this property horribly abused the instant it's supported by any browser; for a few examples of why, see the simulations in Figure 10-14.

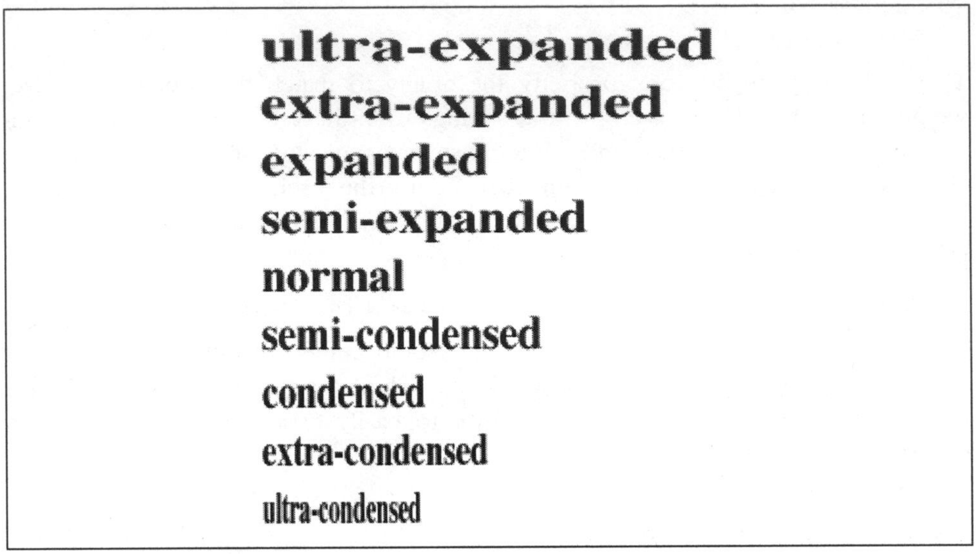

ultra-expanded

extra-expanded

expanded

semi-expanded

normal

semi-condensed

condensed

extra-condensed

ultra-condensed

Figure 10-13. Stretching fonts

Greetings.   Far Shadow.
Coronal Glow

Figure 10-14. Various effects using the text-shadow property

Generated Content

Generated content is a new way of adding things to existing content without having to alter the content itself. It's done by using the pseudo-elements `:before` and
`:after` and the property `content`. Here's a basic example of how it works:

```
P:before, P:after {content: "\""; color: gray;}

<P>This is a quote.</P>
```

The browser will display what's shown in Figure 10-15.

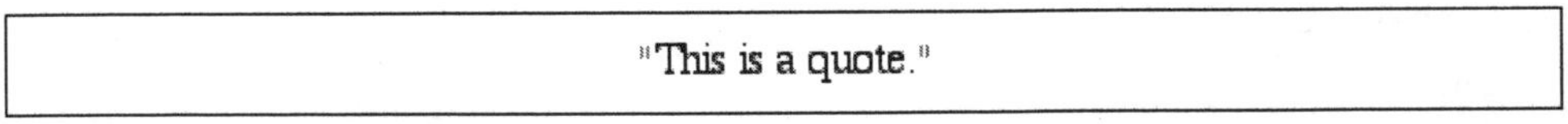

"This is a quote."

Figure 10-15. Adding generated content

Note that the double-quote mark was escaped out—that is, preceded by a back-
slash. This is necessary, since text values for content must be enclosed in double
quotes. You could also place images before (or after) content, using something
like `P:before {content: url(para.gif);}` to put a paragraph symbol at the

beginning of each paragraph. You can even string multiple values together like this (shown in Figure 10-16):

```
P:before {content: url(para.gif) " -- ";}
```

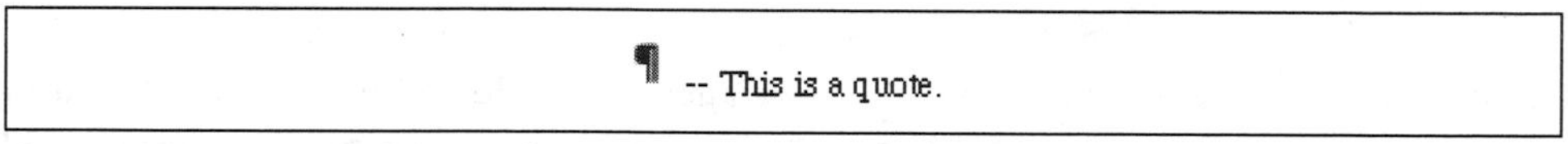

¶ -- This is a quote.

Figure 10-16. Adding an image and text before a paragraph

This would cause each paragraph to be started with a paragraph symbol, a blank space, two dashes, and then another blank space. Note that all of this is considered part of the paragraph and is inlined within it. The spaces appear before and after the double dash because they're included in the string value. If these spaces were omitted, then space would not appear to either side of the dashes.

Let's say, though, that you want to do some real quoting, using real quotation marks—you know, the curly double quotes that are so hard to specify in HTML and which often don't show up even if you do try to specify them. CSS2 has ways to handle this.

content has some other values you can use:

* open-quote, which inserts an opening quotation mark
* close-quote, which inserts a closing quotation mark
* no-open-quote, which prevent the insertion of an opening quotation mark
* no-close-quote, which prevent the insertion of an closing quotation mark

So if you wanted your quotations to begin and end with quotation marks, instead of typing in a literal quotation mark, you could let the browser insert "smart quotes" for you.

```
BLOCKQUOTE:before {content: open-quote;}
BLOCKQUOTE:after {content: close-quote;}
```

Automatic Numbering

In the same vein, CSS2 also includes properties for automatic numbering. First, you can specify a counter as a value of content. This can be a bit tricky, and it would take too long to run through all the possibilities, but here's an example. Say you wanted the chapters and sections of a document numbered 1, 1.1, 1.2, 1.3, and so on. In addition, you're using H1 for your chapters and H2 for your sections. Here are the declarations you would use:

```
H1:before {
   content: "Chapter " counter(chapter) ". ";
   counter-increment: chapter;   /* Add 1 to chapter */
```

```
    counter-reset: section;          /* Set section to 0 */
  }
  H2:before {
    content: counter(chapter) "." counter(section) " ";
    counter-increment: section;
  }
```

As we can see from Figure 10-17, the user agent will add the word "Chapter" and a number at the beginning of H1 text. This number is automatically incremented with each H1, due to the declaration `counter-increment: chapter;`. It also sets the section counter back to zero through `counter-reset: section;`. Then, for each section heading (H2), the browser uses the chapter number, followed by a period (.) followed by the current section number, which is also automatically incremented.

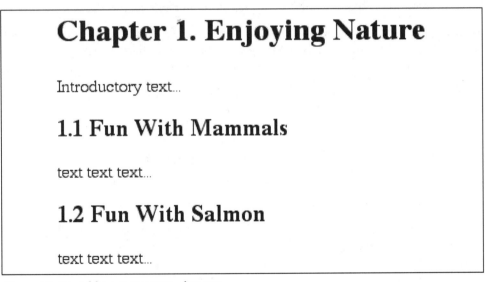

Chapter 1. Enjoying Nature

Introductory text...

1.1 Fun With Mammals

text text text...

1.2 Fun With Salmon

text text text...

Figure 10-17. Adding counters to elements

You don't have to increment by one every time, either. You can define any integer as the increment value, including zero and negative numbers. If you want each section to have an even number, as we see in Figure 10-18, then you can declare the following:

```
  H2:before {
    content: "Section " counter(section) ". ";
    counter-increment: section 2; /* Add 2 to chapter */
  }
```

You can also keep an element from incrementing a counter by setting its `display` to `none`. Of course, that will cause the element to disappear altogether.

Chapter 1. Enjoying Nature

Introductory text...

Section 1.2 Fun With Mammals

text text text...

Section 1.4 Fun With Salmon

text text text...

Figure 10-18. Changing a counter's incremental value

Markers

You can do even more by using the value `marker` for the property `display`, which enables you to define your own marker styles for any element at all. You're already familiar with markers, as it happens—the bullets and numbers at the beginning of list items are markers.

Let's say we want to recreate the way unordered lists behave. For the purposes of this example, we'll use the image *disc.gif* to stand in for the normal bullets. Using marker properties, we would declare:

```
LI:before {display: marker;
   content: url(disc.gif);
   marker-offset: 1em;
}
```

This will insert the disc image before each list item, and set it to be offset from the left edge of the `LI` content by `1em`, as shown in Figure 10-19.

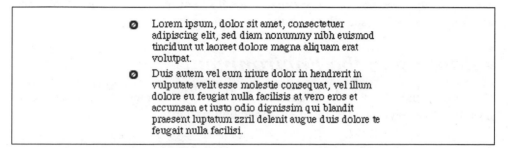

Figure 10-19. Styling list markers

Marker properties are not restricted to list items, however. Let's say that, through-out a document, there are a few paragraphs with a class of `aside`. We wish to call attention to these paragraphs by inserting a small note to the side of each one. Here's one way to do it:

```
BODY {counter-reset: aside-ctr;}
P {margin-left: 10em;}
P.aside:before {display: marker;
   content: "Aside " counter(aside-ctr) " --";
   counter-increment: aside-ctr;
   text-align: right;
   marker-offset: 1em;
   width: 9.5em;
}
```

The effect will be something like that seen in Figure 10-20.

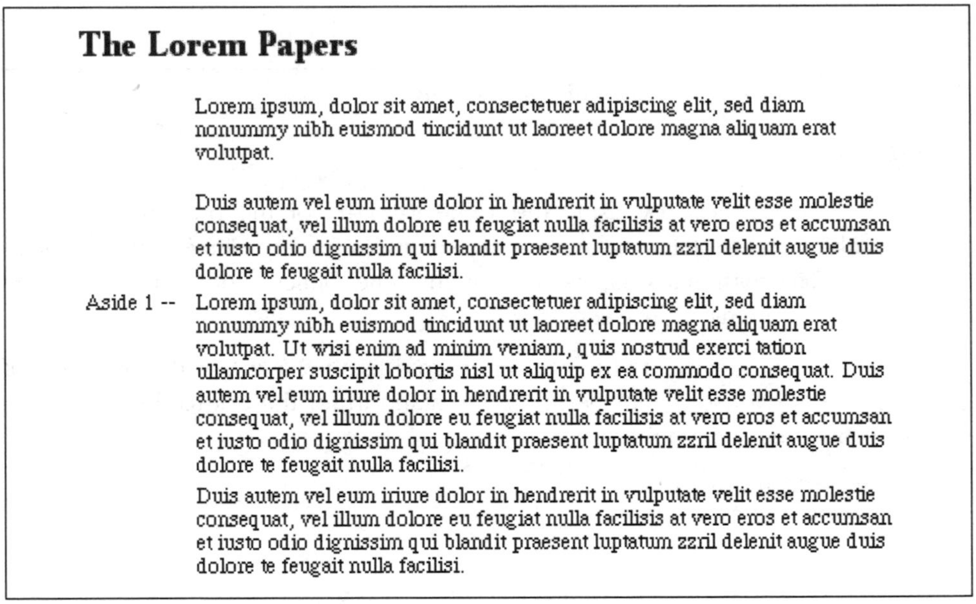

The Lorem Papers

Lorem ipsum, dolor sit amet, consectetuer adipiscing elit, sed diam nonummy nibh euismod tincidunt ut laoreet dolore magna aliquam erat volutpat.

Duis autem vel eum iriure dolor in hendrerit in vulputate velit esse molestie consequat, vel illum dolore eu feugiat nulla facilisis at vero eros et accumsan et iusto odio dignissim qui blandit praesent luptatum zzril delenit augue duis dolore te feugait nulla facilisi.

Aside 1 --   Lorem ipsum, dolor sit amet, consectetuer adipiscing elit, sed diam nonummy nibh euismod tincidunt ut laoreet dolore magna aliquam erat volutpat. Ut wisi enim ad minim veniam, quis nostrud exerci tation ullamcorper suscipit lobortis nisl ut aliquip ex ea commodo consequat. Duis autem vel eum iriure dolor in hendrerit in vulputate velit esse molestie consequat, vel illum dolore eu feugiat nulla facilisis at vero eros et accumsan et iusto odio dignissim qui blandit praesent luptatum zzril delenit augue duis dolore te feugait nulla facilisi.

Duis autem vel eum iriure dolor in hendrerit in vulputate velit esse molestie consequat, vel illum dolore eu feugiat nulla facilisis at vero eros et accumsan et iusto odio dignissim qui blandit praesent luptatum zzril delenit augue duis dolore te feugait nulla facilisi.

Figure 10-20. Automatically numbered asides

This is yet another aspect of CSS2 that, once it's been properly implemented, will allow authors to do quite a bit with their documents.

Adapting to the Environment

CSS2 offers the ability to both alter the browser's environment and integrate its look more closely to that of the user's operating system.

Cursors

To achieve the former, we have the `cursor` property, which lets you declare what shape the browser's cursor will take as it passes over a given element. Want to make a humorous point about download times? Change the cursor to the wait cursor (an hourglass or watch) when the cursor passes over hyperlinks. You can even hook this property up to "cursor files" (which are not defined by the specification), so you could theoretically class your anchors based on where they go and load different icons for each type of link. For example, off-site links could cause the cursor to change into a globe, while links intended to provide help could trigger a question-mark cursor.

Colors

In order to let web pages more closely match the user's desktop environment, there are a whole list of new color keywords like `button-highlight`, `three-d-shadow`, and `gray-text`. These are all intended to use the colors of the user's operating system. In all, there are 27 of these new color keywords. I won't list them all out here, but they're listed in Table 10-1, found at the end of this chapter.

Outlines

While you're moving your cursor around, you might want to show where the focus is set. For example, it might be nice to define a button so that it gets a red box around it when the cursor moves over it. Well, there a number of outline properties, including `outline`, `outline-color`, `outline-style`, and `outline-width`. To use the example of a red box, you might declare:

```
IMG.button:hover {outline: solid red 1px;}
```

This should have the effect described. The outline styles could also be used to set a visible outline for regions in a client-side image map.

Borders

In CSS1, there are quite a few properties devoted to setting borders around element boxes, such as `border-top-width` and `border-color`, not to mention `border` itself. CSS2 adds a even more border properties, most of which are aimed at giving the author even more specific control of the borders. Before, it was difficult to set a specific color or style for a given side of the border, except through properties like `border-left`, and that could require more than one value. The new CSS2 properties address this, and their names are pretty self-explanatory:

```
border-top-color
border-right-color
```

```
border-bottom-color
border-left-color
border-top-style
border-right-style
border-bottom-style
border-left-style
```

Tables

Perhaps as a result of a generic need to be able to describe table layout—something CSS1 lacks—CSS2 includes a handful of features that apply directly to tables and table cells. First, there are 10 new table-related values for `display`:

```
table
inline-table
table-column-group
table-column
table-row-group
table-row
table-cell
table-caption
table-header-group
table-footer-group
```

While the effects of most of these are obvious from their names, at least two may not be familiar to you. `table-header-group` and `table-footer-group` are used to mark the header and footer of a table. These are displayed, respectively, above or below all the rows of the table, but not outside of the table's caption.

Another interesting effect is that you can align text on a character by using the `text-align` property. For example, if you wanted to line up a column of figures on a decimal point, you might declare:

```
TD { text-align: "." }
```

As long as a set of cells are grouped into a column, their content will be aligned so that the periods all line up along a vertical axis.

Far from relying on existing properties, CSS2 provides a whole array of brand-new properties in the table section. Here are a few of them:

- `border-spacing`, which influences the placement of borders around cells
- `border-collapse`, which can be used to influence how the borders of various table elements interact
- `table-layout`, which tells the browser whether or not it can resize the table as necessary

There are also properties describing how `visibility` and `vertical-align` are applied to tables. There is also a `caption-side` property, which functions exactly the same as the `ALIGN` attribute on the `<CAPTION>` tag, and the property `speak-header-cell`, which controls how header cells are handled by speech-generating browsers (more on that later).

Media Types and @-rules

Don't get too excited yet. We aren't talking about media types in the sense of things like audio and video authoring. Well, not exactly, anyway. We're talking about creating rules for presentation within various kinds of media. The defined types of media thus far are:

- `screen`, as in a computer screen
- `print`, for things like printouts and print-preview displays
- `projection`, for projected presentations such as slide shows
- `braille` and `embossed`, for tactile feedback devices and printers
- `aural`, for speech generators
- `tv`, for television-type displays (think WebTV)
- `tty`, for fixed-width character displays
- `handheld`, for palmtop computers
- the ubiquitous `all`

These are all values of `@media`, one of several new @-rules. Some others are:

- `@font-face`, which is used in the definition of a font by manual means
- `@import`, which has more power than under CSS1 by allowing authors to associate media types with `@import` statements; for example, `@import (print.css) print;`
- `@page`, which allows you to define the styles of a page when using paged-media style sheets; for example, `@page {size: 8.5in 11in;}`

Paged Media

Since I just brought up paged media, I should probably mention that there are some new properties that apply to such media. Five of them apply to page breaks and where they appear:

```
page-break-before
page-break-after
page-break-inside
orphans
widows
```

The first two are used to control whether a page break should appear before or after a given element, and the latter two are common desktop publishing terms for the minimum number of lines that can appear at the end or beginning of a page. They mean the same thing in CSS2 as they do in desktop publishing.

`page-break-inside` (first proposed by this author, as it happens) is used to define whether or not page breaks should be placed inside a given element. For example, you might not want unordered lists to have page breaks inside them. You would then declare `UL {page-break-inside: avoid;}`. The rendering agent (your printer, for example) would avoid breaking unordered lists whenever possible.

There is also `size`, which is simply used to define whether a page should be printed in landscape or portrait mode and the length of each axis. If you plan to print your page to a professional printing system, you might want to use `marks`, which can apply either cross or crop marks to your page. Thus you might declare:

```
@page {size: 8.5in 11in; margin: 0.5in; marks: cross;}
```

This will set the pages to be U.S. letter-standard, 8.5 inches wide by 11 inches tall, and place cross marks in the corners of each page.

In addition, there are the new pseudo-classes `:left`, `:right`, and `:first`, all of which are applied only to the `@page` rule. Thus, you could set different margins for left and right pages in double-sided printing:

```
@page:left {margin-left: 0.75in; margin-right: 1in;}
@page:right{margin-left: 1in; margin-right: 0.75in;}
```

The `:first` selector applies only to the first page of a document, so that you could give it a larger top margin or a bigger font size:

```
@page:first {margin-top: 2in; font-size: 150%;}
```

The Spoken Word

To round things out, we'll cover some of the properties in the area of aural style sheets. These are properties that help define how a speaking browser will actually speak the page. This may not be important to many people, but for the visually impaired, these properties are a necessity.

First off, there is `voice-family`, which is much the same as `font-family` in its structure: the author can define both a specific voice and a generic voice family. There are several properties controlling the speed at which the page is read (`speech-rate`), as well as properties for the `pitch`, `pitch-range`, `stress`, `richness`, and `volume` of a given voice. There are also properties that let you control how acronyms, punctuation, dates, numerals, and time are spoken. There are ways to specify audio cues, which can be played before, during, or after a given element (such as a hyperlink), ways to insert pauses before or after elements, and even the ability to control the apparent position in space from which a sound comes via the properties `azimuth` and `elevation`. With these last two properties, you could define a style sheet where the text is read by a voice "in front of" the user, whereas background music comes from "behind" and audio cues come from "above" the user!

Summary

CSS2 obviously covers a lot of ground, and exploring it in detail would probably have added at least four more chapters to this book, not to mention dramatically bulking up some of the chapters that already exist. However, since so little of CSS2 has actually been implemented at this writing, we felt it was better to provide an overview that was light on details. After all, the specification may change as implementations reveal flaws, and we'd rather stick to describing things that are fairly reliable.

For quick reference purposes, Table 10-1 gives a quick summary of everything new in CSS2.

Table 10-1. New Properties in CSS2

New Properties in CSS2		
text-shadow	position	border-spacing
font-size-adjust	direction	empty-cells
font-stretch	top	caption-side
unicode-bidi	right	speak-header-cell
	bottom	
cursor	left	volume
outline	z-index	speak
outline-color		pause-before
outline-style	min-width	pause-after
outline-width	max-width	pause
	min-height	cue-before
content	max-height	cue-after
quotes	overflow	cue
counter-reset	clip	play-during
counter-increment	visibility	azimuth
marker-offset	page-break-before	elevation
	page-break-after	speech-rate
border-top-color	page-break-inside	voice-family
border-right-color	orphans	pitch
border-bottom-color	widows	pitch-range
border-left-color	size	stress
border-top-style	marks	richness
border-right-style		speak-punctuation
border-bottom-style	border-collapse	speak-rate
border-left-style	border-spacing	speak-numeral
	table-layout	speak-time

Table 10-1. New Properties in CSS2 (continued)

New Pseudo-Classes and Pseudo-Elements in CSS2

:hover	:right	:before
:left	:first	:after

New @-rules in CSS2

@media	@font-face	@page

Table 10-2. New Values in CSS2

All Properties

inherit

The display Property

run-in	inline-table	table-footer-group
compact	table-row-group	table-row
marker	table-column-group	table-cell
table	table-header-group	table-caption

The font Property

caption	message-box
icon	small-caption
menu	status-bar

The list-style-type Property

decimal-leading-zero	cjk-ideographic	hiragana-iroha
hebrew	hiragana	katakana-iroha
georgian	katakana	lower-greek
armenian		

The *color* values

active-border	highlight	three-d-dark-shadow
active-caption	highlight-text	three-d-face
app-workspace	inactive-border	three-d-highlight
background	inactive-caption	three-d-lightshadow
button-face	info-background	three-d-shadow
button-highlight	info-text	window
button-text	menu	window-frame
caption-text	menu-text	window-text
gray-text	scrollbar	

The vertical-align Property

length

11

CSS in Action

No instructional work would be complete without a chapter that explores ways to put all that theoretical knowledge into practice, and that's just what we'll be doing here. After we look at three different page (re)design projects using CSS, we'll go through a grab bag of tricks and tips that might help you get around some of your biggest CSS frustrations.

Conversion Projects

Since we've covered the entirety of CSS1, let's exercise that newfound knowledge with three conversion projects. In each of these cases—two of them web pages and one a print magazine article—we'll break down the page into its components and determine the best way to recreate the same effects using CSS1 and structural HTML.

Case 1: Consistent Look and Feel

In this project, we will create an external style sheet that will define a basic, consistent look and feel for an entire corporate web site. Our main goal is to create styles that are as simple as possible, using few (if any) classes or IDs. For the purposes of the project, we will assume there is a standard writing guide for employees of the company: document titles are in H1, subheadings in H2, every page uses standard graphics at the top, and so forth.

Marketing has decreed that all pages shall use a white background with a thin dark green stripe running down the left edge, black body text in a serif font, and hyperlinks that are a dark green when unvisited and dark gray when visited. Furthermore, document titles must be underlined and use a color similar to the standard navigation buttons found at the top of every page, which are gray text against a dark green background—the same dark green you are to use for unvisited hyperlinks and the left edge of the browser window. All headings, including document titles, are to use a sans serif font. The rest is left to our discretion.

A lot of this is fairly straightforward. For the document BODY, we write:

```
BODY {font-family: Times,serif; color: black;
   background: white url(pix/grstripe.gif) repeat-y top left;}
```

For the anchors, among other things, we need to know the color value of the green being used. The art department reports that this particular shade of green uses no red or blue, and just 40% green; someone there has had the foresight to use web-safe colors. (Remember, this is a hypothetical situation.) We want to do the same for the visited links, so we write:

```
A:link {color: rgb(0%,40%,0%);}
A:visited {color: rgb(20%,20%,20%);}
```

This gives us our dark green and dark gray hyperlinks.

Now for headings. They're all supposed to be in a sans serif font, but H1s have some special rules. In order to cover all the bases in a compact manner, we declare:

```
H1, H2, H3, H4, H5, H6 {font-family: Verdana,sans-serif;}
H1 {color: rgb(0%,40%,0%); border-bottom: thin solid; width: 100%;}
```

With the second declaration, not only do we use the standard color, but we enhance the idea of "underlining" by setting a bottom border that will extend from the left edge of the text all the way out to the right edge of the browser window. This line will also inherit the green color of the text and so really punch up the fact that the title and navigation buttons are separate from the rest of the page.

Now that this is all done, we need to link the style sheet into the site's pages. The above declarations are collected into a single file, which is saved to a file with the URL *http://www.mycomp.com/style/site.css*. Then all of the site's pages are modified so that their HEAD element contains the following:

```
<LINK REL="stylesheet" TYPE="text/css"
   HREF="http://www.mycomp.com/style/site.css" >
```

This ensures that all documents—even those without their own style declarations—will use the site's overall style sheet. Figure 11-1 shows one example of how the pages will appear.

Case 2: Library Catalog System Interface

The library of Wattswith University has been using a web-based library catalog system for the last few years, and their web developers have always tried to keep

Figure 11-1. Final results

up with the times. Now that style sheets are gaining currency, the folks in the lab are itching to convert the library system's interface over to use them.

However, the current design has been so popular that a mandate has been handed down from the management: Thou Shalt Not Disrupt The Look And Feel. Annoyed but undaunted, our intrepid websmiths forge ahead. Their mission is to take what's there, then rip it apart and put it all back together again without anyone noticing the difference. (For the purposes of this project, the part of the webmasters will be played by you, the reader.)

The most complicated screen in the system is the record display screen. Composed of three areas—the system navigation bar, a sidebar with current options, and the record display itself—it's structured around a table, with each area being enclosed in a table cell. In addition, there is a fourth table cell between the sidebar and the main part of the page, in order to create some blank space. There are also a lot of FONT tags and a few tables imbedded within the main table that determines the page's layout. The skeleton of the page is expressed as a table, with a border and cell padding added to make the structure more clear:

```
<TABLE CELLSPACING=0 BORDER CELLPADDING="10">
<TR>
<TD ROWSPAN=2>sidebar</TD>
<TD COLSPAN=2>navigation bar</TD>
</TR>
```

```
<TR>
<TD> </TD>
<TD>main display</TD>
</TR>
</TABLE>
```

This has the appearance shown in Figure 11-2. Obviously, there is a lot more in the cells than what's listed above. The actual content was replaced by labels for the sake of brevity and clarity.

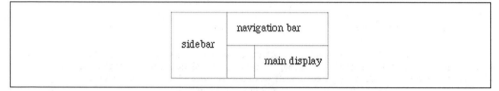

Figure 11-2. A simplified page structure

In order to keep the changes fairly simple, and to avoid stealing a trick I plan to use later in this chapter, for this project we're still going to use a table for the page's overall layout, but we're going to modify it slightly. Instead of four cells, it will only have two: the sidebar and the rest of the screen. The navigation bar will become part of the main display, and the blank "spacing" table cell will be eliminated entirely. This will leave us with the following:

```
<TABLE CELLSPACING=0>
<TR>
<TD>sidebar</TD>
<TD>navigation bar and main display</TD>
</TR>
</TABLE>
```

We'll turn to the sidebar first. Each set of links is grouped into a list under a main heading; these headings look different from the links. Each of the sections uses the following tags:

```
<P>
<FONT FACE="Verdana" COLOR="white" size="+1"><B><U>Heading</U></B></FONT>
<BR>
<FONT FACE="Verdana" SIZE="-1">
<A HREF="link1.html"><FONT COLOR="yellow">Link</FONT></A><BR>
<A HREF="link2.html"><FONT COLOR="yellow">Link</FONT></A><BR>
<A HREF="link3.html"><FONT COLOR="yellow">Link</FONT></A><BR>
</FONT>
</P>
```

Whew! Already we have our work cut out for us.

Probably the easiest thing to do is to assign a class to the sidebar's table cell, so that we can specify certain appearances that are specific to the sidebar. This leads us to enter the tags `<TD CLASS="sidebar">` and `</TD>` for the beginning and end of the cell, respectively.

Now we have the sidebar enclosed in its very own classed table cell. Since the background color for the sidebar is green, we can create our first style:

```
.sidebar {background: green;}
```

Moving on with the sidebar, we want to get rid of all the FONT tags, and hopefully the other style tags as well (like <B> and <U>). Since the entirety of the sidebar uses the font Verdana, we can add that to our style sheet:

```
.sidebar {background: green; font-family: Verdana,sans-serif;}
```

We use `font-family` here because we don't want to specify a `font-size` for the sidebar, so we can't use the shorthand `font`.

Now we *could* put headings and lists of links in separate paragraphs and then mess around with the padding, margin, and line heights of these paragraphs until they match the current look. However, it's probably easier to simply leave the paragraph and line break tags right where they are and simply SPAN the headings:

```
<SPAN CLASS="head">Heading</SPAN><BR>
```

 The danger in using SPAN instead of logical elements like headings is that pre-CSS browsers won't recognize the SPAN element. Also, indexing robots won't be able to make any sense of SPAN as a piece of document structure. On the other hand, using SPAN avoids having to cope with a number of bugs in early CSS implementations, so I've chosen to use SPAN in this case study instead of something a little more structured.

Having done this, we need a style declaration that will recreate the effects of all the tags we just deleted. This should just about do the trick:

```
.sidebar .head {font-size: larger; font-weight: bold;
    text-decoration: underline; color: white;}
```

By using the contextual selector `.sidebar .head`, we ensure only those `.head`s inside a `.sidebar` will receive these styles. Since the entire sidebar is already set to use Verdana, the headings will inherit and use it. As for the links, they need to be yellow, so we declare:

```
.sidebar A:link {color: yellow;}
.sidebar A:visited {color: yellow;}
.sidebar A:active {color: yellow;}
```

This will keep the links yellow no matter what, just as they are now. Figure 11-3 shows us the new, improved, FONT-tag-free sidebar which results from the preceding styles, and this markup:

```
<TD CLASS="sidebar"><P>
<SPAN CLASS="head">Heading</SPAN>
```

```
<BR>
<A HREF="link1.html">Link</A><BR>
<A HREF="link2.html">Link</A><BR>
<A HREF="link3.html">Link</A><BR>
</P>
</TD>
```

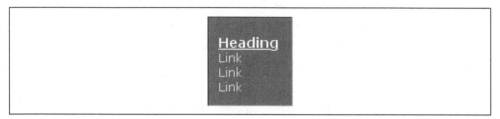

Figure 11-3. The well-styled sidebar

That was pretty easy, eh? Now let's tackle the navigation bar at the top of the main part of the page. This area also has a green background, and within it are a few images. Again, we use a DIV tag with a specific class, like this:

```
<DIV CLASS="navbar">
icons
</DIV>
```

Now all we need is the style `.navbar {background: green;}` and we're set. Or are we?

Not quite, no. In the old page, the navigation bar was separated slightly from the main display, but ran right up against the sidebar, thereby creating a sort of inverted green "L" shape. We want to make sure that this is still the case in the new setup. This is most easily accomplished by making sure that the division has no padding or border set, and that it is guaranteed to be as wide as the table cell in which it's found. Plus, we want the bar to have a little bit of blank space after it, so we need a margin of zero on everything but the bottom, where we just want a few pixels. So we add the following:

```
.navbar {background: green; padding: 0; margin: 0 0 10px 0; width: 100%;}
```

Now everything should be set for the navigation bar, as we can see in Figure 11-4. All we need to do now is make sure the main display has some blank space to its left, and we're done.

Figure 11-4. The greening of the navigational bar

No doubt you already know how this will work. We create another division, this one classed as main and enclosing everything in the main part of the page that isn't the navigation bar. Then we declare:

```
.main {margin-left: 1.5em;}
```

It seems like a reasonable amount of space, so we go with it. We check the result in Figure 11-5, which is based around this skeleton markup:

```
<TABLE CELLPADDING="0" CELLSPACING="0" BORDER>
<TR VALIGN="top">
<TD CLASS="sidebar">
(sidebar)
</TD>
<TD>
<DIV CLASS="navbar">
(icons)
</DIV>
<DIV CLASS="main">
(content)
</DIV>
</TR>
</TABLE>
```

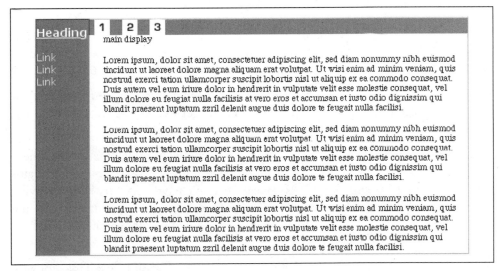

Figure 11-5. Final results

There are a few subtle differences from the original layout, but overall, no significant changes in the document's presentation. We can be quite pleased with the results—and better still, management will never notice the difference.

The advantages of the new design are twofold: the ability to change colors and fonts by editing a small number of styles instead of a bunch of FONT tags and a reduction in size of the HTML source itself. In a case like this, a page's size can shrink by several kilobytes—and in cases where a heavily FONTed page is converted to use CSS instead, the document's file size can decrease by as much as 50%!

Case 3: Putting a Magazine Article Online

Finally, we turn to the situation faced by the editorial offices of *Meerkat Monthly*. This specialist magazine examines the issues of raising a suricate in a domestic environment, away from others of its kind, and also provides general information about the animals themselves. In an effort to boost sales, the editors want to put a few articles online each month.

 This case study ends up using quite a few advanced styles and, as such, may be beyond the capabilities of most older user agents. It's still very instructive, even on a theoretical level, and it should work in a browser that fully and correctly supports CSS1. Just be prepared for one or more errors if you try this in a web browser. You may wish to follow along one step at a time, reloading your page at each step, in order to know when things go wrong—assuming they do.

For their trial run, they decide to use a one-page article that talks about suricates in general terms, examining their life in the wild and their general appeal to humans. The article appears in the magazine as shown in Figure 11-6.

Obviously, the folks at *Meerkat Monthly* have been having some fun with their desktop publishing program. It won't be easy to get everything just the way it is on the page, but we'll see what we can do.

First, let's take apart the page's layout and determine what to eliminate. Since there are no pages on the Web, we can drop the page number. Also, the outer margins can be modified to suit our needs, since we don't have to worry about leaving extra space for the staples and so forth. However, the editors want to keep the two-column layout, the picture placement, and the general appearance of the text, so we'll have to bear that in mind.

First, let's create the two columns. Remember, we don't want to use tables or pro-prietary tags such as `MULTICOL`, so we'll have to resort to something else. In this case, since each column has a number of paragraphs, we can use a `DIV` tag—or, to be more precise, two of them. All we need to do is split the article text roughly in half, and wrap a `DIV` around each half. (By article text, we mean the actual text of the article, excluding the title.) Let's use the place where the column ends on the printed page as our guide to end the first division and start the second:

```
blah blah blah.
</P>
</DIV>
<DIV>
<P>
Blah blah blah
```

Figure 11-6. The original print document

Once that's been done, we modify the first DIV with the following style:

```
<DIV STYLE="float: left; width: 40%; margin-left: 10%; margin-right: 5%;">
```

This causes the entire set of text in the first division to become a floating block on the left margin and the following text to flow past it on the right. In other words, a two-column layout! This first column is declared to be 40% as wide as the browser window, have a left margin 10% as wide as the browser window, and a right margin that is 5% of the window's width. This will cause the second column to automatically calculate its overall width as 45% (40 + 10 + 5 = 55, and 100 − 55 is 45).

Thus, the two columns will be of not-quite-equal width, as we can see in Figure 11-7, but that's the effect we want.

We may eventually have to adjust the point at which the divisions are placed, but for the moment, let's leave things as they are.

Actually, there is one more thing we should add. Here's the markup:

```
<DIV STYLE="float: right; width: 45%;">
```

The meerkat is an animal of endless fascination. Possessed of what seems to be almost human intellect, living in cooperative societies, and undeniably cute, the popularity of these animals is easy to understand. Dolor sit amet, consectetuer adipiscing elit, sed diam nonummy nibh euismod tincidunt ut laoreet dolore magna aliquam erat volutpat. Ut wisi enim ad minim veniam, quis nostrud exerci tation ullamcorper suscipit lobortis nisl ut aliquip ex ea commodo consequat. Duis autem vel eum iriure dolor in hendrerit in vulputate velit esse molestie consequat, vel illum dolore eu feugiat nulla facilisis at vero eros et accumsan et iusto odio dignissim qui blandit praesent luptatum zzril delenit augue duis dolore te feugait nulla facilisi.

Lorem ipsum dolor sit amet, consectetuer adipiscing elit, sed diam nonummy nibh euismod tincidunt ut laoreet dolore magna aliquam erat volutpat. Ut wisi enim ad minim veniam, quis nostrud exerci tation ullamcorper suscipit lobortis nisl ut aliquip ex ea commodo consequat.

Lorem ipsum dolor sit amet, consectetuer adipiscing elit, sed diam nonummy nibh euismod tincidunt ut laoreet dolore magna aliquam erat volutpat. Duis autem vel eum iriure dolor in hendrerit in vulputate velit esse molestie consequat, autem vel eum iriure dolor in hendrerit in vulputate velit esse molestie consequat, vel illum dolore eu feugiat nulla facilisis at vero eros et accumsan et iusto odio dignissim qui blandit praesent luptatum zzril delenit augue duis dolore te feugait nulla facilisi.

Lorem ipsum dolor sit amet, consectetuer adipiscing elit, sed diam nonummy nibh euismod tincidunt ut laoreet dolore magna aliquam erat volutpat. Ut wisi enim ad minim veniam, quis nostrud exerci tation ullamcorper suscipit lobortis nisl ut aliquip ex ea commodo consequat.

Lorem ipsum dolor sit amet, consectetuer adipiscing elit, sed diam nonummy nibh euismod tincidunt ut laoreet dolore magna aliquam erat volutpat. Duis autem vel eum iriure dolor in hendrerit in vulputate velit esse molestie consequat, vel illum dolore eu feugiat nulla facilisis at vero eros et accumsan et iusto odio dignissim qui blandit praesent luptatum zzril delenit augue duis dolore te feugait nulla facilisi.

Lorem ipsum dolor sit amet, consectetuer adipiscing elit, sed diam nonummy nibh euismod tincidunt ut laoreet dolore magna aliquam erat volutpat. Ut wisi enim ad minim veniam, quis nostrud exerci tation ullamcorper suscipit lobortis nisl ut aliquip ex ea commodo consequat. Duis autem vel eum iriure dolor in hendrerit in vulputate velit esse molestie consequat, vel illum dolore eu feugiat nulla facilisis at vero eros et accumsan et iusto odio dignissim qui blandit praesent luptatum zzril delenit augue duis dolore te feugait nulla facilisi.

Figure 11-7. Two columns of text

This is the DIV for the second column. Why have we floated it as well? Assume for a moment that the second column is longer than the first. Without the float for the second column, we'd see a situation like that depicted in Figure 11-8.

This is entirely consistent with the rules for floating, but it obviously isn't what we want. By floating the second column, we avoid this possibility altogether, and the columns stay straight.

Now let's place the pictures. There are two of them, both in the first column, so that makes things a lot easier. Obviously, they're left-floating images. The interesting part will be recreating the way they hang out into the blank space to the left of the column.

If we just give these pictures the style float: left, they'll be completely contained within the column. However, since the first column has a left margin, all we have to do is give images a negative margin-left, like this:

```
IMG {float: left; margin-left: -2.5em;}
```

There is a potential danger here. Our floated images have a left margin of 2.5em, but if you'll recall, the column itself has a left margin of 10%. In a sufficiently nar-

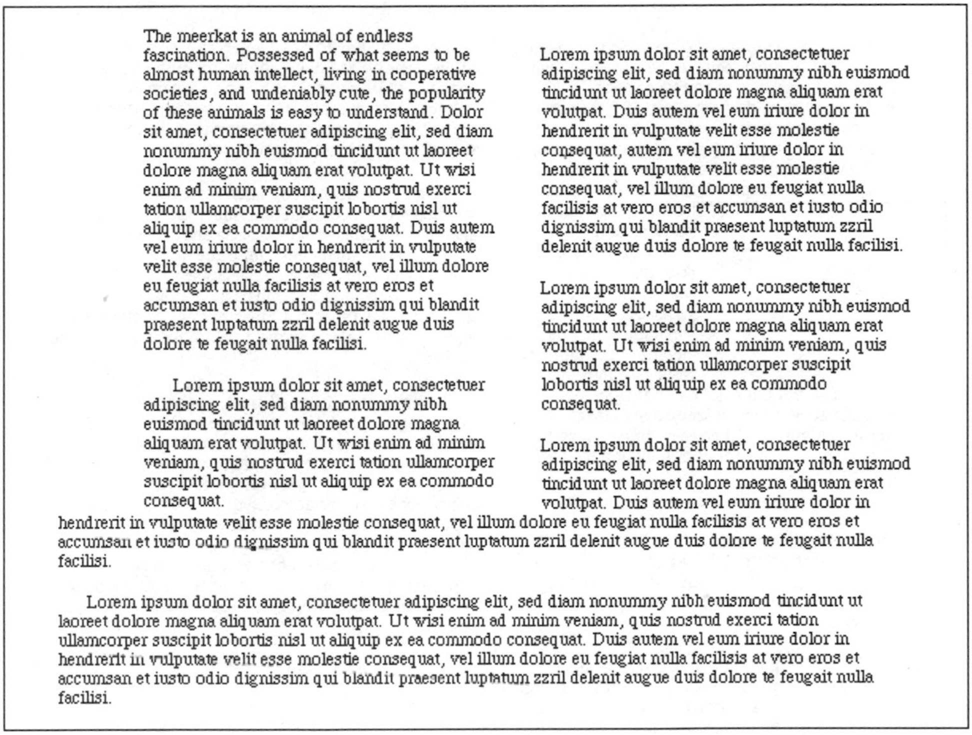

The meerkat is an animal of endless fascination. Possessed of what seems to be almost human intellect, living in cooperative societies, and undeniably cute, the popularity of these animals is easy to understand. Dolor sit amet, consectetuer adipiscing elit, sed diam nonummy nibh euismod tincidunt ut laoreet dolore magna aliquam erat volutpat. Ut wisi enim ad minim veniam, quis nostrud exerci tation ullamcorper suscipit lobortis nisl ut aliquip ex ea commodo consequat. Duis autem vel eum iriure dolor in hendrerit in vulputate velit esse molestie consequat, vel illum dolore eu feugiat nulla facilisis at vero eros et accumsan et iusto odio dignissim qui blandit praesent luptatum zzril delenit augue duis dolore te feugait nulla facilisi.

Lorem ipsum dolor sit amet, consectetuer adipiscing elit, sed diam nonummy nibh euismod tincidunt ut laoreet dolore magna aliquam erat volutpat. Ut wisi enim ad minim veniam, quis nostrud exerci tation ullamcorper suscipit lobortis nisl ut aliquip ex ea commodo consequat.

Lorem ipsum dolor sit amet, consectetuer adipiscing elit, sed diam nonummy nibh euismod tincidunt ut laoreet dolore magna aliquam erat volutpat. Duis autem vel eum iriure dolor in hendrerit in vulputate velit esse molestie consequat, autem vel eum iriure dolor in hendrerit in vulputate velit esse molestie consequat, vel illum dolore eu feugiat nulla facilisis at vero eros et accumsan et iusto odio dignissim qui blandit praesent luptatum zzril delenit augue duis dolore te feugait nulla facilisi.

Lorem ipsum dolor sit amet, consectetuer adipiscing elit, sed diam nonummy nibh euismod tincidunt ut laoreet dolore magna aliquam erat volutpat. Duis autem vel eum iriure dolor in

hendrerit in vulputate velit esse molestie consequat, vel illum dolore eu feugiat nulla facilisis at vero eros et accumsan et iusto odio dignissim qui blandit praesent luptatum zzril delenit augue duis dolore te feugait nulla facilisi.

Lorem ipsum dolor sit amet, consectetuer adipiscing elit, sed diam nonummy nibh euismod tincidunt ut laoreet dolore magna aliquam erat volutpat. Ut wisi enim ad minim veniam, quis nostrud exerci tation ullamcorper suscipit lobortis nisl ut aliquip ex ea commodo consequat. Duis autem vel eum iriure dolor in hendrerit in vulputate velit esse molestie consequat, vel illum dolore eu feugiat nulla facilisis at vero eros et accumsan et iusto odio dignissim qui blandit praesent luptatum zzril delenit augue duis dolore te feugait nulla facilisi.

Figure 11-8. Why we float twice

row browser window, the left margin of the column could end up being much less than 2.5em. If that happens, then the images could get pushed far enough to the left that they go partway "offscreen." Mixing units like this, even indirectly, can be risky. A better choice might be this:

```
IMG{float: left; margin-left: -10%;}
```

This will allow the images' left margins to scale along with the environment.

Since we only have two images, and both of them require the same effect, this declaration will work just fine. Figure 11-9 reveals the result.

As you can see, the first column is now quite a bit longer than the second. However, since we haven't done much of anything to the second column, let's leave things as they are for the moment.

An offset block of text showing a quotation in a larger size is usually called a "pull quote." We have one near the middle of the second column, so let's decide how that will be handled. First, the text is a bit larger than the font size of the main article text, and it's in a sans serif font. Also, it has those nice lines at the top and bottom of the pull quote's box, both of which stretch slightly beyond the right and left boundaries of the text itself. The background is a light gray, and there is a bit

The meerkat is an animal of endless fascination. Possessed of what seems to be almost human intellect, living in cooperative societies, and undeniably cute, the popularity of these animals is easy to understand. Dolor sit amet, consectetuer adipiscing elit, sed diam nonummy nibh euismod tincidunt ut laoreet dolore magna aliquam erat volutpat. Ut wisi enim ad minim

veniam, quis nostrud exerci tation ullamcorper suscipit lobortis nisl ut aliquip ex ea commodo consequat. Duis autem vel eum iriure dolor in hendrerit in vulputate velit esse molestie consequat, vel illum dolore eu feugiat nulla facilisis at vero eros et accumsan et iusto odio dignissim qui blandit praesent luptatum zzril delenit augue duis dolore te feugait nulla facilisi.

Lorem ipsum dolor sit amet, consectetuer adipiscing elit, sed diam nonummy nibh euismod tincidunt ut laoreet dolore magna aliquam erat volutpat. Ut wisi enim ad minim veniam, quis nostrud exerci tation ullamcorper suscipit lobortis nisl ut aliquip ex ea commodo consequat.

Lorem ipsum dolor sit amet, consectetuer adipiscing elit, sed diam nonummy nibh euismod tincidunt ut laoreet dolore magna aliquam erat volutpat. Duis autem vel eum iriure dolor in hendrerit in vulputate velit esse molestie consequat, autem vel eum iriure dolor in hendrerit in vulputate velit esse molestie consequat, vel illum dolore eu feugiat nulla facilisis at vero eros et accumsan et iusto odio dignissim qui blandit praesent luptatum zzril delenit augue duis dolore te feugait nulla facilisi.

Lorem ipsum dolor sit amet, consectetuer adipiscing elit, sed diam nonummy nibh euismod tincidunt ut laoreet dolore magna aliquam erat volutpat. Ut wisi enim ad minim veniam, quis nostrud exerci tation ullamcorper suscipit lobortis nisl ut aliquip ex ea commodo consequat.

Lorem ipsum dolor sit amet, consectetuer adipiscing elit, sed diam nonummy nibh euismod tincidunt ut laoreet dolore magna aliquam erat volutpat. Duis autem vel eum iriure dolor in hendrerit in vulputate velit esse molestie consequat, vel illum dolore eu feugiat nulla facilisis at vero eros et accumsan et iusto odio dignissim qui blandit praesent luptatum zzril delenit augue duis dolore te feugait nulla facilisi.

Lorem ipsum dolor sit amet, consectetuer adipiscing elit, sed diam nonummy nibh euismod tincidunt ut laoreet dolore magna aliquam erat volutpat. Ut wisi enim ad minim veniam, quis nostrud exerci tation ullamcorper suscipit lobortis nisl ut aliquip ex ea commodo consequat. Duis autem vel eum iriure dolor in hendrerit in vulputate velit esse molestie consequat, vel illum dolore eu feugiat nulla facilisis at vero eros et accumsan et iusto odio dignissim qui blandit praesent luptatum zzril delenit augue duis dolore te feugait nulla facilisi.

Figure 11-9. Floating images

of space around the box to separate it from the main body text. The pull quote's text is also centered, the box is about half the width of the column, and it's obviously floating to the right.

Here's what we come up with:

```
.pullq {font: 150% Helvetica,Arial,sans-serif; text-align: center;
   border-top: medium black solid; border-bottom: thin black solid;
   margin: 1em; padding: 0.5em; background: #CCCCCC;
   width: 50%; float: right;}

<P CLASS="pullq">
"The meerkat is a fun, smart, but often exasperating fellow."
</P>
```

Since we've implemented this quote as a paragraph, if we simply float it in place, the top of the pull quote's box will line up with the beginning of the paragraph that comes after the quote in the HTML document. We decide that's okay and end up with what's shown in Figure 11-10.

The meerkat is an animal of endless fascination. Possessed of what seems to be almost human intellect, living in cooperative societies, and undeniably cute, the popularity of these animals is easy to understand. Dolor sit amet, consectetuer adipiscing elit, sed diam nonummy nibh euismod tincidunt ut laoreet dolore magna aliquam erat volutpat. Ut wisi enim ad minim veniam, quis nostrud exerci tation ullamcorper suscipit lobortis nisl ut aliquip ex ea commodo consequat. Duis autem vel eum iriure dolor in hendrerit in vulputate velit esse molestie consequat, vel illum dolore eu feugiat nulla facilisis at vero eros et accumsan et iusto odio dignissim qui blandit praesent luptatum zzril delenit augue duis dolore te feugait nulla facilisi.

Lorem ipsum dolor sit amet, consectetuer adipiscing elit, sed diam nonummy nibh euismod tincidunt ut laoreet dolore magna aliquam erat volutpat. Ut wisi enim ad minim veniam, quis nostrud exerci tation ullamcorper suscipit lobortis nisl ut aliquip ex ea commodo consequat.

Lorem ipsum dolor sit amet, consectetuer adipiscing elit, sed diam nonummy nibh euismod tincidunt ut laoreet dolore magna aliquam erat volutpat. Duis autem vel eum iriure dolor in hendrerit in vulputate velit esse molestie consequat, autem vel eum iriure dolor in hendrerit in vulputate velit esse molestie consequat, vel illum dolore eu feugiat nulla facilisis at vero eros et accumsan et iusto odio dignissim qui blandit praesent luptatum zzril delenit augue duis dolore te feugait nulla facilisi.

Lorem ipsum dolor sit amet, consectetuer adipiscing elit, sed diam nonummy nibh euismod tincidunt ut laoreet dolore magna aliquam erat volutpat. Ut wisi enim ad minim veniam, quis nostrud exerci tation ullamcorper suscipit lobortis nisl ut aliquip ex ea commodo consequat.

Lorem ipsum dolor sit amet, consectetuer adipiscing elit, sed diam nonummy nibh euismod tincidunt ut laoreet dolore magna aliquam erat volutpat. Duis autem vel

"The meerkat is a fun, smart, but often exasperating fellow."

eum iriure dolor in hendrerit in vulputate velit esse molestie consequat, vel illum dolore eu feugiat nulla facilisis at vero eros et accumsan et iusto odio dignissim qui blandit praesent luptatum zzril delenit augue duis dolore te feugait nulla facilisi.

Lorem ipsum dolor sit amet, consectetuer adipiscing elit, sed diam nonummy nibh euismod tincidunt ut laoreet dolore magna aliquam erat volutpat. Ut wisi enim ad minim veniam, quis nostrud exerci tation ullamcorper suscipit lobortis nisl ut aliquip ex ea commodo consequat. Duis autem vel eum iriure dolor in hendrerit in vulputate velit esse molestie consequat, vel illum dolore eu feugiat nulla facilisis at vero eros et accumsan et iusto odio dignissim qui blandit praesent luptatum zzril delenit augue duis dolore te feugait nulla facilisi.

Figure 11-10. A pull quote

Now the document is a bit more even. Adjusting the placement of the DIVs will make it as even as possible, but since we still aren't quite finished, let's put that off yet again.

At the end of the article is a block of text that says a few words about the author of the piece. This is in a smaller text size, italicized, and separated from the rest of the article by a small space and a thin line. We could put a horizontal rule in for the line, but let's stick to CSS1 whenever possible. The following should do quite nicely, as illustrated in Figure 11-11:

```
.author {font: italic x-small Times,serif; border-top: thin black solid;
    padding-top: 0.25em; margin-top: 0.5em;}
```

The meerkat is an animal of endless fascination. Possessed of what seems to be almost human intellect, living in cooperative societies, and undeniably cute, the popularity of these animals is easy to understand. Dolor sit amet, consectetuer adipiscing elit, sed diam nonummy nibh euismod tincidunt ut laoreet dolore magna aliquam erat volutpat. Ut wisi enim ad minim 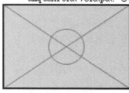veniam, quis nostrud exerci tation ullamcorper suscipit lobortis nisl ut aliquip ex ea commodo consequat. Duis autem vel eum iriure dolor in hendrerit in vulputate velit esse molestie consequat, vel illum dolore eu feugiat nulla facilisis at vero eros et accumsan et iusto odio dignissim qui blandit praesent luptatum zzril delenit augue duis dolore te feugait nulla facilisi.

Lorem ipsum dolor sit amet, consectetuer adipiscing elit, sed diam nonummy nibh euismod tincidunt ut laoreet dolore magna aliquam erat volutpat. Ut wisi enim ad minim veniam, quis nostrud exerci tation ullamcorper suscipit lobortis nisl ut aliquip ex ea commodo consequat.

Lorem ipsum dolor sit amet, consectetuer adipiscing elit, sed diam nonummy nibh euismod tincidunt ut laoreet dolore magna aliquam erat volutpat. Duis autem vel eum iriure dolor in hendrerit in vulputate velit esse molestie consequat, autem vel eum iriure dolor in hendrerit in vulputate velit esse molestie consequat, vel illum dolore eu feugiat nulla facilisis at vero eros et accumsan et iusto odio dignissim qui blandit praesent luptatum zzril delenit augue duis dolore te feugait nulla facilisi.

Lorem ipsum dolor sit amet, consectetuer adipiscing elit, sed diam nonummy nibh euismod tincidunt ut laoreet dolore magna aliquam erat volutpat. Ut wisi enim ad minim veniam, quis nostrud exerci tation ullamcorper suscipit lobortis nisl ut aliquip ex ea commodo consequat.

Lorem ipsum dolor sit amet, consectetuer adipiscing elit, sed diam nonummy nibh euismod tincidunt ut laoreet dolore magna aliquam erat volutpat. Duis autem vel 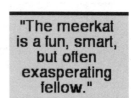eum iriure dolor in hendrerit in vulputate velit esse molestie consequat, vel illum dolore eu feugiat nulla facilisis at vero eros et accumsan et iusto odio dignissim qui blandit praesent luptatum zzril delenit augue duis dolore te feugait nulla facilisi.

Lorem ipsum dolor sit amet, consectetuer adipiscing elit, sed diam nonummy nibh euismod tincidunt ut laoreet dolore magna aliquam erat volutpat. Ut wisi enim ad minim veniam, quis nostrud exerci tation ullamcorper suscipit lobortis nisl ut aliquip ex ea commodo consequat. Duis autem vel eum iriure dolor in hendrerit in vulputate velit esse molestie consequat, vel illum dolore eu feugiat nulla facilisis at vero eros et accumsan et iusto odio dignissim qui blandit praesent luptatum zzril delenit augue duis dolore te feugait nulla facilisi.

Lorem ipsum dolor sit amet, consectetuer adipiscing elit, sed diam nonummy nibh euismod tincidunt ut laoreet dolore magna aliquam erat volutpat.

Figure 11-11. Styling the authorial note

Before we create the title, let's clean up a few last details in the article's body. The overall article has fully justified text in a serif font. We decide that it should be easily readable, so we go with Times. We also want the article to have black text on a white background, thereby mimicking the appearance of printed text. Each paragraph has its first line indented about half an inch, but we'll reduce that to a quarter-inch for the web version. We can handle this with the following:

```
BODY {color: black; background: white;}
P {font-family: Times,serif; text-align: justify; text-indent: 0.25in;}
```

Figure 11-12 shows the appearance of a paragraph.

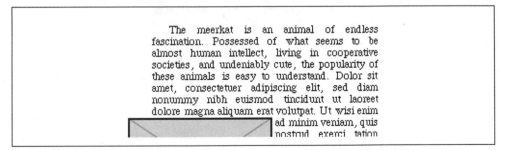

Figure 11-12. Paragraph indenting

The last rule will give us about the correct amount of indenting for each paragraph, no matter the resolution to which the user's monitor has been set. However, the very first letter of the first paragraph of the article is a "drop cap," which means that it's larger and extends down from the first line, with subsequent lines flowing past it. This first paragraph has no indentation of the first line, so we'll have to counteract it somehow. This leads us to the following:

```
.initial {text-indent: 0;}
P.initial:first-letter {font-size: 200%; float: left;}
```

These rules will, obviously, require us to add the attribute `class="initial"` to the first paragraph tag. The declaration of `text-indent: 0;` overrides previously declared values, as long as this block of declarations comes later in the style sheet. They're also more specific than the other styles we're using, due to the presence of a class selector, so that also helps these rules win out. The values for `:first-letter` will cause the first letter of the initial paragraph to be twice normal size, and floated left, as shown in Figure 11-13.

Under CSS2, the same effect can be achieved without the use of a class on the first paragraph. This is done by using new CSS2 selectors, such as the adjacent-sibling selector:

```
H1 + P {text-indent: 0;}
```

In a CSS2-aware user agent, this will set a `text-indent` of 0 for any paragraph which immediately follows any `H1` element. However, since the paragraph here is the child of a `DIV`, it doesn't immediately follow the `H1`. Therefore, we would need to add a child selector and a first-child pseudo-class:

```
H1 + DIV > P:first-child {text-indent: 0;}
```

This will match any paragraph that is the first child of a `DIV` that immediately follows an `H1` element. See Chapter 10, *CSS2: A Look Ahead*, for more details.

The meerkat is an animal of endless fascination. Possessed of what seems to be almost human intellect, living in cooperative societies, and undeniably cute, the popularity of these animals is easy to understand. Dolor sit amet, consectetuer adipiscing elit, sed diam nonummy nibh euismod tincidunt ut laoreet dolore magna aliquam erat

Figure 11-13. First-letter styling

Having set the article's body to the appearance we want, all that remains is to adjust the placement of the divisions so that the columns are of roughly equal length. We can do this now because regardless of what we do to the title, the columns will be the same length. So we move the divisions appropriately. Note that we may not get an exact balance because of the need to break the divisions between paragraphs. Whether the longer column should be the first or the second is up to you.

With all that done, all that remains is for us to recreate the document's title. Looking at it closely in Figure 11-14, we see that this is an interesting specimen: it's right-justified and yet not aligned with the right margin of the document; the letters are spaced rather far apart; the text is small caps, and yet the first letter is much bigger than the others; finally, the entire thing is set in a large sans serif font.

Figure 11-14. The original document's title

Rather than dream up a new class for the title, let's just put it into an H1 and set styles on that element. At a rough visual guess, the text is about three times larger than the body text, and the space between each letter is about the size of one of the letters. Starting with the easy stuff, here's what we have for the title H1:

```
H1 {font: 300% Helvetica,sans-serif; font-variant: small-caps;
    letter-spacing: 0.75em;}
```

As was already observed, the title is right-justified but isn't up against the right margin. The easiest thing to do is insert some padding to the H1's right side, which leads us to the following declarations:

```
H1 {font: 300% Helvetica,sans-serif; font-variant: small-caps;
    letter-spacing: 0.75em; text-align: right; padding-right: 1em;}
```

Figure 11-15 shows us our progress so far.

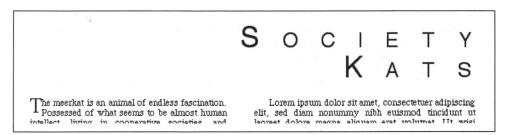

Figure 11-15. The styled title: a work in progress

We're getting close; in fact, the only thing left is that first letter of the title. We can easily handle it with a `:first-letter` selector, so let's do that. The "S" is about twice the size of the "K" in "Kats," so we set the following:

```
H1 {font: 300% Helvetica,sans-serif; font-variant: small-caps;
    letter-spacing: 0.75em; text-align: right; padding-right: 1em;
    line-height: 1em;}
H1:first-letter {font-size: 200%; line-height: 1px; vertical-align: -100%;}
```

Consulting Figure 11-16, we see that it looks about right!

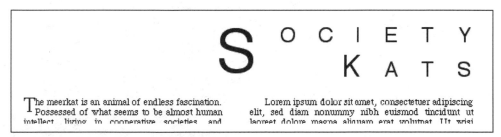

Figure 11-16. The final styled title

The `line-height` and `vertical-align` values deserve a small discussion. What's been done is that the inline box of the "S" has been reduced so that it's only one pixel tall. (We could have used almost any length value here, so long as it was a very small amount.) This inline box, as we saw in Chapter 8, is centered vertically inside the "S" itself. Then the baseline of the "S" is lowered so that it's as far down as the baseline of the next line of text (since a `-100%` vertical alignment will lower the baseline the same distance as the `font-size` of the parent element). Ordinarily, this would make the first line box correspondingly taller, but since we're declared `line-height: 1px` for the "S", the actual inline box is so small that it has almost no effect on the height of the line box. While the title shown in Figure 11-16 may not precisely match the title in Figure 11-14, they're very close to each other.

So, put together, here's the entire style sheet:

```
BODY {color: black; background: white;}
P {font-family: Times,serif; text-align: justify; text-indent: 6em;}
```

```
IMG{float: left; margin: 0.5em 0.5em 0.5em -10%;}
.pullq {font: 200% Helvetica,Arial,sans-serif; text-align: center;
  border-top: medium black solid; border-bottom: thin black solid;
  margin: 1em; padding: 0.5em; background: #CCCCCC;
  width: 50%; float: right;}
.author {font: italic x-small Times,serif; border-top: thin black solid;
  padding-top: 0.25em; margin-top: 0.5em;}
.initial {text-indent: 0;}
P.initial:first-letter {font-size: 200%; float: left;}
H1 {font: 300% Helvetica,sans-serif; font-variant: small-caps;
  letter-spacing: 0.75em; text-align: right; padding-right: 1em;
  line-height: 1em;}
H1:first-letter {font-size: 200%; line-height: 1px;vertical-align: -100%;}
```

Figure 11-17 shows a side-by-side comparison of the original article and its online cousin.

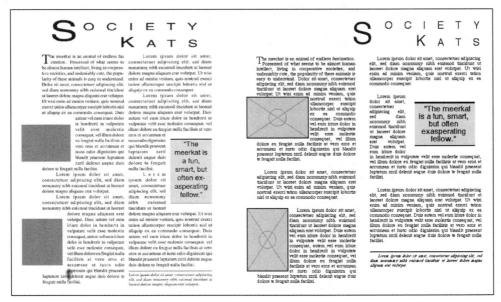

Figure 11-17. A comparison

Furthermore, if we view the web page using a browser without style sheets, it will come out looking like Figure 11-18. It may not be as pretty, but it's still quite readable.

Cleaning up

There are a few places where the CSS version isn't quite the same as the printed version, as a detailed study of Figure 11-17 reveals, and of course the creation of the columns is a bit of a hack. How can these be addressed?

The title of the article is the most obvious visual difference between the two layouts. The printed version of the article has a title which is stretched out, so to

Society Kats

The meerkat is an animal of endless fascination. Possessed of what seems to be almost human intellect, living in cooperative societies, and undeniably cute, the popularity of these animals is easy to understand. Dolor sit amet, consectetuer adipiscing elit, sed diam nonummy nibh euismod tincidunt ut laoreet dolore magna aliquam erat volutpat.

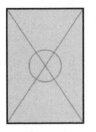 Ut wisi enim ad minim veniam, quis nostrud exerci tation ullamcorper suscipit lobortis nisl ut aliquip ex ea commodo consequat. Duis autem vel eum iriure dolor in hendrerit in vulputate velit esse molestie consequat, vel illum dolore eu feugiat nulla facilisis at vero eros et accumsan et iusto odio dignissim qui blandit praesent luptatum zzril delenit augue duis dolore te feugait nulla facilisi.

Lorem ipsum dolor sit amet, consectetuer adipiscing elit, sed diam nonummy nibh euismod tincidunt ut laoreet dolore magna aliquam erat volutpat. Ut wisi enim ad minim veniam, quis nostrud exerci tation ullamcorper suscipit lobortis nisl ut aliquip ex ea commodo consequat.

Lorem ipsum dolor sit amet, consectetuer adipiscing elit, sed diam nonummy nibh euismod tincidunt ut laoreet dolore magna aliquam erat volutpat. Duis autem vel eum iriure dolor in hendrerit in vulputate velit esse molestie consequat, autem vel eum iriure dolor in hendrerit in vulputate velit esse molestie consequat, vel illum dolore eu feugiat nulla

Figure 11-18. The styled page without any styles

speak. This could be easily recreated using the CSS2 property `font-stretch`, but sadly, this property was not supported at the time of this writing. See Chapter 10 for a look at `font-stretch`.

The opening dropped capital "T" also doesn't seem to quite match up. This might also be addressed using `font-stretch`, or perhaps by giving the letter a `font-weight` of 900. However, it might be best to leave things as they are, since this is a small effect and not too important.

How about those columns, though? In order to get these columns to display properly, we were forced to enclose each column in its own DIV. While this approach is certainly preferable to using tables, it still requires us to do some small violence to the structure of the page—and trying to create visual effects by adding elements is never a good idea. It would be far better to simply set the BODY contents to be flowed into two columns. Unfortunately, CSS2 contains no provisions for columns or column flow. There have been discussions in the CSS community about adding such behaviors to CSS, and perhaps they will be added in the future. For now, we're forced to do things like add DIVs to represent columns.

This assumes that you wish to create columns at all, of course. We went to a great deal of effort to get those columns, but was it really worth it? Multiple-column layouts can be very difficult to read on a monitor, since the user may be forced to scroll downward to read the first column, then back up to the top of the second, then down again. Adding the columns was an interesting theoretical exercise, but it may not be the best approach for the Web.

Tips & Tricks

Here we present a handful of quick tips and workarounds which might save you a lot of time and hassles. Some are related to ways of making buggy browsers behave, while others describe ways to write completely correct CSS and HTML and still mangle the document display, simply by not thinking about the consequences of one's actions.

Making Styles Work

This is an easy one. If you want Navigator 4 to use CSS at all, you have to go to the preferences dialog and check the boxes for both style sheets and JavaScript. If JavaScript is disabled, Navigator will not apply styles. Why? In the early days of style sheets, there were a number of proposals for styling. One of these was Java-Script Style Sheets (JSSS), an interesting hybrid of early CSS and JavaScript. It probably won't surprise you to learn that JSSS was promoted by Netscape. Although JSSS was never adopted, Navigator 4's rendering engine uses it, and so CSS doesn't work without JavaScript.

Hiding Styles with @import

The fact that Navigator 4.x understands `LINK` but doesn't recognize `@import` statements can be turned to your advantage. Since any styles you place in an external style sheet must be brought in via either `LINK` or `@import`, you can group all of the styles that will cause Navigator problems and put them into a style sheet that you then import. Since Navigator will refuse to import this style sheet, it won't have to deal with styles it can't deal with. This simple trick can save you a lot of headaches, but there is one drawback: a very few early versions of Navigator 4.x could crash when trying to process an `@import` statement. This was quickly fixed, and very few of these versions are still in use.

Fighting Margin Problems with @import

If you want to use `margin` rules which you know won't work in Navigator, use the previous trick and the cascade to your advantage. Let's say you want a document where a paragraph has no vertical space between its top and the bottom of a preceding `H1` element, as illustrated in Figure 11-19.

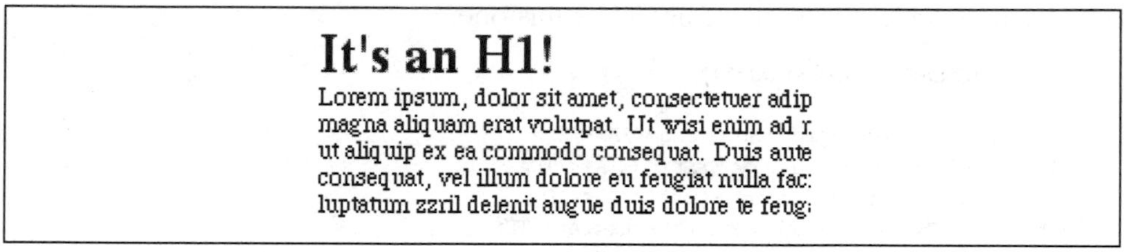

Figure 11-19. Closing up the usual gap

In Explorer, this can be done with these rules:

```
H1 {margin-bottom: 0;}
P {margin-top: 0;}
```

For Navigator, though, you have to set the top margin of the paragraph to be -1em to get the same effect, which will hopelessly mangle Explorer's display of the document. How to resolve the conflict?

First, place all your Navigator-unfriendly rules into an external style sheet and hook that up using an @import statement. Then place all of your Navigator-friendly margin rules into another external style sheet and LINK it in. (Just make sure your LINK comes before the @import statement.) You'll end up with something like this:

```
/* file 'link-styles.css' */        /* file 'import-styles.css' */
H1 {margin-bottom: 0;}              H1 {margin-bottom: 0;}
P {margin-top: -1em;}               P {margin-top: 0;}


<LINK REL="stylesheet" TYPE="text/css" HREF="link-styles.css"
   TITLE="Linked">
<STYLE TYPE="text/css">
@import url(import-styles.css);
</STYLE>
```

Because Explorer will read in both style sheets, it will use the cascade to determine which rules should actually be applied. If you've ordered things correctly, and the imported style sheet comes after the linked style sheet, its rules will win out over the rules in the linked style sheet.

Therefore, Explorer will use the styles from **import-styles.css**. Navigator, on the other hand, won't even read the styles that are supposed to be imported, so it will only have the styles from **link-styles.css** available and will therefore use them.

Styling Common Elements

If you have documents in which there is a certain block of common markup—say, a table that holds links to the main pages of your site—it's easy to style them without having to change the HTML markup on each page.

Let's assume we have a table of links like this one:

```
<TABLE BORDER CELLPADDING="4">
<TR>
<TD><A HREF="home.html">Home Page</A></TD>
<TD><A HREF="read.html">My Writing</A></TD>
<TD><A HREF="fun.html">Fun Stuff!</A></TD>
<TD><A HREF="links.html">Other Links</A></TD>
<TD><A HREF="write.html">Contact Me</A></TD>
</TR>
</TABLE>
```

However, on each page, we want the cell containing the current page to be highlighted in some fashion. This is really easy. All we have to do is add a class to each table cell, like this:

```
<TABLE border cellpadding="4">
<TR>
<TD CLASS="home"><A HREF="home.html">Home Page</A></TD>
<TD CLASS="read"><A HREF="read.html">My Writing</A></TD>
<TD CLASS="fun"><A HREF="fun.html">Fun Stuff!</A></TD>
<TD CLASS="links"><A HREF="links.html">Other Links</A></TD>
<TD CLASS="write"><A HREF="write.html">Contact Me</A></TD>
</TR>
</TABLE>
```

Then, on each page, we simply write an appropriate style. If the highlighted link should have a yellow background, then on the "Other Links" page, we would add this to the style sheet, leading to the result depicted in Figure 11-20:

```
TD.links {background: yellow;}
```

Figure 11-20. Highlighting the current page

Similarly, on the site's home page, we would find this style at the top of the page:

```
TD.home {background: yellow;}
```

This is a fast, easy way to make a "toolbar" a little more active, without the need for fitting BGCOLOR attributes on to specific table cells.

By taking this approach, it's possible to take the toolbar and split it into a separate file, and then include that file on every page by means of a *server-side include*. Includes are described in much greater detail in *Web Design in a Nutshell,* by Jennifer Niederst, and *Apache: The Definitive Guide,* by Ben Laurie and Peter Laurie, both published by O'Reilly and Associates.

Getting Full Content Backgrounds in Navigator

We covered this in Chapter 6, *Colors and Backgrounds*, but it bears some repetition. We assume you want people using Navigator 4.x to see full background colors in text elements, not just behind the text. If you've applied a background color to a text element, add the following declaration: `border: 0.1px solid none`. This will have no visual effect, but in the course of telling Navigator to draw a 0.1-pixel, solid, nonexistent border, the background color will usually fill the entire content area and the padding. If you set a visible border, then there will still be a gap between the padding and the border, but otherwise you should get roughly the correct effect.

Nonetheless, if you leave out this statement, every version of Navigator 4.x will not extend the background color throughout the entire content box but will only place it behind the element's text.

The Incredible Shrinking Text!

Here's a fun thing to do: make your document text so small that it can't be read by the human eye. You can do this using completely correct CSS and a bug-free browser. Here's the easiest way to see it:

```
UL {font-size: 75%;}
```

This seems simple enough: the text in unordered lists should be 75% normal size. Ah, but what happens if you have unordered lists nested inside unordered lists? You get the results shown in Figure 11-21, that's what.

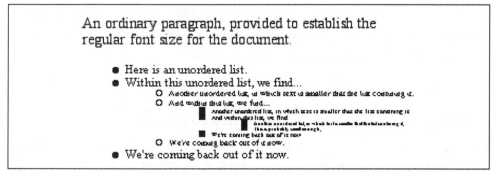

Figure 11-21. Help me

Wow! What happened? Simply put, each nested list cuts the font size by a quarter. Let's assume the document's base `font-size` is 12pt. Therefore, at the top level, the font's size will be three-quarters of that, or 9pt. All well and good, except the next level down will see a reduction to 6pt, and the next level to 4pt, and so on.

Once the text goes below 7pt, it will become unreadably small on most monitors (and will be tough to read even on most printouts).

You're probably thinking to yourself, "Ha! How dumb do you have to be to shrink text in lists like that?" True, it's easy to spot this with lists. However, think about how most of your pages are structured (with nested tables) and then consider this rule:

```
BODY {font-size: 12pt;}
TD {font-size: 80%;}
```

All it takes is three levels of nesting in your tables, and you end up with 6-point text (12 × 0.8 × 0.8 × 0.8 = 6.144). Many complicated pages have at least three levels of nesting, and sometimes even more.

Preserving Boldness

Here's a similar trick that helps work around a bug in most versions of Navigator 4. In situations where `font-weight: normal` has been set on an element, this value will be inherited by all the descendants of the element. That's as it should be, of course, but Navigator takes it one step too far. Given the following:

```
<P STYLE="font-weight: normal;">This is a paragraph which contains a
<B>boldface element</B>, but Navigator 4 won't make the text bold.</P>
```

That's right: all of the text in the example paragraph will have a normal font weight. For some reason, Navigator 4 doesn't know that it should assign a `font-weight` of `bold` (or `bolder`) to B elements. Similar problems can arise when using STRONG, or any other element that would ordinarily call for boldface text.

The solution is simple enough. Just make sure that you set an explicit `font-weight` for these elements. A good rule to include in your style sheet would be:

```
STRONG, B {font-weight: bolder;}
```

This should overcome any reluctance on Navigator 4's part.

Floating Text Elements in Internet Explorer

In Internet Explorer 4.x for Windows, in order to get `float` to work with text elements, you need to explicitly declare a `width` as well, like so: `width: 10em`. To be honest, I'm not sure why this should permit floating where it wouldn't otherwise happen. It does make some sense, given the usual desire for declaring a `width` on floated text elements in any case, but the specification does not *require* that a `width` be declared in order to make a text element float successfully. Internet Explorer 4.x for Windows does.

Also, you must have the final version of Explorer 4.x for this to work—so if you're still using a preview release, you'll need to upgrade it, which is probably a good idea anyway. (Thanks to Howard Marvel for discovering and sharing this trick.)

Drop Caps With and Without :first-letter

Drop caps are a very common, and much-requested, typographical effect. A typical drop cap looks like the illustration in Figure 11-22.

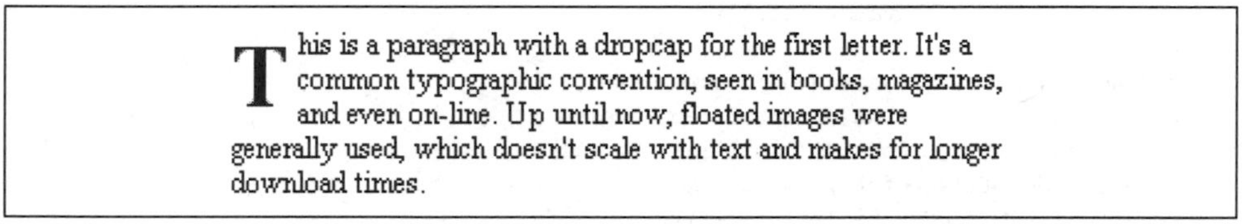

> T his is a paragraph with a dropcap for the first letter. It's a common typographic convention, seen in books, magazines, and even on-line. Up until now, floated images were generally used, which doesn't scale with text and makes for longer download times.

Figure 11-22. A drop cap

There's an easy way to do this, and that is of course to use the `:first-letter` pseudo-element. The style would look something like this:

```
P.intro:first-letter {font-size: 300%; font-weight: bold; float: left;
    width: 1em;}
```

This will result in approximately what is seen in Figure 11-22.

However, as you probably know, older browsers don't support the `:first-letter` pseudo-element. In many of these—Internet Explorer 3.x and Navigator 4.x, for example—there is no alternative. In Internet Explorer 4.x and 5.0, however, you can use a `SPAN` element to fake your way around the lack of support for `:first-letter`. Here's how it works:

```
SPAN.dropcap {font-size: 300%; font-weight: bold; float: left;
    width: 0.75em;}

<P><SPAN CLASS="dropcap">T</SPAN>his is a paragraph with...</P>
```

Since this is very similar to the fictional tag sequence used to describe the behavior of `:first-letter` anyway, it works fairly well. It's less elegant, granted, but it does work. We use a `width` of `0.75em` because most letters are not as wide as they are tall, but of course you may use other values; experiment to see what you like best.

Disappearing Styles

Here's a rather obscure Navigator bug which is utterly baffling when encountered. Under whatever circumstances trigger the bug (frames seem to be a major cause), resizing the browser window can cause all of the styles to go away, leaving plain text in their wake.

Reloading the page will get the styles back, but that's hardly a satisfactory solution. Slightly better is the inclusion of a small bit of JavaScript that will fix the problem for you. This widget should cause any JavaScript-enabled version of Navigator to reapply the styles after the window is resized—and if JavaScript is turned off, then CSS won't work at all, which is another thing to remember when you try to figure out why styles don't work.

In the meantime, however, here's the script:

```
<SCRIPT LANGUAGE="JavaScript1.2">
<!--
var agt = navigator.userAgent.toLowerCase();
var is_major = parseInt(navigator.appVersion);
var is_nav = ((agt.indexOf('mozilla') != -1) &&
  (agt.indexOf('spoofer') == -1) &&
  (agt.indexOf('compatible') == -1));
var is_nav4 = (is_nav && (is_major == 4));


if (is_nav4) {onresize = location.reload();}
//-->
</SCRIPT>
```

This should cause the document to be reloaded whenever the browser window is resized in any version of Navigator 4.

The script used for this trick was adopted from a technique presented in the Netscape Developer's Edge article "Determining Browser Type and Version with JavaScript" at (*http://developer.netscape.com:80/docs/examples/javascript/browser_type.html*).

Serving CSS Up Correctly

Finally, a problem related to, but not exactly about, CSS. Some authors have reported trouble with getting their web hosts to correctly serve up external style sheets. Apparently, with some web servers, the file extension *.css* is mapped to the MIME type `x-application/css`, or "Continuous Slide Show," instead of the MIME type `text/css`. Even older servers may not have any mapping for *.css*, and so will serve up the files as `text/plain`.

When it comes right down to it, the extension isn't actually the important part. What matters is the MIME type the server uses when sending a file. However, since the vast majority of web servers use a file's extension to decide which MIME type to use when sending the file, it obviously becomes important to have a friendly server configuration.

If an external style sheet is sent using the wrong MIME type, the style sheet gets mangled into something unusable. If you find that you're having this problem, then you'll need to contact your ISP and explain the problem. If they refuse to fix it, try explaining to them that IANA (the Internet Assigned Numbers Authority, which also approves MIME types) has approved *.css* as the extension for the MIME type `text/css`, and the slideshow mapping is not a recognized IANA MIME type.

If they still refuse to correct the problem, then you may be able to fix it yourself with a directive file in your web space. If your web server runs using an NCSA-based web server like that sold by Netscape, add the following line to a file called `.htaccess` (that's all, nothing more) in the top level of your web space:

```
AddType "text/css; charset=iso-8859-1" .css
```

If none of this works, and you really need (or even want) to use external style sheets, you may have to consider switching ISPs.

A

CSS Resources

There are a number of very good CSS-related resources available on the Web. Here are some of them.

General Information

These resources provide a good overview of what's happening in the world of CSS or otherwise provide you with a broad look at CSS.

CSS Recommendations

> *http://www.w3.org/TR/REC-CSS1*
> *http://www.w3.org/TR/REC-CSS2*

When all else fails, you can always use the source, Luke. The specifications contain, albeit in a somewhat terse and not always easily decipherable form, the complete description of how conforming user agents should handle CSS. They also contain a complete CSS parsing grammar and forward-compatible parsing rules, both of which are invaluable to the people who write user agents but of minimal interest to almost everyone else.

W3C CSS Activity Page

> *http://www.w3.org/Style/CSS*

This is, officially speaking, the online center of the CSS universe. There are links to the CSS Recommendations, to new ideas under consideration, and to other sites about CSS. There are links to historical style sheet proposals, to information about current usage and implementations of CSS, and more. There are also lists of books about CSS, news of new CSS tools, and many other useful bits of information.

W3C CSS Test Suite

http://www.w3.org/Style/CSS/Test/

This presents a fairly complete set of pages designed to test any CSS implementation. Each page of the suite tests various aspects of CSS properties, one property per page. The tests were largely developed by the author of this book, Håkon Lie (Opera Software), and Tim Boland (NIST), with many contributions from the CSS community and even the browser vendors themselves. If you're wondering how good your browser is at handling CSS1, this is the place to find out. As of this writing, the Test Suite covers only CSS1, but a CSS2 Test Suite is expected in the near future.

Error Checkers

You can save a lot of time and effort simply by running your CSS through a validity checker. This is particularly recommended if you're thinking about asking for help online, because if your CSS contains errors, the first thing the experts will tell you to do is to use a validator. May as well get into the practice first.

W3C CSS Validator

http://jigsaw.w3.org/css-validator/

If you're having trouble getting your style sheets to work, it might be the result of a typographical error, or some other basic error that is difficult to diagnose. You could spend a long time combing through your styles, exhaustively checking each rule for correctness—and that's a good exercise, of course—but you could also have a program do it for you, and simply tell you if it found any errors. The W3C CSS Validator will do exactly that. You can supply it with the URL of a style sheet or document containing styles, or simply paste a block of styles into an input field, and let the validator tell you if your problems are the result of a misspelled color name (or something similar). The chief drawback, for most people, is the technical nature of its reporting. Unless you're already familiar with HTML and CSS, the results you get back may be somewhat confusing.

WDG CSScheck

http://www.htmlhelp.com/tools/csscheck/

Similar in nature to the W3C's validator, CSScheck offers much friendlier error messages, which makes it more useful to the beginning author. In addition to indicating the severity of the error with whimsical icons (American-style traffic signals, at last check), CSScheck provides a message detailing each problem, as well as the reason it is a problem. It is possible to learn a great deal about good document authoring practices simply by running a few style sheets through CSScheck and carefully reading its responses.

Tips, Pointers, and Other Practical Advice

Once you've gotten through all the general information and checked your documents for errors, you'll probably be looking for some real-world advice on how to use CSS, where some pitfalls may be, and why your letter-perfect CSS isn't displaying in quite the way you think it should.

Style Sheets Reference Guide (SSRG)

http://style.webreview.com/

This site is home of the Browser Compatibility Charts, which is its main claim to fame. The Chart is a listing of every property and value in CSS1 and the status of its support in each of several major browsers, with notes explaining the ratings. As of this writing, the Chart covered 10 major browser versions, with more expected, and there were plans afoot to add CSS2 support tracking to the charts as well.

The SSRG is also the home of the *Web Review* column "A Sense of Style," with archives of all the articles, and sections devoted to CSS question and answers, common mistakes with CSS, cool ways to use styles, and more. *(Disclaimer: the SSRG is edited and maintained by the author of this book.)*

CSS Pointers Group (CPG)

http://css.nu/

Maintained by CSS gurus Sue Sims and Jan Roland Eriksson, the CPG is a wonderful collection of articles, bug reports, workarounds, and literally hundreds of other resources. Many of the pointers listed are simply links to material generated by various people throughout the Web, but some of the best articles are the work of Sue and Roland themselves. The site can be a little difficult to navigate at first, but the enormous wealth of information available through these pages makes the effort well worth it.

WSP CSS Samurai Reports

http://www.webstandards.org/css/

A series of documents detailing the major failings in CSS support in available web browsers, written by the CSS Action Committee—or, as they are sometimes called, the "CSS Samurai"—of the Web Standards Project (WSP). As of this writing, there were reports covering Internet Explorer for both Windows and Macintosh, and Opera for Windows. These reports offer an interesting insight into what can go wrong in browser support, what designers want to see, and how to test for CSS support problems.

Agitprop

> *http://www.metrius.com/agitprop/*

A small collection of articles and observations written by Todd Fahrner, this site is a gold mine of detailed information. Each and every one of the articles here contains information CSS authors can use and should know by heart, from "The Amazing em Unit" to "Why Points Suck." This site should be visited by anyone serious about understanding the design trade-offs inherent in any design project, and the special issues surrounding CSS design in particular.

Online Communities

One can read only so much before it comes time to join a discussion and ask some questions. There are two major venues for discussions about CSS, but each is concerned with a specific type of discussion—so make sure you go to the right place.

comp.infosystems.www.authoring.stylesheets

This Usenet group, often abbreviated as *ciwas* (pronounced "see-wass"), is *the* gathering place for CSS authors. A number of experts in the field check this newsgroup regularly, this author among them, and all are there for one primary reason: to help new CSS authors over the hurdles that learning any new language will generate. The secondary reason is for the spirited debates that occasionally erupt over some aspect of CSS, or a browser's implementation thereof. Rather unusually for a newsgroup, the signal-to-noise ratio stayed fairly high for the last few years of the 1990s, and will with any luck continue in that vein.

www-style@w3.org

Anyone who wishes to be involved in discussing the future course of CSS, and to clearing up ambiguities in the specifications, should subscribe to this list. The members of the list are all, in one fashion or another, interested in making CSS better than it is already. Please note: *www-style* is *not* the place to ask for assistance with writing CSS. For help with CSS authoring problems, visit *ciwas* instead. Questions beginning with "How do I...?" are frowned upon by the regulars of *www-style* and are usually redirected to a more appropriate forum such as *ciwas*. On the other hand, questions that begin "Why can't I…?" or "Wouldn't it be cool if…?" are generally welcome, so long as they relate to some ability that appears to be missing from CSS.

Messages to *www-style* are only accepted if the sender is already subscribed to the list. In order to subscribe, send email to *www-style-request@w3.org* with the word *subscribe* in the subject of the message; to unsubscribe, send email to *www-style-request@w3.org* with the word *unsubscribe* in the subject of the message.

Bug Reporting

So you've validated your styles, checked for browser support, talked with experts, and it turns out that you've found a new bug in your web browser—one that nobody has yet mentioned online, and that you suspect may have been previously unknown. Here's how to let the browser manufacturer know.

Vendor	Reporting page
Microsoft	*http://register.microsoft.com/contactus/contactus.asp* (Select "Reporting a product bug" from the Microsoft Products menu.)
Netscape	*http://help.netscape.com/forms/bug-client.html*
Opera	*http://www.operasoftware.com/bugreport.html*

B

HTML 2.0 Style Sheet

The style sheet provided in this chapter was excerpted from the CSS1 specification and is included here to give authors an idea of how legacy browser behavior in handling HTML can be reproduced, or at least approximated, using CSS1 rules. A thorough understanding of this style sheet is a good first step to understanding how CSS1 operates. The simpler HTML 2.0 style sheet is reproduced here in order to minimize complexity and possible confusion. A suggested style sheet for HTML 3.2 is also available on the W3C web site, as part of the CSS2 specification.

This HTML 2.0 style sheet was written by Todd Fahrner, in accordance with the suggested rendering in the HTML 2.0 specification:

```
BODY {
 margin: 1em;
 font-family: serif;
 line-height: 1.1;
 background: white;
 color: black;
}

H1, H2, H3, H4, H5, H6, P, UL, OL, DIR, MENU, DIV,
DT, DD, ADDRESS, BLOCKQUOTE, PRE, BR, HR { display: block }

B, STRONG, I, EM, CITE, VAR, TT, CODE, KBD, SAMP,
IMG, SPAN { display: inline }

LI { display: list-item }

H1, H2, H3, H4 { margin-top: 1em; margin-bottom: 1em }
H5, H6 { margin-top: 1em }
H1 { text-align: center }
H1, H2, H4, H6 { font-weight: bold }
H3, H5 { font-style: italic }
```

```
H1 { font-size: xx-large }
H2 { font-size: x-large }
H3 { font-size: large }

B, STRONG { font-weight: bolder } /* relative to the parent */
I, CITE, EM, VAR, ADDRESS, BLOCKQUOTE { font-style: italic }
PRE, TT, CODE, KBD, SAMP { font-family: monospace }

PRE { white-space: pre }

ADDRESS { margin-left: 3em }
BLOCKQUOTE { margin-left: 3em; margin-right: 3em }

UL, DIR { list-style: disc }
OL { list-style: decimal }
MENU { margin: 0 }       /* tight formatting */
LI { margin-left: 3em }

DT { margin-bottom: 0 }
DD { margin-top: 0; margin-left: 3em }

HR { border-top: solid }    /* 'border-bottom' could also have been used */

A:link { color: blue }    /* unvisited link */
A:visited { color: red }   /* visited links */
A:active { color: lime }   /* active links */

/* setting the anchor border around IMG elements
   requires contextual selectors */

A:link IMG { border: 2px solid blue }
A:visited IMG { border: 2px solid red }
A:active IMG { border: 2px solid lime }
```

C

CSS1 Properties

This appendix lists all CSS1 properties, plus the CSS1 pseudo-elements and pseudo-classes. The values to the right of a property name show the browser compatibility information for that property. They will look something like this:

IE4 Y/N   IE5 Y/Y   NN4 N/N   Op3 Y/-

The browsers listed are:

NN4

Netscape Navigator 4

IE4

Internet Explorer 4 (IE4.5 for Macintosh)

IE5

Internet Explorer 5

Op3

Opera 3.6

The first value in each pair is for the Windows version; the second value is for the Macintosh version. (Sorry, Macintosh folks, but we are in the minority.) For instance, IE4 Y/N means that the property is supported in IE4 for Windows, but not IE4 for Macintosh. The possible support values are:

Y   Supported

N   Not Supported

P   Partial Support (may mean that some values are supported and others are not)

Q   Quirky Support (close to the letter of the specification)

B   Buggy Support (may mangle display, or even crash the browser)

-   Not Applicable (browser doesn't exist)

For more detailed information about browser support, including notes on the support ratings, see Appendix D, *CSS Support Chart*.

:active   IE4 Y/Y   IE5 Y/Y   NN4 N/N   Op3 N/-

This pseudo-class applies to hyperlinks, but not named anchors. It sets the styles to be used at the moment a hyperlink is being selected (e.g., clicked).

Example   `A:active {color: red; background: yellow;}`

Values   n/a

Default   n/a

Inherited   yes

Applies to   anchor elements with an HREF attribute

:first-letter   IE4 N/N   IE5 N/Y   NN4 N/N   Op3 Y/-

Applies styles to the first letter of an element. This pseudo-class can be used to generate drop-cap effects, among other things.

Example
```
P:first-letter {color: purple;}
    <P>The capital 'T' at the beginning of this paragraph is purple.</P>
```

Values   n/a

Default   n/a

Inherited   yes

Applies to   block

:first-line   IE4 N/N   IE5 N/Y   NN4 N/N   Op3 Y/-

Applies styles to the first line of an element. The styles are applied even if the window is resized; the text is simply restyled to encompass only the first line of the element.

Example
```
P:first-line {color: red;}
    <P>The first line of this paragraph is red. blah blah blah...</P>
```

Values   n/a

Default   n/a

Inherited   yes

Applies to   block

!important   IE4 Y/N   IE5 Y/Y   NN4 N/N   Op3 Y/-

Style declaration is made important, thereby raising its weight in the cascade. Important declarations override all others. In CSS1, important author styles override all reader styles, even important ones. In CSS2, this is reversed, so that important reader styles always win out over the author's styles, important or otherwise.

Example
```
H1 {color: maroon !important;}
P.warning {color: rgb(100%,20%,20%) !important; font-weight: bold;}
```

Values   n/a

Default   n/a

Inherited   yes

Applies to   style rules

:link   IE4 Y/Y   IE5 Y/Y   NN4 Y/Y   Op3 Y/-

This pseudo-class applies to hyperlinks, but not named anchors. It sets the styles to be used for a hyperlink that points to a URI that has not yet been visited (i.e., is not listed in the browser's history).

Example   `A:link {color: blue;}`

Values   n/a

Default   n/a

Inherited   yes

Applies to   anchor elements with an `HREF` attribute

:visited   IE4 Y/Y   IE5 Y/Y   NN4 N/N   Op3 Y/-

This pseudo-class applies to hyperlinks, but not named anchors. It sets the styles to be used for a hyperlink that points to a URI that has already been visited (i.e., is listed in the browser's history).

Example   `A:visited {color: navy;}`

Values   n/a

Default   n/a

Inherited   yes

Applies to   anchor elements with an HREF attribute

background

IE4 P/Y   IE5 Y/Y   NN4 P/P   Op3 P/-

A shorthand way of expressing the various background properties using a single rule. Use of this property is encouraged over the other background properties because it is more widely supported and doesn't take as long to type.

Example
```
BODY {background: white url(bg41.gif) fixed center repeat-x;}
P {background: #555 url(http://www.pix.org/stone.png);}
PRE {background: yellow;}
```

Values
<background-color> || <background-image> || <background-repeat> || <background-attachment> || <background-position>

Default   refer to individual properties

Inherited   no

Applies to   all elements

Percentage values allowed on <background-position>.

background-attachment

IE4 Y/Y   IE5 Y/Y   NN4 N/N   Op3 N/-

This property defines whether or not the background image scrolls along with the element. This is generally applied to BODY only, and in fact is largely supported only for that element. It is theoretically possible to create "aligned" backgrounds in multiple elements using this property; see Chapter 6, *Colors and Backgrounds*, for more details.

Example
```
BODY {background-attachment: scroll;}
DIV.fixbg {background-attachment: fixed;}
```

Values   scroll | fixed

Default   scroll

Inherited   no

Applies to   all elements

background-color

IE4 Y/Y   IE5 Y/Y   NN4 B/B   Op3 Y/-

This sets the background color of an element. The color fills the content area and padding, and extends out to the outer edge of the element's border. The value transparent trips across a nasty bug in Navigator 4.x, which interprets it as black.

Example
```
H4 {background-color: white;}
P {background-color: rgb(50%,50%,50%);}
PRE {background-color: #FFFF99;}
```

Values   <color> | transparent

Default   transparent

Inherited   no

Applies to   all elements

---

background-image   IE4 Y/Y   IE5 Y/Y   NN4 Y/Y   Op3 Y/-

Sets an image to be the background pattern. Depending on the value of
background-repeat, the background image may tile indefinitely, or only along
one axis, or not at all, and the starting position of the tiling is dependent on the
value of background-position.

Example
```
BODY {background-image: url(bg41.gif);}
H2 {background-image: url(http://www.pix.org/dots.png);}
```

Values   <url> | none

Default   none

Inherited   no

Applies to   all elements

---

background-position   IE4 Y/Y   IE5 Y/Y   NN4 N/N   Op3 Y/-

This sets the starting position of a background image (defined by the value of
background-image). background-position is used to set the origin of the
background's tiling, or its position if there is no tiling. Percentage values define
not only a point within the element, but also the same point in the origin image
itself; see Chapter 6 for more details.

Example   BODY {background-position: top center;}

Values
[<percentage> | <length>]{1,2} | [top | center | bottom] || [left | center
| right]

Default   0% 0%

Inherited   no

Applies to   block-level and replaced

Percentage values refer to the size of the element itself as well as the size of the origin image.

---

background-repeat   IE4 P/Y   IE5 Y/Y   NN4 P/B   Op3 Y/-

Sets the repeat style for a background image. Note that the axis-related repeats actually repeat in *both* directions along the specified axis. The repeating of a background image begins with the origin image, whose position is defined by the value of `background-position`.

Example	BODY {background-repeat: no-repeat;}
Values	repeat | repeat-x | repeat-y | no-repeat
Default	repeat
Inherited	no
Applies to	all elements

---

border   IE4 P/P   IE5 P/Y   NN4 P/P   Op3 P/-

This is a shorthand property that defines the width, color, and style of the border of an element. Note that while none of the values are required, omitting the `<border-style>` value will result in no border being applied, since the default of `border-style` is `none.`

Example	H1 {border: 2px dashed maroon;}
Values	<border-width> || <border-style> || <color>
Default	not defined for shorthand properties
Inherited	no
Applies to	all elements

---

border-bottom   IE4 P/P   IE5 P/Y   NN4 N/N   Op3 P/-

This shorthand property defines the width, color, and style of the bottom border of an element. The same caveats about `border-style` apply.

Example	UL {border-bottom: 0.5in inset green;}
Values	<border-bottom> || <border-style> || <color>
Default	not defined for shorthand properties
Inherited	no
Applies to	all elements

border-bottom-width   IE4 P/P   IE5 P/Y   NN4 B/B   Op3 Y/-

Sets the width of the bottom border of an element, which will inherit the element's background, and may have a foreground of its own (see `border-style`). Negative length values are not permitted.

Example   UL {border-bottom-width: 0.5in;}

Values   thin | medium | thick | <length>

Default   medium

Inherited   no

Applies to   all elements

border-color   IE4 Y/Y   IE5 Y/Y   NN4 P/P   Op3 Y/-

Sets the color of the foreground of the overall border of an element (see `border-style`).

Example   H1 {border-color: purple; border-style: solid;}

Values   <color>{1,4}

Default   the value of `color` for the element itself

Inherited   no

Applies to   all elements

border-left   IE4 P/P   IE5 P/Y   NN4 N/N   Op3 P/-

This shorthand property defines the width, color, and style of the left border of an element. The usual caveats about `border-style` apply.

Example   P {border-left: 3em solid gray;}

Values   <border-left> || <border-style> || <color>

Default   not defined for shorthand properties

Inherited   no

Applies to   all elements

border-left-width   IE4 P/P   IE5 P/Y   NN4 B/B   Op3 Y/-

Sets the width of the left border of an element, which will inherit the element's background, and may have a foreground of its own (see `border-style`). Negative length values are not permitted.

Example	P {border-left-width: 3em;}
Values	thin | medium | thick | <length>
Default	medium
Inherited	no
Applies to	all elements

---

border-right   IE4 P/P   IE5 P/Y   NN4 N/N   Op3 P/-

This shorthand property defines the width, color, and style of the right border of an element. The usual caveats about border-style apply.

Example	IMG {border-right: 30px dotted blue;}
Values	<border-right> || <border-style> || <color>
Default	not defined for shorthand properties
Inherited	no
Applies to	all elements

---

border-right-width   IE4 P/P   IE5 P/Y   NN4 B/B   Op3 Y/-

Sets the width of the right border of an element, which will inherit the element's background, and may have a foreground of its own (see border-style). Negative length values are not permitted.

Example	IMG {border-right-width: 30px;}
Values	thin | medium | thick | <length>
Default	medium
Inherited	no
Applies to	all elements

---

border-style   IE4 P/Y   IE5 P/Y   NN4 P/P   Op3 Y/-

Sets the style of the overall border of an element, using the color set by border-color or the foreground of the element itself if no border-color has been defined. CSS1 does not require recognition of any values besides none and solid. Any unrecognized value from the list of values should be reinterpreted as solid.

Example	H1 {border-style: solid; border-color: purple;}

Values

none I dotted I dashed I solid I double I groove I ridge I inset I outset

Default   none

Inherited   no

Applies to   all elements

---

border-top   IE4 P/P   IE5 P/Y   NN4 N/N   Op3 P/-

This shorthand property defines the width, color, and style of the top border of an element. The usual caveats about `border-style` apply.

Example   UL {border-top: 0.5in solid black;}

Values   <border-top> || <border-style> || <color>

Default   not defined for shorthand properties

Inherited   no

Applies to   all elements

---

border-top-width   IE4 P/P   IE5 P/Y   NN4 B/B   Op3 Y/-

Sets the width of the top border of an element, which will inherit the element's background, and may have a foreground of its own (see `border-style`). Negative length values are not permitted.

Example   UL {border-top-width: 0.5in;}

Values   thin I medium I thick I <length>

Default   medium

Inherited   no

Applies to   all elements

---

border-width   IE4 P/P   IE5 P/Y   NN4 B/B   Op3 Y/-

Sets the width of the overall border of an element, which will inherit the element's background, and may have a foreground of its own (see `border-style`). Negative length values are not permitted.

Example   H1 {border-width: 2ex;}

Values   [thin I medium I thick I <length>]{1,4}

Default   not defined for shorthand properties

Inherited	no
Applies to	all elements

---

clear IE4 P/Y IE5 P/Y NN4 P/P Op3 B/-

Defines the sides of an element on which no floating images may be placed. The effect of this is to move the element downward until the top of its border-edge is below the bottom edge of the floated element.

Example	H1 {clear: right;}
Values	none | left | right | both
Default	none
Inherited	no
Applies to	all elements

---

color IE4 Y/Y IE5 Y/Y NN4 Y/Y Op3 Y/-

Sets the foreground color of a given element. For text, this sets the text color. The value of color is inherited by any borders of an element, unless they have had a color set `border-color`.

Example	STRONG {color: rgb(255,128,128);}
Values	\<color\>
Default	UA specific
Inherited	yes
Applies to	all elements

---

display IE4 P/P IE5 P/Y NN4 P/P Op3 P/-

Used to classify elements into broad categories. The most popular value is probably `none`, which suppresses the display of an element altogether. Gratuitous use of `display` with a document type such as HTML can be dangerous, since HTML already has a `display` hierarchy defined. However, in the case of XML, which has no such hierarchy, display is indispensable.

In CSS2, the range of values for display is dramatically expanded. See Chapter 10, *CSS2: A Look Ahead*, for more details.

Example	.hide {display: none;}
Values	block | inline | list-item | none

Default	block
Inherited	no
Applies to	all elements

---

float   IE4 P/B   IE5 P/Q   NN4 P/P   Op3 B/-

Sets the float direction for an element. This is generally applied to images in order to allow text to flow around them, but under CSS1 any element may be floated. Note that, for elements such as paragraph, floating the element will cause its width to tend toward zero unless an explicit width is assigned; thus, width assignment is a crucial part of floating any nonreplaced element.

Example	`IMG {float: left;}`
Values	left | right | none
Default	none
Inherited	no
Applies to	all elements

---

font   IE4 P/Q   IE5 P/Y   NN4 P/P   Op3 Y/-

This is a shorthand property for the other font properties. Any of these values may be omitted except for `font-size` and `font-family`, which are always required for a valid font declaration. Note the following incorrect examples.

Example

```
P {font: bold 12pt/14pt Helvetica,sans-serif;}
P.wrong {font: bold Helvetica,sans-serif;} /* missing a font-size */
P.wrong {font: 12pt Times,serif bold;}   /* font-weight must come before others */
P.wrong {font: 12pt italic Times;}   /* font-style must come before font-size */
P.fancy {font: 14pt Author;}   /* technically correct, although generic font-
families are encouraged for fallback purposes */
```

Values

[<font-style> || <font-variant> || <font-weight>]? <font-size>
[/ <line-height>]? <font-family>

Default	refer to individual properties
Inherited	yes
Applies to	all elements

---

font-family   IE4 Y/Y   IE5 Y/Y   NN4 Y/Y   Op3 Y/-

This is used to declare a specific font to be used, or a generic font family, or both. Note that the use of a specific font family is dependent on the user having said font installed on the system. Thus the use of generic font families is strongly encouraged, since this will cause the user agent to attempt to substitute a similar font.

Example   `P {font-family: Helvetica,sans-serif;}`

Values

    [[<family-name> | <generic-family>],]* [<family-name> | <generic-family>]

Default   UA specific

Inherited   yes

Applies to   all elements

---

font-size   IE4 P/Q   IE5 P/Y   NN4 Y/Y   Op3 Y/-

This sets the size of the font. This can be defined as an absolute size, a relative size, a length value, or a percentage value. Negative length and percentage values are not permitted. The dangers of font-size assignment are many and varied. Some of these dangers are covered in Chapter 4, *Text Properties.*

Example

    `H2 {font-size: 200%;}`
    `H3 {font-size: 36pt;}`

Values

    `xx-small | x-small | small | medium | large | x-large | xx-large | larger | smaller |` <length> | <percentage>

Default   `medium`

Inherited   yes

Applies to   all elements

Percentage values are relative to the parent element's font size.

---

font-style   IE4 Y/Y   IE5 Y/Y   NN4 P/P   Op3 Y/-

This set the font to use either italic, oblique, or normal text. Italic text is generally a defined font face within the font itself, whereas oblique text is less often so. In the latter case, the user agent can compute a slanted font face.

Example   `EM {font-style: oblique;}`

Values   `normal | italic | oblique`

Default	normal
Inherited	yes
Applies to	all elements

---

font-variant   IE4 Q/Y   IE5 Q/Y   NN4 N/N   Op3 Y/-

This property currently has two values: `small-caps` and `normal`. The `small-caps` variant can either be applied as a face of the selected font or computed by the user agent.

Example	H3 {font-variant: small-caps;}
Values	normal | small-caps
Default	normal
Inherited	yes
Applies to	all elements

---

font-weight   IE4 Y/Y   IE5 Y/Y   NN4 P/P   Op3 Y/-

This is used to set the weight of a font, making it heavier or lighter. The numeric value 400 is equivalent to the value `normal`, and 700 is equal to `bold`. Each numeric value is at least as heavy as the next-lower value, and at least as light as the next-higher number.

| *Example* | B {font-weight: 700;} |
| *Values* | |

normal \| bold \| bolder \| lighter \| 100 \| 200 \| 300 \| 400 \| 500 \| 600 \| 700 \| 800 \| 900

Default	normal
Inherited	yes
Applies to	all elements

---

height   IE4 Y/Y   IE5 Y/Y   NN4 N/N   Op3 Y/-

This is used to set the height of an element. Height is most often applied to images, but can be used on any block-level or replaced element, although support for such behavior is not widespread as of this writing. Negative length values are not permitted.

| *Example* | IMG.icon {height: 50px;} |
| *Values* | <length> \| auto |

Default   auto

Inherited   no

Applies to block-level and replaced

---

letter-spacing   IE4 Y/Y   IE5 Y/Y   NN4 N/N   Op3 Y/-

Used to set the amount of whitespace between letters. A letter is defined as any displayed character, including numbers, symbols, and other font glyphs. Length values are used to define a modifier to the usual spacing, not the entire space itself; thus, `normal` is synonymous with 0 (zero). Negative values are permitted, and cause the letters to bunch closer together.

Example   `P {letter-spacing: 0.5em;}`

Values   normal | <length>

Default   normal

Inherited   yes

Applies to all elements

---

line-height   IE4 P/P   IE5 P/Y   NN4 P/P   Op3 Q/-

This influences the layout of line boxes. The difference between the value of `line-height` and the value of `font-size` is called leading, and half of the leading (otherwise known as half-leading) is applied above and below the content of an element or line of text. Negative values are not permitted. Using a number defines a scaling factor that is multiplied by the font-size, and the number itself is inherited, not the computed value. This allows for much more intelligent page layout, and is strongly preferred over other methods of setting `line-height`.

The drawback to using a number value is that IE3 will interpret it as a number of pixels. See Chapter 8 for a detailed discussion of `line-height` and line boxes.

Example
```
P {line-height: 18pt;}
H2 {line-height: 200%;}
```

Values   normal | <number> | <length> | <percentage>

Default   normal

Inherited   yes

Applies to all elements

Percentage values relative to the font size of the element itself

list-style   IE4 P/P   IE5 Y/Y   NN4 P/P   Op3 Y/-

A shorthand property condensing all other `list-style` properties. It applies to all elements with a display value of `list-item`; in ordinary HTML, this is any `<LI>` element.

Example

```
UL {list-style: square url(bullet3.gif) outer;}  /* values are inherited by LI
elements */
```

Values

[disc | circle | square | decimal | lower-roman | upper-roman | lower-alpha | upper-alpha | none] || [inside | outside] || [<url> | none]

Default   not defined for shorthand properties

Inherited   yes

Applies to   elements with display of `list-item`

---

list-style-image   IE4 Y/Y   IE5 Y/Y   NN4 N/N   Op3 Y/-

Used to declare an image which is to be used as the "bullet" in an unordered or ordered list. This style applies to elements with a `display` value of `list-item` (e. g., `<LI>` elements). The position of the image with respect to the content of the list item is defined using `list-style-position`.

Example   `UL {list-style-image: url(bullet3.gif);}`

Values   <url> | none

Default   none

Inherited   yes

Applies to elements with display of `list-item`

---

list-style-position   IE4 Y/Y   IE5 Y/Y   NN4 N/N   Op3 Y/-

This property is used to declare the position of the bullet or number in an unordered or ordered list with respect to the content of the list item. Applies to elements with a `display` value of `list-item`. If the bullet is set to be `outside`, then it is placed in the margin of the list-item element. The exact behavior in this circumstance is not defined in CSS.

Example   `LI {list-style-position: outer;}`

Values   inside | outside

Default	outside
Inherited	yes
Applies to	elements with display of `list-item`

list-style-type   IE4 Y/Y   IE5 Y/Y   NN4 Y/P   Op3 Y/-

This is used to declare the type of bullet numbering system to be used in either an unordered or ordered list, depending on the value specified. This property applies to elements with a `display` value of `list-item`.

Example
```
UL {list-style-type: square;}
OL {list-style-type: lower-roman;}
```

Values
> disc | circle | square | decimal | lower-roman | upper-roman | lower-alpha | upper-alpha | none

Default	disc
Inherited	yes
Applies to	elements with display of list-item

margin   IE4 P/P   IE5 P/Y   NN4 B/B   Op3 Y/-

This sets the size of the overall margin of an element. Vertically adjacent margins of block-level elements are collapsed to be as large as the largest margin, whereas inline elements effectively do not take margins (they are allowed, but have no effect on page layout). Only the left and right margins of inline elements have any effect, and are not collapsed. Margins set on floated elements are not collapsed with other margins under any circumstance. Negative values are permitted, but caution is recommended.

Example	H1 {margin: 2ex;}
Values	[<length>	<percentage>	auto]{1,4}
Default	not defined for shorthand properties
Inherited	no
Applies to	all elements

Percentage values refer to width of the closest block-level ancestor.

---

margin-bottom   IE4 P/P   IE5 P/Y   NN4 N/N   Op3 Y/-

This sets the size of the bottom margin of an element. Negative values are permitted, but caution is recommended.

Example   UL {margin-bottom: 0.5in;}

Values   <length> | <percentage> | auto

Default   0

Inherited   no

Applies to   all elements

Percentage values refer to the width of the closest block-level ancestor.

---

margin-left   IE4 P/P   IE5 P/Y   NN4 B/B   Op3 Y/-

This sets the size of the left margin of an element. Negative values are permitted, but caution is recommended.

Example   P {margin-left: 3em;}

Values   <length> | <percentage> | auto

Default   0

Inherited   no

Applies to   all elements

Percentage values refer to width of the closest block-level ancestor.

---

margin-right   IE4 P/P   IE5 P/Y   NN4 B/B   Op3 Y/-

This sets the size of the right margin of an element. Negative values are permitted, but caution is recommended.

Example   IMG {margin-right: 30px;}

Values   <length> | <percentage> | auto

Default   0

Inherited   no

Applies to   all elements

Percentage values refer to width of the closest block-level ancestor.

margin-top   IE4 P/P   IE5 P/Y   NN4 P/P   Op3 Y/-

This sets the size of the top margin of an element. Negative values are permitted, but caution is recommended.

Example   UL {margin-top: 0.5in;}

Values   <length> | <percentage> | auto

Default   0

Inherited no

Applies to all elements

Percentage values refer to the width of the closest block-level ancestor.

padding   IE4 P/P   IE5 P/Y   NN4 B/B   Op3 B/-

This sets the size of the overall padding of an element. The padding will "inherit" the element's background; in other words, the background of an element fills its content area and padding. Padding set on inline elements does not affect line-height calculations, but will be applied to the right and left ends of the element. If an inline element has both padding and a background, the background may be extended above and below the edges of the line-box in which the inline element appears, but user agents are not required to support this behavior. There is also no defined behavior to say whether the foreground content of a previous line appears above the background of a succeeding line, or is overwritten by that background. Negative values are not permitted.

Example   H1 {padding: 2ex;}

Values   [<length> | <percentage>]{1,4}

Default   not defined for shorthand properties

Inherited no

Applies to all elements

Percentage values refer to the width of closest block-level ancestor.

padding-bottom   IE4 P/P   IE5 P/Y   NN4 B/B   Op3 Y/-

This property sets the size of the bottom padding of an element, and this padding will "inherit" the element's background. Negative values are not permitted.

Example   UL {padding-bottom: 0.5in;}

Values   <length> | <percentage>

Default   0

Inherited   no

Applies to   all elements

Percentage values refer to the width of closest block-level ancestor.

---

padding-left   IE4 P/P   IE5 P/Y   NN4 B/B   Op3 Y/-

This property sets the size of the left padding of an element, and this padding will "inherit" the element's background. Negative values are not permitted.

Example   `P {padding-left: 3em;}`

Values   <length> | <percentage>

Default   0

Inherited   no

Applies to   all elements

Percentage values refer to the width of closest block-level ancestor.

---

padding-right   IE4 P/P   IE5 P/Y   NN4 B/B   Op3 Y/-

This property sets the size of the right padding of an element, and this padding will "inherit" the element's background. Negative values are not permitted.

Example   `IMG {padding-right: 30px;}`

Values   <length> | <percentage>

Default   0

Inherited   no

Applies to   all elements

Percentage values refer to the width of closest block-level ancestor.

---

padding-top   IE4 P/P   IE5 P/Y   NN4 B/B   Op3 Y/-

This property sets the size of the top padding of an element, and this padding will "inherit" the element's background. Negative values are not permitted.

Example   `UL {padding-top: 0.5in;}`

Values   <length> | <percentage>

Default   0

Inherited	no
Applies to	all elements

Percentage values refer to the width of the closest block-level ancestor.

---

text-align   IE4 Y/P   IE5 Y/Y   NN4 Y/P   Op3 Y/-

This sets the horizontal alignment of the text in an element, or more precisely, defines to which side of the element the line-boxes are aligned. The value `justify` is supported by programmatically adjusting the letter- and word-spacing of the line's content, and results may vary by user agent.

Example

```
P {text-align: justify;}
H4 {text-align: center;}
```

Values	left | right | center | justify
Default	UA specific
Inherited	yes
Applies to	block

---

text-decoration   IE4 P/P   IE5 P/P   NN4 Q/Q   Op3 P/-

This property sets certain effects on the text, such as `underline` and `blink`. These decorations will "span" child elements that do not have text decoration defined; see Chapter 4 for more details. Combinations of the values are legal.

User agents are not required to support the value `blink`, and in fact only Netscape Navigator 4.x does so.

Example

```
U {text-decoration: underline;}
.old {text-decoration: line-through;}
U.old {text-decoration: line-through underline;}
```

Values	none | [underline || overline || line-through || blink]
Default	none
Inherited	no
Applies to	all elements

text-indent   IE4 Y/Y   IE5 Y/Y   NN4 Y/Y   Op3 Y/-

Used to set the indentation of the first line of an element. This is most often used to create a tab effect for Negative values are permitted, and cause "hanging indents."

Example
```
P {text-indent: 5em;}
H2 {text-indent: -25px;}
```

Values   <length> | <percentage>

Default   0

Inherited   yes

Applies to   block

Percentage values refer to parent element's width.

---

text-transform   IE4 Y/Y   IE5 Y/Y   NN4 Y/Y   Op3 P/-

This property changes the case of the letters in the element, regardless of the case of the original text. The selection of letters to be capitalized by the value `capitalize` is not a precisely defined behavior, depending as it does on "words," which are difficult to define in a programmatic way.

Example
```
H1 {text-transform: uppercase;}
.title {text-transform: capitalize;}
```

Values   `capitalize` | `uppercase` | `lowercase` | `none`

Default   `none`

Inherited   yes

Applies to   all elements

---

vertical-align   IE4 P/P   IE5 P/Y   NN4 N/N   Op3 P/-

Used to set the vertical alignment of an element's baseline with respect to its line-height. Negative percentage values are permitted, and will cause the element to be lowered, not raised.

Example
```
SUP {vertical-align: super;}
.fnote {vertical-align: 50%;}
```

Values

baseline | sub | super | top | text-top | middle | bottom |
text-bottom | <percentage>

Default   baseline

Inherited   no

Applies to   inline

Percentage values refer to the line height of the element itself.

---

white-space   IE4 N/N   IE5 N/Y   NN4 P/P   Op3 N/-

This property defines how whitespace within the element is treated. normal acts
like traditional web browsers, in that it reduces any sequence of whitespace to a
single space. pre causes whitespace to be treated as it is in the HTML element
PRE, with whitespace and returns preserved. nowrap prevents an element from
line breaking.

Example

```
TD {white-space: nowrap;}
TT {white-space: pre;}
```

Values   normal | pre | nowrap

Default   normal

Inherited   yes

Applies to   block

---

width   IE4 P/Y   IE5 P/Y   NN4 P/P   Op3 Q/-

Used to set the width of an element. This is most often applied to images, but can
be used on any block-level or replaced element. Negative values are not permitted.

Example   TABLE {width: 80%;}

Values   <length> | <percentage> | auto

Default   auto

Inherited   no

Applies to   block-level and replaced

Percentage values refer to the parent element's width.

---

word-spacing IE4 N/Y   IE5 N/Y   NN4 N/N   Op3 Y/-

Used to set the amount of whitespace between words. A "word" is defined as a string of characters surrounded by whitespace. Length values are used to define a modifier to the usual spacing, not the entire space itself; thus, `normal` is synonymous with 0 (zero). Negative values are permitted, and cause the words to bunch closer together.

Example	`P {word-spacing: 0.5em;}`
Values	normal | <length>
Default	normal
Inherited	yes
Applies to	all elements

D

CSS Support Chart

As we've seen, browser compatibility—or a lack thereof—is the biggest obstacle to adoption of CSS. This appendix provides a comprehensive guide to how the browsers have implemented support for CSS1. Check this master list to get a rough idea of how well a given property and its values are supported.

This appendix uses the following key:

Y   Yes

N   No

P   Partial

B   Buggy

Q   Quirky

"Buggy" can refer to anything from mangled display to an actual browser crash. "Quirky" means that, while the browser is technically compliant with the specification, it acts in a fashion which authors may not expect.

This list and the notes that follow are current as of April 2000. For the latest information, please visit *http://style.webreview.com/*.

| Spec Reference | Property or Value | Windows 95 | | | | | Macintosh | | | | Notes |
		NN4	IE3	IE4	IE5	Op3	NN4	IE3	IE4	IE5	
1.1	Containment in HTML	P	P	P	P	Y	P	B	Y	Y	
	LINK	Y	Y	Y	Y	Y	Y	B	Y	Y	
	\<STYLE>...\</STYLE>	Y	Y	Y	Y	Y	Y	Y	Y	Y	
	@import	N	N	Q	Q	Y	N	N	Y	Y	*
	\<x STYLE="dec;">	B	Y	Y	Y	Y	B	Y	Y	Y	*

Spec Reference	Property or Value	Windows 95					Macintosh				Notes
		NN4	IE3	IE4	IE5	Op3	NN4	IE3	IE4	IE5	
1.2	Grouping	Y	N	Y	Y	Y	Y	Y	Y	Y	
	x, y, z {dec;}	Y	N	Y	Y	Y	Y	Y	Y	Y	
1.3	Inheritance	B	P	Y	Y	Y	B	B	Y	Y	*
	(inherited values)	B	P	Y	Y	Y	B	B	Y	Y	
1.4	Class selector	Y	B	Q	Q	Y	Y	B	Y	Y	*
	.class	Y	B	Q	Q	Y	Y	B	Y	Y	
1.5	ID selector	B	B	B	B	Y	B	B	B	Y	*
	#ID	B	B	B	B	B	B	B	B	Y	
1.6	Contextual selectors	Y	Y	Y	Y	Y	B	P	Y	Y	
	x y z {dec;}	Y	Y	Y	Y	Y	B	P	Y	Y	*
1.7	Comments	Y	B	Y	Y	Y	Y	Y	Y	Y	
	/* comment */	Y	B	Y	Y	Y	Y	Y	Y	Y	
2.1	anchor	P	N	Y	Y	P	P	B	Y	Y	
	A:link	Y	N	Y	Y	Y	Y	B	Y	Y	
	A:active	N	N	Y	Y	N	N	N	Y	Y	
	A:visited	N	N	Y	Y	Y	N	B	Y	Y	
2.3	first-line	N	N	N	N	Y	N	B	N	Y	*
	:first-line	N	N	N	N	Y	N	B	N	Y	
2.4	first-letter	N	N	N	N	Y	N	B	N	Y	*
	:first-letter	N	N	N	N	Y	N	B	N	Y	
3.1	important	N	N	Y	Y	Y	N	N	N	Y	
	!important	N	N	Y	Y	Y	N	N	N	Y	
3.2	Cascading Order	B	P	Y	Y	Y	B	P	Y	Y	*
	Weight sorting	B	Y	Y	Y	Y	B	Y	Y	Y	
	Origin sorting	B	Y	Y	Y	Y	B	B	Y	Y	
	Specificity sorting	B	P	Y	Y	Y	B	B	Y	Y	
	Order sorting	B	N	Y	Y	Y	B	N	Y	Y	
5.2.2	font-family	Y	P	Y	Y	Y	Y	P	Y	Y	
	<family-name>	Y	Y	Y	Y	Y	Y	P	Y	Y	
	<generic-family>	P	P	Y	Y	P	Y	P	Y	Y	
	serif	Y	Y	Y	Y	Y	Y	Y	Y	Y	
	sans-serif	Y	Y	Y	Y	Y	Y	N	Y	Y	
	cursive	N	B	Y	Y	N	Y	N	Y	Y	*
	fantasy	N	B	Y	Y	Y	Y	N	Y	Y	
	monospace	Y	Y	Y	Y	Y	Y	Y	Y	Y	

Spec Reference	Property or Value	Windows 95					Macintosh				Notes
		NN4	IE3	IE4	IE5	Op3	NN4	IE3	IE4	IE5	
5.2.3	font-style	P	P	Y	Y	Y	P	P	Y	Y	
	normal	Y	Y	Y	Y	Y	Y	N	Y	Y	
	italic	Y	N	Y	Y	Y	Y	Y	Y	Y	
	oblique	N	N	Y	Y	Y	N	N	Y	Y	
5.2.4	font-variant	N	N	P	P	Y	N	N	Y	Y	
	normal	N	N	Y	Y	Y	N	N	Y	Y	
	small-caps	N	N	Q	Q	Y	N	N	Q	Y	*
5.2.5	font-weight	P	P	Y	Y	Y	P	P	Y	Y	
	normal	Y	N	Y	Y	Y	Y	N	Y	Y	
	bold	Y	Y	Y	Y	Y	Y	Y	Y	Y	
	bolder	Y	Y	Y	Y	Y	N	N	Y	Y	
	lighter	N	Y	Y	Y	Y	N	N	Y	Y	
	100–900	Y	N	Y	Y	Y	Y	N	Y	Y	
5.2.6	font-size	Y	P	P	P	Y	Y	P	Q	Y	
	<absolute-size>	Y	Y	Q	Q	Y	Y	B	Q	Y	
	xx-small – xx-large	Y	Y	Q	Q	Y	Y	B	Q	Y	*
	<relative-size>	Y	Y	Y	Y	Y	Y	N	Y	Y	
	larger	Y	Y	Y	Y	Y	Y	N	Y	Y	
	smaller	Y	Y	Y	Y	Y	Y	N	Y	Y	
	<length>	Y	P	Y	Y	Y	Y	B	Y	Y	
	<percentage>	Y	Y	Y	Y	Y	Y	P	Y	Y	
5.2.7	font	P	P	P	P	Y	P	P	Q	Y	
	<font-family>	P	Y	Y	Y	Y	Y	P	Y	Y	
	<font-style>	P	P	Y	Y	Y	Y	P	Y	Y	
	<font-variant>	N	N	P	P	Y	N	N	Q	Y	
	<font-weight>	P	Y	Y	Y	Y	Y	N	Y	Y	
	<font-size>	Y	B	Q	Q	Y	Y	B	Y	Y	
	<line-height>	B	Y	Y	Y	Y	B	B	Y	Y	
5.3.1	color	Y	Y	Y	Y	Y	Y	Y	Y	Y	
	<color>	Y	Y	Y	Y	Y	Y	Y	Y	Y	
5.3.2	background-color	B	P	Y	Y	Y	B	N	Y	Y	
	<color>	B	B	Y	Y	Y	B	N	Y	Y	*
	transparent	B	N	Y	Y	Y	B	N	Y	Y	*
5.3.3	background-image	Y	N	Y	Y	Y	Y	N	Y	Y	
	<url>	Y	N	Y	Y	Y	Y	N	Y	Y	
	none	Y	N	Y	Y	Y	Y	N	Y	Y	

Spec Reference	Property or Value	Windows 95					Macintosh				Notes
		NN4	IE3	IE4	IE5	Op3	NN4	IE3	IE4	IE5	
5.3.4	background-repeat	P	N	P	Y	Y	B	N	Y	Y	
	repeat	Y	N	B	Y	Y	Y	N	Y	Y	*
	repeat-x	P	N	B	Y	Y	P	N	Y	Y	*
	repeat-y	P	N	B	Y	Y	P	N	Y	Y	*
	no-repeat	Y	N	Y	Y	Y	Y	N	Y	Y	
5.3.5	background-attachment	N	N	Y	Y	N	N	N	Y	Y	
	scroll	N	N	Y	Y	N	N	N	Y	Y	
	fixed	N	N	Y	Y	N	N	N	Y	Y	
5.3.6	background-position	N	N	Y	Y	Y	N	N	Y	Y	
	\<percentage>	N	N	Y	Y	Y	N	N	Y	Y	
	\<length>	N	N	Y	Y	Y	N	N	Y	Y	
	top	N	N	Y	Y	Y	N	N	Y	Y	
	center	N	N	Y	Y	Y	N	N	Y	Y	
	bottom	N	N	Y	Y	Y	N	N	Y	Y	
	left	N	N	Y	Y	Y	N	N	Y	Y	
	right	N	N	Y	Y	Y	N	N	Y	Y	
5.3.7	background	P	P	P	Y	P	P	P	Y	Y	
	\<background-color>	B	P	Y	Y	Y	P	P	Y	Y	
	\<background-image>	P	Y	Y	Y	Y	P	Y	Y	Y	
	\<background-repeat>	P	B	B	Y	Y	P	B	Y	Y	
	\<background-attachment>	N	N	Y	Y	N	N	Y	Y	Y	
	\<background-position>	N	N	Y	Y	Y	N	P	Y	Y	
5.4.1	word-spacing	N	N	N	N	Y	N	N	Y	Y	
	normal	N	N	N	N	Y	N	N	Y	Y	
	\<length>	N	N	N	N	Y	N	N	Y	Y	
5.4.2	letter-spacing	N	N	Y	Y	Y	N	N	Y	Y	
	normal	N	N	Y	Y	Y	N	N	Y	Y	
	\<length>	N	N	Y	Y	Y	N	N	Y	Y	
5.4.3	text-decoration	Q	P	P	P	P	Q	P	P	P	
	none	Q	N	Q	Q	Y	Q	Y	Q	Y	*
	underline	Q	B	Q	Q	Y	Q	B	Q	Y	
	overline	N	N	Y	Y	Y	N	N	Y	Y	
	line-through	Y	Y	Y	Y	Y	Y	Y	Y	Y	
	blink	Y	N	N	N	N	Y	N	N	N	*
5.4.4	vertical-align	N	N	P	P	P	N	N	P	Y	
	baseline	N	N	Y	Y	Y	N	N	Y	Y	
	sub	N	N	Y	Y	Y	N	N	Y	Y	

Spec Reference	Property or Value	Windows 95					Macintosh				Notes
		NN4	IE3	IE4	IE5	Op3	NN4	IE3	IE4	IE5	
	super	N	N	Y	Y	Y	N	N	Y	Y	
	top	N	N	N	N	B	N	N	Y	Y	
	text-top	N	N	N	N	N	N	N	Y	Y	
	middle	N	N	B	N	B	N	N	Y	Y	
	bottom	N	N	N	N	B	N	N	B	Y	
	text-bottom	N	N	N	N	N	N	N	B	Y	
	<percentage>	N	N	N	N	Y	N	N	B	Y	
5.4.5	text-transform	Y	N	Y	Y	P	Y	N	Y	Y	
	capitalize	Y	N	Y	Y	Y	Y	N	Y	Y	
	uppercase	Y	N	Y	Y	B	Y	N	Y	Y	*
	lowercase	Y	N	Y	Y	Y	Y	N	Y	Y	
	none	Y	N	Y	Y	Y	Y	N	Y	Y	
5.4.6	text-align	Y	P	Y	Y	Y	P	P	P	Y	
	left	Y	Y	Y	Y	Y	Y	Y	Y	Y	
	right	Y	Y	Y	Y	Y	Y	Y	Y	Y	
	center	Y	Y	Y	Y	Y	Y	Y	Y	Y	
	justify	B	N	Y	Y	Y	B	N	N	Y	*
5.4.7	text-indent	Y	Y	Y	Y	Y	Y	Y	Y	Y	
	<length>	Y	Y	Y	Y	Y	Y	Y	Y	Y	
	<percentage>	Y	Y	Y	Y	Y	Y	Y	Y	Y	
5.4.8	line-height	P	P	Y	Y	Q	P	P	Y	Y	*
	normal	Y	Y	Y	Y	Y	Y	Y	Y	Y	
	<number>	P	N	Y	Y	Y	P	B	Y	Y	
	<length>	B	Y	Y	Y	Y	B	B	Y	Y	*
	<percentage>	P	Y	Y	Y	Y	P	B	Y	Y	
5.5.01	margin-top	P	B	P	P	Y	P	B	P	Y	*
	<length>	P	B	P	P	Y	P	B	P	Y	
	<percentage>	P	Y	P	P	Y	P	B	P	Y	
	auto	P	Y	P	P	Y	P	B	P	Y	
5.5.02	margin-right	B	P	P	P	Y	B	P	P	Y	*
	<length>	B	Y	P	P	Y	B	Y	P	Y	
	<percentage>	B	N	P	P	Y	B	Y	P	Y	
	auto	N	N	N	N	Y	N	N	P	Y	
5.5.03	margin-bottom	N	Y	P	P	Y	N	N	P	Y	*
	<length>	N	N	P	P	Y	N	N	P	Y	
	<percentage>	N	N	P	P	Y	N	N	P	Y	
	auto	N	N	P	P	Y	N	N	P	Y	

Spec Reference	Property or Value	Windows 95					Macintosh				Notes
		NN4	IE3	IE4	IE5	Op3	NN4	IE3	IE4	IE5	
5.5.04	margin-left	B	P	P	P	Y	B	P	P	Y	*
	<length>	B	Y	P	P	Y	Y	Y	P	Y	
	<percentage>	B	Y	P	P	Y	B	Y	P	Y	
	auto	N	N	N	N	Y	B	N	P	Y	
5.5.05	margin	B	B	P	P	Y	B	B	P	Y	*
	<length>	B	B	P	P	Y	B	B	P	Y	
	<percentage>	B	Y	P	P	Y	B	B	P	Y	
	auto	N	Y	P	P	Y	N	B	P	Y	
5.5.06	padding-top	B	N	P	P	Y	B	N	P	Y	*
	<length>	B	N	P	P	Y	B	N	P	Y	
	<percentage>	B	N	P	P	Y	B	N	P	Y	
5.5.07	padding-right	B	N	P	P	Y	B	N	P	Y	*
	<length>	B	N	P	P	Y	B	N	P	Y	
	<percentage>	B	N	P	P	Y	B	N	P	Y	
5.5.08	padding-bottom	B	N	P	P	Y	B	N	P	Y	*
	<length>	B	N	P	P	Y	B	N	P	Y	
	<percentage>	B	N	P	P	Y	B	N	P	Y	
5.5.09	padding-left	B	N	P	P	Y	B	N	P	Y	*
	<length>	B	N	P	P	Y	B	N	P	Y	
	<percentage>	B	N	P	P	Y	B	N	P	Y	
5.5.10	padding	B	N	P	P	B	B	N	P	Y	*
	<length>	B	N	P	P	B	B	N	P	Y	
	<percentage>	B	N	P	P	B	B	N	P	Y	
5.5.11	border-top-width	B	N	P	P	Y	B	N	P	Y	*
	thin	Y	N	P	P	Y	Y	N	P	Y	
	medium	Y	N	P	P	Y	Y	N	P	Y	
	thick	Y	N	P	P	Y	Y	N	P	Y	
	<length>	Y	N	P	P	Y	Y	N	P	Y	
5.5.12	border-right-width	B	N	P	P	Y	B	N	P	Y	*
	thin	Y	N	P	P	Y	Y	N	P	Y	
	medium	Y	N	P	P	Y	Y	N	P	Y	
	thick	Y	N	P	P	Y	Y	N	P	Y	
	<length>	Y	N	P	P	Y	Y	N	P	Y	
5.5.13	border-bottom-width	B	N	P	P	Y	B	N	P	Y	*
	thin	B	N	P	P	Y	B	N	P	Y	
	medium	B	N	P	P	Y	B	N	P	Y	

Spec Reference	Property or Value	Windows 95					Macintosh				Notes
		NN4	IE3	IE4	IE5	Op3	NN4	IE3	IE4	IE5	
	thick	B	N	P	P	Y	B	N	P	Y	
	<length>	B	N	P	P	Y	B	N	P	Y	
5.5.14	border-left-width	B	N	P	P	Y	B	N	P	Y	*
	thin	Y	N	P	P	Y	Y	N	P	Y	
	medium	Y	N	P	P	Y	Y	N	P	Y	
	thick	Y	N	P	P	Y	Y	N	P	Y	
	<length>	Y	N	P	P	Y	Y	N	P	Y	
5.5.15	border-width	B	N	P	P	Y	B	N	P	Y	*
	thin	Y	N	P	P	Y	Y	N	P	Y	
	medium	Y	N	P	P	Y	Y	N	P	Y	
	thick	Y	N	P	P	Y	Y	N	P	Y	
	<length>	Y	N	P	P	Y	Y	N	P	Y	
5.5.16	border-color	P	N	Y	Y	Y	P	N	Y	Y	*
	<color>	P	N	Y	Y	Y	P	N	Y	Y	
5.5.17	border-style	P	N	P	P	Y	P	N	Y	Y	
	none	Y	N	Y	Y	Y	Y	N	Y	Y	
	dotted	N	N	N	N	Y	N	N	Y	Y	
	dashed	N	N	N	N	Y	N	N	Y	Y	
	solid	Y	N	Y	Y	Y	Y	N	Y	Y	
	double	Y	N	Y	Y	Y	Y	N	Y	Y	
	groove	Y	N	Y	Y	Y	Y	N	Y	Y	
	ridge	Y	N	Y	Y	Y	Y	N	Y	Y	
	inset	Y	N	Y	Y	Y	Y	N	Y	Y	
	outset	Y	N	Y	Y	Y	Y	N	Y	Y	
5.5.18	border-top	N	N	P	P	Y	N	N	P	Y	*
	<border-top-width>	N	N	P	P	Y	N	N	P	Y	
	<border-style>	N	N	P	P	Y	N	N	P	Y	
	<color>	N	N	P	P	Y	N	N	P	Y	
5.5.19	border-right	N	N	P	P	Y	N	N	P	Y	*
	<border-right-width>	N	N	P	P	Y	N	N	P	Y	
	<border-style>	N	N	P	P	Y	N	N	P	Y	
	<color>	N	N	P	P	Y	N	N	P	Y	
5.5.20	border-bottom	N	N	P	P	Y	N	N	P	Y	*
	<border-bottom-width>	N	N	P	P	Y	N	N	P	Y	
	<border-style>	N	N	P	P	Y	N	N	P	Y	
	<color>	N	N	P	P	Y	N	N	P	Y	

Spec Reference	Property or Value	Windows 95					Macintosh				Notes
		NN4	IE3	IE4	IE5	Op3	NN4	IE3	IE4	IE5	
5.5.21	border-left	N	N	P	P	Y	N	N	P	Y	*
	<border-left-width>	N	N	P	P	Y	N	N	P	Y	
	<border-style>	N	N	P	P	Y	N	N	P	Y	
	<color>	N	N	P	P	Y	N	N	P	Y	
5.5.22	border	P	N	P	P	Y	P	N	P	Y	*
	<border-width>	B	N	P	P	Y	B	N	P	Y	
	<border-style>	P	N	P	P	Y	P	N	P	Y	
	<color>	Y	N	P	P	Y	Y	N	P	Y	
5.5.23	width	P	N	P	P	Q	P	N	Y	Y	*
	<length>	P	N	P	P	Q	P	N	Y	Y	
	<percentage>	P	N	P	P	Q	P	N	Y	Y	
	auto	P	N	P	P	Q	P	N	Y	Y	
5.5.24	height	N	N	Y	Y	Y	N	N	Y	Y	
	<length>	N	N	Y	Y	Y	N	N	Y	Y	
	auto	N	N	Y	Y	Y	N	N	Y	Y	
5.5.25	float	P	N	P	P	B	P	N	B	Q	*
	left	B	N	B	B	Y	B	N	Y	Y	
	right	B	N	B	B	Y	B	N	Y	Y	
	none	Y	N	Y	Y	Y	Y	N	Y	Y	
5.5.26	clear	P	N	P	P	B	P	N	Y	Y	*
	none	Y	Y	Y	Y	Y	Y	Y	Y	Y	
	left	B	N	B	B	N	B	N	Y	Y	
	right	B	N	B	B	Y	B	N	Y	Y	
	both	Y	N	Y	Y	Y	Y	N	Y	Y	
5.6.1	display	P	N	P	P	P	P	N	P	Y	
	block	B	N	N	Y	Y	B	N	P	Y	
	inline	N	N	N	Y	B	N	N	N	Y	*
	list-item	B	N	N	N	N	P	N	P	Y	
	none	Y	N	Y	Y	Y	Y	N	Y	Y	
5.6.2	white-space	P	N	N	N	N	P	N	N	Y	
	normal	Y	N	N	N	N	Y	N	N	Y	
	pre	Y	N	N	N	N	Y	N	N	Y	
	nowrap	N	N	N	N	N	N	N	N	Y	
5.6.3	list-style-type	Y	N	Y	Y	Y	P	N	Y	Y	
	disc	Y	N	Y	Y	Y	Y	N	Y	Y	
	circle	Y	N	Y	Y	Y	Y	N	Y	Y	

Spec Reference	Property or Value	Windows 95					Macintosh				Notes
		NN4	IE3	IE4	IE5	Op3	NN4	IE3	IE4	IE5	
	square	Y	N	Y	Y	Y	Y	N	Y	Y	
	decimal	Y	N	Y	Y	Y	Y	N	Y	Y	
	lower-roman	Y	N	Y	Y	Y	Y	N	Y	Y	
	upper-roman	Y	N	Y	Y	Y	Y	N	Y	Y	
	lower-alpha	Y	N	Y	Y	Y	Y	N	Y	Y	
	upper-alpha	Y	N	Y	Y	Y	Y	N	Y	Y	
	none	Y	N	Y	Y	Y	B	N	Y	Y	*
5.6.4	list-style-image	N	N	Y	Y	Y	N	N	Y	Y	
	<url>	N	N	Y	Y	Y	N	N	Y	Y	
	none	N	N	Y	Y	Y	N	N	Y	Y	
5.6.5	list-style-position	N	N	Y	Y	Y	N	N	Y	Y	
	inside	N	N	Y	Y	Y	N	N	Q	Y	*
	outside	N	N	Y	Y	Y	N	N	Y	Y	
5.6.6	list-style	P	N	P	Y	Y	P	N	P	Y	
	<keyword>	Y	N	Y	Y	Y	P	N	Y	Y	
	<position>	N	N	Q	Q	Y	N	N	Q	Y	
	<url>	N	N	Y	Y	Y	N	N	Y	Y	
6.1	Length Units	P	P	Y	Y	Y	Y	B	Y	Y	
	em	Y	N	Y	Y	Y	Y	Y	Y	Y	
	ex	Q	N	Q	Q	Q	Q	Q	Q	Y	*
	px	Y	Y	Y	Y	Y	Y	Y	Y	Y	
	in	Y	Y	Y	Y	Y	Y	Y	Y	Y	
	cm	Y	Y	Y	Y	Y	Y	Y	Y	Y	
	mm	Y	Y	Y	Y	Y	Y	Y	Y	Y	
	pt	Y	Y	Y	Y	Y	Y	Y	Y	Y	
	pc	Y	Y	Y	Y	Y	Y	Y	Y	Y	
6.2	Percentage Units	Y	Y	Y	Y	Y	Y	Y	Y	Y	
	<percentage>	Y	Y	Y	Y	Y	Y	Y	Y	Y	
6.3	Color Units	P	P	Y	Y	Y	P	P	Y	Y	
	#000	Y	Y	Y	Y	Y	Y	B	Y	Y	
	#000000	Y	Y	Y	Y	Y	Y	B	Y	Y	
	(RRR,GGG,BBB)	Y	N	Y	Y	Y	Y	N	Y	Y	
	(R%,G%,B%)	Y	N	Y	Y	Y	Y	N	Y	Y	
	<keyword>	B	Y	Y	Y	Y	B	Y	Y	Y	*
6.4	URLs	B	Y	Y	Y	Y	B	B	Y	Y	
	<url>	B	Y	Y	Y	Y	B	B	Y	Y	*

Notes

1.1 Containment in HTML: `@import`

WinIE4 and WinIE5 both import files even when the `@import` statement is at the end of the document style sheet. This is technically in violation of the CSS1 specification, although not a major failing; thus the "Quirk" rating.

1.1 Containment in HTML: `<x STYLE="dec;">`

Navigator 4 has particular trouble with list items, which is most of the reason for the "Buggy" rating.

1.3 Inheritance

Navigator 4's inheritance is unstable at best, and fatally flawed at worst. It would take too long to list all occurrences, but particularly troublesome areas include tables and lists.

1.4 Class selector

WinIE4/5 allows class names to begin with digits; this is not permitted under CSS1. It is allowed in CSS2.

1.5 ID selector

WinIE4/5 allows ID names to begin with digits; this is not permitted under CSS1. All browsers apply the style for a given ID to more than one instance of that ID in an HTML document, which is not permitted. This is properly an error-checking problem, not a failing of the CSS implementations, but I feel it is significant enough to warrant the ratings shown.

1.6 Contextual selectors: `x y z {dec;}`

MacNav4 has the most trouble with contextual selectors involving tables. For example, `HTML BODY TABLE P` is not properly handled.

2.3 `:first-line`

IE3 incorrectly applies styles to the entire element.

2.4 `:first-letter`

IE3 incorrectly applies styles to the entire element.

3.2 Cascading Order

Again, there are simply far too many instances of problems to list here.

5.2.2 `font-family: cursive`

Despite a preferences setting for cursive fonts, Opera does not seem to apply the preference, but instead substitutes another font. This may vary by system, as others have reported no trouble with this feature.

5.2.4 `font-variant: small-caps`

IE4/5 approximates the `small-caps` style by making all such text uppercase. While this can be justified under the CSS1 specification, visually, it does not render the text in small caps.

5.2.6 font-size: xx-small through xx-large

IE4/5's values for absolute sizes assigns small to be the same size as unstyled text, instead of medium, as one might expect. Thus, declaring an absolute font size (such as font-size: medium) will almost certainly lead to different size fonts in Navigator and Explorer. While this is not incorrect under the specification, it is confusing to many authors.

5.3.2 background-color: <color>

Nav4 does not apply the background color to the entire content box and padding, but rather just to the text in the element. This can be worked around by declaring a near-zero-width border.

5.3.2 background-color: transparent

Nav4 insists on applying this value to the parent of an element, not the element itself. This can lead to "holes" in the parent element's background.

5.3.4 background-repeat: repeat

WinIE4 only repeats down and to the right. The correct behavior is for the background image to be tiled in both vertical directions for repeat-y, and both horizontal for repeat-x. Nav4 gets this property correct on a technicality: since it does not support background-position, there is no way to know whether or not it would tile in all four directions if given the chance, or instead emulate WinIE4's behavior. Opera 3.6, MacIE4.5, and WinIE5 all behave correctly.

5.3.4 background-repeat: repeat-x

WinIE4 only repeats to the right, instead of both left and right.

5.3.4 background-repeat: repeat-y

WinIE4 only repeats down, instead of both up and down.

5.4.3 text-decoration: none

According to the specification, if an element is decorated, but one of its children is not, the parent's effect will still be visible on the child; in a certain sense, it "shines through." Thus, if a paragraph is underlined, but a STRONG element within it is set to have no underlining, the paragraph underline will still "span" the STRONG element. This also means that the underlining of child elements should be the same color as the parent element, unless the child element has also been set to be underlined. In practice, however, setting an inline element to none will turn off all decorations, regardless of the parent's decoration. The only exception to this is Opera, which implements the specification correctly.

5.4.3 text-decoration: blink

Since this value is not required under CSS1, only Navigator supports it (surprise).

5.4.5 `text-transform: uppercase`

Opera 3.6 uppercases the first letter in each inline element within a word, which (according to the CSS1 Test Suite) it should not do.

5.4.6 `text-align: justify`

In Nav4, this value has a tendency to break down in tables, but generally works in other circumstances.

5.4.8 `line-height: <length>`

Nav4 incorrectly permits negative values for this property.

5.4.8 `line-height`

Opera 3.6 applies background colors to the space between lines, as opposed to just the text itself, when the background is set for an inline element within the text. (See the CSS1 Test Suite for more details.)

5.5.01 `margin-top`

All margin properties seem to be problematic, or else completely unsupported, on inline elements. In the case of `margin-top`, support is pretty good on block-level elements in Nav4 and IE4/IE5, and appears to be perfect in Opera 3.6.

5.5.02 `margin-right`

All margin properties seem to be problematic, or else completely unsupported, on inline elements. In the case of `margin-right`, support is pretty good on block-level elements in IE4 and IE5, while with inline elements, IE4 and IE5 ignore this property completely. Navigator does fairly well so long as margins are not applied to floating or inline elements, in which case major bugs can be tripped.

5.5.03 `margin-bottom`

All margin properties seem to be problematic, or else completely unsupported, on inline elements. In the case of `margin-bottom`, support is pretty good on block-level elements in IE4 and IE5, while with inline elements, IE4 and IE5 ignore this property completely. Navigator does fairly well so long as margins are not applied to floating or inline elements, in which case major bugs can be tripped.

5.5.04 `margin-left`

All margin properties seem to be problematic, or else completely unsupported, on inline elements. In the case of `margin-left`, support is pretty good on block-level elements in IE4 and IE5, while with inline elements, IE4 and IE5 ignore this property completely. Navigator does fairly well so long as margins are not applied to floating or inline elements, in which case major bugs can be tripped.

5.5.05 `margin`

All margin properties seem to be problematic, or else completely unsupported, on inline elements. In the case of `margin`, support is pretty good on block-level elements in IE4 and IE5, while with inline elements, IE4 and IE5 ignore this property completely. Navigator does fairly well so long as margins are not applied to floating or inline elements, in which case major bugs can be tripped.

5.5.06 `padding-top`

All padding properties seem to be problematic, or else completely unsupported, on inline elements. In the case of `padding-top`, support is pretty good on block-level elements in IE4 and IE5. Navigator does fairly well so long as margins are not applied to floating or inline elements, in which case major bugs can be tripped.

5.5.07 `padding-right`

All padding properties seem to be problematic, or else completely unsupported, on inline elements. In the case of `padding-right`, support is pretty good on block-level elements in IE4 and IE5. Navigator does fairly well so long as margins are not applied to floating or inline elements, in which case major bugs can be tripped.

5.5.08 `padding-bottom`

All padding properties seem to be problematic, or else completely unsupported, on inline elements. Navigator does fairly well so long as padding is not applied to floating or inline elements, in which case major bugs can be tripped.

5.5.09 `padding-left`

All padding properties seem to be problematic, or else completely unsupported, on inline elements. Navigator does fairly well so long as padding is not applied to floating or inline elements, in which case major bugs can be tripped.

5.5.10 `padding`

All padding properties seem to be problematic, or else completely unsupported, on inline elements. Opera correctly ignores negative padding values (although Opera 3.5 applied negative padding), but will alter the line height based on values of `padding` applied to inline elements, which is incorrect. Navigator does fairly well so long as padding is not applied to floating or inline elements, in which case major bugs can be tripped.

5.5.11 `border-top-width`

Navigator will create visible borders even when no `border-style` is set, and does not set borders on all sides when a style is set. Things get really ugly when borders are applied to inline styles. IE4 and IE5 correctly handle borders on block-level elements, but ignore them for inlines.

5.5.12 `border-right-width`

Navigator will create visible borders even when no `border-style` is set, and does not set borders on all sides when a style is set. Things get really ugly when borders are applied to inline styles. IE4 and IE5 correctly handle borders on block-level elements, but ignore them for inlines.

5.5.13 `border-bottom-width`

Navigator will create visible borders even when no `border-style` is set, and does not set borders on all sides when a style is set. Things get really ugly when borders are applied to inline styles. IE4 and IE5 correctly handle borders on block-level elements, but ignore them for inlines.

5.5.14 `border-left-width`

Navigator will create visible borders even when no `border-style` is set, and does not set borders on all sides when a style is set. Things get really ugly when borders are applied to inline styles. IE4 and IE5 correctly handle borders on block-level elements, but ignore them for inlines.

5.5.15 `border-width`

Navigator will create visible borders even when no `border-style` is set, and does not set borders on all sides when a style is set. Things get really ugly when borders are applied to inline styles. IE4 and IE5 correctly handle borders on block-level elements, but ignore them for inlines.

5.5.16 `border-color`

Nav4 and Opera do not set colors on individual sides, as in `border-color: red blue green purple;`. Explorer cannot apply border colors to inline elements, since it does not apply borders to inlines, but this is not penalized here.

5.5.18 `border-top`

IE4 and IE5 do not apply borders to inline elements.

5.5.19 `border-right`

IE4 and IE5 do not apply borders to inline elements.

5.5.20 `border-bottom`

IE4 and IE5 do not apply borders to inline elements.

5.5.21 `border-left`

IE4 and IE5 do not apply borders to inline elements.

5.5.22 `border`

IE4 and IE5 do not apply borders to inline elements.

5.5.23 `width`

Navigator applies `width` in an inconsistent fashion, but appears to honor it on most simple text elements and images. WinIE4/5 applies it to images and tables, but ignores it for most text elements like P and headings. Opera 3.6, weirdly, seems to set the width of images to 100%, but this is largely an illusion, since minimizing the window and then maximizing it again will reveal correctly sized images.

5.5.25 `float`

`float` is one of the most complicated and hardest-to-implement aspects of the entire CSS1 specification. Basic floating is generally supported by all browsers, especially on images, but when the specification is closely tested, or the document structure becomes complicated, floating most often happens incorrectly, or not at all. The floating of text elements is especially inconsistent, although IE5 and Opera have cleaned up their act to a large degree, leaving WinIE4 and Nav4 the major transgressors in this respect. Authors should use `float` with some care, and thoroughly test any pages employing it with great care.

5.5.26 `clear`

Like `float`, `clear` is not a simple thing to support. Again, basic support is there, but as things get more complicated, browser behavior breaks down. Thoroughly test pages using this property.

5.6.1 `display: inline`

Opera 3.6 almost gets `inline` right, but seems to honor the occasional carriage return as though it were a BR element, instead of plain whitespace.

5.6.3 `list-style-type: none`

MacNav4 displays question marks for bullets when using this value.

5.6.5 `list-style-position: inside`

The positioning and formatting of list-items when set to this value are a bit odd under MacIE4.

6.1 Length Units: ex

All supporting browsers appear to calculate ex as one-half em. This is arguably a reasonable approximation, but it is technically incorrect.

6.3 Color Units: <keyword>

Navigator will generate a color for any apparent keyword. For example, `color: invalidValue` will yield a dark blue, and `color: inherit` (a valid declaration under CSS2) comes out as a vaguely nauseous green.

6.4 URLs: <url>

Navigator determines relative URLs with respect to the HTML document, not the style sheet.

Index

X

Z

About the Author

Eric A. Meyer has been working with the Web since late 1993. Although he spent most of that time as Hypermedia Systems Manager for Digital Media Services at Case Western Reserve University (*http://www.cwru.edu/*), he left CWRU in March 2000 to join an information technology firm in Cleveland, Ohio, which is a much nicer city than you've been led to believe. Eric has been called "an internationally recognized expert on the subjects of HTML and Cascading Style Sheets (CSS)." He is an invited expert and member of the W3C CSS&FP Working Group, coordinated the authoring and creation of the W3C's CSS Test Suite (*http://www.w3.org/Style/CSS/Test/*), remains active on CSS newsgroups, and edits Web Review's "Style Sheets Reference Guide" (*http://style.webreview.com/*). He does as much writing as he can without burning out, and also does his best to keep up with CSS support in popular web browsers. If you have a taste for early jazz and swing, you can catch his weekly big band radio show over the Internet via WRUW-FM 91.1 (*http://radio.cwru.edu/*) in Cleveland. When not otherwise busy, Eric is usually bothering his wife Kat in some fashion.

Colophon

Our look is the result of reader comments, our own experimentation, and feedback from distribution channels. Distinctive covers complement our distinctive approach to technical topics, breathing personality and life into potentially dry subjects.

The animals on the cover of *Cascading Style Sheets: The Definitive Guide* are salmon (*salmonidae*), which is a family of fish consisting of many different species. Two of the most common salmon are the Pacific salmon and the Atlantic salmon.

Pacific salmon live in the northern Pacific Ocean off the coasts of North America and Asia. There are five subspecies of Pacific salmon, with an average weight of ten to thirty pounds and an average age of five years. Pacific salmon are born in the fall in freshwater stream gravel beds, where they incubate through the winter and emerge as inch-long fish. They live for a year or two in the stream or lake, and then head downstream to the ocean. There they live for a few years, before heading back upstream to their exact place of birth to spawn and then die.

Atlantic salmon live in the northern Atlantic Ocean off the coasts of North America and Europe. There are many subspecies of Atlantic salmon, including the trout and the char. Their typical size is ten to twenty pounds, with an average age of seven to ten years. The Atlantic salmon family has a similar life cycle to its Pacific cousins, from freshwater gravel beds to the sea. A major difference between the two, however, is that the Atlantic salmon does not die after spawning; it can return to the ocean and then return to the stream to spawn again, usually two or three times.

Salmon, in general, are graceful, silver-colored fish with spots on their backs and fins. Their diet consists of plankton, insect larvae, shrimp, and smaller fish. Their unusually keen sense of smell is thought to be what helps them navigate from the ocean back to the exact spot of their birth, upstream past many obstacles. Some species of salmon remain landlocked, living their entire lives in freshwater.

Salmon are an important part of the ecosystem, as their decaying bodies provide fertilizer for streambeds. Their numbers have been dwindling over the years, however. Factors in the declining salmon population include habitat destruction, fishing, dams that block spawning paths, acid rain, droughts, floods, and pollution.

Melanie Wang was the production editor and copyeditor for *Cascading Style Sheets: The Definitive Guide*. Madeleine Newell was the proofreader, and Jeff Holcomb and Colleen Gorman provided quality control. Maeve O'Meara, Mary Sheehan, Emily Quill, Ann Schirmer, Jeff Holcomb, and Colleen Gorman provided production support. Brenda Miller wrote the index.

Ellie Volckhausen designed the cover of this book, based on a series design by Edie Freedman. The cover image is a 19th-century engraving from the Dover Pictorial Archive. Emma Colby produced the cover layout with QuarkXPress 3.32 using Adobe's ITC Garamond font.

Alicia Cech designed the interior layout based on a series design by Nancy Priest. Mike Sierra implemented the design in FrameMaker 5.5.6. The text and heading fonts are ITC Garamond Light and Garamond Book. The illustrations that appear in the book were produced by Robert Romano and Rhon Porter using Macromedia FreeHand 8 and Adobe Photoshop 5. This colophon was written by Nicole Arigo.

Whenever possible, our books use RepKover™, a durable and flexible lay-flat binding. If the page count exceeds RepKover's limit, perfect binding is used.

How to stay in touch with O'Reilly

1. Visit Our Award-Winning Web Site

http://www.oreilly.com/

★ "Top 100 Sites on the Web" —*PC Magazine*
★ "Top 5% Web sites" —*Point Communications*
★ "3-Star site" —*The McKinley Group*

Our web site contains a library of comprehensive product information (including book excerpts and tables of contents), downloadable software, background articles, interviews with technology leaders, links to relevant sites, book cover art, and more. File us in your Bookmarks or Hotlist!

2. Join Our Email Mailing Lists

New Product Releases

To receive automatic email with brief descriptions of all new O'Reilly products as they are released, send email to:
listproc@online.oreilly.com
Put the following information in the first line of your message (*not* in the Subject field):
subscribe oreilly-news

O'Reilly Events

If you'd also like us to send information about trade show events, special promotions, and other O'Reilly events, send email to:
listproc@online.oreilly.com
Put the following information in the first line of your message (*not* in the Subject field):
subscribe oreilly-events

3. Get Examples from Our Books via FTP

There are two ways to access an archive of example files from our books:

Regular FTP

- ftp to:
  ftp.oreilly.com
  (login: anonymous
  password: your email address)
- Point your web browser to:
  ftp://ftp.oreilly.com/

FTPMAIL

- Send an email message to:
  ftpmail@online.oreilly.com
  (Write "help" in the message body)

4. Contact Us via Email

order@oreilly.com
To place a book or software order online. Good for North American and international customers.

subscriptions@oreilly.com
To place an order for any of our newsletters or periodicals.

books@oreilly.com
General questions about any of our books.

software@oreilly.com
For general questions and product information about our software. Check out O'Reilly Software Online at **http://software.oreilly.com/** for software and technical support information. Registered O'Reilly software users send your questions to: **website-support@oreilly.com**

cs@oreilly.com
For answers to problems regarding your order or our products.

booktech@oreilly.com
For book content technical questions or corrections.

proposals@oreilly.com
To submit new book or software proposals to our editors and product managers.

international@oreilly.com
For information about our international distributors or translation queries. For a list of our distributors outside of North America check out:
http://www.oreilly.com/www/order/country.html

5. Work with Us

Check out our website for current employment opportunites:
www.jobs@oreilly.com
Click on "Work with Us"

O'Reilly & Associates, Inc.
101 Morris Street, Sebastopol, CA 95472 USA
TEL   707-829-0515 or 800-998-9938
        (6am to 5pm PST)
FAX   707-829-0104

International Distributors

UK, EUROPE, MIDDLE EAST AND AFRICA (EXCEPT FRANCE, GERMANY, AUSTRIA, SWITZERLAND, LUXEMBOURG, LIECHTENSTEIN, AND EASTERN EUROPE)

INQUIRIES
O'Reilly UK Limited
4 Castle Street
Farnham
Surrey, GU9 7HS
United Kingdom
Telephone: 44-1252-711776
Fax: 44-1252-734211
Email: information@oreilly.co.uk

ORDERS
Wiley Distribution Services Ltd.
1 Oldlands Way
Bognor Regis
West Sussex PO22 9SA
United Kingdom
Telephone: 44-1243-779777
Fax: 44-1243-820250
Email: cs-books@wiley.co.uk

FRANCE

INQUIRIES
Éditions O'Reilly
18 rue Séguier
75006 Paris, France
Tel: 33-1-40-51-52-30
Fax: 33-1-40-51-52-31
Email: france@editions-oreilly.fr

ORDERS
GEODIF
61, Bd Saint-Germain
75240 Paris Cedex 05, France
Tel: 33-1-44-41-46-16 (French books)
Tel: 33-1-44-41-11-87 (English books)
Fax: 33-1-44-41-11-44
Email: distribution@eyrolles.com

GERMANY, SWITZERLAND, AUSTRIA, EASTERN EUROPE, LUXEMBOURG, AND LIECHTENSTEIN

INQUIRIES & ORDERS
O'Reilly Verlag
Balthasarstr. 81
D-50670 Köln
Germany
Telephone: 49-221-973160-91
Fax: 49-221-973160-8
Email: anfragen@oreilly.de (inquiries)
Emäil: order@oreilly.de (orders)

CANADA (FRENCH LANGUAGE BOOKS)
Les Éditions Flammarion ltée
375, Avenue Laurier Ouest
Montréal (Québec) H2V 2K3
Tel: 00-1-514-277-8807
Fax: 00-1-514-278-2085
Email: info@flammarion.qc.ca

HONG KONG
City Discount Subscription Service, Ltd.
Unit D, 3rd Floor, Yan's Tower
27 Wong Chuk Hang Road
Aberdeen, Hong Kong
Tel: 852-2580-3539
Fax: 852-2580-6463
Email: citydis@ppn.com.hk

KOREA
Hanbit Media, Inc.
Chungmu Bldg. 201
Yonnam-dong 568-33
Mapo-gu
Seoul, Korea
Tel: 822-325-0397
Fax: 822-325-9697
Email: hant93@chollian.dacom.co.kr

PHILIPPINES
Global Publishing
G/F Benavides Garden
1186 Benavides Street
Manila, Philippines
Tel: 632-254-8949/637-252-2582
Fax: 632-734-5060/632-252-2733
Email: globalp@pacific.net.ph

TAIWAN
O'Reilly Taiwan
No. 3, Lane 131
Hang-Chow South Road
Section 1, Taipei, Taiwan
Tel: 886-2-23968990
Fax: 886-2-23968916
Email: taiwan@oreilly.com

CHINA
O'Reilly Beijing
Room 2410
160, FuXingMenNeiDaJie
XiCheng District
Beijing, China PR 100031
Tel: 86-10-66412305
Fax: 86-10-86631007
Email: beijing@oreilly.com

INDIA
Computer Bookshop (India) Pvt. Ltd.
190 Dr. D.N. Road, Fort
Bombay 400 001 India
Tel: 91-22-207-0989
Fax: 91-22-262-3551
Email: cbsbom@giasbm01.vsnl.net.in

JAPAN
O'Reilly Japan, Inc.
Yotsuya Y's Building
7 Banch 6, Honshio-cho
Shinjuku-ku
Tokyo 160-0003 Japan
Tel: 81-3-3356-5227
Fax: 81-3-3356-5261
Email: japan@oreilly.com

ALL OTHER ASIAN COUNTRIES
O'Reilly & Associates, Inc.
101 Morris Street
Sebastopol, CA 95472 USA
Tel: 707-829-0515
Fax: 707-829-0104
Email: order@oreilly.com

AUSTRALIA
Woodslane Pty., Ltd.
7/5 Vuko Place
Warriewood NSW 2102
Australia
Tel: 61-2-9970-5111
Fax: 61-2-9970-5002
Email: info@woodslane.com.au

NEW ZEALAND
Woodslane New Zealand, Ltd.
21 Cooks Street (P.O. Box 575)
Waganui, New Zealand
Tel: 64-6-347-6543
Fax: 64-6-345-4840
Email: info@woodslane.com.au

LATIN AMERICA
McGraw-Hill Interamericana
Editores, S.A. de C.V.
Cedro No. 512
Col. Atlampa
06450, Mexico, D.F.
Tel: 52-5-547-6777
Fax: 52-5-547-3336
Email: mcgraw-hill@infosel.net.mx

O'REILLY®